Phil Jackson's professional background is of a teacher and dyslexia tutor. He has had a lifelong passion for music (listening, playing and reviewing) and literature, especially science fiction. It has taken him a long time to realise his life-long ambition to become a professional writer, although he has been writing and reviewing for magazines all over the world for twenty years, principally *Acid Dragon* magazine, published in Lyon. During that time, he has had the privilege of reviewing and interviewing many famous players in the music industry. Happily, the coalescence of his interest in music, sociology, history and writing has finally found its ultimate expression in *Within You, Without You*. Phil lives in rural Angus, Scotland, with his wife, Maureen, and his son, Benedict.

This book is dedicated to the countless musicians and writers who have inspired me over the years.

# Phil Jackson

# WITHIN YOU, WITHOUT YOU

## A Sociological, Cultural and Musical History of Great Britain, 1945–1967

AUSTIN MACAULEY PUBLISHERS™

LONDON • CAMBRIDGE • NEW YORK • SHARJAH

A CIP catalogue record for this title is available from the British Library.

ISBN 9781788789363 (Paperback)
ISBN 9781788789370 (Hardback)
ISBN 9781528956444 (ePub e-book)

www.austinmacauley.com

First Published (2020)
Austin Macauley Publishers Ltd
25 Canada Square
Canary Wharf
London
E14 5LQ

I would like to acknowledge the help given by the numerous artists I have interviewed and the labels whose music I have reviewed over the past decades, especially Gary Brooker, Dave Greenslade and Wally Waller, for agreeing to provide some commentary on the book and Vicky and Mark Powell of the Esoteric label whose reissues have proved illuminating in providing a complete story of popular music in the 1960s. I am deeply indebted to the various magazines, books and websites to which I have subscribed and have done my best to give due reference to them. My special thanks go to my friend, Thierry Sportouche, the editor of *Acid Dragon* magazine, for publishing thousands of my reviews, articles and interviews over more than two decades. Without all of these people, and more, this book would not have been possible.

# Table of Content

# Overture

The explicit aim of this book is to consider 'Sergeant Pepper's Lonely Hearts Club Band' as a 'high water mark' in pop/rock music, and to examine its impact and influence in the context of the times in which it was conceived. Meanwhile, a certain Jimi Hendrix was crossing the Atlantic Ocean in the opposite direction to the Brit pop invasion which had ignited the States in 1964 to impress his own lasting legacy on a cultural scene that was flowing with idealism and creativity. The result was 'Are You Experienced?', 'Axis: Bold as Love' which were to have a parallel impact to 'Sergeant Pepper's', 'The Magical Mystery Tour' and, in 1968, 'The Beatles' known as 'The White Album'.

Why 'Sergeant Pepper'?

Because it is consistently and persistently regarded as the yardstick by which all other albums are measured, illogical as this might seem, as critical analysis and opinion polls, which it must be remembered are just that, people's opinions, regularly confirm. I might add also that this position is unlikely to change.

As Gerard DeGroot put it *"the reason the Beatles phenomenon has not been repeated is perhaps that the industry today could never accommodate a band so creative, autonomous and progressive."* **(1)**

This is not a book about the Beatles. Nor is it a book about Jimi Hendrix. Nor is it a book exclusively about music although a lifelong passion for music is the motivating force behind it.

Music, although a sublime art form existing for itself and within itself, cannot exist within a vacuum. The context is all important for it is the thoughts, words and events of the past and the present, and predictions of the future that inform and inspire the music. This is why I outline significant historical events during the lifetimes of the group's main protagonists. While some of the post-war years will only be dimly remembered or not even recalled at all, it is important to consider the historical, social and cultural events that helped shape attitudes and artistic responses. Our nadir year of 1967 is quite arbitrary in many ways but there is a good reason for its selection.

1967 was a prolific year for The Beatles and music in general, the year not only of 'Sergeant Pepper' but also of The Doors debut album (January), The Velvet Underground and Nico's 'Andy Warhol', and Jefferson Airplane's 'Surrealistic Pillow' (March); The Jimi Hendrix's Experience's 'Are You Experienced?' (May); and, post 'Sergeant Pepper', Pink Floyd's 'Piper at the Gates of Dawn' (August), Love's 'Forever Changes', Cream's 'Disraeli Gears' (November) and 'Songs of Leonard Cohen' (December). As we will discover, these albums were merely the tip of the iceberg. There was also 'The Magical Mystery Tour' to take the bus towards 1968 and new musical horizons.

A romanticised view of 'Sergeant Pepper' does not reflect the reality of its anfractuous creation. Not only was there an awful lot of other great music being conceived by other artists but also, the group considered by many to be the leaders and trendsetters, was by no means finished. Even before the new year bells heralded the end of 1967, The Beatles had laid the foundations for albums like 'The Beatles' and 'Abbey

Road' before a slow mortification in the early months of 1970 ghosted them away for ever.

W. Fraser Sandercombe quoting Derek Taylor in the Disc and Music Echo paper says:

*"No one left the Beatles. The Beatles left them. Now they were Paul McCartney, John Lennon, George Harrison and Ringo Starr, all trying to make their own way through a harsh world that judged them as Beatles."* **(2)**

The Beatles, along with 'the swinging sixties', may have ended in chronological terms but this must be seen as a false dichotomy for the world of progressive rock, that 'Sergeant Pepper' pre-empted, was just about to bloom.

So the book you hold in your hands or glimpse on your Kindle, tablet, e-reader or computer reaches its nadir in the time of 'Sergeant Pepper' with the gradual descent of the most famous group on planet Earth towards extinction as the sixties unfolded. From a personal point of view, I hope it serves as an appreciation and a thank you to those wonderful minds that changed my life, and the life of millions like me through the late sixties and early seventies with a music that seemed to appear from another dimension. And after all, many of the records under discussion here were works of art that even softened the hearts of the most hard-nosed critics who doubted whether rock 'n' roll would survive beyond the early sixties.

I hope also that this book informs, reminds, explains and contextualises just what happened when 'pop' and 'rock' emerged from the grim years of post-war austerity.

One final aim is to encourage people of all ages but especially the young to explore the magic and mystery of what is related here. It is a life long journey. If I achieve that then I will have succeeded.

Meanwhile, enjoy the descriptions, explore the links and please do not take the recommendations as gospel (I'm sure you won't – you will have your own ideas!) but as a rich source of where to start if you are starting on the journey or returning to it. Whether you like to download, buy CDs or my preferred medium vinyl, I would be very flattered if you could let 'Within You, Without You' be your guide.

Phil Jackson
Angus, Scotland

# Part One

# Chapter One
## Setting the Scene

Kurt Cobain of Nirvana, Noel Gallagher of Oasis and Steven Wilson were all 'born in 1967'.

War babies: the Britain that four young lads from Liverpool grew up in:

- Richard Starkey, born 7 July 1940
- John Lennon, born 9 October 1940
- Paul McCartney, born 18 June 1942
- George Harrison, born 25 February 1943

**"1950s Britain was an authoritarian, illiberal, puritanical society. Not entirely, of course, but the cumulative evidence is overwhelming." (1)**
**"Food, jobs, homes: such was the holy trinity of the 1950s." (2)**

The post Second World War years saw music change from big band to trad jazz to skiffle to rockabilly, and rock 'n' roll to rock with increasing degrees of revolution, evolution and retrogression. As Tony Judt's masterful account of those post-war years reminds us, it is a sobering thought that "proud, victorious Britain seemed somehow tighter, poorer, greyer and grimmer than any of the erstwhile defeated, occupied and ravished lands across the water. Everything was rationed, restricted, controlled." **(3)**

Post-war planning had, of course, originated before the conflict had ended. In the final month of 1942, Sir William Beveridge had in his report set out post-war social security provisions thus laying the foundations of the 'welfare state'. At last, a concerted political attempt was to be made to liquidate the five evils of disease, idleness, ignorance, squalor and want.

There was great interest in Beveridge's report amongst the public, and sales would soon reach half a million copies. Apparently a copy had even been found in Hitler's bunker. Progress was not fast as the report worked its way through the political system and it was not until 1948 that a new National Insurance system was put into place. Even so it failed to address the role of women of society, despite their great efforts and sacrifices in the war, and married women were still treated as dependents.

The Labour party manifesto for 1945 was entitled 'Let Us Face the Future' and demanded full employment, the nationalisation of industry, a programme for building new houses and the formation of a national health service. A Labour majority of 146 seats in the ensuing General Election saw Clement Attlee become only the second Labour Prime Minister in history (after Ramsay MacDonald). This outcome was perhaps a surprise, given Winston Churchill's war hero status but probably a reaction against the ruling elite's failure to provide for working class people and the appeasement politics of the 1930s that had allowed Adolf Hitler's brand of fascism (under the disguise of national socialism) to progress to a point where it had nearly engulfed the world in its genocidal fanaticism. People had had enough of war, now they wanted to build peace from the ruins of the past six years.

In 1946, a National Insurance Act was passed which came into operation (with the National Health Service) on 5 July, 1948 to offer protection against sickness, unemployment and old age. 16 to 65-years-olds (or 60, if you were a woman) made flat-rate contributions for benefits. In that same year, a National Assistance Act that did not involve the paying of contributions was passed to assist the poorest people. Within fifteen months, Minister of Health Aneurin (Nye) Bevan and the Labour government could take pride in the statistics that 5.25 million pairs of free spectacles had been supplied, as well as 187 million free prescriptions, and free dental treatment for 8.5 million people. **(4)**

Despite such admirable progress, writers such as J.B. Priestley and Eric Blair (pen name George Orwell) provided a touch of sobriety in lamenting the plight of the poor and the slowness of the British establishment to seriously address the issues of poverty and inequality **(5)**

Removed from the slow process of domestic rebuilding, the wider world was still an insecure place. The constant deadly threat of the atomic bomb following Hiroshima and Nagasaki moved J.R.R. Tolkien to comment that 'lunatic physicists' were 'calmly plotting the destruction of the world', and a Soviet coup in Czechoslovakia in February, 1948 did little to settle observers' nerves. The dilemma of how to gain retribution without reigniting the spark of Fascism or igniting Communism, the dilemma also of how to deal with displaced people, rebuild shattered lives and devastated cities, provide security and a reasonable standard of living exercised many minds in the years immediately following the ending of hostilities.

There was also a dreadful realisation that for many, the immediate post-war period was, in terms of deprivation, as bad, if not worse, than wartime and while there might be an acceptance that progress had been made in difficult circumstances, a pyrrhic victory among the ruins might be a good way to describe the resulting chaos and devastation of six years of bloody fighting, first use of atomic bombs as well as genocide and cruelty beyond belief.[1]

Fear of Russian expansionism, of German recidivism, the inability of the European nations to find a European solution led inevitably to the USA leading the bailout. In 1947, the Marshall Plan, named after US Secretary of State George Marshall, gave surety in the form of grants and loans to a large number of European countries including Britain and Germany. Later, in 1947, following a breakdown in discussions in London between the political leaders of Russia, Britain, the US and France (Molotov, Bevan, Marshall and Bidault), France, Britain and the Benelux countries formed a defensive alliance, the Brussels Pact, in March, 1948.

Gradually, Europe did begin to move from instability towards a limited form of prosperity. Nobel laureate Günter Grass[2], still an outspoken critic of German government (in particular Angela Merkel's austerity measures in response to a worldwide failure of

---

[1] Bread supply, never rationed during the war, was restricted until the summer of 1948. The rationing of basic food like meat and sugar didn't end until 1954. Above all, despite the sacrifices made by millions of working class people both at home and abroad during the war, Britain remained, in Judt's words, "a deferential, class-divided society." **(6)**

[2] A poem by an 84-year-old Grass in the daily 'Süeddeutsche Zeitung' lambasted some of the major European powers, including Germany, for their austerity programmes saying that Greece, without whose spirit Europe would not have been conceived, has been "pilloried naked as a debtor". **(8)**

banking institutions), is paraphrased by Tony Judt as thinking that "Its (Germany's) citizens had vaulted with shocking ease from Hitler to consumerism" as its population disengaged from politics to build a shiny new future based on 'private accumulation'. **(7)**

Labour was returned to power in 1949 with Clement Attlee Prime Minister once again on a reduced majority gaining 46.1% of the popular vote and a narrow majority of 17 seats over the Conservatives (43.5%). Very quickly, a major international challenge presented itself in the form of Communist North Korea invading South Korea. Britain joined the US in supporting the United Nations resolution of condemnation and President Truman's offer of military aid to South Korea was immediately backed by the British fleet in the Pacific. China would join the war on the side of North Korea further inflaming an already difficult international situation. Although 78% of the population backed British involvement in a Gallup poll (at a time when national service had been extended from 18 months to 2 years) the Korean War, apart from stoking the Cold War fire, hindered post-war recovery by deflecting industry from exports and diverting spending needed for social reform to defence. Its effects were long lasting – it would not end until 1953.

Away from serious international affairs, 1946 saw a peak in cinema-going which continued into the fifties (in 1950, the average person went to the cinema 28 times per year). By 1956, this fell to the still respectable figure of 22 times a year, mostly to see American films.

Radio (or the wireless as it was known as back then) was in the ascendancy. The pilot episode of 'The Archers' was broadcast on 1 January, 1951 and a staggering 11.7 million listened to the account of Queen Elizabeth II's coronation on the radio with an estimated 20.4 million on TV either watching their own sets (mostly on 'hire purchase') or at neighbours, shops or in cinemas.

A historic date for the development of TV sci-fi came on 18th July, 1953 when the first episode of Nigel Kneale's six-part sci-fi drama 'The Quatermass Experiment' was screened. Kneale's dramatization capitalised on a post-war paranoia that would persist right through to the Cuban missile crisis and beyond.

Kneale also produced an adaptation of George Orwell's '1984' the following year which was broadcast live with orchestral backing and featured Peter Cushing in the lead role of Winston Smith. The drama provoked a House of Commons motion claiming it put householders in a state of alarm with particular criticism of the decision to broadcast it on a Sunday. Dr Who was still to come while 'Star Trek' followed in the grand tradition of sci-fi/ horror series like 'The Twilight Zone' and 'The Outer Limits' as well as films like 'It Came from Outer Space', and 'The Forbidden Planet'.

Large numbers of people regularly danced to the music of Billy Cotton, Henry Hall or Ted Heath, and around half a million people attended the 1948 Earls Court Motor Show over its 10-day duration. If people wanted to look much further afield, Fred Hoyle coined the term 'big bang' for the first time during a radio show on 'The Nature of the Universe'. All of this helped to take peoples' minds off the bad housing situation (notwithstanding that there was a commitment to do something about it), the continuing rationing of bread and clothes, and the shortage of fuel at a time when there was less travel by tram and more by car. Indeed, as a new decade dawned, there were roughly 2 million cars on the road. Particularly telling is the account of a Czech woman's impressions of London as she speaks of bombed-out ruins, post-war 'drabness, sloppily dressed English women, disappointing shops and an ambience that was overall 'worse than Prague'. **(9)**

Nor was there much to hearten people on the sporting front. The 1950 World Cup in Brazil was the first to which England accepted an invitation and a 1-0 defeat by the USA, a nation not renowned for soccer as opposed to its own brand of American football, would not be a major shock now but certainly was back then.[3] In the same year, the English cricket team suffered ignominy in its first defeat by the West Indies on their own soil.

That there was still much to do in terms of basic health care is illustrated by the tragic contraction of polio by Ian Dury, set to become the linguistically astute leader of the Blockheads, in an open-air swimming pool at Southend. In 1956, for the first time, a polio vaccine was made widely available (although it had been created in 1952), alas, too late for Dury.

Another major threat was presented by smoking, still seen as socially acceptable and even desirable. The Health Minister in the mid-fifties, Robin Turton, while accepting a probable link between smoking and lung cancer (a report was published in 1954) was neither prepared to personally give up smoking nor to countenance a public information campaign warning against the dangers of smoking. The prevailing orthodoxy was that it was up to individuals to decide (even if not readily provided with the full facts), and it was axiomatic that the government of the day would prefer to 'keep in' with the tobacco companies and continue to raise significant amounts of tax revenue from the nation's die-hard smokers.

A staggering number of newspapers were sold, according to available statistics to the extent of 18.6 million morning, 10.4 million evening and 31.7 million Sunday. This was a level of interest that would dwindle as we moved towards a new millennium but the scale of it was not lost on newspaper proprietors like Rupert Murdoch. Although the 'News of the World' has now been expunged, 55% of working-class people read it in 1952.

Agatha Christie's 'The Mouse Trap', based on a radio production, 'Three Blind Mice', opened on 25th November, 1952 at the Ambassador Theatre (until 23rd March, 1974) then moved to the larger St. Martin's Theatre, just next door, in the Cambridge Circus area of central London and is still running breaking all world records (and indeed touring the country for the first time) with the audience still sworn to secrecy about the resolution. Ian Fleming's durable creation James Bond made his fictional debut in April 1953 with 'Casino Royale', followed by 'Live and Let Die' in 1954 and 'Moonraker' in 1955.

The first popular music chart also appeared in the New Musical Express in 1953 and, before he came to prominence with 'Juke Box Jury', David Jacobs, in 1954, hosted a TV panel game 'Music! Music! Music!' described at the time as a 'musical battle of wits'.

By that time, the honeymoon period of the Conservative government was already ending with the citizens of Glasgow still complaining of rats, no proper place to deposit refuge or to do or hang their washing. A Swiss architect Le Corbusier's showpiece 'city in the sky', the 'unité d'habitation' was completed in the vicinity of Marseilles in 1952. This was a 20-storey block housing, 1600 workers and their families. Le Corbusier was invited to London to be presented with the Royal Gold Medal by the Royal Institute of

---

[3] Nearly as big a shock came four years later when West Germany defied the odds and defeated the all-conquering Hungarians in the World Cup Final in Berne. As Kynaston wryly remarks, "The German economic miracle was already under way, and this outcome was richly symbolic, especially after the recent British football humiliations (including a 7-3 defeat of England by Hungary). As yet, however, there was only the barest perception in the old country that we had won the war, but—for all the material easement—were losing the peace." **(10)**

British Architects. Multi-storey blocks and soulless housing estates would later face demolition, and the 'high rise' idea was to be brutally satirised, later in 1975, in J G Ballard's brilliant novel 'High Rise'.

1953 is demarcated as the year when people began to emerge from the scourge of austerity to spend more on food, especially meat, clothes and cars. The first Gaggia coffee machine also made its appearance in the Moka café in Soho's Frith Street (number 29), opened by film star Gina Lollobrigida. Books absorbed over a cup of foaming coffee might have included the poems of Dylan Thomas whose posthumous play, 'Under Milk Wood', was premiered on the BBC Third Programme on 25th January, 1954 with up and coming actor, Richard Burton, playing Thomas's parts. Or perhaps Kingsley Amis's first novel, 'Lucky Jim', was the book of choice. The most iconic work to emerge in 1954 was 'The Fellowship of the Ring', the first volume of J.R.R. Tolkien's 'The Lord of the Rings' trilogy. And it was no sleeping giant. Before the year was out, the second volume, 'The Two Towers', was published with equal commercial success. There were many popular comics around for those too young to visit coffee shops and on the fantasy football front, Roy Race made his debut for Melchester Rovers as 'Roy of the Rovers' in the 'Tiger' boys' comic.

Leading entertainers of the day included Max Bygraves, Eddie Calvert, Tony Hancock (whose 'Half Hour' would appear on TV for the first time in 1956), Michael Redgrave, Beryl Reid and Terry Thomas. The above list, with the possible exception of Hancock, hardly boded well for countercultural developments in the 'swinging sixties' but it should not be forgotten that the popular appeal of mainstream middle of the road entertainers and 'easy listening' artists like Des O'Connor and Engelbert Humperdinck (who famously kept The Beatles 'Strawberry Fields Forever/ Penny Lane' single from reaching the top of his chart with his 'Release Me' record) would continue into the sixties.

Scripted by Ray Galton, Hancock brilliantly portrayed an irascible middle-aged bachelor who lived at 23 Railway Cuttings, East Cheam whose fantasy world often collided with reality, and who thrived on febrile and sardonic self-pity with top comedians like Sid James and Kenneth Williams providing perfect 'foils'. Hancock had a particularly expressive face that the camera angles took full advantage of with close-up 'full facials'. His most famous episodes are probably 'The Blood Donor' and 'The Bed Sitter', and these drew massive viewing figures.[4]

'Light entertainment' was also well served by game shows like 'Take Your Pick' presented by New Zealander, Michael Miles, and 'Double Your Money' presented by Hughie Green; real-life dramas like 'Dixon of Dock Green' and variety shows like 'Sunday Night at the London Palladium'. Amidst this escapism, though there was still a demand for war films with 'The Dam Busters' starring Michael Redgrave and Richard Todd in 1954, stoking the dying embers of nostalgia, and Kenneth More portraying war hero Douglas Bader in 'Reach for the Sky' two years later. Indeed, war films have never gone out of popularity.

While the debate about selective education continued to rage, Mike Jagger started his secondary education at Dartford Grammar School on 15th September, 1954, having successfully passed his '11-plus' examination. His friend, Keith Richards, was consigned to the technical school in Dartford. That same week London's first purpose-built comprehensive school, Kidbrooke, was opened.

---

[4] Sadly, Hancock, in real life disenchanted with his lot, and increasingly frustrated at his inability to further his career in film and other television, took his own life in 1968.

Meanwhile, John Lennon was picking up the 'lingo' of Bluebottle, Neddie Seagoon, Eccles et al from listening to 'The Goons' (Spike Milligan, Michael Bentine, Harry Secombe and Peter Sellars) which took sideways swipes at the church, army, politicians and the establishment. 'The Goons' was the first broadcast on the long extinct London Home Service radio station, and this zany, satirical show was especially relevant for The Beatles and hosts of other '60s' artistes turned onto an alternative form of comedy that would find ultimate expression in the BBC series, 'Monty Python's Flying Circus'.

Escaping into films, stage, TV, radio and literature may have provided a temporary distraction for some but many took extreme measures to escape from the grim reality of working life, emigrating to seek out better lives in Australia, Canada and America. The challenge of providing decent sized houses, inside toilets, baths or a wage sufficient to provide anything beyond modest living let alone a refrigerator or a car (which were still very much the preserve of the upper or middle classes) meant progress was frustratingly slow for a generation who had sacrificed so much during wartime.

Nor should another group be forgotten: the politically disenchanted 'white settlers' who in the ten years between 1945 and 1955 increased the white population of Northern and Southern Rhodesia dramatically. These were the people that Dominic Sandbrook refers to as "middle or upper-middle class Britons who found life in Attlee's austere new world intolerable." **(11)**

David Kynaston describes in detail in his book, 'Austerity Britain 1945-1951', life in the immediate post-war period drawing on recollections and diaries of a spectrum of citizens as well as surveys, especially the so-called Mass-Observation national interviews. It is a bleak picture. Three-quarter of a million homes destroyed or damaged, debt, dislocation and the legacy of Victorian slums among the properties that were still standing.

Racism was still rampant and 'no coloured' signs were still prevalent on the windows of rooms to let in the 1950s. A variation on this often seen in London was 'No Blacks, No Irish'.

Immigrants were often associated with the damp and dingy conditions they lived in but, of course, the decline and deprivation were already there before they arrived. Often, the rent for immigrants was not cheap, as in Notting Hill where one effect of the 1957 Rent Act was to facilitate unscrupulous landlords to evict standing tenants and replace them in rooms now containing some basic furniture at higher rents. Clichéd, stereotypical descriptions of West Indians as flashy, party-loving sexual predators (a perception perhaps reinforced by the dearth of West Indian women compared to men) were, of course, unfounded but racial tension was simmering. During the summer of 1958, things boiled over in the St Ann's area of Nottingham and also in North Kensington in what became known as the Notting Hill riots. Although some chose to return to their native land, the riots had a strangely galvanising effect on many West Indians with the formation of vigilante groups but more positively with an increased sense of community and commonality, and the instigation of the first carnival in St Pancras Town Hall in 1959, now known as the world famous Notting Hill carnival. Anyone wandering to the Portobello market nowadays would be amazed at the 'melting pot' of food and music, and how natural and vibrant it all seems.

The political response was both positive and negative with the foundation of the Institute for Race Relations in 1958, and a report by James Wickenden on 'Colour in Britain' which while well-intentioned, unfortunately, came to the misguided conclusion that the ultimate solution was in restriction rather than integration which inadvertently added fuel to the fire that was to manifest itself in the openly racist expostulations of the likes of Enoch Powell in the following decade.

A film was also made in 1959 called 'Sapphire' that escapes the often-lashing tongue of the Halliwell film guide to gain a respectable review. It is summarised as "Scotland Yard solves the murder of a black music student" with praise for its "strong race angle" (12)The film was set in Notting Hill in response to the recent riots and showed the West Indian community in a positive light. Colin MacInnes' trilogy of novels, 'City of Spades', 'Absolute Beginners', and 'Mr Love and Justice', published between 1957 and 1960, took a rather idealistic view of events in a changing, multi-racial society where immigrants, Vespa scooters, angry young men, coffee bars and record shops were to be celebrated as harbingers of diversity and innovation. MacInnes goes on to describe black immigrants as 'the new English' in his 1961 book, 'England, Half English'.

A very significant film appeared in 1967: 'Look Who's Coming to Dinner?' a 'comedy' (with not many laughs) characterised by the slick dialogue between the main protagonists, Sidney Poitier, Spencer Tracey and Katharine Hepburn. When it is revealed that Poitier is planning to get married to a white girl played by Katharine Houghton, the Draytons' long-serving black maid, Tilly, predicts that all hell will break loose. In a heart to heart with his prospective father-in-law, Poitier comes out with the brilliant line, "You can do the watusi, I am the watusi." Tracey replies, "Have you given any thought to the problems your children will have?" Poitier gets the last word, "Everyone will be Presidents of the USA. No, that's a bit optimistic. I'd settle for Secretaries of State. You think of yourself as a coloured man, I think of myself as a man." Eventually, Mr Drayton gives his blessing but the celebration is subdued given his warning that "100 million people in this country will be shocked, offended and appalled."

Of course, as a seafaring nation, Great Britain was, in fact, a multi-cultural society for a long time before the Second World War with many next generations of black and Asian people qualifying as British citizens, and not just because of Commonwealth status as Crown subjects under the terms of the 1948 British Nationality Act.

A landmark event, depicted in the opening ceremony to the 2012 London Olympic Games, was the arrival of S.S. Empire Windrush at Tilbury Docks on 23rd June, 1948 (to be followed by the S.S. Orbita and the S.S. Georgic) with its 492 fare paying Caribbean passengers and 18 stowaways soon to be sheltered on Clapham Common before visiting the Brixton labour exchange to find gainful employment. This wave of mostly Jamaican immigrants, many of them ex-servicemen, paid £24 a head for the privilege. The incomers occupied the semi-derelict streets of Notting Hill and Harlesden, and by 1954, an estimated 10,000 people from the West Indies had settled in big cities like London, Birmingham and Bristol. That was nothing compared to the population explosion over the ensuing four years by which time the number had risen to 125,000 and the immigrants became a scapegoat for the far right as nationwide unemployment reached half a million (that would be a perfectly acceptable figure to many economists nowadays!) as opportunistic fascists such as Oswald Mosley exploited any opportunity to set race against race and render division within the people. Fortunately, Oswald Mosley's 'Keep Britain White' movement was not endorsed by the electorate in his quest for the parliamentary seat of North Kensington in the 1959 general election where he lost his deposit.

In 1956, London Transport began to recruit staff for the buses and tube trains from, first of all, Barbados, and then Jamaica and Trinidad, with assistance with travel fares and accommodation provided. An estimated 4,500 Barbadians were to make the journey between 1955 and 1961 to take up low-skilled, low paid jobs mostly in various industries including hospitals, hotels, restaurants and the railways. The population impact on places like London and Birmingham was significant especially in the latter where cheap labour was needed for manufacturing companies. It was no secret that restrictions on immigration would come into force and, indeed, in 1962, the Commonwealth Immigrants Act did set strict controls with preference given to skilled workers.

Of course, The Beatles could not understand or accept racism in any way, shape or form, nor could the multitude of 'beat' groups so inspired by black blues and soul. With the release of director Ron Howard's film 'The Beatles: Eight Days a Week: The Touring Years', The Big Issue magazine was not alone in taking the opportunity to front their early September, 2016 issue with *'Meet The Beatles: Back Better Than Ever Again!'* and remind us that the film "shows the unsung role they played politically in America by insisting on the desegregation of concert venues in the South during their US tours" **(13)**Quoting Larry Kane, newsman and Beatles author: "They changed a lot of things – fashion, the music industry, how women expressed themselves in public, and they did have a big impact on segregation. They couldn't believe someone would be banned from certain seating areas because their skin had a different colour. They fought that and they won." **(14)**

Although the press was largely biased towards the Conservative party, Eric Blair AKA George Orwell nailed his political colours to the mast following the publication of '1984' in 1949. The story, he said, "is NOT intended as an attack on Socialism or the British Labour Party (of which I am a supporter) but as a show-up of the perversions to which a centralised economy is liable and which have already been partly realised in Communism and Fascism."[5]

In 'Family Britain', the second of four projected books David Kynaston covers the period 1951 to 1957. Kynaston's biographical approach drawing on eyewitness accounts is brilliantly demonstrated in his section on the Festival of Britain and includes an account by a young Welsh poet named Dylan Thomas who waxes eloquently in a style that was uniquely his. Ray Davies of the Kinks was six years old at the time when he famously asked his dad what all the fuss was about to be greeted with the reply, "It's the future."

---

[5] In Thomas Pynchon's introduction to the 2003 edition of '1984', he explores the links between Orwell's political persuasions, and the themes and characters in his epic book. "Orwell, being a perpetual dissident, must have been delighted to help the (Labour) party confront its contradictions, notably those arising from its wartime acquiescence to, and participation in, a repressive, Tory-led government. Once having enjoyed and exerted that sort of power, how likely would Labour be to choose not to extend its scope, rather than stick to the ideals of its founders, and go back to fighting on the side of the oppressed? Project this will to power four decades into the future, and you could easily end up with Ingsoc, Oceania and Big Brother", and "Nearly the whole of the English left has been driven to accept the Russian regime as 'Socialist', while silently recognising that its spirit and practice are quite alien... we recognise this 'sort of schizophrenic manner of thinking' as a source for the idea of 'doublethink' so central to the book". **(15)**Additionally, I recommend Orwell's 'The Lion and the Unicorn', a readable collection of essays on 'socialism and the English genius' with a detailed introduction by Bernard Crick. **(16)** Of course, the Stalinist gulags were also beginning to exercise people's minds especially that of Alexander Solzhenitsyn and his harrowing short novel, 'One Day in the Life of Ivan Denisovich' with its depiction of life in a Siberian labour camp first published in the UK in 1963.

In 1951, in an incredulous 'volte-face' by the British electorate, Winston Churchill once again found himself Prime Minister, ironically, the same year that President Truman officially ended World War II by signing a peace treaty with Japan. This outcome might have been avoided if the Liberal Party had fielded more candidates (back then their votes tended to go to the Tories) but in the end, the electorate were seduced by a small majority to opt for what was touted as 'progressive Conservativism', as incongruous a concept as 'New Labour'. Instead of being accorded recognition for the progress made under difficult circumstances the Labour Party flew too close to the Sun of the 'hard times' (to paraphrase Dickens) of post-war reconstruction. A Gallup Poll revealed the deep-rooted prejudice within some of the British electorates with patronising statements like "bringing the working classes power they are not fitted to use". As Kynaston puts it, "there lingered in many middle-class breasts a visceral satisfaction that Britain had at last expelled its Socialist rulers." **(17)**

Meanwhile, Churchill showed how out of touch he was when expressing the thought that the working class food ration for a week was actually for a day! Harold Macmillan was appointed Minister of Housing whose primary task was to deliver the pledged 300,000 new houses a year in the Conservative party's manifesto. What this meant in practice was smaller houses with virtually no storage space, demonstrating once again the impotence of Government to look after, at the most basic level, the very people who entrusted them with power in the first place.[6] The 'returning war heroes' discovered how vacuous an expression that really was.

While the Conservative government was denationalising industries that were previously state-controlled like steel and road haulage, Anthony Crosland's 'The Transition from Capitalism' identified ways of moving towards a classless society A three-pronged plan was proposed: to fiscally attack the skewered ownership of wealth and 'the maldistribution of property'; to reform education to stop a hierarchical school system; to transform the psychology of industrial relations to afford the working classes 'social status', rights and the ability to participate without the fear of class hostility. The age-old dichotomy evident in 1952, with the Tories concerned with diminishing public expenditure, and Labour advocating greater social and economic equality, still remains, although it has blurred at the edges through the Blair, Brown and Milliband eras of 'New Labour', and the so-called 'caring Conservatism' of the modern Conservative party.

With the welfare state barely out of its nappies, a Conservative economist called Colin Clark wrote an essay entitled 'Welfare and Taxation' in which he referred to a moral and economic imperative to reduce taxation, and reduce dependence on a centralised provision of social services which, he argued, should be the responsibility of

---

[6] A 1951 housing census in England and Wales revealed that 1.9 million people had three rooms or less, 4.8 million had no fixed bath, and 2.8 million shared a lavatory. There were still 2½ million houses that were 100 years old or more. Regional variations were also startling. A Glasgow 1957 census revealed that 50.8% of houses had only 1 or 2 rooms compared with 5.5% in greater London. New towns would eventually emerge but hearts were ripped out of city centres as residents were decanted, sometimes reluctantly, into the suburbs. There has been a steady reversal of town planning decisions made in the 1950s to the 1970s as soul-less multi-storey blocks (first built in Liverpool and known as 'multis'), and housing schemes with no community focus are hauled down, town centres and riversides redeveloped. If only the politicians of the time had listened to visionaries like Michael Young as he argued against 'forcing them (people) to move to housing estates on the outskirts' in his 1952 report 'For Richer or Poorer', advocating instead houses with gardens, not flats. Most people were, of course, so desperate to get away from the squalor they had endured through centuries of misrule that they would have moved anywhere with basic facilities.

local Councils and voluntary organisations. This view would find a prescient echo in the 'nanny state' arguments of Future Conservative politicians brought to ultimate expression by Prime Minister Margaret Thatcher. David Cameron would later talk of a 'big society' approach and vacuously claim that 'we are all in it together'. 'Welfare and Taxation' was swiftly followed by essays by the One Nation Conservative pressure group entitled 'Change is Our Ally' in which the benefits of free-market competition were espoused. One of the authors was Enoch Powell who would gain notoriety with his 'rivers of blood' speech satirised by The Beatles in their 'Get Back' record in 1968. This free market dogma has endured to this day with Margaret Thatcher and her cabinet adopting the fringe economics of monetarism advocated by Milton Friedman, and the Chicago School of Economics and successive 'new Labour' and Conservative/ Liberal Democrat 'coalition' governments doing little to question this approach.

As a riposte to one nation Conservatism in 1956, Anthony Crosland wrote a paper called 'The Future of Socialism' which has become the 'blueprint' for New Labour and was republished in 2006 with a foreword by the Chancellor of the Exchequer of the time, Gordon Brown. In it, a number of principles were espoused: high social expenditure, curbs on unfettered 'laissez-faire' capitalism; state schools and hospitals the equal of privately funded provisions, and comprehensive secondary school education; less puritanism and more social liberalism; a 'canny' approach to nationalisation with regard to economic consequences; more industrial democracy and finally, the redistribution of wealth through the fiscal system.

# Chapter Two
## "You've Never Had It So Good"

**"At the end of 1955, Britain went through a period of sudden dramatic change: commercial television made its debut, the Angry Young Men suddenly filled the newspapers and radio waves, The Suez crisis marked the end of Empire and rock 'n' roll reached Britain." (18)**

1955 was the start of a 'consumer boom'. Rationing had ended in 1954. It would be two years though before the Prime Minister of the day, Harold Macmillan, would be confident enough to pronounce that "most of our people have never had it so good." According to Tony Judt, it would be "by the end of the 1950s, the European economy was beginning to feel the full commercial impact of the baby boom." Most of this commercial impact is self-evident but a less obvious fact that emerged around 1957 was that, for the first time, young people started buying things for themselves and started to become consumers in their own right." **(19)**

In 1955, also, there was another election as Churchill abdicated on health grounds to be succeeded by Anthony Eden, already a knight of the realm. 21 was the minimum voting age and the turnout was a disappointing one for the times: 76%, down from 82% in 1951! Shirley Catin (later Williams) said during the election campaign, "Out of the 600 Tory candidates, 80 went to Eton and 80% went to public schools." One might be justified in asking oneself just how much have changed in the ensuing period!

Eden's tenancy of 10 Downing Street didn't last long, mired by his involvement in the Suez crisis in 1956, and forced into a humiliating climb down on an invasion of Egypt in a cack-handed attempt to depose ruling President Nasser in the face of opposition from the American President Dwight Eisenhower. The implications of the Suez crisis were manifold as Israel saw its own interests best protected by aligning with the USA and Nasser's reputation was enhanced by his successful resistance of attack by two colonial powers, Britain and France. Consequently, Nasser's influence on Arab nationalists increased and, finally, the ramifications of the opposition of Washington, the seat of American government, to Britain and France putting their own interests above those of the western alliance as a whole at a time when its main concern was the Soviet occupation of Hungary was a hard pill to swallow for the British government. Further, because Russia, led by Nikita Khrushchev, by now into his fourth year as Stalin's successor had managed to stay on the sidelines and oversee a desirable outcome to the Suez crisis, the divisive Cold War chill was inadvertently exported deep into the Middle East and Africa. Despite public dismay in the UK, when the details of the conspiracy against President Nasser were revealed and the humiliation became clear, the Conservative party went on to win the general election of 1959 under the leadership of Harold Macmillan.

Tony Judt asserted, "The first lesson of Suez was that Britain could no longer maintain a global colonial presence." Having been shown to lack the economic or military capability to sustain 'the days of Empire' the inevitability of a rise in demands by the colonies to become independent was palpable and increased levels of de-colonisation irresistible. **(20)**

The response of the daily newspapers to the Suez crisis is interesting. The Daily Sketch with a circulation of around 70,000 put on a 'survival or ruin' spin and led with 'IT'S ON – AND EDEN STICKS TO HIS GUNS!' The Telegraph, Express and Financial Times, by and large, went with this approach but The Mail and The Times were not so jingoistic. The Mail with a circulation nearer 280,000 proclaimed 'EDEN's WAR – NO! NO! NO!' and The Spectator and The Economist took a similar line. The Observer newspaper's view was that the folly of attacking Nasser and Egypt was to "endanger the American alliance and NATO, split the Commonwealth, flout the UN, shock and overwhelm the majority of world opinion, and dishonour the name of Britain." Bertrand Russell, in a letter to The Guardian, wrote of "the criminal lunacy of the British and French governments' actions fills me with deep shame for my country," while Peter Ustinov and Michael Foot also condemned the action, Foot describing it in The Tribune as an act of "brutal contempt" comparable to "Chamberlain presenting Hitler's terms to the Czechs in 1938." A 'Stop the War' rally in Trafalgar Square had as its slogan "LAW NOT WAR". The Mirror adopted the rather sensationalist view that "Once the British bombs fell on Egypt, the fate of Hungary was sealed" (a reference to Russian tanks rolling into Budapest). There is an element of truth in this as there is little doubt that Khrushchev, despite his '(not so) secret speech' to the Congress of the Soviet Union's Communist Party in which he condemned certain acts authorised by his predecessor, Josef Stalin, would have acted anyway but Suez did provide him with a welcome distraction. It is difficult to take the moral high ground if you, yourself, are an aggressor. An interesting footnote to the Soviet invasion of Hungary was the outbreak of a fight between players that spilled into the crowd during a water polo match between the two countries at the 1956 Melbourne Olympic Games.

At home, trade union membership was at twice the level it is today, at around 12 million. Public opinion was generally favourable. 67% of responses to a 1957 Gallup poll thought that trade unions were a good thing. The 1955 Gallup responses also suggested that professional workers like teachers and engineers were paid too little, and lawyers and civil servants too much.

The 1955 gathering of the six member states of the European Coal and Steel Community (formed in 1951) at the Messina Conference set up the parameters for the inception of a European Economic Community on 1 January, 1958. There were plenty of new consumers as the UK population rose substantially by 17% between 1950 and 1970. The Treaty of Rome was signed on 25th March, 1957 and also established an atomic energy authority (Euratom) but it would not be until 1973 that the UK would join. In the interim period, a European Free Trade Association of seven countries (later to be expanded to ten) including the UK was set up in Stockholm. In November, 1959, Prime Minister Macmillan had applied to join the EEC in July, 1961, and Britain had tried again in 1963 and yet again, in 1967 but was rejected on each occasion.

Ruth Ellis was hanged for murder on 13th July, 1955 at Holloway Prison and within days, a ghoulish effigy of her was standing in Blackpool's Chamber of Horrors. On 16 February, 1956, the House of Commons voted for an experimental suspension of the death penalty. Women's lib and the sexual liberation of the '60s were still a long way off. According to 'Woman's Own' magazine, a woman's place was at home. How un-hip and un-liberated it all was, is demonstrated by articles such as 'How to Dress to Please Men' series in another 1950s women's magazine while the Women's institute provided assistance with the development of the art of housewifery. In addition to a women's institute, there was also a Good Housekeeping Institute. Cleaning, washing, ironing, cooking (also being a good hostess) were all part of many 1950s women's remits. Advertising was all about getting the house sparkling clean, the most effective washing powders and kitchen gadgets, and there was a distinct whiff of the 'pipe and slippers' mentality.

The giveaway budget of Chancellor of the Exchequer Derick Heathcoat Amory had doubtless been a factor in Harold MacMillan's electoral success in 1959. Notwithstanding MacMillan's commitment to 'you've never had it so good' expansionist economics, there is no getting away from the fact that such policies inevitably produce inflationary pressures, and threaten the balance of payments and the stability of pounds sterling. With imports increasing by 10% and exports by only 4% in 1959, the trade gap widened. Amory was dissuaded by his old friend MacMillan from resigning but trouble was on the way with MacMillan's micromanaged meddling causing serious economic problems as the 1960s got under way.

The first 45 revolutions per minute single vinyl record had been released by RCA in 1949. Each musical genre had its own colour of vinyl, and because the first '45' was a country record ('Texarkana Baby' by Eddy Arnold) it was pressed on green vinyl. Among the other colours used were black for 'popular', red for classical and, in keeping with a time when racial stereotyping and prejudice were still rife, orange for 'race' records, basically rhythm and blues and gospel music. Previously records had been released on noisy, brittle Bakelite, which was a synthetic plastic compound named after the chemist Leo Baekeland who developed the product in 1907, and then came an equally noisy and brittle format, shellac, which contained a resin secreted by Asian lac tree insects, which fell into short supply when the Japanese invaded Malysia during World War Two.

V-discs were produced on 12" vinyl 78 R.P.M. records between 1943 and 1949, at first specifically ro raise the morale of American servicemen with big band music and jazz concerts by artists such as Louis Armstrong and Glenn Miller. RCA also developed records which rotated at 33 R.P.M. featuring artists such as Duke Ellington and Frank Sinatra, which were restricted at first to 6½ minutes per side then extended to 22½ minutes to accommodate classical music. The first such album to be released on the Columbia Masterworks label ('non-breakable microgroove LP') was 'Mendelssohn's Concerto in E minor for Violin and Orchestra' in 1948. Within a year a hundred more titles followed, including 'Frank Sinatra Sings'.

The rise in popularity of popular music or 'pop' can be traced from the 1956 film 'Rock Around the Clock' starring Bill Haley and The Platters, first aired in Britain in September, 1956, which although paling in comparison to Elvis Presley's swaggering 'Jailhouse Rock', captured the imagination of young people throughout the country, especially Haley's 45 hit that gave its name to the film. Music journalist Nick Johnstone describes 1956 as the 'ground zero' year for pop and rock, the year in which "popular music had its greatest musical upheaval, revolution and transformation." **(21)**[7]

The advent of 'teddy boys', or 'Edwardians' as they were then known, can be traced back even earlier, to 1954. The activities of this social grouping were fuelled by films like 'Rebel without a Cause' starring James Dean and 'The Wild One' starring Marlon Brando. The Teds' reaction to the 'Rock Around the Clock' film was hormonal with cinema seats ripped, shop windows smashed with dancing in cinema aisles and even streets! The soundtrack to the times was provided by Haley, Elvis Presley, Lonnie

---

[7] Johnstone also identifies his 5 'holy grails' of 1956: Elvis Presley's 'Heartbreak Hotel', Little Richard's 'Tutti Frutti'; CB; Chuck Berry's 'Roll Over Beethoven'; Janis Martin's 'Drugstore Rock and Roll' and the 'Rock Around the Clock' film.

Donegan (who came up through the trad jazz scene and was credited as the originator of 'skiffle' music, so influential on a nascent John Lennon and his Quarrymen in Liverpool), Tommy Steele, Gene Vincent, Eddie Cochran and many others documented in the next chapter. This was also the era of Levi jeans first sold in Paris in 1963, motorbikes, Coca Cola, beehive hairstyles (or ponytails if you were a 'teddy girl') and jukeboxes.

So how are the post-war years to be summed up so far? Barry Miles provides an absorbing insight into the microcosm that was London, and Soho in particular, a city that proved to be the magnet for runaways and wannabe rock stars as the 1960s approached. He begins his account with an all-night VJ day party on the rooftop bar of the Gargoyle Club at 69 Dean Street, Soho, a Bohemian mecca for the 'bright young things' who had inhabited its corridors in the years before the war. Dylan Thomas, Francis Bacon, Antonia Fraser and Lucian Freud counted themselves as members and customers but, at 4 guineas a head, it was a pretty exclusive place. Anyone walking around the streets of Soho and visiting its pubs or cafes, as I certainly do whenever in London, will find themselves steeped in literary, comedic and musical history: for instance, the Grafton Arms (now the Stratton Arms) where Harry Secombe, Michael Bentine and Spike Milligan met Peter Sellers, and hatched the idea for a radio show originally known as 'Crazy People' but, on 22 June, 1952, changed to 'The Goon Show'. As Miles reminds us, "This anarchic, surrealist and very British Humour has permeated British comedy ever since." **(22)**Then there is Ronnie Scott's jazz club, still there today on Frith Street but originally on Gerrard Street. The cultural oasis that is Soho is a great relief from the shoulder-to-shoulder mass consumerism of Oxford Street just minutes away. And the bookshops! Charing Cross Road into Shaftesbury Avenue, some remain as if caught in a time warp but it was David Archer's bookshop at 34 Greek Street that would provide a refuge for down at heel writers and enthusiastic browsers. Archer's reputed attitude to business reminds me of the character in one of Agatha Christie's books, 'Murder is Easy', published in the year the Second World War started, Mr Ellsworthy who says, "I love my bits and pieces, you know, hate to sell them."

The sign that the great damage inflicted by the war was at last beginning to recede lies in the statistic that there was less demand for allotments by 1956 as more food was available, more people had jobs, credit (the 'never never') was easier to obtain (even mail order was beginning to take off) with young earners in particular having more spending power. Advertising was also beginning to take off not only on TV (remember 'snap, crackle and pop'?) but also in popular magazines like 'Homes and Gardens' and 'Woman'. The products that started to appear are still household names: for Do It Yourself cue Dulux paint, and Black and Decker drills. Every householder's dream was a new kitchen with a brand new Kenwood Chef food mixer, some cookery books, Rice Krispies for breakfast, Birds Eye fish fingers for tea and Nescafé coffee – or Maxwell House (branded as 'America's favourite). This was a time that marked the advent of the 'celebrity chef' as Johnny and Fanny Craddock filled out the Albert Hall. Off-licence sales increased, as more people started to drink wine and beer at home with a corresponding drop in pub sales. To get around, there was the Mini car, to get away, caravans. For the fashion conscious, Mary Quant's bazaar opened on the King's Road in 1955. It is a sure sign that consumerism is on the rise then Marks and Spencer's star also starts to ascend!

All was not cosy or comfortable though. This was the age of the 'angry young men' who would congregate in David Archer's bookshop and in Better books on the Charing Cross Road. These counted among their number John Osborne who was living in a houseboat on the Thames when his play 'Look Back in Anger' caught the eye of the English Stage Company's artistic director George Devine. 'Look Back in Anger' followed Arthur Miller's 'The Crucible' onto the stage of the Royal Court Theatre in Sloan Square on 8 May, 1956. Despite initial critical reviews, BBC TV, with a 20-minute excerpt and Granada with a screening of the entire play, helped to raise its profile, and eventually, it came to be regarded rather differently.

Kingsley Amis was another considered an 'angry young man'. His 'Lucky Jim' was first published in 1954 and has been re-printed many times, and was also made into a film in 1957 with Ian Carmichael in the starring role. 'Lucky Jim' tells the story of Jimmy Dixon, a social misfit, accident-prone young lecturer in medieval history at a provincial university. "Above all, 'Lucky Jim' was controversial. For many conservative literary figures, it seemed to encapsulate, not only the new lower-middle class challenge to Modernist orthodoxy, but also the degrading effects of the post-war welfare state," comments Dominic Sandbrook. **(23)**

The right wing reaction was venomous showing the deeply entrenched attitudes existing within certain members of the establishment. An extreme example of this was in a letter written on Christmas Day, 1954 to The Sunday Times by English playwright and author Somerset Maugham, who was clearly not full of Christmas spirit when he complained about young students with "no manners" who "scamp it" and "drink too much beer", calling them "mean, malicious, envious" and "scum". Maugham obviously felt that this new generation of University undergraduates would not only undermine the establishment but society itself and looked forward to them sinking back "into the modest class from which they emerged," It deeply troubled him that these young people would go on to become schoolmasters or journalists or, perish the thought, "go into Parliament to become Cabinet Ministers and rule the country."

Colin Wilson was the third member of the 'angry young men' (although there were more depending on whose account you read). Wilson slept in Hampstead Heath in a tent and spent his day writing in the British Museum. Positive reviews of his book 'The Outsider' by the likes of Philip Toynbee for The Observer gave him overnight fame which was probably the worst thing to happen as he already had a well-developed ego (with delusions of grandeur) as was graphically revealed when the parents of his girlfriend, Joy Stewart, burst into his flat upset at discovering one of Wilson's 'pornographic' diaries. Wilson, in an attempt, to 'come clean' handed over his diaries to The Daily Mail and soon the world would know that he had written, "The day must come when I'm hailed as a major prophet" and "I am the major literary genius of our century". **(24)**

Unrest could also manifest itself in the aspirations of working class people. Henry Phelps-Brown wrote a definitive book, at that time, called 'The Origins of Trade Union Power' in which he acknowledged the self-control of trade union activists in what amounted to a moratorium on pay claims between 1948 and 1950. This did not continue into the 1950s, a decade in which, while there were no major strikes there was an increased incidence of unofficial ones.

The unions' steadily worsening relationship with the Conservative government saw a steady rise in lost working days, and meteoric rise in 'wildcat' strikes particularly between 1955 and the end of the decade, lasting right into the next decade. The Ford car plant in Dagenham became a hotbed of strike activity, with over two hundred stoppages in just two years culminating a decade later, in 1968, in industrial action by women claiming equal treatment with men, so brilliantly depicted in the film 'Made in Dagenham'. More militant union leaders rose up including Frank Cousins, another 'angry man' with a cause, who became General Secretary of the Transport and General Workers' Union in May, 1956. His keynote message might succinctly read something like this "While prices rise, wages must rise with them. Wage increases that result from rising output are the worker's share of the extra wealth they are helping to create. We are not prepared to stand still while the government continually hands out largesses to those more favourably placed."

A few months later, on 17 October, the first nuclear reactor to feed power into the National Grid opened at Calder Hall, Windscale in Northumbria and Cousins was an implacable opponent of Britain entering the 'atomic age'. He had other immediate priorities though, and a fight on his hands with the management of the British Midland Company who had sacked 6,000 workers without warning and put countless others on reduced working weeks. The Longbridge plant was the worst affected and although strike action did not succeed in reversing the changes, management did agree that compensation needed to be provided to sacked workers and consultation entered into before any more redundancies could be contemplated.

John and Roy Boulting, whose films included 'Brighton Rock' and 'Lucky Jim', reunited the cast of their 'Private's Progress' film and made 'I'm Alright, Jack' starring Peter Sellars as shop steward Fred Kite and Ian Carmichael as the naïve nephew of the boss of an arms factory who uncovers a fraud, and is caught up in a world of disgruntled workers described by personnel officer Major Hitchcock (Terry Thomas) as 'rotters' and 'stinkers'. The film contains the classic line by the time and motion inspector (played by John Le Mesurier): "The natural rhythm of the British worker is neither natural, rhythmic or much to do with work." The world that is the subject of pastiche is one of cynical self-seeking degeneracy. Interestingly, the Boultings were not members of the Labour Party as is often thought but were actually members of the Liberal Party.[8] Another film 'The Angry Silence' with David Attenborough playing a determined worker who is persecuted by his old friends on the shop floor for not participating in an unofficial strike, was predictably praised by the Conservative right and lambasted by supporters of the unions like 'The Daily Worker'.

---

[8] They once described Big Business and Organised Labour as 'two sacred cows' with both 'deep in an organised conspiracy against the individual—to force us to accept certain things for what they are not. (14th August, 1959)

# Chapter Three
## "Context Is Everything"

This was the period in which four young lads from Liverpool assumed a collective identity as The Beatles and would rise higher than any in popular music are ever likely to do. The 1950s shaped their culture, their politics and most of all, their music.

John Lennon was born on 9th October, 1940. Recounting his childhood days in 'The Beatles Anthology', he says: "We all knew America. All those movies: whether it was Disneyland or Doris Day, Rock Hudson, James Dean or Marilyn (Monroe). Everything was American: Coco-Cola, Heinz ketchup. The music was mainly American before rock 'n' roll. We still had our own artists but the big artists were American." **(25)** Lennon's main musical inspirations were Carl Perkins, Elvis Presley, Buddy Holly ("He could play and sing at the same time."), Jerry Lee Lewis, Chuck Berry ("a rock poet – we all owe a lot to him including Dylan"), Eddie Cochran, Gene Vincent and Little Richard. **(26)**

Paul McCartney was born on 18th June, 1942. On 6th July, 1957, John heard Paul play 'Whole Lotta Shakin' Goin' On' and 'Twenty Flight Rock' with his guitar upside down, and his whole world changed as history was about to be made. Paul cites Bill Haley, Elvis (but not after he left the army), Chuck Berry, Eddie Cochran and Buddy Holly as major influences but has always had eclectic, explorative tastes.

George Harrison was born on 25th February, 1943. In The Beatles Anthology, he acknowledges the influence of "the crap music that we hated", the schmaltzy and the novelty on "the comic aspect of our songs like the middle of 'Yellow Submarine" **(27)**In saying this, Harrison makes an important point, that you cannot divorce yourself from your formative years and the influence they have on you in later life. The first rock 'n' roll record he ever heard was Fats Domino's 'I'm in Love Again' and he remembers Ray Charles' 'What'd I Say' as one of the best. Harrison says that the music of Elvis, Little Richard and Buddy Holly endured as his favourite rock 'n' roll music.)**(28)**. He recalls going to the Liverpool Empire in 1956 to see Lonnie Donegan ("a big hero"), Danny and the Juniors, and The Crew Cuts. Later, he saw Eddie Cochran play his Gretsch guitar and George's destiny too was sealed.

Richard Starkey AKA Ringo Starr was born on 7th July, 1940. The first record he remembers hearing was Gene Autry's 'South of the Border'. Aged 14, he bought three records: The Four Aces 'Love is a Many Splendoured Thing', Eddie Calvert's 'Oh Mein Papa' and David Whitfield's 'Mama'. "The Four Aces still holds up," he says) **(29)**. Ringo developed a love of country music and was a Johnny Ray fan, and in 1956, his idols were Frankie Laine and Bill Haley. Like many other budding musicians, the 'Rock Around the Clock' film made a big impact on him and he cut his drumming teeth on old-time records revisited on his 1970 'Sentimental Journey' album. He discovered the blues (Lightnin' Hopkins) and skiffle (Lonnie Donegan and The Vipers), playing in different local skiffle groups before joining Rory and the Hurricanes, played a residency at Butlin's and would later star as a Teddy Boy in the film 'That'll Be the Day'.

The Beatles were all 'war babies'.

As we leave the 1950s, it is interesting to reflect, as this book is ostensibly about music above all things, on what the most popular recordings were in the UK and the US, remembering that while being the most popular, these were not necessarily the best or most influential.

This is reflected by the fact (looking at the top 100 US artists between 1950 and 1959) **(30)** that while Elvis Presley (*1*), Les Paul (*6*), Ricky Nelson (*8*) and The Everly Brothers (*19*) from the top 20 could be legitimately counted as influential on the nascent rock movement that produced The Beatles as its most famous protagonists, most of the entries in the top 20 were 'middle of the road' artists whose recordings would now be found in the 'easy listening' section of record stores e.g. Perry Como (*2*), Nat 'King' Cole (*7*) and Tony Bennett (*16*) while others would be little known to audiences of today e.g. Kay Starr (*10*) and Gordon Jenkins (*20*) in the US list, and David Whitfield (*4*) in the UK.

More influential artists on the development of music in the 1960s would be found outside the US top 20 e.g. Fats Domino (*24*), Chuck Berry (*38*), and Bill Haley and His Comets (*45*). Little Richard is to be found at #83. Elvis is ousted from top spot by Frankie Laine in the UK (with the period 1952–1959 only covered because of the lack of availability of chart information prior to that time).

The UK top 20 includes many artists not in the US 100 (e.g. Lonnie Donegan at 5, Cliff Richard at 22, Tommy Steele at 26) and some artists who had more sales impact in the UK than the US (e.g. Bill Haley and His Comets at 11, Little Richard at 41). The complete absence of Buddy Holly and The Crickets (45 and 44 respectively in the UK ratings) from the US list goes at least part of the way towards explaining why it may have taken a 'British invasion' to kick start rock music in the States. Some artists' success straddled both countries like Jerry Lee Lewis who occupies a similar position in both lists just outside the top 50. There are also some US artists whose music was arguably even more 'middle of the road' than it was in the UK. Quintessentially, American and English artists exclusive to each list included Crew-Cuts and Four Lads, some novelty acts (e.g. Chipmunks and Goons), a fair sprinkling of 'crooners' and operatic singers/ orchestral or big band acts: Bing Crosby, Frank Sinatra – with Paul Anka just as popular – Mario Lanza, Mantovani and Billy Cotton and his Band. All in all, a 'mixed bag' and it is interesting to reflect on to what extent this changed in the 'swinging sixties'. Nor should we forget the influence of Les Paul real name Lester Polsfuss cannot be underestimated, not only in the pioneering music he produced but in technological development. A child performer in Waukesha, Wisconsin, he developed the famous Les Paul Model electric guitar which went into production in 1952 and, as Record Collector's Jonathan Wingate pointed out in the last major interview with Polsfuss, "His signature Gibson Les Paul immediately changed the sound of rock 'n' roll forever and became one of the most iconic instruments in musical history." Polsfuss had 'cut his teeth' with artists like Art Tatum, Nat King Cole and Django Reinhardt, and had several hits for the Decca label as The Les Paul Trio, also backing Judy Garland. He adapted the first Ampex reel-to-reel tape recorder (which Bing Crosby had invested $50,000 in) and "went on to revolutionise modern recording in the 1950s and early 1960s". He invented 'The New Sound' which multi-layered as many as eight electric guitars. He also collaborated with his wife, who assumed the name Mary Ford, and together, they had many hit records until their divorce in 1964, after which Polsfuss went into semi-retirement. As remarkable as his musical achievements, is the fact that he continued playing after a serious car accident in 1948 with his right arm set at a permanent right angle.

Perhaps, more enduring than the artists themselves are some of the songs they produced. The proliferation of '50s and 'rock n roll era' compilations allow easy and affordable access to the music on CD.

*'A sound to jump right out of the jukebox'*

# Elvis Presley

A perusal of what was successful in the UK and the US reveals a pattern of top 30 hits (most of them top 10, many of them number ones) that shows why Elvis Presley became known as 'the King'. Consider this: *Heartbreak Hotel, Blue Suede Shoes, I Want You, I Need You I Love You, Hound Dog/ Don't Be Cruel, Blue Moon, Love Me Tender, I Don't Care If the Sun Don't Shine, Love Me Tender* (and this is 1956 alone); *Mystery Train, Rip It Up, Too Much, All Shook Up* (his first UK #1), *Teddy Bear, Paralysed, Jailhouse Rock, Party, Got a Lot O' Livin' To Do', Trying to Get to You, Loving You, Lawdy Miss Clawdy, Santa, Bring My Baby Back to Me* (This is 1957). By now, the point is already made. Paul McCartney said, "If we were feeling lousy, we'd play an Elvis 78 – *'Don't Be Cruel'* – it could cure any blues". **(31)**

Before the '50s gave way to the '60s, Elvis would enjoy further #1 hits in the UK: *One Night/ I Got Stung, A Fool Such as I/ I Need Your Love Tonight and Jailhouse Rock* (lagging behind the States by 3 months) with other memorable records like *Don't, Wear You Ring Around My Neck, Heard headed Woman* and *King Creole* just failing short of the number one spot *Big Hunk of Love* also reached #1 in the US and #4 in the UK,

Carl Perkins' *'Blue Suede Shoes'* competed for a time with it head-to-head in a race with Elvis's version towards the top of the American charts, eventually, stalling at number 10. For Elvis *'Heartbreak Hotel'* wouldn't quite make it all the way to the top reaching number 2 in both the US and the UK. However, Elvis was rapidly establishing himself as "the hottest artist on the RCA Victor label" according to Billboard magazine who reported: "Presley has six singles in the company's list of top 25 best sellers, five of which have been previously been issued on the Sun label." Closing in on a million sales by the end of March, 1956, *'Heartbreak Hotel'* was also doing well in the country and R&B charts. By the end of 1956, Presley had sold an unprecedented 10 million singles accounting for approximately 60% of the RCA label's total sales.

Elvis's' first album was also in its way to being RCA's first million-dollar LP. As if that were not achievement enough, an EP spearheaded by Perkins' *'Blue Suede Shoes'*\* would reach #9 in the UK and #10 Stateside. To add injury to insult, Perkins was recuperating in hospital following a car accident along with his two brothers. The LP, in fact, opened with *'Blue Suede Shoes'*, had covers of songs by Little Richard (*'Tutti Frutti'*) and Ray Charles (*'I Got a Woman'*) and also included three ballads, *'Blue Moon', 'I Love You Because'* and *'I'll Never Let You Go'* that were recorded at Presley's first label Sun Records but were never released by label supremo Sam Phillips, the man who had discovered Presley in the first place. The LP did not include *'Heartbreak Hotel'*, chosen as the lead single. The iconic cover was famously adapted by The Clash for their 'London Calling' album.

Shortly after the album sessions, a screen test with Paramount Studios reaped a three picture deal for Elvis and the shooting for the first movie 'Love Me Tender' would begin in late August, just before the start of the sessions for his second album which this time included three Little Richard songs, *'Rip It Up, 'Long Tall Sally',* and *'Ready Teddy'* with the emerging song-writing partnership of Jerry Leiber and Mike Stoller providing *'Love Me'* written in hillbilly style, which reached the US top ten as a single. The inclusion of the Red Foley song *'Old Shep'* was a large slice of nostalgia taking Elvis right back to the Mississippi-Alabama Fair in 1945 when he first came to the public's attention. Again, his next massive hit *'Hound Dog'*, originally recorded by Big Mama Thornton, coupled with *'Don't Be Cruel'* were omitted from the album. *'Love Me Tender'*, a rewrite of an old American Civil War ballad *'Aura Lee'*, would prove an enduring number in Elvis's back catalogue and was included on the film soundtrack.

Elvis had come a long way in a short time since his first tentative moments in the recording studio when he would have to use a felt pick to mute the sound of his high held strummed guitar and stop it bleeding into the microphone.Greil Marcus in his seminal book 'Mystery Train' described in great detail precisely what took place in that Sun Studios session on 5 July,1954, when the record often described as the one that changed the world was recorded. The record in question was 'Big Boy' Arthur Crudup's 'That's Alright, Mama', a faster rendition than the original, that just appeared as if out of nowhere as Elvis, Bill Black and Scotty Moore, his bass player and guitarist respectively, deliberated on what to play, having come into the studio with no agreed material. Producer Sam Phillips was somewhat baffled and worried that white disc jockeys wouldn't play it because it was black blues music and black audiences would be put off by the hillbilly beat. The rest, in the words of the old cliché, is history.[9]

The tectonic plates in popular music started to shift. As Drew Heatley put it in his liner notes to the 'Sun Record Company Essential Collection' box. **(32)**

"The Sun Studios at 706 Union Avenue, Memphis, Tennessee, was quite simply, the birthplace of rock 'n' roll."

## Bill Haley

As I have already touched on another defining moment, some would say the defining moment in the development of rock 'n' roll, and, by default, popular music came in 1956 with the impact of Bill Haley and his influence on teenager consumers of the time. In 1955, Elvis Presley had told legendary radio DJ Bill Randle that he counted Pat Boone and Bill Haley among his idols.

Pennsylvanian Haley had been recording country and western style since 1946, and in 1951, had recorded 'Rocket 88', originally performed by Jackie Brenston and Ike Turner when it topped the R&B chart in 1951 on lease from Sam Phillips to Chess Records. This was a turning point for Phillips: "In the sense of the term, rock 'n' roll – which to me wrapped up black and white youth, and vitality it really was the first rock 'n' roll record."

Haley's output over the period to 1954 has been variously described as swing, big band (because of the sax, steel guitar and accordion), boogie and hillbilly. As Pete Guralnick remarks, "It was a mix that defied categorisation". **(33)**The big commercial breakthrough came for Haley when his *'Rock Around the Clock'* played over the opening credits of the 1955 film 'The Blackboard Jungle', a surprise considering the record had

---

[9] By 1954, Philips had installed two Ampex 350 recorders in his studio thus facilitating tape delay echo and adding to the vibrancy of the Sun sound. Big Boy Arthur Crudup's song, originally a blues, is reckoned to have been the foundation stone of rockabilly, with a rapid metamorphosis to rock 'n' roll just over the horizon. Phillips sold Presley's contract to RCA Victor for $35,000 plus $5,000 in back royalties (a record at the time) with *'I Forgot to Remember/ Mystery Train'* the last Elvis hit on Sun in 1956.

achieved only modest success on first release but went on to sell many millions of copies and become influential in the development of rock 'n' roll music.

The 'Bill Haley Story' film that followed might have born only passing relation to reality but helped to perpetuate the legend. By Haley's own account, he also advised a young Elvis that he was leaning too much on ballads and should put more rhythm into his music.

Bill Haley and His Comets also made quite an impact on the charts (especially in the UK) *with See You Later Alligator, Rockin' Through the Rye, The Saints Rock 'n' Roll, Rip It Up* and *Shake, Rattle and Rock.* Paul McCartney apparently saw Haley play live when still in short trousers!

## Buddy Holly

As for Buddy Holly and the Crickets, *'That'll Be the Day'* (the Crickets) and *'Peggy Sue'* both made the US charts, the former being the first song the early Beatles recorded along with Paul McCartney's original *'In Spite of all the Danger'* while UK record buyers opted for Holly's *'It Doesn't Matter Anymore'* (it made top 40) and The Crickets *'Oh, Boy!'* (This scraped into the top 200).

The world that Buddy Holly grew up in is vividly described by Spencer Leigh in his 2009 book 'Everyday: Getting Closer to Buddy Holly'. It tells a fascinating tale of Holly (actually Holley, thanks to a misspelling on his birth certificate) singing first tenor in his school choir in Lubbock, a Bible belt settlement in west Texas steeped in UFO folklore (the Lubbock lights of 1951). Lubbock also had a 10% black population living in ghettos with separate toilets and drinking fountains. Buddy started playing banjo, mandolin, and singing harmony vocals with Jack Neal, a singer, guitarist and pianist, Bob Montgomery, a singer and guitarist joined sometimes by Don Guess on bass and steel guitar (Larry Welborn was to become the regular double bass player).

Holly started writing songs with Graham Turnbull, called Scotty because he was born in Nova Scotia.[10] Holly saw Elvis perform at the Cotton Club in Lubbock early in 1955 and was inspired to record some demos. By 14th October, 1955, he was opening for Bill Haley and his Comets at the Fair Park Auditorium in Lubbock (Elvis would play on a stellar bill including Johnny Cash and Carl Perkins the next day). Buddy was impressed by Elvis's addition of a drummer DJ Fontana and his hybrid of blues and country, and started to play Elvis numbers like *'I Forgot to Remember to Forget'*. By the end of October, Holly was back at the Auditorium for a 'Grand Ole Opry' show.

In December, it was Big Joe Turner's and Fats Domino's turn to play in Lubbock, another milestone in Holly's musical journey. By this time, Holly's potential as a star in his own right was being recognised and Decca record company executive Paul Cohen signed him up, providing him with a song *'Midnight Shift'* to record. His first single though was *'Blue Days-Black Nights/ Love Me'* released on 16th April, 1956. Holly got the idea for the line in the song *'That'll Be the Day'* from the film 'The Searchers' (as uttered by John Wayne). Both Decca and Roulette Records rejected the song. The line-up at this time is Sonny Curtis, Don Guess and Jerry Allison on drums. The Nashville sessions produced *'Rock Around with Ollie Vee'*, another song that is reckoned to be a rockabilly into rock and roll transition point.

In August, 1956, Holly and his group supported Little Richard, and Holly started to record songs of his like *'Ready Teddy'* and *'Rip It Up'* just as Elvis had done. A third

---

[10] Indeed, one of these songs 'My Baby's Comin' Home' was recorded by Harry Nilsson in 1962.

and final recording session saw the inclusion of more musicians including a saxophone whose playing on 'Modern Don Juan' has been much commented upon. It was released on Christmas Eve, 1956 as the next single A-side. Another film that would prove influential on Holly's early development was 'The Girl Can't Help It'. Holly next recorded in Norman Petty's studio in Clovis, laying down covers of Chuck Berry's 'Brown Eyed Handsome Man' and Bo Diddley's eponymous song. By this time, Holly had a comprehensive repertoire of songs that could be played live, by artists like Presley, Berry, Ray Charles, Haley and Little Richard, and a modified version of 'That'll Be the Day' was recorded at the Clovis studio. His Decca contract prevented him from releasing any previously recorded songs and Holly's way of getting around this, on the advice of Norman Petty, was to put it out under a group name, the Beetles being rejected in favour of The Crickets. Eventually, 'That'll Be the Day/ I'm Lookin' for Someone to Love' was released on 27 May, 1957. It is also reckoned that 'Not Fade Away' was originally penned by Holly and Jerry Allison only for it to be assimilated in fine style by The Rolling Stones.[11]

## Chuck Berry

In a chapter entitled 'The Creation of My Recordings' in his autobiography Charles 'Chuck' Berry describes the origin of his songs: To give just three examples, 'Roll Over Beethoven' was "written based on the feelings I had when my sister would monopolise the piano at home… telling Mother in an attempt to get support for my kind of music did no good but writing a letter and mailing it to a local DJ might have"; 'Reelin' and Rockin'' was inspired by seeing Big Joe Turner in Chicago when Berry was 16 "singing the song that Bill Haley covered for the then so-called white market, 'Rock Around the Clock'. If ever I was inspired as a teenager, I was then. What I then heard and felt, I tried to reprovoke (sic) in the song.". 'Johnny B Goode', originally intended as a song for piano player Johnnie Johnson but 'more or less about himself' with his mother, who instinctively knew her son was bound for success, inspiring the 'go Johnny go' part. "I had driven through New Orleans on tour and I'd been told my great Grandfather lived 'way back up in the woods among the evergreens' in a log cabin. I thought it seemed biased to white fans to say 'coloured boy' and changed it to 'country boy' **(34)**

It is difficult to understate the significance of Chuck Berry. As he says himself, "In 1971, the great John Lennon mentioned once that I was his hero. This was one of the most stimulating statements that had ever been bestowed upon me. On my forty-fifth birthday, the only time we stood side by side performing together, the music we both loved so well, though sixteen years apart in age, we stood sixteen inches apart, sharing the lyrics of 'Johnny B. Goode'" **(35)**

He would also play the same number with Keith Richards in Chicago on 6th June, 1986 at a Rock 'n' Roll Induction Day ceremony.

It is a remarkable fact that, on Carl Sagan's suggestion, the song *'Johnny B. Goode'* was chosen as part of the music aboard Voyager 1 as it took off on its journey across the solar system.

If ever there was an artist that was truly ahead of his time, that artist was Chuck Berry.[12]

---

[11] Apparently, Bo Diddley also had a claim to writing it but has since deferred to Holly and Allison.

[12] These are a selection of the recordings Berry made for Chess (all re-recordings are on Mercury): Maybellene (21/5/55 -re-recorded 21/9/66); Roll Over Beethoven (recording date

# Popular 1950s records in the US and the UK

The nascent Beatles would have been exposed to an eclectic collection of songs on the radio that would all have left an impact of some kind or another.

Records like Les Paul and Mary Ford's '*Vaya Con Dios*' [13] and '*Goodnight Irene*' (Gordon Jenkins and the Weavers) were most popular in the US Bobby Darin's '*Mack the Knife*' would prove popular across both side of the Atlantic, and continue to be a juke box favourite as would Danny and The Juniors '*At the Hop*'. Wilbert Harrison's 1959 recording '*Kansas City*' would assume a special significance for the early Beatles (as would '*Let's Work Together*' for Canned Head in the sixties). Fats Domino's '*Blueberry Hill*' remains a perennial favourite much beloved of local radio stations while Carl Perkins and Elvis Presley both had hits with Perkins' '*Blue Suede Shoes*' in 1956.

Later that same year, Guy Mitchell would gain a massive hit with '*Singing the Blues*' (Tommy Steele also having a UK hit with the same song), another one that has seldom left the airwaves. Jerry Lee Lewis had two enduring hits in 1957, '*Great Balls of Fire*' and '*Whole Lot of Shakin' Going On*' while, as we have seen, Chuck Berry had a succession of hits over 1957 and 1958 with '*School Day*', '*Rock & Roll Music*', '*Sweet Little Sixteen*', and '*Johnny B. Goode*' to follow his 1955 success with '*Maybelline*'. Little Richard was another artist with a pervasive influence on the development of 'rock 'n' roll', his most memorable numbers along with '*Tutti Frutti*' which Elvis covered on his first LP included '*Long Tall Sally*' from 1956, and '*Good Golly Miss Molly*' and '*Lucille*' from 1957.

Frankie Laine's '*I Believe*' was a major UK hit, which not quite so successful in the US, a similar story to Doris Day's '*Secret Love*'. Uniquely, British artists like Cliff Richard had success with '*Living Doll*', '*Travellin' Light*' and '*Move It*', of which John Lennon famously said, "I think the first English record that was anywhere near anything was '*Move It*' by Cliff Richard" **(36)**. Lonnie Donegan was similarly successful with a succession of hits like '*Rock Island Line*' (1956) and '*Cumberland Gap*', '*Gamblin' Man/ Putting on the Style*' from 1957, and as the decade drew to a close '*Tom Dooley*', '*Battle of New Orleans*' and the execrable novelty record '*Does Your Chewing Gum Lose Its Flavour?*'. Just as the decade was ending Neil Sedaka broke into the UK charts with '*Oh! Carol*', written for prolific songwriter Carole King.

Other successful records and artists in the 1950s included Lionel Hampton who in 1950 released '*Rag Mop*'. Hampton, a jazz vibraphonist and his boogie-woogie band is reckoned to have laid the foundation of rock 'n' roll as early as 1943 with '*Flying Home*', and three years later with '*Hey! Ba-Ba-Re-Bop*'.

In 1951, Tennessee Ernie Ford is regarded as an early pioneer in the country boogie style which would feature in the DNA of rockabilly, and subsequently, rock 'n' roll with his '*The Shot Gun Boogie*'. The following year, The Four Aces: '*Tell Me Why*' was an early example of doo-wop. They also sang '*Mr Sandman*' in 1954 but were pipped to the hit by The Chordettes. In 1955, The Penguins released '*Earth Angel (Will You Be*

---

16/4/56 -re-recorded 21/9/66); Brown Eyed Handsome Man (16/4/56 -re-recorded 27/10/66); School Days (21/1/57 – re-recorded 21/9/66); Reelin' and Rockin' (6/5/57 – re-recorded 27/10/66); Rock and Roll Music (6/5/57 -re-recorded 21/9/66); Sweet Little Sixteen (6/1/58 – re-recorded 21/9/66); Johnny B. Goode (28/2/58 – re-recorded 21/9/66); Around and Around 28/2/58-re-recorded 26/10/66); Carol (12/6/58 – re-recorded 27/10/66); Memphis (28/9/58 – re-recorded 21/9/66); Route 66 (19/1/61); Nadine (14/1/64) and No Particular Place to Go (26/3/64)

[13] Among other duo records well worth checking out are '*The World is Waiting for the Sunrise*' and '*Tiger Rag* (1951/52)

Mine?)', recorded in a garage but turning out to be a multi-million doo-wop sellerand one of a teenage Frank Zappa's favourites.

Lloyd Price's 'Lawdy Miss Clawdy' topped the R&B charts in 1953.[14] While in 1954, Gale Storm released 'I Hear You Knocking' which would become a #1 UK hit for Dave Edmunds 16 years later. Edmunds pretty much milked this scene dry scoring again, in irresistible style with a top 10 cover of The Chordettes 'Born to Be With You' from 1956. This was also the year that Gene Vincent (Vincent Eugene Craddock) & His Blue Caps' 'Be-Bop-A-Lula' entered the rock 'n' roll arena. This song is still much played and imitated with Ian Dury paying the ultimate tribute with his own tribute 'Sweet Gene Vincent'.

It is a little known fact also that Frankie Abelson AKA Vaughan's 'Green Door', a big hit in 1956 was produced by a young Joe Meek. That ultimate piece of teenage angst, Frankie Lymon and the Teenagers: 'Why Do Fools Fall in Love?' was also very successful in 1956 along with The Platters 'The Great Pretender', a much copied song, notably by Freddie Mercury of Queen. 1956 was also the year of Screaming Jay Hawkins' much copied 'I Put a Spell On You' which is still heard on TV advertisements to this day, and was covered by Nina Simone and many others.

In 1957, Sam Cooke reached a milestone in releasing his first secular single, 'You Send Me'. In the same year, Jackie Wilson's 'Reet Petite' (a bigger hit in the UK than in Detroit!) was Berry Gordy Jr. of Motown fame's first hit as a composer, returning to the charts in 1986.

The Everly Brothers, Phil and Don (Isaac Donald) straddled country music and rock 'n' roll' (although the guys themselves told the New Musical Express in 1960 that they were "not Grand Ole Opry, obviously not Perry Como, we're just pop music but you could call us an American skiffle group"). 'Bye, Bye, Love', written by Felice and Boudleaux Bryant, reached #2 in the US pop charts and #1 on the country charts, becoming the group's first million-seller. Despite the fact the song had already been rejected by dozens of artists, it was good enough for Simon and Garfunkel to include on their 'Bridge Over Troubled Water' album. Their self-composed 'Cathy's Clown' was the first record Warner Brothers issued in the UK and sold eight million copies worldwide. Other great songs included Wake Up Little Susie and All I Have to Do is Dream. While their success had waned in the US by the time of the 'British invasion' in 1964, they remained popular in the UK (and remain both popular and influential to musicians to this day). They actually recorded an album in 1966 with The Hollies entitled 'Two Yanks in England'.

In 1958, The Crickets had a big hit with 'Maybe Baby', written by Buddy Holly. Don Gibson's 'Oh, Lonesome Me' also originates from this year. Gibson is thought to be the originator of the 'Nashville sound' and has been covered by over 700 artists including Johnny Cash on his 'American Recordings'. The Coasters: 'Yakety Yak' (Don't talk back!) was a great novelty record while Bobby Freeman: 'Do You Want to Dance?' would be the San Franciscan ex doo-wopper's finest three minutes and prove an enduring crowd pleaser.

Duane Eddy, the originator of the 'twangy' guitar sound remains, enormously influential releasing a series of catchy instrumentals including 'Rebel Rouser' in 1958. That same year, The Johnny Otis Show had success with 'Willie and the Hand Jive' later revived by Eric Clapton on his '461 Ocean Boulevard' album.

---

[14] Joe Cocker's version of 'Lawdy Miss Clawdy' coupled with The Beatles' 'She Came in Through the Bathroom Window' is stunning and an ingenuous link of 'past to present'.

Also, in 1958, there was Peggy Lee: with *'Fever'* which has become a finger-snapping standard, Eddie Cochran's *'Summertime Blues'* (ahead of its time, cue Blue Cheer and The Who!) and Big Bopper's big ballad *'Chantilly Lace'* which reached the UK top 20 on the fateful night he perished with Richie Valens and Buddy Holly on an ill-fated aeroplane journey. As early rock music developed and intensified, Chuck Berry would score with *'Johnny B. Goode'* and *'Sweet Little Sixteen',* and Little Richard with *'Good, Golly Miss Molly'.* Early rock music history was being written.

In 1959, The Coasters released another excellent novelty record *'Charlie Brown'* (I found this old record lying about the house as a child and played it to extinction); Ricky Nelson released *'It's Late',* revived by Shakin' Stevens in 1983; and Eddie Cochran provided another classic with *'C'mon Everybody'* but tragically died in a car accident less than a year later. Also, in 1959, Francis's *'Lipstick on Your Collar'* (the first record I remember hearing – I must have been crawling!) came out, along with Bert Weedon's *'Guitar Boogie Shuffle'* (His tutorial books inspired many young aspiring guitarists); and Duane Eddy's 'Peter Gunn Theme'. Ray Robinson AKA Ray Charles sang *'What'd I Say?'* and would assume legendary proportions influencing great singers like Gary Brooker of Procol Harum. Johnny & The Hurricanes' released *'Red River Rock'* (The Beatles supported them in Hamburg in 1962); also released were Sandy Nelson's *'Teen Beat'* (This established Nelson as rock's best known drummer and featured Barney Kessell and Bruce Johnson) and Frank Sinatra's *'High Hopes'* (There has to be something by old blue eyes and this was his last hit of the last decade before the sixties).

Once the '60s dawned, youngsters were primed to hear all this exciting new music that had emerged in the '50s to be taken to new levels in the years ahead by equally thirsty and adventurous musicians who saw 'pop music' as a road to fame and fortune. The problem was, as Bob Stanley, author of 'Yeah, Yeah, Yeah: The Story of Modern Pop' put it in an excellent article for the Big Issue. **(37)** BBC Radio was 'starchy' in the early '60s and 'pop' was restricted to a daily hour on The Light Programme. The USA became the oasis to the UK's desert with 24-hour rock 'n' roll radio. Listeners had access to Radio Luxembourg which even had its own weekly 'Fab 2008' magazine but had to wait until 1964 for Radio Caroline followed by London, England and Sutch each with their own chart and based in old ships, and, in the case of Radio Sutch, an abandoned World War II fort in the North Sea called Shivering Sands. Easter Sunday, 1964 was the historic date for Caroline, Simon Dee was the first DJ, The Rolling Stones the first record with *'Not Fade Away'.* With an estimated 20 million people listening to pirate radio by 1967, the Labour government took the decision to shut down the pirates and the Marine Offences Act was passed with the aid of other parliamentarians with Tony Benn, then postmaster general tasked with being the enforcer.[15] All was not lost though as Radio 1 was up and running a month later in November, 1967.

The musical 'revolution' thus ignited was further advanced by the development of technology. The possibilities of new and not so new instruments like the Moog synthesiser (after Robert Moog its creator in 1964), the theremin (named after Leon Theremin, a Russian cellist and actually originating in 1917, Vladimir Iyich Lenin owned one!) and the mellotron, and a more 'arty', fashion based approach epitomised in a

---

[15] As a postscript Pirate Beat Boat Cruise, organised by British promoter Stuart Lyon, set sail in 2014 with veteran pirate broadcasters Dave Cash, Emperor Rosko and Johnny Walker on-board, destined for the shipping routes frequented by the original pirate ships, and docking in Amsterdam and Antwerp. This brought to real life the brilliant dramatisation in the film 'The Boat That Rocked' though not in such lurid or satirical comic detail one would suppose. Times have changed after all, even if the music has endured!

photograph in Mo Foster's book showing the quantum leap that occurred in one musician, Roger Glover then of Episode Six, later of Deep Purple whose image took a 360 degree turn as the suits disappeared in favour of a 'floral adornment'. **(38)** Political sloganising e.g. make love, not war and drug experimentation would also characterise the era.[16]

In the case of artists like Donovan and The Beatles, of course, there was also the quest for spiritual advancement. As far as the music was concerned, a bolder, more ambitious approach based on myriad influences (including classical) as in progressive rock or more 'popular' influences with more of a kindred spirit to US groups (the west coast in particular) as in psychedelic[17] each of which had its own preferred instrumentation (with much overlap!), in the case of progressive rock in particular, the increased use of keyboards. The three minute 'hit and run' of a basic guitar, bass and drum line-up would return in the punk era but, for now, it was 'all systems go'.

**"The Beatles wrote songs that appear to have always existed. Like all the best ideas you cannot imagine a world without them."**
**(Will Hodgkinson) (40)**

---

[16] Albert Hoffman's famous 'bad trip' in 1943 while riding his bike is referenced in at least three songs: Pink Floyd's *'Bike'*, Tomorrow's *'My White Bicycle'* and The Beach Boys *'I Just Wasn't Made for These Times'*.

[17] De Rogatis and others have noted that English groups were more 'whimsically psychedelic' **(39)** whereas typical examples of American psych might be the 'bad trip' psychedelia of Count 5's 'Psychotic Reaction' and the explicit 'trip psych' of The Seeds (e.g. 'Mr Farmer', an ode to marijuana growers and 'Pushin' Too Hard', self-explanatory). Of course, the quickest way to explore American psych is through 'Nuggets: Original Artyfacts from the First Psych Era: 1965 to 1968' compiled by Lenny Kaye and familiar to many as the 1998 Rhino 4 CD box set. Nuggets were followed by Pebbles, Boulders and Rubble!

# Chapter Four

## The Beatles: Part One – Conception to the American Breakthrough

The Beatles' family history is well documented. Predictably, there was already some musical tradition in the families: Paul McCartney's Dad was an amateur musician on guitar and piano, John Lennon's Mum played a ukulele, Ringo's Mum liked to sing *'Little Drummer Boy'*. (I am sure there were other songs in her repertoire). But it was listening to records, especially American imports that provided the main impetus.

Unknown to one another, the die was already cast and all four of what became the established line-up of The Beatles had been impressed by the revolutionary widescreen colour film 'The Girl Can't Help It' starring Jayne Mansfield about whom Little Richard sings "she's got a lot of what they call the most."

It was a historic day when Paul McCartney saw a group called The Quarrymen playing at a local church fete at St Peter's Field in the Woolton area of Liverpool. The thing that left the most indelible mark on the 16-year-old McCartney was John Lennon's ad libbing of the Del Vikings *'Congo with Me,* lobbing in random blues lyrics with absurdist abandon. For his part, Paul impressed John, by not only playing but knowing all the words to Eddie Cochran's *'25 Rock'* and was invited to join the group. George Harrison, who lived a bus stop way from Paul, was auditioned on the top deck of a Liverpool bus and so it was that, a 78 rpm record was recorded at the Phillips Sound Recording Service in Liverpool in 1958 for 17s 6d (£0.87½) with the Buddy Holly and the Crickets number *'That'll Be the Day'* on one side and a McCartney/ Harrison original *'In Spite of all the Danger'* on the other.[18] Lennon took the lead vocal on each song and also in the line-up were Quarrymen members John Lowe (piano) and Colin Hanton (drums), both of whom left the group shortly afterwards. The three remaining 'Beatles' continued to play at the Jacaranda Club near the Art College and recruited John's friend Stuart Sutcliffe, who was persuaded to spend the £75 he had earned from selling one of his paintings on a Hofner bass guitar. Sutcliffe's lack of prowess on this particular instrument was illustrated by him turning his back on the audience during live performances to disguise the fact. On 'The Beatles Anthology 1' CD (Apple Records), three songs recorded in 1960 in Paul's house, can be heard. These are Ray Charles' *'Hallelujah, I Love Her So'* (based on the Eddie Cochran version), *'You'll Be Mine'*, one of the first credited McCartney/ Lennon compositions [19], a tongue in cheek ditty

---

[18] This was actually run by local electrical goods shop owner Percy Phillips and was located in a living room in his Victorian terraced house.

[19] The honour may well go to *'The One After 909'*, a snatch of which can be heard on The Beatles Anthology video. This song originally dates to 1957 written as Lennon/ McCartney at McCartney's house shortly after the Woolton church fete. It was tried out again at the *'From Me to You'* session in 1963 and finally recorded in January, 1969 before appearing on the 'Let It Be' album released in May, 1970. The group also played it on the Abbey Road

reminiscent of American vocal group The Ink Spots and an early example of John Lennon's mischievous word play, and *'Cayenne'*, a fair if slightly laboured attempt at a multi-part guitar instrumental established in the 1950s and popularised in the UK by groups like The Shadows in the '60s. Paul sang lead vocals on both numbers and composed the instrumental.

The group briefly adopted the name Long John and the Silver Beetles (shortened to The Beetles) for a Scottish tour in the tradition of artists with pseudonyms, apparently, a prerequisite for artists in the stable of well-known promoter Larry Parnes whose roster at the Blue Angel club included Marty Wilde, Billy Fury and Storm Tempest none of whom used their actual birth names. The group expanded once again to a five piece as this was a condition of their first Hamburg residency and thus Pete Best was recruited for their infamous stay in the St Pauli Reeperbahn district where 'uppers' were recommended by waiters struggling to cope with long shifts and combined with beer served to keep the musicians awake through arduous musical shifts. It was in Hamburg that Ringo Starr, then the drummer with Rory and the Hurricanes, would request *'3.30 Blues'* after most of the crowd had departed.

The Hamburg experience was brought to an abrupt end when George Harrison was deported for being under age (there was a curfew for anyone under 18 and George was just 17) and the remaining Beatles were unceremoniously sent packing after a prank involving setting fire to a condom in the Kaiserkeller where they played. This act was no more than an adolescent act of revenge in the knowledge that they were about to secure a better gig at the more prestigious rival club The Top Ten. The group did return to Hamburg in April, 1961. While there, on 22nd June, they backed English rocker Tony Sheridan on a revved up, over the top version of old traditional favourite *'My Bonnie'* produced by famous orchestra leader Bert Kaempfert, which became a top 10 record in Germany and demonstrates Harrison's developing prowess on lead guitar. The *'My Bonnie'* record was to be significant in one other way in renaming the group The Beatles, most likely a calculated decision in deference to The Crickets. [20] The group was brought to the attention of NEMS Enterprises entrepreneur Brian Epstein following a request for *'My Bonnie'* in his record store. This prompted Epstein to check the group out when they returned to Liverpool where they now played at The Cavern Club. On The Beatles Anthology 1 collection, Epstein takes up the story, "I secured them an audition at Decca on New Year's Day, 1962, and they came to London to stay at The Royal Hotel at 27 shillings a night for bed and breakfast. They were poor and I wasn't rich but we all celebrated with rum and Scotch, and coke which was becoming a Beatles drink even then." During this session, the group laid down fifteen songs in total including McCartney's old favourite, the Jerry Lieber/ Mike Stoller composition *'Searchin'* which had been a hit for The Coasters, another Lieber/ Stoller song *'Three Cool Cats'* (delivered with their customary wry sense of humour) and a Joe Brown inspired version of a number dating to back to the 1940 musical 'Tin Pan Alley', *'The Sheik of Araby'* with lead vocal

---

rooftop. That it took so long for the track to be successfully laid down reflects the tight schedule in 1963 and the finger can literally be heard being pointed at McCartney as takes broke down. The Beatles Anthology 1 CD illustrates how a composite could have been produced from the aborted five takes at the 1963 session.

[20] Other songs were also recorded during this session including another well-known song *'Ain't She Sweet'* with Lennon on lead vocal. *'Cry for a Shadow'* followed *'Cayenne'* as an early instrumental number but this time credited to Harrison/ Lennon, a unique occurrence in Beatles history.

by Harrison.[21] Two other songs of note during this session, for different reasons, are the first Lennon original *'Hello, Little Girl'*, later, a hit for The Fourmost in 1963 and the McCartney song *'Like Dreamers Do'* which brought success to Birmingham group The Applejacks in 1964.[22]

Despite this early promise, it is hard to believe that the group that would be heard on the Polydor LP of 'The Early Tapes of the Beatles: The Beatles with Tony Sheridan and The Beat Brothers' with standards like *'When the Saints Go Marching In'* and *'Nobody's Child'* would develop into planet Earth's most revered pop group! Before all of this could happen, of course, the group needed a recording contract. Disappointed but undeterred by the rejection of The Beatles by head of Decca Records Dick Rowe, Epstein stayed on in London until, acting on a lead by a member of staff of the HMV record store on Oxford Street, he caught the interest of George Martin, then A&R man for EMI's Parlophone label. So it was that on the historic date of 6th June, 1962, the group went to 3 Abbey Road, St John's Wood to record a number of songs only four of which made it onto tape: *'Besame Mucho'*, *'Love Me Do'* (a McCartney song which dated back to his school days at the Liverpool Institute in 1958), *'PS I Love You'* and *'Ask Me Why'*. Two have survived, *'Besumo Mucho'* based on the second part of The Coasters' version (the B-side of their 1960 single), and a nervy slower and longer version than the two versions of *'Love Me Do'* eventually issued. Pete Best was the drummer at these sessions.

A second EMI session was arranged for 4th September, 1962. Two songs were recorded, another version of *'Love Me Do'* with Ringo Starr (who had accepted Brian Epstein's invitation to join The Beatles giving a few days' notice to Rory and the Hurricanes) on drums and a Mitch Murray number *'How Do You Do It?'* which would provide fellow Liverpudlians Gerry and the Pacemakers with a #1 hit. It was originally George Martin's intention to release *'How Do You Do It?'* as the Beatles' first single but succumbed to the group's desire to give one of their own songs, *'Love Me Do'* precedence. Martin also had a hunch that *'Love Me Do'* was something a bit fresh and different with Lennon's harmonica influenced by Delbert McClinton's playing on the Bruce Channel hit *'Hey! Baby'* while *'How Do You Do It?'* might provide a hit for somebody else (as it did) and was, in Ian MacDonald's words, "stylistically passé". **(42)**

Exactly a week later, another session occurred with their new drummer Ringo Starr. Unfortunately, Martin was apparently dissatisfied with Ringo's drumming and had booked Andy White for the session, and it was he who can be heard on later releases of *'Love Me Do'* and the track that opened side two of the group's debut LP *'Please, Please Me'*. *'Love Me Do'* was released on 5th October, 1962, around the same time as the first James Bond movie 'Dr No' starring Sean Connery but would not be released in the US until 27th April, 1964. The Beatles' first A-side reached a respectable #17 in December, 1962, at a time that Elvis Presley's *'Return to Sender'* was #1. Its B-side, *'PS I Love You'*

---

[21] Alistair Taylor had known Brian Epstein since 1960 after successfully applying for a job in the NEMS record shop in Liverpool city centre. He quickly discovered that Epstein had an instinct for selling records, and after repeated orders of a record by Tony Sheridan and the Beat Brothers (*'My Bonnie'*) and, on a hunch, the pair went to see The Beatles play at the Cavern Club one lunchtime. Despite jazz buff, Taylor opining "They sang *Money, 'Til There Was You, A Taste of Honey* and *Twist and Shout* and, in a way, they were all equally terrible." He concluded, "It was mind-blowing for both of us. They were loud and they weren't very good but there was just this special ingredient. It was beyond charisma. It was beyond musicianship. It was beyond anything you could easily define." **(41)**

[22] It was this song that finally convinced the sceptical Alistair Taylor who could now see the potential—little did he realise how immense this would be!

with its cha-cha groove and *'Please, Please Me'* which was eventually to provide (in a different version recorded on 26th November) their first #1 single, but, on this occasion, was a work in progress, were also recorded at this session.

*'Please, Please Me'* was conceived by John Lennon who cited inspiration from Roy Orbison's *'Only The Lonely'* and lyrical inspiration from Bing Crosby's 1930s hit *'Please'* but as the song developed, The Everly Brothers' *'Cathy's Clown'* asserted more influence. George Martin's prudent and prescient guidance of The Beatles is illustrated in his famous statement: "Congratulations, gentlemen, you've just made your first number one." Indeed, the record did reach #1 on the Melody Maker, NME and Disc charts. It was issued on the Vee Jay label in the United States but only impacted significantly on the charts there on re-issue in June, 1964. Its B-side *'Ask Me Why'* was in the style of Smokey Robinson and the Miracles.[23] According to Iain MacDonald, "*I Saw Her Standing There* may have been The Beatles' first attempt at writing something 'off' *'Some Other Guy'*. Both songs were influenced by the prototype English rock 'n' roller Tony Sheridan whom The Beatles backed at the Top Ten Club in Hamburg and whose Eddie Cochran guitar style suggested the bluesy sevenths which litter their early output. (In The Beatles Anthology DVD 1, an ecstatic Cavern audience can be seen tapping their feet along to a rousing version of *'Some Other Guy'*). Recording of the first Beatles album began on 11th February, 1963 with *'There's A Place'* and *'I Saw Her Standing There'* featuring Harrison's first officially released guitar solo. Basically, it was a compilation of the best of what the group were performing live so they had a ready-made 'stock' of material. A 'left over' from the 11th September, 1962 session, *'A Taste of Honey'*, was a cover of a song that appeared in a film starring Liverpudlian actress Rita Tushingham with whom Paul McCartney was particularly captivated by at the time. Trad jazz clarinettist Acker Bilk would have a UK hit with it, and Herb Alpert and his Tijuana Brass would make it their own. *'Do You Want to Know a Secret'* provided a #1 hit for Bill J Kramer and the Dakotas, and indeed, a #2 US hit for The Beatles themselves in May, 1964. *'Misery'* was one of eight original songs on the debut LP, an unusually high number for these times. The covers were of Alabama singer Arthur Alexander's *'Anna (Go to Him)'* *, *'Boys'*, a 12-bar written by the Dixon-Farrell song writing team for The Shirelles and the B-side of *'Will You Love Me Tomorrow'*. (*'Boys'* was Ringo's featured vocal live spot when he played with Rory Storm and The Hurricanes). *'Chains'* a Gerry Goffin and Carole King number with Harrison on lead vocal, *'Baby It's You'*, another Shirelles song written by David-Williams and Burt Bacharach, and *'Twist and Shout'* written by Bert Berns (who also wrote *'Here Comes The Night'* popularised by Them, *'Hang On Sloopy'* for The McCoys and *'Piece of My Heart'* for Janis Joplin) and was already a hit for The Isley Brothers.[24] "The result," says Ian MacDonald, "is remarkable for its time, raw to a degree unmatched by other white artists."**(43)**

The 'Please Please Me' LP, completed on 20th February, 1963, was released in the UK on 22nd March, 1963 and in the US as 'Introducing The Beatles' on 22nd July, 1963. Needless to say, it went to number one on both sides of the Atlantic. The year 1963 was epochal for The Beatles. What was left to accomplish after successful touring with Helen Shapiro, Tommy Roe and Chris Montez, and record making? "Radio" is the answer on The Beatles Anthology 'racing up the ladder' segment, the Saturday Club show in particular and the greatly missed Bryan Mathew's voice has been prominent for many

---

[23] The Beatles also used Alexander's *'A Shot of Rhythm and Blues'* – which surfaced on the 1994 CD 'Live at the BBC'. The Rolling Stones recorded its a-side *'You Better Move'*.

[24] The Isley Brothers' *'Shout (Part One)'* was also in the repertoire, emerging on 'The Beatles Anthology 1'.

years (on Radio 2's 'Sounds of The Sixties'). But there were also TV and appearances on comedy shows like those hosted by Mike and Bernie Winters, and Morecambe and Wise. As far as the interminable touring was concerned, by Ringo's account, "We never stopped, we'd just go anywhere" with Neil Aspinall, to be joined by Mal Evans as 'roadie' and driver of their Bedford van. (The touring extended from as far north as Elgin to as far south as Portsmouth). "It could well be three number ones in a row for the Liverpool boys," speculated Bryan Mathew and he was right. Driven on by the likes of Roy Orbison and his *'Pretty Women'* to become better song writers (Paul cites the chord change in the middle as a sign of advancement), *'From Me You;'* (B-side *'Thank You Girl'*) knocked *'How Do You Do It?'* off the top of the charts to provide their second chart topper. *'She Loves You'* (b/w *'I'll Get You'*), released on 23rd August, 1963 in the UK, completed the hat trick of number ones. This would be the number chosen to complete their appearance on Sunday Night at the London Palladium on 13th October, a key occasion for The Beatles to transit from 'they'll never last' to being accepted by 'the establishment', the parents and even the grandparents perhaps.

To follow that, there was the Royal Variety Performance at the Prince of Wales Theatre on 4th November during which Lennon came out with the famous line about those in the stalls clapping and the rest rattling their jewellery. (The Queen Mother seemed to take it in good spirit). The three song set comprised *'She Loves You'*, *'Til There Was You'* (a Meredith Wilson song from the Broadway show 'The Music Man' which Peggy Lee had a hit with), included to widen audience appeal, and *'Twist and Shout'*. The performance was sound with Harrison holding his nerve well on the guitar break on *'Til There Was You'*. The group had not long returned from a successful tour of Sweden and the strength of their performance can be heard on The Beatles Anthology 1 CD.

Sessions for the second Beatles album began on 18th July, 1963. The group always had a policy of trying to give their fans value for money and included 14 songs none of them hit singles. George Martin describes the album (*'With The Beatles'* in the UK and *'The Beatles Second Album'* in the US) as their "first songbook". The cover was designed by Robert Freeman based on Astrid Kircher's photographs of the group taken in Hamburg and the album broke the previous record for advance sales set by Elvis Presley's 'Blue Hawaii' with a quarter of a million early orders put in. The songs on the album were, cover versions first: *'You Really Got a Hold on Me'*, already a top 10 US hit for Smokey Robinson and The Miracles, a superior version of a Bradford-Gordy song *'Money (That's What I Want)'*, a hit for Barrett Strong in 1959; a little known song called *'Devil in Her Heart'* which was originally sung by American girl group The Donays in 1962; the aforementioned *'Till There Was You'*; and *'Please Mr Postman'*, a song that had given the Tamla Motown label its first US #1 hit for The Marvelettes in 1961 and was later a big hit for The Carpenters.; and, finally, Chuck Berry's *'Roll Over Beethoven'* which, despite Harrison doing a reasonable job on the vocal and guitar break doesn't advance the song in a way that Beatles nut Jeff Lynne would years later in ELO's *'10357 Overture'*. The originals were: *'It Won't Be Long'*, *'All My Loving'*, *'I Wanna Be Your Man'* (with Ringo on vocals), originally given to The Rolling Stones who had a big hit with it; the little remembered *'Little Child'*, *'All I've Got to Do'*, *'Not a Second Time'* and a first Harrison original *'Don't Bother Me'*. The American version had just 11 songs and lasted only 22 minutes. Dave Dexter Junior was the Capitol Records executive who was slightly cynical about the status of rock 'n' roll as a legitimate music form who put the album together. It wasn't really representative of the force The Beatles had become and was poorly mastered in contrast to the Parlophone UK version 'With The Beatles' which had 14 tracks (8 originals, 6 covers). Despite all that, it has become for Dave

Marsh, former editor of Creem and Rolling Stone it has become, in his own words, a 'lodestone'. He has even written a whole book about it. **(44)**

## 1964 to 1966: The Times They are a Changin'

Before the New Year bells of 1964 had rung, The Beatles had committed to vinyl the record that would at last ensure their breakthrough in the United States. So far, American audiences had resisted four records, three of which had been number ones in the UK and, ironically, EMI owned Capitol Records, had not released them, leaving it to smaller labels like Swan and Vee Jay. With advance orders of more than a million, it was no surprise when *'I Want to Hold Your Hold'* became a Christmas number one. The Beatles' performance on the Ed Sullivan show on 9th February, 1964 'sealed the deal' and by the first week of April, they held the top 5 positions on the US chart, a week later, creating a seemingly unsurpassable record of having 14 records in the top 100 at the same time. The scale of the breakthrough is illustrated by the fact that the A&R supremo of The Beatles' US label Capitol, Dave Dexter Junior had turned down the group's first four singles for EMI. John Lennon would refer to American apathy in his apprehensive comment about Cliff Richard being fourteenth on the bill when he appeared in North America. Lack of promotion and the eventual release of the records on a gospel/ R&B label Vee-Jay, and, in the case of *'She Loves You',* the small Swan imprint, guaranteed low sales. It was to be the million advance orders for *'I Want to Hold Your Hand'* that finally persuaded Capitol's president Alan Livingston to pledge $50,000 promotion for the record. It is also thought that an article in Variety magazine about The Beatles appearing on three Ed Sullivan shows helped.

Prior to *'I Want to Hold Your Hand'* only Acker Bilk with *'Strangers on the Shore'* and The Tornados with *'Telstar'* had made number one in the USA. This was about to change. The successful gig at the 18,000 seat Washington Coliseum and an estimated audience of over 70 million for the Ed Sullivan Show precipitated the coining of the phrase 'British invasion' by news presenter Walter Cronkite. Prior to that, the defiance of an embargo by The Musicians Union on American artists appearing in the UK (in response to the closed shop of the US in not allowing British acts to perform there) when Chet Baker played at London's Flamingo Club on 23 October, 1955 after the MU and the American Federation of Musicians agreed to lift their mutual ban, and after The Beatles had performed two further gigs at New York's Carnegie Hall the floodgates began to open: The Animals, The Dave Clark Five, The Kinks, The Searchers, The

Rolling Stones and The Zombies were among the acts crossing the Atlantic. This was 'the British invasion' Walter Cronkite was referring to.[25]/[26]/[27]

The B-side of *'I Want to Hold Your Hand'*, *'This Boy'* is a great demonstration, if one were needed, of what great vocal harmonists The Beatles were and, of their ability to perform 'middle of the road' music, of great appeal to TV shows, variety performances and those less than convinced by rock 'n' roll. (*'Til There Was You'* is another excellent example).

1964 began with the recording of *'Can't Buy Me Love'*, soon to be their fourth UK number one, on 29th January. It was perhaps the group's jazziest (certainly most swinging) song to date prompting a cover by Ella Fitzgerald and was backed by another equally hip, percussive song strong enough to have been the A-side, *'You Can't Do That'*. Following the breakthrough provided by *'I Want to Hold Your Hand'*, the group that the US, and EMI Capitol, had staunchly held out against were now on the front cover of magazines like 'Time', 'Life' and 'Newsweek'. Big stars in the UK were often relegated to a bit part on American concert hall bills but now truth was becoming stranger than fiction and limousines and decoy cars part of the routine. The group had to play on a revolving stage at the Washington Coliseum with the drums on the turntable, and the mikes and equipment being repositioned after every song so that the appropriate quarter of the crowd could get a full frontal view. There is a lady taking photographs with what looks suspiciously like the Kodak used by my parents as The Beatles ripped into *'She Loves You'*, *'Please Please Me'* and an especially dynamic performance of *'I Saw Her Standing There'*.

---

[25] There was also a US 'invasion' of Britain in October, 1963 with the likes of Little Richard on a package tour headlined by The Everly Brothers, later joined by Bo Diddley and The Rolling Stones.

[26] It is also interesting to note that there were not many indigenous British artists active in the soul/ R&B scene in the sixties which was predominately an American preserve. Despite that, the Northern Soul scene was established by the middle of the sixties with the likes of Roger Eagle of Manchester's Twisted Wheel Club on 6 Whitfield Street searching for obscure records from the States. Peter Shapiro explains: "Most of these (records) that really moved the dance floor, shared the monolithic stomping 4/4 Holland-Dozier-Holland Motown backbeat and up tempo, uplifting chords usually masking the pain of the lyrics." The Blackpool Mecca and Wigan Casino were two other popular venues. While the focus of this book is primarily pop and rock, British soul did establish itself to a degree in the late '60s with The Foundations (with their Trinidadian lead singer), Johnny Johnson and The Bandwagon (Americans who had relocated to the UK), The Equals (an authentically multi-racial group from north London led by a Guyanese Eddy Grant). And, of course, there was Dusty Springfield. A woman of high principle she was deported from South Africa in 1964 for refusing to perform in front of segregated audiences and became a worldwide critically acclaimed soul singer when she moved away from the big production style of *'I Only Want to Be With You'* to angst ridden songs like *'What's It Gonna Be'* and *'Don't Forget About Me'*, releasing two creditable LPs in our target year of 1967 but reaching her apotheosis in 1968 with 'Dusty in Memphis'. **(45)**

[27] The impact of *I Want to Hold Your Hand* was such that there was suddenly an obsession with 'English' groups after years of ambivalence.

Larry Kane who was the only American journalist in the official Beatles press group in 1964 has written a book about The Beatles' 1964 tour called 'Ticket to Ride'. This is all the more fascinating as it includes an hour long CD of interviews with the four main protagonists. Kane had previously been unconvinced about the staying power of the group considering them to be a bit of a flash in the pan despite the frenzied scene in Miami International Airport on 13 February, six days after The Beatles landed on American soil for the first time to a New York welcome from an estimated 3,000 fans and onlookers. In between times, the group had achieved unprecedented TV exposure on the Ed Sullivan show, and played live before ecstatic crowds in the aforementioned Coliseum Theatre in Washington DC and New York's Carnegie Hall. Kane's first involvement proper with the group came after an invitation from Brian Epstein to join the travelling press party for a summer tour beginning in the Cow Palace, San Francisco on 19 August before around 17,000 fans, the start of a whistle stop tour of 26 gigs[28] ending in New York's Paramount Theatre on 20 September. This was pretty much 'spills and thrills' as Kane's eye witness account attests with George Martin's famous phrase about the noise being like putting a microphone in front of a Boeing 747, not much about the music, more about hysteria and celebrity. Underneath all the tumult and hubbub though, Kane, at first sceptical, could hear the beauty of the songs and the consummate professionalism of the musicians.

There was also a film to be made called 'A Hard Day's Night', named after one of Ringo's endearingly frequent malpropisms. This was to be masterminded by Dick Lester, an amateur jazz pianist, who had worked with Spike Milligan and The Goons, and Alan Owen, the Welsh playwright. There was also a soundtrack LP in 1964 and another album before the end of the year.

---

[28] including four gigs over the border in Canada, one in Vancouver and Toronto, and two on the same night in a smaller venue in Montreal.

# Chapter Five

## The Beatles: Part Two – A Hard Day's Night / Help / For Sale / Rubber Soul / Revolver

The Beatles also toured the Netherlands in 1964. Unfortunately, Ringo couldn't make it as he was recovering from having his tonsils removed, not an easy operation at the best of times but worse for adults and smokers.[29] His replacement for the Hong Kong leg of the tour was Jimmy Nichol[30] and Ringo returned for the Australian leg where The Beatles occupied the top six places on the chart. There were also tours de France in 1964 including the Olympia Theatre, Paris where they shared a bill with Trini Lopez. There is some fabulous footage on the Beatles Anthology 4 DVD which shows what a great frontman George Harrison could be (*'Everybody's Tryin' to Be My Baby'*) and Paul McCartney trying to get his tongue round: "*Et maintenant... chanson... qui s'apelle...* I'm A Loser'!

By the time of the filming of the second Dick Lester produced film, the group were smoking 'herbal jazz cigarettes' (McCartney's epithet) and "smoking marijuana for breakfast" (Lennon's). The film itself was a classic of self-indulgence. Ringo's lauded canal side scene in 'A Hard Day's Night' was actually totally improvised, Charlie Chaplin-like with George Martin's orchestrated version of *'This Boy'* renamed *'Ringo's Theme'* added, after returning from an all-night bender at the Ad-Lib club. Members of the group would say, "We've never been to the Bahamas" or "We've never been skiing" and a scene would be written to accommodate their fantasies. It could be argued that the guys deserved some self-indulgence as they had played 32 venues in 34 days in 24 different cities only to return to the road when they returned to the UK where their adoring fans were getting a bit jealous and possessive, even displaying banners with proclamations of loyalty such as "We love you more than the US".

The LP soundtrack to 'A Hard Day's Night' was recorded between February and June, 1964, and released on 10th July in the UK (but earlier in the US on 26th June). It was made up of *'And I Love Her'* (a McCartney song about Jane Asher), Lennon's *'I Should Have Known Better'* (influenced by Bob Dylan), *'Any Time at All'* and *'I'll Be Back'*, reckoned by some to be one of their finest songs and described by MacDonald as "a melancholy essay in major/minor uncertainty mirrored in the emotional instability of its lyric" **(47)**. The other songs on the album were *'Tell Me Why'*, *'I'm Happy Just to Dance with You, 'When I Get Home'* and, two songs which would become much admired and covered, Lennon's *'If I Fell'* and McCartney's *'Things We Said Today'*. An EP 'Long Tall Sally' was also released on 19th June, 1964. This included the title track (co-written by 'Little' Richard Penniman and a 1956

---

[29] As Alan Clayson relates in 'Ringo: A Life' despite attempts at being incognito in his hospital ward (as 'Mr Jackson), "Starr's whereabouts had been rumbled and Covent Garden exchange burned with concerned calls. Many were from the States, where, even as they spoke, *'What's Wrong with Ringo?'* – a 45 by The Bon-Bons – was being pressed." **(46)**

[30] Nicol was chosen because he 'looked like a Beatle' (Brian Epstein) and had been a 'ghost' musician on a budget Pye LP of Beatles covers called 'This is Merseybeat'.

hit for him), a staple in Beatles' live performances; *'I Call Your Name'* (with a touch of Kingston ska); and covers of Carl Perkins' rockabilly song *'Matchbox'* and Larry Williams' *'Slow Down'* (Williams main claim to fame is as the writer of rock 'n' roll standard *'Bony Maronie'*). *'Long Tall Sally'* and *'I Call Your Name'* were included on 'The Beatles Second Album' in the US while *'Matchbox/ Slow Down'* was released as a single. Such variations are a constant source of fascination to discographers and record collectors all over the world. The fourth album 'Beatles for Sale' came out in December, 1964 and in the US was called 'Beatles '65' by the time it was released. The gruelling schedule The Beatles were on is illustrated by the fact that the sessions began shortly after the chart topping *'A Hard Day's Night'* (on both sides of the Atlantic). The album included *'Baby's in Black'* which would become a staple of the group's live act, another Dylan influenced song *'I'm a Loser'*; *'Eight Days a Week'*, the title from another of Ringo Starr's malapropisms; McCartney's *'I'll Follow the Sun'* written in Hamburg in 1960; and covers of Lieber /Stoller /Penniman's *'Kansas City/ Hey, Hey, Hey'* medley (recorded by Little Richard himself as *Hey-Hey-Hey-Hey (Going Back to Birmingham)* the B-side of *'Good Golly Miss Molly'*; Chuck Berry's *'Rock and Roll Music'*, Buddy Holly's *Words of Love'* and two Carl Perkins numbers *'Honey Don't* and *'Everybody's Trying to Be My Baby'*. Lennon's *'I Feel Fine'* was reserved as a single and his Rickenbacker, he claimed, produced the first guitar feedback on record. Philip Norman's summation of the 'Beatles for Sale' album from a Lennon perspective was the contrast between upbeat Paul songs like *'Things We Said Today'* and *'I'll Follow the Sun'*, and John exploring "greyer areas of self-doubt, mourning and embarrassment" such as on *'No Reply'*, *'Baby's in Black'* and *'I Don't Want to Spoil the Party'*, John's 'darkness' to Paul's 'lightness' with "his spirits seeming highest in the cover versions." **(48)**

A second American tour followed in 1965 which gave The Beatles an opportunity to meet Bob Dylan whose 'Freewheeling' album they 'played constantly', being quickly transported upon arrival at Kennedy Airport to the 33rd floor of the Warwick Hotel on 6th Avenue. This tour started dramatically. Larry Kane takes up the story: "Almost at the same hour of their touchdown in New York, Los Angeles exploded in a wave of racial violence and terror that would rock the foundations of urban America". **(49)** (The Watts riots)

Another two appearances on the Ed Sullivan Show at which they performed well on six numbers: *'Ticket to Ride, Act Naturally, Help, Yesterday, I Feel Fine and I'm Down'* helped to take their minds off the events unfolding in Watts. *'Twist and Shout, Dizzy Miss Lizzie, Everybody's Trying to Be My Baby, Can't Buy Me Love, Baby's in Black and A Hard Day's Night* as well as all of the 'Sullivan songs' except for Paul's *'Yesterday'* were performed at the first concert of the 1965 tour at the Shea Stadium where the official attendance was 55,600, and, by all accounts, everyone connected with the groups seemed pleased. Ten more dates followed with two nights at the Hollywood Bowl ending up where they had started on their second tour a year before at the Cow Palace. It was in Hollywood that The Beatles would meet Elvis.

Tony Barrow related to Larry Kane (who had to wait outside the Presley complex on Perugia Road in Bel Air) that: "When they got there, it was almost anti-climactic until the music. Before that, they were talking a great deal of small talk. It was very meaningless until Elvis called for guitars and turned the sound on the television down, and they all sat around this crescent-shaped sofa and started to have a jam session, and sparkling conversation that had been missing in speech was now replaced by sparkling conversation in music." **(50)**

Awkward as it was, after the three-hour meeting, the group left with some nice memorabilia including Elvis LPs and sequined jackets. "However carefully phrased his best wishes for the Beatles' success, he saw the Beatles and the whole British invasion as a threat, and it galled him to be widely perceived as passé." **(51)**(Elvis had his very first UK #1 with *'Crying in the Chapel'* around the time of the Beatles visit, and he felt restricted and creatively and artistically dissatisfied with the music released in his name. Once the rock 'n' roll revolutionary, he was fast becoming an establishment figure as The Beatles, The Rolling Stones and Bob Dylan pushed the boundaries. Having a big hit with a gospel number recorded five years before which Elvis himself did not think matched up to the original, certainly did not help his image). There had been some horse trading between the respective managers, Brian Epstein and 'Colonel' Tom Parker which did not help to ease the tension of the well-publicised meeting. Elvis's group of close buddies, the 'Memphis Mafia', were all excited about the meeting but Elvis openly displayed his indifference by making brief introductions and some small talk until returning to the soundless TV in his 'den', plugging a bass into an amp, and playing along with Charlie Rich's *'Mohair Sam'*.

In the second of Peter Guralnick's beautifully written books on Elvis, he has more to say on this subject: "The Beatles' overall reaction was one of disappointment, their response to Elvis a prickly mix of anger and disillusion. Nonetheless, they reciprocated with an invitation of their own (for Elvis and his 'gang' to visit them at the weekend), Elvis almost immediately demurred, he didn't know what his schedule was like."[31] **(52)** Albert Goldman in his book 'Elvis' claims that Elvis played Paul's bass part on *'I Feel Fine'* but 'The Beatles Anthology' recollections make no specific reference to that, only that Paul showed Elvis 'a thing or two'**(53)**

As a postscript, 'The Beatles Live at Hollywood Bowl' was issued on vinyl and CD on 9 September, 2016 with Ron Howard's film 'Eight Days a Week-The Touring Years' due in cinemas on 15 September (now on DVD).

Following a UK tour and a Christmas season at Hammersmith Odeon, the first song The Beatles recorded in 1965 was *'Ticket to Ride'* on 15 February. *'Eight Days a Week'* had just hit #1 in the US and *'Ticket to Ride'* would follow it, if only for one week. Ian Macdonald reckoned that: "*Ticket to Ride* was psychologically deeper than anything The Beatles had recorded before. Yet, there was more to the record than unusual emotional depth. As sheer sound, *Ticket to Ride* is extraordinary for its time – massive with chiming electric guitars, weighty rhythm, and rumbling floor tom-toms" (the heavier sound possibly in response to The Who, The Kinks and The Yardbirds while there is a 'narcotic passivity' about Lennon's lyric). **(54)**

The McCartney song *'Another Girl'* (subject matter – secret assignations in his London flat) was next. This, along with Lennon's *'Yes It Is'*, the B-side to *'Ticket to Ride'* and another song that would appear on the 'Help!' soundtrack, George Harrison's *'I Need You'* written with Patti Boyd in mind, were recorded at Abbey Road between 15 and 16 February. These were followed over the next few days by *'The Night Before'*, Harrison's *'You Like Me Too Much'*, the Dylan influenced *'You've Got to Hide Your Love Way'*, *'Tell Me What You See'*, all destined for the 'Help!' soundtrack with *'You're Going to Lose That Girl'* the last track laid down before departing to the Bahamas to start filming for 'Help!'

The film project was still called 'Eight Arms to Hold You' until the group reassembled on 13 April to record Lennon's highly personal, mid-tempo ballad, soon to be revved up, *'Help!'*. Thus octopoidal visions were banished and *'Help!'* as a 45 became a great success hitting #1 in the charts on both sides of the Atlantic. The 'Help!' sessions

---

[31] Some of the 'Memphis Mafia' did visit The Beatles' house in Benedict Canyon the following night but there was no Elvis.

continued until August with notable songs like *'I'm Down'*, the B-side of *'Help!'*, a 12-bar rock 'n' roller with a searing Paul vocal and Lennon adding Hammond organ; *'Yesterday'*, a McCartney solo number written early in 1964 in Paris which became a #1 hit in the US (and also much covered by easy listening artists) and benefited from an empathetic George Martin string arrangement; and *'Act Naturally'*, actually a cover version which became a country and western hit for Buck Owens in 1963 (this provided the B-side for *'Yesterday'*). To expand its length towards half an hour, a version of Larry Williams' *'Dizzy Miss Lizzy'* was recorded with Paul on electric piano. This would appear on 'Beatles VI' in the US as would a cover of Williams' *'Bad Boy'* and *'You Like Me too Much'* and *'Tell Me What You See'*. The song *'Wait'*, a Beatles rarity as it is reckoned to be a genuine 50/50 composition, was recorded during the 'Help!' sessions but would have to wait until the next LP 'Rubber Soul', released in December, 1965.

The 'Rubber Soul' sessions would start in October, 1965, following a tour of France, Italy and Spain, a holiday, and another US summer tour. The first song to be recorded was *'Run for Your Life'* followed by *'Norwegian Wood (The Bird Has Flown)'* whose origins are mysterious although Lennon claimed ownership in the interview with Playboy magazine in 1980. In any event, it's a lovely song, much covered by folk singers and featuring double tracked sitar played by Harrison with Ringo on percussion only. *'Drive My Car'*, thought to be inspired by Otis Redding's Memphis sound, particularly *'Respect'*, is a strong opening track while Harrison's own Byrds influenced *'If I Needed Someone'* had the 'fifth Beatle' George Martin on harmonium. Lennon's autobiographical song *'In My Life'* has Martin playing again, on electric piano this time. Also, in October, *'Day Tripper'*, a dig at part-time hippies for want of a better description (the term had not yet surfaced), was a refreshing 12-bar of sorts with a memorable riff and drumming inspired by Al Jackson of Booker T and The MGs (The number was later covered by Otis Redding for Stax in 1967). *'We Can Work It Out'* (the theme is reckoned to be Paul's on the oft repeated subject of his relationship with Jane Asher, the song a collaboration), the other side of the 45, once again hit #1 on both sides of the Atlantic. Returning to the 'Rubber Soul' album itself, there was also Lennon's *'Nowhere Man'* with its 'drag beat' which would become a folk favourite (just like *'Norwegian Wood'*) and *'Michelle'* which borrowed a line from *'I Put a Spell on You'* and provided The Overlanders with a #1 hit in February, 1966. The others songs were *'The Word'*, *'You Won't See Me'* (again about Asher) and Lennon's *'Girl'* which had an interesting guitar sound produced by guitars with capos suggesting the sound of mandolins and accordions. Again, there were variations between the UK and the US releases'. For example, *'It's Only Love'* was on 'Help!' in the UK and 'Rubber Soul' in the US; *'Drive My Car'* and *'If I Needed Someone'* (which would provide The Hollies with a hit) were on 'Yesterday and Today' in the US, and *'What Goes On'* was the B-side of *'Nowhere Man'* for a US single released in February, 1966.

'Rubber Soul' marked the start of an era when The Beatles would be considered an 'albums' band. This is not to disparage earlier LPs but few are likely to figure in all-time greats lists the way that 'Rubber Soul' and its successors did. Clearly, the 1966 LPs that preceded 'Sergeant Pepper' are worthy of further analysis. Here is some of what was said: Rolling Stone described 'Rubber Soul' as a "real breakthrough" calling it a "folk-rock masterpiece" under the influence of Dylan. **(55)**Colin Larkin recognises 'Rubber Soul' as "not a collection of would be hits or cover versions but a startlingly diverse collection ranging from the pointed satire of *'Nowhere Man'* to the intensely reflective *'In My Life'*."**(56)**. Larkin also comments on the innovative use of sitar on the "punningly titled tale of Lennon's infidelity, *'Norwegian Wood'*." He also uses the analogy of growing up and appealing to a new audience of middle class as opposed to working class listeners as "the art and literary worlds moved away from polo-necked bohemian jazz" as "The Beatles wooed them with simple melodies and clever lyrics" singling out *'Norwegian Wood'*, *'I'm Looking Through You'*, *'Think for Yourself'* and *'In My Life'* as the key tracks **(57)**

A final tour of Britain followed 'Rubber Soul' and then the luxury of three months off. Musically, Harrison was soaking up Indian music, McCartney classical. During the first week of April, work began on a track that would change popular music history. *'Tomorrow Never Knows'* used tape loops and, as Ian Macdonald describes some 'musique concrete' – a 'seagull/ Red Indian effect' loop (apparently McCartney laughing) at 0:07; a B flat major orchestral chord at 0:19; a mellotron flute at 0:22; a mellotron string oscillation at 0:38; an accelerated rising sitar scalar phase at 0:56**(58)**. Macdonald goes on to explain that 'the most salient of these five effects is the sitar and mellotron flute setting with the second half of the instrumental break McCartney's guitar break for *'Taxman'* "slowed down a tone, cut up and run backwards."**(59)**. Lennon's desire to sound like the Dalai Lami and Tibetan monks chanting on a mountain top was achieved by putting the voice through a Leslie cabinet. He concludes: "The soundscape of *'Tomorrow Never Knows'* is a riveting blend of anarchy and awe, its loops crisscrossing in a random pattern of colliding circles."

While the like of this had not been heard before, the next track had a more traditional focus. *'Got to Get You into My Life'* was also started in early April but not completed until 20 June. Thought to be inspired by The Supremes *'I Hear a Symphony'* or perhaps earlier hits like *'Where Did Our Love Go'*. Jane Asher and Paul were regular attendees of the Bag O' Nails in Soho, and were familiar with Georgie Fame's music and the trumpeter and alto saxophonist both of whom were hired for this recording (with three other brass players, all session men). So what is it about: relationships or LSD? Paul states in The Beatles Anthology book, "It was a song about pot, actually"**(60)**. Either way, John Lennon thought it had one of Paul's better lyrics (He was not that enthusiastic about some of Paul's lyrics also saying "he could write lyrics if he took the effort")**(61)**, and it provided hits for Cliff Bennett and the Rebel Rousers and Earth, Wind and Fire.

In the second week of April, the group entered the studio again to record Harrison's *'Love You To'*, a philosophical/ love song written on sitar and, as far as The Beatles' involvement was concerned, effectively a solo number with a tabla player and other members of the North London Asian Music Circle on sitar and tambura.[32]

---

[32] Sandy Pearlman wrote an interesting article in 'Crawdaddy' issue 7 on 'Patterns and Sounds: The Uses of Raga in Rock' which first appeared in the spring of 1966, the 'raga rock' phrase used by Roger McGuinn with reference to *'Eight Miles High'*. The term 'appropriation of the Indian sound' is used to describe its use on *'Norwegian Wood'* followed by The Rolling Stones' *'Paint It Black'* (the spring of '66) Donovan's *'Three King Fishers'* and The Beatles' *'Love You to'* (the summer of '66) while the term 'The 'Indian' sound' as produced through tuning etc. is exemplified by The Rolling Stones on *'Tell Me'* (summer '64) and The Yardbirds on *'Heart Full of Soul'* (autumn, '65). Sandy Bull was the first to assimilate the Indian drone sound on his 1963 LP 'Fantasia' by adapting a banjo tuning for guitar (tuned to B with the next string a fourth down with B as the lowest string, the melody played on one string, the neighbouring string producing the drone). Pearlman says Sandy Bull's *'Memphis, Tennessee'* is an 'organic' raga while *'Norwegian Wood'* is merely an 'exotic accompaniment'. NB. This article was written for the January, 1967 issue of 'Crawdaddy', therefore, preceding *'Within You, Without You'*. **(62)**

Also recorded was the excellent 45, McCartney's *'Paperback Writer'*, perhaps inspired by time spent assisting John Dunbar in the Indica Bookshop in Southampton Row, and its superlative B-side *'Rain'* written by Lennon. The rest of April produced two more songs: Lennon's *'Dr Robert'* about a real-life New York Doctor who mixed his patients' vitamin shots with methedrine and *'And Your Bird Can Sing'* while Harrison's diatribe about the high income tax rate for high earners in Labour Britain *'Taxman'*; Lennon's *'I'm Only Sleeping'* (another piece of sonic architecture featuring Harrison's backwards guitar) and *'Eleanor Rigby'* which had to wait until May and June for completion. Originally called *'Why Did It Die?,'* McCartney's *'For No One'* is another song about Jane Asher (the end of the relationship) with French horn by Alan Civil and was completed in May while his other songs *'Yellow Submarine'*[33], *'Good Day Sunshine'*, and *'Here, There and Everywhere'* (another favourite of John's); and Lennon's *'She Said, She Said'*[34] all came to fruition in June along with the swiftly completed Harrison song *'I Want to Tell You'*. Regarding one of The Beatles' best-loved songs *'Eleanor Rigby'*, Paul's explanation of the name was that Eleanor was after Eleanor Bron, a collaborator on 'Help!', Rigby named after a shop in Bristol's Docklands. However, in Woolton Cemetery, there is a gravestone on which the name Eleanor Rigby appears "beloved wife of Thomas Woods and grand daughter of John Rigby, died 10th October, 1939, aged 44, asleep". Paul reckons one of the most famous names in pop history was already there subconsciously from his youth having 'fly fags' in the graveyard **(63)**.

The 'Revolver' LP was issued on 5 August in the UK and 8 August in the US. Rolling Stone said, "It was with 'Revolver' that the group left virtually all their contemporaries behind." (The use of the word 'virtually' is unqualified)**(64)**. *'Eleanor Rigby'*, *'Tomorrow Never Knows'* and *'Love You to'* are singled out, each showing different aspects of Beatles music "and 'Revolver' was only the prelude to 'Sergeant Pepper'". On 9 July, 1966, Melody Maker said that 'Revolver' would 'change the direction of pop music'. "Were The Beatles re-defining pop music? Had the group found the way to remove themselves from the pop scene into a scene of their very own?"

The Beatles congregated in the studio on 24 November, 1966, following a turbulent period in which the group had undertaken a tour of Germany and Japan, including gigs in Munich, Essen and Hamburg the city where they had 'cut their teeth, almost immediately after the final grooves of their 'Revolver' album had been cut'. Manager Brian Epstein's insistence on such a heavy touring schedule did not go down too well with the group and things came to head during a tour of the Philippines in the events following their refusal to pay due dotage to the wishes of the wife of the Philippine President Ferdinand, Imelda Marcos. It was policy for the group to refuse to attend official functions and despite the insistence of uniformed aides from the presidential palace in Malancanang, they stuck to their guns. A state-run TV programme spoke the following day of the dishonour of The Beatles who had let down 300 children (including the Marcos's) many of whom were war orphans or cripples. The headline in the Manila newspaper read 'Beatles Snub President'. The limousines and room service promptly disappeared as the group, their manager Brian Epstein and their entourage were publicly ostracised. Things didn't get any better at the airport where the party were manhandled

---

[33] Paul's mind turned to childhood in a twilight moment, Donovan and John helped with the lyrics, Ringo delivered the vocal, and one of the group's most widely appealing and recognisable, and repeated (e.g. at sporting events) was delivered.

[34] A Lennon song that John recalls writing after an acid trip in LA when hanging out with The Byrds.

and had to endure an angry mob pounding on the glass of the terminal. Epstein was pushed over in the melee, and the crazed overreaction of the Fillipinos temporarily soured the relationships between manager and group, and did little to help the fragile state of mind of the Beatles' manager. As George Harrison sardonically remarked, "We'll take a couple of weeks to recuperate before we go and get beaten up by the Americans." Harrison had every right to be concerned, for John Lennon had said in an interview with journalist Maureen Cleave that appeared in the London 'Evening Standard' newspaper on 4 March, 1966: "I don't know which will go first – rock n, roll or Christianity" and also voiced the opinion that it was likely to be Christianity that would 'vanish and shrink' because The Beatles were 'more popular than Jesus now'. The reaction in the UK was muted but when the same remarks were reprinted in American teen magazine *Datebook,* the Beatles headed into the eye of a Bible belt backlash.

As Jonathan Gould puts in his 'Can't Buy Me Love: The Beatles, Britain and America' book: "The *New York Times Magazine* published an article by Maureen Cleave titled 'Old Beatles-A Study in Paradox'. This was mainly a rewrite of her *Evening Standard* series (of articles)… This provoked no more response from *Times* readers in July than it had from *Evening Standard* readers in March. But when Lennon's words were yet again reprinted in the August issue of the American teen magazine *Datebook*, Judgement Day was at hand." **(65)**

Despite Cleave's attempt to put the record straight by putting Lennon's remarks into the context and spirit in which they were intended ("John was certainly not comparing The Beatles and Christ. He was simply observing that so weak was the state of Christianity that The Beatles were to many people better known. He was deploring rather than approving."), Beatles records and memorabilia were sacrificially put to the fire. While refusing to make an outright, unqualified apology, Lennon did at least go some way to appeasing public opinion on 11 August on arriving at O'Hare Airport, Chicago in his statements, "I'm not anti-God, anti-Christ or anti-religion" and "If I had said television was more popular than Jesus, I might have got away with it". Brian Epstein in a press conference in advance of the tour had already explained that Lennon's remarks were made in relation to his "astonishment at the fact that in the last fifty years, the Church of England had declined so much" and that "John Lennon is deeply concerned about the publication of his remarks out of context in America and regrets any offence to people with certain religious beliefs." *The Disc and Music Echo* paper came to Lennon's aid on 13 August saying that he was deeply interested in religion and was not boasting that the Beatles were more popular than Jesus but lamenting the fact. (The Melody Maker also leapt to Lennon's defence in an article on the same date).

Derek Taylor writing for Disc and Music Echo from Hollywood spoke of America being 'unsettled, violent, crazy and paranoid' and that 'it was a dangerous time for The Beatles to visit'. Fans did try to charge the stage tearing down barricades in the process in Cleveland, Ohio, and the group had to be escorted by police and security men to a nearby caravan in a temporary abatement of the concert. This was actually an enthusiastic rather than aggressive response by 'fans' as Kenny Everett reported for the Melody Maker. (Everett, a Radio London deejay at the time, also reported on police coming to the group's rescue when fans also stormed towards the stage in Los Angeles). As it turned out, the group were generally well received and the Ban the Beatles campaign started by Alabama deejay Tommy Charles (but which he retreated from after John Lennon's press conference in Chicago) became a bit of a non-event. This analysis must, of course, be tempered by the fact that death threats were made during the tour and there was the continuing fear of snipers in the audience, although nothing worse happened than a firecracker being thrown towards the stage at the Memphis Coliseum. The tour concluded with a date at Candlestick Park in San Francisco which was to turn out to be the last time The Beatles gave an official public performance to paying customers. [35]

As Ringo Starr once said, "Four years of Beatlemania was enough for anyone". George Harrison made a remark about not being a Beatle any more after this concert but Brian Epstein's promise that there would be no more touring, and the critical and commercial success of the 'Revolver' album helped establish a welcome degree of equilibrium.

Overall though, the 'runes' were not looking good in the year of 1966 as The Beatles started work on their next step towards musical pop perfection. They had not only to endure difficult tours in Germany, the Philippines and the USA, but George Harrison was growing apart musically from the rest, and the growing insinuation of LSD and its relatively unknown and unpredictable effects would certainly affect their creativity, and could have jeopardised their discipline and self-control if not their very sanity. Even an album cover caused a furore. Derek Taylor writing for 'Disc and Music Echo' on 25 June, 2011, reported that Capitol Records, the US distributors of Beatles music, had recalled the infamous 'butcher' covers of their LP 'Yesterday and Today'.[36]

So this was the context in which the Beatles reconvened to decide their next move. As far as the next album was concerned, the gauntlet had already been thrown down by LPs like The Who's 'A Quick One' and The Rolling Stones 'Aftermath' on one side of the Atlantic, and Bob Dylan's double LP 'Blonde on Blonde' (avidly listened to by the group) and The Mothers of Invention's 'Freak Out' on the other. It was The Beach Boys 'Pet Sounds', Brian Wilson's response to 'Rubber Soul' and the ground breaking single *'Good Vibrations'*, though that provided the yardstick against which the success of Lennon/ McCartney and co would both measure themselves and be measured. By the time The Beatles began the sessions that led to the release of 'Sergeant Pepper's', Brian Wilson was already in a state of creative depression on hearing 'Revolver'. Following a motor cycle accident, and in state of drug and excessive touring induced breakdown and burnout, Dylan was about to embark on a 'gap year' in which he retreated to Woodstock and, during which time, he recorded The Basement Tapes' with The Band while The Stones had recorded 'Between The Buttons' which could hardly be considered an artistic triumph.

Clearly, The Beatles were now in a position to fully realise their potential creatively and artistically. The seeds were also sown and a major breakthrough in The Beatles progressing from 'mop top' pop stars to serious composers and musicians came as early as 1963 when the esteemed Times newspaper music critic William Mann eulogised about the LP 'With The Beatles' referring to Aeolian cadences in the song *It Won't Be Long,* and praising the band in technical terms normally reserved for a world class orchestra.[37]

---

[35] Coincidentally, this was to be the meeting point some five months later where thousands would converge on Golden Gate Park for the 'First Human Be-In: A Gathering of the Tribes'.

[36] Apparently, it cost Capitol $75,000 to recover 500,000 albums.

[37] It is interesting to note that, while John Lennon was never one to overplay The Beatles' contribution to rock 'n' roll, nor was he a big fan of Bill Haley. "There have only been two great albums that I listened to all the way through when I was about sixteen. One by Carl Perkins and Elvis's first." (my annotation) **(66)**

# Chapter Six

## The Beatles: Part Three – To Sergeant Pepper and Beyond

One fateful night, Paul McCartney, in the company of Tara Browne (the subject of the song '*A Day in the Life*'), distracted by a picturesque full moon, fell off his hired moped and split his lip. Little did he realise it at the time but this incident precipitated a large symbolic step towards the idea of **'Sergeant Pepper'**: the relatively mundane cultivation of a moustache to cover his wounded lip.

Moustaches were also a way of trying to seek anonymity (ironically, Paul himself was prone to donning disguises to escape being noticed including one famous instance during the Beatles' appearances at the Budokan Theatre, Tokyo, when he and Mal Evans, the Beatles 'roadie' donned wide brimmed hats and false moustaches to slip out of the service entrance of the Hilton Hotel) and Harrison, who although unconvinced by Ravi Shankar's exhortation for George to disguise himself by growing a moustache when visiting Bombay, decided to grow one anyway. And as Beatles insider Alistair Taylor reminds us in his book **'With the Beatles'**, John Lennon had to wear a disguise on visits to see his wife, Cynthia, and his newly born son, Julian, in hospital. Ringo was convinced that "We were gradually turning into Sergeant Peppers. It was as if we were going through a metamorphosis." **(67)**

In fact, the four Beatles had been taking sabbaticals with the intention of reconvening towards the end of 1966 to start work on a new album after the commercial and critical success of the **'Revolver'** album released on 5 August, 1966 in the UK and 8 August, 1966 in the US. **'Revolver'** and its predecessor **'Rubber Soul'** (3 and 6 December, 1965 respectively) had been well received by fans and reviewers, and, most importantly, had marked significant steps forward musically. By the time the Beatles did reconvene, they had coincidentally all cultivated moustaches and grown their hair longer.

After his marriage to Maureen Cox, Ringo Starr was enjoying being a father following the birth of his first child, Zak. Ringo seemed to be adept at keeping out of the spotlight. When asked on 2 December, 1967 about his daily routine by Melody Maker's Jack Hutton, he replied: "Very quiet, I get up at nine and come up to town every day. It's like an office job really. I get home about half past seven, have my dinner, chat, do whatever you do, then go to bed. I drive in with John, and see Paul and George in town." Prior to 'Sergeant Pepper' Ringo, in rare interviews, comes across as equally 'down to earth', enjoying country life, although he does allude to future ambitions when he says to Melody Maker's Alan Walsh in response to a question about the Beach Boys and recording techniques: "It's a natural step to try to make the next thing better than the last. The Beach Boys do the same." **(68)**

Paul McCartney took advantage of the 'time out' to enjoy London night life with girlfriend, Jane Asher, from his new Georgian town house in Cavendish Avenue, St John's Wood and to work on the soundtrack for a movie entitled 'The Family Way' starring Hayley Mills.

George and Pattie Harrison were on a 'study leave' in Ravi Shankar's Himalayan retreat studying Indian beliefs, and George was mastering the sitar he had previously played on two Beatles songs, *'Norwegian Wood'* and *'Rain'*.

John Lennon was in Almeria, Spain with his wife, Cynthia, and the Beatles' head roadie, Neil Aspinall, acting as Private Gripweed, batman to platoon Commander Michael Crawford (who would later be the hapless star of the TV comedy sitcom 'Some Mothers Do Have Them') in the Richard Lester directed satire **'How I Won the War'**. During this time, John also started wearing the 'National Health Service' or 'granny' glasses that became his trademark.

A large still photograph of Lennon in full combat camouflage dominated the front cover of the very first Rolling Stone magazine (Volume 1 #1 9 November, 1967, price 25 cents)[38].

The review inside the magazine reads as follows: "The primary mood of the film is morbid. There's a lot of bleeding and amputating, and one person gets run over by a tank. It's all pointless… that's the point of the film." Lennon comes across as good actor and the final scene is particularly effective as "Michael Crawford's face ages 30 years in 2 seconds."

On returning to London, Lennon made the acquaintance of John Dunbar and Barry Miles[39], the former a Bohemian artist and entrepreneur, the latter a bookseller and childhood contemporary of Brian Jones of The Rolling Stones. It was at the Indica art gallery and bookshop established in 1965 with £2,000 starting capital from Paul's girlfriend Jane's brother, Peter Asher, that John was to meet Yoko Ono for the first time.

LSD or 'acid' as it was popularly known was also playing a bigger and bigger part in Lennon's life. Lennon and Harrisons' introduction to LSD had been when it was slipped into their coffee by their dentist (of all people!) at the end of a dinner party. (George subsequently referred to this as 'The Dental Experience'). The Independent newspaper in an article by Ian Herbert entitled 'Revealed: Dentist who introduced Beatles to LSD' portrayed the scene and its significance, referring to the "profound consequences of one evening spent at an unprepossessing two bedroom flat near Bayswater in April, 1965" where George Harrison, John Lennon and their wives Patti and Cynthia were spending an evening with George's dentist who, allegedly, slipped LSD into their coffee. .[40] **(69)** This first experience with LSD is one that brought George closer to John although relationships between the men subsequently chilled with Lennon taking particular offence by his apparent airbrushing out in Harrison's semi-autobiographical book 'I Me Mine'.

---

[38] It is illuminating to dwell for a moment on the other features in the magazine with articles about the "high cost of music and love: where's the money from Monterey?", the impending release of a new Jefferson Airplane LP, an interview with Donovan, and articles on The Grateful Dead and the sacking of David Crosby from The Byrds.

[39] It was apparently Miles who introduced Lennon to a book called 'The Psychedelic Experience' co-written by Timothy Leary, the LSD 'guru'.

[40] Incomprehensibly, it took until the publication of Steve Turner's book 'The Fab Four: The Gospel According to the Beatles' in 2006 to identify the mystery dentist who was revealed as John Riley, the son of a Metropolitan Police Officer and a former cosmetic dentist in Chicago. However, the story doesn't end there. A further refinement is contained in Philip Norman's book 'John Lennon: The Life'. Norman says that it was not the dentist's wife but his 22-year-old girlfriend, Cindy Bury, who worked at the Playboy Club in Park Lane, who 'was the only other person present' (and not Riley's wife). Norman is also at pains to stress that Riley was no drug pusher, and that Lennon and Harrison had previously expressed curiosity about LSD. For a full account of what took place, the reader should refer to Norman's book**(70)**.

It was in The Ad Lib club situated in a penthouse above Leicester Square entered by a door next to the Prince Charles Theatre (with views of The Post Office Tower) that the LSD administered by the dentist in the sugar cubes his guests added to their after dinner coffee took full effect. In The Beatles' Anthology book, Harrison vividly recalled the LSD experience: "It felt as though the elevator was on fire and we were going into Hell, but at the same time, we were all in hysterics and crazy. Eventually, we got out at the Ad Lib, on the top floor, and sat there, probably for hours and hours." **(71)**

McCartney, after initial resistance, finally succumbed to taking the drug with his friend, Tara Browne (his companion the night he fell off his moped), after a night out at the Bag o' Nails' pub. McCartney had tried cocaine and heroin rejecting both but despite some bad 'trips' with LSD, he became somewhat of a 'convert'. The Sunday People newspaper picked up on this in an article published on 18 June, 1967, the day of McCartney's 25th birthday, with the headline 'Beatle Paul's Amazing Confession – Yes – I took LSD.'[41] Lennon was so dependent upon LSD that, when he arrived in Greece to follow up an interest the Beatles had in purchasing some remote Greek islands suggested to them by John Alexis Mardis ('Magic Alex'), a friend of the group at the time, and discovered he had left his LSD supply in London, he panicked. "What good is the Parthenon without LSD?" he supposedly exclaimed.**(72)** Also there was Lennon's famous remark to George Harrison who, disillusioned after a trip to the Haight-Ashbury district of San Francisco when his limousine was mobbed by an angry crowd when he refused to play for them in Golden Gate Park, had decided to give up drugs (which he didn't): "Well, it's not doing me any harm!" Philip Norman claims that the strength of the Sgt Pepper's period is that "to all four Beatles, the vision was the same, all four were now converted to LSD." **(73)**

Lest I give the wrong impression it must be pointed out, that apart from the growing development of a 'recreational drugs' culture, there were also a lot of other things going in year of Sergeant Pepper.

---

[41] Although a check on the number of references to each of the other Beatles perhaps suggests otherwise. This 'confession' also appeared in Life Magazine on 19 June although some accounts suggest that Paul had been taking LSD in 1966.

# Chapter Seven
## The Year 1967: The Year of Sergeant Pepper

## The Six Day War

**"Netanyahu tells Obama, we can't go back to 1967"** ran the headline for an article by David Usborne, the Independent newspaper US editor. Benjamin Netanyahu expressed his hope for "a peace that will be genuine and endure, and is based on reality." This was in response to US President Barrack Obama's suggestion that a peace settlement with the Palestinians should be based on Israel's borders as they were before the 6 Day War.

1967 was demarcated, in world affairs, by serious political and environmental issues that still dominate the world stage today: The Middle East and the Arab-Israeli war which, while it only lasted for six days, stirred up a bitter resentment among the Palestinians displaced by a crushing Israeli victory. Jordan lost a significant part of the West Bank and Israel also captured the Golan Heights, the Gaza Strip and the east part of Jerusalem, including the Wailing Wall.

President Nasser of Egypt had ordered the United Nations to remove its forces from Sinai, a desert area that had been under Egyptian rule since 1948 (A United Nations Emergency Force had been established after the Israeli-Egyptian war of 1956). The Gaza Strip, a buffer zone between Israel and Egypt, had also been controlled by Egypt since 1948. A blockade of Israeli shipping in the Straits of Tiran, a safe passage that had been guaranteed by the US, the UK and France after the Suez War in 1956, was announced by Nasser.

Martin Gilbert takes up the story: "Anxious to avoid a drawing in of any of the nuclear powers into any Middle Eastern war, (President) Johnson and (Soviet Premier) Kosygin made use, for the first time, of the Washington-Moscow hot-line. Both men agreed that there would be no direct military intervention by the United States or the Soviet Union. The Israelis were on their own." **(74)**

When King Hussein of Jordan committed his country to enter into hostilities against Israel, the writing really was on the wall. Israel felt it had to act alone and quickly, and on 5th June, the Israeli air force carried out a pre-emptive strike against more than twenty Egyptian air bases, destroying one third of Egypt's air force. Syrian, Iraqi and Jordanian aircraft attacked military targets inside Israel in retaliation. Israeli forces were gaining the upper hand on the ground and in the air, and the Soviet Union wisely did not respond to Egypt's call for assistance, realising that Egypt's claims that the US and Britain were actively helping Israel were unsubstantiated. By 7th June, Israeli forces had occupied the former Jordanian stronghold of Jerusalem and within six days had driven the Egyptians out of the Sinai region, the Jordanians out of the West Bank and the Syrians from the Golan Heights.

9th June was a crucial day for world affairs and for the ideology fuelling the 'cold war' as Communist leaders from eastern countries assembled in Moscow where they joined the Russian Communist party in condemning Israeli aggression. Russia also broke off diplomatic relations with Israel. However, no troops were committed to the Arab side which led to condemnation of the Soviet Union from China as well as the Arab states. By the next day, the war was over with Israeli territory tripled in size with a million Arabs on the West Bank and the Gaza Strip outcast.

The six-day war might have been over but its legacy remained. Before the year was out, the first shots of real anger were fired when an Israeli ship, The Eilat, was sunk by Egyptian missiles on 21st October. Israel retaliated by the firing of heavy artillery along the Suez Canal and Suez City was set on fire during the bombardment. Israeli casualties in the 'War of Attrition' almost equalled the lives lost in the six days' war itself.

The United Nations mediated a cease-fire on 10th June and Israel annexed east Jerusalem as payback for Jordan's participation in the war. In November, the United Nations Security Council approved Resolution 242 calling upon Israel to withdraw from the territories it captured during the Six Days War.

Palestinians point the finger at Israelis aiming missiles indiscriminately at targets including schools and holidays. Israel says Hamas terrorists use members of the public as human shields. In 2018, a diplomatic solution seems no nearer.

## Environmental Issues and Atomic Bombs

The worst global environmental disaster to that point, the scuppering of the oil tanker, the 'Torrey Canyon', and subsequent devastation to wildlife and the hitherto unspoilt beaches of the English west-country occurred on 18 March, 1967. The super tanker hit a rock in a reef between the Scilly Isles and Land's End. What to do to stop the 120,000 tons of crude oil spread its poison was a unique challenge at the time and attempts to bomb the ship to the bottom of the sea before the 56 by 32 km slick got any bigger failed, not helped by the high spring tides that doused the inferno. The Torrey Canyon was sunk a day later but not before 112 km of Cornish coastline was contaminated.

Lesser known are two other events that occurred in the same year, the partial meltdown of a nuclear reactor in the Chapelcross plant in Annan, Scotland which produced plutonium for nuclear weapons and a reactor meltdown in the nuclear-powered ice breaker Soviet ship Lenin which had to be abandoned in the Arctic. It was to be 19 years until events in Chernobyl and a further 25 until events in Japan reminded us once again that, while nuclear power may be cheaper and 'cleaner', it is not without its risks, and, if you'll pardon the pun, fuelled the debate as to whether the risks to human health are acceptable when natural resources like wind and water power provide alternative sources of energy.

J Robert Oppenheimer, the US physicist who contributed much to the development of the atomic bomb, departed this mortal coil in 1967. Oppenheimer had been suspected of having 'past associations with Communists' during the McCarthy era in the '50s. In fact, his ostracism from work for the United States Atomic Energy Commission was more to do with doubts about the hydrogen bomb and the terrible legacy he had helped to create, seen with horrific effect in the bombing of Hiroshima and Nagasaki, than with any supposed allegiance to an extreme left wing ideology. Ironically, in the same year that he died, China tested its first hydrogen bomb.

## You Say You Want a Revolution? Cold War and Protest

In China, there was turmoil as factions warred over the precepts enshrined in Mao Tse-tung's Little Red Book.

"By September, Mao Tse-tung realised that the cultural revolution had gone too far... Workers' organisations were called upon to combat the Red Guards, whose internal divisions were leading to internecine fighting and – fortunately for the authorities that had originally called them into being – weakening their collective strength." **(75)**

It took until the summer of 1968 for order to be restored by a 'Three-Way Alliance' of the army; the workers' organisations; and the revolutionary masses. Before 1967 was over, Mao Tse-tung had launched a 'Campaign to Purify Class Ranks' and established Workers Mao-Thought Propaganda Teams. It is easy to ridicule this as some Orwellian nightmare but the implications of not 'confessing' could be imprisonment or an extended spell in a labour camp.

On 21st April, Josef Stalin's daughter, Svetlana Alliluyeva, caused quite a stir when she defected to the United States to the chagrin of the KGB chief Yuri Andropov who accused the US of exploiting Alliluyeva for propaganda purposes. It would not have been lost on Andropov that this blow to Soviet prestige occurred on the 50th anniversary of the Russian Revolution. Alexander Solzhenitsyn attacked the Soviet censorship of literature in an article published by the French newspaper 'Le Monde' on 31st May.

To match the Soviet Union's own 'Fractional Orbital Bombardment System' then in development, US Secretary of Defence Robert McNamara announced in September that the US was spending $5,000 million on an anti-ballistic missile defence system. To reassure the hawks or the just plain paranoid members of the American government, the Pentagon gave reassurances that the relative force of the US and the Soviet Union were as follows:

US: 1,710 intercontinental ballistic missiles (including 656 Polaris missiles in submarines)
Versus
Soviet Union: 500 (maximum) ICBMs

A couple of weeks before Christmas, the Pentagon also announced that a new system called the Multiple Independent Re-entry Vehicle had been developed, a space age weapon of mass destruction that demonstrated that spending on research into technology required for a moon landing could be used for a far more evil and destructive purpose.

Peter Doggett devotes a whole chapter to the year 1967 in his book 'There's a Riot Going On'. Quoting the alternative publication, the 'Berkeley Barb', the significance of the 'Human-Be-In' on 14th January is mapped out: "When the Berkeley political activists, and the love generation of the Haight-Ashbury and thousands of young men and women from every state in the nation embrace at the Gathering of the Tribes for a Human Be-In at the Polo Field in Golden Gate Park, the spiritual revolution will be manifest and proven. In unity we shall shower the country with waves of ecstasy and purification. Fear will be washed away; ignorance will be exposed to sunlight; profits and empire will lie drying on deserted beaches; violence will be submerged, and transmuted in rhythm and dancing; racism will be purified by the salt of forgiveness."

Nowadays, many people reflecting on this would consider that such a statement was the result of too many designer drugs but it must not be forgotten that many of the participants were deadly serious. Yes, there was a hedonistic element, a seeking of love, joy and free sex, an enhanced state of being through drugs but there was also a seeking of spiritual freedom, of altruistic enlightenment a world apart from the suffocating prison of a failed establishment model based on capitalist corruption. There was a genuine feeling that the world could change away from the failed pursuit of wealth and power based on exploitation and greed, and war to a higher plane where opportunity would be genuinely equal, where peace and love would prevail, and music, writing, poetry and all aesthetically driven art forms would carry the message. Deep down inside though, there was a realisation that the forces aligned against such a spiritual and cultural revolution were almost insurmountable, and that the revolution, to paraphrase Gil Scott Heron, while it could not be televised could also not last. The acid dream was constantly in danger of interruption and eventual extinction by the face of harsh reality. Following Timothy Leary's advice and turning onto the 'scene' and 'tuning in' (to drugs, music, whatever raised the consciousness to a different plane), were relatively easy and short term, 'dropping out' could inevitably ruin prospects and derail lives. Unless you were lucky enough to be a member of a band like The Grateful Dead, most of the counterculture in 1967 were not in a position to 'live the dream' and had to return to their schools, colleges, offices etc. once the party was over. The hippies and counter-culturalists had to seize the moment, and what a moment it was!

A chapter of Isaac and Downing's book 'Cold War' is starkly entitled 'MAD'. It begins with Nikita Kruschev's reference at the Communist Party Congress on 31st October, 1961 that on the day before, the Soviet Union had detonated the largest bomb the world had ever seen. (It was reported that the flash was seen 600 miles away). The Campaign for Nuclear Disarmament had been established in 1958, and the following year the Aldermaston March was a mass demonstration and also the subject of a documentary film. The world had been brought to the edge of the abyss during the Cuban Missile Crisis in October, 1962 and in the summer of 1963, the Nuclear Test Ban Treaty, by which only underground nuclear testing was allowed, was signed by the USA, USSR and the UK but not by France. China was undeterred and exploded their first atom bomb on 16 October, 1964. Becoming the fifth power to have thermonuclear capability, China went on to explode their first Hydrogen Bomb on 17th June, 1967. 'Accidents' and systems failures around the world and the spectre of 'mutually assured destruction' stoked up the fear and paranoia. This was satirised in the black comedy 'Dr Strangelove or How I Started to Stop Worrying and Love The Bomb' directed by a young Stanley Kubrick. In January, 1967, US Home Secretary Robert McNamara persuaded President Lyndon Johnson to postpone the development of US anti-ballistic missiles and give diplomacy a try. From the Kremlin Kosygin disagreed, claiming that 'defence is moral' and noting that the US had more missiles than the USSR. **(76)** (as we have seen).

As Isaacs/ Downing pointed out: "The arms race now meant that the two superpowers spending more than $550 million per day between them on nuclear armaments negotiations to limit this intolerable burden became inevitable." **(77)**

By the summer of 1968, the US, USSR and UK had all signed the Nuclear Non Proliferation Treaty but France and China abstained.

Of course, British eyes were also on mass protests in Washington in October, 1967 against the Vietnam War and as the number of US troops in Vietnam approached, half a million with the US economy sinking into deficit many, like Country Joe Macdonald, was asking 'what the hell are we fighting for?'

There were other problems identified by Doggett. Musicians like Paul Kantner of Jefferson Airplane were turned off by the politics as they saw this as restricting their freedom. Indeed, the Airplane, in common with many other psychedelic artists of the time participated in advertisements for companies like Levi jeans. Abbie Hoffman writing in The Village Voice was not impressed. "While the Jefferson Airplane grooves, over 100 workers in the Levi Strauss factory on the Tennessee-Georgia border are doing their thing, which consists of being on strike to protest deplorable working conditions."

Gerald DeGroot puts it this way: "Hippies espoused an alternative culture, but in reality, created a parallel universe in which power, though differently distributed, was still crucially important."(78) (It must, of course, be remembered that 'hippies' was a term originally coined by black musicians to describe white beatnik 'hangers-on' at music gigs). In a chapter entitled 'Everybody Get Together', DeGroot cites the case of the moral dilemma confronting the staff of the International Times underground magazine by anarchists and Hell Angels from the 'London Street Commune' who occupied their offices chanting 'property is theft', and would not go away, not that is until the police were called. (79)

Richard Neville, editor of another underground magazine, Oz is even more to the point in his book 'Playpower' "Revolution became the most popular consumer product since the T-Model Ford"(80). You can choose from three models quipped Neville:

1. "Student Internationale: with New Left drive, collapsible steering and comfy sit-in support for fellow travellers.
2. Acid-cool Underground model: On full 'speed', the only sound you can hear is the top 40 and:
3. Ghetto Guerilla: Black powered, brakeless, best used when destination seems impossible." (81)

There was indeed quite a bit of hype, hyperbole and hypocrisy surrounding 1967, and 'the summer of love', the 'halcyon era' of 'Sergeant Pepper', flower power et al as "the energy was poised precariously on the edge of an inferno."(82). The acid dream could quickly become a nightmare.

So the establishment prevailed and at Royal Variety Performances, the boldest The Beatles would get was an exhortation by John Lennon for those in the cheap seats to clap their hands and those in the boxes to rattle their jewellery. Rolling Stones guitarist Keith Richards was somewhat less tolerant when he ordered the band to stop playing during a concert in The Palace of Culture in Warsaw on observing the ruling elite who occupied the front rows "sitting there with their diamonds and their pearls, and their fingers in their ears." The 'rock 'n' roll revolutionaries' did not, in fact, join with the British literati (Iris Murdoch, J B Priestley etc.) in exhorting the British Prime Minister Harold Wilson to condemn the American government for their war in Vietnam. That is not to say that The Beatles et al agreed with it but perhaps there is a sense in which they could see on which side their 'bread was buttered', and to ply their trade out with the forces of establishment would merely alienate them and deprive them of the oxygen necessary to convey any message at all to an eager listening public. It is the age old dilemma of staying out of the tent and adopting an idealistic position with no influence or getting your sleeves rolled up, and getting involved in the dirty work and compromise involved of operating within the tent (or more accurately pissing in or out of the tent as Lyndon B Johnson famously said).

George Harrison was another who was less than impressed by what he saw when visiting the Haight-Ashbury district of San Francisco, supposed home of the Californian counter-culture in the summer of 1967 which he saw as more about alcohol and drugs than about spiritual awakening and high art. Of course, Harrison's search for truth and meaning led him down another cul-de-sac in the form of the Maharishi Mahesh Yogi's Transcendental Meditation. The Maharishi's comment about it being a man's duty to serve his country enraged many including pacifist poet and activist, Allen Ginsberg, who saw the Indian guru as one who cosied up to the establishment to avoid trouble.

As Peter Doggett dryly observed: "It was a recipe not for pacifism, but for passive-ism: another invitation to maintain a crucial distance from political commitment; another excuse not to confront the men behind the war."(83) In July, 1967, The Beatles had flown to Greece in the hope of buying a remote island named Leslo for £90,000 and turning it into a hippie haven. It became obvious before John Lennon confirmed it in an interview with Beatles' biographer Hunter Davies that the band had little interest in the morality of the military regime that had taken control of Greece. "I'm not worried about the political situation in Greece, as long as it doesn't affect us. I don't care if the government is all fascist or Communist. I don't care," said Lennon. As Gerard DeGroot in his '60s Unplugged' book says: "Revolution was never on the cards. The door of idealism opened briefly and was then slammed shut, for fear of what might enter. Chauvinism and cynicism got the better of hope and tolerance." **(84)**

That is not to say that all musicians stayed aloof. Nearby the site of The Gathering of the Tribes Human Be-In, an estimated 25,000 people gathered in San Francisco's Kezar Stadium to protest about the Vietnam War. Judy Collins, Big Brother and the Holding Company, and Country Joe and The Fish joined celebrities like Robert Vaughan of 'Man from Uncle' fame to swell the numbers determined to publicly demonstrate their anger and frustration. Later, Phil Ochs would sing 'The War is Over' during an 'Angry Arts Festival' that lasted 11 days, and also featured groups like Canned Heat, Kaleidoscope and Taj Mahal.

Although The Beatles remained aloof, across the channel in The Roundhouse, London on 1st July, 1967, Procol Harum topped an anti-war benefit bill that also included The Crazy World of Arthur Brown and The Yardbirds. The most telling protest perhaps came from the magnificent oratory of Martin Luther King at the same Kezar Stadium when before a crowd with banners proclaiming Muhammad Ali's slogan 'No Viet Cong ever called me nigger': "Let us save our national honour – stop the bombing. Let us save American lives and Vietnamese lives – stop the bombing. Let us take a single instantaneous step to the peace table – stop the bombing. Let our voices ring out across the land to say the American people are not vainglorious conquerors – stop the bombing."

Keith Richards mostly refrains from political comment in his 2011 autobiography 'Life'. You will find references to B B King and Albert King but nothing about Martin Luther King. "1967 was the watershed year," he says. "The year the seams gave way. There was that feeling that trouble was coming which it did later, with all the riots, street fighting and all of that. There was a tension in the air. It's like negative and positive ions before a storm, you get that breathlessness that something's got to break." **(85)**

Richards was, of course, mainly referring to tensions within the band especially in relationships with Brian Jones but could just as easily have been referring to the political and cultural scene. 'Sex and drugs and rock 'n' roll' are, however, Richards' main preoccupations even to the extent of mapping out the years the development of the drug culture with Mandrax and grass giving way to acid in late 1966, coke in 1967 then smack.

## Vietnam – "Turning a Small Country into a Charnel House"

1967 had not long started when 16,000 American troops and an equal number of South Vietnamese mounted an offensive against the Vietcong in the Mekong Delta. After trying to evacuate the residents, villages were bombed and burnt to the ground. Whenever this tactic was used, the Vietcong troops just kept reappearing from the incinerated trees, and charred countryside with an almost kamikaze like determination and durability. There was a temporary respite in the bombing while Ho Chi Minh and Lyndon Johnson entered into some negotiations but despite the positive intentions of UK Prime Minister Harold Wilson and Soviet Premier Kosygin, the truce ended and the bombing resumed again 11 days later.

The anti-war protests gained in ferocity following the killing of eighty South Vietnamese civilians on 2 March in the village of Lang Vei. In New York, there was a mass demonstration against the Vietnam War as an estimated 400,000 protestors marched from Central Park to the United Nations building. There were also demonstrations outside the US Embassy in London. In Washington DC, an estimated 100,000 protestors led in chant by Allen Ginsberg tried to levitate the Pentagon in protest. According to the account of Richard Neville, editor of Oz magazine, in his book 'Playpower', this coincided with the formation of what became known as the 'Youth International Party' (codenamed yippees). The scene planned for the day is mapped out by Marshall Bloom for the 'Liberation News Service': "Swamis, Indian men, people with water pistols (passed out free), noise makers, hundreds of skulls on poles, flower banners and groups. The Jefferson Airplane, Mother Earth, Mad River, The Fugs, C.I.A Change and Rhinoceros, and thirty theatre groups, including the Bread and Puppet Theatre, and the Surrealist Minority all stopping along the way to do guerrilla play-fare."(86) By the way, the yippies are described by Neville as 'politicised acid freaks' or as Paul Krassner once put it, 'they're hippies who've been hit on the head by a policeman'.(87) Norman Mailer, author of the classic anti-war novel 'The Naked and the Dead' and inventor of the term 'fug' for 'GI' (hence the group 'The Fugs'), was arrested on the steps of the Pentagon that day.

President Lyndon Johnson came up with one of his less subtle ideas in conscription into the army by lottery, a practice also employed by Australia which sent 15,000 conscripts to Vietnam, a controversial and insensitive act by Prime Minister Robert Menzies. 'Draft dodging' became popular as conscriptees fled across the border into Canada and public burnings of draft notices became commonplace. American citizens were also feeling the war in their pockets when a 6% tax increase was raised to 10% by the end of the year as endless resources were committed to no discernible purpose. The determination of the North Vietnamese, likened by some to Londoners in the blitz ensured that the war would prolong and intensify. By August, the commitment of American troops had reached 500,000 with 9,000 fatalities to that point in 1967. While Defence Secretary Robert McNamara started to have second thoughts about how the war could be won without the 'virtual annihilation' of North Vietnam and its people (so poignantly depicted in the confessional film 'The Fog of War'), Johnson renewed his commitment in a speech in San Antonio where he argued that a Communist conquest of South Vietnam would lead to domination of south-east Asia and lay open the stark possibility of a third world war. Of course, we had all heard this kind of talk before, during the Cuban Missile Crisis. Anti-war protestors' concerns reached fever pitch when it was revealed that chemical warfare units had been deployed to drop napalm bombs and terms like 'agent orange' entered modern parlance.

By October, Johnson was being branded a war criminal by the peace movement which grew to include 'straights' appalled not only at the futility of the war but also the cost. The North Vietnamese continued to prove stubbornly resistant helped by food supplies from China and Russia and by December Senator Fulbright's patience had run out: "The United States is using its B-52s, its napalm, and all those other ingenuous weapons of counter-insurgency to turn a small country into a charnel house." (88)

The world was shocked by the eye witness account of Ho Thanh Dam, a resident of Vinh Quang village, in an interview with Pulitzer Prize winning historian and journalist Stanley Karnow. The harrowing and graphic detail of the terror and destruction, and the effect on the victims of napalm, turned public opinion even more against the inhuman tactics employed by the U.S. during the Vietnam War.As a footnote how much has been actually learned about waging war from the air. No matter what the intelligence or how much stealth there will inevitably be non-military casualties (or 'collateral damage' in its cruelly sanitised form) which, in time, will turn public opinion against what may seem like even the most just cause for conflict (which did not apply in this case for as far as Vietnam is concerned, it seemed a war as much against ideology and fear of Communism threatening the 'free' western world). As Draft Week became Peace Week, Senator Eugene McCarthy announced his intention to stand as an anti-war candidate in the 1968 presidential elections, a decision supported by one of the presidential candidates JFK's brother, Robert Kennedy.

## The Counterculture/ Acid Daze

*"When the power of love overcomes the love of power, the world will know peace."*
*(Jimi Hendrix)*

The first human 'be-in' held in San Francisco and Golden Gate Park became a hippy paradise while the Haight-Ashbury district became a 'Mecca' for young devotees of flower power, and a new era of experimental drugs and music. Alternative poet Alan Ginsberg coined the phrase 'flower power' and the 'ban the bomb' sign, and 'two fingered salute' (or peace sign) symbolised passive resistance and non-violence with the Vietnam War as the catalyst to a movement based on peace and love, and hippies 'wearing flowers in their hair'.

London hosted its own major hippy event, the 14-Hour Technicolour Dream at Alexandra Palace and Jimi Hendrix, an American who had relocated in Britain, uttered the immortal words, "When the power of love overcomes the love of power, the world will know peace."

Tom Wolfe's 'The Electric Kool-Aid Acid Test', published in 1967, has been described by Newsweek magazine as 'an American classic'. Wolfe was a Virginia boy who went on to earn a doctorate in American studies at Yale University. He worked as a reporter for the Washington Post and New York Tribune, and his first book, exotically entitled 'The Kandy-Kolored Tangerine-Flake Streamline Baby' was published in 1965. He went on to win a nonfiction American book award for his 'The Right Stuff' in 1979 and is perhaps most famous for his 'Bonfire of the Vanities' book in 1987. Wolfe offered some wonderful insights into the sixties counterculture: "The acid tests were the *epoch* of the psychedelic style; mixed media entertainment came straight out of the Acid Tests' combination of light and movie projections, strobes, tapes, rock 'n' roll, black light. 'Acid rock' – the sound of The Beatles 'Sergeant Pepper' album and the high vibrato electronic sounds of The Jefferson Airplane, the Mothers of Invention (etc.) – the mothers of it all were The Grateful Dead (who) were the *audio* counterpart of Roy Seburn's light projections." **(89)**

In this era of mind expanding drugs, there were campaigns for the legalisation of cannabis with the patronage of the likes of Bernard Crick, and Graham Greene and the Release organisation was founded to help people arrested for drug possession (two famous examples are Mick Jagger and Keith Richards of the Rolling Stones).

The 'Big Issue', a much respected journal of concise articles about topical issues as well as an estimable philanthropic endeavour, published an article 'THE BEAT LIVES ON' by John Kercher in its April 4 – 10, 2011 edition. In it, Kercher writes about the City Lights Bookshop opened by writer/ poet Lawrence Ferlinghetti in 1953. His first major brush with the establishment came three years later when he had the temerity to publish Allen Ginsberg's poem 'Howl', copies of which were seized by the San Francisco police as evidence for an obscenity charge. The passage of time writes an alternative history and 44 years after Ferlinghetti's acquittal, a film (entitled 'Howl') dramatising the trial was first screened in February, 2011 to be followed later that year by a screen version of Jack Kerouac's beat novel 'On The Road'.

Looking back on the significance of these events at the age of 92, Ferlinghetti says: "It (Judge Clayton Horn's decision) opened the floodgates for American writers and poets. It allowed books like Henry Miller's 'Tropic of Cancer', DH Lawrence's 'Lady Chatterley's Lover' and William Burroughs 'Naked Lunch' to be published." Ferlinghetti, in a revealing interview, remembers Jack Kerouac and Neal Cassady, the inspiration for the character Dean Moriarty in 'On The Road' staying at his log cabin at Big Sur. Ferenghetti himself features as the character Lorenzo Monsanto in 'Big Sur'. Kerouac frequented the City Lights Bookstore as did Ginsberg who lived just around the corner when he moved to San Francisco in 1954. Ferenghetti described Gregory Corso as "the last great voice of the original Beat rebellion." **(90)**

Drug cartography aside, 1967 was, of course, the year that Richards, Mick Jagger and gallery owner Robert Fraser (or Strawberry Bob as he was known) stood trial on 27 June after the busts at the house at Redlands in February. After demonstrations outside the News of the World offices ("the bust was a collusion between the News of the World and the cops" maintains Richards) and a protest in Piccadilly, the sentences were quashed on appeal. The Beatles showed their solidarity by being among the signatories of an advertisement in The Times newspaper calling for the legislation of cannabis resin.

The development of lysergic acid diethylamide, or LSD as it became known in 1938 by Swiss chemist Albert Hoffman as a cure for migraine changed everything, of course. Both Robert Hunter who was to become a lyricist for The Grateful Dead and Ken Kesey, a successful novelist participated in drug experiments that included trials of so-called 'psychomimetic drugs'. Indeed, Kesey conceived the idea for the award winning 'One Flew Over the Cuckoo's Nest' when working as a night attendant in a hospital 'psych ward'. With the royalty money, Kesey purchased a log house in the hills of La Honda, north-west of Palo Alto. Neal Cassady, the inspiration for Jack Kerouac's character Dean Moriarty, became a kind of 'aide-de-camp' to Kesey. The two men would, along with returning Vietnam helicopter pilot Ken Babbs, become part of the 'Merry Pranksters' who would tour around the country in a 1939 'International Harvester' bus adapted by its previous owner to accommodate his wife and eleven children. (The word 'magic' was subsequently painted on the bus fender). In the summer of 1964, the 'magic bus' visited Texas, New Orleans and New York City where Kesey's follow-up to 'One Flew Over the Cuckoo's Nest', 'Sometimes a Great Notion' was to be published. The Pranksters visited Timothy Leary and Richard Alpert (who had just seen their 'The Psychedelic Experience' book published) in Millbrook, New York but found the scene in New York "too solemn and precious about the business of psychedelic liberation". As Barney Hoskins observed, "Acid changed everything in San Francisco and the Pranksters were evangelical to the point of zealotry in their attempts to turn people onto it." **(91)** The first 'acid test' as such took place in Ken Babb's house in Santa Cruz in the autumn of 1965 with Tom Wolfe present and The Warlocks, forerunners of The Grateful Dead as the house band. The second acid test took place on 4 December in San Jose and acid tests reached San Francisco eight days into January, 1966. It is merely stating the obvious to suggest that rave culture began here. On 6th October, 1966, LSD was declared illegal. A 'Love Pageant Rally' including a free concert featuring The Grateful Dead and Big Brother, and the Holding Company, took place at the Panhandle, an area of parkland running parallel from Haight Street to the Golden Gate Park. It was organised by Allen Cohen and Michael Bowen of the San Francisco Oracle but Richard Alpert was concerned that Haight-Ashbury would be frowned upon by the Berkeley radicals who advocated political activism as opposed to 'dropping out', and 'peace and love'. The 'Diggers' were formed in October, 1966 after a meeting of the Artist Liberation Front who distributed free food, usually donations from local supermarkets, in the Panhandle every afternoon. An 'Acid Test Graduation' was held on Halloween, 1966 with the 'Diggers' wearing large animal masks and carrying a coffin symbolising the death of money. Ken Kesey was advocating 'going beyond acid', alienating The Grateful Dead and others who felt he had gone too far. Neil Cassady was on stage wearing a mortar board, and handing out diplomas while Kesey would spend 90 days in jail and 5 months on a work farm before moving back to Oregon. By February, 1968, the other Pranksters scattered to New Mexico and Los Angeles. The way was open for entrepreneurs like Bill Graham. As Hoskyns put it, "a more efficient marketing of flower power would now replace the outrageous chaos of the Acid tests." **(92)**

The Human Be-In was held in the polo grounds of Golden Gate Park on 14 January, 1967. The press was told that 'the Berkeley political activists and the love generation of Haight-Ashbury will join together with members of the new nation who will be coming from every state in the nation, every tribe of the young to <POW-WOW, CELEBRATE, AND PROPHESY THE EPOCH OF LIBERATION, LOVE, PEACE, COMPASSION AND UNITY OF MANKIND>.' A Rick Griffin poster showed a guitar toting Native American warrior on a horse. The 'pow-wow' was a line-up of bands, Beat legends as well as 'psychedelic gurus' like Ginsberg, Leary, Ferlinghetti and Rabin.

Barney Hoskins in his beautifully illustrated and highly informative book 'Beneath The Diamond Sky: Haight-Ashbury 1965-1970', centres on San Francisco as he maps out the progress of the 'revolution' in the mid to late sixties. Setting the scene in San Francisco, a port city with a chequered past "the tension between its picturesqueness and its hedonism; between its culture and its dissipation, was one that played out throughout the 60's"**(93)** As the 'beats' gravitated towards SF's North Beach to listen to bebop jazz in the Blackhawk club, hang around the City Lights Store or Vesuvio's coffee house, visit the world's first 'head shop' ('Magic Theatre for Madmen Only!') or hear Lenny Bruce's rarified brand of satirical comedy, musicians like Paul Kantner were not alone in pilgrimaging from his home in San Jose to seek out the 'happening scene'. Folk clubs like The Drinking Gourd in Union Street or Tangent in Palo Alto also attracted 'immigrants'. Indeed, Jerry Garcia, later to front The Grateful Dead started off as a bluegrass banjo player there.

Perhaps the attitude of the 'counterculture' might be best summed up in the words of D.H. Lawrence: "If you make a revolution, make it for fun, don't make it in ghastly seriousness, don't do it in deadly earnest, do it for fun."

But more serious and potentially deadly events were unfolding as black power movements jostled for position. A summit meeting was called between the Revolutionary Action Movement and the Black Panther Party in February, 1967. Out of all the confusion, the seeds of the idea of a 'Black Cultural Revolution' were being born. Figures like Leroi Jones saw in music and poetry the spirit of revolution, even exhorting black people to listen exclusively to black artists and championing the likes of John Coltrane who apparently did not reciprocate the politicisation of 'the arts' that Jones, who had been violently beaten by the police following unrest in the Newark district of New Jersey, purveyed. There was also Ron Everett who reinvented himself as Ron Karenga. Karenga's message was similar to Jones' in advocating that 'all art must reflect the Black Revolution'. Whereas Jones saw the blues as something still pure and sacred, and pilloried the likes of The Rolling Stones for stealing the blues from black people, Karenga saw the blues as a millstone from the past. Nevertheless, the two men did envisage a common purpose and, under Karenga's influence, Jones took the Swahili name of Amiri Baraka. Baraka continued to search for iconic musical figures of 'African-American music' and alongside the aforementioned, John Coltrane, who sadly did not survive beyond the summer of 1967, championed Sun Ra, whose otherworldly musical explorations might have suggested a less than comfortable fit with Jones/ Baraka's vision of the 'African-American musician' and Albert Ayler, another free jazz artist from another riot afflicted town, Newark, New Jersey. Rap Brown completed a triumvirat of black activists, famous for the amendment named after him when an act was passed making it illegal to cross state lines with the intention of provoking a riot. This came about when Brown was accused of inciting delegates to riot at a National Conference on Black Power.

The worst riots were yet to come in Detroit, the spark being a police raid on an afterhours drinking den ('a blind pig') precipitating unrest spanning six days between 22nd and 27th July, and resulted in over 2,000 casualties, 43 deaths and an estimated 5,000 homeless after devastating fires started during the unrest. Martha Reeves and the Vandellas' 1964 hit *'Dancing in the Streets'* became the unofficial anthem of the riots. The song was recorded by the Detroit label Tamla Motown whose supremo Berry Gordy also issued some of Martin Luther King's speeches on LP records. John Lee Hooker would record *'Motor City is Burning'* in September. The group MC5 incorporated the number into their repertoire and The Doors would receive an unlikely boost in sales for the unrelated *'Light My Fire'*. In total, there were race riots in over a hundred American cities.

The significance of music to protest and that of John Coltrane in particular, is well put by Martin Smith in his fascinating little volume 'John Coltrane: Jazz, Racism and Resistance': "There has always been a tradition in jazz of conscious rebellion and resistance to the indignities of racism. Duke Ellington was a standard bearer for black pride and on many occasions played benefits for organisations linked to the US Communist party. In 1931, trumpet player Louis Armstrong was arrested for refusing to give up his seat to a white person on a bus in Memphis. Twenty-five years later, when Martin Luther King was leading the civil rights movement, many in the jazz community rallied to his support. Then when the black power movement swept across the US in the late 1960s, it was John Coltrane's driving music with which many of these revolutionaries identified." **(94)** With the advent of television and the mass media, The Beatles and other '60s' British groups would not be oblivious to what a momentous year 1967 was, and, subliminally at least, world events would influence the creative process, sometimes overtly in the themes and lyrics.

## The Final Frontier

The first Moon landing was still two years away but, on 27 January, three astronauts, Roger Chaffee, Gus Grissom and Edward White, tragically lost their lives in a launch pad fire in Apollo 1 at Cape Canaveral before they even got off the ground. Space race rivals Russia also lost a cosmonaut, Colonel Vladimir Komarov who did not survive the crash landing of Soyuz 1 on Earth when his parachute failed to open.

On 19th April, a tentative step towards an actual human landing on the Moon was taken when the US probe Surveyor 3 made a soft landing on the Moon's surface. In so doing, it confirmed with the help of a mechanical shovel that the lunar surface was firm enough to land on. Even more significant perhaps was the successful launching of the most powerful rocket to date, Saturn 5, and the safe return to the Pacific Ocean of the unmanned space probe accompanying it.

In May of 1967, the first British satellite 'Ariel III' went into orbit. The first live international satellite television show was broadcast in June with The Beatles performing '*All You Need is Love*' in the same month as the Monterey Pop Festival.

The space race was well and truly on and it soon became apparent that the Soviet scientists did not quite appreciate the density of the Venusian atmosphere. Their ambitious aim was to land on the surface and send back pictures. Moscow had already claimed that the Venera 3 probe had actually landed on the surface in 1966 but it was in reality crushed by the atmospheric pressure as it descended. Venera 4 was mainly designed to study the planet's atmosphere which it did enter on 18th October, 1967 but contact was lost about sixteen miles above the surface although it was established that the probe did land in an area known as Eistla Regio.

The American response to the Russians, Mariner 5 had been launched two days after Venera 4 (on 14 June), and flew by the planet and sent back some useful data. The first views of the planet's surface would be transmitted from Veneras 9 and 10 in October, 1975, and put paid to any more speculation about life as we understand it on Venus.

# Departing this Mortal Coil

On 3th Feb, record producer Joe Meek took his own life after killing his land lady, and on 6th March baritone singer and actor Nelson Eddy famous for his role in 'Phantom of the Opera' passed. On 29th April, it was blues singer and political commentator J B Lenoir. John Coltrane died on 17th July, 1967, only forty years old. Other musical casualties followed: The Beatles manager Brian Epstein died aged 32 on 27th August while the group were providing an audience for the Mahirishi Yogi in Marikesh (more on this later).

Woody Guthrie, died aged 52 on 3rd October, the same day as Malcolm Sergeant, the famous conductor; Otis Redding is half Woody Guthrie's age when he perishes in a plane crash in Wisconsin along with the entire Bar Keys group: Carl Cunningham, Jimmy King, Phalin Jones and Ron Caldwell on 10 October. Bert Berns, producer and writer of 'Twist and Shout' died on 30th December.

Away from music, on 3rd January, Jack Ruby, Lee Harvey Oswald's assassin died; the following day, Donald Campbell's life was taken at 300 mph attempting to break the world speed record on water. On February 8th, it was Robert Oppenheimer, the creator of the first atomic bomb; on 10th June, actor Spencer Tracy, most famous for his role in 'Father of The Bride' and on 11th July, Basil Rathbone, famous for his portrayal of Sherlock Holmes; on 29th June and 7th July, actresses Jayne Mansfield and Julian Leigh forever known for her role as Scarlet O'Hara in 'Gone with the Wind' passed. Vladimir Komanov, a cosmonaut in Soyuz 1 died on 24th April, and the tragic fire which took the lives of US astronauts White, Chaffee and Grisson will never be forgotten. Prominent political figures who died in 1967 included Konrad Adenauer, the West German Chancellor between 1949 and 1963 (19th April), Clement Attlee, British Prime Minister between 1954 and 1951 (8th October); Ernesto 'Che' Guevara, Argentinian Marxist, physician and revolutionary, executed in Bolivia (9th October), and Harold Holt, the Australian Prime Minister who drowned on 17th December.

In the world of the arts, Rene Magritte, the Belgian surrealist painter died on 15th August while cult writer Carson McCullers died tragically young on 29th September.

# Pirate Radio, Che Guevara and Rolling Stone

As already observed, Britain's offshore pirate radio stations were closed down in 1967, an event dramatised to hilarious effect in the film 'The Boat That Rocked'. The prosecution of the Marine Broadcasting Offences Act associated with right wing Conservative Home Secretary Reginald Maudling (but 'enforced' by Tony Benn) was a pyrrhic victory at best and the name Radio Caroline is still with us today in crystal clear digital sound but not broadcasting from a boat. On dry land, the BBC wasted no time in launching Radio 1 in the wake of the sinking of the pirates.

1967 was also the year in which Che Guevara was captured and killed in Bolivia by US trained troops. He remains, to this day, an iconic figure, and a recent search of leading bookshops revealed it can be easier to find books about Guevara and Cuba than it is about the Kennedys.

Rolling Stone magazine began publication in San Francisco. It was a much more radical journal then than it is today. There was a period in the late seventies when it was 'lost in punk' but it still produced many leading and influential writers on 'rock music'. The underground magazine Oz was published in London for the first time.

In 1967, Police raiding the laboratory of Californian acid head Augustus Owsley Stanley III found enough doses of LSD to send an estimated ¾ of a million people on a trip. In 2011, Mojo published his obituary describing him as "the first mass provider of the era's finest LSD. The self-taught chemist supplied large quantities of his concoctions – featuring names like Blue Cheer – to the Beatles, Jimi Hendrix and Jefferson Airplane, but was also an early financial backer of the Grateful Dead. He devised sound systems, revolutionising concert sound, and later released state-of-the-art live recordings of numerous Bay Area groups. Stanley, who provided the chemicals for Ken Kesey's electric Kool-Aid acid tests and was immortalised in song by the Dead, Steely Dan and Frank Zappa, died in a car crash in Australia on March 13th."

Tom Wolfe says that, "Owsley had snapped back from his great freak-out and started pouring money into The Grateful Dead, and thereby, the tests. Maybe he figured the Tests were the wave of the future. Maybe he thought 'Acid Rock' was the sound of the future and he would become a kind of Brian Epstein for The Grateful Dead. In any case, he started buying The Grateful Dead equipment such as no rock 'n' roll band ever had before, Beatles included. There was something wholly new and deliriously weird in The Dead's sound, and practically everything new in rock 'n' roll, rock jazz I have heard it called, came out of it." **(95)**

# Furniture, Fashion and Pop Art

The book 'Ready Steady Go – the Smashing Rise and Giddy Fall of Swinging London' by Shawn Levy talks of "the explosion of creativity, in art, music and fashion, and the sexual, social and political revolution," that re-shaped the world pointing to iconic names like Mary Quant, Vidal Sassoon, David Bailey, Michael Caine, Terence Stamp and Lester Roeg. By the end of 1967, The Beatles had opened their clothes boutique, Apple, on the corner of Baker Street and Paddington Street, its famous logo inspired by a painting by Rene Magritte (unfortunately he did not live to see it), and aided and abetted by The Fool, an artistic collective mainly from Holland.

Furniture was also important, as much of a statement as a convenience.

Stacking chairs – where would offices be without them? 1967 saw the arrival of 'Universale' moulded plastic stacking chairs designed by Joe Columbo and mass produced by the Kartell company, ABS Plastic. The legs were detachable and the maximum stacking height was three chairs. Joe Columbo (1931–1970) was a Milanese designer who pioneered easily self-assembled and space saving pop art furniture designs such as the Elda chair. Columbo was so influential and successful his work was commissioned by the national Italian airline Airitalia. His less than alluring 'Tube' chair is even more collectable but didn't arrive on the market until 1969. There were numerous weird and innovative seats and tables developed in the sixties, too many to go into here. Habitat paper shades were popular as were mushroom shaped lamps and lava lamps (introduced in 1963). The Italian brothers Castiglioni introduced the 'Arco' lamp and, of course, space age lighting was all the rage with Danish designer Verner Panton, famous for his 'moon light' in the forefront of innovative design. A 'sputnik' or 'videosphere' television if you can find one would be worth as much as £400 nowadays.

Fashion designer Mary Quant lent her name to gimmicks like the lipstick radio and more practical appliances such as the Morphy Richards stainless steel pop art 'Carnaby' daisy motif pop up toaster.

1967 was also the year when 'For mash get Smash' was the slogan in one of the most popular advertisements ever. Despite the smirking superiority of the 'tin cans' in the advert, 'smash', as a product, was merely an updated version of 'pom', the powdered potato used during World War II.

Anyone still possessing a set of four colour posters featuring each member of The Beatles created by fashion photographer Richard Avedon in 1967 could expect to get upwards of £600 for them now. For around the same price, you could get Martin Sharp's sensational foil print 'Mister Tambourine Man' created in homage to Bob Dylan. (Sharp was director of the counterculture magazine Oz).

Back to the fashion world where Mary Quant and her Chelsea look was 'all the rage', the 'Twiggy' range made Lesley Hornby a fortune. The iconic Biba shop opened in Kensington High Street in 1964, and was famous for its cheap, fashionable clothes and its roof garden (I should know. I worked in the loading bay there during the summer of 1976). Ossie Clark, the 'King of the King's Road' and his Quorom boutique was another trendy place to go, and Clark's jumpsuits were worn by Mick Jagger. Two famous names operating around this time associated more with after shave, nowadays, were Parisian Pierre Cardin (who designed the men's collarless jacket in 1960, popularised by the Beatles in 1963) and Spaniard Paco Rabanne. Harriet Walker writing for the Independent newspaper reported on 5th May (paraphrasing parts of the Paul Anka song 'My Way') that Cardin, increasingly conscious of his own mortality, had put his one billion euro empire up for sale. The paper also reminds us that "Cardin was one of the first designers to diversify beyond mere clothing. Although he never designed curtains as such, he did lend his name to products such as radios and alarm clocks." Relevant to the fashion conscious sixties, also, was Cardin's pioneering of the mini skirt and trouser combinations for women called 'Ensemble.'.(96) Another newspaper, the Guardian, asked Mary Quant in 1967, "What is the erogenous zone of our present time period?" "The crotch," she replied without hesitation. Clothes are designed to lead the eye to it." And so it was that the sixties became the age of geometric patterns, bikini dresses, paper dresses, crochet dresses and mini suits and skirts, and in Cardin's case, 'slinkies' and 'bubble dresses'. Quant also pioneered the use of PVC in fashion and the plastic mac became another fashion icon. Boldly patterned silk Pucci designs were also influential, thanks to the patronage of Mick Jagger and Jackie Kennedy.

The space age, of course, influenced clothes designs as well as furniture, for example, Barbara Hulanicki's gold and silver brocade waistcoats sold in Biba, and shiny, metallic sequinned tops were also becoming increasingly popular. Kaftans, Afghans, cheesecloth shirts, suede jackets popularised by John Lennon and Bob Dylan, Mexican ponchos, Levi jackets and jeans, sandals, polka dot shirts, shoulder bags, beads, flowerpot hats, patchwork bags, frock coats, kipper ties, paisley patterns, flares, bell bottoms, loons, chokers, kinetic art, 'costume jewellery' (which New York designer Kenneth J Lane laid first claim to inventing) with pendants worn by men and women. Anything went in the esoteric sixties. Ironically, in an era of 'peace and love', regimental jackets were in vogue, many of them coming from the 'I Was Lord Kitchener's Valet' shop. Tommy Roberts opened his first shop Kleptomania in Carnaby Street, London in 1966, specialising in Indian fashions before moving to the Kings Road in 1969 under the name 'Mr Freedom'. Wendy Ramshaw, the celebrated British jeweller began her career producing items in Perspex and paper that were sold through shops such as Quant's Bazaar and 'Way in', the trendy boutique opened on the top floor of Harrods in 1967." Perspex rings and badges were also popular as well as 'Op Art' sunglasses.

Across the Atlantic, The United States and the Haight-Ashbury area of San Francisco in particular were not slow in responding to a growing demand for artefacts symbolising affiliation to the 'hippy cause'. Perhaps, the weirdest shop to open there was one called 'The Magic Theatre for Madmen Only!', reckoned to be the first 'head shop' and one that sold items like dope pipes and musty Edwardian garments. Mike Ferguson, the 'businessman' behind this venture would later become the pianist in The Charlatans, a group that was not 'backwards in coming forwards' in terms of chic image. In 1966, The Psychedelic Shop opened on 1535 Haight Street.

Tom Wolfe, an avid chronicler of the sixties also points to the significance of psychedelic poster art, with its 'nouveau swirls of lettering, design, and vibrating colours, electro-pastels and spectral Day-Glo'. Nothing much from the year 1967 makes it into most collections of 'modern art' with one notable exception, Patrick Caulfield whose 'Street Bowl' seems a rather undemonstrative piece of art more renowned for its use of colour and its place within the 'pop art' pantheon. Michael Kerrigan explains: "The term pop art was first used in 1958, anticipating the 1960s revolution in pop music by some years. The phrase was coined by critic Lawrence Alloway; it neatly encapsulated the inspiration, sometimes, but by no means invariably, found in commercial art of every kind, from children's cartoons to advertising posters."(97) Artwork such as Caulfield's and Roy Lichtenstein's 'Eddie Diptych' from 1962 would influence sleeve designs for pop and rock years for many years to come including The Beatles, with 'Yellow Submarine' as a prime example. Peter Blake was another famous exponent of pop art, his most famous work prior to the album cover of The Beatles 'Sergeant Pepper's Lonely Hearts Club Band', 'Got a Girl' incorporated within its design were pop stars of the early '60s, Fabian, Avalon, Ricky Nelson, Bobby Rydell and Elvis Presley.

LP sales surpassed those of 45 revolutions per minutes for the first time in 1967 with over $1 billion a year spent on records in the US. Cassette tapes were on the market in the UK and, with initial prices of 40s (£2), only affordable by the few.

The big rock 'n' roll celebrity event occurred on 1st May when Elvis Presley married Priscilla Beaulieu in the Aladdin Hotel, Las Vegas.

## Films and Books

"I am not a number, I'm a free man," declared Patrick McGoohan, star of Danger Man in his self-created cult TV series 'The Prisoner', set in the village of Portmeiron in north Wales, an idyllic wonderland that can still be walked around today, immaculately preserved as a piece of living history.

The 'At Last the 1948 Show', a brilliant and ground breaking comedy show following on from the scathing satire of The Goons and Peter Cook and Dudley Moore, was broadcast in glorious black and white on Redifusion in the UK. Lasting only 13 episodes, it starred a young John Cleese and formed the blueprint for Monty Python's Flying Circus. In the US, Rowan and Martin's Laugh-In is first screened proving that the British and Americans had very different senses of humour.

American and British audiences already familiar with sci-fi series 'The Twilight Zone' and 'The Outer Limits' would soon become familiar with 'Dr Who', a series starring veteran actor William Hartnell that began in 1963, the day after JFK was assassinated in Dallas (at least, the British would as the series was not syndicated in America) and 'Star Trek', an altogether more sophisticated affair employing renowned science fiction authors as script writers. 1967 demonstrates the sharp contrast vividly with Dr Who screening episodes like 'The Evil of the Daleks' over seven episodes (20 May–1 July) followed by 'Tomb of the Cybermen' (2–23 September) in black and white while 'Star Trek' was screening classic episodes like 'The City on the Edge of Forever' (broadcast in the States on 4th June) regularly nominated by fans as their favourite episode. This was a saga fit for the times. Dr McCoy played by DeForest Kelley, overdoses accidentally on an experimental drug[42] and transports to a planet where he visits the past through a portal in a sentient machine named the 'guardian of forever'. Captain Kirk (William Shatner), and First Officer Spock (Leonard Nimoy) follow and find themselves in Depression era New York. Long before alternative histories became fashionable, two possible futures are mapped out: Edith Keeler, who is played by Joan Collins, runs a homeless shelter and her destiny is either to begin a pacifist movement that will delay US entry into World War II or be hit by a truck. 29 episodes in, all were aired in the US in 1967, many of them classics like 'The Doomsday Machine' (20th October) in which the crew tangle with a genuinely chilling adversary that devours entire planets and 'Journey to Babel' (17th November) in which a murder mystery develops, the Starship Enterprise is pursued by a suicide mission and Spock finds an unusual way to reconcile a 20-year stand-off with his father, Ambassador Jarek. Alan Asherman's verdict was writer "DC Fontana, utilising her customary attention to characterisation, sensitivity and continuity, created a 'Trek' masterpiece." **(98)**

Mark Harris in his book 'Scenes from a Revolution' describes 'the extraordinary story of the year that changed film'. Five movies were nominated in the best picture category. Harris tells the story of each film in great detail, and regards 1967 as a watershed year for the film industry and "as a second golden age of studio moviemaking that lasted roughly until the late 1970s." **(99)**

Bob Hope compered the awards ceremony at the Santa Monica Civic Auditorium, Los Angeles. Hope was introduced by Gregory Peck who paid his respects to Dr Martin Luther King Junior. 'In The Heat of the Night' was voted best film overcoming some tough opposition in 'Bonnie and Clyde', 'Doctor Dolittle', 'The Graduate' and 'Guess Who's Coming to Dinner'. Rod Steiger saw off competition from Warren Beatty ('Bonnie and Clyde'), Dustin Hoffman ('The Graduate'), Spencer Tracy ('Guess, Who's Coming to Dinner') and also Paul Newman in 'Cool Hand Luke' to win the best actor award (Katherine Hepburn won best actress for 'Guess Who's Coming to Dinner'). Other films winning awards were 'Camelot' (best art direction and set decoration and best costume design and best scoring); 'Thoroughly Modern Millie' (best original score); 'The Dirty Dozen' (best sound effects); the intense 'Closely Watched Trains' (best foreign language film). 'Talk to the Animals' won the best original score with Bacharach/ David's 'The Look of Love' for 'Casino Royale' and 'The Bare Necessities' from 'The Jungle

---

[42] Originally, Harlan Ellison's script envisaged another character who was a drug addict but this was deemed unacceptable for family viewing at the time.

Book'. Other famous films being screened in 1967 were '2001: A Space Odyssey' and 'Planet of the Apes'. Michelangelo Antonioni's 'Blow-Up' 1967 starring David Hemmings, a fashion photographer who accidentally snaps a murder, also starred Vanessa Redgrave, Sarah Miles and Jane Birkin.

Halliwell's famous guide, a forensic arbiter of taste in moving pictures, doesn't award many films four stars but there was one in 1967 that didn't feature in the Academy Awards and that was the French/ Italian made film 'Belle de Jour'. 'La Chinoise', 'In Cold Blood', 'The Samurai', 'War and Peace' and, even a film by an insanely talented comedy duo: 'The Further Perils of Laurel and Hardy', all gain three stars. Mark Cousins' insightful book on the history of film is seen as much from the perspective of the film maker as the viewer 'The Story of Film' offers an alternative choice for a classic film from 1967, Polish Director Roman Polanski's 'The Fearless Vampire Killers': "Set in a castle somewhere in Jewish Middle-Europe, Polanski himself played the lead. Opposite him, his producer cast a beautiful young actress called Sharon Tate. She and Polanski dined, and took LSD together, fell in love, married and conceived a child, and set up home in the Hollywood hills."**(100)** This film would tame in comparison with Polanski's 'Rosemary's Baby' (rejected by Alfred Hitchcock), in which Mia Farrow played a New York woman impregnated by the devil, which hit the cinemas the following year

Among the best-selling books in 1967, were the popular social psychology text 'The Games People Play' by Eric Berne, a standard text in further education courses to this day. The catchy title was put to good use by Joe South with the hit song 'Games People Play' the following year. 'The Death of a President' by William Manchester; 'The Ghost in the Machine' by Arthur Koestler and the Penguin Modern Poets series all originated in 1967. 1967 was also the year of publication of Gabriel Garcia Marquez's 'One Hundred Years of Solitude'. Described by Simon Mason in The Rough Guide to Classic Novels as "like the Creation myth of a family in which everything – including the world at large – is marvellously new (the book is) famous as the first best-selling example of 'Magic Realism', a literary style that combines realism with surreal imaginative flights, 'One Hundred Years of Solitude' is a hugely entertaining and emotive novel about the corruption of power, the wizardries of love and the desolation of despair."**(101)** 'Love in the Time of Cholera' written in 1985 is often described as Marquez's second masterpiece.

Science-fiction books were still avidly read and episodes of Star Trek, Dr Who, Fireball XL5 etc. were eagerly awaited. Roger Zelazny's 'Lord of Light' won a Hugo for best SF novel of the year. Zelazny, born in 1937 in Ohio, was a resident of Sante Fe, New Mexico for most of his writing life (He died in 1995). 'Lord of Light' is a complex book with Eastern religion and mythology central to its theme. Adam Roberts explains in his introduction for the 2009 SF Masterworks edition. It is, he says, "a superb example of High Fantasy, in which gods and demons mingle with mortals, and powerful magic is loosed upon the world." The mythology is Hindu; and that is enough to situate the novel in its era. The year of its publication was the year that The Beatles put out *Sergeant Pepper* after sojourning in India and absorbing a quantity of Indian culture. Samuel R Delaney's 'Babel 17' was also published in 1967. Delany was just 23-years-old when he wrote this extraordinary book which won a Nebula Award, and concerns a time in the far future when human beings have colonised the galaxy and messages start to arrive in an alien language (Babel 17) which must be decoded to determine whether the aliens' intentions are hostile or benevolent.

Sword and sorcery also emerged as a popular form of fiction: "The Earth grew old, its landscapes mellowing and showing signs of age, its ways becoming whimsical and strange in the manner of a man in his last years." Thus wrote Michael Moorcock in 'The Jewel in the Skull' in 1967. **(102)** This quote is from the 1979 Hart-Davis 4 volume compilation of Panther Books 'The High History of the Runestaff', my original copy is long gone. I remember reading it and books like it in a graveyard dating back to Mary, Queen of Scots – it seemed fitting at the time. Moorcock would go on to a long and distinguished career, recently authoring a book in the Dr Who series, and also dabbling in music with Robert Calvert and Hawkwind. His early examples of sword and sorcery, an increasingly popular genre of science fiction, earned the author praise from The Times newspaper as 'a myth-maker, an epic fantasist'. The story of the destiny of Dorian Hawkmoon, Duke of Koln, eternal champion, forever bound by the Runestaff and his adversary Count Brass in whose skull is embedded the black jewel, an evil eye through which the enemies of the Dark Empire can see everything he sees, would become an enduring piece of fantasy.

1967 was also the year in which Oz magazine was first published. This would gain notoriety and polarise opinion when charged under the Obscene Publications Act. In 1970, Paladin would publish a book of reminiscences which also served as a guide to the 'counterculture' and its principles, principals and issue. It was written by its editor Richard Neville, the aforementioned 'Playpower'. This also polarised opinion drawing out comments ranging from 'almost totally devoid of intellectual content' by his native Sydney Morning Herald'; 'contains the germs of a new fascism' (The Sunday Times) to 'a deeply+ felt and honourable book' (The Guardian). Its value nowadays is to chronicle Neville's wide ranging take on a turbulent period in artistic, political and cultural history (without his ever offering a rationale for his book which, while fascinating, is steeped in cynicism). Thus, he reminds his readers of the significance of "the explosion of Arts Laboratories" since Jim Haynes had opened his first experimental workshop in Drury Lane, London in July, 1967, with over 150 Art Labs in operation by the end of 1969. "These centres, like the art college sit-ins, are a rejection of the chic gallery, dilettantish, whiz-kid, polka-dotted art-as-a-commodity philosophy and, in the case of Guildford Art College, student sitters-in have their ranks swelled by visitors from the local Arts Lab, Hare Krishna chanters *et al*." **(103)**

The musical 'Hair' opened in Broadway in October, 1967. It tells the story of the 'Hippies of the Age of Aquarius' who live an anti-war bohemian lifestyle. It is not until almost a year later that the show opened in Shaftesbury Avenue, London where it ran for five years.

### *"The games people play, every night and every day." (and so on and so forth)*

In sport, the World Boxing Association stripped Cassius Clay (Muhammad Ali) of his heavyweight boxing title because of his refusal to be drafted to fight in Vietnam and he was later sentenced to five years' imprisonment for draft evasion. Edward W Brooke became the first black person to be elected to the US Senate by popular vote and Thurgood Marshall became the first African American justice of the United States Supreme Court. The dark flipside of this was the inauguration of segregationist Lester Maddox as Governor of Georgia. This all went to show that so long after the conclusion of the American Civil War and four years after the struggle to get James Meredith enrolled into University, a serious early watershed in John Fitzgerald Kennedy's Presidency, that America still had a long way to go to overcome its racial divisions and to seriously challenge the notion of white supremacy. This was not confined to the US, of course, and it was also in 1967 that the Bahamas elected its first black prime minister,

Lynden Oscar Pindling. In Rhodesia, things headed in the opposite direction as pro-Apartheid laws are passed.

Devoted followers of satellite TV coverage of American football may be amazed to learn that the very first American Superbowl final was in 1967 and was won by the Green Bay Packers. Glasgow Celtic became the first British team to win the European Cup, now the Champions League, when they defeated Inter Milan 2–1 in the final. They achieved this one year before Manchester United and it remains the club's greatest achievement. The tennis match between Cliff Drysdale and Roger Taylor with commentary from David Vine is the first to be broadcast in colour television on BBC2 in July in the UK. In an anti-climactic men's singles final, Australian John Newcombe defeated W G Wilhelm Bungert 6–3, 6–1, 6–1 while American Billie Jean King defeated Britain's Ann Jones 6–3, 6–4.

Nine executives of the German pharmaceutical company Gruenenthal were charged for supplying the thalidomide drug which was taken by pregnant mothers and caused birth defects in children. Also in 1967, Christiaan Barnard carried out the first human heart transplant. The recipient, Louis Washkansky, survived for only 18 days but plays his part in pioneering work that would go on to save countless lives. Coronary by-pass and the use of lasers in surgery were also pioneering events in medicine in 1967. The term 'black hole' was used for the first time by Professor John Archibald Wheeler, a collaborator of Albert Einstein and the world's first supersonic airliner Concorde, a British-French project was unveiled in Toulouse. While we take bank machines for granted nowadays and it seems there is one on every urban street corner, the first Automatic Teller Machine (ATM) was, in fact, installed at a branch of Barclay's Bank in Enfield, North London in the year 1967. By 1967, nine in ten UK households had a television set. Those who didn't survive the sixties would marvel at the technological developments in lightweight flat screen TVs and the head spinning choice of channels available nowadays. Despite the introduction of colour TV in July, 1967, one of the most popular BBC programmes, as we have seen, the long running sci-fi drama series 'Dr Who' (as popular as ever following a new millennium renaissance) did not broadcast in colour until 1970. 'Danger Man' ended in 1967 and Partick McGoogan effortlessly transmogrified into 'The Prisoner' in the same year. Future James Bond, Roger Moore, was starring as Simon Templar 'the Saint' and 'the Avengers' with Honour Blackman then Diana Rigg as Emma Peel, and the debonaire umbrella and bowler hat toting Patrick Macnee as Patrick Steed was also a popular show in 1967. Dominic Sandbrook in his book 'White Heat' asserts that the Avengers was the more significant of the two, not just because of its more international appeal but because it "tended to skirt around controversial contemporary issues, preferring to take careful refuge in a careful blend of nostalgia and modernity" so much so that "by the time the Avengers switched to colour in 1967, its ethos was becoming increasingly surreal. Its designers were clearly inspired by Pop Art... and the action was shot in an increasingly comic-book fashion."(104) [43] 'The Saint' was by comparison rather po-faced with Simon Templar on a one man quest to protect innocents from injustice, usually accompanied by a pretty accomplice and, occasionally, a moral twist or two! The vintage Bentley and Lotus Elan cars also proved appealing.

It is difficult to sum up a year, let alone a decade, in pictures but many books have attempted to do just that. 'The Sixties in Pictures' starts with the dramatic beginning to

[43] Pierre Cardin was the wardrobe designer for 'the Avengers' and Diana Rigg had eight jump suits made out of crimplene. McNee wrote a book 'the Avengers (And Me)' in which he reveals some fashion secrets.

1967 as "On 5th January, 1967, millions of TV viewers watched in horror as Donald Campbell's attempt to break his own water-speed record of 276.33 miles per hour ended in tragedy". Coniston Water in Cumbria, England was the scene of this disaster as Campbell's hydroplane lift from the water at 300 mph before somersaulting backwards to certain death. Moving into March, the Torrey Canyon oil spill is documented. Elvis Presley's marriage to Priscilla Beaulieu is commemorated by a photograph of the cutting of the cake at the Aladdin Hotel in Las Vegas. There is a photograph of Paul McCartney sitting beside Jane Asher holding up a copy of the Evening Standard newspaper with the bold headline 'Stones won't go to Jail' after Mick Jagger and Keith Richards were released by Chichester Magistrates' Court on 10 May. The Six Day War is next. The Israeli Prime Minister is shown visiting the Wailing Wall in Jerusalem on 12th June. Middle East unrest, and US and Israel talks in particular are constantly under the microscope. "The Prime Minister, Benjamin Netanyahu, said yesterday that it would be 'indefensible' if his country's 1967 borders were to become the basis of a peace deal with the Palestinians as proposed by President Barack Obama in a wide-ranging speech. But after a White House meeting which some expected to be frosty, Mr Natanyahu said Israel was ready to make concessions to bring about a settlement," reported David Usborne for The Independent newspaper on 13th May, 2011. The riots in Detroit are depicted by pictures of national guardsmen patrolling the streets in July while on the following page, there is close-up picture of a propeller of the Queen Elizabeth II, the last of the Cunard transatlantic superliners launched from the Clyde, Glasgow shipyard on 20th September. A photograph of the dead body of Ernesto Che Guevara surrounded by the press corps and military operatives serves as a ghoulish reminder of his assassination on 9th October in Bolivia. A bitter Fidel Castro is also pictured holding up a photograph of General Ovanda Candia and members of the Bolivian Army Command celebrating Guevara's death. By the time we get to 1968, another kind of war, Vietnam, was dominating the headlines.

In 1967, sixty of the nations of planet Earth signed a treaty banning nuclear weapons from space. The UK began negotiations for membership of the European Economic Community eventually blocked by French President De Gaulle because of doubts about whether Britain was serious about being 'European' with the Commonwealth and the special relationship with the US compromising our commitment to our near neighbours. Now, the citizens of the UK and the European Union face an altogether different set of possibilities!

The first Human Be-In contrasted with the US and South Vietnamese attack on the Mekong Delta. The first North Sea gas was pumped ashore at Easington, County Durham. This was April and in May, Australia began to recognise the rights of its indigenous people, and Francis Chichester completed the first solo navigation of the planet in Gypsy Moth IV.

The Sexual Offences Act in July decriminalised homosexuality. The breathalyser was introduced for motorists in October. The £ was devalued by 14.3% but was still worth $2.40 (at the time of writing around $1.3 if you are lucky!). IKEA began with beanbag chairs and inflatable PVC armchairs particularly popular.

Before we go on, the last word is about Brian Epstein. Following an admission to the Priory Hospital in Roehampton, he was not much present during the 'Sergeant Pepper' sessions and, in fact, his contract to manage The Beatles was to expire at the end of 1967. He never repeated his success with The Beatles. However entertaining Gerry and The Pacemakers, Billy J Kramer and The Dakotas, The Fourmost and Sounds Incorporated were, they were not The Beatles. Epstein had, before his tragic death, teamed up with Australian Robert Stigwood who reputedly got 50% of NEMS for £0.5

million. Nevertheless, without Epstein's backing, would The Beatles have gone on to achieve what they did, hypothetical I admit, but perhaps if history had taken a different turn, the history and culture of popular music would have been very different.

# Chapter Eight
## Sergeant Pepper Beckons

So it was against this backdrop: struggles in the middle East, environmental issues, space exploration the 'cultural revolution' in China, and 'countercultural revolution' in the US and parts of Europe (a different kind of revolution altogether!), the cold war, race riots, the civil rights movement, the rise of 'black power' and 'flower power', Vietnam, the growing importance of TV and the mass media, fashion and music, much of which would reverberate into the 21st century, that The Beatles would enter the studio on 19th January, 1967 to begin recording *'A Day in the Life',* and herald a prolific year of recording spanning 26 original songs culminating in *'Hello, Goodbye'* completed on 2nd November, 1967.

One song was already in the can for what would become the 'Sergeant Pepper's Lonely Hearts Club Band' album; Paul McCartney's *'When I'm 64',* written when he was 16 and completed four days before Christmas Day in 1966. Over a period stretching to April Fool's Day, The Beatles would put together what would become regarded as the greatest 'concept' album of all time (although the term 'concept' is debatable when applied here) and change the face of popular music forever.

### *"Let me take you down": a visit to Strawberry Field and Penny Lane*

In an interview with Playboy magazine John Lennon supplied a comprehensive answer on the location and significance of Strawberry Fields : "It's a Salvation Army home that was near the house I lived in with my auntie in the suburbs. There were two famous houses there. One was owned by Gladstone which was a reformatory home for boys, which I could see out my window. And Strawberry Fields was just round the corner from that," he said. Lennon went on to refer to the old Victorian house which had been converted for Salvation Army orphans. where he used to go to garden parties with his childhood friends, and that they would "hang out" and sell lemonade bottles for a penny." **(105)** (Paul referred to Strawberry Fields as John's 'secret garden')

James Alexander reporting for BBC Radio Scotland on Tuesday, 10th May, 2011, broke the news that the gates to 'Strawberry Field', the legendary forbidden playground of John Lennon's childhood, were to be removed. Tour guide Paul Beasley lamented that the entrance to Strawberry Field was "one place on the tour that creates real emotion." This was, of course, no ordinary gate and no ordinary field. It was the entrance to a place that inspired the line 'nothing to get hung up about' in the song that was to become known as *'Strawberry Fields Forever'* (referring to Lennon's chasing after rabbits and generally invading the privacy of an area that then contained a Salvation Army home). As Alexander wryly commented in the conclusion to his report, "A bit of musical history will be lost." The Independent newspaper of 14th May also picked up the story under the headline 'Strawberry Fields' Gates Are Not Forever'. It transpired that local metal work specialist Jim Bennett had made replica gates to replace the original red ones that had fallen into disrepair. The Salvation Army children's home contained within the gates was demolished in the 1970s, and was replaced by a new building which now serves as a prayer venue and art studio.

'Strawberry Fields Forever' was, in fact, the first song recorded during the 'Sergeant Pepper sessions', and George Martin was so moved by John's original acoustic guitar rendition he described it as 'magic' and 'absolutely lovely' almost in the same breath. The finished product he described as 'like a modern Debussy'. Reflecting on the song in 2011 Martin's admiration is undiminished, saying to Mojo magazine writer Jim Irvin that (Strawberry Fields) opened a completely new field of dreams. Philip Norman in his book 'John Lennon: The Life' deconstructs the song: "The song that subsequently evolved in the studio was at first simple, light and literal. Where John had originally begun with the first verse, 'Living is easy with eyes closed', (George) Martin suggested going straight into the chorus, 'Let me take you down', that misleadingly plainspoken invitation to accompany him back to boyhood. Paul McCartney provided a crucial atmospheric touch, playing a mellotron (actually sampled flute) intro like some creaky, dusty harmonium in a 1950s church hall." **(106)**

On reflection, Martin decided that the 'nostalgic, folksy' early version needed a heavier treatment, changing the key to accommodate a cello score for three players, and adding four trumpets and a swarmandel, a type of Indian zither played by George Harrison, who had learned about the instrument under the tutelage of Ravi Shankar. As a compromise between the earlier, simpler version favoured by Lennon and Martin's arrangement the two versions were spliced together. It was a stroke of genius but Martin also struck lucky in the sense that the difference in tempi between the two takes was in almost perfect ratio to the difference in their keys.

The development of the song is documented on 'The Beatles Anthology Volume 2' on Apple in 1996 with the inclusion of the song's acoustic beginnings on take one recorded on 24th November, 1966 and a mono version (take seven) which along with take 26th would provide the final master. The 'dramatic change' in the song is astonishing. 'Strawberry Fields Forever' took 55 hours of studio time to finish, being completed just 3 days before Christmas, 1966. It was released on 13th February, 1967 in the US and the UK 4 days later.

Ian MacDonald rates the song's all pervasive influence on other musicians: "the song effectively inaugurated the English pop-pastoral mood explored in the late sixties by groups like Pink Floyd, Traffic, Family and Fairport Convention' identifying 'the true subject of English psychedelia'" as "neither love nor drugs, but nostalgia for the innocent vision of the child." **(107)** Clinton Heylin compares Lennon's vision for the song to the likes of William Blake and Bob Dylan who "when adults referred to a similar dislocation from the world first experienced through the eyes of a child" (with specific reference to the line 'No one I think is in my tree'). **(108)** Howard Sounes in his 'An Intimate Life of Paul McCartney' also alludes to Dylan and, indeed the difference between McCartney and Lennon's approach to song writing: "Like Dylan, Lennon had the knack of writing couplets like this ('Living is easy with eyes closed/ Misunderstanding all you see') that seem to contain an essential truth. Paul was rarely such a philosopher." **(109)** The next song from the session to be released (although not completed until 17th January, 1967) was also about a suburban district in Liverpool with a bus terminal where John Lennon lived with his mum and dad, and where his aunt Mimi used to see him safely off to Dovedale Primary School. The 'Barney's' referred to in the song was St Barnabus Church Hall, the hall where an embryonic form of the Beatles, The Quarry Men played. The barbers in the little parade is where Paul and his brother Mike would go for their 'short back and sides' and 'the barber showing photographs' was an Italian named Bioletti. The shop is still there opposite Lloyd's Bank although no longer run by the Bioletti family. Also mentioned in the lyrics is the chip shop ('four of fish' meant four old pennies worth of cod or hake – remember this was the pre decimal era). The 'pretty nurse selling poppies from a tray' was probably a reference to John's friend Pete Shotton's wife who used to sell poppies for Remembrance Sunday. In fact, Penny Lane was woven into the Lennon family psychi as Philip Norman details in his book 'John Lennon: The Life', Norman relates the story of the significance Penny Lane had for John's father Alf who was educated nearby, his mother Julia who worked at cafe in Penny Lane itself and in an eerie instance of 'lightning strikes twice' Julia's former partner Bobby Dykins who died in a car accident eight years after Lennon's Mum was knocked down by a car. **(110)** Norman also wryly points out that "No pop song had ever smuggled such arrant smut onto a million turntables", a reference, of course, to the 'finger pie', 'the olfactory reward for groping inside a girl's crotch.' (or 'heavy petting')**(111)**. In an earlier book about The Beatles, Norman describes *'Penny Lane'* as "surrealism from a rational mind (Paul's)" whereas *'Strawberry Fields'* was written under the influence of LSD. **(112)** The piccolo trumpet (Its use in Bach's Brandenberg Concerto was not lost on Paul) was played by David Mason of the London Symphony Orchestra.

Ian MacDonald pretty well sums up the significance of *'Penny Lane'* with his customary insight: "Anyone unlucky enough not to have been aged between 14 and 30 during 1966–1967 will never know the excitement of those years in popular culture. A sunny optimism permeated everything and possibilities seemed limitless. Bestriding a British scene that embraced music, poetry, fashion and film, The Beatles were at their peak, and were looked up to in awe as arbiters of a positive new age in which the dead customs of the older generation would be refreshed and remade through the creative energy of the classless young. With its vision of 'blue suburban skies' and boundlessly confident vigour, *'Penny Lane'* distils the spirit of that time more perfectly than any other creative produce of the mid-sixties. Crouched in the primary colours of a picture book, yet observed with the slyness of a gang of kids straggling home from school, *'Penny Lane'* is both naive and knowing – but above all thrilled to be alive." **(113)**

McCartney was well conversant with the scenes and characters portrayed in *'Penny Lane'* having travelled in the number 86 bus fom Mather Avenue to the Liverpool Institute High School for Boys in Mount Road, passing the bus and tram stop at the corner of Smithdown Road and Penny Lane. The level of nostalgia McCartney felt was revealed in 1996 when the school was re-opened as the Liverpool Institute for the Performing Arts by McCartney himself, soon to become a Knight of the Realm. Apart from George Harrison other famous contemporaneous alumni included Peter Sissons who became a news presenter for the BBC, the ITV and Channel 4.

*'Strawberry Fields Forever'* and *'Penny Lane'* might have been on the 'Sergeant Pepper' album if it weren't for the fact that the band had a set of unwritten rules about including singles on their LPs (These were released in two volumes as 'Past Masters' instead). As it turned out, there was no shortage of inspiration for the songs yet to come. With a delicious sense of irony, the generous double A-side 'Strawberry Fields/ Penny Lane' never made #1, kept off the top spot by a moustachioed Engelbert Humperdinck singing *'Release Me'*. But let's not dwell too much on that! At least, *'Penny Lane'* did make #1 on Billboard and Cash Box charts in the States.

A popular misconception is that 'Sergeant Pepper's' was a concept album. John Lennon put paid to that notion when he said that, in fact, Sergeant Pepper was "a bunch of songs, and you stick bits of Pepper in it and it's a concept."(11) Having said that, as George Martin said at the time of the 20th anniversary CD, "Sergeant Pepper's didn't start out life as a concept album but it very soon developed a life of its own."

Indeed, George Martin was more a galvanising force than a mere producer. In an interview with Mojo magazine's Jim Irvin, he describes it as 'the freedom album': "It was about giving themselves the freedom to experiment and grow up. It was also about adopting a new guise, to rid themselves once and for all of what Paul McCartney later described as 'the four fucking mop tops'. He (Martin) says that the idea for the album came on a flight back from a Kenyan holiday in November, 1966 when McCartney reflected on how enjoyable it had been to wander around incognito on a stopover in France wearing spectacles and a false moustache. John Lennon concurs with the 'coming of age' idea in the famous Playboy interview. However, given everything the band had gone through together, one would expect the gestation and realisation of 'Sergeant Pepper's' to be a unifying and cathartic experience but not every Beatle was equally enthusiastic about the project. Referring to the 1993 documentary on the making of 'Sergeant Pepper's', Clinton Heylin wryly comments, "The participation of every surviving Beatle could have ensured a fascinating insight into the *Pepper* process. However, everyone carefully skirted the issue of whether those perpetual onlookers Harrison and Starkey were really blown away by the results." (115)

George Harrison actually does set the record straight in The Beatles Anthology: "It was becoming difficult for me because I wasn't really that into it." He goes on to explain that previously The Beatles had worked more as a band but now "it became an assembly process – just little parts and then overdubbing – and for me, it became a bit tiring and a bit boring."(116) Harrison also remarked, "Everybody else thought that Sgt Pepper was a revolutionary record – but for me, it was not as enjoyable as *Rubber Soul* or *Revolver*."(117) Harrison also experienced the usual difficulties of coming up with material considered strong enough for the album. '*Only a Northern Song*' was recorded as part of the sessions but failed to impress George Martin and had to wait until it was used to fill up the second side of the 'Yellow Submarine; soundtrack album before it was heard. Marc Shapiro in his book 'All Things Must Pass: The Life of George Harrison' maintains that despite his low level of contribution in terms of songs, Harrison "had a definite impact on the ground breaking, heavily psychedelicised (sic) music of *Sergeant Pepper'*(118) and attributes much of this to his immersion in Krishna philosophy (It was George, of course, who encouraged The Beatles to attend a lecture by the Maharishi Mahesh Yogi in London on 24 August, 1967 which led to the group's visit to Rishikesh, India). It is equally arguable that Harrison's predilection for Indian music and exploring more experimental forms of music could have headed him in an entirely different direction.

'Sergeant Pepper' was certainly good for George Martin who was encouraged to 'pull every trick out of the bag' with electronics, musique concrete and string arrangements all requiring his magic touch. In fact, there was so much attention to detail that Ringo was taught how to play chess by Neil Aspinall "while he was waiting".

# Chapter Nine
## Sergeant Pepper's Lonely Hearts Club Band
## Track by Track

## Side One Track One

*'Sergeant Pepper's Lonely Hearts Club Band'*
*(Recorded between 1st February and 6th March, 1967)*
*(43 known cover versions and counting)*

The first track on the actual album was, of course, the title track itself, and Paul McCartney somehow came up with *'Sergeant Pepper's Lonely Hearts Club Band'* and an idea for a song that was to become the overture to the album. The popular story about the origins of the title is that McCartney and Mal Evans, The Beatles' roadie and personal assistant, were joking about the 'S' and 'P' on the salt and pepper sachets and McCartney came up with 'Sergeant Pepper' instead of 'salt and pepper'. Dating agencies were growing in popularity at the time so the idea for the 'lonely hearts' club band' was born. The title could also have been influenced by the exotic names of some west coast Ameican bands like Big Brother and the Holding Company or even the names of popular London boutiques like Lord Kitchener's Valet.

The title track *'Sgt Pepper's Lonely Hearts Club Band'* opens with the expectant murmur of a theatre audience and the muted cacophony of an orchestra tuning up. After a few seconds, the band eases into a lethargic rock 'n' roll vamp, the rhythm demarked by piercing squawks on the offbeats from a strident lead guitar. There comes a rest, then a leaden drum fill, whereupon McCartney bursts in with the excited, occupationally breathless voice of a master of ceremonies, setting the scene for the crowd in the theatre and everyone listening at home to enjoy a fictional band enjoying its twentieth anniversary. . Described by Ian MacDonald as "a shrewd fusion of Edwardian variety orchestra and contemporary heavy rock"**(119)** the heavy guitar by McCartney (which replaced an earlier solo by Harrison) was obviously influenced by Jimi Hendrix whose exciting new blend of heavy blues rock he and John Lennon admired. Hendrix returned the compliment playing the number live only days after the album's release.

By all accounts, Paul McCartney, who attended the gig with George and Patti Harrison, and his new love interest photographer Linda Eastman, was apparently flabbergasted when Jimi Hendrix and his Experience group opened their set with the song at the Saville Theatre on Shaftesbury Avenue. He began to get an idea of what the album would come to mean to people as Hendrix had only heard the number a few days before.

## Side One Track Two

*'With a Little Help from My Friends'*
*(Recorded between 29th and 30th March, 1967)*
*(50 known cover versions and counting)*

*'With a Little Help from My Friends'*, later immortalised by Joe Cocker and so stirringly performed at Woodstock, was written specifically for Ringo to accompany his alter ego as Billy Shears. It is, in fact, the only song on the album that in any way develops the theme set out in the title track. The song features a rare vocal from Ringo and George Martin on Hammond organ. It started off as an idea by McCartney under the working title of *'Bad Finger Boogie'*. Ian Macdonald's verdict was: "At once communal and personal, it's a song of comfort, an acid lullaby, meant as gesture of inclusivity."**(120)** The reference to getting high escaped the censors. While they probably didn't realise it at the time, it is likely that the line is another one of those 'in-jokes' referred to by Paul McCartney in the book 'Many Years from Now' with its origin in Bob Dylan's admiration for the middle-eight from *'I Wanna Hold Your Hand'*!

## Side One Track Three

*'Lucy in the Sky with Diamonds'*
*(Recorded between 28th February and 2nd March, 1967)*
*(65 known cover versions and counting)*

Life is full of confusing acronyms and the title of the next song *'Lucy in the Sky with Diamonds'* is another case in point. Although easily construed as referring to an acid trip, the accidental acronym LSD in the title was as innocent as an imaginative phrase used by a child (Julian Lennon) to describe his painting of a girl (Lucy O'Donnell) who sat next to him at nursery school. John said the images were from the landscape inhabited by the likes of 'Alice in Wonderland' (or the 'Wool and Water' chapter of 'Through the Looking Glass' to be precise).

John Lennon squashes all suggestions that the song was about LSD in The Beatles Anthology: "I swear to God, or swear to Mao, or to anybody you like. I had no idea it spelt LSD. *This* is the *truth*: my son came home with a drawing and showed me this strange looking woman flying around. I said, 'What is it?' and he said, 'It's Lucy in the Sky with Diamonds.' **(121)** In 'The Beatles Anthology' Paul refers to the influence of psychedelics and his memory of the writing of the lyrics is untarnished by the years: "I offered cellophane flowers and newspaper taxis, and John replied with kaleidoscope eyes.' **(122)**

George, while having reservations about the way 'Sergeant Pepper' came about, was obviously proud to be associated with songs like *'Lucy in the Sky'* where he could be an integral part of the creative process superimposing an eastern fixed tamboura drone on top of modulating western psychedelic music.

Irish comedian and writer Spike Milligan may have unwittingly inspired some of the whimsical lines in the song as John Lennon had told him that he was an avid fan of the Goon Show. In particular, the line 'plasticine porters with looking glass ties' establishes a clear link between the 'plasticine ties' referred to in the Goon Show and Lewis Carrol's famous book. Bob Dylan is another likely inspiration. "On a very basic level, *'Lucy in the Sky'* was an attempt to write a pastoral British equivalent of Dylan's *'Mr Tambourine Man'*, a song both Lennon and McCartney adored. Even the boat on the river is as much

Dylan's 'magic swirlin' ship' (itself a homage to Rimbaud's 'bateau ivre') as Alice's daydream." **(123)**

*'Lucy in the Sky'* is, of course, also singled out for praise as one of the most sonically innovative songs on 'Sergeant Pepper' with George Harrison's Fender Stratocaster in chorus put through a Leslie speaker with added tremolo and the use of a Lowrey theatre organ which provides the opening keyboard arpeggios.

## Side One Track Four

### *'Getting Better'*
*(Recorded between 9th and 23rd March, 1967)*
*(13 known cover versions and counting)*

'It's Getting Better' was a phrase used by Jimmy Nichol. Drum stool deputy for Ringo during his illness when the Beatles were in tour in 1964, an often overlooked gem of a song referring among other things to the feelings of an 'angry young man' about reactionary school teachers (fast forward to Pink Floyd's *'Another Brick in the Wall'* and you will find similar sentiments). It is also autobiographical.

John Lennon: "It is a diary form of writing… I was a hitter. I couldn't express myself and I hit. I fought men and I hit women. That's why I am always on about peace… I am a violent man who has learned not to be violent and regrets his violence." **(124)**

With its insidious beat, it is the strident lyric, and unusual embellishments like the plucked piano strings by George Martin and McCartney's double tracked bass help to define the number. It was while recording vocal parts for *'Getting Better'* that John Lennon took some acid, mistaking it for an amphetamine. George Martin took John up to the roof of the recording studio for some fresh air and was mystified at his enthusiasm for a perfectly familiar London skyline. (The Beatles were also introduced to the Pink Floyd, who were working on their 'Piper at the Gates of Dawn' album elsewhere in Abbey Road, during one of the '*Getting Better*' recording sessions).

## Side One Track Five

### *'Fixing a Hole'*
*(Recorded between 9th and 21st February, 1967)*
*(10 known cover versions and counting)*

'Fixing a Hole' has nothing to do with drugs – or has it?

Paul McCartney from 1967: "(*'Fixing A Hole'*) is about… the hole in your make-up which lets the rain in, and stops your mind going where it will… if you're a junkie sitting in a room fixing a hole then that's what it will mean to you, but when I wrote it, I meant if there's a crack or the room is uncolourful (sic), then I'll paint it."**(125)** It is much more likely, therefore, to represent McCartney's musings while fixing up his remote Scottish cottage!

The song was actually recorded not at Abbey Road but in Regent Sound Studio in Denmark Place creating a sound much more similar to that produced by Andrew Loog Oldham for The Rolling Stones. The guitar solo was played on a Fender Stratocaster with a high treble setting. George Martin played the harpsichord. John Lennon didn't play anything but did sing backing vocals.

## Side One Track Six

*'She's Leaving Home'*
*(Recorded between 17th and 20th March, 1967)*
*(59 known cover versions and counting)*

Paul's *'She's Leaving Home'*, is the mundane counterpart to the more 'trippy' songs on the album, just a simple tale that in its own way perfectly encapsulates the rebelliousness of the times as a young lady abandons her parents to go to London to meet a motor salesman (a character based on a real car dealer Terry Dolan who was a friend of Brian Epstein) and fulfils the desire to experience life to the full, away from the security of comfortable but boring 'semi suburban' lives (Melanie Coe's father actually told a reporter, "I cannot imagine why she should run away. She has everything here. She is very keen on clothes but she left them all, even her fur coat."). The song was actually inspired by a story in the Daily Mail newspaper on 27th February, 1967 published under the title, 'A' Level Girl Dumps Car and Vanishes'.

Clinton Heylin puts his finger on the pulse of the song: "Despite its detached viewpoint (the writer did not actually know the main protagonist, unlike Tara Browne, the subject *of 'A Day in the Life')*, McCartney manages to seamlessly weave the feelings of the two parties – the girl and the parents – so successfully that Melanie Coe herself later admitted, 'The amazing thing about the song was how much it got right about my life'**(126)**. Heylin also makes the important point that the song chimed well with the 'gritty realism' of dramatised semi documentaries popular in the BBC television's 'Play for Today' series.

The critic Wilfred Mellers shrewdly observed that McCartney avoided taking sides in contrasting 'the muddled hope, apprehension and fear in the girl's heart' with 'the fuddled incomprehension of the parents'. The whole Beatles do not actually play on the song: it is John and Paul singing to a backing of harp, violins, violas, cellos and a double bass. Mike Leander's score for harp and strings was praised by musical theorist Walter Everett, referring to it as a 'vivid characterisation (of) a lonely girl and her selfish parents.' **(127)**

While *'She's Leaving Home'* was clearly Paul's song, John enthusiastically contributed background vocals, adding a dash of vinegar to the honey as Philip Norman would put it.

## Side One Track Seven

*'Being for the Benefit of Mr Kite'*
*(Recorded between 17th February and 31st March, 1967)*
*(9 known cover versions and counting)*

*'Being for The Benefit of Mr Kite'* was written by John with some inspiration coming from an 1843 circus poster advertising a travelling troupe who appeared in Rochdale, Lancashire, and, depending on which source you read, bought in an antique shop in Sevenoaks, Kent. The fire leaper Mr Henderson was one of the characters who appeared on the poster with, curiously, 'summersets' (rather than somersaults) being performed and, as a special big top attraction, a horse called Henry dancing a waltz.

John Lennon was especially pleased with the studio effects producer George Martin created to, as Martin himself once said, make the listener smell the sawdust in the circus ring and be dazzled by the swirling lights of the fairground. The organ effects were particularly effective, old calliope, or steam organ recordings, being copied onto tape, spliced and mixed up. Lennon also collaborated with Martin in playing one organ while Martin played the other, speeded up as he couldn't play it fast enough, to create a rotary effect. Martin also gave a lot of credit to studio engineer Geoff Emerick especially in "the use of unusual room ambience and big reverbs, making even the apparent locations of these performances sound exotic and, occasionally chilly." **(128)** (Emerick was indeed a precocious talent having been only 19 years old when he engineered the sessions for the 'Revolver' album).

'Mr Kite' also includes one of those rarities in British rock/ pop: a drum roll!

## Side Two Track One

*'Within You Without You'*
*(Recorded between 15th March and 4th April, 1967)*
*(13 known cover versions and counting)*

The only George Harrison song to make the album was *'Within You, Without You'*. Originally composed on Klaus Voorman's harmonium, *'Within You, Without You'* not only had Harrison playing sitar, tambura and acoustic guitar (as well as singing) but also additional unnamed Indian musicians from the Asian Music Centre on dilrubas, tabla, more tambura and svarmandal. Eight violinists and three cellists provided a full string sound and Neil Aspinall contributed additional tambura. The song, reflecting Harrison's fascination with Indian culture and the playing of Indian musicians like Ravi Shankar (whose daughter Anoushka would appear in the tribute 'Concert for George') was recorded over four separate days from 15th March to 4th April which was the final day of the 'Sergeant Pepper' sessions. Ian Macdonald seems at first sight to be unimpressed with the song commenting on the 'lack of harmonic interest', and the 'didactic' and 'dated' lyric and 'air of superiority and sanctimonious 'finger-wagging' at those who 'gain the world and lose their soul'. On closer reading though, he projects these misgivings towards other critics and commentators, and chastises them for considering *'Within You, Without You'* to be a blot on the Sergeant Pepper landscape. Instead, he points to the 'ethos of 1967' and affirms it as an expression of 'inner revolution against materialism' and scathing condemnation of the 'spiritual aridity of modern life'. **(129)**

In the closest Harrison came to writing an autobiography, 'I, Me, Mine', published in 1980, he describes the etymology of the song: "The tune came first then the first sentence... *we were talking*... I finished the words later. I had been taking sitar lessons with Ravi Shankar for some time... I was continually playing Indian music, the melodies of which were called Sargams, which are the bases of the different Ragas."
The effectiveness of the instrumental solo in 5/4 time in the middle of the piece is also commented on by Harrison. **(130)**

A totally instrumental version of 'Within You, Without You' can be heard on 'The Beatles Anthology 2'.

## Side Two Track Two

*'When I'm Sixty-Four'*
*(Recorded between 6th and 21st December, 1966)*
*(50 known cover versions and counting)*

The first 'Sergeant Pepper's song to be completed was *'When I'm 64'*, a tune originally conceived by Paul when he was just 16 during the days when the group had a residency at The Cavern Club in Mathew Street, Liverpool and returned to when Paul's father Jim turned 64 in the summer of 1966. It featured no less than three clarinet players, and recalled the pastiche of The Temperance Seven and The New Vaudeville Band, popular at the time.

The song was actually considered as the double A-side companion to *'Strawberry Fields Forever'* but, as McCartney was to tell 'Uncut' magazine many years later, Lennon had thrown down the gauntlet with 'Strawberry Fields; and 'upped the ante' for Paul to come up with the idea for *'Penny Lane'*.

## Side Two Track Three

*'Lovely Rita'*
*(Recorded between 23rd February and 21st March, 1967)*
*(8 known cover versions and counting)*

*'Lovely Rita'* was based on an encounter between Paul McCartney and a traffic warden called Meta Davis in Garden Road, St John's Wood. It is a typical example of Paul's penchant for 'third party' songs (a 'paperback writer!) as opposed to John's preference for writing from personal experience. In a neat little critique, Iain Macdonald distils the essence of the approach taken on the song: "Plastered with the ubiquitous *Sergeant Pepper* repeat echo, the track was subjected to much vari-speeding, ending up in E flat major, a brass band key not much used in pop." **(131)** George Martin opened his box of tricks by weighing the capstan of the tape recorder with sticky tape to simulate the sound of a honky tonk piano It was Lennon who made the "percussive mouth noises", a trick repeated later on *'I Am The* Walrus'. Ringo's drums were noticeably separated in the stereo mix, isolating McCartney's strolling bass line.

An even cheaper alternative to a kazoo, a comb and paper with added reverb was also used on this song.

## Side Two Track Four

*'Good Morning, Good Morning'*
*(Recorded between 8th February and 29th March, 1967)*
*(8 known cover versions and counting)*

Jon Wiener reckons that *'Good Morning, Good Morning'* "hinted at his (John Lennon's) dark feelings and then denied them' – 'I've got nothing to say but it's OK'**(132)** It's difficult to find much comment on *'Good Morning, Good Morning'* which is a pity as it fits into the album so well but Ian Macdonald does comment in some detail: "Later dismissed by Lennon as 'a throwaway, a piece of garbage', *'Good Morning, Good Morning'* is a bilious riposte to McCartney's blithe *'Good Day Sunshine'*. Born from its author's habit of working with the television on in the background, it was inspired by an irritating Kellogg's cornflakes commercial and contains a sneering reference to a middlebrow British sitcom of the period 'Meet the Wife' (Lennon's tastes were more programmes like 'The Power Game' and 'Danger Man')... A disgusted canter through the muck, mayhem and mundanity of the human farmyard, *'Good Morning, Good Morning'* belies the airy-fairy reputation Sergeant Pepper has acquired in hindsight, being one of the earthiest things The Beatles ever made." **(133)** Macdonald goes on to talk about the 'mighty pugilistic smashes on the crash cymbals', and George Martin's maximising the aggression' by 'vicious compression' with brass backing from Sounds Incorporated The whole demented thing is 'whipped to a climax by a coruscating pseudo-Indian guitar solo from McCartney'. **(134)**

One final thing that must be elucidated is that the farmyard noises were programmed in a specific order at John's insistence so that each successive animal is capable of eating its predecessor – clever!

## Side Two Track Five

*'Sergeant Pepper's Lonely Hearts Club Band (reprise)'*
*(Recorded on 1st April, 1967)*

There was no April fool's joke about a masterstroke of sequencing which was actually suggested by Neil Aspinall much to John Lennon's sardonic chagrin – he probably wished he'd thought of it first. Side two sounded incomplete so Aspinall suggested an abbreviated reprise of the 'signature tune' and it was decided to segue this into *'A Day in the Life'*. This worked brilliantly yielding a dramatic and stunning transition between a triad of songs starting with *'Good Morning, Good Morning'*.

## Side Two Track Six

*'A Day in the Life'*
(Recorded between 19th January and 22nd February, 1967)
(35 known cover versions and counting)

The real 'coup de grace' on 'Sergeant Pepper's' was *'A Day in the Life'* which started off life as a collage of newspaper stories culled by John Lennon from 'The Daily Mail' and put together in the cut up style of William Burroughs. The car crash reference was about Guinness heir Tara driving his Lotus sports car through a red light and colliding with a van in South Kensington with fatal consequences with a story lamenting the large number of pot holes on Blackburn roads catching John's attention on the very next page. Paul and John worked together on the song with Paul contributing the memorable bridge about turning people on and also the part about a reluctant worker who has perhaps overslept and immediately reaches for a comb. Again, drug reference was denied as turning on could just as easily be about turning on a light switch, sex (or anything at all). John added the surrealistic reference to the Albert Hall (also in South Kensington) and the reference to the 'English army has just won the war', presumably with his part in the film 'How I Won the War' in mind. Paul also had the idea of giving the orchestra 15 bars to do anything they liked, starting on the lowest notes on their instruments and ending up on the highest notes producing what he described as 'a crazy big swing storm' with the trumpets totally freaked out.

Chatting with the sound engineers about frequencies and their capabilities, they decided to have a bit at the end of *'A Day in The Life'* at the frequency that only a dog could hear. The Beatles were also exploring the possibilities of stereo panning, and in using the 3 second gap between tracks to put sound effects in and even using the run off groove to capture some 'chit chat'. A composite mix reckoned by the compilers to be a combination of the best outtakes can be heard on 'The Beatles Anthology' volume 2 on Apple Records. One fascinating aspect of this is Mal Evans counting towards 24, later to be filled by orchestral crescendos.

Clinton Heylin traces the gestation of ideas that coalesced in the experimental orchestral passages on *'A Day in the Life'*: "He (McCartney) made a habit of putting on some particularly atonal Albert Ayler LP like **Spirits** or **Bells,** and gauging (George) Martin's reaction. Though Martin went along with McCartney's notion of an orchestra playing not as one but as many, he did rein in at least one aspect of Macca's vision." **(135)** Thus, ninety musicians were whittled down to forty although because the orchestra was recorded on four tracks of tape mixed down to one "he had the equivalent of 160 musicians." In fact, Paul had been corresponding with Stockhausen, and he and John were also familiar with the music of experimental composers such as John Cage all of which had big influence in their quest for something 'different' and out with the normal parameters of 'pop'. The climax to *'A Day in the Life'* was, of course, not just a piece of music but a 'happening' with the group's flower power outfits contrasting with the formal evening dress of George Martin and the orchestra. Masks and fancy dress were handed out with perhaps the most memorable being the violinist with the gorilla paw! Guests at the 'happening' which was recorded for posterity included Donovan Leitch, the Glaswegian singer, Mike Nesmith of the Monkees and members of The Rolling Stones.

## The Run off Groove

And so, we are nearing the end of 129 days of blood, sweat and tears but it was worth it in the end as the most influential pop rock recording of all times was in the final stages of its creation. All that remained was for The Beatles to pose for the sleeve pictures on Tuesday, March 30th, to finish off *'With a Little Help from My Friends'* in the Abbey Road Studio tape the title track's reprise that Saturday, before Paul McCartney left for America, the following Monday, and add eight violins and three cellos to *'Within You, Without You'*. The final act occurred on April 21st when all four Beatles assembled at Abbey Road to record the gibberish that would be cut – along with a sound audible only to dogs – into side two's run-out groove. (Appended to the last embers of the crashing piano chord that ends *'A Day in the Life'* a few seconds of sound at 15 kilocycles were added at the request of John Lennon. This frequency was only heard by and could be intensely annoying to the poor unsuspecting canines!)

Geoff Emerick, the recording engineer for the album, looking back on it all in the liner notes for the 20th anniversary CD edition, recalled, "The Beatles insisted that everything on 'Sergeant Pepper' had to be different so everything was either distorted, limited, heavily compressed or treated with excessive equalisation. We had microphones right down in the bells of the brass instruments and headphones turned into microphones attached to violins. We plastered vast amounts of echo onto vocals, and sent them through the circuitry of the revolving Leslie speaker inside a Hammond organ. We used giant primitive oscillators to vary the speed of instruments and vocals, and we had tapes chopped to pieces and stuck together upside down and the wrong way round."

One interesting thought when choosing which version of 'Sergeant Pepper' to listen to is George Martin's recommendation of the mono version which he considered to be "more rock 'n' roll" than the stereo version. Tim Sommer, writing for the Observer newspaper, goes into great detail to explain why: "The mono **Sergeant Pepper's** sounds like a cynical, often aggressive burlesque of the dawning Age of Aquarius, instead of a heraldic celebration of it." The stereo mix, on the other hand, sounds like "an over large bouquet of sickeningly sweet aromatic flowers."**(136).**

## Peter Blake and That sleeve!

Of course, the costuming and sleeve design of 'Sergeant Pepper' do suggest a unifying concept for the music and take us back to Ringo Starr's opening remarks near the beginning of this chapter about the Beatles becoming Sergeant Pepper. Procuring their military tunics from Berman's, the theatrical costumers, was quite a spontaneous thing and The Beatles made no particular claims to setting trends. "It was just another psychedelic image," said John. "Kids were already wearing army jackets on the King's Road. All we did was make them famous." Indeed, Victorian militaria, was sold in shops like 'I Was Lord Kitchener's Valet'. With most permissions granted, the 'heroes/ villains' of The Beatles/ Sgt Pepper's band took their positions on one of the most-bold and iconic album sleeves in the history of rock music. Designed by Peter Blake who at the time of writing is still an obsessive collector of paraphernalia and exhibitor of his own (and others) 'Pop Art'. It was Robert Fraser, known as 'Groovy Bob', a famous London art dealer, who suggested painter Peter Blake, who had already included The Beatles among his subjects.

As Paul McCartney describes in The Beatles Anthology, the group took album sleeves very seriously even to the extent of reading them from 'cover to cover'. Consulting books available in Bermans, the theatrical costumers on old military tunics from the Edwardian or Crimean eras the group members chose their own colours, bright psychedelic colours, "a bit like the fluorescent socks you used to get in the fifties"[44] (137) As far as who was to appear on the front cover, the group members wrote a list.[45] As Neil Aspinall recalls, the whole process became very eclectic, "everybody was asking, who do you want in the band?" Peter Blake's recollection is that lists were to be made of people in an imaginary audience. The art dealer Robert Fraser joined Blake in compiling a list but Ringo declined.[46]

This was not because he didn't take the idea seriously. In fact he has since said that everyone participated enthusiastically in the dressing up as 'the Peppers', like Flower Power, and, of course, his legendary peace sign is still flashed at the cameras to this current day.

As for Paul, as related in 'The Beatles Anthology'. it was his initial drawing that started the project off with the idea of a presentation where The Beatles are given the keys to an unspecified northern city beside a floral clock with the group sitting inside the cover with their favourite icons. (138) McCartney arrived with a vanload of brass-band instruments. Lennon brought his favourite TV. Blake's wife, the artist Jill Haworth, contributed a debauched looking doll in a sweatshirt inscribed 'WELCOME THE ROLLING STONES'. Revelling in the influence that came with working on behalf of a national institution, Blake had requisitioned a number of waxworks from Madame Tussaud's London Museum to stand in front and flesh out the crowd. (139)

As Clinton Heylin observed: "The sleeve would become the most famous album cover in Rock, an image so iconic, it still spawns a never ending variety of parodies, a process that would begin before the year was out with The Mothers of Invention's *We're Only in it for the Money'.*" (140)

---

[44] Actress Mae West changed her mind when asked by letter to reconsider. Her initial response had been, "What would I be doing in a lonely hearts club?"

[45] On the day of the photo session, Blake asked everyone involved in the project to bring along a few props or possessions that held some special significance for them.

[46] Robert Fraser, as Andy Warhol's London art dealer knew that Blake had been commissioned to design the cover for the first Velvet Underground LP.

### The impact of 'Sergeant Pepper's Lonely Hearts Club Band'

How did the world respond to such an apotheosis?

**"Listen without prejudice and you'll hear good reasons why Sgt Pepper tilted the world on its axis"** (John Harris) **(141)** The impact of 'Sergeant Peppers' was immediate. As Paul McCartney observed, "It certainly got noticed. It was released on the Friday, and on the Sunday Jimi Hendrix opened with 'Sgt Pepper' when we saw him at the Saville Theatre." **(142)** Sergeant Pepper's quickly became the iconic album of the age, a prototype for the future direction of psych/pop/rock. Mama Cass Elliot was the first to hear an original acetate in her flat in Luna Street off the King's Road as did all her neighbours as the album blasted out at full volume from speakers on her window ledge. Neil Aspinall, another school friend of George and Paul, and an associate of the group, recalled that it was six o'clock in the morning when an entourage arrived in cars at Cass Elliot's house, and that windows started opening and people leaned out giving the thumbs up. History was truly in the making. The album soon began to dominate the American airwaves, and Paul Kantner of Jefferson Airplane and David Crosby were early 'Sergeant Pepper' devotees. Crosby was a visitor to Abbey Road on the evening when the finishing touches were being put to '*A Day in the Life*'. He had been in London with The Byrds promoting his last album with them (Younger Than Yesterday) at a fan convention in the Roundhouse in Camden Town. He is quoted in Mojo magazine as saying: "They *knew* what they had created. They sat me down in the middle of a room on a stool and then they played me '*A Day in the Life*'. And when they got to the end of the piano chord, man, I was a dish rag. I was floored. It took me several minutes to be able to talk after that." **(143)** Crosby returned to the States armed with a reel-to-reel copy of '*A Day in the Life*' and 'became a Sgt Pepper evangelist'. **(144).** Like Brian Wilson, Crosby found the bar the Beatles had set was so high that it would be impossible to top it. In fact he once comented that The Beatles were so far ahead of everybody else that they had not only stretched the envelope but they had thrown the envelope away.

Kenneth Tynan, writing in The Times (in an echo of William Mann's acceptance of The Beatles as serious artists in 1963), described 'Sergeant Pepper' as 'a decisive moment in the history of western civilisation'.

Barry Miles calls it 'the soundtrack to that summer, and that winter for that matter'. "You just could *not* get away from it. It was playing everywhere. If you went down the King's Road, it was coming out of every shop. Anywhere that played music, had it on. And it was the same in New York." **(145)**

Ian Macdonald goes as far as considering the 'Sergeant Pepper' album to be 'a distillation of the spirit of 1967', not a bad accolade for a suite of music! **(146)** Across the Atlantic, writers and critics were equally enthusiastic. Rolling Stone writers called it "the most astonishing single record of popular music ever released", "They fused orchestral and electronic arts in unprecedented ways. If '*She's Leaving Home*' was a song as structurally sound as any Schubert lieder, '*A Day in the Life*' was music that only studio technology made possible. **(147)** Crawdaddy's Don McNeill also had plenty to say. Comparing it to Dylan's 'Blonde on Blonde': "Both are monuments; both are manifestos. Dylan was the model for the movement last summer, when the world had hardly heard of hippies. Sgt Pepper may be the looking glass through which hippies can disappear". Once all the allegorical analysis has disappeared through the mirror, McNeill gets to the point: "Sgt Pepper is a monument in rock... It is such a dramatic break with the past that it is best examined as the first album of a new group. A parallel may be found in The Beach Boys' 'Pet Sounds'. Another may be coming in the Stones' next album." **(148)** What 'Sergeant Pepper' didn't do was say much about the momentous times they were living, with no social or political comment despite the turbulence of the times. . The Rolling Stones' 'response' referred to by Don McNeil was 'Their Satanic Majesties Request', recorded between June and September and released in November, 1967 where "the Stones' attempt to be more psychedelic than Sergeant Pepper and it was a failure." (148)[47] Indeed, it is evident from the 'response' to *'All You Need is Love'*, *'Sing This All Together'* that the Stones were trying to be more like The Beatles than like themselves and the mellotron flute sample [48]at the beginning of the *'Sing This All Together'*'s reprise sounds suspiciously familiar! Overall, 'Their Satanic Majesties' Request' is a bold but strange album showcasing little[49] of the strong songwriting that Jagger and Richards were capable of. Bob Dylan's response to 'Sergeant Pepper' (if it can be called that, I doubt whether Dylan worried about artistic competition too much!) came in January of 1968 with the comparatively austere 'John Wesley Harding' drawing on American roots music and sporting a distinctly plain cover in contrast with the extravagance of the 'Pepper' sleeve.

Brian Epstein first heard 'Sergeant Pepper' during his rehabilitation at the private Priory Hospital in Roehampton. He was discharged on 19th May, the day of the press party to unveil the Beatles' long awaited opus. The official release date was 1st June in the UK and 2nd June in the US. On 27th August, the BBC announced that Epstein had been found dead in his Belgravia home. He had been planning to join the Beatles at a meeting of the International Mediation Society with the Maharishi in Bangor, Wales the following day.

### *"The Magical Mystery Tour: step right this way!"*

The Beatles were by no means finished with the year 1967. A mere four days after 'Sergeant Pepper's' was completed, the band was back in the Abbey Road studio to record the title track for the 'Magical Mystery Tour' double EP. It was now 25th April and the genesis of the 'Magical Mystery Tour' concept had already been fashioned in California when Paul joined Jane Asher on her theatre tour, and was impressed by how serious the west coast hippies were compared with their British counterparts.

. Ian Macdonald recalls that as "A cinema fan and a maker of 'underground' home-movies, McCartney saw the motif of a psychedelic roadshow as the basis for a film, which he accordingly roughed out on a sheet of paper while flying back to Britain." (149) The next song recorded for the project was *'Your Mother Should Know'*, its title borrowed from the song *'A Taste of Honey'* and the music would not have sounded out of place in a vaudevillian music hall. Then, in the month of September, came George Harrison's *'Blue Jay Way'* which is often described as gloomy and monotonous (indeed legend has it the song was written in a fog-bound Hollywood Hills, Los Angeles). To me, this is rather a harsh judgement for it captures a mood perfectly. Thepassage in which the protagonist becomes impatient to the point of exhaustion is a classic piece of soporific

---

[47] The title was a parody of the phrase 'Her Britannic Majesty' on British passports and a sardonic comment on restrictions on travel imposed as part of the sentence resulting from the drug busts referred to in chapter one which prompted The Times newspaper to ask 'Who breaks a butterfly on a wheel?'

[48] Mellotron (with synthesiser) was also used copiously on the penultimate track '*2,000 Light Years from Home.*'

[49] On '*She's a Rainbow*', the Stones get back to what they were good at. Their '*Within You, Without You*' was called '*Gomper*' and is on the second side which is better than the first. To be fair, it is a pretty good 'psych' album. '*On with the Show*' was an obvious 'cop-off' of The Beatles. Another group might well have got away with it!

psychedelia. *'Flying'* was a genuine group collaboration and is described by Ian Macdonald as "a sleepy C blues decorated with pseudo-Indian melismas and some beautiful varispeeded Mellotron by Lennon, gently doodled in two casual sessions at either end of a chaotic fortnight's filming for the (Magical Mystery) programme." **(150)** Finally, recorded over three days in September and completed on 20th October, there was the beautiful and wistful *'The Fool on the Hill'*, written by Paul McCartney during the 'Sergeant Pepper' sessions in March, 1967. It is thought that McCartney may have been thinking about the fool in a Tarot pack which would be consistent with his (and others) interest in eastern religions and western occultism.

There was, of course, a film as well. As the magical mystery tour weaved a serpentine path through Devon, Teignmouth and Brighton with a collection of characters like some wayward travelling circus, and Paul, still dissatisfied with the film footage at West Morley airbase and suchlike, sojourned to Nice to be filmed on top of a picturesque hill, it was quickly becoming evident that the wheels were coming off the bus. The London Evening Standard printed a story with the headline, 'We've Goofed, says Paul'. However, 'Magical Mystery Tour' was not just about the pictures, for there were some memorable words and music as well. Referring to this very music, the veteran Beatles biographer Philip Norman reckons that it "certainly reaches *Sergeant Pepper* standard and several times goes a step higher." **(151)** This is not a universal view but I must say that I agree with it. Finally, John Lennon has quite a lot to say on 'Magical Mystery Tour' in 'The Beatles Anthology' even going so far as to say it's one of his favourite albums.

In the UK, 'Magical Mystery Tour' was issued on 8th December, 1967 in an elegantly packaged double EP. In the US, the tracks were incorporated into an LP released on 27th November. The critical response to the film, when it was transmitted on BBC TV on Boxing Day, was in some cases rather savage not helped by its screening in black 'n' white but history has been kinder in its assessment and it has been hailed variously as an early countercultural movie, an 'art film' that inspired Steven Spielberg in film school, a forerunner of the road movie (two years before 'Easy Rider'), and a bold subversion of image from the comparatively twee days of 'Help' and 'A Hard Day's Night.' Alistair Taylor certainly enjoyed the experience: "I thought 'Magical Mystery Tour' was great," he says in his book 'With the Beatles', "and years ahead of its time." **(152)** Regardless of opinions on the merits or demerits of the film, if there were any lingering doubts that the Beatles had cast off their family friendly 'mop top' image then 'Magical Mystery Tour' dispelled them. As Ringo Starr put it in The Beatles Anthology: "You have to remember that anything we did in the early days was a love song and now suddenly *'I Am the Walrus'* and 'you let your knickers down'. **(153)**[50]

There was yet more to come. *'Baby, You're a Rich Man'* was recorded on 11th May and issued as the B-side to *'All You Need is Love'*. While the song ostensibly mocks hippies, it was also a thinly disguised dig at the Beatles' manager, Brian Epstein. The next day, the jaunty sing-along *'All Together Now'* was recorded (but would not appear on vinyl until 1969 on the 'Yellow Submarine' LP). Work also began on the sleazy *'You Know My Name (Look Up the Number)'* which would not be completed until the end of April, 1969 and released until 1970 as the B-side to the *'Let It Be'* single.[51] George

---

[50] The use of the word 'knickers' was the reason the record was banned by the BBC.

[51] The six-minute version on 'The Beatles Anthology 2' is well-worth checking out as it is in stereo as opposed to the monaural sound of the shorter single version and captures all the hilarity to great effect including Brian Jones of The Rolling Stones making a cameo appearance on saxophone. In many respects, it resembles the zany musical approach taken by

Harrison's *'It's All Too Much'* was recorded over three days and completed on 2nd June, having to wait, like *'All Together Now'* for a 'filler' place on the 'Yellow Submarine' album. George Harrison's *'Only a Northern Song'* had been completed in April, but also had to wait.

Ian Macdonald does a biopsy on all these songs describing Harrison's (and the others) as 'dismal rejects' and describing: *'It's All Too Much'* as "marked by hamfisted feedback guitar, a trumpet quotation from Jeremiah Clarke's *Prince of Denmark's March* and a meaningless snatch of The Merseys' 1966 hit *Sorrow*." **(154)** MacDonald's dismissive view didn't put off acid guitarist extraordinaire Steve Hillage. veteran of groups like Gong, who included an extended version of the song on his best-selling album 'L'. Nor was Macdonald too keen on *'All You Need is Love'*, in his words, 'thrown together for *Our World*, a live TV broadcast linking twenty-four countries by global satellite on 25th June, 1967, the song is an inelegant structure in alternating bars of 4/4 and ¾, capped by a chorus'. **(155)** Although many critics shared some of Macdonald's sentiments, few railed against it with such invective, confining their misgivings to ambivalence. It is right to set the highest standards but, perhaps in the Beatles case, too much was expected of them. 'All You Need is Love' was a global television event. On 25th June at Studio One in Abbey Road, Mick Jagger, Keith Richards, Marianne Faithful, Eric Clapton, Keith Moon and Graham Nash all sang in the chorus to a pre-recorded backing track. It was a #1 hit on both sides of the Atlantic and personally, although it is irrefutably 'corny', I like it. I never thought it was that serious. The *'La Marseillaise'* and the boozy *'She Loves You'* sing-along sound like great fun to me. It might sound as naïve as *'Give Peace a Chance'* and as crass as having a bed-in (at least deejay John Peel thought so), but maybe I never thought the Beatles were ever going to change the world anyway!

There can be no such doubts, even in the most rigorous and sceptical critic's mind about *'I Am the Walrus'*, a song birthed from adversity, the death of the group's manager Brian Epstein. John Lennon conceived the song on the piano in his Weybridge home absorbing the distant two-note siren of a distant police car. The music, based on an unconventional sequence of ascending and descending major chords defied logic, while the words were carefully constructed under the influence of acid. As a response to finding out through a letter from an ex-pupil at Lennon's old school, Quarry Bank, that some of the English teachers were analysing Beatles' lyrics with their classes, Lennon and his pal Pete Shotton recalled an old playground chant, 'Yellow matter custard, green slop pie/ All mixed together with a dead dog's eye' which informed some of the lyrics. Further inspiration came from poking fun at establishment figures 'expert texpert choking smokers, don't you know the joker laughs at you', 'smiling pigs in a sty, pretty little policemen in a row', and a rant against censorship and prudishness in the catchphrases 'pornographic priestess' and 'you've been a naughty girl, you let your knickers down'. There is even a reference to the surrealistic horror writer and opium addict Edgar Allen Poe. Other inspirations for *'I Am the Walrus'* were Procol Harum's *'A Whiter Shade of Pale'*, a particular favourite of Lennon's especially Keith Reid's abstract lyrics and as a literary inspiration, Lewis Carroll who leant the song its title (from 'the walrus and the carpenter'). Lennon famously said, "Oh, shit, I picked the wrong guy" on realising that the walrus was the 'baddie' in Lewis Carroll's story! The 'I am the egg man' line was allegedly inspired by Eric Burdon's obsession with cracking eggs on the bodies of his lovers. Crazy though it seems even phrases like 'crabalocker fishwife', 'corporation T-

---

the Bonzo Dog Doo-Dah Band who, of course, had a major hit record with the Paul McCartney produced *'I'm the Urban Spaceman'* in 1968.

shirt', 'elementary penguin' and 'sitting on a cornflake' became indelibly edged on the psychi and, as I can testify, are hard to shake off still appearing in ones' thoughts over four decades later! It is illogical to try to look for deeper meanings. As John Lennon said in 'The Beatles Anthology', "Walrus is just saying a dream – the words don't mean a lot. People draw so many conclusions and it's ridiculous. I've had tongue-in-cheek all along." **(156)** Despite that, in his next sentence, the ever enigmatic Lennon suggests that perhaps 'the egg-man' refers to Allen Ginsberg or that, "the words elementary penguin meant that it's naïve to just go around chanting Hare Krishna or just putting your faith in one idol." He likens his lyrics for *'I Am the Walrus'* to "writing obscurely àla Dylan, never saying what you mean but giving the *impression* of something, where more or less can be read into it." Of course, the approach is similar to his works of poetry like 'A Spaniard in the Works' or 'In His Own Write'. Everything works on the song, right down to the infantile talk of 'Goo-goo G'joob' and 'Oompah, oompah stick up yer jumpah' (a lyrical message lacking in profundity reinforced by an unlikely source, the Mike Sammes Singers). Hidden inside *'I Am the Walrus',* there is even a brief snippet of a BBC recording of Shakespeare's King Lear. Ian Macdonald was certainly satisfied: "Representing Lennon's final high-tide of inspiration for The Beatles, *I Am the Walrus* is (apart perhaps from Dylan's surrealistic anti-nuclear nightmare *A Hard Rain's a Gonna Fall* ) the most idiosyncratic protest song ever written. Though its author continued to write exceptional songs for the group, he never rose to this stunning level again.' **(157)**

Philip Norman describes *'I Am the Walrus'* as "a string of random images, fulminating against the repressive forces of law and order, with a sideswipe at credulous souls who poured over his words as if they were holy writ. By the time he was finished, the lyric was almost a miniature *'Oh! Calcutta!'* in the number of taboos it sought to shatter." **(158)** In *'I Am the Walrus',* Lennon and the Beatles really did give the English teachers something to analyse!

Still the creative power of the most prolific songwriting machine in musical history was not exhausted, for on 2nd November, the last of four days in the studio that had begun on 2nd October, The Beatles bagged themselves another #1 hit with *'Hello, Goodbye'*. Clever though the song was, I suspect its B-side *'I Am the Walrus'* got even more plays on most record players befitting its bona fide classic status.

In October, it had been announced that Ringo Starr was to emulate John Lennon's achievement of the year before by securing a role in an 'X' rated film (18 or over at the time) 'Candy' alongside Marlon Brando, Richard Burton and Walter Matthau. As Christmas approached, the Beatles were hosting parties, at least some of them were. The fan club secretaries were given screenings of 'Magical Mystery Tour', and 'The Beatles at Shea Stadium' at the Hanover Grand Film and Art Theatre in London. There was another party, a fancy dress one at a 'secret location' for the staff of NEMS, and the cast and crew of 'Magical Mystery Tour'. By the time the bells rung at New Year, the LP 'Magical Mystery Tour' had sold 1,600,000 in the three weeks since its release in the USA and *'Hello, Goodbye'* was still #1 in the US music charts.

On 30th December, 1967, George Harrison completed a two-part interview with Nick Jones of Melody Maker. Predictably, this is mostly concerned with Harrison's growing spirituality and interest in Indian music but on 'Sergeant Pepper', he says: "With 'Pepper', it's just that anybody who wants to be in pepper's band is in it. Anybody who feels any identification. And this all gets back again to God. But at the same time, we're all responsible, in a way, because a lot of people are following us, we're influencing a lot of people, so really, it's to influence them in the right way." **(159)** Marianne Faithful spoke of an edge to the music in 'Sergeant Pepper', the darkening process beginning with

'Revolver' and 'Rubber Soul., The Beach Boys 'Pet Sounds' sounding innocent in comparison. **(160)**

# Part Two
### Band Digest: The Main Course:
### Major Groups, Artists and Records of 1967

# Contents: Artist/ Important Albums of 1967

NB The star ratings are based on my personal opinion (although others' opinions of the music are quoted). The meaning of the ratings is explained in the Appendix to this book. The term 'Excellent' when referring to collectible records is as per the 'Record Collector' Rare Record Price Guide. When I am not 100% sure of the release date of albums, I have indicated so by the use of '?'.

Numbers in brackets refer to an alphabetacised selection of 1967 LPs.

"I turned 20 in 1967, the year of *Sgt Pepper* and *The Piper at the Gates of Dawn*. Those two game-changing moments were the precursors of progressive rock. And while not entirely conceptual, they contained many brave departures from the traditional way of writing and presenting songs, and used the studio more creatively with effects and dramatic motifs. All that was radical and new." Ian Anderson (MOJO, year of Homo Erraticus)

(NB for an explanation of the ***** rating system please refer to the appendix).

## Eric Burdon and the Animals

Eric Burdon and the Animals in 1967: '*Good Times*' 45*****; '*San Franciscan Nights*' 45*****; '*Monterey*' **** 45 (all MGM); 'The Winds of Change' LP (MGM) ***½ – the start of Burdon's conversion from blues and R&B based singer to the 'Sergeant Pepper' era.

THE MUSICIANS: Detailed below.

RECOMMENDED LISTENING/ COLLECTING: The key 45s, or alternatively, 'We're Gonna Howl Tonight' (mono compilation of early music) (R & B Records) (April, 2015); 'The Mickie Most Years and More' (4 x CD plus 4 track EP) (Abuco) (US, 2013); 'As and Bs and EPs' (24 track compilation with booklet) (EMI Gold) (2003); 'The Animals with Sonny Boy Williamson' (Charly CD) (1990); 'The Most of the Animals' (Australian 20 track compilation) (EMI) (1993); Animals Anthology' (2 x vinyl LP) (EMI France). The group's first 1964 LP 'The Animals' was issued in mono on Columbia in the UK and MGM in the US, and excellent playing copies will cost between £30 and £100. Reissues are relatively inexpensive, and there is a plethora of Animals records and compilations from various countries although it is difficult to find their 45s in excellent playing condition and even the big selling '*House of the Rising Sun*' will be valued at over £10.

THE MUSICAL HISTORY: Eric Victor Burdon, born 11th May, 1941, was a Geordie who suffered the post-war austerity that afflicted Newcastle, like most places in the country. He studied Art at Newcastle College which is where he met John Steel who would become The Animals drummer. Burdon's biggest vocal influences were Ray Charles, Chuck Berry, Billie Holiday, Big Joe Turner and Jimmy Witherspoon (with whom he would later make an album). (1) Pianist Alan Price was the next to be recruited then bass player Chas Chandler who was a couple of years older than the other three. Chandler was less into jazz and rhythm and blues than the others, and more into popular music especially The Beatles. Guitarist Hilton Valentine completed the original Animals line-up, although at that time it was known as the Alan Price Rhythm and Blues Combo.

A 4 track EP '*I Just Wanna Make Love to You*' (the Muddy Waters song) was the first to be recorded in September, 1963. The other tracks were covers of John Lee Hooker's '*Boom Boom*', Jimmy Reed's '*Big Boss Man*' and Bo Diddley's '*Pretty Thing*'. Graham Bond suggested the name The Animals and the group went on to record some songs with bluesman Sonny Boy Williamson.

Recording for Columbia in the UK and MGM in the US, The Animals' nearly reached the UK top 20 with their first single '*Baby, Let Me Take You Home/ Gonna Send You Back to Walker*' in 1964 but it was a version of the traditional song '*House of the Rising Sun*' which also featured on Bob Dylan's first album (a big influence on the group), that propelled them into the limelight reaching #1 in both the US and the UK. *'House of the Rising Sun'* is prominent on commercial radio stations throughout the world to this day and as prolifically covered as ever. [52]

The Animals were not exactly renowned for their writing skills, a point acknowledged by Eric Burdon in an interview with MOJO magazine **(2)** and the B-side was a cover of Ray Charles' *'Talkin' Bout You'*. A rare original *'I'm Crying b/w Take It Easy'* (written by Alan Price and Eric Burdon) did provide a successful follow-up to *'House of the Rising Sun'* however, making the top 10 in the UK and the top 20 in US.

The group's first album **'The Animals'** (1964) made top 10 on both sides of the Atlantic with different track listings, and covers of songs by the likes of Bo Diddley, John Lee Hooker, Fats Domino and Chuck Berry. A cover of Hooker's *'Boom Boom'* didn't make much impact but The Animals struck gold once again with a brilliant version of a number sung by but not written by Nina Simone and another that still garners considerable radio air play. I refer, of course, to *'Don't Let Me Be Misunderstood'* which made #3 in the UK.

Early in 1965, Burdon and Price were beginning to write a little more with *'Club A-Gogo'* on the B-side of *'Don't Let Me Be Misunderstood'* and Burdon's *'For Miss Caulker'* on the B-side of the group's next hit, a cover of **Sam Cooke**'s *'Bring It On Home to Me'* which made #7 in the UK. Other albums, **'Animal Tracks'** in the UK and **'The Animals On Tour'** in the US, followed in the spring of 1965. **'Animal Tracks'** made #6 in the UK but barely scraped the top 100 Stateside. Again, there were lots of covers. The Animals struck gold for the third time with a Barry Mann/ Cynthia Weil song *'We Gotta Get Out of This Place'* which reached #2 in the UK and #13 in the US. The US version of **'Animal Tracks'** came out in the fall of 1965. There were four more singles (on Decca this time in the UK), two of them released under the name Eric Burdon and the Animals, which were actually recorded in New York by Eric Burdon and session men, the most successful of which was *'Don't Bring Me Down'*, peaking at #6 in the UK. Further albums **'Animalisms'** (1966) in the UK (#40) and US (#20), and **'Animalisation'** (in the US only – #33) were released in 1966, again with variations in track listings.

In March, 1967, Burdon released a US album **'Eric is Here'** which included covers of no less than three Randy Newman songs. It was as **The New Animals** in San Francisco though that Burdon reached a creative height. Peace and love was one thing but, as Sean Egan pointed out, there were bands like The Grateful Dead, Jefferson Airplane and Quicksilver Messenger Service that espoused a radical political progressivism and pushed musical boundaries with extended and improvisational playing. Burdon signed up to this new direction. (3) [53] A single *'When I Was Young'* was released in the spring of 1967 to much acclaim and some commercial success (reaching the US top 20). It was backed with an ode to LSD, *'A Girl Named Sandoz'*. [54]

As this book is ostensibly about the influence of Sergeant Pepper and a comparison with that milestone, and what else was going on at the time, it is timely now to reflect on

---

[52] It is also an early recorded example of the Vox Continental electric piano played in the solo.

[53] Burdon was also impressed by the ambitious approach taken by Frank Zappa and Zappa's song *'How Could I Be Such a Fool'* was included in New Animals' setlists.

[54] Sandoz was the name of the company that Albert Hoffman was working for when he discovered LSD. The love story about a girl called Sandoz was merely a cover. George Harrison endorsed the song which prompted Burdon to say, "I felt very confident that we were going to be around for a while".

to what extent The Animals were part of that 'scene'. The answer is, of course, that, while The Animals were a blues and R&B based group albeit a highly influential one who tried to push boundaries, The New Animals (Eric Burdon and The Animals) were in tune with the times and did push boundaries. In 1967, they released a classic summer of love song *'San Franciscan Nights'* preceded by another classic *'Good Times'*, an uplifting, if doleful, song of nostalgia about growing up in the 1950s. Also, in 1967, they released a perplexing album **'Winds of Change'** which amazes and bewilders in equal measure and is analysed below.

Of course, the original Animals followed a different trajectory altogether to The Beatles: indeed, they wrote none of their three major songs *'House of the Rising Sun'*, *'Don't Let Me Be Misunderstood'* and *'We Gotta Get Out of this Place'*, and were influenced largely by blues and R&B singers. The only comparison might possibly be with the early Beatles. They were a bit too early to do the remarkable things that, for example, Gary Brooker, also much influenced by the likes of Ray Charles, did with R&B and blues in Procol Harum. The New Animals were another beast altogether! In the song *'Monterey'*, they distilled the essence of the 'summer of love' even going so far as to refer to "religion being born", citing The Byrds, The Airplane, Ravi Shankar, The Who, Hugh Masakela, The Grateful Dead. Jimi Hendrix and 'His Majesty Prince Jones', referring to Brian Jones of The Rolling Stones… to a rousing 'mover' with bluesy guitar runs, brass and sitar. A dose of reality does creep in near the end of the song as Burdon reflects, "I think that maybe I'm dreaming".

Sean Egan, in the afterword to his book, also reflects on the place of The Animals in popular music: "The original line-up were hampered by their blues purism: the blues – whether 12-bar or R&B – gets repetitive when stretched over an entire album, even in the case of a band far more capable than most of transcending the genre's rigid conventions." **(4)** Egan acknowledges that The Animals wrote so little that was original and by his own admission, their music could be 'repetitive' as a reason for relegating them to "the ranks of minor artists". This is true but there were limitations in the original Animals that the New Animals tried to transcend and did, on occasion, do so magnificently.

The influence of The Animals extends beyond their own musical landscape. They certainly blew Bob Dylan away when he first heard their take of *'House of the Rising Sun'* and Bruce Springsteen has cited the group as an influence on his own music.

At the time of writing this part, Burdon was back in business doing talk shows, interviews, recording and making a cameo appearance on stage with Bruce Springsteen. He had just completed an album entitled *'Til Your River Runs Dry'*, garnering 4-star reviews in the likes of UNCUT and MOJO magazines. He tells Alan Light in a revealing interview how he dislikes the term' British Invasion', dismissing it as a business scam while acknowledging that he still earns a living doing Brit Invasion tours. He repeats the oft told story that The Animals, mismanaged (by Mike Jeffrey), were ripped off (they had £500 in their bank account when Chas Chandler became involved in managing the group), drinking heavily and touring excessively (Alan Price said that in his 15 months with The Animals, they completed 3 US tours and 2 European tours as well as recording 4 LPs and 6 singles). It was, in every sense of the words, a case of 'blood, sweat and tears'. Inevitably, they were rent asunder, and Burdon went on to front a new Animals with **John Weider** and **Vic Briggs** on guitar, **Danny McCulloch** on bass and **Barry Jenkins** on drums. He would also go on to have 4 top 20 US hits, *'When I Was Young'*, *'San Franciscan Nights'*, *'Monterey'* and *'Sky Pilot'*.

Two further albums were released in the UK and three in the US in 1968 before they called it a day. The first of these was **'The Twain Shall Meet'** which began with the aforementioned *'Monterey'* in honour of the Monterey Pop Festival the year before and also contained *'Sky Pilot'* (also a minor UK hit) and the flower power psych of *'Orange and Red Beams'*. *'No Self Pity'* is another self-revelatory song while *'All is One'* continues Burdon's penchant for the unusual in its use of bagpipes in the introduction. The US only album **'Every One of Us'** failed to impress while Andy Summers played guitar on **'Love is'**, a double LP in the US and a single LP in the UK. *'Ring of Fire'* provided their final top 40 hit while much use was made of cover versions including The Bee Gees *'To Love Somebody'*, Ike and Tina Turner's *'River Deep Mountain High'*, and Traffic's *'Coloured Rain'*. *'Madman'* was an old song by Dantalion's Chariot.

Burdon went on to further success with **War** and discovered a new musical path when he famously remarked, 'It's white groups that love the blues, not black guys'. Two albums were released in 1970 **'Eric Burdon Declares War'** and the double LP **'The Black Man's Burdon'** and *'Spill The Wine'* provided them with an unlikely US #3 hit (versions of *'Tobacco Road'* and *'Paint It Black'* providing lesser hits). The most famous story about Burdon and War is probably Jimi Hendrix jamming with them on two successive nights before departing this mortal coil two-days later, on 18 September, 1970, in Monika Dannemann's Notting Hill flat. In 1971, War unceremoniously asked Burdon to leave the group. A claim to fame (or notoriety!) may be that Eric Burdon is thought to be the 'egg man' in The Beatles' classic *'I Am the Walrus'* because of his apparent penchant for cracking raw eggs over his sexual partners.

Reviewing The Animals' recording legacy, 4 singles stand out: *'The House of the Rising Sun'* (Columbia, 1964) is a 4½ minute dramatic milestone in '60s' pop; *'Don't Let Me Be Misunderstood'* (Columbia, 1965), Burdon's anguished singing is just brilliant although it didn't please Nina Simone that The Animals had usurped, for a second time, a song that she had also recorded. Joe Cocker's version on the *'With a Little Help from My Friends'* album is the nearest you will get to this perfection of pleading; *'We've Gotta Get Out of the Place'* (Columbia, 1965) – a Brill Building Mann-Weil song that transfers seamlessly from the grim working class Newcastle neighbourhood of Burdon's youth to the insane cruelty and pointlessness of the Vietnam war; and, finally, *'It's My Life'* (Columbia, 1965) – "and I'll do what I want", classic 'angry young man' rock.

**IMPORTANT ALBUMS oF 1967 (1):**
**WINDS oF CHANGE by ERIC BURDON**

**MUSICIANS: Eric Burdon: Vocals; Vic Briggs: Guitar, Piano, Vibes; John Weider: Guitar, Violin; Danny McCulloch: Bass; Barry Jenkins: Drums; PRODUCER: Tom Wilson; SLEEVE DESIGN: Paragon Publicity; RELEASE DATE: 1st September, 1967; LABEL: MGM; CHART: (US – September #42; UK – October) – (Did not chart).**

# Tracks/ Writing Credits

1. **Winds of Change 4:00**
2. **Poem by the Sea 2:15**
3. **Paint It Black 6:20**
4. **The Black Plague 6:05**
5. **Yes, I Am Experienced 3:40**

6. **San Franciscan Nights 3:24**
7. **Man – Woman 5:25**
8. **Hotel Hell 4:20**
9. **Good Times 2:50**
10. **Anything 3:20**
11. **It's All Meat 2:50**

**All songs credited to Jenkins/ McCulloch/ Burdon/ Weider/ Briggs**

## The Music:

On the title track, Eric Burdon name checks all kinds of influential blues, soul, jazz and rock 'n' roll legends through Chuck Berry and Elvis Presley to what he obviously regards as a pinnacle when he half speaks, half sings *'then came The Beatles and the Rolling Stones – a whole new thing was going on'*. When he refers to Ravi Shankar, the sitar gets louder, Frank Zappa gets a mention then *'now we got Jimi Hendrix we know where we are.'* He concludes with *'Bobby Dylan sang about the winds of change blowing.'* There is also violin and a strange electronic depiction of wind which could be mistaken for waves. Opener *'Poem by the Sea'* is followed by the only non-original on the album, a lengthy, tortured evocation of Jagger/ Richards' *'Paint It Black'* improvising the lyrics proclaiming he is colour blind at one stage but it mostly seems to be about the darkness of depression. *'The Black Plague'*, complete with mourning monks is narrated, poetic, and compares the likely fate of the rich and the poor (with a twist at the end). The message on the sleeve opens a window on Burdon's state of mind at the time referring to 'the recognition of existence of pain and ecstasy to know that they are both there in the pit of my stomach, and can be turned on or off as easily as a stereo colour TV set. I love you all and want you to gain something from these new sounds as I gain listening to my saints in past years.' He concludes, "I'm only human after all and still a student of life. Maybe the next production will be *all* games of love, but by then, I could be in another world." And, *'Yes, I Am Experienced'* is a reference to Hendrix.

The album was released along with no less than four singles that year, *'When I Was Young'/ A Girl Named Sandoz'; 'Good Times'/ 'Ain't That So'; 'San Franciscan Nights'/ 'Gratefully Dead'* (interesting title!) and *'Sky Pilot Parts 1&2'* which would appear on the next album released in 1968, **'The Twain Shall Meet'**.

*'San Franciscan Nights'* is a classic starting in similar vein to **The Doors'** *'Texas Radio and the Big Beat'*, it suddenly changes into a pretty and nostalgic song. "*I wasn't born there, perhaps I'll die, there's no other place to go*" sings Burdon reflectively with more than a touch of fatalism. This song isn't what it seems though with Burdon having a dig at the establishment especially the 'cops'. *'Man – Woman'* has congas and Burdon repeating a mantra 'man-woman-desire-love', very tribal, and is probably one of the reasons why Vernon Joynson says, "Many of his fans back in England were disappointed by an album they did not understand." **(5)**. *'Hotel Hell'* is rather lachrymose and has a Mexican feel with lots of wistful trumpet while the confessional *'Good Times'* is a definite high point in Burdon's career deserving better than its #20 chart placing in the UK. with the 'Wild West' barroom sequence adding a tongue in cheek element as Burdon bares his soul. *'Anything'* is a sentimental ballad while album closer *'It's All Meat'* is a heavy song that, like the opener, name checks blues and soul artists as *'all meat on the same bone',* and another Hendrix feel with added strings. Burdon was now living in San Francisco and started to make music with a risky, acid rock and psychedelic edge endorsing the 'peace and love' message completely.

# Brian Auger/ Julie Driscoll/The Trinity (6(7))

Brian Auger and Julie Driscoll in 1967: *Save Me* (Marmalade 45); \*\*\*\*\* *'Open'* (with The Trinity) (Marmalade LP #12 UK) \*\*\*\*; Brian Auger and The Trinity in 1967: *'Tiger'* (Columbia 45) \*\*\*; *'Red Beans and Rice parts 1 & 2'* \*\*\* (Marmalade 45); *Julie Driscoll & Brian Auger London 1964–1967* (Charly, 2004) (retrospective compilation) \*\*\*

THE MUSICIANS: See below (Herbie Hancock described Auger as 'one of the best B-3 artists I've ever heard in my life').

RECOMMENDED LISTENING/ COLLECTING: Marmalade is a collectible label although the better selling singles shouldn't cost too much. The **'Open'** LP will not be easy to find in prime condition (US copies may be easier to come by) but is well worth tracking down on CD, the latest edition being the Fresh Fruit edition in 2011 (stickered 'original recording remastered') with 4 great bonus tracks: *'I've Gotta Go Now'*, *'Save Me'*, *'Road to Cairo'* and *'This Wheel's on Fire'*. The Ricordi Italian original LP with the 'dayglo' colour sleeve and shot of Julie Driscoll in front, Brian Auger at the back will set you back around £150 in mint condition as there are not many of these around. The only mint/ mint mono or stereo copy of the original Maramalade LP on Discogs cost £90.00 with that price doubling with insert (and that was a VG+/ Near Mint copy!) In the US, **'Open'** was released on Atco in 1968, and has a vivid photo of 'Jools' on the front with floppy hat and fur, and is very hard to find in excellent+ condition. The 2nd pressing is much cheaper and should be bought in near mint condition for around £25 (although don't expect to find many pristine copies!) I've seen a copy of *'Save Me'* on Discogs that plays through fairly noiselessly for around £15 with shipping. That is definitely the '45' I would have on my jukebox! If it's The Trinity's early Columbia 45s you're after (*'Fool Killer'*, *'Green Onions '65'*, *'Tiger'*) these are valued at £50 upwards while the Marmalade LPs **'Don't Send Me No Flowers'** and **'Definitely What'** usually clock in at over three figures in excellent condition.

THE MUSICAL HISTORY: One of Brain Auger's first recorded works was on the 1965 Sonny Boy Williamson album **'Don't Send Me Flowers'**. The band also included Jimmy Page. Between 1965 and 1966, Auger played in **Steampacket** with Long John Baldry, Rod Stewart, Peter Green, Mick Fleetwood and Julie Driscoll. Steampacket were basically an R&B roadshow playing clubs and ballrooms but did record some music that was finally released in 1977 on the Charly label as 'Steampacket: The First Supergroup'. There is also a Repertoire CD, 'The Steampacket featuring Long John Baldry, Rod Stewart, Brian Auger and Julie Driscoll: First R&B Festival, 1964'. Working (and personal in the case of Rod Stewart and Julie Driscoll) relationships and a disastrous US tour expedited the demise of the group which split up in July, 1966. Vic Briggs left to join Eric Burdon and The Animals. Driscoll and Auger (who did maintain a working relationship in Steampacket) went on to form **The Trinity** whose 1967 album 'Open' had **Gary Boyle**, later of Isotope, on guitar and a rhythm section of **Roger Sutton** and **Clive Thacker** (Sutton was replaced by **Dave Ambrose**). Auger's ambition with The Trinity was to create a "jazz rock bridge". The group released some singles in 1967, *'Tiger'* (**Clem Cattini** was the drummer), *'Save Me (Parts 1 & 2)/ Red Beans and Rice'*. *'Save Me'* topped the charts in France and another single *'Black Cat'* was a #4 hit in Italy (Auger actually did an Italian version). Auger's singles are compiled on the Disconforme CD 'Brain Auger: The Mod Years 1965-1969: Complete Singles, B-Sides and Rare Tracks'. Driscoll, who had been the Secretary of the Yardbirds fan club and a protégé of Giogio Gomelsky, famous for his association with both The Rolling Stones and The Yardbirds, had released her first 45 *'Take Me by the Hand'* for Columbia in 1963, another for Parlophone in 1966 *'Don't do it No More'*, a cover of The Lovin'

Spoonful's *'Didn't Want to Have to Do it'*, and, finally and most creditable of all, a number written by Brian Godding of Blossom Toes, *'I Know You Love Me Not'*. The original (and short lived) Trinity line-up was actually **John McLaughlin** and **Rick Laird**, later of The Mahavishnu Orchestra on guitar and bass, respectively. The line-up was completed by drummer **Phil Kimora** and sax player **Glen Hughes**. This quickly changed to **Vic Briggs** on guitar, **Rick Brown** on bass and **Mickey Waller** on drums. Auger switched from piano to organ and history started to be made. **'Definitely What'** followed in 1968 with the same line-up minus Julie Driscoll. This album had some strings and brass, and was a not altogether successful attempt to fuse traditional jazz tracks like *'John Brown's Body'* with 'pop' classics like *'A Day in the Life'*. **'Street-noise'** (1969) was the 'coming of age' album with Driscoll back on board. Of course, **Julie Driscoll, Brian Auger and The Trinity** is probably best known for having a major UK hit single with a Bob Dylan song plucked from the then unreleased 'Basement Tapes' – *'This Wheel's On Fire'*.

There have been many other Brian Auger albums down the years and I refer you to the excellent www.brainauger.com website for more information[55]. There was a retrospective compilation album released on Charly Records in 2004. Side one has six songs from 1967. This includes covers of songs by Randy Newman, Brian Godding (of Blossom Toes) and John Sebastian. Auger comes in on the last two numbers Giorgio Gomelsky's sleeve notes are illuminating: "The last two tracks are examples of what Julie sounded like on stage with Brian Auger and the Trinity. It was during Brian's solo on *'Shadows of You'* that Julie started doing her 'gyrations' later to be seen by millions on TV and throughout the world." Side two of the Charly compilation is from 1964 and includes the song *'Tiger'*.

### IMPORTANT ALBUMS oF 1967 (2)
### 'OPEN' by JULIE DRISCOLL, BRIAN AUGER and the TRINITY

**MUSICIANS: Brian Auger (Organ, Piano, Vocals); Julie Driscoll (Vocals, Acoustic Guitar); Gary Boyle (Electric Guitar); Dave Ambrose (Bass); Clive Thacker (Drums) with uncredited brass players; ARRANGERS: Brian Auger and Richard Hill; ENGINEER: John Timperly; DESIGN: Paragon Publicity; RELEASE DATE: 11/67 – mono (France); LABEL: Polydor (UK); CHART (Did not chart).**

## Track Listing / Writing Credits

1. **In and Out (Wes Montgomery) 3:06**
2. **Isola Natale (Brian Auger) 5:28**
3. **Black Cat (Brian Auger) 3:25**
4. **Lament for Miss Baker (Brian Auger) 2:37**
5. **Goodbye, Jungle Telegraph (Brian Auger) 6:12**
6. **Tramp (Lowell Fulsom/ Jimmy McCrackin) 4:04**
7. **Why (Am I Treated So Bad)? (Roebuck 'Pops' Staples) 3:33**

---

[55] In fact, it has been claimed that 'Streetnoise' was the first jazz fusion album, years before the term was invented.

8.   **A Kind of Love-In (Brian Auger/ Julie Driscoll) 2:32**
9.   **Break it Up (Brian Auger/ Sutton) 3:00**
10.  **Season of the Witch (Donovan Leitch) 7:50**

## The Music: Track by Track

1.   **In and Out** is a groovy jazz tune come 12 bar with nice jazzy guitar and a fluent Hammond solo by Auger, and brass backing;
2.   An Auger original, **Isola Natale** continues in similar vein, smooth jazz with a familiar organ chord progression and a fluid guitar solo by the estimable Gary Boyle who picks out the tune nicely, and an inevitable but welcome Auger organ solo;
3.   **Black Cat**, the Italian hit, is counted in and a frantic vocal from Auger, powerhouse drumming and brass, and a passing similarity to the Spencer Davis group number 'I'm a Man' showing why it was such a popular number in music clubs;
4.   **Lament for Miss Baker** has Auger solo on piano, a beautiful 'filmic' composition;
5.   **Goodbye, Jungle Telegraph** is a different style altogether, a loose early example of what we might call 'world music' (or 'skronk') now with congas, whistle, sax, chunky guitar and Auger simmering away in the background, reminiscent of what Steve Winwood would later do with Third World on the 'Aiye Keta' album;
6.   **Tramp:** While side one was all instrumental, side two sees the introduction of Julie Driscoll's unforgettable soul vocal style of this Kent Records 1967 US 'R&B' song, again, a 12 bar variation that chugs along nicely with sax and a great 'in your face' vocal performance;
7.   **Why (Am I Treated So Bad)?** continues in similar vein showing another side to Driscoll's singing, more Dusty Springfield than Janis Joplin this time perhaps (although she was never a screamer!);
8.   **A Kind of Love-In** has a nice little tune but gets a bit messy in the organ/ brass section;
9.   **Break it Up:** While the last song started with a baby crying this one starts with Big Ben or some such with Auger on piano and a not altogether successful vocal two-parter;
10.  **Season of the Witch**: The album ends in real style with a great Donovan cover; the 'mysterious' brings out the best in Driscoll as the song simmers away nicely only lacking a big climax.

Overall, while not quite the 'finished album' and an uneasy amalgam of Rhythm and Blues, Jazz, Mod and Soul, a tremendous potential is unleashed, hinting at Brian Auger's development as a prodigious B-3 player, his 'open' (pun intended!) approach to music, and Julie Driscoll's nascent brilliance (leading to the jazz field with husband Keith Tippetts, working with the likes of Martin Archer).

# Jeff Beck

**Jeff Beck in 1967:** *Hi Ho Silver Lining* \*\*\*\*\*/ *Beck's Bolero* **45** \*\*\*\*\* **(Columbia, March, 1967);** *Tallyman* \*\*\*\* / *Rock My Plimsoul* \*\*\*\* **(Columbia, July, 1967)**

**MUSICIANS: See below.**

**RECOMMENDED LISTENING/ COLLECTING:** There are many compilations including **'Yardbirds Featuring Eric Clapton and Jeff Beck – Immortal Yardbirds'** (Odeon LP, 1969); **'The Best of Jeff Beck'** (Columbia, 1972'); **'Truth/ Beck-Ola'** (Epic) CDs; **'Then and Now'** (Epic) 2 LP; and most recently, **'Original Album Classics'** 5 CD sets (2008/2010) with cheaper options such as **'The Collection'** (Camden/ Sony) (CD compilation) Jeff Beck's most collectible records are first pressings of **'Truth'** (Columbia, 1968) (three figures) and **'Beck-Ola'** the following year (around £50).

**THE MUSICAL HISTORY:** Geoffrey Arnold Beck was born in Wallington, Surrey, on 24th June, 1944. He was highly regarded by fellow musicians, courted by many, spurning the advances of John Mayall and The Rolling Stones to pursue a solo career, and, as if that weren't sufficient, inspiring the character Nigel Turnell in 'This is Spinal Tap'. At school, Beck was playing piano, singing in the church choir, and learning to drum as well as playing the violin and the cello. Gene Vincent, whom he saw live in 1959, was an early hero, and he enjoyed the playing of Elvis guitarist Scotty Moore and Ricky Nelson's 'axe man' James Burton. In 1960, he started his studies at Wimbledon Art School, joined a group called **The Deltones** and worked his way through the repertoire of Shadows' guitarist Hank Marvin. He left Art School and cut a demo record with The Deltones (now **The Crescents**) [56]entitled *'Wedding Bells'*. In 1962, he founded **The Nightshift** who released two 45s on the Piccadilly label *'Corrina, Corrina'* and *'That's My Story'*.

In 1963, after seeing Buddy Guy and Howling Wolf, Beck discovered the blues, and set about producing his own guitar sound, messing around with slackening off strings, echoes, loops, and making heavy use of distortion, feedback and fuzz. By 1964, he was playing in rhythm and blues quartet **The Tridents** and jamming with Jimmy Page and The Rolling Stones. He also played on the Screaming Lord Sutch and The Savages single *'Dracula's Daughter'*, now highly collectible. In March, 1965, Beck became a member of **The Yardbirds** following the departure of Eric Clapton (Jimmy Page being otherwise engaged). He played on the **'Five Yardbirds'** EP which was recorded in London's Advision Studios and released in August, 1965. This record made US #6 and was followed by an American tour. While there, The Yardbirds recorded at the legendary Memphis studio, Sun, and Chicago's Chess Studio. *'Heart Full of Soul'* was released in June, 1965 and made #2 UK. In September, 1965, Beck played on the Chris Andrews' hit single *'Yesterday Man'*, released on Decca. *'Evil Hearted You'* provided The Yardbirds with a #3 hit in the UK in October and the group appeared in the 'Blow Up!' movie.

The Yardbirds' manager Georgio Gomelsky had plans for solo albums from each of the group members but the plan was shelved. After a spell of illness, Beck jammed with John Paul Jones, Nicky Hopkins, Jimmy Page and Keith Moon, and the excellent *'Beck's Bolero'* was cut. In February, 1966, *'Shapes of Things'* was released and made #3 UK.

---

[56] As a member of Phil Ryan and the Crescents, a 1964 '45' was released on Columbia called *'Mary, Don't You Weep'*.

In May, *'Over, Under, Sideways, Down'* was released, backed by *'Jeff's Boogie'* and made #10 UK. In July of 1966 'The Yardbirds' LP made #12 UK.

Bassist Paul Samwell-Smith became increasingly frustrated with singer Keith Relf's 'antics' and new Yardbirds' manager Simon Napier-Bell brought in Jimmy Page to play bass. Beck himself had problems with Relf's behaviour and succumbed to a bout of tonsillitis. By November, Page had taken the role of lead guitarist and Jeff signed a solo record deal with Columbia. By January, 1967, after Beck left The Yardbirds in November, 1966, The Jeff Beck Group was born. Before that though, *'Happenings Ten Years' Time Ago'* was the first of six consecutive singles not to make the UK top 10 for The Yardbirds (settling at #43)

Membership of the Jeff Beck Group was like a set of revolving doors but the recordings were mostly superb with the dance floor filler *'Hi Ho Silver Lining',* effectively, a solo Beck plus session musicians, securing a #14 hit only, which surprises many nowadays! The B-side was a very significant piece in terms of his solo career, and one of Beck's best, *'Beck's Bolero'* with the 'supergroup' described earlier. By March, 1967, the line-up settled to **Rod Stewart** (vocals), **Ron Wood** (ex **The Birds** on bass), **Aynsley Dunbar** on drums and, of course, Beck on lead guitar. A tour supporting Roy Orbison and The Small Faces followed, and in August, the group played the Reading Festival followed by the Windsor International Jazz & Blues Festival. The Graham Gouldman penned *'Tallyman'*, performed by Beck and session men (like *'Hi Ho Silver Lining'*), made UK #30, and in September, Dunbar left to be replaced by **Micky Waller** (ex Brian Auger). They began work on what would become their first album in December at Abbey Road.

Alas, the rest of the story is not within our timeframe. However, to briefly summarise Beck's subsequent career, MOJO's Peter Makowski spoke to Beck **(8)**, aged 64, on a tour of Japan (with Eric Clapton) about his 1973 group **Beck, Bogert and Appice**, a loud and heavy metal/ funk supergroup (Bogert and Appice were the rhythm section of **Vanilla Fudge**) that had taken Japan by storm. [57]

On reflection, Beck's self-nominated five biggest guitar influences were Chet Atkins, Cliff Gallup (Gene Vincent's guitarist on recordings like *'Be Bop a Lula'*), Les Paul, Django Reinhardt and Lonnie Mack.

---

[57] The concert on the night of Makowski's interview opened with *'Beck's Bolero'* followed by John McLaughlin's *'Eternity Breath'* then a résumé of tracks from his previous nine albums including Stevie Wonder's *'Cause We Ended as Lovers'* from one of Beck's most accomplished albums **'Blow by Blow'** (1975), a gold disc #4 album in the US charts, which was produced by George Martin. This album included a reading of Lennon and McCartney's *'She's a Woman'* which was released as a single. Intriguingly, just four months earlier in November, 1974, Beck had been asked to replace Mick Taylor in The Rolling Stones. In terms of Beatles connections, Beck also appeared in Robert Stigwood's 1978 film '**Sergeant Pepper'**. **Jan Hammer** (ex Mahavishnu Orchestra and considerable solo artist in his own right) was recruited to play on 1976's **'Wired'**, a top 40 UK album in the UK and top 20 in the US. This included an interpretation of Charlie Mingus' *'Goodbye Pork Pie Hat'* and even some reggae influences to add to the funk/ jazz/ rock fusion **'There and Back'** was another successful recording with **Jan Hammer, Simon Philips, Tony Hymas** and **Mo Foster** in the group. His *'Star Cycle'* single became the theme tune to Channel 4 TV show 'The Tube'. Beck eventually succumbed to overtures to play at Ronnie Scott's and a CD was released on the Eagle label in 2008 which includes a version of The Beatles' *'A Day in the Life'*. Beck's collaborations and achievements are too many to list here.

# The Bee Gees

**THE BEE GEES in 1967:** *New York Mining Disaster, 1941* (45) \*\*\*\*\*; *To Love Somebody* (45) \*\*\*\*\*; *World* (45) \*\*\*\*; *Bee Gees First* (LP) \*\*\*\* (Polydor)

**RECOMMENDED LISTENING/ COLLECTING:** The Bee Gees first album has been released no fewer than 62 times, according to the latest Discogs statistics. An original Polydor LP might be difficult to track down in excellent or mint condition. The first CD reissue was in 1985, on RSO (the cassette edition came first in 1978). These were released again on Polydor in 1991 and 1995. The Reprise remastered CD (2007) with stereo and mono versions of the album, and 14 previously unissued tracks comes highly recommended. There are many compilations with tracks from 1967, and before and the more famous songs are staples on compilations of '60s' music. None of their records are particularly collectible except the 2 LP **'Odessa'** with the red felt cover released on Polydor in 1969.

**THE MUSICAL HISTORY: Barry Gibb** was the elder brother; **Robin** and **Maurice**, the twins, were born three years later, in 1949. Born into a musical family on The Isle of Man, the brothers grew up in Manchester before migrating to Brisbane, Australia in 1958. It was in Sydney that the first 'Bee Gees' recordings were made. In 1966, they had a number one Australian single *'Spicks and Specks'*.

Returning to Britain in January, 1967, **Robert Stigwood** tracked them down and signed them up on a five-year contract to Polydor rushing out *'Spicks and Specks'* to little reaction in the UK. Australian musicians **Vince Melouney** (guitar – through his hanging around with **The Easybeats** who just happened to mention the new kids on the block) and **Colin Peterson** (drums) were brought in. Midway through recording their first album, The Bee Gees made their UK debut at the Saville Theatre in London at a series of shows promoted by The Beatles' manager **Brian Epstein**, opening for Gerry and The Pacemakers and Fats Domino. Two classic 45s followed, *'New York Mining Disaster 1941'* (possibly with the dreadful 1966 Aberfan disaster in mind, although there had been a mining disaster in New York State in 1935), made clever use of cellos, and was a big success on both sides of the Atlantic (In the US, it was subtitled *'Have you seen my wife, Mr Jones?'* and peaked at #7 (UK' #12)) while *'To Love Somebody'* showcasing the boys' vocal harmonies, should have done better in the UK but did reach the US top 20.

The **'Bee Gees 1st'** LP was released in the UK on 12th August, 1967, stayed on the charts for six months and peaked at #8. On 26th August, it was released in the US on the Atco label and remained in the charts for a whole year peaking at #7. The sleeve design is by **Klaus Voormann** who also designed The Beatles' **'Revolver'** sleeve. The first number one hit was not long in coming but took a while to reach #1. In the US, the record only stayed in the charts for 8 weeks reaching #11. Robin said, "What it means is that anyone who wants to turn to LSD and leave solid things behind is a maniac. Fantasy is fantasy and reality is reality, so which is it going to be?" The song was, of course, *'Massachusetts (The Lights Went Out in)'* backed with *'Barker of the UFO'*. The Bee Gees returned to IBC Studios to record two other excellent songs *'World'* and *'Words'* (the latter augmented by French horn), and by the end of October, most of the mixes were ready for the next album **'Horizontal'**. *'World'* didn't repeat the chart topping success of *'Massachusetts'* although it did reach the top 10 but not until 1968, having entered the chart in November, 1967. Some excellent work was to follow on singles like *'I've Got to Get a Message to You'* and *'First of May'* (1968), and in albums like **'Idea'** (1968) and **'Odessa'** (1969 – the group's masterpiece) before The Bee Gees reinvented themselves as kings of the disco but at this point, we reach the limit to our timeframe and the rest would probably take up a whole book!

## IMPORTANT ALBUMS oF 1967 (3)
### 1ST by the BEE GEES

MUSICIANS: Barry Gibb: Vocals, Rhythm Guitar; Robin Gibb: Vocals, Organ; Maurice Gibb: Vocals, Bass Guitar, Guitar, Piano, Organ, Mellotron; Vince Melouney: Lead Guitar; Colin Petersen: Drums with orchestral arrangements by Phil Dennys/ Bill Shepherd; PRODUCER: Robert Stigwood/ Ossie Byrne; SLEEVE DESIGN: Klaus Voormann; LABEL: MGM; RELEASE DATE: 14th July, 1967; CHART: (US – September #7; UK #8))

## Tracks/ Writing Credits

1. **Turn of the Century 2:25**
2. **Holiday 2:58**
3. **Red Chair Fade Away 2:20**
4. **One Minute Woman 2:21**
5. **In My Own Time 2:18**
6. **Every Christian Lion-Hearted Man Will Show You 3:40 ***
7. **Craise Finton Kirk Royal Academy of Arts 2:20**
8. **New York Mining Disaster 1941 2:15**
9. **Cucumber Castle 2:08**
10. **To Love Somebody 3:04**
11. **I Close My Eyes 2:27 ***
12. **I Can't See Nobody 3:48**
13. **Please Read Me 2:20**
14. **Close Another Door 3:34 ***

All songs credited to Barry Gibb and Robin Gibb except * Barry Gibb/ Robin Gibb/ Maurice Gibb

## The Music: Track by Track

1. *Turn of the Century*: The origins of this song were on the ship during the Gibb family's migration to England. "The Beatles changed lyric forms of pop songs," said Barry. "Most of their songs were very picturesque and lyrical. So we were influenced by that heavily." **(9);**
2. *Holiday* was the last track to be completed and one of the best. It eventually reached #16 in the US with his brothers crediting Maurice, although not yet an established songwriter as such, for his inspirational organ chords on the record;
3. *Red Chair, Fade Away* A splendid psych number was about the Gibbs' father's recollection of his father's favourite chair;
4. *One Minute Woman* This song was inspired by the Stax label and **Otis Redding** in particular;
5. *In My Own Time* This is another very strong track with an infectious rhythmic beat, close to songs like *'Taxman'* from The Beatles' **'Revolver'** album;

6. *Every Christian Lion-Hearted Man Will Show You* was another standout track with Maurice on Mellotron and the brothers as monks chanting 'O Solo Dominique';

7. *Craise Finton Kirk Royal Academy of Arts* A piano based ad lib like one of **The Beatles**' more whimsical songs;

8. *New York Mining Disaster 1941* was originally going to be orchestrated but the stripped down approach with cello as the only orchestral instrument worked brilliantly. There was a strong rumour that this song had been written by **Lennon and McCartney**;

9. *Cucumber Castle* had a psychedelic medieval kind of theme;

10. *To Love Somebody* was written for **Otis Redding**, an outstanding ballad much imitated and copied;

11. *I Close My Eyes*, a very good pop number;

12. *I Can't See Nobody*: This was released as the B-side of their first US 45 and refers to the embarrassing experience of sharing a dressing room with the opposite sex;

13. *Please Read Me*: The subject matter is a spell on the psychiatrist's couch featuring falsetto vocals with **The Beach Boys** in mind;

14. *Close Another Door* provided the B-side of '*To Love Somebody*'.

The interesting point has been made that songs like' *New York Mining Disaster'*, *'To Love Somebody'* and *'Holiday'* were "gorgeous but relatively sombre, this giving *The Bee Gees 1st* a melancholy cast" **(10).** During these sessions in the spring of 1967 at London's IBC Studios, other tracks were laid down as follows: The **Beatles** influenced *'House of Lords'* with a baroque arrangement of brass, harpsichord and strings and a more basic guitar-based version; *'Henry Braff'*, passed over as a single release in favour of *'To Love Somebody'*; *'I've Got to Learn'* (a rocker), the whimsical *'All Around My Clock'* and *'Gilbert Green'*.

## Blossom Toes

MUSICIANS: Brian Godding: guitar/ vocals; Alan Kensley: lead guitar then Eddie Lynch: guitar/ vocals (ex Cheynes with Pete Bardens and Mick Fleetwood) then Jim Cregan; Brian Belshaw (bass) and Kevin Westlake (drums)

BLOSSOM TOES IN 1967: *Look at Me, I'm You* (45) ****; We are Ever So Clean *(LP) ****; What on Earth?/ Mrs Murphy's Budgerigar/ Look at Me, I'm You **** (EP) (Marmalade)

RECOMMENDED LISTENING/ COLLECTING: You may not get much change out of £1,000 if you are looking for mint copies of the first two albums but should be able to obtain a copy of their Marmalade 1967 '45' in a picture sleeve for around £70 (half of that without picture sleeve). The '**We are Ever So Clean**' album was reissued on Polydor in 1968. It was also reissued on the Ricordi label as '**The Psychedelic Sounds of Blossom Toes**' in 1968. The 1967 LP was first reissued on CD by Polydor in 1992 but the better option is the Sunbeam 2007 reissue with 10 bonus tracks while the LP was reissued on Akarma in 2006 (and again in 2014) and also, as a 2 LP set, by Sunbeam in 2007. The '**Love Bomb 1967–69**' double CD (also available as a 3 LP set) on Sunbeam is worth checking out.

"*Every inch as kaleidoscopically vivid, inviting and redolent of a rarefied time and place as Sergeant Pepper.*" **(11)**

**THE MUSICAL HISTORY**: Blossom Toes started off life as **The Ingoes** (after the Chuck Berry instrumental 'Ingo' on a 1958 LP 'One Dozen Berrys') [58], an R&B, soul and rock conglomerate who decanted to Paris where Salvador Dali and Sean Connery allegedly used to attend their gigs at Le Bus Palladium, a disused tram depot. The two **Brians, Godding** and **Belshaw**, originated from Highbury, Islington, and were in a group called **The Grave Diggers**. While in Paris, The Ingoes recorded an EP for the Riviera label with The Beatles' *'Help'* sung in Italian. Under the tutelage of Giorgio Gomelsky, they also recorded a football chant dance craze number called *'Viens Danser Le Monkiss'*, much to their discomfit! They played a mixture of Stax label soul, rhythm, and blues and rock covering songs like Otis Redding's *'Mr Pitiful'* and Wilson Pickett's *'Midnight Hour'*, and also played at La Locomotive adjacent to the Moulin Rouge and appeared on 'Ready, Steady, Allez!' alongside The Who and The Yardbirds. [59] By early 1967, the line-up had stabilised to **Brian Godding** (guitar, vocals), **Jim Cregan** (guitar, vocals), **Brian Belshaw** (bass) and **Kevin Westlake** (drums), their name had changed to Blossom Toes, and they were signed to Giorgio Gomelsky's Marmalade label[60] Under Gomelsky's management, they did a three week stint in Dortmund, backed Sonny Boy Williamson in London, and were regulars at The Crawdaddy and The Marquee.

The live debut of Blossom Toes was at the Alexandra Palace on 29 July, 1967 alongside Pink Floyd, Arthur Brown and Tomorrow. "It wasn't very nice," recalled Brian Godding later. In August, 1967, the group also appeared at the Windsor Jazz and Blues Festival. A soundtrack for a 1967 French film '**La Collectionneuse**' was not exactly a high-water mark in the group's history. More soundtrack work followed – '**Popdown**' was a US made film about swinging London which also featured the music of Idle Race and Dantalian's Chariot. In August, 1967, Blossom Toes also played at Klubb Filips in Stockholm captured on a double CD released on the Sunbeam label, '**Love Bomb Live 67/69**,' which includes a version of Captain Beefheart's *'Electricity'*.

---

[58] The group would support Berry at the Paris Olympia where, cutting their teeth in France unlike many others who honed their skills in Germany!

[59] Indeed, Godding and John Entwistle of The Who briefly became drinking buddies, and Godding recollects The Who drummer Keith Moon 'going berserk'.

[60] Gomelsky was very keen on the group, and described Godding as 'one of the most original and underrated songwriters of his generation'. The Marmalade label had been launched in August, 1966 with a gimmick number *'We Love the Pirates'* by The Roaring Sixties. They were a natural fit for the label, Gomelsky suggesting the name Blossom Toes on their return from France to the UK where they decanted to a communal house at 6 Holmead Road, Fulham in which house parties were attended by the likes of Captain Beefheart, Eric Clapton, Eric Burdon and members of Family and Traffic. Godding was, in fact, Julie Driscoll's brother-in-law and Driscoll recorded his *'I Know You Love Me Not'* in 1967.

MUSICIANS: Brian Godding (guitar/ vocals), Jim Cregan (guitar), Brian Belshaw (bass) and Kevin Westlake (drums); PRODUCER: Giorgio Gomelsky; SLEEVE DESIGN: Paragon Publicity; RELEASE DATE: 24th October, 1967; LABEL: Marmalade; CHART: Did not chart.

## Tracks/ Writing Credits

1. Look at Me, I'm You (Godding/ Gomelsky) 4:09
2. I'll Be Late for Tea (Godding) 2:38
3. The Remarkable Saga of the Frozen Dog (Westlake) 2:35
4. Telegram Tuesday (Godding) 2:28
5. Love Is (Godding) 2:22
6. What's it for (Cregan) 2:49
7. People of the Royal Parks (Westlake) 2:12
8. What on Earth? (Godding) 2:47
9. Mrs Murphy's Budgerigar (Cregan/ Westlake) 2:34
10. I Will Bring You This and That (Godding) 2:50
11. Mister Watchmaker (Godding) 2:12
12. When the Alarm Clock Rings (Cregan) 2:15
13. The Intrepid Balloonist's Handbook, Volume One (Cregan) 2:05

## The Music

In October, 1967, Blossom Toes released their first album, '**We are Ever So Clean**'. There was snide social comment à la The Kinks, what seemed to be a pharmaceutically induced and utterly 'out there' unpredictability, sometimes risky, often sublime with interesting string, xylophone and brass arrangements that almost made the backwards, and bowed guitars deployed by others seem passé. '***Look at Me, I'm You***' was not only a stunning single but a perfect album opener for '**We're Ever So Clean**' (the trite title a giveaway for where Blossom Toes were at) with its atonal riffing and backwards guitar, and air of degeneration, decay and dislocation. Glorious melodies and hooks abound such as on '***What On Earth?***' and '***Telegram Tuesday***', and '*Love is*' with its wonderful cello works as a ballad. You wouldn't guess listening to the album that, by Brian Godding's admission, Blossom Toes were fledgling musicians, "we were learning to play" he says, **(12)** and had to rely on session musicians to play some of the parts and instruments which is why he reflects, "It wasn't our product. It was like a joint venture between us and Giorgio, and the arranger." (David Whittaker) **(13)**

Richie Unterberger gave '**We are Ever So Clean**' a five-star review in the All Music Guide **(14)**. He refers to their 'droll charm' sitting somewhere between The Kinks and the 'absurdist wit' of the Bonzo Dog Doo Dah Band. "With its references to royal parks, tea time, watchmakers, intrepid balloon makers, '***Mrs Murphy's Budgerigar***' and the like, it's a distinctly British brand of whimsy which conjured images of a sun-drenched Summer of Love." The mysterious Oregano Rathbone employs his customary eloquent and floral language to describe the LP. Songs like '***When the Alarm Clock Rings***' and '***Telegram Tuesday***' are depicted as 'elliptically melodious vignettes' while 'the immense weariness of '***Mr Watchmaker***', '***What on Earth?***' and '*Love is*' constitutes the album's emotional core." '***People of the Royal Parks***' and '***The Intrepid Balloonist's Handbook Volume One***' are 'capricious fresh-air exultations', and '***The Remarkable***

*Saga of the Dog...* ' is "a springboard for wry live experimentation." As for *'Look at Me, I'm You'*, the song "can genuinely duke it out with *'Strawberry Fields'* as the era's most obliquely affecting evocation of rainy-day surrealist melancholia." **(15)** Finally, it is worth noting that Brian Godding gives a lot of the credit for the enduring listenability of **'We are Ever So Clean'** to in-house engineer John Timperley.

During 1967, Blossom Toes also played a three-week residency at a Stockholm psychedelic club, and a bootleg recording exists on LP and CD. Despite the variable sound quality and chaotic extemporisation, the diversity and inventiveness of this criminally under-regarded group is very much evident [61] with original numbers, and a preview of the classic *'Listen to the Silence'* which ended up on their second and arguably even better album, **'If Only for a Moment'** (1969). Their sophomore album includes psych/ rock classics like the anti-war song *'Peace Loving Man'* and *'Confusion'* with its unforgettable guitar riff. This album has all the confidence and cohesion that its predecessor lacked (despite its daringness), and is demarcated by wonderful guitar interplay between principal writers Brian Godding and Jim Cregan, and increasingly confident vocal harmonies. The bootleg also prefaces the growing influence of Californian psychedelic music and Captain Beefheart (a few of whose numbers they played) which infiltrated their music, transforming it from a peculiarly British confection into an American west coast heavy psych rock.[62]

In late 1967, Westlake left and was replaced by **Poli Palmer** (from Deep Feeling), later to join Family, who added flute, harpsichord and vibes to the eclectic mix. Palmer would in turn leave to be replaced by **Barry Reeves** from Ferris Wheel. Two further singles were released in 1968, including a cover of Bob Dylan's *'I'll Be Your Baby Tonight'* and *'Postcard'* which was later recorded by Harry Nilsson but never released. Another two followed in 1969 but by then, the race was run for Blossom Toes. The two Brians (Goddard and Belshaw) with Westlake did release another album in 1971 called *'Workers' Playtime'* using the nom be plume **B B Blunder** which was released on United Artists and was quite progressive in style. Jim Cregan went on to play in Stud, then Family, Cockney Rebel and with Rod Stewart. Godding moved in a jazz direction and was a member of Centipede. Belshaw and Westlake joined Ronnie Lane's Slim Chance.

Jimi Hendrix was a fan but, sadly, Blossom Toes were largely ignored by the record buying public. They never made The Rough Guide's 'The Best Music You've Never Heard' but probably should have done. Their LPs and CDs are easy to get now through Sunbeam reissues.

## The Bonzo Dog Doo Dah Band

**THE BONZOS in 1967**: *Equestrian Statue/ The Intro and the Outro* (45) ****; **Gorilla (LP) ***** (Liberty)**

MUSICIANS (line-up on first LP): **Neil Innes (piano, harpsichord, guitar); Vivian Stanshall (vocals, trumpet, euphonium, tuba, ukulele); Roger Ruskin Spear (tenor sax, trumpet, xylophone, bells, 'electrical props'); Sam Spoons (acoustic/ string bass; percussion, spoons); Legs 'Larry' Smith (drums, tuba); Vernon Dudley**

---

[61] The fact is that Blossom Toes had difficulty reproducing their first album, chamber orchestra et al live and, therefore, their concerts only bore a tenuous resemblance to their music at that time. They had no such trouble playing their second album after extensive touring to place like Prague where 10,000 people turned up to see them.

[62] Another American icon Frank Zappa jammed with them in Belgium in 1969.

Bohay-Nowell (bass guitar, baritone and bass sax, banjo, whistle) and Rodney Slater (alto, baritone and bass sax, clarinet and bass clarinet, trombone).

RECOMMENDED LISTENING/ COLLECTING: An original 'Gorilla' album on Liberty (SLYL-932,826 and LYL 1093 in mono) will be hard to find in decent condition. The same applies to second pressings on Liberty and Imperial in 1967. The LP was reissued on Sunset in 1976 then United Artists in 1980 then, in limited edition, on Timeless in 1986 and again on BGO in 1990. The most recent LP reissues are on the Sunset and Liberty labels. The recommended CD reissue of 'Gorilla' is the 2007 Liberty remaster with 7 bonus tracks. If you prefer an overview, 'The History of the Bonzos' double LP on United Artists (1974) is quite comprehensive and well presented (This was reissued on CD on BGO). There was a revival of interest in the 'Bonzos' in 2007 with a new CD 'Songs the Bonzo Dog Band Taught Us' on Lightning Tree Records and a reissue of their CDs.

THE MUSICAL HISTORY: Originally called The Bonzo Dog Dada Band, The Bonzo Dog Doo Dah Band was a possé of art students formed in 1966 in London with obvious immediate comparisons to Vaudevillian group the Temperance Seven, who had enjoyed much success in the early 1960s, and The New Vaudeville Band, then enjoying contemporaneous success. But as their first LP 'Gorilla' demonstrated, the 'Bonzos' proved to be "gifted beyond all competition." (16). By the time 'The Doughnut in Granny's Greenhouse' came out in 1968, Rob Chapman of MOJO magazine was not the first to notice that only The Mothers of Invention were taking parody to this level of musicality and invention. The way Chapman describes the music is as 'complete irreverence' and 'taking a flamethrower to trad jazz'! (17) Colin Larkin points out that "initially viewed as a 20s revival act, they quickly developed into one of the pop era's most virulent satirists." (18) I would add there is also more than a touch of The Goons and Spike Milligan, and in Monty Python's Flying Circus yet to come.

Percussionist 'Legs' Larry Smith, as told to Uncut magazine (19), recalls how the group used to search for old 78s in old junkyards and collectors' stores in London, and even fans used to show up at gigs with a clutch of old 78s under their arms! John Lewis points out in his article that "It becomes clear that the Bonzos' curiously subversive take on pre-War jazz had little to do with the late-50s trad revival of Acker Bilk and co." (20) 'Legs' Smith further points out that "None of these English bands could really swing like the American bands but that was all part of the charm to dandies like Viv Stanshall," referring to artists like The Jack Hylton Orchestra and the Garber Davis Orchestra "whose deliciously clumsy 'jazz' owed more to English music hall and P.G. Woodhouse than Louis Armstrong". (21)

The 'Bonzos' were feted by rock stars of the era and were invited to tour with Cream in 1967 and appear in the Beatles' 'Magical Mystery Tour' film performing 'Death Cab for Cutie'. Their 'Gorilla' album is a classic deserving of a track by track analysis.

## IMPORTANT ALBUMS of 1967 (5)

### GORILLA (Dedicated to Kong) by THE BONZO DOG DOO DAH BAND

MUSICIANS: Vivian Stanshall (vocals, trumpet, tuba, euphonium, ukulele); Neil Innes (piano, harpsichord, guitar); Rodney Slater (alto/ baritone. bass saxophone, trombone, clarinet and bass clarinet); Vernon Dudley Bohay-Nowell (bass guitar, baritone and bass saxophone, banjo and whistle); Sam Spoons (double bass, percussion, spoons); 'Legs' Larry Smith (drums, tuba, tap-dancing); Roger Ruskin Spear (technician – creator of electrical props); PRODUCERS: Gerry

Bron/ Lyn Birkbeck; MUSICAL DIRECTOR: Neil Innes; COVER DESIGN: Vivian Stanshall; RELEASE DATE: October, 1967; LABEL: Liberty

## Tracks/ Writing Credits

| | | |
|---|---|---|
| 1. | Cool Britannia (Traditional/ Innes, Stanshall) | 1:00 |
| 2. | The Equestrian Statue (Innes) | 2:49 |
| 3. | Jollity Farm (Leslie Sarony) | 2:30 |
| 4. | I Left My Heart in San Francisco (George Cory/ Doug Cross) | 1:05 |
| 5. | Look Out, There's a Monster Coming (Stanshall) | 2:55 |
| 6. | Jazz Delicious Hot, Disgusting Cold (Bonzos) | 3:10 |
| 7. | Death Cab for Cutie (Innes/ Stanshall) | 2:56 |
| 8. | Narcissus (Ethelbert Nevin) | 0:27 |
| 9. | The Intro and the Outro (Stanshall) | 3:05 |
| 10. | Micky's Son and Daughter (Lisbona/ Connor) | 3:43 |
| 11. | Big Shot (Stanshall) | 3:30 |
| 12. | Music for the Head Ballet (Innes) | 1:45 |
| 13. | Piggy Bank Love (Innes) | 3:05 |
| 14. | I'm Bored (Stanshall) | 3:06 |
| 15. | The Sound of Music (Rogers/ Hammerstein) | 1:20 |

## The Music:

1. *Cool Britannia*: "Britons never, never shall be fools", an irresistibly 'hip' piece;
2. *The Equestrian Statue*: A Neil Innes song to express his disgust at Jean-Paul Sartre's 'Nausea' as out of a bus in Liverpool, he spies a statue whose life is presumably more important than his (according to Sartre, according to Innes). It is a catchy little number too;
3. *Jollity Farm*: credited to one Leslie Sarony who sang a song by Jay Wallis called 'Misery Farm'! Super – I dare you not to sing along!
4. *I Left My Heart in San Francisco*: Yes, the song Tony Bennett made famous, mercilessly satirised!
5. *Look Out, There's a Monster Coming!* A Viv Stanshall song adopting Edmundo Ros's accent; about attracting the opposite sex on the dance floor apparently!
6. *Jazz, Delicious Hot, Disgusting Cold:* first take, swapping instruments, whole group improvisation, chaotic as intended;
7. *Death Cab for Cutie:* Viv Stanshall, as Elvis, written with Neil Innes with a little help from a pile of 'Crime' magazines. Who would have thought it would have given the name to a Seattle group?
8. *Narcissus*: I see you have the same trouble with your trousers as I do! A classic, salutary tale of spending too much time looking in the mirror;
9. *The Intro and the Outro*: Eric Clapton on ukulele, Val Doonican as himself ('Hallo dare!'), Lord Snooty and his pals tap dancing – sheer genius!
10. *Mickey's Son and Daughter*: Origin: The BBC Dance Orchestra conducted by Henry Hall, the moving story of Mr and Mrs Mickey Mouse, and being 'happy, bright and gay';
11. *Big Shot*: A Viv song, Roger Ruskin Spear manages to get a sax to swear – listen carefully!

12. *Music for the Head Ballet*: a Neil Innes piece making full use of the plethora of keyboard type instruments in Abbey Road including a harpsichord!
13. *Piggy Bank Love*: another Innes spoof song;
14. *I'm Bored:* This is boredom you can afford by Cyril Bored! [63] A rare bird, a classic song of ennui!
15. *The Sound of Music*: As the theme song to the famous musical is unsentimentally decapitated, this shows Viv at his comic best. [64]

Sophomore album, *'The Doughnut in Granny's Greenhouse'* (Liberty, 1968) was no disappointment despite the high bar set by its predecessor. It was more rock-based, and all the songs were written by Innes and Stanshall. Who could resist an opening line like 'We are normal and we want our freedom', titles like *'Can Blue Men Sing the Whites?'* which did have its serious side, asking the question 'Is the fact that white men have never felt more like singing the blues necessarily a good thing?', a new dance (**'The Trouser Press'**); and a closing piece Frank Zappa may have been proud of *'Eleven Moustachioed Daughters.'* (its title anyway) *'Tadpoles'* (Liberty, 1969) is equally good with such eccentric brilliance as Innes' *'I'm the Urban Spaceman'* with Paul McCartney ghosting as Apollo C Vermouth. Bonus tracks on this include Carl Perkins' *'Blue Suede Shoes'*, the single version of *'Canyons of Your Mind'* and a German version of *'Mr Apollo'*. Stanshall's *'Canyons of Your Mind'* was a catchy piece of existential quirk sending-up rock 'n' roll in an endearing and enduring way; and Innes/ Stanshall's *Mr Apollo.* was an exquisite parody of bodybuilding (and Charles Atlas), 'Add to that Roger Ruskin Spear's *'Shirt'*, a satire on one hour cleaners who take three days; and inspired picks from the old 78s mentioned earlier like *'Hunting Tigers Out in Indiah'* ('a comedy eastern song foxtrot') and *'Ali Baba's Camel'*. Add in a nifty cover of Bobby 'Boris' Picket and his Crypt Kickers 1962 #1 hit *'Monster Mash',* and you've got a winner on your hands. **'Tadpoles'** was also a compilation of the songs performed on the children's Thames ITV show 'Do Not Adjust Your Set' on which they had a residency. [65] 'Keynsham' was released in 1969 but not generally considered to be as good and that, coupled, with the obligatory contractual fulfilment album **'Let's Make Up and Be Friendly'** (1972) completes the story – almost. One other highly significant event to report is the 40th anniversary tour in 2006 with special guests Adrian Edmondson, Stephen Fry, Phil Jupitus and Paul Merton if you were lucky enough to catch it. If not, it was released on a Classic Rock Distribution DVD.

---

[63] Cyril Bored is a reference to Cyril Lord, a famous London tailor often advertised on TV in the '60s.

[64] The EMI digital remaster also has some very important bonus tracks including *'I'm Gonna Bring a Watermelon to My Girl Tonight'* (music-Con Conrad; lyrics-Billy Rose) 'with ukulele accompaniment' performed originally by Jan Garber and his Garber Davis Orchestra; *Ali Baba's Camel'* by Noel Gay and 'Hulbert'; and a hilarious Stanshall/ Innes send-up *'The Craig Torso Show'* with extracts from the likes of *'I Remember You'*, a big hit for Frank Ifield, and *'With a Little Help from My Friends'*. Also included is the first Bonzos' single *'My Brother Makes the Noises for the Talkies'*.

[65] The B-side of *'Mr Apollo'*, *'Readymades'* was added as one of five bonus tracks.

# The Dave Clark Five

NOTABLE RECORDINGS: (all Columbia): *Glad All Over* (1963) #1 UK, *Bits and Pieces* (1964) #2 UK; *Catch Us If You Can* (1965) #5 UK; in 1967 *You Got What It Takes* \*\*\* / *Sitting Here Baby* \*\*\* #28 UK; *Tabatha Twitchit* \*\*\* / *Man in a Pinstriped Suit* \*\*\*\*; *Everybody Knows* \*\*\*\* / *Concentration Baby* \*\*\*\* #2 UK

THE MUSICIANS: Drummer **Dave Clark**'s five were completed by guitarist/ singer **Lenny Davidson**, keyboard player/ singer **Mike Smith**, saxophonist **Denny Payton** and bass player **Rick Huxley**.

RECOMMENDED LISTENING: As they were not really an albums band, the best way to listen to The Dave Clark Five is by listening to their '45s'. On CD, there is **'The Dave Clark Five: The Hits'**, a 28 tracker on Universal (2008).

THE MUSICAL HISTORY: The group originated in Tottenham, London in 1958, and early recordings were on the Ember and Piccadilly labels. Their first top 30 single, in 1963 was a cover of The Contours' *Do You Love Me?* (Brian Poole and The Tremeloes did a lot better scoring a #1 hit). *'Glad All Over'* was a pounding beat record that knocked The Beatles' *'I Want to Hold Your Hand'* off the top of the charts in 1964. They were part of the British invasion appearing at New York's Carnegie Hall on 30th May, 1964 and on the Ed Sullivan Show the following day. Proving to be real rivals to The Beatles in the short term their US discography, like The Beatles, differed from the UK variety. Emulating The Beatles again, they made a film **'Catch Us If You Can'** in 1965 with Dave Clark forming his own film company Big Five Films, in 1967. Although they existed contemporaneously with The Beatles, comparison in their numerous greatest hits repackaging is as much a public relations exercise as anything else. Indeed, Clark, who owned the rights to the songs, was an astute businessman. Their last big hits were with *'The Red Balloon'*, a novelty song in much the same way as 'Yellow Submarine' but neither as compelling or as enduring a song and a *'Good Old Rock 'n' Roll Medley'* in 1969. I hope I am not being too unkind when I say that the Dave Clark Five made a little go a very long way (although their 1970 cover of Neil Young's *'Southern Man'* is worth a listen, the devotion of their fan base is not to be taken lightly and they did release a series of infectious and enduring singles in the early days).

In 1967, *'You Got What It Takes'* is a rather overwrought version with throaty vocals and brass while its B-side sounds like more like The Lovin' Spoonful with harmonica, a little bass solo and guitar played banjo style. *'Tabatha Twitchit'* is a rather awkward attempt at a more psychedelic form of pop. Its B-side *'Man in a Pin Striped Suit'* is an attempt to inhabit Kinks/ Beatles territory, and actually succeeds quite well with harpsichord and an endearingly lachrymose lyric, pity it's so short. *'Everybody Knows'* is a rather cloying Reed/ Mason penned ballad with strings which probably would have been a number one if it had been sung by Engelbert Humperdinck (although Lenny Davidson sings it well). You'd never believe its B-side *'Concentration Baby'* is the same group, psychedelic pop with a 'shouty' vocal in true Stax soul style.

# Cream

CREAM in 1967: *Strange Brew/ Tales of Brave Ulysses* (45) \*\*\*\*\*; **Disraeli Gears** *(LP)* \*\*\*\*\* (#5 UK; #4 US); US: *I Feel Free/ NSU* (45) \*\*\*\*\*; *Spoonful/ Spoonful Part 2* (45) \*\*\*\* (Reaction label in UK; Atco in US)

THE MUSICIANS: **Eric Clapton (Guitar, Vocals); Jack Bruce (Bass, Harmonica, Cello, Keyboards, Vocals); Ginger Baker (Drums, Percussion, Vocals)**

RECOMMENDED LISTENING/ COLLECTING: According to Discogs, at last count, there were 184 versions of **'Disraeli Gears'**, Cream's classic album from our pivotal year of 1967. While it shouldn't be difficult to find a repressed LP, an original or early pressing will be more difficult as it is one that tended to get played a lot! Indeed, first and second pressings will attract three figures in excellent condition. It is a similar story for their first, 1966, LP **'Fresh Cream'** with the mono version being more collectible. The latest LP version of **'Disraeli Gears'**, at the time of writing was the limited edition, half speed remastered mono version on Reaction. This has an OBI strip and an Abbey Road certificate. In the same year, Polydor issued a Japanese SACD mono limited edition album. A stereo 180-gram reissue was released on LP by Polydor in 2015, while in 2013, there was a Japanese CD reissue with the stereo and mono version, and 6 bonus tracks. The CD version I would recommend is the Polydor 2004/ 2008/ 2010 deluxe edition 2 CD as these have stereo and mono versions, and some cracking demos like *'Weird of Hermiston'* and *'The Clear-out'* which would emerge as 'standouts' on Jack Bruce's first solo LP **'Songs for a Tailor'**. There are also some BBC sessions on this release. Prior to **'Disraeli Gears'**, there was **'Fresh Cream'** in 1966, a first step with the group not yet having found its blues psych creative mojo and relying on blues covers like *'Spoonful', 'Rollin' and Tumblin' and 'I'm So Glad'* with only *'N.S.U.'* pointing the way to *'Strange Brew'* etcetera. The double LP set in 1968 was released also as two single LPs: **'In the Studio'** and **'Live at the Fillmore'** with the former at least a match for **'Disraeli Gears'** with classics like *'White Room'* and *'Deserted Cities of the Heart'* while the live set has a brilliant version of *'Crossroads'*. Eric Clapton's soloing on these last two numbers is simply breath-taking! The group's farewell album **'Goodbye'** was a mixture of live and studio again, and disappointed many on its release, especially the sound but it has gained in status, and included the wonderful *'Badge'* with George Harrison on guitar and its memorable clattering B-side *'What a Bringdown'*. Two posthumous live albums were released in 1970 and 1972, **'Live Cream'** not being held in particularly high regard by Cream connoisseurs while **'Volume II'** is more reflective of the progressive psych blues direction of the group which manifested itself on their two best LPs **'Disraeli Gears'** and **'Wheels of Fire'**.

Returning to Cream's 'goodbye', on 26th November, 1968, Cream played their final concert at the Royal Albert Hall in London. It was only 33 days earlier in Texas as part of a North American tour that Eric Clapton announced he was quitting in a desire to move on musically, and to free himself from the constant personal squabbles between bass player Jack Bruce and drummer Ginger Baker. There were actually two shows that night with the same set list: *'White Room', 'Politician', 'I'm So Glad', 'Sitting on Top of the World', 'Crossroads', 'Toad', 'Spoonful', 'Sunshine of Your Love'* and *'Stepping Out'*. The compere was DJ John Peel, and Cream was supported by Yes and Taste. The concert was shown on the BBC Arts programme 'Omnibus'. Tony Palmer's film was broadcast on 5th January, 1969, and the BBC1 TV audience may have been a little bemused to see costumes change midway through a number, some vertiginous zoom shots and a screening in black and white. Even two of the songs were missing and were finally seen in 1969 in a showing at the Rainbow Theatre in Finsbury Park, London. The full 90-minute cut as opposed to the 48-minute edit and the album **'Goodbye'**, a mixture of live and studio marked the end of the official Polydor recorded output from this legendary group apart from some posthumous live albums and compilations as detailed above.

It would not be until 11th January, 1993 that Cream would reunite for a one off performance of three numbers in Los Angeles to mark their inauguration into the Rock 'n' Roll Hall of Fame. A further 12 years would pass before the Cream appeared once again at London's Royal Albert Hall, on May 23rd, 25th and 26th May, 2005. Three shows at New York's Madison Square Garden followed in October. The 24th October show can be seen in full on You Tube.

## Cream: The Sum of the Parts: Eric Clapton

Now in his seventies, Eric Clapton, formerly given the somewhat sacrilegious title of 'God' is still releasing music albums, defying the odds, a survivor of a life ravaged by drink, drugs and personal tragedy. It has been a long time since his first venture into the recording studio as a teenager in May, 1964 when he played on The Yardbirds' single *'I Wish You Would'* with his first guitar solo appearing on its flip side *'A Certain Girl'*.[66] The Yardbirds' most famous single *'For Your Love'* (and more or less the only one that still garners airplay in the reductionist minds of commercial radio stations) features Clapton in a more marginal way and it is at this point that he left the group but not before contributing his first composition *'Got to Hurry'* as its B-side in March, 1965. Clapton's playing on *'Got to Hurry'* so impressed John Mayall that, without further ado, he recruited him into his Bluesbreakers. His first recording with his new group was *'I'm Your Witch Doctor/ Telephone Blues'* produced by Jimmy Page then an in-house producer for Immediate Records. It is on the album **'John Mayall's Bluesbreakers with Eric Clapton'**, otherwise known as 'the Beano album', a reference to Clapton's absorption in the pages of the famous comic on its cover, that Clapton first came to prominence in a major way. The album consists mostly of cover versions drawn from Mayall's own comprehensive record collection. It was more than that though and broke new ground with *'Steppin' Out'*, which became not only a Cream staple but also a blues standard for groups up and down the country. Of the covers, Freddie King's *'Hideaway'* was given a particularly outstanding makeover and would be revisited on Cream's 1968 tour. *'Double Crossing Time'* is a strong original, a Clapton/ Mayall co-write while Clapton's solo on *'Have You Heard?'* is among his finest.

Clapton also sang his first studio lead vocal on the traditional *'Ramblin' on My Mind'*. On Ray Charles' *'What'd I Say'*, Clapton cheekily incorporates the riff from The Beatles' *'Day Tripper'*. Wishing to broaden his musical horizons, Clapton joined forces with Jack Bruce, who was disillusioned with the straight forward pop approach of Manfred Mann's group, and Ginger Baker, formerly his rhythm partner in the Graham Bond Organisation.

## Cream: The Sum of the Parts

## Jack Bruce

I am listening to the first of the 6 CDs in the retrospective **'Can You Follow?'** issued in a box set by Esoteric Recordings, part of the Cherry Red group, in 2011. This amazing document traces Bruce's pre Cream career in:

➤ Rock 'n' roll (an anaemic version of *'I Saw Her Standing There'* with Duffy Power'; the *'Long Tall Shorty'* is much better);
➤ Blues (*'I'm Your Hoochie Coochie Man'* from 1962 with Alexis Korner's Blues Incorporated – Charlie Watts is the drummer – and a live (from the

---

[66] Clapton also played on two Otis Spann tracks *'Pretty Girls Everywhere'* and *'Stir Me Up'*, recorded in the Decca Studios in London on 4th May, 1964. The first of these can be heard on **'The Blues World of Eric Clapton'** a Decca 1975 compilation LP of cuts mostly with John Mayall and Champion Jack Dupree, that, personally, I wouldn't part with.

Flamingo Club, London, 1965) version of T Bone Walker's *'They Call It Stormy Monday'* with John Mayall's Bluesbreakers featuring great Clapton guitar and Bruce on Fender bass, a worthy inclusion on Mayall's **'Looking Back'** LP in 1969);

➢ Jazz (Sonny Rollins' *'Doxy'*, more of which later');

➢ Boogie woogie (a live *'Rockin'*); and his early prowess as a:

➢ Bass player (witness his double bass on Alexis Korner's *'Early in the Morning'* and more extensively on *'Doxy'*, an 11-minute long live 'Klooks Kleek' track produced by a young Jon Heisman that appeared the **'Solid Bond'** album).

➢ The company he keeps on these recordings illuminates the pedigree of the young Glaswegian musician: Graham Bond (on alto sax), Dick Heckstall-Smith, Cyril Davies, John McLaughlin (listen to his guitar playing on *'Doxy'*). The rock 'n' roll numbers reveal Bruce singing backing vocals and playing harmonica for the first time, and this material with Alexis Korner was issued as either 45s or an EP in 1964).

The real breakthrough musically came with the tracks from Graham Bond's Columbia LP **'The Sound of '65'**. Bond's organ sound and playing are much advanced with even a little classical twist at the end of an energising version of *'Wade in the Water'*. *'Train Time'* was to be revived later on the live **'Wheels of Fire'** album, and this particular trip shows an early Bruce harmonica [67] and vocal excursion. Bruce is starting to write now (with his girlfriend, later wife, Janet Godfrey), and, if you disregard the sleazy lyrics, *'Baby Make Love to Me'* points to early Cream and early signs of Baker's Afro/ Latin American drumming can be heard on *'Spanish Blues'*. There are also some tracks from The Graham Bond Organisation's second album **'There's a Bond Between Us'**, released at the end of 1965 including a charged up version of Booker T and the MG's *'Last Night'* and an early Bruce composition *'Hear Me Calling Your Name'*, in a territory that would be fully explored by Georgie Fame. [68]

It's fascinating to hear the Jack Bruce voice we've all come to know and love appear for the first time on *'I'm Getting Tired (Of Drinking and Gambling)*. This is now Bruce's group with Don Rendall on sax and John Stevens on drums. Bruce plays bass, piano, sings and also plays harmonica on the B-side of the 1965 Polydor single, entitled *'Rootin' Tootin'*.

CD 2 of the retrospective takes us to the formation of Cream. There are two tracks from Manfred Mann's album **'Mann Made[69]'**: *'Spirit Feel'* (with a great Henry Lowther trumpet solo) and an intriguing instrumental(ish) version of Jagger/ Richard's *'I Can't Get No Satisfaction'*. These were recorded in February, 1966 but not released until 1967. There are three tracks from Eric Clapton's Powerhouse from March, 1966 eventually released on an Elektra album *'What's Shakin'* later that year, *'Steppin' Out'*, *'I Want to Know'* (with harmonica and backing vocals by Paul Jones) and *'Crossroads'* (it's a faltering version and a pity you can hardly hear Jones' harmonica buried deep in the

---

[67] Stepping into Cyril Davies' shoes after his premature and untimely death was always awkward for Bruce but he rose to the challenge with *'Train Time'*;

[68] An interesting footnote to The Graham Bond Organisation's second LP – in the original sleeve notes Vicki Wickham says, "They (the group) took me to a hideaway in Chalk Farm to show me a new instrument called a mellotron (She goes on to describe its workings) – pretty impressive for 1965!";

[69] Manfred Mann's best days, like Bruce, are still to come with some brilliant pop singles before a metamorphosis into an outstanding progressive rock group with his Earth Band.

mix), and by this stage, we are coming ever closer to Cream. **Stevie Winwood** is the singer in this group. It only needs Ginger Baker to now step from behind the curtain. Before he does, **Dick Heckstall-Smith** relays some great memories of his life on the road with Jack Bruce and others in the days before Cream in his book, written with Pete Grant, 'Blowing The Blues': "One Thursday night at the Marquee at the corner of Poland Street and Oxford Street, Charlie Watts, who already dug Ginger's playing, was quite happy to step out for a bit, and the sit-in went in all night." **(22)** (Jack Bruce was the bass player.) [70]

After Cream, Bruce went on to have a highly successful solo career beginning with the splendid **'Songs for a Tailor'** in 1969, a #6 LP in the UK and nearly breeching the top 50 in the US. This included *'Theme for an Imaginary Western'*, which would be much covered by the likes of Colosseum; *'Rope Ladder to the Moon'*; and older numbers like *'Weird of Hermiston'* and *'The Clear-out'*. 1971 brought two albums: **'Things We Like'** (an instrumental jazz album reuniting him with Dick Heckstall-Smith and John McLaughlin) and **'Harmony Row'**. Inexplicably, neither of them charted. It would be three years until the next album **'Out of the Storm'**, also a strong work. Considering their past differences, it was a surprise that a new 'Cream' emerged in 1994, **BBM**, Baker, Bruce and Gary Moore which made the top 10 album charts in the UK. [71]Bruce also recorded a fine album with Robin Trower and Bill Lordan ('**BLT**')

## Cream: The Sum of the Parts:

### GINGER (PETER) BAKER
Ginger Baker, **'Hell-raiser'** reads the title of the 2010, autobiography of 'the world's greatest drummer'. His early drum hero was Phil Seaman and their first encounter was less than fortuitous when Baker was told in no uncertain terms where to go. Their next meeting, during an all-nighter at London's Flamingo Club, was an improvement as Seaman realised the boy could really play. In the film 'Beware of Mr Baker' Ginger relates how he ended up in Seaman's flat in Maida Vale listening to The Watusi Drummers on a 78 r.p.m. record with Seaman. Baker's other drum heroes would include Max Roach and Art Blakey

"For the first time, I felt the pulse of Africa," recalls Baker**(27)**. We have already tracked Ginger's progress in the Graham Bond ORGANisation. His candour about his days with Cream is not unexpected describing the first 45 *'Wrapping Paper'* as "the most awful song and nothing to with what Cream was doing"**(28)**. It was not all bad though. He does recall a largely enjoyable time recording the first album **'Fresh Cream'**.

---

[70] At that time, Watts didn't want to turn professional and was quite happy to give way to Baker but ended up in Alexis Korner's interval band, The Rolling Stones, despite his protestations! Smith also considered the Korner/Smith/Davies/Bruce/ Baker line-up with Johnny Parker on piano to be the Blues Incorporated's best. **(23)**. However, when Davies left because the group was too 'jazzy' (although a more likely explanation is that he was very ill and later succumbed to pleurisy), Smith was impressed by the one who stepped in, Graham Bond. Smith **(24)** was invited to join The Graham Bond ORGANisation when John McLaughlin was allegedly sacked by Ginger Baker for not keeping time and 'speeding up'! **(25)** Smith went on to record a fine album with Graham Bond in 1972 called *'A Story Ended'*.
[71] Ginger Baker's version of events was that he got a call from Jack Bruce making it clear that Baker was working for him. To add insult to injury Baker, concerned about his deteriorating hearing, asked the others to keep the volume at a reasonable level. They did so at rehearsals but not apparently at the first gig. Baker walked out but returned after the police came knocking on his door to persuade him to return to the tour! **(26)**

During the sessions for **'Disraeli Gears'**, Baker's relationship with Bruce began to deteriorate further and Baker felt he didn't always get the credit for the suggestions he made, for example, the backwards drum beat on *'Sunshine of Your Love'* (and later changing *'White Room'* into a 5/4 bolero). He further resented the fact that he had formed the group with Eric, and now Bruce and Pete Brown were doing most of the writing and getting most of the royalties.

Propelled by his beloved sport, polo, various addictions and excesses but most of all by a love of rock and jazz drumming and African beats in particular Baker went on, post Cream, to have an Air force, an Army, a Band, an African Force, a Trio and, simply '& Friends'. His first (live) double LP with Air force charted top 40 on both sides of the Atlantic but his only other album to chart was as the Baker Gurvitz Army (with ex Gun members and brothers Adrian and Paul Gurvitz). This included a tribute to Phil Seaman *'4 Phil'*. Speaking to Mark Paytress, Baker opined, "Cream was always a jazz thing. It was 80% or more totally improvised and never the same two nights running. Jazz and blues are like that. There's not really any difference."**(29)**

Ginger was not inclined to recommend any album he had drummed on except Fela Kuti and the Afrika **'70 Live'**, Masters of Reality's **'Sunrise of the Sufferbus.'** and his own trio's **'Going Back Home'**. Never a shrinking violet, Ginger is not afraid to say that he was the original rock drummer ("I was a big hero to Keith Moon") **(30)** and also to disparage 'pop'. Thus the scene was set for the coming of the first rock super group, neither short of talent nor of self-belief – and not without justification. [72]

### CREAM: THE WHOLE

Cream released their first single *'Wrapping Paper/ Cat's Squirrel'* in October, 1966. The B-side would prove more representative of Cream's oeuvre in contrast to the light pop of *'Wrapping Paper'*. A second 'poppy' but edgier single *'I Feel Free'* was released in December and a debut album **'Fresh Cream'** swiftly followed. *'N.S.U'*, also the B-side of *'I Feel Free'*, leads off the album in rousing style. Also on the album were enduring Cream favourites like *'Sleepy Time Time'*. It was also the start of the 'sleight of hand' approach that transformed blues songs like *'4 Until Late'* (credited as 'traditional' but actually written by Robert Johnson), *'Spoonful'* and *'Rollin' and Tumblin'* (often credited to Muddy Waters but first recorded by Hambone Willie Newbern in 1929 on Okeh Records, although Jas Obrecht states that its melody first appeared a year earlier on a record by Cannon's Jug Stompers called 'Minglewood Blues'[73]) into a gargantuan form of 'blues rock'. Skip James' *'I'm So Glad'* and a self-penned vehicle for Baker's drum solo *'Toad'* would also become Cream live standards. The album made #6 UK and breached the top 40 in the US. The album has been reissued, in truncated form as **'Full Cream'** in 1970, as part of Polydor's Rock Flashback series with *'Wrapping Paper'*[74] and *'The Coffee Song'* as additional tracks and as a budget price LP in 1983. Having toured in the UK and Europe, including being supported by a nascent Jimi Hendrix Experience in late 1966 at the Central Polytechnic in London,

---

[72] A two CD retrospective CD book was released in 2015 on Nova UK entitled 'A Drummer's Tale'.

[73] I highly recommend that you visit the Jas Obrecht Music Archive and in this context, *'Rollin' and Tumblin'*: The Story of a Song' where you can hear early versions of the song. jasobrecht.com music archive

[74] *'Wrapping Paper'* was the first number Jack Bruce wrote with lyricist Pete Brown. Bruce always considered it to be a 'tongue-in-cheek' good time song even if it did have a 12-bar blues format.

Cream undertook their first US tour between 25th March and 3rd April, 1967 alongside The Who, Wilson Pickett and The Lovin' Spoonful as part of the Murray the K package show. [75] Also in 1967, in July, the sessions began at IBC Recording Studios in London for the **'Wheels of Fire'** album which would not be released until the following summer. The group's first 'solo' US tour started on 20th August with a gig at the Whiskey a Go-Go in Los Angeles. Cream also did a lot of BBC radio sessions compiled on the 1996 Polydor CD **'Cream: BBC Sessions'**. It was while in the US that the group recorded their classic **'Disraeli Gears'** album at Atlantic's New York studio with engineer Tom Dowd and producer Felix Pappalardi. The album's status as a 'classic' has been questioned by some – Mark Paytress calls it 'inconsistent, poorly recorded and doing little to justify its inviting acid-drenched Martin Sharp sleeve design' **(31)** The tracks he cites as displaying the group at their best are *'Sunshine of Your Love'*, *'Tales of Brave Ulysses'* and *'We're Going Wrong'*.

While Cream's second album does have its detractors, I do not count myself among them. I do agree that the studio album **'Wheels of Fire'** is stronger but still feel that, at a time when The Beatles had set the bar so high, **'Disraeli Gears'** is a significant achievement for its time. It rarely fails to appear in all time classic compilations such as 'Albums: 50 Years of Great Recordings' whose anonymous contributor points to songs like *'SWALBR'* describing Clapton's fuzzy front pick-ups 'one of the definitive tones in rock guitar'. He also points out that the album influenced legions of guitarists including Eddie Van Halen and Buddy Guy whose favourite song was *'Strange Brew'*. **(32)**

Eric Clapton's remembered the group being excited about what they considered to be a ground-breaking cross-genre album. However, he quickly came down to earth: "Unfortunately for us, Jimi (Hendrix) had just released **'Are You Experienced?'** and that was all anybody wanted to listen to. He kicked everybody into touch really, and he was flavour, not just of the month, but of the year. Everywhere you went, it was wall-to-wall Jimi, and I felt really down. I thought we had made our definitive album, only to find that nobody was interested."**(33)** Of course, this was understandable as an initial reaction but something of an overstatement by Clapton as the album did go on to sell well and stand the test of time. Indeed, it probably would have reached higher than #5 on the UK album chart if Cream still had the energy left to go on a promotional tour. Having completed a couple of US tours, it was back to more mundane matters in the UK. As Dave Thompson relates, "Their itinerary continued on the same sporadic pathway as it had through the summer." The group returned to the Saville Theatre at the end of November, to share the bill with their good friends, the Bonzo Dog Doo Dah Band. They headlined the correspondingly unglamorous Silver Blades Ice Rink in Streatham, south London. There was a short burst of gigging through Scandinavia, and a couple of dates in the English north. And every single one of them reminded the band why America was

---

[75] Murray the K (Murray Kaufman) was a DJ who presented a show called 'The Swingin' Soiree' on WINS-AM in New York, and soon inherited the prime evening show after Alan Freed (who was indicted for tax evasion) and Bruce Morrow. Apparently, Tom Wolfe called him 'the hysterical disc jockey' because of his use of jingles, sound effects, antics and theatrics. He became friendly with the Beatles, who were familiar with Kaufman because of his radio show and his patronage of Harlem singing trio The Ronettes. One of his radio shows was broadcast from the Plaza Hotel where The Beatles were staying. Kaufman was later a supporter of Bob Dylan during his controversial 'electric conversion' and during the difficult year of 1967, the year of **'The Basement Tapes'** when his recording career went into temporary abeyance following a motorcycle accident.

so exciting." **(37)** Clapton also recalls playing in the Marine Ballroom at the end of Morecambe pier. "The whole thing was like being in another era." **(34)**

So Cream left 1967 in great shape with **'Wheels of Fire** studio/ live and **'Goodbye'** still to come. Retrospective releases inevitably followed, including two live albums as we have seen, when the group eventually split, Jack Bruce would release some distinguished solo albums, and would also join two musicians from American power rock outfit **Mountain** in **West, Bruce and Laing** and pursue his love of jazz on albums like **'Things We Like'**. Up until his sad death on 25th October, 2014, Bruce continued to record with 2014's **'Silver Rails'** on the Esoteric Antenna label attracting rave reviews. Also, as we have seen, Baker would form various groups of his own and, more surprisingly, become part of **Hawkwind** for their **'Levitation'** album, an experience he didn't particularly enjoy.

Of the three, Clapton has had the most varied and prolific post Cream career (and certainly the most successful). After the break-up of Cream, he became a part of supergroup **Blind Faith**, made a splendid double album **'Layla and Assorted Love Songs'** incognito as **Derek and the Dominoes**, released acclaimed solo albums like **'461 Ocean Boulevard', 'Slowhand'** and **'Me and Mr Johnson'**, a CD/ documentary re-examining Clapton's musical roots and collaborated with Michael Kamen on the soundtrack to the wonderful BBC drama starring Bob Peck and Joanne Whaley, **'The Edge of Darkness'**.

Clapton was also engaged in much session work for artists like Aretha Franklin, The Beatles *('Yer Blues'* on **'The White Album'**), John Lennon's Plastic Ono Band, the Rolling Stones' **'Rock 'n' Roll Circus'**, George Harrison's **'All Things Must Pass'**, and his Beatles connection was further extended by his appearing on Apple LPs by **Jackie Lomax** and **Billy Preston**. [76]

Important Albums of 1967 (6):

Disraeli Gears by Cream

(The Title is a Pun on 'Derailleur Gears')

**MUSICIANS: Eric Clapton (Guitar, Vocals); Jack Bruce (Bass, Vocals); Ginger Baker (Drums, Percussion, Vocals); PRODUCER: Felix Pappalardi; ENGINEER: Tom Dowd; COVER DESIGN: Martin Sharp (artwork); Robert Whitaker (cover montage images); RELEASE DATE: 2 November, 1967; LABEL: Reaction; CHART: #5 UK; #4 US (in 1968)**

## Tracks/ Writing Credits

| | | |
|---|---|---|
| 1. | **Strange Brew (Clapton/ Collins/ Pappalardi)** | **2:45** |
| 2. | **Sunshine of Your Love (Bruce/ Brown/ Clapton)** | **4:08** |
| 3. | **World of Pain (Pappalardi/ Collins)** | **3:05** |
| 4. | **Dance the Night Away (Bruce/ Brown)** | **3:30** |
| 5. | **Blue Condition (Baker)** | **3:26** |
| 6. | **Tales of Brave Ulysses (Clapton/ Sharp)** | **2:50** |
| 7. | **Swlabr (Bruce/ Brown)** | **2:32** |

[76] In a long and distinguished career, Clapton had also appeared on, among others, The Who's **'Tommy'** and Bob Dylan's **'Desire'**.

| 8. | We're Going Wrong (Bruce) | 3:25 |
|---|---|---|
| 9. | Outside Woman Blues (Reynolds) | 2:20 |
| 10. | Take It Back (Bruce/ Brown) | 3:05 |
| 11. | Mother's Lament (Traditional/ arranged by Cream) | 1:48 |

There has been a whole book written about this one album by John Platt but it is my own personal experience of all the albums selected for our essential listening in the year 1967 that colours the words that follow. First of all, it has one of the most, if not the most, astounding covers of the psychedelic era. While Peter Blake's collage for 'Sergeant Pepper' set a new standard for LP art, Martin Sharp's vivid, detailed, colourful, oh so psychedelic sleeve, incorporating a group portrait by photographer Bob Whittaker, is equally well remembered. The photo shoot took place at Ben Nevis, much enjoyed by Ginger Baker, as related in his book 'Hell Raiser'.

In the build-up to **'Disraeli Gears'**, a demo tape was made in Ryemuse Studio, Mayfair on 15th March, 1967 with four of the songs that appeared on 'Disraeli Gears': *'Blue Condition'. 'SWLABR', 'Take It Back'* and *'We're Going Wrong'*. Three Bruce/ Brown songs were also recorded: *'The Clear-out'* and *'Weird of Hermiston'* which were never released by Cream and, as we have seen, ended up on Bruce's seminal **'Songs for a Tailor'** solo album; and *'Look Now Princess'* which eventually appeared on Bruce's 1990 album **'A Question of Time'**.

## The Music Track by Track

1. **Strange Brew** (Clapton/ Collins/ Pappalardi) Originally to be called 'Brain Stew', this classic record is an alternative take on an Albert King style *'Hey Lawdy Mama'* with guitar overdubs and the extraordinary lyrics of producer Felix Pappalardi's wife Gail (née Collins) sung over the top (much to the chagrin of Jack Bruce who complained that his bass part wasn't a perfect fit and that there is a bum note in there). Baker's opinion was that mixing minor with major was standard in jazz and absolutely fine!

2. **Sunshine of Your Love** (Clapton/ Bruce/ Brown) This song was to become one of the most covered in rock history and the one with the most famous riff constructed by Bruce (and inspired by a Jimi Hendrix gig who returned the compliment by including the song as part of his repertoire) on a double bass, with Ginger Baker adopting a tribal rhythm to slow down what began at a rather frenetic piece. Bruce and Pete Brown had spent a sleepless night trying to come up with a lyric which is where the 'It's getting near dawn where lights close a tired eye' come from. Eric Clapton came up with the bridge, 'I've been waiting so long'. After all that, it nearly never made the album, Ahmet Ertegun, Head of Atlantic Records described it as 'psychedelic hogwash' with Booker T Jones, of Booker T and the MGs, saving the day by recommending it to the record company bosses. A classic case of serendipity facilitated one of the all-time rock standards!

3. **World of Pain** (Clapton/ Collins/ Pappalardi): With lyrics by Gail Pappalardi (nee Collins), subtle wah-wah underlines the subject matter of a lone tree 'in the pouring rain' mirroring the human condition of dislocation in a big city with Bruce and Clapton both singing.

4. **Dance the Night Away** (Pappalardi/ Brown): This song was a rare case of an autobiographical Pete Brown lyric: "It was a very dreamlike time, made more so by my state of mind… I felt in danger of literally floating off the planet."**(35)**

(). Eric Clapton told the 'Record Mirror' weekly paper that it was a tribute to The Byrds.

5.  **Blue Condition:** Ginger Baker's only composition on the album which was unjustly savaged in some of the reviews. It is lethargic and I can even understand why some might found it annoying but there is something about it that depicts a mind in turmoil (Baker was spending a lot of time in the bar near the studio) so graphically, it is hard not to respond to its pathos.

6.  **Tales of Brave Ulysses** (Clapton/ Sharp): While reservations were expressed about 'Blue Condition', none were expressed about this. This song was inspired by the lyrics of sleeve designer Martin Sharp based on a visit to the island of Formentera, and passing the rock where the sirens allegedly sung. Clapton put music to it and, aided by his newly purchased Vox wah-wah pedal, helped Cream to another rock classic. In an interview with Nigel Williamson for Uncut magazine, Eric Clapton says, "It's got this guitar line I thought no one had ever done before, but, in fact, it's exactly the same as *'Summer in the City'*. Maybe I subliminally ripped it off from that because I adored The Lovin' Spoonful. I felt like I'd really made some kind of a breakthrough there." **(36)**

7.  **SWLABR (She walks like a bearded rainbow)** (Bruce/ Brown): There is nothing more typical of the 'anything goes' freedom of the psychedelic era even if Bruce said it had elements of The Monkees in it!

8.  **We're Going Wrong** (Bruce): "It doesn't follow the usual verse-chorus-verse structure. Rather, it relies on its shimmering texture and sheer intensity to succeed, not to mention Ginger's hypnotic tom-tom pattern," says John Platt**(37)**. The words could apply to any relationship going wrong but it was actually Jack Bruce singing about his song writing partner Pete Brown and based on a Gil Evans number. It was one of the highlights of the Royal Albert Hall reunion concert.

9.  **Outside Woman Blues**: A Blind Willie Reynolds' number dug out and sung by Clapton it may have satisfied some of those critics who thought Cream should have produced a blues album.

10. **Take It Back** (Bruce/ Brown): The thing that Jack Bruce suggests is taken back ("get that thing right out of here") is the draft card. Pete Brown recalls it as an anti-Vietnam war song about 'sexuality being destroyed by war'. A Vaudevillian atmosphere pervades it despite the serious subject with the 'party atmosphere' supplied by a well-known New York groupie and friends. Instead of a guitar solo there is a harmonica solo.

11. **Mother's Lament** (Traditional): This track has been much vilified by some but the inclusion of it to me is perfectly appropriate as a coda for **'Disraeli Gears'** at a time when Zappa's question about humour belonging in music was answered in the affirmative by bands like the 'Bonzos' (one of Clapton's favourite groups – indeed, he was name checked in their famous *'Into and Outro'* with 'Eric Clapton on ukulele'!). Clapton and Baker were both familiar with this old music hall comedy song, and sang it inebriated in the studio bar in broad Cockney accents, of course!

# The Spencer Davis Group

The Spencer Davis Group in 1967: I'm A Man (45) *****/ I Can't Get Enough of It **** (Fontana); 'Gimme Some Lovin' LP (US, United Artists) **** and 'I'm a Man' LP (US, United Artists) ****

MUSICIANS: Spencer Davis (Guitar, Vocals), Steve Winwood (Keyboards, Guitar, Vocals), Muff Winwood (Steve's brother on Bass and Vocals) and Pete York (Drums).

RECOMMENDED LISTENING/ COLLECTING: The best way to appreciate the music is to listen to the 45s or a compilation CD, the most recent and comprehensive of which is 'Taking Out Time: Complete Recordings 1967–1969 (RPM 3 CD, 2016). Their most collectible records are their early singles (1964–1967) especially the first 'Dimples' (1964), 'I Can't Stand It' (1964), 'Every Little Bit Hurts' (1965), 'Strong Love' (1965), 'I'm a Man' (1966) and 'Time Seller' (1967): in the region of £12–£25 if in excellent condition. 'Their First LP' and 'The Second Album' from 1965 and 1966 nudge up towards three figures in original excellent condition but they have been reissued. The same applies to 'Autumn '66' (1966) which is valued at £50+. These were all on the Fontana label. Their United Artists 1967 soundtrack with **Traffic** attracts similar value.

THE MUSICAL HISTORY: Can white men sing the blues? Well, they sure can sing soul if Stevie Winwood, then in his teens, was anything to go by. The Spencer Davis Group formed in Birmingham in 1963. After four singles on Fontana, the group hit #1 twice in a row with songs written by Jamaican Jackie Edwards, 'Keep on Running' and 'Somebody Help Me',in 1965 and 1966. Two Winwood songs: 'Gimme Some Loving' and 'I'm a Man' provided two more top 10 hits in 1966 and 1967 (#2 and #9 respectively). 'I'm a Man' has been covered many times notably, in extended form, by Chicago Transit Authority on their debut double LP. Its B-side 'I Can't Get Enough of It' is well-worth checking out, a Winwood/ Miller song led off by 'barrelhouse' piano, a soulful, hip swinging clap-along number with great multi-part vocals. The group also had three top ten LPs in 1965 ('Their First LP') and 1966 ('The Second Album) and 'Autumn '66', and released three EPs. Winwood left in 1967 to form Traffic. One final 45 was released on Fontana: 'Time Seller', then a switch of labels to United Artists yielded three more with a final three on Vertigo which takes us to 1973. Five further new albums, a best of and the group's appearance on the 'Here We Go Round the Mulberry Bush' soundtrack, completes their recording history. The Spencer Davis Group was never quite the same without their talisman. Although Eddie Hardin was an accomplished keyboard player (and indeed teamed up with Peter York to form Hardin and York), and guitarist Phil Sawyer had played in the highly rated The Fleur De Lys, Winwood's unmistakeable voice and song writing ability was sorely missed. Dee Murray and Nigel Olsson played in the final manifestation of the band, and would become Elton John's rhythm section. As far as Stevie Winwood is concerned, Spencer Davis' loss was Traffic's gain.

# Donovan (Donovan Leitch)

Donovan in 1967: Mellow Yellow (45) *****; There is a Mountain (45) ***** (all Pye); Sunshine Superman (LP) **** (recorded 1966 but not released in UK until July, 1967 composited with the 'Mellow Yellow' LP. (US release key tracks **released September, 1966**: 'Sunshine Superman'; 'Three Kingfishers'; 'Season of the Witch'; 'Celeste'); Mellow Yellow (LP) **** (recorded in 1967* and released in both the UK and the US that year) (US release key tracks: 'Mellow Yellow'; 'Hampstead Incident' and '*Sunny South Kensington*'); **A Gift from a Flower to a Garden (Single LPs and LP box consisting of 'A Gift from a Flower to a Garden' \*\*\***; key tracks – '*Wear Your Love Like Heaven*', '*Mad John's Escape*', '*The Land of Doesn't Have to Be*'; and '*For Little Ones*' \*\*\*\*; key tracks – should be listened to as a whole but if time is tight – '*The Enchanted Gypsy*', '*Voyage into the Golden Screen*'; '*Widow with Shawl (A Portrait)*, '*The Lullaby of Spring*', '*The Magpie*'); **Universal Soldier (LP) \*\*\*\* (Marble Arch)**

**MUSICIANS:** As described in narrative below

**RECOMMENDED LISTENING/ COLLECTING:** Ideally, '45s' which are not that difficult to acquire; as far as albums go, 'greatest hits' are fine but I think that does a disservice to Mr Leitch and I recommend you check out at least one of his early albums. '**Sunshine Superman**' was first issued on CD as part of 'Four Donovan Originals' on EMI in 1994 although Epic had released the US version in the US in 1990. Commonly available and highly recommended CDs, now easily tracked down at very reasonable prices, were released by EMI in 2005 with generous bonus tracks, and include '**Sunshine Superman**' and '**Mellow Yellow**'. If you are looking for original LPs, an original '**Sunshine Superman**' in excellent condition could cost £50, while the 2 LP box set '**A Gift from a Flower to a Garden**' could cost a three figure sum, with the mono version more expensive. Another highly collectible Donovan LP is the first pressing of '**HMS Donovan**' on Dawn Records with the fold-out poster.

**THE MUSICAL HISTORY:** Glaswegian Donovan was a 'one-off'. Some called him 'Britain's answer to Bob Dylan', not entirely fair, although there seemed to be some kind of mild rivalry going on if the appearance of the two in the Dylan film 'Don't Look Back' is anything to go by and certainly Dylan influenced Donovan (along with a lot of other people) but not necessarily the other way around.[77] (I remember as a young teenager playing one of his Marble Arch LPs into a frazzled state and pretending I was a DJ (I did have a few other albums as well!) with the old Bush record player with the enormous tone arm plugged precariously into the light bulb socket above!). Donovan is also unique in writing one of the best popular musical biographies ever called 'The Hurdy Gurdy Man', published by Arrow Books in 2006. It is like a '60s' time capsule. In an interview with John Naish of the Times newspaper, Donovan, then a sprightly 60, pays tribute to the influence of his father, "a working class bohemian factory worker (He worked for Rolls Royce) with elevated thoughts of poetry and great poets. At 15, I was reading Alan Watts, Allen Ginsberg and Jack Kerouac, which led me to discover alternative health and living through Zen meditation." By the time Donovan was 18, in 1965, he had hit the charts with '*Catch the Wind*'. The following year, Donovan and his best friend Gypsy Dave returned from the Greek island of Paros in good spirits as '*Sunshine Superman*' topped the US singles chart. In October and November, he was back in the studio. It was then announced that '*Sunshine Superman*' was to be released as a single on 2nd December in the UK. Donovan explains that the superman depicted in the song is the full potential we can all discover within. It mostly concerns Donovan's tempestuous relationship with and subsequent pursuit of Linda Lawrence, one-time girlfriend of Brian Jones of The Rolling Stones, with no doubt in the writer's mind that the lady "is going to be mine" and that "any trick in the book" will be used to ensure this outcome. Donovan eventually realised his ambition by marrying Linda Lawrence in 1969 after the death of her husband Brian Jones. According to Donovan himself, "*Sunshine Superman* was a three-chord Latin rocker, scored for two basses, one acoustic and one

---

[77] Although in the 'Don't Look Back' film Dylan is seen reading Melody Maker with the headline 'Dylan Digs Donovan'.

electric." The drummer was **Bobby Orr** and the percussionist **Tony 'The Maltese Falcon' Carr**. The electric guitars were **Jimmy (Page)** and **Eric (Ford)**. The new sound of rock harpsichord was played by **John Cameron**." (Donovan played his Gibson J-45 acoustic)**(38)** [78] "It's not a normal love song," Donovan told *Mojo* magazine in June 2011. "On the face of it, the song is about being with Linda again. But sunshine is a nickname for acid. The Superman is the person capable of entering higher states because it's not easy to go into the fourth dimension and see the matrix of the universe in which everything is connected."

### IMPORTANT ALBUMS of 1967: (7)
### SUNSHINE SUPERMAN by DONOVAN

The complicated logistics of record releases leave us with a rather confusing picture. Released in the US in August, 1966, **'Sunshine Superman'** had to wait until a June, 1967 release in the UK, composited with the **'Mellow Yellow'** album. This situation has since been rectified by the release of the two albums with copious bonus tracks on CD. First of all, we'll take a look at the US album which was only released in Europe in Holland and Italy as a separate entity.

**SUNSHINE SUPERMAN by DONOVAN US VERSION** (Originally released in 1966 in the US but delayed until 1967 in the UK because of a contractual dispute between the Pye and Epic labels)

**MUSICIANS (including guests): Donovan Leitch (Vocals, Acoustic Guitar); Harold McNair (Sax, Flute); Shawn Phillips (Sitar); Lenny Maitlin (Keyboards); Don Brown (Electric Guitar); Lorne Faryar (Bouzouki); Peter Pilafian (Viola); Bobby Ray (Bass); 'Fast' Eddy Hoh (Drums) with Jimmy Page & Eric Ford (Electric Guitars); John Cameron (Keyboards); Spike Healey (Bass); Bobby Orr (Drums) and Tony Carr (Percussion) on the track 'Sunshine Superman'; PRODUCER: Mickie Most; RELEASE DATE: 26 August, 1966 (in US); LABEL: Epic.**

---

[78] As per Donovan's recollection, the consensus seems to be that *Jimmy Page,* in fact, played guitar on *'Sunshine Superman'*. The liner notes to the CD reissue suggest that guitar was also played by *Eric Ford* by moving a foot pedal swiftly between the bass and treble settings like on the weeping effect on Dave Berry's *'The Crying Game'*—the number described as a 'pioneering slice of psychedelic pop, with its catchy bass quickly echoed by harpsichord and nagging electric guitar. The Byrds' first attempt to record *'Eight Miles High'* took place in Hollywood on December 22, 1965, just three days after *'Sunshine Superman'* was recorded. The song was originally subtitled *'For John and Paul'*.

# Tracks/ Writing Credits

| | | |
|---|---|---|
| 1. | Sunshine Superman | 3:15 |
| 2. | Legend of a Girl Called Linda | 6:50 |
| 3. | Three Kingfishers | 3:15 |
| 4. | Ferris Wheel | 4:10 |
| 5. | Bert's Blues | 3:55 |
| 6. | Season of the Witch | 4:55 |
| 7. | The Trip | 4:35 |
| 8. | Guinevere | 3:40 |
| 9. | The Fat Angel | 4:10 |
| 10. | Celeste | 4:08 |

## The Music

A change in style from rock to folk is evident on the near seven-minute long *'Legend of a Girl Child Linda'*, the second track on the album, Linda Lawrence once again the focus. *'Three Kingfishers'*, later covered by The Jefferson Airplane on their 'Bless Its Pointed Little Head' LP, has sitar by **Shawn Phillips** and tabla, and is a trippy, swaying and calming piece as is *'Ferris Wheel'*, another acoustic number with a bass foundation and sitar/ tabla. *'Bert's Blues'* which may have had Jansch vocal mannerisms but as Donovan later admitted was another "a song for Linda" with orchestration/ woodwind/ cello/ sax with harpsichord particularly prominent. Once again, **Harold McNair**'s contribution on sax and flute is key but 'Bert's Blues' ends a rather chaotic mish-mash of folk and jazz.

Side two opens with the much covered classic, *'Season of the Witch'*, [79], a study of paranoia based on the, at this point, prophetic and undesirable experience Donovan had, which he said was Britain's first drug bust. His sleeve note referred to "Mr Plod in action with a daughter of the evil land of Mordor." The electric guitar is riveting – it may be Donovan himself on his white Fender Stratocaster and the bass playing has **Bobbie Ray** hitting red on the four-track tape machine.

*'The Trip'* was heavily influenced by Bob Dylan especially *'Rainy Day Women'* and was the B-side of the *'Sunshine Superman'* single. The title refers to the Los Angeles Club of the same name, and Dylan, Joan Baez and Alice in Wonderland are all name-checked. Apparently, **Lorne Murdoch Cyrus Faryar** of the Modern Folk Quartet guests on electric violin (Donovan himself says Faryar was on bouzouki with **Peter Pilafian** on viola). *'Guinevere'* is another piece of 'new age' Arthurian folk which featured sitar, electric violin and bongos and prompted girls to give Donovan gifts of crystals, flowers and hand-sewn pouches at his concerts **(39)** while the opening of drug song *'The Fat Angel'* (written about Mama Cass) is also stylistically reminiscent of The

---

[79] There have been many fine covers of **'Season of the Witch'**. My personal favourites are Julie Driscoll/ Brian Auger and The Trinity's fairly straight cover and Vanilla Fudge's extended excursion which appears on their 1968 album **'Renaissance'**.

Mamas and The Papas with whom Donovan was friendly at that time – "fly Jefferson Airplane airways" (the song was later recorded by The Jefferson Airplane as *'Trans-love Airways'*) and a whisper of 'Cass' confirms that the 'fat angel' is indeed Cass Elliott. The album ends with one of Donovan's most beautiful songs, a 'torch' classic of the '60s, you could imagine The Walker Brothers or any number of similar vocal combos having a major hit with and that is *'Celeste',* with extensive harpsichord once again.

Referring to the LA sessions, Donovan recalls that "**John 'Candy' Carr** flew in to play percussion. **Shawn Phillips** (sitar) was already with me. We wanted a rock-combo sound on some tracks and picked up two young guys in the clubs, **Lenny Maitlin** on keyboards and **Don Brown** on electric lead guitar. The Mamas and Papas had been recording with **'Fast Eddie' (Hoh),** a drummer from Chicago, and he came down to play too, **Bobbie Ray** from LA was on electric bass." **(40)**

The bonus tracks on the CD reissue are most worthwhile with *'Breezes of Patchouli'* having similarities to *'Celeste'* and, most definitely, Dylan influenced – it had already appeared as a 45 by a group called Trisha in 1965 with the title *'The Darkness of My Night'*; first versions of *'Museum'* (similar to *'Sunshine Superman'*) and *'Superlungs'* with its heavy bass and Ray Manzarek like organ. There's *'The Land of Doesn't Have to Be'* sounding like a Ray Davies 'beat' number which was to end up on **'A Gift from a Flower to a Garden'** sounding very different. The stereo version of *'Sunshine Superman'* is also there, a minute and a half longer than the album track. There are also two short demos of *'Good Trip'* and *'House of Jansch'.*

**SUNSHINE SUPERMAN by DONOVAN UK VERSION** (Playing catch-up after the contractual dispute Pye Records finally released the LP in June, 1967).

**MUSICIANS (including guests): Donovan Leitch (Vocals, Acoustic Guitar); Harold McNair (Sax, Flute); Shawn Phillips (Sitar); Lenny Maitlin (Keyboards); Don Brown (Electric Guitar); Lorne Faryar (Bouzouki); Peter Pilafian (Viola); Bobby Ray (Bass); 'Fast' Eddy Hoh (Drums) with Jimmy Page & Eric Ford (Electric Guitars); John Cameron (Keyboards); Spike Healey (Bass); Bobby Orr (Drums) and Tony Carr (Percussion) on the track 'Sunshine Superman'; PRODUCER: Mickie Most; COVER DESIGN: Mick Taylor/ Sheena McCall** (different sleeve to the US release); **RELEASE DATE: June, 1967; LABEL: Pye Records; CHART #25.**

# Tracks/ Writing Credits (All Credited to Donovan Leitch)

|    |                               |      |
|----|-------------------------------|------|
| 1. | Sunshine Superman             | 3:15 |
| 2. | Legend of a Girl Called Linda | 6:50 |
| 3. | The Observation               | 2:23 |
| 4. | Guinevere                     | 3:40 |
| 5. | Celeste                       | 4:08 |
| 6. | Writer in the Sun             | 4:33 |
| 7. | Season of the Witch           | 4:55 |
| 8. | Hampstead Incident            | 4:40 |
| 9. | Sand and Foam                 | 3:20 |
| 10.| Young Girl Blues              | 3:45 |
| 11.| Three Kingfishers             | 3:15 |
| 12.| Bert's Blues                  | 3:55 |

**FOR THE RECORD: MELLOW YELLOW by DONOVAN** (Released in March, 1967 in the US only)

**MUSICIANS (including guests):** Donovan (Acoustic Guitar, Vocals); John Cameron (Piano, Harpsichord, Organ, Celeste. Arrangements); Big Jim Sullivan (Electric Guitar – 5); Eric Ford (Electric Guitar – 10); Danny Moss (Tenor Sax, Clarinet); Ronnie Ross (Sax – 1); Danny Thompson/ Spike Heatley (Bass) (John Paul Jones –(Bass and arrangement on 1); Phil Seaman/ Bobby Orr (Drums); Harold McNair (Flute, Alto & Tenor Sax); Shawn Phillips (Sitar); Pat Halling (Violin); John McLaughlin and Joe Moretti (Rhythm Guitar – 1); PRODUCER: Mickie Most; RELEASE DATE: March, 1967; LABEL: Epic

## Tracks/ Writing Credits (All Credited to Donovan Leitch)

| | | |
|---|---|---|
| 1. | Mellow Yellow | 3:45 |
| 2. | Writer in the Sun | 4:38 |
| 3. | Sand and Foam | 3:20 |
| 4. | The Observation | 2:23 |
| 5. | Bleak City Woman | 2:25 |
| 6. | House of Jansch | 2:45 |
| 7. | Young Girl Blues | 3:45 |
| 8. | Museum | 2:55 |
| 9. | Hampstead Incident | 4:40 |
| 10. | Sunny South Kensington | 3:48 |

*'Mellow Yellow'*, arranged by John Paul Jones, later of Led Zeppelin, nearly repeated the success of its predecessor reaching #2 in the US charts in December and yielded a gold disc. In the UK, it achieved the same maximum position in January, 1967. This burlesque sing-along includes the famous line 'electrical banana' which referred to a vibrator and not to drugs, a story that started with Country Joe Macdonald who found a giant banana skin and released a story to radio that you could get high smoking a dried banana skin! All Donovan had intended was to express in the song is that he was a laid back fellow who enjoyed a bit of 'weed' and a good party – the party atmosphere included Paul McCartney. Musically, he was looking for a New Orleans jazz sound with horns muted at the suggestion of Mickie Most. It was also the lead-off track on the **'Mellow Yellow'** album. Track 2 *'Writer in the Sun'*, written on sabbatical in Greece, had prominent woodwind; *'Sand and Foam'* was inspired by a journey to Puerto Vallarta in west Mexico, and covered by Julie Felix, with a **John Cameron** string arrangement, on her album **'Flowers'**. *'The Observation'* is a close relative of *'Mellow Yellow'* (also called *'The Sidewalk'*) but more jazzy with legendary jazz man Phil Seaman on drums. *'Bleak City Woman'* is a basic blues with lots of brass and electric guitar played by renowned session man **Big Jim Sullivan**. The 'bleak house' referred to

in the song was his partner Enid's birthplace, New York. *'House of Jansch'* describes a ménage à trois with folk singer Beverley Kutner.[80] It has been said that *'Young Girl Blues'* (covered by Marianne Faithful and Julie Felix) is set in London's bedsitter land but Donovan himself says it's about a disillusioned Linda Lawrence in Los Angeles ('your friends are still taking one or two pop stars each evening'). Whatever, it is a sensitive, solo acoustic portrayal of dislocation. The re-recorded *'Museum'*, with Jimmy Page on guitar, still close to *'Sunshine, Superman'*, was to be covered by Herman's Hermits in the summer of love. The opening chords to *'Hampstead Incident'* sound very much like the opening to Led Zeppelin's interpretation of *'Babe, I'm Gonna Leave You'* from their first album, with strings and harpsichord creating a magical atmosphere. 'Gothic melancholy' as it has been described although the jazzy twist seems a little out of place as the coda restores the acoustic magic. *'Sunny South Kensington'*, the B-side of the single, has a trippy Dylan like narrative, describing how John-Paul Demondo and Mary Quant got stoned but Allan Ginsberg had to do the driving! Donovan cites the main inspirations for this song as Nina Simone and Davy Graham's *'Anji'*. It was later covered by Marianne Faithful.

The bonus tracks to the 2005 CD reissue start with *'Epistle to Dippy'*, released as a 45 in the US, with a raga guitar riff and a **John Cameron** scored string quartet part. [81] *'Preachin' Love'* is a 'hip' jazz number resembling *'Fever'* in places with sax solo and another 'little big band jazz number, and *'Good Time'*, are from a November, 1966 session. *'Superlungs'* has more emphasis on guitar and brass. The classic *'There is a Mountain'* is also there, along with a second version of *'Superlungs'*, an alternative version of *'Epistle To Dippy'* and four demos.

Apart from all these recordings, a lot was happening for Donovan in our target year of 1967. In the same week that Donovan watched The Jimi Hendrix Experience at the Bag O' Nails pub, he played a sell-out concert at the Royal Albert Hall in London with 5,000 fans watching including, as a vindication of his growing status, two Beatles, George Harrison and Paul McCartney, who would have noted the adventurous nature of Donovan's music and kept it in mind, no doubt, for the future 'Sergeant Pepper's Lonely Hearts Club Band' project. In February, he got the news he was to be a father. Things were getting claustrophobic in the house he shared in Wimbledon Common with best friend Gypsy Dave and his girlfriend, and Donovan bought Bucks Alley Cottage, Hertfordshire for £12,000. An accolade was to come in an invitation by Laurence Olivier to compose for a new production of Shakespeare's **'As You Like It'** in the National Theatre. *'Under the Greenwood Tree'* resulted. Donovan's music became aligned with Brian Epstein's NEMS publishing company and Donovan appeared in Epstein's recently acquired Saville Theatre for a week long residency. There were also tours of Scandinavia, Germany, Australia, the Far East and North America. Nearer to home, Donovan was on the bill at The Windsor Festival. The Animals (Eric Burdon's new version), The Crazy World of Arthur Brown, Cream, Dantalian's Chariot, The Move and The Small Faces were among the others on the bill. Chris Barber and his wife Ottilie, Jeff Beck and Steve Winwood and Traffic were among those in the audience.

In August, the paths of Donovan and The Beatles crossed once again when the Maharishi Mahesh Yogi came to the UK. George Harrison had been learning sitar with

---

[80] For trivia fans, it is Beverly Kutner who utters the words 'Good morning, Mr Leitch, have you had a busy day?' on Simon and Garfunkel's *'Faking It'* released during the summer of love.

[81] *'Epistle to Dippy'* was, rather prosaically dedicated to Donovan's old school friend Ron 'Dippy' Gale whom he ended up bailing out of the army!

Ravi Shankar with his wife Patti occupying herself learning transcendental meditation, enrolling into the grandly titled Spiritual Regeneration Movement. As Donovan would put it, a whole new universe was opening up for, while the reading had been done and the theory was known, a yogi was needed to put it into practice and show them the way to meditate. So it was that eventually the four Beatles, Gyp and Donovan attended a ten-day course in Bangor, Wales. Tragically, as has already been related, Brian Epstein was found dead on the Sunday of that bank holiday weekend, the news breaking when the Beatles were in Bangor.

The next project for Donovan was one he initiated himself, at the time of his strained relationship with Mickie Most. Epic Records weren't too impressed either at his idea of a double LP box set with poetry and illustrations, expensive, and normally, the domain of classical records, the project that was known as **'Wear Your Love Like Heaven'**. A compromise of sorts was reached with two single albums to be released (titles **'For Little Ones'** and **'Gift from a Flower to a Garden')** followed by a double box. Donovan's original idea was vindicated when the box went on to be more successful than the two individual albums going gold and becoming a collector's item. There are no problems identifying the musicians on *'A Gift from a Flower to a Garden'*. 'These were: **Eric Leese** (electric guitar); **Mike O'Neil** (organ, piano and harpsichord); **Harold McNair** (flute); **Mike Carr** (vibraphone); **Cliff Barton** (electric bass – **Jack Bruce** on 'Someone Singing'); **Keith Webb** (drums); and **Candy John Carr** (congas and bongo).

The first song *'Wear Your Love Like Heaven'* is about Donovan's love of painting and colour, and is basically a peace song totally in tune with the 'vibes' of 1967. *'Mad John's Escape',* in contrast, is an edgy tale about an escapee from a Borstal in Birmingham who flees to Torquay where he meets Jill, who becomes the object of his affections, in a transport café. *'Skip-Along-Sam'* is a straight tempo light swing jazz number. The album goes along pleasantly with *'Under the Greenwood Tree',* the song Donovan wrote for the Olivier production of **'As You Like It'**. *'The Land of Doesn't Have to Be'* with its dreamy fairground organ is also there in final form but it's all very understated. *'Someone Singing'* starts with sea birds and sounds a bit like early Bee Gees or mid-sixties Beatles.

The line-up on *'For the Little Ones'* was: **Harold McNair** (flute); **Ken Baldock** (string bass); **Tony Carr** (drums, bells, conga, Turkish and finger cymbals); **Candy John Carr** (bongos) with Donovan on acoustic guitar and harmonica. *'Song of the Naturalist's Wife'* is the one that starts with the cries of Donovan's new born baby and some more sea birds, a poignant musical sketch. *'The Enchanted Gypsy'* is a splendid 'Arabic' folk piece. *'Voyage into the Golden Screen'* is a solo song that starts with bird song. The lyrics were inspired by a crystal methylene trip in which Donovan experienced 'symphonies of seaweed dance and swoon, God's celestial shore beneath the moon' as stinging Mexican ants crawled over his feet! It is one of Donovan's most affecting songs. There follows the breath-taking *'Isle of Islay'* and a lovely song about a travelling minstrel *'The Mandolin Man and His Secret'*. The enigmatic *'Lay of the Last Tinker'* contains the intriguing repeated line "Break cheese with me, won't you, break bread and have some wine" and McNair's playful flute. *'The Tinker and the Crab'* has more expansive McNair flute while *'Widow with Shawl (A Portrait)',* surely, must have influenced Nick Drake. *'The Lullaby of Spring'* was written about the garden of the first house he owned, Bucks Alley Cottage. *'The Magpie'* is a beautiful little song starting with, naturally enough, the recording of a magpie singing. Final song *'Epistle to Derroll'* is a long narrative song. Derroll is Derroll Adams, a US banjo player who taught Donovan the Zen poem on which he based the lyrics of *'There is a Mountain'*. This particular 'epistle' is musically a stylistic departure with an exotic Caribbean touch, an infectious rhythm and **Harold McNair**'s glorious flute providing a key element. *'There is a Mountain'* would shoot up the UK and US charts before the year was out. It's nice to hear Donovan in such fine voice on this album and playing his acoustic guitar largely unadorned just like in the beginning.

In 2006, EMI released another recording from 1967, the complete live concert from the Anaheim Convention Centre on 17th November. The line-up is: **Donovan** on guitar and vocals; **Lorin Newkirk** on piano; **Harold McNair** on flute; **Andy Toncosco** on bass; **Tony Carr** on drums and **'Candy' John Carr** on bongos and finger cymbals. The material was taken from **'A Gift from a Flower to a Garden'** (6 songs); the 'hits' (*'There is a Mountain', 'Mellow Yellow'* but no *'Sunshine Superman'*), 'the **'Mellow Yellow'** album (7 songs) as well as 'blasts from the past' like *'Catch The Wind'* which unfortunately is clipped after 1:16 and *'Sunny Goodge Street'*. The fascinating part is listening to extended versions of songs: *'Young Girl Blues'* extends to 6:22; *'Preachin' Love'* to 9:38 and the space provided for the expansive playing of the likes of **Harold McNair**, an integral part of Donovan's sound at this stage.

There is much, much more to tell about Donovan but as 1967 comes to a close, this must be left for another time.

In summary, apart from the wonderful musical legacy that Donovan Leitch has left, the thing I admire about him most is his unrepentant and un-reconstituted devotion to the hippy philosophy of the sixties, and transcendental meditation in particular. In fact, at the end of the sixties, Donovan, looking back, reflected in his book about how displaced he felt, bemoaning the fact that The Beatles had stopped playing live and wondering what else there was to do. "The liberal attitude of the 1960s opened many doors of perception, not mainly through the use of mind-expanding drugs (though they played a good part), but through the deliberate spreading of ideas and the new ways of seeing which flooded popular culture in those days."**(41)** Although the re-building process was not complete there was hope in the '60s. "My parents had given me a loving upbringing, yet, being a young boy with polio had been hard, and although the wee tenement flat had been warm and cosy, the streets of Glasgow outside were full of poverty and oppression." **(42)**

Perhaps it is best to see Donovan Leitch the way he saw himself: as a Celtic musician, Bohemian, poet and actor, and, at the time of writing, still performing and attracting legions of new fans.

## The Hollies

**The Hollies in 1967:** *On a Carousel* (Parlophone/ Liberty 45, #4/11 (UK/US) ****; *Pay You Back with Interest Liberty* 45 #28 US ***; *Carrie-Anne* #3/9 (UK/US) ****; *Evolution LP #13/43* ***; *King Midas in Reverse 45 #18 UK* ****; *Butterfly LP* – *** ½; *Dear Eloise 45 #50 US* ***

**MUSICIANS:** As detailed below

**RECOMMENDED LISTENING/ COLLECTING:** Never really thought of as an albums band the best option is to track down 45s or listen to their songs on compilations (there are plenty of them), the extensiveness of which depends upon your level of interest. My own recommendation would be: **'The Hollies: Clarke, Hicks & Nash Years, April, 1963 – October, 1968** (Parlophone, 2011 6 CD box set) with songs in chronological order. Early Parlophone LPs from 1964–1966 like **'Stay with the Hollies'**, **'The Hollies'** and **'Would You Believe?'** have great value to collectors fetching £100 or more (stereo copies will be even more expensive). Prices come down a bit as we reach **'For Certain Because'** (1966), **'Butterfly'** and **'Evolution'** (1967) with stereo copies again having the most value.

**THE MUSICAL HISTORY:** Reckoned by some to be second only to The Beatles and The Rolling Stones in British pop, all of The Hollies' 45s between 1963 and 1973 got into the UK charts bar one. Formed in Manchester in 1961 by school pals **Allan Clarke** and **Graham Nash** (who formed a group called The Two Teens), they added bass player **Eric Haydock** and drummer **Don Rathbone** to become The Fourtones, The Deltas and, finally, The Hollies. Starting off with a cover of The Coasters' *'(Ain't That) Just Like Me'* for Parlophone in 1963 after being discovered at Liverpool's Cavern Club, its follow up, also a Coasters' cover *'Searchin'*, an unusual song about private detectives, almost made the top 10. Rathbone was replaced by **Bobby Elliot**, later to marry Cilla Black (Priscilla White). Another cover, this time of a number by Maurice Williams and The Zodiacs *'Stay',* made #8 then came their first classic harmony pop single, Doris Troy's *'Just One Look'* which made #2 UK and just made the top 100 Stateside. It is now 1964 and the first LP called *'Stay with The Hollies'* is released reaching #2 UK. *'Here I Go Again'*, their first original song, written by Clarke, Hicks and Nash, made the top 10 but their second album **'In the Hollies Style'** was largely ignored, certainly in comparison to their first LP.

In 1965, further progress was made with a Goffin/ King song *'(I'll be True to You) Yes I Will'* which provided a top 10 UK hit then the group topped the UK and US charts for the first time with a sparkling cover of Clint Ballard Junior's *'I'm Alive'*. Graham Gouldman's *'Look Through Any Window'* also provided them with a big UK hit and their third album **'The Hollies'** made the UK top 10. They also embarked on their first US tour playing with Little Richard. Despite a highly successful year, their next 45, a cover of George Harrison's *'If I Needed Someone'* didn't ignite the record buying public, making #20 UK, considered disappointing by this stage.

1966 started with a strong cover of Chip Taylor's *'I Can't Let Go'* which finished just one place short of the top of the charts. Haydock left the group to be replaced by **Bernie Calvert** of The Dolphins and he played on one of The Hollies' most famous songs, *'Bus Stop'*. Then came *'Stop, Stop, Stop'*, with its distinctive banjo riff which reached #2 UK. Two albums were released in 1966, the second **'For Certain Because'**, the harbinger of a more orchestrated, psychedelic approach and Graham Nash's growing ability as a song writer.

It would be 1967 though that The Hollies would enter the world of 'flower power' as an album as well as singles group starting with **'Evolution'** (with **Clem Cattini, Mitch Mitchell** and **Dougie Wright** deputising for Elliot on drums when he suffered a burst appendix on tour in Germany). It got to #13 in the UK and #43 in the US. This album was followed by **'Butterfly'**, under the spell of The Beatles' **'Sergeant Pepper'**.

The *'On a Carousel'* 45 had got 1967 to a good start providing them with a top 10 hit in the UK (and as close as you can get to one in the US). A US only top 30 '45' *'Pay You Back with Interest'* was released and *'Carrie-Anne'*, another of their most popular songs, reached #3 in the UK and #9 in the US. By now, The Hollies were well established in the US as well as the UK. The experimental *'King Midas in Reverse'* would be a prime example of how they would try to emulate The Beatles but the new approach didn't catch on with all Hollies fans, just making the top 20. **'Butterfly'** was a very interesting album including key tracks *'Dear Eloise'*, *'Elevated Observations'* and *'Lullaby to Tim'* but didn't chart. During a visit to a Mamas and Papas recording session in Los Angeles, Nash met David Crosby, fell in love with LA and the seeds were sown for Crosby, Stills, Nash (and later Neil Young).

1968 began well with another of their regularly played songs *'Jennifer Eccles'* which would have placated fans unsure about the new experimental/ psychedelic approach but we are now beyond our timeframe. Graham Nash left for sunnier climes as

'The Hollies Greatest Hits' LP was enjoying an extended stay at #1 in the UK charts. His replacement **Terry Sylvester** (ex The Escorts and The Swinging Blue Jeans) would play on another of the group's best known songs '*He Ain't Heavy, He's My Brother*' and, in the same year, the top 3 album **'The Hollies Sing Dylan'**.

In summarising their achievements, The Hollies will be remembered as masters of vocal harmony pop who did some great interpretations but also wrote some memorable originals, still regularly on playlists to this day. Their brave attempt to move in a more psychedelic direction had its moments but is ultimately not the way they will be remembered. In that sense, they did not develop in the way The Beatles did but then again, few groups from the sixties did!

## The Incredible String Band

'The folk Sergeant Pepper': Paul McCartney named 'The 5,000 Spirits' his favourite album of 1967'

The Incredible String Band in 1967: '*Way Back in the 1960s* \*\*\*\*/ *Chinese White*' (Elektra 45) \*\*\*\*; 'The 5,000 Spirits of the Layers of the Onion' (Elektra LP, 1967 #26 UK) \*\*\*\*

MUSICIANS: As detailed below

RECOMMENDED LISTENING/ COLLECTING: 'The 5,000 Spirits or The Layers of the Onion' (Fledgling Records remastered CD, 2010); reissued or original/ early press vinyl should be readily available at record shops, fairs etc. Personally, I treasure the early vinyl pressings if you are lucky enough to track one down with the group really flourishing on classics like **'The Hangman's Beautiful Daughter'** and **Big Tam and the Wee Huge'**. **'The Chelsea Sessions'** is highly recommending for tracing the group's early development (see below). A pristine copy of the group's first '45' *'Way Back in the 1960s'* could cost £50 upwards while a first pressing of their first (1966) self-titled LP could cost £200 or more. A mono **'5,000 Spirits'** first pressing will cost over £100 mono but less than that in stereo while **'The Hangman's Beautiful Daughter',** despite its great success, will cost £50 or so.

THE MUSICAL HISTORY: Most people would cite Fairport Convention as prime movers of folk-rock, and I don't disagree with this as I have been a long-time fan of the Fairports and Sandy Denny but The Incredible String Band were in many ways more experimental and invented what I call 'progressive folk', others call 'acid folk' (probably a more accurate description) loved by folkees, lovers of underground music and progressive rock in equal measure. While Fairport Convention had their **'Unhalfbricking'**, The ISB had **'The Hangman's Beautiful Daughter'**; and while the Fairports broke new ground with **'Liege and Lief'** so did ISB especially with the 'Wee Tam' part of the **'Wee Tam and the Big Huge'**, still, to my ears, one of the greatest albums of music ever released.

But as 1967 is our target year, I must not stray far beyond that to tell this story. It is true to say that The Incredible String Band were off the starter's block slightly ahead of the Fairports with two fine albums and a 45 under their belt even breaking into the UK top 30 with what some described as 'the folk **Sergeant Pepper'** (I agree with this analogy only in as much as 'Sergeant Pepper' set a challenge for all makers of serious albums): '*The 5,000 Spirits or the Layers of the Onion'*.

A good introduction to The Incredible String Band for the unacquainted or distant is to read Joe Boyd's account of meeting and signing the group. Boyd believed: "The sixties began in the summer of 1956, ended in October, 1973 and peaked just before dawn on 1 July, 1967 during a set by Tomorrow at the UFO Club in London."**(43)** But it was his association with the likes of The Incredible String Band, Fairport Convention, and Nick Drake that laid out Boyd's route map and success in the record industry. In his search for talent for Jan Holzman's Elektra label, he visited Scotland on two occasions, and on a visit to an Edinburgh pub, was impressed by **Robin Williamson**: "Robin conversed engagingly in a lilting, heavily elocuted, burred Scots accent. His manner was somewhere between a hippy and a nineteenth-century parlour bard and he glowed with self-assurance. I was convinced I had found a star."**(44)** He went to see Williamson and Englishman **Clive Palmer**, then a folk duo a second time in Glasgow only to find the Incredible Folk Club, which they had founded, closed. He tracked them down the following morning to Temple Cottage, Balmore, north of Glasgow, only to discover they had a third recruit, **Mike Heron**, of Edinburgh local band Rock Bottom and The Deadbeats. They played Boyd some of this new folk/ rock fusion and Boyd recalls: "I was astounded: the songs were completely original, influenced by American folk and Scottish ballads, but full of flavour from the Balkans, ragtime, North Africa, music hall and William Blake. The combination of Mike's Dylan-tinged vocals and Robin's keening glissandos created harmonies both exotic and commercial." It only took an acetate of Williamson's *'October Song'* for Holzman to agree to signing them, just ahead of Transatlantic Records. **(45)**

The first album was recorded over one weekend, released in 1966 to critical acclaim but no commercial success although their first major gig was to be an illustrious one, at London's Royal Albert Hall, in November, with Judy Collins and Tom Paxton. Rob Young, in his 'Electric Eden' book, waxed eloquent on The Incredible String Band's "visionary mystique", established prior to 'Sergeant Pepper's Lonely Hearts Club Band', and "the fertile mulch of their music, riddling, pagan poetry, multi-instrumental sorcery and complex song structures." **(46)**

In 1966, The Incredible String Band, still a trio of Heron, Williamson and Palmer, released their eponymous debut on Elektra Records. True 'outsiders', Williamson was brought up on a diet of traditional Scottish and Irish music, and shared a flat with Bert Jansch, meeting Palmer, who plucked a banjo to half remembered tunes of old time, vaudeville, blues, gospel and jug band music as collected by Uncle Dave Macon, or played and sang on the stages of Edwardian music halls. When Jansch left for the 'big lights' of London, Palmer and Williamson founded The Incredible Folk Club in Sauchiehall Street, Glasgow (with Billy Connolly who was in The Humblebums with Gerry Rafferty at the time appearing to watch gigs) which, as we have seen, was shut when Joe Boyd tried to catch the men in musical action on that fateful night in Glasgow.

Not a lot has been written about the ISB's first album and it seems at first a slightly schizophrenic outing as Heron takes the lead on songs like *'How Happy I Am'*, Williamson on the ballad *'Womankind'* and Palmer on *'Empty Pocket Blues'*. There's a jig, a 'whistle tune' even a 'smoke shovelling song' but the LP is very much a young group feeling its way and trying to create something unique which they certainly did on their sophomore album. After the album's recording, Palmer apparently walked from Dover to Delhi and disappeared to Afghanistan never to return to the group which he had co-founded while Williamson spent four months in Morocco with girlfriend Christine McKechnie (Licorice), who later joined the group, returning to Scotland with a variety of obscure Moroccan instruments.

'The 5,000 Spirits or the Layers of the Onion'/ 'The Chelsea Sessions, 1967' by the Incredible String Band

THE MUSICIANS: Robin Williamson (Vocals, Guitar, Flute, Sitar, Oud, Percussion, Bowed Gimbri, Tamboura, Bass); Mike Heron (Vocals, Guitar, Harmonica); Danny Thompson: Bass (2–4; 7–9; 10; 13); John Hopkins (Piano); 'Licorice' McKechnie: (Vocals (3,6,12); Nazir Jairazbhoy – AKA Soma (Sitar, Tampura); PRODUCER: Joe Boyd; ENGINEER: John Wood; DATE: July, 1967; SLEEVE DESIGN: The Fool (Simon Postuma and Marijke Koger), LABEL: Elektra; CHART: #25 UK

## Track Listing/ Writing Credits for '5,000 Spirits'

| | | |
|---|---|---|
| 1. | Chinese White (Mike Heron) | 3:40 |
| 2. | No Sleep Blues (Robin Williamson) | 3:52 |
| 3. | Painting Box (Mike Heron) | 4:05 |
| 4. | The Mad Hatter's Song (Robin Williamson) | 5:40 |
| 5. | Little Cloud (Mike Heron) | 4:05 |
| 6. | The Eyes of Fate (Robin Williamson) | 4:00 |
| 7. | Blues for the Muse (Robin Williamson) | 2:50 |
| 8. | The Hedgehog's Song (Mike Heron) | 3:30 |
| 9. | First Girl I Loved (Robin Williamson) | 4:55 |
| 10. | You Know What You Could Be (Mike Heron) | 2:45 |
| 11. | My Name is Death (Robin Williamson) | 2:45 |
| 12. | Gently Tender (Mike Heron) | 4:10 |
| 13. | Way Back in the '60s (Robin Williamson) | 3:30 |

## The Chelsea Sessions, 1967 Track Listing/ Writing Credits

| | | |
|---|---|---|
| 1. | Lover Man (Mike Heron) | 3:00 |
| 2. | Born In Your Town (Robin Williamson) | 4:30 |
| 3. | First Girl I Loved (Robin Williamson) | 5:00 |
| 4. | Gently Tender (Mike Heron) | 4:45 |
| 5. | Little Cloud (Mike Heron) | 4:00 |
| 6. | Blues for the Muse (Robin Williamson) | 3:50 |
| 7. | The Eyes of Fate (Robin Williamson) | 4:00 |
| 8. | The Mad Hatter's Song (Robin Williamson) | 5:00 |
| 9. | Alice is a Long Time Gone (Robin Williamson) | 2:55 |
| 10. | See Your Face and Know You (Robin Williamson) | 2:37 |
| 11. | Frutch (Mike Heron) | 3:55 |
| 12. | The Iron Stone (Robin Williamson) | 3:30 |
| 13. | God Dog (Robin Williamson) | 2:40 |

# The Music

A good way to start listening to The Incredible String Band is through the Chelsea Demo Sessions, 1967 which provided some signposts to '*The 5,000 Spirits or the Layers of the Onion*'. With particular reference to '*The Mad Hatter's Song*', Rob Young comments on the variety of instrumentation, with no drum kit as such, and the variety of styles from folk saga fusion to bar room blues to Celtic psychedelia to Jacobean minstrelsy. **(47).**

The music is also very impressionistic and Young pretty much says it all when he talks of 'the sound-shape' of a plucked sitar or oud note as suggestive of a leaf or flame. Or to paraphrase Robin Williamson, "Interesting instruments make interesting sounds".

With Danny Thompson, then with Pentangle on double bass, and '**Licorice**' **McKechnie** on backing vocals, Heron's '*Chinese White*', about a shade of paint and not a butterfly, is an arresting start to the LP as, following an acoustic guitar intro a gimbri is sawn by a double-bass bow, a 'cycle of growth' or 'regeneration' song, a common motif in ISB's musical imagery' or, to take the analysis further, "an awakening of the spirit, from the whitewash of routine to a tinsel illumination of the soul." **(48)** '*No Sleep Blues*', describing the squat land in Scotland's two biggest cities, Glasgow and Edinburgh[82], and '*Blues for the Muse*' (more so the latter) are a large tip of the hat to Dylan; '*Painting Box*', '*Way Back in the 1960's*' and (especially) '*The First Girl I Loved*', surely, one of the best love songs, or more accurately, 'age of innocence' songs ever, are most often referred to as the key songs on the LP. I had never really thought of '*Way Back in the 1960s*' as a riposte to the cosy retirement story in McCartney's '*When I'm 64*' from 'Sgt Pepper' until I read Young's book. No 'pipe and slippers' as a third world war has been fought and "the song embodied everything that made the ISB simultaneously of their time and hovering gloriously above it". **(49)** No romance, only reality but '*The Hedgehog's Song*' points to the whimsical psych that was to follow in abundance. As Young points out, there is much going on at dawn or the middle of the night in ISB songs and he describes side two as the 'twilight side'.

Much has been said about the cover of '5,000 Spirits', one of the best of the psychedelic era. Will Hodgkinson devoted a whole page to it in 'Shindig' magazine. Designed by Dutch artists The Fool (Simon Postuma and Marijke Koger), painter of the 'wonder-wall' in Notting Hill whose design for '**Sergeant Pepper**' was rejected, it has a two headed angel with the planet Earth rotating in its womb, a serpent in the woman (Eve's) hand, a crescent red moon, an unidentified green planet and an all-seeing eye at the centre, variously copied throughout the history of modern art (some X-Files t-shirts for example). You strain to read the band's name as it melts as if into acid, and underneath it lies the onion sprouting with arterial roots and budding flowers above the

---

[82] A BBC TV documentary had, at the time of writing this section, been broadcasting a series of films about Scotland's streets including one about Duke Street in Glasgow. It is interesting to note Williamson's earlier remarks as he and Heron obviously had much direct experience of life in Edinburgh and Glasgow, the former having the highest level of heroin addiction in the UK at one point. Many people who were around at the time (with reference mainly to the 1970s) shared the same view that, while the slums needed to be cleared, the decanting of people to soulless housing estates like Glasgow's Easterhouse, which had a population of 40,000 at one point, and no social amenities was misguided. Housing associations sprung up to do the job that the City Council was clearly neglecting to do, restore perfectly good Victorian houses to a live-in state and get rid of the hideous multi-storeys surrounding them. As one survivor said, the easiest thing to get in the housing estate or the multi was drugs. In the Thatcher era, of course, things didn't get any better.

soil. Eyes are also a recurring theme on the album and, indeed, there is a song called *'The Eyes of Fate'*.

With regard to **'The Chelsea Sessions'**, the story behind this is quite remarkable. Frank Kornelussen, later a producer for Joe Boyd's Hannibal Records, on searching the Island archives, found what became known as **'The Chelsea Sessions'** which was a mystery because, at the time, the ISB were, of course, signed to Elektra. New Yorker Edward Haber articulates the differences between **'The 5,000 Spirits'** and the demos in his liner notes to the 'Pig's Whisker Music' CD released in the same year: "Robin Williamson's *First Girl I Loved* and *Eyes of Fate* are more relaxed than on the more aggressive performances on '5,000 Spirits'." *The Mad Hatter's Song* provides a spare Williamson solo, without **John Hopkins'** blues piano, **Danny Thompson**'s bass, or **Soma**'s sitar and tamboura overdub. Perhaps best of all are some of the unreleased songs: Robin's superb *Born in Your Town* which would have sat easily on the finished album; Mike Heron's *Lover Man* (which is known from Al Stewart's recording for the 1970 re-issue of his first album) and Robin's *God Dog* with **Dolly Collins'** organ arrangement that she would subsequently recycle on Shirley and Dolly Collins' **Anthems In Eden** in 1969. **'The Iron Man'** ended up on **'The Big Huge'** part of the group's 1968 double/two single LPs **'Wee Tam and the Big Huge'**. The most important thing to note is the dominance of Robin Williamson songs some of which are presented solo.

And Raymond Greenoaken writing from Sheffield on the thirtieth anniversary of '5,000 Spirits' summarises the context well as he continues the liner notes of '**The Chelsea Sessions**': "It was thirty years ago today – or thereabouts – and The Beatles were assembling *Sergeant Pepper* in the white-coated soutterains of Abbey Road. As the world held its breath in collective anticipation, across the city in Chelsea's Sound Techniques Studio, two young Scotsmen were creating music of a very different stripe. It was a music full of muezzin wails, choppy Bahamian guitars, thrumming ouds and a strange skirling thing called a gimbri. Odd stuff, even in those eclectic times. But when it emerged on vinyl in July of 1967, it supplied a soundtrack for the Summer of Love every bit as potent as *Pepper*. The record was *The 5,000 Spirits or the Layers of the Onion*. It was by The Incredible String Band."

There is much more to say about The Incredible String Band with the advancement into '**The Hangman's Beautiful Daughter'**, their most popular album commercially and '**Wee Tam and the Big Huge'**, also in 1968 which I would argue is their high water mark, creatively, artistically and musically (especially the **'Wee Tam'** album which was released separately). Then there are years of relative creative decline (with many great moments as is inevitable with such talented writers and musicians), starting with the uneven '**Changing Horses'** LP in 1969.

When all is said and done, The Incredible String Band was a massively creative and influential group who carved a unique niche for themselves. As a postscript, I had the great pleasure to see Mike Heron, in his seventieth year, on tour with Trembling Bells in 2013. I quote from a review I did of the Concert in the Electric Circus, Edinburgh. "What struck me was the togetherness of the music and the myriad of instruments, and twists and turns as two complimentary forces worked their way through the set. I was literally spellbound by the intricacy, humanity and attention to detail (a finger bell here, there a finger bell there)… as they were playing their magical mini symphonies, I was thinking of who had taken folk music forward, and I thought primarily of Fairport Convention (who Trembling Bells very much resemble stylistically) and The Incredible String Band." **(50)**

# Bert Jansch

**Bert Jansch in 1967: 45 *'Life Depends on Love'* \*\*\*½/ *'A Little Sweet Sunshine* \*\*\*\* (Big T); LP Nicola \*\*\*½ (Transatlantic Records)**

**MUSICIANS:** Mostly, Bert Jansch solo on acoustic guitar and vocals but sometimes playing electric guitar 12-string guitar, banjo. dulcimer, recorder, concertina.

**RECOMMENDED LISTENING/ COLLECTING:** At the time of writing this final entry in the book, a career spanning Bert Jansch collection had just been announced, a 2CD/ 2 LP collection called **'Just a Simple Soul'** with liner notes by Bernard Butler of Suede who also appeared in the 'Celebration of Bert Jansch' concert at The Royal Festival Hall with Robert Plant. Bert did not release many singles, the most collectible at around £10 being the one he released in 1967 (see below). His LPs are a different story hard to find in excellent condition with his albums to 1967 all attracting ing a value of £35 upwards, the same applies to his **'Needle of Death'** EP from 1966 but this has been reissued on the Sanctuary label. For reissues, there is **'A Man I'd Rather Be: Part 1/2'** two 4 LP/ 4CD sets on the Earth label with his first 4 LPs on part 1 and the LPs from 1967 to 1973 on part 2. A more affordable alternative is a good early LP compilation **'The Bert Jansch Sampler'** (1969). As far as CD compilations go, if you want to hear Bert playing live, there is **'Fresh as a Sweet Sunday Morning'**, a 2 CD set on Mooncrest (2007) which is repackaged with a DVD as **'Strolling Down The Highway'** (Secret Records, 2016).

**THE MUSICAL HISTORY:** Bert Jansch was born in Glasgow but brought up in Edinburgh. While there, he frequented a folk club called 'The Howff' and shared a flat with Robin Williamson of **The Incredible String Band**. Between 1963 and 1965, he hitch-hiked through Europe and to Morocco then moved to London where he met engineer/ producer Bill Leader who recorded his early songs on a reel-to-reel tape which were subsequently sold to Transatlantic Records for £100. Two LPs were released by Transatlantic in 1965 **'Bert Jansch'** and **'It Don't Bother Me'**. The former contained one of his most famous songs *'Needle of Death'*, about folk singer Buck Polly, covered by Neil Young and many others, and other fine songs like the protest number *'Do You Hear Me Now'* (which was covered by **Donovan** on his best-selling EP 'Universal Soldier')**,** *'Strolling Down the Highway'* and *'Anjy'* written by **Davy Graham** which was recorded by **Simon and Garfunkel** as *'Anji'* on their **'Sounds of Silence'** album. **'Jack Orion'**, the first of two 1966 LPs, had *'Black Waterside'* with John Renbourn on guitar – this was the subject of a potential legal case (that was not pursued) due to its remarkable similarity to *'Black Mountainside'* on **Led Zeppelin**'s first album (Jimmy Page was a Jansch fan) and a cover of Ewan McColl's *'The First Time Ever I Saw Your Face'*. The other LP was with **John Renbourn** (**'Bert and John'**) and was termed a kind of 'folk baroque'. Jansch shared a flat with Renbourn in Kilburn, and would meet **Roy Harper** and **Paul Simon** in clubs like 'The Troubadour' in Old Brompton Road and 'Les Cousins' club in Greek Street, Soho. Eventually, Jansch, tired with the peripatetic gigging, got a residency in the Horseshoe Pub in Tottenham Court Road, also frequented by Sandy Denny. Jansch was a protogee of **Anne Briggs** who inspired the number *'Black Waterside'*. He was also much taken by diverse folk, blues and jazz influences like **Davy Graham, Big Bill Broonzy** and **Charles Mingus**, covering the latter's *Goodbye Pork Pie Hat* on his LP with John Renbourn. In turn, Jansch influenced the likes of **Jimmy Page, Neil Young** and **Donovan** who wrote two songs in his honour, *'Bert's Blues'* and *'House of Jansch'*. In our target year of 1967, **'Nicola'** has lots of good songs on it but suffers a bit from the mixture of Jansch's acoustic music with an uncharacteristic stab at '60s' pop on *'Life Depends On Love'* with its nice piano motif and swirling strings, and its B-side which was quite Donovan like and 'hip' with electric guitar and sax. This contrasts with the lovely acoustic album opener *'Go Your Way My Love',* later sung by Robert Plant in tribute. The title track straddles both styles starting as a 'medieval troubadour' kind of folk before becoming a strident '60s' style soundtrack piece with flute. Still this a lovely track and, on balance the orchestral arrangements by David G Palmer are successful. *'Woe is Love My Dear'* also works well in this vein and was covered by **The Koobas** (see separate entry). The sound of Jansch duetting with himself is risky but powerful on the well observed blues folk of *'Rabbit Run'* and there are also two uncredited blues tunes. 1968 was to be a big year for both Jansch and Renbourn. **Jacqui McShee** had already sung them when **Pentangle** came into being in 1968. With a rhythm section of Danny Thompson and Terry Cox, they found critical acclaim and fame with their #5 UK LP **'Basket of Light'** (1969). Sadly, **'The Black Swan'** (2006) would be Bert's last LP as a new group of devotees like Devendra Banhart and Beth Orton joined in. Perhaps, the final words should go to Johnny Marr when he described Bert Jansch as "one of the most influential and intriguing musicians to have come out of the British music scene."

## The Kinks

The Kinks in 1967: **'Waterloo Sunset'** (Pye 45 #2 UK) *****; **'Autumn Almanac'** (Pye 45 #3 UK) ****; Something Else by The Kinks (Pye LP #35) ****

MUSICIANS: As detailed below

RECOMMENDED LISTENING/ COLLECTING: Decent early pressings of classic 45s, EPs and LPs might be hard to come by but there is no shortage of LP and CDs with nearly 6,000 listings on Discogs! In 2012, Sanctuary released LP versions of **'Something Else by The Kinks'** in mono and stereo. A cheaper option is the 2 CD remastered deluxe edition on Universal/ Sanctuary (2011) with the original stereo and mono albums and 9 tracks recorded for the BBC and 10 bonus tracks. **'The Kinks Anthology 1964–1971'** box set with bonus 45 on BGM/ Sony, 2014, gives you pretty much everything you would ever need. The 45 has *'You Really Got Me'* recorded live at Twickenham TV Studios on 16 December, 1964 b/w *'Milk Cow Blues'* recorded in the same venue on 4 August, 1965. A good alternative is the 6 CD box set **'Picture Book'** released by Universal in 2008. This includes proto Kinks tracks by The Ravens but not any rehearsals with Rod Stewart on vocals which Ray Davies told MOJO magazine weren't recorded and, anyway, his connection with Stewart was more on the football field! The Dave Davies' compilation **'Hidden Treasures'** (Universal) has previously unreleased (to 2011) songs scheduled for his legendary aborted 1969 album. If it is vinyl you seek, The Kinks is a highly collectible group. Their first two Pye '45's *'Long Tall Sally'* and *'You Still Want Me'* fetching between £100 and £200 in excellent condition. Export singles between 1965 and 1967 are also very collectible. Whereas the Pye 7N 15981 single *''Til the End of the Day/ Where Have All the Good Times Gone'* would not have much value between 5 or 10 pounds, the same catalogue number with picture sleeve would net well over £100. Others had different catalogue numbers and B-sides to the UK releases. EPs are also highly desirable with **'Dedicated Kinks'** and **'The Kinks'**, from 1966 and 1968 respectively, being valued at between £100 and £200 (at least!). It will come as no surprise to know that their early LPs are also highly valued: **'The Kinks'** (Pye, 1964) at between £150 and £200+ for an excellent copy depending on whether it is mono or stereo (stereo copies were all for export); **'Kinda Kinks'** (Pye, 1965) at £100+; **'The Kink Kontroversy'** (also Pye, 1965) slightly less but twice as much as 'Kinda Kinks' for a stereo export copy; **'Face To Face'**, a similar story with the stereo export copy twice as valued; **'Live at Kelvin Hall'** (Pye, 1967) (up to £100 for mono, more for stereo); **'Something Else by the Kinks'** (£125+ for stereo but more for mono as more and more people were listening in stereo); **'The Kinks are the Village Preservation Society'** (Surprisingly, high value for their 1968 LP – up to £200, again more for a mono copy) and the last of the 'high enders', **'Arthur'** (Pye, 1969), gatefold mono with Queen Victoria insert over £100 in mono but less in stereo.

**THE MUSICAL HISTORY: Ray Davies** and his brother **Dave** were raised in the Muswell Hill area of London, and would later, in 1971, release an album called '**Muswell Hillbillies'**. The group was formed when a chance meeting with Alexis Korner led to the brothers playing together in The Ravens who caught the attention of Larry Page, and in turn, American producer Shel Talmy, who signed them to Pye. They adopted the name The Kinks in 1963 and **Mick Avory** joined on drums. An old school acquaintance of Ray Davies, **Jeff Quaife** (they met up again later at Hornsby Art College), also joined. The Kinks made an early breakthrough with *'You Really Got Me'*, an acknowledged classic to this day which made #1 UK and #7 in the US. It took an extra session in the studio to perfect the guitar sound that may well have started off the 'riff' guitar (and perhaps heavy metal!) and Ray has confirmed that it was not Jimmy Page who played the solo by saying that "If Dave plays another note, his performance on *'You Really Got Me'* will always get him a special place among guitar players." [83]

The Kinks' first LP **'Kinks'** was mostly Chuck Berry, Bo Diddley/ R&B covers but one song, *'Stop Your Sobbing'*, endured to be successfully recorded by The Pretenders. The group dealt with the difficulty of following a #1 by producing another that fell just one place short of that exalted position in the UK and emulated the success of *'You Really Got Me'* in the US. This was *'All Day and All of the Night'*, another enduring classic demarcated by a memorable guitar riff. *'Tired of Waiting'* hit #1 again (#6 US) and, by now, The Kinks were well established international stars, and part of the pop/ rock elite. Their albums also sold well from the offset, even if they were afterthoughts, and despite the lack of original material, **'Kinks'**, released in 1964, made #3 and so did '**Kinda Kinks'** released in 1965, despite Johnny Rogan justifiably describing it as 'terribly rushed and unfocused'. Further strong 45s followed: *'Set Me Free'* (#9 UK; #23 US); *'Till the End of the Day'* (#8 UK; #50 US where they were banned from touring for failing to turn up at a gig).

1966 was an epic year with the ingenuous prose of *'Dedicated Follower of Fashion'* (#4 UK; #36 US) and the acerbic *'Well Respected Man'* establishing them in the US top 20 again. Then came another classic *'Sunny Afternoon'* (#1 UK/ #14 US) with its equally brilliant B-side *'I'm Not Like Everybody Else'* and, of course, *'Waterloo Sunset'*. The increased development of satirical lyrical phrases, and social observation, criticising conservatism and flamboyance in equal measure, showed in the first real album The Kinks made: **'Face to Face'**. Alas, as we have seen, an opportunity was

---

[83] This is confirmed in a Robert Chalmers interview with Ray Davies for The Independent on Sunday newspaper 27 March, 2011, when he is asked whether he watched the Julian Temple film **Imaginary Man**. In it, Bruce Springsteen asks, "Just tell me one thing: where did that riff come from?" Davies tells Chalmers its origin is actually Ray's piano Stockhausen style 'tinkering'. "But it was Dave, with the help of an old amplifier cone, that he'd deliberately slashed with a razor blade, and a battered Harmony Meteor guitar, who invented the sound whose influence would be publicly acknowledged by The Who, The Clash, Paul Weller (etc.)" (as the successful and long overdue 2016 'Sunny Afternoon' stage show further confirmed). Two books to refer to for the real story of The Kinks are, Ray's **X-Ray** (1996, revised 2008) and Dave's **Kink** (1997). Dave has also released a revealing DVD, **Kronikles/ Mystical Journey**.

missed, as it would be with 'Something Else' the following year, as the expansiveness and experimentation that would drive The Beach Boys with their 'Pet Sounds', and in the following year, 'Sgt Pepper' to create a unified, 'conceptual' work was absent. An idea to link songs with sound montages was shelved. At least, the long player was now at last recognised as a means for the group to express their artistic intentions. 'Face to Face' was a landmark in that it was the first album with no covers and notable songs like 'Party Line' (pointing to 'Lola' in the future with its line "Is she a she at all?"); 'Fancy', a song about sexual ambiguity to a lesser extent; 'Dandy', a US hit for Herman's Hermits; Ray Davies' candid song on Obsessive Compulsive Disorder 'Too Much on My Mind'; a dig at mercenary session musicians 'Session Man'; 'House in the Country', a satire on the nouveau riche, its title adopted by Kinks fan Damon Albarn of Blur in the mid-1990s; and 'Most Exclusive Residence For Sale' (no explanation necessary).

The year 1967 also produced 'Autumn Almanac', another classic to follow the timeless 'Waterloo Sunset', described by Neville Marten and Jeff Hudson in the second edition of their book 'The Kinks' as, "Both lyrically and musically graced with pure pop genius." (51)

In 1968, the critically acclaimed 'Kinks are the Village Green Preservation Society' album and the timeless 45 'Days', covered so well by Kirsty McColl, would emerge, and in 1969, there was 'Shangri-La' and my own favourite Kinks album 'Arthur (Or the Decline and Fall of the British Empire)' with its brilliant rocking single 'Victoria' and its acerbic satirical B-side 'Mr Churchill Says', deserving much better than a finish outside the top 30 of the UK chart. Transexual encounter tale 'Lola' was also still to come in 1970 as was 'Celluloid Heroes' in 1972 when The Kinks had moved to RCA Records.

To an extent, The Kinks did not really fit into 1967. As Peter Quaife said, "It was a fad and I wanted nothing to do with it at all. We all conformed for a few seconds by wearing multi-coloured gear, but we knew we didn't fit into all of this, especially Mick Avory – just think of it Mick Avory as a flower-power child." (52)

### IMPORTANT ALBUMS oF 1967 (9)
### 'SOMETHING ELSE' by THE KINKS

**MUSICIANS: Ray Davies (Lead Vocals, Rhythm Guitar, Harmonica, Harpsichord, Organ, Tuba, Maracas); Dave Davies: (Lead Guitar, 12 string Guitar, Backing Vocals, Lead on 2,8,11); Pete Quaife (Bass, Backing Vocals); Mick Avory (Drums, Percussion); Nicky Hopkins (Keyboards); Rasa Davies (Backing Vocals); PRODUCER: Shel Talmy/ Ray Davies; DATE: 15 September, 1967; LABEL: Pye; CHART #35 UK**

# Tracklist/ Credits:

| | | |
|---|---|---|
| 1. | David Watts (Ray Davies) | 2:30 |
| 2. | Death of a Clown (Dave Davies/ Ray Davies) | 3:05 |
| 3. | Two Sisters (Ray Davies) | 2:00 |
| 4. | No Return (Ray Davies) | 2:04 |
| 5. | Harry Rag (Ray Davies) | 2:15 |

| 6. | Tin Soldier Man (Ray Davies) | 2:50 |
| 7. | Situation Vacant (Ray Davies) | 3:15 |
| 8. | Love Me Till the Sun Shines (Dave Davies) | 3:16 |
| 9. | Lazy Old Sun (Ray Davies) | 2:48 |
| 10. | Afternoon Tea (Ray Davies) | 3:25 |
| 11. | Funny Face (Dave Davies) | 2:18 |
| 12. | End of the Season (Ray Davies) | 2:58 |
| 13. | Waterloo Sunset (Ray Davies) | 3:15 |

## The Music

'*David Watts*' (later covered by The Jam) was a controversial opener for those times, the name coming from a retired army major of the same name who booked them for a gig in Rutland and in which Dave Davies, Ray's younger brother was propositioned. The lyric depicts a disparaging envy expressed towards a head boy at school who is 'gay and fancy free' with the wish that 'all his money belonged to me'. The rhythm section of **Pete Quaife** and **Mick Avory** do a particularly great job on this number. '*Death of a Clown*' marked Dave Davies' coming out from under the shadow of his brother Ray (Dave started the lyric and he and Ray completed the song together) in a successful foray into songwriting, and also providing Dave with a solo hit. The subject matter is coming of age through marriage as the wild years of clubbing are muzzled. '*Two Sisters*' has a related theme with Ray looking on enviously as his brother 'Dave the Rave' continues his free, single life while he faces up to the responsibilities of marriage and parenthood. The elder sister eventually comes to terms with this at the end of this salutary tale. The cello and viola backing along with guest **Nicky Hopkins**' harpsichord add a musical gravitas to the song. '*No Return*' is another example of what The Kinks did best – nostalgia – as reflections of first love are delivered bossa nova style. '*Harry Rag*' sounds like an old World War One song or possibly a sea shanty, the 'Harry rag' referred to is Cockney rhyming slang for a cigarette. '*Tin Soldier Man*' has a brass section and a song that fitted the psychedelic sixties being explored by the likes of Donovan and The Small Faces. Ray Davies' songs often sounded like mini-plays, and '*Situation Vacant*' tells of a disillusioned 'Johnny' leaving a secure job in search of pastures new but his gamble doesn't pay off, and he ends up losing his home and his wife. Davies' wrote many satirical songs about the perils of upward social mobility, '*Well Respected Man*' being one that springs to mind. The guitar/ drums coda and brief fade out at the end are a sign that The Kinks are getting a grip of the little tricks that make a good album. '*Love Me till the Sun Shines*' was another Dave Davies song, stylistically more from the early Kinks 'R&B' era but an effective piece of rock 'n' roll with more good work from the rhythm section which continues, more imaginatively, on a raga ballad '*Lazy Old Sun*', unmistakably, one of Ray's, with mellotron and brass. Ray Davies liked using his Noel Coward persona and '*Afternoon Tea*' is another example, rather corny, nostalgia making one think of Battenburg cake and china tea sets. '*Funny Face*' was another case of Dave emerging as a songwriter in his own right and injecting some rock into brother Ray's pop. The subject matter was deadly serious: the 'funny face', "eyes that don't smile, all they do is cry" looking out from a mental home yearning for his love lying beyond the 'frosted window'. Melodically, it had similarities in places to '*Where Have All the Good Times Gone*' from 1965. It ends rather abruptly unfortunately. Johnny Rogan refers to Dave Davies' 'psychotic humour' in this song. '*End of the Season*' dates back to the '**Face to Face**' sessions, a Vaudevillian Ray Davies' melancholy take on the end of summer and a relationship using the end of the cricket season as an analogy. The song was covered by The Uglys who had a young Steve Gibbons and Dave Pegg (later of Fairport Convention and Procol Harum) in its ranks. The album ends with the all-time classic *'Waterloo Sunset'*, to this day, one of The Kink's most loved songs. It was originally going to be called 'Liverpool Sunset' and only the presence of Sandie Shaw's Eurovision song contest winning *'Puppet on a String'*, The Tremeloes *'Silence is Golden'* and The Beatles' *'All You Need is Love'* kept it off the top of the charts. The descending bass line and vocal harmonies, some marvellous twangy guitar and Pete Townshend ripped chords all embellish a lovely piece of music unfortunately all too short. By Ray's own account, it was a substitute for a painting of Waterloo Bridge and, therefore, not about anything in particular. [84]

Completed around the same time as **'Sergeant Pepper'**, **'Something Else'** falls short of that particular classic as a landmark recording but shows progress that would be developed on the conceptual **'Village Green'** LP in 1968. The Kinks' difficulty was always that they were such a prolific singles group that they were never seen as an 'albums' group. Indeed, their most significant albums chart successes came with two budget LPs on the Marble Arch label: 'Well Respected Man' and 'Sunny Afternoon'. Also, The Kinks never quite had the production quality, imaginative arrangements or consistency of song writing to sustain an album or achieve a coherent programme of music. Opportunities were also missed on 'Something Else' such as at the end of *'Funny Face'* which could have been a much longer piece and extending *'Waterloo Sunset'* to end it in true style. Having said all that, comparing The Beatles and The Kinks is to compare 'apples and pears', no Cockney rhyming slang is intended here, and The Kinks were definitely the best at what they did. I suspect their intense English nostalgia puzzled and possibly alienated some listeners, and sometimes sat uneasily with their heavier, rock leanings. Troubled by fighting and extroverted behaviour that didn't always impress others, The Kinks' cause in the US wasn't helped by a ban between 1966 and the summer of 1969 allegedly emanating from Ray Davies manhandling a TV studio technician. Peter Doggett pretty well sums them up: "The Kinks had the uncanny ability to be very much of their own times, and yet exist completely outside them too."

The anthology box set must be seen as the current definitive starting point, its 42-page booklet is crammed full of photos, press clippings etcetera with five CDs and a 7" vinyl single (details in recommended listening).

**CD 1** has 33 mono tracks scanning the period between 1964 and 1965. Alongside 45s, EP and LP tracks, there are three previously unreleased including a New York TV interview.

**CD 2** concentrates mostly on 1965, has 27 tracks, mostly mono, with 4 previously unreleased including takes 1 to 3 of *'Dedicated Follower of Fashion'* recorded at Pye Studios on 7 February, 1966 and clocking in at 7:14.

**CD 3** focuses on **1966–1967** with 29 tracks in stereo/ mono with seven different mixes, four previously unreleased. As far as our target year is concerned, of particular interest are: *Mr Pleasant* (a '45' released on 21 April); *Act Nice and Gentle* (15 May); alternative stereo mixes of *Afternoon Tea* and *Lazy Old Sun*; and

---

[84] "Words are just like pieces of plasticine that you mould. But it's only words and there are no rules." Also, speaking on a 1995 BBC Documentary, "Today, it really is a dirty old river. But I imagined it… (then – now) I do it as if it's a new song based on what I feel… it's like an actor, doing Hamlet every night." (Ray Davies is obviously enormously proud of the song and rightly so).

a version of John A Koerner's **Good Luck Charm** from August and first released on **'Hidden Treasures'** (Sanctuary/ Universal 2011).

**CD 4** has 31 tracks and continues through 1967 into 1968. It includes **Rosemary Rose** (June, '67 which first appeared on **The Great Lost Kinks Album** in 1973) and **Polly**, recorded in March, '67 but not released until 5th April, 1968 as a '45'.

**CD 5** has 20 tracks, effectively a compendium from 1969 to 1971.

A 'Kink', of course, could refer literally to an eccentric individual, usually a flamboyant dresser. Indeed, Honor Blackman, who played Emma Peel in The Avengers TV series, wore 'kinky' boots and the 'kinky' behaviour of call girls like Christine Keeler triggered one of the biggest political outrages of the time, the 'Profumo scandal'.

## John Mayall and His Bluesbreakers in 1967

*'Sittin' in the Rain' (*Decca 45) *****; *'Double Trouble ***/ It Hurts Me Too'* ****(Decca 45); *'Suspicions Parts 1 & 2* (Decca 45) ***; 'A Hard Road' (Decca LP) ****; 'Crusade' (Decca LP) ***; 'Raw Blues' (Ace of Clubs LP) ***; 'The Blues Alone' ***(Ace of Clubs LP)

**MUSICIANS:** John Mayall, similarly to Alexis Korner's Blues Incorporated, recruited many musicians who later achieve stardom for his Bluesbreakers group. Some of these are detailed below.

**RECOMMENDED LISTENING/ COLLECTING:** The 2006 Decca 2 CD remasters are recommended and *'A Hard Road'* is well worth finding on vinyl (it has been reissued). The better selling 45s shouldn't be too difficult to find. However, if you are a vinyl collector the 45s, *'Crawling Up a Hill'* and *'Crocodile Walk'* on the Decca label (1964/1965) may prove elusive unless you have at least £30 to spend on each. *'I'm a Witch-doctor'* is also a popular target for collectors but was reissued in 1967 as 'John Mayall with Eric Clapton' for half of what an original Immediate copy from 1965 will cost (£20/£40). Mayall's 1967 Decca EP **'The Bluesbreakers with Paul Butterfield'** could cost £50 or more if you can find a copy. As for Mayall's LPs, **'Plays John Mayall – Live at Klooks Kleek'** (Decca, 1965) and **'Bluesbreakers with Eric Clapton'** (mono 'Beano' cover, Decca, 1966) are the most sought after attracting prices of £100+.

**THE MUSICAL HISTORY:** At the time of writing this part of the book, John Mayall had already completed his 50th anniversary tour at the age of 81. Born in Macclesfield, Cheshire, Mayall went to school in Manchester and studied at the Regional College of Art. After a succession of local bands, he went to London to work as a draughtsman and by 1964, had a recording contract with Decca. He was 31 years old so a relative latecomer to the music scene. His first single release was *'Crawling Up a Hill/ Mr James'* in 1964 with a **'Live at Klooks Kleek'** album the same year. Already beginning to acquire a father figure status within blues music, he recruited **Eric Clapton** who'd left The Yardbirds. After Decca didn't renew his contract, Mayall recorded one splendid single *'I'm Your Witch-doctor/ Telephone Blues'* for the Immediate label and another 45 *'Lonely Years/ Bernard Jenkins'* for the Purdah label. Decca saw the error of their ways and took Mayall back. It's just as well they did for a line-up of **Mayall** (vocals, organ), **Eric Clapton** (guitar), **Jack Bruce** and **John McVie** (bass), and **Hughie Flint** (drums) recorded the seminal **'Bluesbreakers with Eric Clapton'**, affectionately known as the 'Beano album' which made #6 in the UK album chart.

Before the end of 1966, Clapton had left to form Cream and Flint also left. **Aynsley Dunbar** was Flint's replacement, and an EP and a fine album **'A Hard Road'** (see below) was made with Peter Green, soon to be Fleetwood Mac's talismanic guitarist. An

EP was also made with Paul Butterfield on guitar and harmonica on *'Little by Little'* and on the classic single *'Sitting in the Rain'*. Dunbar left for The Jeff Beck Group being replaced briefly by **Micky Waller** (ex Steampacket and Brian Auger and the Trinity) before **Mick Fleetwood** joined. He, like his other famous rhythm partner in Fleetwood Mac, John McVie before him was fired by Mayall for boozing. **Keef Hartley** was Fleetwood's replacement and he would not fare any better as depicted on the track *'Sacked'* on the Keef Hartley album **'Halfbreed'**.

A fourth album **'Crusade'**, released in 1967, featuring sax for the first time, broke into the American charts and made the UK top 10. Many famous musicians came and went, and many landmark recordings followed: the LPs **'Bare Wires'** (1968 #3 UK; #59 US); **'Blues from Laurel Canyon'** (1969 only #33 but should have fared better; #68 US) with its 45 *'The Bear'* (about Canned Heat singer Bob Hite and surely the inspiration for Norman Greenbaum's *'Spirit in the Sky'*); and **'The Turning Point'** (1970). John Mayall's legacy has just gone on and on and his contribution to the credible development of the blues in the UK is inestimable.

### IMPORTANT ALBUMS oF 1967 (10)
### 'A HARD ROAD' by JOHN MAYALL

**MUSICIANS: John Mayall (Vocals, Guitar, Harmonica, Piano, Organ); Peter Green (Guitar); John McVie (Bass); Aynsley Dunbar/ Hughie Flint (Drums); Alan Skidmore, Ray Warleigh, Johnny Almond (Brass); PRODUCER: Mike Vernon; RELEASED: February, 1967; LABEL: Decca; CHART #10 UK**

## Track List and Credits

1. **A Hard Road (John Mayall) 3:12**
2. **It's Over (John Mayall) 2:50**
3. **You Don't Love Me (Willie Cobbs) 2:50**
4. **The Stumble (Freddy King/ Sonny Thompson) 2:55**
5. **Another Kind of Love (John Mayall) 3:05**
6. **Hit The Highway (John Mayall) 2:17**
7. **Leaping Christine (John Mayall) 2:15**
8. **Dust My Blues (Elmore James) 2:50**
9. **There's Always Work (John Mayall) 1:40**
10. **The Same Way (Peter Green) 2:10**
11. **The Super-natural (Peter Green) 2:58**
12. **Top of the Hill (John Mayall) 2:40**
13. **Someday After a While (You'll Be Sorry) (Freddy King/ Sonny Thompson) 3:02**
14. **Living Alone (John Mayall) 2:25**

15. **THE MUSIC**
16. **'A Hard Road'**, a classic opener with Mayall's rolling piano, fine falsetto and Peter Green's exquisite guitar licks;
17. **'It's Over'**, the album stalls a wee bit with fairly standard blues ballad fayre, however, picks up again in style on;
18. **'You Don't Love Me'** with great harmonica and drumming, a lead vocal by Green and:
19. **'The Stumble',** a fine instrumental showcase for Green's fluent guitar playing;

155

20. **'Another Kind of Love'**, a slow blues with organ augmented by a brass section of Alan Skidmore, Ray Warleigh and Johnny Almond who would play on **'The Turning Point'** and the **'Empty Rooms'** albums in 1970; Green's incisive guitar cutting through the mix;

21. **'Hit The Highway'** features Mayall's barrelhouse boogie piano with great interplay between him and Green, no rhythm section, great fun, then there's;

22. **'Leaping Christine'**, an uptempo boogie number with lashings of Mayall's harmonica, a neat little Hammond break and nice harmony vocals (Mayall and Green);

23. **'Dust My Blues'**, the Elmore James classic with Mayall playing slide on 5-string guitar, a ripping Green solo, otherwise known as 'Dust My Broom' Taj Mahal way;

24. **'There's Always Work',** with harmonica and a lot of moaning and groaning in the background;

25. **'The Same Way'** with Peter Green's distinctive lead vocal (He wrote it) and Mayall on 9-string guitar (why have 6 strings when you can have 5 or 9?)

26. **'The Super-natural'**, Green's use of soaring sustain is undemonstrative but brilliant bringing 'Black Magic Woman' and 'Albatross' (later) with Fleetwood Mac to mind, (Mayall described it as "one of the most meaningful instrumentals I've heard") with Mayall's organ softly in the background and nice rolling drums and steady drums not invading on Green's space – this one is all his!

27. **'Top of the Hill'** fine but doesn't really ignite;

28. **'Someday After a While (You'll Be Sorry)',** the brass is back for this classic slow soul blues reminiscent of 'It Hurts Me Too' and thought to be the prototype for Fleetwood Mac's 'Need Your Love So Bad', once again Green lifts it and;

29. **'Living Alone'** is an effective, quirky blues (due to the choppy guitar chords and slide perhaps) with harmonica, a fine ending to a fine album.

John Mayall said in the sleeve notes for the album: "The music contained here means far more to me than anything we've recorded before," and if there were any doubts about Clapton's successor, these were quickly dispelled by Peter Green's virtuoso performance. The 2006 Decca CD remaster features the album's 14 tracks with 14 bonus tracks: the **'*Looking Back/ So Many Roads*'** 45; J.B. Lenoir's **'*Mama, Talk to Your Daughter'*** and **'*Alabama Blues'*** recorded in the Autumn of 1966; the 4 track EP with Paul Butterfield; and a Saturday Club session for the BBC Light Programme in January, 1967.

Nigel Williamson's summation of Mayall's contribution to the blues is that he "can rightly claim to be the father of the British blues. Alexis Korner and Cyril Davies, among others, preceded him as musical pioneers, while several of those employed, like Eric Clapton and Peter Green, went on to greater commercial success. But Mayall was the catalyst. Almost every significant British blues player passed through his band, and his influence was immeasurable." **(53)**

# The Moody Blues:

The Moody Blues in 1967: *'Life's Not Life'* (Decca 45) ***; *'Fly Me High'* *** (Decca 45); *'Love and Beauty'* (Decca 45) ****; *'Nights in White Satin'* (Decca 45 # 19 UK; reissued Deram 45 in 1972 #9 UK) *****; *'Days of Future Past'* (Deram, 1967) ***

# The Musicians:

The first line-up was **Denny Laine (Guitar, Vocals); Mike Pinder (Keyboards, Vocals); Ray Thomas (Brass, Vocals); Clint Warwick (Bass) and Graeme Edge (Drums)** and **Justin Hayward and John Lodge** figure prominently in the history of the group (see below).

# Recommended Listening / Collecting:

If you want to delve into the history of The Moody Blues, the most recent vinyl release (2016) is **'Go Now – Moody Blues #1'**, a 12 track 180-gram reissue on the Varese Vintage label (USA/ Canada). The same album, under the name, **'The Magnificent Moodies'**, was released on vinyl by Esoteric Recordings in 2015, in mono. This was an 'official 50th anniversary remastered edition Record Store Day release'. A two CD set was also released by Esoteric in 2014. This has the original album with no fewer than 15 bonus tracks, seven previously unreleased tracks from 1964 to 1966, 12 tracks from 'Saturday Club' sessions, an interview with Ray Thomas and Graeme Edge, a Coca Cola radio commercial from 1965, and nine 'Denny Cordell Session' tracks from 1966. Early pressings of the **'Days of Future Passed'** LP are not too hard to find. It was remastered for CD by Deram in 1997 and there is a Japanese CD remaster from 2016 with ten bonus tracks and a 50th anniversary 'deluxe' edition from 2017, a high quality 'needle drop' (transferred from vinyl to digital audio – the master tapes of the album had deteriorated so much that reissues from 1978 were remixed, the differences are noted in detail on Wikipedia). There is also a 2006 SACD quadrophonic mix by Mark Powell and Paschal Byrne. For vinyl lovers, their first 45 as **Moody Blues, *'Steal Your Heart Away/ Lose your Money (But Don't Lose Your Mind)'*** (Decca, 1964) doesn't show up that often and is valued at around £40 in excellent condition. The unboxed **'The Magnificent Moodies'** (Decca, 1965) is their most valuable LP at around £50. Mostly, Moody Blues records are reasonably affordable.

# The Musical History:

Formed in Birmingham in 1964, The Moody Blues made a quick breakthrough with the #1 single **'Go Now'** in 1964 which also made #10 in the US charts. Their early songs were mostly covers and an album modestly (!) entitled **'The Magnificent Moodies'** was released in 1966 in similar R&B format. Denny Laine left to go solo, eventually, surfacing in Wings in 1973 and Warwick quit the music business. **John Lodge** and **Justin Hayward** were then recruited. They soldiered on and even the appointment of Brian Epstein as manager failed to halt their declining fortunes.

1967 was a key year for them as they discovered the mellotron and worked on poetic, classically based music recording the album **'Days of Future Passed'** with the London Festival Orchestra. (See 'Important Albums of 1967'). **'In Search of a Lost Chord'** followed in 1968 with the group playing all the instruments themselves, more than 30 of them! Then, in 1969, came the brilliant **'On the Threshold of a Dream'** which topped the charts and reached #20 in the US. There is much more to tell but, as far as 1967 is concerned, The Moody Blues were just beginning to lift from the launch pad as a group who strode between the progressive rock and general rock like a colossus going on to have two further #1 albums 'A Question of Balance' (1970) and 'Every Good Boy Deserves Favour' (1971), both on the Threshold subsidiary of Decca.

### IMPORTANT ALBUMS of 1967 (11)
### DAYS oF FUTURE PASSED by THE MOODY BLUES

"*Days of Future Passed* almost singlehandedly established the concept of symphonic rock." (54) Ed Macan

MUSICIANS: Justin Hayward (Vocals, Acoustic and Electric Guitar, Piano, Electric Piano, Sitar); Mike Pinder (Vocals, Piano, Mellotron, Tamboura, Spoken parts); Ray Thomas (Flute, Piano, Percussion, Vocals), John Lodge (Bass, Vocals), Graeme Edge (Drums, Percussion, Backing Vocals); London Festival Orchestra conducted by Peter Knight; PRODUCERS/ ENGINEER: Tony Clarke, Michael Dacre-Barclay; Derek Varnals (High Mendl Executive Producer); SLEEVE: David Anstey; DATE: 10 November, 1967; LABEL : Deram; CHART: #27 UK

## Tracklist/ Credits
1. a. The Day Begins (Peter Knight) 4:05; b. Morning Glory (Graeme Edge) 1:40
2. Dawn is a Feeling (Mike Pinder) 3:50
3. The Morning: Another Morning (Ray Thomas) 3:40
4. Lunch Break: Peak Hour (John Lodge) 5:30
5. The Afternoon: a. Forever Afternoon (Tuesday?); b. Time to Get Away 8:25
6. Evening: a. The Sunset; b. Twilight Time 6:40
7. The Night: Nights in White Satin 7:30

## The Music
An original plan to record Dvorak's 'New World Symphony' was dropped in favour of a concept album about time and night and day. The group and orchestra worked around one another and '*Nights in White Satin*' provided a fine centre piece. Indeed, given its status as a '60s' classic most people assume the '45' went to #1 whereas it barely scraped the top 20 in the UK. Another fine track '*Tuesday Afternoon*' was released as a single in the US and made the top 50 there. There was little indication of all this prior to the album, apart from some nice flute, with the first 45 '*Life's Not Life*', a straightforward but jaunty vocal harmony ballad with the chorus 'Life's not life no more' (sic!) There is a clip from French TV on YouTube of a trademark Justin Hayward vocal performance of the second single '*Fly Me High*'. You do get an indication of what was coming on the ambitious '*Love and Beauty*', a pretty, thoughtful ballad with big vocal harmonies, a big arrangement and mellotron.

As Vernon Joynson says, "The significance of 'Days of Future Passed' should not be underestimated – not only did it represent a drastic change of musical direction for the band it also helped to encourage the avalanche of concept albums that followed."(55) Ed Macan's analysis suggests that The Beatles and 'Sergeant Pepper' in particular influenced groups like The Nice, Pink Floyd, Procol Harum and The Moody Blues (in effect, a first wave of proto progressive rock), the difference being that on albums like **'Days of Future Passed'** there was a "more through exploration of purely instrumental music".**(56)**[85]

The album starts off with a rather disconcerting 'rumble' but all is harmonious when the 'romantic' strings 'kick in' and 'the day begins', the *'Nights in White Satin'* theme is introduced at this point and the narration sounds a bit contrived although the lyrics and narrations, with elements of myth and magic (and quite poetic), provide interest and coherence as we go through the day. The first bit of real pop/ rock appears on 'Lunch Break: Peak Hour'. Mellotron appears on 'The Afternoon' and there are some memorable orchestral passages and themes taking us to the climax and closing narration. The difficulty I have always had with this album is that *'Nights in White Satin'* stands head and shoulders above the rest.

As a first step, **'Days of Future Passed'** is a significant one although it does sound an uneasy amalgamation of group, orchestra, mellotron and narration in places. However, it was more the direction of travel than this particular excursion that demarcates the album as a landmark moment in the development of popular and progressive music.

# The Move

The Move in 1967: *'I Can Hear the Grass Grow'* **(Deram 45 #5 UK) \*\*\*\*;** *'Flowers in the Rain'* **(Regal Zonophone #45 #2 UK) \*\*\*\*;** *'Fire Brigade'* **(Regal Zonophone LP track in 1967; 45 #3 UK in 1968) \*\*\*\*\*;** *'Cherry Blossom Clinic'* **(Regal Zonophone 45); \*\*\*\*;** 'Move' **(Regal Zonophone LP #15 UK) \*\*\*\*** – while released in 1968, it took over two years to complete and, as most of it was familiar to fans in 1967, it is arguably valid to the year 1967**) THE MUSICIANS: first line-up: Carl Wayne (Vocals); Roy Wood and Trevor Burton (Guitar and Vocals); Ace Kefford (Bass) and Bev Bevan (Drums).**

**RECOMMENDED LISTENING/ COLLECTING:** The Salvo CD reissues (see below). Esoteric has also recently released remastered editions. The Move released a lot of fine singles which is not to detract from some fine albums, and this may be a collector's preferred route (Why not both?) and the 'sellers' should be readily available, condition may be an issue but it should be possible to track down 'pre loved' 45s and LPs. A copy of an original **'Move'** LP on Regal Zonophone with a laminated, flip back cover, could cost three figures in excellent condition assuming you can find one.

**THE MUSICAL HISTORY:** Like The Moody Blues, The Move hails from Birmingham but three years later in early 1966. The Move was an innovative pop psych group who hit the ground running with a great debut single *'Night of Fear'* with its quotation from Tchaikovsky's *'1812 Overture'* which nearly made #1 in the UK. They appeared at the 14-Hour Technicolour Dream event on 29 July, 1967 and shortly afterwards, enjoyed success with *'I Can Hear the Grass Grow'*, acknowledged as a psych classic appearing on Nuggets compilations and the like. *'Flowers in the Rain'* was also a psych classic and the first record to be played on BBC Radio 1 on 30 September, 1967. Believe it or not, all royalties from the record were ordered to be given to charity as a result of a successful legal action by the government against the promotional postcard showing Prime Minister Harold Wilson in his bath (as a protest against the shutting down of the pirate radio stations). "That really scared us," said Trevor Burton,

---

[85] While light classical music in the vein of Dvorak was at its roots, there is narration by Mike Pinder and singing.

"when you f*** with the Prime Minister, you've got to watch your step. MI5 were outside Tony's place (Tony Visconti) and we were being followed by God knows who, it was like being in a James Bond movie (Not that The Move was shy to publicity.)" They engaged in a 'demolition' of the Marquee Club stage and some car wrecking at The Roundhouse on New Year's Eve, 1966. Also, their signing of a contract with Decca's 'hip' subsidiary Deram with Moody Blues producer Denny Cordell and Essex Music production was signed on the back of a topless model Liz Wilson. The next proposed 45 (and a brave move), *'Cherry Blossom Clinic'* was withdrawn because of its lyric about a mental asylum but appeared to good effect on the first Move album which made #15 on the UK album chart so plenty of people heard it anyway.

### IMPORTANT ALBUMS of 1967 (12)
### 'MOVE' by THE MOVE

**MUSICIANS: Roy Wood (Vocals, Guitar); Carl Wayne (Vocals); Trevor Burton (Guitar, Vocals); Ace Kefford (Bass, Vocals); Bev Bevan (Drums, Percussion, Vocals) with Nicky Hopkins (Piano – 7, Harpsichord – 12); ARRANGEMENTS: Tony Visconti (Strings, Brass, Wind); PRODUCER: Denny Cordell: SLEEVE DESIGN: The Fool with photography by Bobby Davidson; DATE OF RELEASE: March, 1968** (but completed in 1967); **LABEL: Regal Zonophone; CHART: UK #15 (1968)**

## Track Listing / Credits

| | | |
|---|---|---|
| 1. | Yellow Rainbow (Roy Wood) | 2:35 |
| 2. | Kilroy was Here (Roy Wood) | 2:45 |
| 3. | (Here We Go Round) The Mulberry Bush (Roy Wood) | 3:00 |
| 4. | Weekend (Bill and Doree Post) | 1:45 |
| 5. | Walk Upon the Water (Roy Wood) | 3:20 |
| 6. | Flowers in the Rain (Roy Wood) | 2:30 |
| 7. | Hey Grandma (Don Stevenson/ Jerry Miller) | 3:10 |
| 8. | Useless Information (Roy Wood) | 2:55 |
| 9. | Zing Went the Strings of My Heart (James F Hanley) | 2:50 |
| 10. | The Girl Outside (Roy Wood) | 2:55 |
| 11. | Fire Brigade (Roy Wood) | 2:22 |
| 12. | Mist on a Monday Morning (Roy Wood) | 2:30 |
| 13. | Cherry Blossom Clinic (Roy Wood) | 2:30 |

## The Music Track by Track

1. **'Yellow Rainbow'** is a sizzling powerhouse of a psych number written by Roy Wood (as were all the originals) dealing with the uncomfortable subject of nuclear war with frenetic bass and drums;
2. **'Kilroy Was Here'** (although I've never seen his face) is more folky but also enigmatic including a line about an insane dustman;
3. **'(Here We Go Round) The Lemon Tree'** is orchestrated, was the flip side of *'Flowers in the Rain'* and was part of the repertoire of The Idle Race

with Jeff Lynne, future collaborator with Wood in the Electric Light Orchestra;

4. **'Weekend'**, the Eddie Cochran rock 'n' roller with Trevor Burton on vocals;

5. **'Walk Upon the Water':** Recorded in January, 1967. The Beatles saw The Move play in brightly coloured regalia at the Marquee Club and the trippy ending and phased drums (and costumes) might just have caught their ears that night as they were devising the musical project to end all projects;

6. **'Flowers in the Rain'**, with its classic rhyming couplets, Mendelssohn inspired Tony Visconti wind quartet arrangement, thunder claps, a classic as befitting the summer of love;

7. **'Hey Grandma'** (you're so young, your old man's just a boy), the classic opening to the Moby Grape song chugs along with old time piano and a two neat guitar breaks, the second wilder than the first;

8. **'Useless Information'** began side two and is one of Wood's personal favourites with its multi-layered vocals and lead bass line, The Move was musically a very good group indeed and this is an oft neglected gem;

9. **'Zing Went the Strings of My Heart'**, a Coasters song with Bev Bevan on deep throat vocal, sounds like a bit of a 'Monster Mash' Frank Zappa tribute/ send-up with deep bass as a lead instrument once again, definitely out of place;

10. **'The Girl Outside'**, a string quartet introduces what seems to be Tony Visconti's failed attempt to replicate the pop baroque of *'Eleanor Rigby'* with Trevor Burton on vocal with a cold and bottle of brandy, sounds like a Zombies song that didn't quite work;

11. **'Fire Brigade'**, an all-time classic which should have been #1 (and nearly was) about a schoolboy flirtation needing a fire brigade to put the heat out; 'compromise' and 'exercise' and 'surprise' who else would produce rhyming triplets like these;– brilliant with Eddie Cochran type guitar;

12. **'Mist on a Monday Morning'**, an early indication of ELO perhaps, a folk song and a baroque arrangement with harpsichord, strings and pipes;

13. **'Cherry Blossom Clinic':** Memorable for its haunting words, , the strings a bit overdone and discordant with the thumping bass and wah-wah guitar but suitably chaotic given the fragile state of mind of the subject who thinks he might be better off dead, a strong ending in more ways than one and ambitious even for those heady days.

The best way to explore 'The Move' LP is through the Salvo two CD mono expanded edition with five bonus tracks *'Vote for Me'*, the B-side of the withdrawn 45 *'Cherry Blossom Clinic'* which would be almost impossible to find on vinyl, with the group railing against the *'Flowers in the Rain'* court case. *'The Night of Fear'* is there, inspired by hearing noises during the night and suffering insomnia as a consequence with reference to shadows, mind tripping and green and purple lights– (too many drugs or time spent at the disco perhaps?) along with its B-side *'The Disturbance'* with a horror riff at the end that winds forward to another Birmingham group, Black Sabbath. The B-side of *'I Can Hear the Grass Grow'* is also included *'Wave the Flag and Stop the Train'*, apparently, an attempt to emulate (or is that emasculate?) The Monkees: subject matter – the attempted suicide of a girl.

The second CD is an intriguing recreation in stereo of mixes from the original four-track session tapes. It's entitled *'New Movement'* and reveals 'The Move as you've never, ever heard them before.' *'The Move Intro'*, the aborted original B-side to *'I Can Hear the Grass Grow'*, their unofficial Stax inspired theme song starts the CD. *'Cherry Blossom Clinic'* is promoted to first track after the intro with newly restored strings and the very first version of *'Fire Brigade'* is promoted to track 3. Tracks 2–4 on the album originally released become tracks 4–6 but are taken from an Advision Studios session on 23 March, 1967. *'Don't Throw Stones at Me'*, a Detroit sound Tamla-inspired number is restored as track 7. *'Mist on a Monday Morning'* rises 4 places to #8, a 19th December acoustic version by Roy Wood, strings, flute and harpsichord. *'Vote for Me'* is included as is *'Night of Fear'*. An alternate take on *'The Girl Outside'* is track 13, an original stereo mix of *'Walk Upon the Water'* from January, 1967 is lower down the order at 14 while *'Useless Information'* and *'Flowers in the Rain'* conclude this fascinating re-conceptualisation, the latter recorded on 6 July, 1967 and found in a forgotten tape vault near London Bridge railway station.

What marked The Move apart from most groups of the time was their fascination with uncomfortable subject matter, danger, nightmares, mental illness, paranoia with songs' lyrics sometimes reading a bit like a horror novel. They seemed to live on the edge and bass player Chris 'Ace' Kefford, a Syd Barrett figure who dabbled in acid, was nicknamed 'The Singing Skull' by pop writer Nik Cohn for his habit of chewing endlessly on gum with a bored expression on his face. The drummer Bev Bevan would give Keith Moon of The Who a run for his money in beating the living daylights out of his kit and once said to Mark Paytress that "To this day, no one believes that Roy didn't take drugs. Once in a while, we'd lock him in a hotel room with a bottle of vodka and say, write a new single!"

The relevance to 1967 of an album not released until the spring of 1968 might raise a few eyebrows but as Mark Paytress says in his concluding liner notes to the Salvo two CD set: "Bev Bevan says the album was far too late in coming out and he's probably right. By spring '68, the pop scene had changed dramatically, with a discernible gap appearing between 'singles and 'albums' artists. Groups such as The Small Faces, The Herd and The Move found themselves caught awkwardly between the two. For a songwriter such as Roy Wood, who was already being pulled in several directions, and a band as quirkily individual as The Move, that would present huge problems over the next couple of years."

Nevertheless, the group went on to produce some very creditable singles like *'Blackberry Way'* (#1, 1968); *'Brontosaurus'* (#7, 1970) and *'California Man'* (1972). ELO was on the horizon and, tellingly, the B-side of *'California Man'*, Jeff Lynne's *'Do Ya'* would become part of the ELO repertoire. *'Shazam'* was a strong second album even if it didn't sell that well and Lynne had joined the group in time to record the **'Looking On'** and **'Message from the Country'** albums in 1971 and 1972.

The dilemma in which The Move found themselves in 1967 is well put by Mark Paytress: "When it came to finishing their much delayed debut album, **Sergeant Pepper** had changed everything, and no one – not least a bunch of Tamla enthusiasts decked out in floral shirts – quite knew which way to turn."

## The Nice

The Nice in 1967: *'Thoughts of Emerlist Davjack/ Angel of Death'* (Immediate 45) ****/****; 'Thoughts of Emerlist Davjack' (Immediate LP) ****

THE MUSICIANS: Keith Emerson (Organ, Piano, Harpsichord, Vocals); Lee Jackson (Bass, Vocals); David O'List (Guitar, Trumpet, Flute, Vocals) and Brian Davison (Drums, Timpani, Bells) reverting to a 3 piece without O'List.

**RECOMMENDED RELEASES/ COLLECTING:** 'The Thoughts of Emerlist Davjack' was reissued, in gatefold sleeve, by Let Them Eat Vinyl in 2014. The Nice was a big selling band, and shouldn't be too difficult to find on LP and, if you want bonus tracks, CD. Personally (and straying beyond 1967), while **'The Thoughts'** should not be missed, I think **'Ars Longa, Vita Brevis', 'The Nice', 'Elegy'** and **'Five Bridges'** are all essential listening. As far as CDs go **'The Swedish Radio Sessions'** (2001, Castle Music) and **'Live at the Fillmore East, December, 1969'** (2009. EMI) are not to be missed. It is very difficult to find a copy of their single in excellent to mint condition and a picture sleeve German pressing will cost around £50 in VG+ condition. LPs tend to be readily available at record fairs and not too expensive.

## The Musical History:

Fronted by Keith Emerson, brandy imbibing, leather clad virtuoso, who repaid the complement of inspiration (JS Bach, Lionel Hampton, Thelonious Monk, Dave Brubeck and Jimmy Smith) by, in his own inimitable style, inspiring countless others to push keyboards to centre stage. Classically trained as a child, Emerson cut his teeth with British blues band Gary and the T-Bones in the mid-60s but it was as member of the **VIPs** (who evolved into Spooky Tooth) that he first attacked his Hammond C-100 with knives while on tour in France and Germany.

The Nice were arguably the first true 'proto' prog band with an insistent neoclassicism and plundering of modern folk music (Bob Dylan and Tim Hardin), jazz and blues with impunity and equanimity. The group played their first gig backing **P.P. Arnold** at the Windsor Jazz and Blues Festival in a 30-minute spot which included Arnold's hit song **'The First Cut is the Deepest'**. Next stop was the famous Marquee Club in Soho, London where the group unleashed their version of The Beatles' **'A Day in the Life'** on an unsuspecting audience.

The Nice's first album for Immediate Records **'The Thoughts of Emerlist Davjack'** was released in December, 1967, featuring a line-up of Emerson, Davy O'List on guitar (O'List would 'sub' for Syd Barrett in Pink Floyd when he was incapacitated and was a member of The Attack and once mooted for a spot in John Mayall's Bluesbreakers) but his 'psychedelic noodling' guitar style sat uneasily with Emerson's increasing virtuosity and he left after just one LP. [86] **Brian 'Blinky'** (after renowned jazz drummer Art Blakey) **Davison**, an excellent drummer in the jazz style, the replacement for Ian Hague during the PP Arnold days, and the Newcastle 'Geordie' **Lee Jackson** [87] with his rather strained, but immediately recognisable vocals, completed the line-up.

The group's debut album was preceded by a single with the LP title track on the A side and **'Azrial' (Angel of Death)** on the flip, a song that would be 'revisited' in fine, expanded form as the lead-off track on **'The Nice'** LP in 1969. Keith Emerson recalls that he "created **Azrael**, a heavy 5/4 motif that melted into Rachmaninoff changes from his prelude in C# minor. Lee wrote the lyrics based on the mythical personification of the Grim Reaper, otherwise referred to as the Angel of Death." Rachmaninoff's prelude itself dealt with most people's ultimate fear of struggling to get out of a coffin after being buried alive – cheery stuff!

---

[86] Later, in 1971, he became Phil Manzanera's successor as Roxy Music guitarist. He had actually been Bryan Ferry's original choice for his group.
[87] Like Davison with his Every Which Way, Jackson would go on to form his own band, Jackson Heights.

# Important Albums of 1967 (13)
## 'The Thoughts of Emerson Davjack' by The Nice

THE MUSICIANS: Keith Emerson (Organ, Piano, Harpsichord, Vocals); Davy O' List (Guitar, Trumpet, Flute, Vocals); Lee Jackson (Vocals, Bass, Guitar, Timpani); Brian Davison (Drums, Tubular Bells, Timpani) with Bill Nicholls (Harmony Vocals on the title track); PRODUCER: Group; COVER DESIGN: Derek Burton, Gered Mankowitz; LABEL: Immediate; DATE: December, 1967; CHART: Did not chart.

## Tracklist/Credits

| | | |
|---|---|---|
| 1. | Flower King of Flies (Keith Emerson/ Lee Jackson) | 3:56 |
| 2. | The Thoughts of Emerlist Davjack (Keith Emerson, Davy O'List) | 2:47 |
| 3. | Bonnie K (Lee Jackson, Davy O' List) | 3:22 |
| 4. | Rondo (Dave Brubeck arranged by group) | 8:25 |
| 5. | War and Peace (Group) | 5:13 |
| 6. | Tantalising Maggie (Keith Emerson, Lee Jackson) | 4:30 |
| 7. | Dawn (Brian Davison, Keith Emerson, Lee Jackson) | 5:07 |
| 8. | Cry of Eugene (Keith Emerson, Lee Jackson, Davy O'List) | 4:30 |

The album was named after a mythical figure which was, in fact, four parts or, more prosaically, on a suggestion by Andrew Oldham's accountant Tony Calder that it would be to the group's advantage to register all songs under one name, a practice later abandoned. **'The Thoughts'** part came from Lee Jackson's antipathy towards The Musician's Union and his habit of carrying Chairman Mao's 'Little Red Book' around with him. The album featured the group's first version of a Dave Brubeck piano piece *'Blue Rondo a La Turk'*, the opening track of his highly acclaimed and successful LP *'Time Out'* released in 1959. The 9/8 rhythms are translated into 4/4 to suit the rock genre, and the mid 'blues' section of the piece is transformed from swing blues with piano and sax (Paul Desmond on the original) to what Ed Macan describes as "a throbbing, hypnotic drone in 4/4 iterated in a 'galloping' 8th-16th-16th-note pattern." Instead of piano and sax solos, we have guitar, then organ incorporating a snatch of JS Bach's *'Toccata and Fugue in D Minor'*. "At this time, only one other rock musician, Jimi Hendrix, was soloing at this level of virtuosity," says Macan.(57) This was the first Nice track that Emerson pronounced himself satisfied with and was to become a concert favourite and revived as *'Rondo '69'* on **'The Nice'** album. Of The Nice's first recording adventure as a whole, Macan says that the album is "a classic of British psychedelic rock, all the more impressive for being the creation of a group that had been together not quite five months when it was recorded. About the worst that can be said is that some of its tracks are products of their period, and while exemplifying the music of the period well enough, fail to transcend it. This is especially true of the title track and *'Flower King of Flies'*, both of which can be described as flower-power anthems that owe something to The Beatles circa 1966–67."(58) [88] with some slight abridgement.

---

[88] Macan bases The Beatles comparison in the case of *'The Thoughts of Emerlist Davjack'* on its similarity to *'Penny Lane'*, "with its cheerful rock march rhythm and Brandenburg

The authors of **'Emerson, Lake and Palmer: The Show That Never Ends'** share Macan's view on the importance of the Nice's first album saying that "this ground-breaking album would exert a major influence on the flood of European heavy rock and progressive bands that would emerge in the 1970s." **(59)**

The third track on the album was **'Bonnie K'**, a new breed of distorted and feedback psych R&B to some ears that owed much to the Memphis Stax sound. **'War and Peace'** was based on an unreleased T-Bones recording and lurches between 12-bar and a more baroque style. **'Tantalising Maggie'** is another fusion of blues and baroque while *'The Cry of Eugene'* and **'Dawn'** are also mature pieces for the time, the former rightly described by Ed Macan as a "flower-power anthem that transcends its period, the latter predating the captivating organ riffs that would emerge in full force on tracks like *'Knife-Edge'* with **Emerson, Lake and Palmer**. The effects used and whispered Emerson vocal on 'dawn' give it an air of mystery that verges on 'musique concrète'." **(60)**

1967 was also a seminal year for the development of popular music and The Nice in particular in other ways. Apart from their intensive British touring, they embarked on an immediate package tour of Europe from 6th to 20th October billed alongside P P Arnold, Chris Farlowe and The Small Faces, and a recording of The Nice's performance in Stockholm was released in 2001 by Sanctuary Records. The numbers captured on tape for posterity were: Bob Dylan's **'She Belongs to Me'** (which would not be recorded on album until 1969), interesting for O'List's edgy guitar; a version of **'Flower King of Flies'** that is heavier than the studio one; a rocked-up cover of The Charles Lloyd Quartet's. [89] **'Sombrero Sam'**; a sloppy, overlong version of The Supremes' *'You Keep Me Hanging On'* done Vanilla Fudge style; a short and snappy **'Thoughts of Emerlist Davjack'** and a triumphant 12-minute version of *'Rondo'* to end.

The Jimi Hendrix Package Tour opened at London's Royal Albert Hall in November, and on the bill were The Amen Corner, The Move, Pink Floyd and The Nice, all for the equivalent of 75p! Our story stops in 1967 but many fine, if eclectic, records followed: an irreverent rendition of Leonard Bernstein's *'America'* from West Side Story nearly made the UK top 20 and was a prelude to the highly successful **'Ars Longa Vita Brevis'** album. **'The Nice'** LP, one side studio, one side live, was their most successful yet reaching #3 in the UK. 1970's **'Five Bridges Suite'**, partly, a live recording of a concept work on the five bridges that crossed the River Tyne at that point in time and partly a studio album, that while critically panned by some at the time, was even more successful going one place higher. **'Elegy'** was a posthumous album, released the year after they split up but a worthwhile rounding off.

I have a soft spot for The Nice for they were the first group I saw live, and they made an enormous impression on me (Emerson in particular) in wanting to develop my own keyboard skills and my own music. They were truly pioneers of 'classical rock' (and much more besides) in much the same way as The Moody Blues might be considered the pioneers of 'symphonic rock'. The mighty supergroup Emerson, Lake and Palmer brought the whole project to an end in 1970 but not before The Nice made a major impact on the development of sixties music.

---

Concerto-style obligato, played by Davy O'List and in the case of **'Flower King of Flies'** with discerned 'wisps' of the chorus to **'Lucy in the Sky with Diamonds'**." O'List sang his only lead vocal on **'Thoughts'**. It should be noted that the album was released in the UK in December, 1967 but not until 1st March, 1968 in the US after the group had completed its US tour.

[89] Flautist Lloyd's Quartet with Keith Jarrett on piano went down very well at the 1966 Monterey Jazz Festival.

# Pink Floyd

**Pink Floyd in 1967:** 'Arnold Layne' (March, Columbia 45 #20) \*\*\*\*; 'See Emily Play' (June, Columbia 45 #6) \*\*\*\*\*; 'Apples and Oranges' (November, Columbia 45) \*\*\*; 'The Piper at the Gates of Dawn' (August, Columbia LP) \*\*\*\*

**THE MUSICIANS:** Syd Barrett then Dave Gilmour (Guitar/ Vocals); Roger Waters (Bass/ Vocals); Richard Wright (Keyboards); Nick Mason (Drums, Timpani, Percussion)

**RECOMMENDED LISTENING/ COLLECTING:** Pink Floyd has been comprehensively reissued, remastered and recompiled with new vinyl releases continuing to appear in 2016. Probably best listened to on vinyl, early pristine copies will set you back a bit but there are plenty of alternatives. It is best to look at Discogs or Music Stack or read Record Collector magazine to keep up-to-date. Pink Floyd 45s can easily run towards £100 with *'Apples and Oranges'* (Columbia, 1967) and *'Point Me at the Sky'* and *'It Would Be So Nice'* (Columbia, 1968) the priciest. Even *'See Emily Play'* (Columbia, 1967) will probably cost £50 in excellent shape. The figures become quite mind-boggling when considering their LPs: a first pressing of **'The Piper at the Gates of Dawn'** mono copy (Columbia, 1967) will likely figure in auctions and specialist shops, and command prices well in excess of £500, stereo £300+. It is a similar story with second LP **'A Saucerful of Secrets'** (Columbia, 1968). Most Pink Floyd records are highly desired by collectors with first pressings of **'Dark Side of the Moon'** complete with two posters and stickers commanding £500 upwards. Even as late as 1975 **'Wish You Were Here'** sealed copy originals would be around £200. Much more recently those who bought **'Pulse'** in a four LP box with book, at a time when vinyl was unfashionable, will find it is worth around £150. Although we have strayed way beyond our time zone, this serves as an illustration of how gigantic Pink Floyd is in terms of collecting, perhaps second only to The Beatles.

## The Musical History

The story of Pink Floyd has filled many, many volumes and, after The Beatles, they seem to be the most written about group. Why is that? Let's go back to 1967 to see. "A song about a fetishist whose 'strange hobby' involves stealing women's underwear,"**(61)** Pink Floyd's debut single *'Arnold Layne'* was released on 11th March, 1967. The Kinks and The Who were already dabbling with more outlandish lyrical ideas as well as blazing a trail for quirkily English bands. The music employed a woozy, merry-go-round rhythm, with (Syd) Barrett's vocals sounding defiantly English. Bordering on deadpan, it is Richard Wright's Farfisa organ that provides the clearest link to psychedelia, splashing colour in place of a traditional guitar solo, and dominating the song.(62) *'Arnold Layne'* was banned by the BBC, who also had difficulty with its B-side *'Let's Roll Another One'* which was hastily retitled *'Candy and a Currant Bun'* (!) but eventually, made #20 in the UK, not bad for a debut, and a strange one at that! At the time Pink Floyd, named after two relatively obscure bluesmen Pink Anderson and Floyd Council, were the resident band at London's UFO Club. Nick Mason does a pretty good period piece on the founding of the group and their early days in his entertaining book '**Inside Out: A Personal History of Pink Floyd'** published in paperback a couple of months after the surprise one-off reunion for the Live 8 concert at Hyde Park on 2nd July, 2005. It certainly doesn't seem fifteen years since I sat down with a beer or two to watch the live feed of this momentous occasion on TV!

Mason's chronology of 1967 is interesting listing the recordings released by the group and Pink Floyd gigs that year and referring to the police raid on Keith Richards'

Redlands home in February; the release of The Jimi Hendrix Experience's '*Purple Haze*' 45 on 17th March; Procol Harum's '*A Whiter Shade of Pale*' topping the charts in May; The Beatles **'Sergeant Pepper's Lonely Hearts Club Band'** topping the album charts in June (of course!); the Monterey International Pop Festival on 16th–18th June; the first automated cash machine (was it really that long ago?); the National Jazz and Blues Festival in Windsor on 12th August; the launch of BBC Radio 1 (30th September); the killing of Che Guevara on 3rd November; Pink Floyd's first (ill-fated) tour of the US in November; the first issue of 'Rolling Stone' magazine the same month (still going strong!); and, perhaps most significant for Pink Floyd historians, the Apollo 8 astronauts becoming the first to see the dark side of the moon on Christmas eve. Some of these events were very near but others very far to the Regent Street Polytechnic in Little Titchfield Street, just off Oxford Street, where Nick (brought up on an early musical diet of Bill Haley and Elvis Presley), Roger Waters and Richard Wright were in the first year of an architecture course.

Rick Wright had been brought up in Hatch End, just outside London, and was a trad jazz and R&B fan going to see the likes of Humphrey Lyttelton and Cyril Davies at the Railway Tavern in Harrow. Roger Waters' early musical influences included Bob Dylan's '*Sad Eyed Lady of the Lowlands*' which he saw as a radical departure from the norm of three to four minute songs: He is also on record as saying that he had to pull his Zephyr 4 car over to the lay by when hearing **'Sergeant Pepper'** as he was so amazed at the staggering wealth of ideas, opening up possibilities far removed from reliance on Tin Pan Alley songwriters. Syd (born Roger Keith) Barrett arrived from Cambridge to study at Camberwell Art College, having studied art at Cambridge Technical College where he would have musical jams with David Gilmour. Barrett considered himself first and foremost to be a painter, and one of his drawings can be seen on the back of Pink Floyd's first LP **'The Piper at the Gates of Dawn'.** We know that he had albums by Pink Anderson and Floyd Council in his collection, and that he was in various local R&B groups (including The Abdabs with Waters) before he became a founding member of Pink Floyd (or The Pink Floyd Sound to be precise). His main early guitar heroes were Booker T's Steve Cropper and Bo Diddley.

On 12th May, 1967, Pink Floyd premiered what was to be their next 45, then called '*Games for May*' at a concert in London's newly opened Queen Elizabeth Hall on the South Bank. '*See Emily Play*' was finally released on 16 June, 1967 to enthusiastic response from the New Musical Express: "It's full of weird oscillations, reverberations, electronic vibrations, fuzzy rumblings and appealing harmonies," the reviewer commented. Mark Blake reflects that '*See Emily Play*' was "the perfect amalgam of psychedelic excess and pure pop, brighter than '*Arnold Layne*' on all levels, but with just enough of Wright's spooked-sounding keyboards and Syd's fey, disengaged vocals to prevent a complete slip into easy listening pop."(63) At the time that **'See *Emily Play*'** was making an impact, Barrett's addictions and health problems were peaking and he appeared to some as 'completely off his head', and BBC's 'Top of the Pops' performances capture his deterioration. Barrett had always seemed an unstable and otherworldly individual, and things came to a head during the group's first US tour as, on TV appearances such as Dick Clark's Bandstand and The Pat Boone Show, Syd simply could not function, when it came to singing and answering questions as he seemed constantly spaced out. By December, 1967, Barrett's intake of LSD [90] was such that his mental state had deteriorated to the extent that the other group members felt impelled to

---

[90] Despite the deceptively cheery title, the lyrics of the song were eerie, if not schizophrenic: "It's clear that I am not here and I'm wondering who could be writing this song."

bring in an old friend from Cambridge, **David Gilmour**, to leave his current group Joker's Wild to play guitar. Richard Wright later described Gilmour as "much more of a blues guitarist". **(64)**

Syd hung around for a little longer playing his final gig with them, at Hastings Pier, Sussex on 18th January, 1968, as the group continued as a five piece and he contributed '*Jugband Blues*' [91] to Pink Floyd's second LP '**A Saucerful of Secrets**' before going on to release solo albums like '**The Madcap Laughs**'. He lived as a bit of a recluse in Cambridge indulging in his passions of art and gardening, briefly appearing in the studio during the recording of Pink Floyd's '*Wish You Were Here*' album [92] before passing, aged 60, in 2006. Rick Wright would pass two years later. Dave Gilmour and Roger Waters are, at the time of writing, still recording.

## Important Albums of 1967 (14)

## The Piper at the Gates of Dawn by Pink Floyd

MUSICIANS: Syd Barrett (Guitar, Vocals); Rick Wright (Organ, Piano); Roger Waters (Bass, Vocals); Nick Mason (Drums); PRODUCER: Norman Smith; ENGINEER: Peter Bown; SLEEVE DESIGN: Vic Singh (Front photograph), Syd Barrett (Rear); RELEASE DATE: 5th August, 1967; LABEL: Columbia; CHART: #6 (UK); #131 (US Billboard)

## Tracklisting/ Writing Credits

1.  **Astronomy Domine (Syd Barrett) 4:10**
2.  **Lucifer Sam (Syd Barrett) 3:08**
3.  **Matilda Mother (Syd Barrett) 3:10**
4.  **Flaming (Syd Barrett) 2:45**
5.  **Pow R Toc H (Syd Barrett/ Rick Wright/ Roger Waters/ Nick Mason) 4:25**
6.  **Take Up Thy Stethoscope and Walk (Roger Waters) 3:05**
7.  **Interstellar Overdrive (Syd Barrett/ Rick Wright/ Roger Waters/ Nick Mason) 9:40**
8.  **The Gnome (Syd Barrett) 2:15**
9.  **Chapter 24 (Syd Barrett) 3:40**
10. **The Scarecrow (Syd Barrett) 2:10**
11. **Bike (Syd Barrett) 3:20**

## The Music

Sessions for what would become Pink Floyd's first album '**The Piper at the Gates of Dawn**' began in January, 1967 in Abbey Road's Studio Three, with The Beatles occasionally next door in Studio Two working on '**Sergeant Pepper**'. The album can

---

[91] Two numbers '*Vegetable Man*' and '*Scream Thy Last Scream*' were declined for being too 'dark', the former eventually achieving cult status, and being covered by Jesus and the Mary Chain.

[92] The songs '*Shine on You Crazy Diamond*' and '*Wish You Were Here*' were written specifically with Syd in mind.

truly be described as an authentic early piece of acid rock in the most literal of senses. "Most of the songs on **Piper** had been written during a concerted burst of creativity when (Syd) Barrett was living in an apartment on Earlham Street in central London. In the recollection of his flat-mate, the group's lighting technician Peter Wynne-Wilson 'Those were halcyon days. He (Syd) would sit around with copious amounts of hash and grass and write these incredible songs." **(65)** Steve Huey in the All Music Guide, rankingthe album as one of the best psychedelic albums of all time, said it, "successfully captures both sides of psychedelic experimentation – the pleasures of expanding one's mind and perception, and an underlying threat of mental disorder and even lunacy" **(66)**

"A kaleidoscopic trawl through the various talismans of the era **The Piper at the Gates of Dawn** was split between Syd Barrett's bedtime tales of kings, gnomes and scarecrows and the epic *Interstellar Overdrive.*"**(67)** (The free-form instrumental to which Hoey refers was the kind of long 'space rock' creation that constituted most of Pink Floyd's live performances in the early days).

Kenneth Graham's famous book, '**The Wind in the Willows'**, in which the 'piper at the gates of dawn' appeared, provided the album title.

It was big advantage for the group to be recording in Abbey Road with its wide selection of keyboard and percussion instruments and a sound-effects library. As Mark Blake points out, "With Peter Jenner reciting astronomical co-ordinates from a children's book of the planets through a megaphone and Roger Waters' primitive bass runs, it sounded like pop art and science fiction condensed into a rock song."**(68)** , the number became a staple in live sets. Space as subject matter was, of course, nothing new. The Tornadoes had a big hit five years before with Joe Meek's *'Telstar'* and, in the following year with Meek's *'Robot/ Life on Venus'*.

*Interstellar Overdrive* was based around a straightforward Barrett riff, and could extend to 20 minutes live but is only 9:40 on the album. The Who's Pete Townshend was disappointed at the time that the album failed to capture Floyd's live sound and you could see his point as most songs were in the 2 to 4 minute bracket As Dave Thompson and others have pointed out Floyd were already well versed in "extending and extemporising on sundry themes' (the likes of Junior Walker and the Allstars *'Roadrunner')*"**(69)** and *'Interstellar Overdrive'* itself may well qualify as a development of brass roots rock 'n' roll and beat music or as Thompson puts it, "They were still turning out traditional R&B, but it has mutated even further, and so skilfully that the transition from the standard *'Cops and Robbers'* to *'Interstellar Overdrive'* was barely noticeable."**(70)** [93]

Most of the tracks were written by Barrett with *Chapter 24* taking the I Ching as its subject matter and *The Scarecrow* widely considered to have been influenced by The Incredible String Band. The exceptions were the intriguingly entitled *Pow R Toc H* which was, like *Astronomy Domine* and *Interstellar Overdrive,* a group composed instrumental, and *Take Up Thy Stethoscope and Walk'*, the first Waters' composition to make an album, the references to madness and the howling to be revisited later on '**Dark Side of the Moon'**. The catchiest song was *Bike*, a fanciful ditty not just about a bike but also other 'gifts' including a pet mouse called Gerald.

---

[93] EMI A&R man Norman Smith (who later released records under the name Hurricane Smith) decided not to replicate the group's sprawling live sound for commercial reasons. Thus there was less improvisation than usual on an album which was crafted over three months next door to The Beatles recording '**Sergeant Pepper'**.

The US would have to wait until October for an official release with a different track listing and running order omitting certain songs like '*Bike*' and inserting '*See Emily Play*'.

## The 14 Hour Technicolor Dream

This seems as good a point as any, as Pink Floyd is most closely associated with the event, to mention 'The 14 Hour Technicolor Dream'. One of the most comprehensive articles I have seen on the subject can be read in the re-launch issue of 'Shindig!' This article is particularly interesting as it sets the event in the context of the 'scene' at the time. Musically, this means that the pioneering jazz of Chris Barber, Ken Colyer and Humphrey Lyttelton had become 'passé and labelled' trad jazz', in stark contrast with the daring, expansive approach of American artists like John Coltrane and reflected in the changing roster of talent on show at Ronnie Scott's famous Soho club.

Also the folk traditionalists were being regarded as 'stuffy' as the concert going and record listening public cried out for more experimentation and got that, to a degree, in the 'neu-folk' of Donovan, Davy Graham ("adding flamenco, ragas, gospel and post-bop jazz") and Bert Jansch.**(71)** The ultimate manifestation of this would come in Bob Dylan's 'electric conversion', witnessed by many at the Royal Albert Hall, which sent shock waves through the folk world, alienating the 'purists' but exciting those who saw traditional folk as something of a 'private members' club'. Those not present to see Dylan's conversion live could listen to it on the 'Highway 61 Revisited' album. Finally, this was the time of beat poetry (and the 'sixties modern poets'), 'performance art' (the Indica Gallery, for example) and drug experimentation with The Beatles at its epicentre. And so it was that the Indica became a gathering place for the 'underground'. As Dellar puts it, "International Times – or – *I T*, as it was universally known – became the notice – board and rant line for all those caught up in the currents and eddies sweeping through the city's underbelly."**(72))**. The benefit gig that took place at the Alexandra Palace (or the Ally Pally as it was affectionately known) was organised for 'I.T.' following a police bust in April.

Those rumoured to play but who did not include The Beatles, The Who, The Mothers of Invention and The Velvet Underground. Those who did appear included: The Exploding Galaxy Dancers, Arthur Brown and his Crazy World, The Pretty Things, The Soft Machine, The Purple Gang, Champion Jack Dupree, Alexis Korner and, of course, Pink Floyd, part of whose 5 a.m. set, features in Peter Whitehead's **'Let's All Make Love in London'**. The famous photograph of 'revellers' crashing out among the detritus on the floor sums up, the end of the 'hippy dream', confirmation that the revolution had not started and that the Technicolor Dream was a mere symbol and that reality rapidly kicked in, the dark underbelly exposed as 700 tickets were stolen prior to the event, people without tickets stormed the door, most of the takings disappeared (the popular view is that it was 'liberated' by Malcolm X) and the venue was never paid for the hire!

What lay ahead for Pink Floyd was the ground-breaking album **'A Saucerful of Secrets'**[94], the title track itself having already been conceived in 1967; and future classics like **'Dark Side of the Moon'**, **'Wish You Were Here'** and **'The Wall'**, not to mention my own personal favourites '**Atom Heart Mother'**, '**Meddle'** and '**Animals'**.

---

[94] Klaus Schulze, famous for his work with Tangerine Dream and as a solo artist, nominated **'A Saucerful of Secrets'** in the 'Last Night a Record Changed My Life' section of MOJO magazine. Schulze enjoyed the abstractness and expansiveness of the music.

# The Pretty Things

The Pretty Things in 1967: 'Children/ My Time (April, Fontana 45) ****; 'Defecting Grey/ Mr. Evasion' (November, Columbia 45) *****/****; 'Emotions' LP (May, Fontana LP) *** (key tracks: 'Death of a Socialite'; 'Children'; 'The Sun'; 'There Will Never Be Another Day'; 'One Long Glance'; 'Photographer'; 'My Time')

THE MUSICIANS: Original line-up: **Phil May (Vocals), Dick Taylor (Lead Guitar), Brian Pendleton (Rhythm Guitar), John Stax (Bass), Viv Prince (Drums)**

RECOMMENDED RELEASES/ COLLECTING: The Pretty Things' 1967 album **'Emotions'** was released on 180-gram mono LP in 2015 by Madfish Records. A remastered CD edition with 11 bonus including singles was released on Repertoire in 2002 as **The Collectible Pretty Things.** The 45s are pretty expensive, the Dutch picture sleeve copy of *'Defecting Grey'* selling for well over £100. The last time I looked there was only one copy of the 45 for sale on Discogs costing around £50 and only in Good+ condition. You might be able to track down a German picture sleeve of *'Death of A Socialite/ Photographer'* for around £30 in near mint condition. The Spanish picture sleeve edition of *'Come See Me/ L.S.D./ Children/ My Time'* does appear on Discogs occasionally but costs a small fortune in decent condition (as much as £150). The June, 1967 *'Road Runner' EP* is a Yugoslavian release in picture sleeve with a price tag of around £15 in decent, playable condition. There was also a '45' released in Holland, *My Time/ Trippin'* which occasionally appears for sale at around £50. The Spanish *'A House in The Country/ Me Needing You'* picture sleeve 4 track EP is usually valued around £100 in near mint condition. Remastered CDs or reissued LPs seem to be the best option unless you are a serious collector.

## The Musical History:

In 1967 The Pretty Things were in a state of transition, with membership changes, and uncertainty about the future. As Mark Andrews, writing in 'Progression' magazine, put it, "they were struggling commercially and floundering for direction musically. The R&B movement that had spawned them three years earlier had all but faded, and the band was considered by many to be a spent force." **(73)**

However, as Mike Stax, the editor of Ugly Things magazine, relates in the liner notes to the Snapper reissue of The Pretty Things' 1967 album **'Emotions'**, rightly states: **"Emotions** has undergone something of a critical re-evaluation". **(74) Wally Waller**, who had been brought into the group in 1967 to replace the departed bass player John Stax, and had written the highly regarded song *'Rejected'* for his previous group The Fenmen, told 'Shindig' magazine, "I am not sure I have any vivid memories from the **Emotions** sessions, but if you pressed me, I would have to say it was listening in utter disbelief at the sheer inappropriateness of most of the orchestral arrangements." **(75)** I spoke to Wally myself in 2016 when he said, "Almost overnight, everyone decided it was cool to use orchestrations on things. Fontana (Phonogram) decided to impose some orchestrations 'Emotions' but to my mind it was no 'magic bullet', it was, instead, an unmitigated disaster." So we are left to reflect on what might have been and a re-evaluation of the good intentions on the album certainly vindicates 'Emotions'as an interesting and important album of 1967.

**THE MUSICIANS: Phil May (Vocals); Dick Taylor (Lead Guitar); Brian Pendleton (Rhythm Guitar – quit during sessions); Wally Waller (Bass, Vocals); John Stax (Bass – quit during sessions); Skip Allan or Joe Povey (Drums) with guest players on saxes, cello, trombones, trumpet, double bass. CONDUCTOR: Reg Tilsley; PRODUCER: Steve Rowland; DATE: 18 April, 1967; LABEL: Fontana**

## The Music Track by Track

1. **'Death of a Socialite'**, a step forward in song writing, the West coast American influence, especially Love, can be heard and the brass 'parps' add an idiosyncratic touch – the phased drumming is nice too;
2. **'Children'**, a salutary tale of inappropriate play and growing up;
3. **'The Sun'**, a psych song with strings;
4. **'There Will Never Be Another Day'**, a return to R&B roots, forcefully done with drug references;
5. **'House of Ten'**, introduced by piano and syrupy strings, an odd but well delivered little song;
6. **'Out in The Night'** is unremarkable and over produced;
7. **'One Long Glance'** as it should be with rasping guitar and diverse multi-part vocal harmonies and a marvellous, all too short, coda;
8. **'Growing in My Mind'**, one of the best psych tracks;
9. **'Photographer'** could easily have provided them with a hit, great drumming from Skip Allan and neat little piano break depicting the seedy side of London;
10. **'Bright Lights of the City'** has a measured vocal performance by Phil May with some West Coast influence (although the brass is a bit suffocating sitting uneasily alongside the guitar strumming);
11. **'Tripping'**, a snarling Mick Jagger type delivery, basic group format, Dick Taylor's guitar to the fore, back to roots, not about going on holiday;
12. **'My Time'**, the strongest song on the album in this writer's humble opinion, perhaps the snatches of harp and brass may seem a bit 'James Bond' but the breathless emotion of the song is not lost, it would have been better done acoustically but still;
13. **'A House in The Country'**, a Ray Davies song (see The Kinks), typical Davies' cynicism about the 'upwardly mobile' or just plain corrupt, a good version with a nice 'retro' guitar break and;
14. **'Progress'**, another cover, distant sounding, subdued and unconvincing. Why try to drown the guitar break with brass?

## More on the Music

Hailing from Kent, England, The Pretty Things took their name from a Bo Diddley song and began life with an aspiration to be a dirtier, grittier version of The Rolling Stones. Hell-raising seemed part of the image although as with John Mayall, there was discipline as well as original drummer Viv Prince paid the price by getting sacked for being thrown off a plane during an Australasian tour. They hit the group running with a top 50 hit *'Rosalyn'* backed by *'Big Boss Man'*, which would also be covered by The

Grateful Dead on their debut LP in 1967 and by Elvis Presley in the same year. This was accompanied by a self-titled debut album, also in 1964, which made the top 50 album chart. (Two further LPs in 1965 and 1966 fared less well) *'Don't Let Me Down'* gave the group their only top 10 hit, in 1964 while *'Honey, I Need'* reached #13 the following year. Four further top 50 records followed, the last of them being a cover of Ray Davies' *'House in the Country'* with the B-side of their *Come See Me'* '45 *('LSD')* signalling times ahead.

Once their contract with Fontana Records was exhausted they struck a deal with EMI and teamed up with Norman Smith, who had produced The Pink Floyd's debut album **'The Piper at the Gates of Dawn'**. Things got off to a great start with a 45, *'Defecting Grey'*, released in November, 1967. Lenny Helsing is not alone in considering *'Defecting Grey'* to be "a four-minute all-encompassing 'tour de force' and possibly the greatest Brit psych 45 of all time."(76) [95] Mike Stax, who also waxed lyrical about the "extraordinary creation" that was *'Defecting Grey'*, with its shifting moods, "swirling" sitar passages and "storming pedal-to-the-metal fuzz-wah breaks", is also correct in pointing out the longevity of the band right up to 'Balboa Island' (2007), their eleventh studio album to that point. (77) Perhaps there was just too much in it to impact on the record buying public as it failed to chart, another one that 'got away'. Its B-side *'Mr Evasion'* has attracted similarly favourable comment for its acerbic vocals and harmonies, fuzz guitar and strident rock beat. Another 45 *'Turn My Head'* was recorded but shelved. The brilliant **'S.F. Sorrow'** and **'Parachute'** albums were still to come but that is another story.

## Procol Harum

**Procol Harum in 1967: 'A Whiter Shade of Pale' (Deram, May, #1 UK; A&M, #5 US) *****; 'Homburg' (Regal Zonophone, September #6 UK; #34 US) *****; 'Procol Harum (US version with the two 45s, A&M, September, #47) *****; 'Procol Harum' (UK version, Regal Zonophone, December) *****

THE MUSICIANS:** Perhaps the most famous line-up: **Gary Brooker (Piano, Vocals), Matthew Fisher (Organ), Chris Copping (Bass), Robin Trower (Guitar), B J Wilson (Drums)** (See below for the whole story)

## Recommended Listening/ Collecting:

Procol Harum vinyl is not hard to find although copies of early originals may command a significant price. There are loads of compilations and some good CD reissues most recently on Salvo and Esoteric. Their first four albums are, in my humble opinion, bona fide classics compiled together on a West Side box set with bonuses and rarities. Their 45s don't attract much value as they sold well and it is their LPs that are collectible: their most valuable album being the mono edition of **'Shine On Brightly'**. An original copy of their 1967 LP may also change hands for £100 or more. In fact, their first four albums are the most sought after.

---

[95] Helsing even went as far as to describe *'Strawberry Fields Forever'* and *'See Emily Play'* as 'relatively benign in comparison.'

# The Musical History: getting beyond 'A Whiter Shade of Pale'

To many people Procol Harum is synonymous with *'A Whiter Shade of Pale'*, with its strange, impressionistic lyrics, the subject of prolonged legal proceedings by Matthew Fisher on writing credits **(78)** and the most played record on radio in the past fifty years. Keith Reid, the group's lyricist, actually posted the lyrics to Gary Brooker, the group's talismanic vocalist, song writer and keyboard player then Brooker, heavily influenced by adaptations of the works of Johann Sebastian Bach by the Jacques Loussier Trio and The Swingle Sisters and the Bach pieces *'Air On a G String'* and *'Sleepers Awake'* in particular, worked on a melody. *A Whiter Shade of Pale'* while not unrepresentative of the group's canon does inadvertently create a misconception that kept the 'iceberg' (as a metaphor for Procol Harum as the most extraordinarily gifted and creative architect of albums that are among the finest of their period) submerged with only the 'tip' making its way into mass public consciousness the way their '45s' did. Listeners to local and popular radio stations hear only their first '45', its follow-up *'Homburg'* and successful '45s' like *'Conquistador'* and *'Pandora's Box'*. Clearly there was life after *'A Whiter Shade of Pale'* and to some, Procol Harum appear like Orson Welles in *'Citizen Kane'*, to have started at the top and then worked their way steadily downhill. As Rob Chapman put it, "It was the Citizen Kane Syndrome that did it. Reckoned by many to have put their most splendid eggs in their very first basket. Procol Harum, as Gary Brooker will admit, have rarely been in danger of hitting fashionability head on. And all because of THAT record."**(79)** In actual fact, in the decade between that landmark 1967 single and their split in 1977, Procol went on to record some stunning albums. In an interview with Gary Brooker for Acid Dragon magazine, Gary explained, "Sometimes people think about who they are going to appeal to but we never did that. The reason we cross over and are considered in the progressive rock genre is that we always wanted to progress our music. There was no such word as progressive rock at the time of *'Shine on Brightly.'* Also, "Perhaps there is a misconception, it's hard to be objective about Procol Harum because it all seems perfectly logical and perfectly reachable but I suppose you have to have an open musical mind to take that all in. Many groups wish they could have *'A Whiter Shade of Pale'* as their first record and suddenly be well known all over the world. It was so big that perhaps some people find it hard to get beyond it."**(80)**, Many people around the world did, though, and a sub-culture has grown up around Procol Harum. Its members even have a name – the Palers and a first class website.

Starting off life as The Paramounts in Southend-on-Sea, an area that became known as 'The Essex Delta', an hour from London, and boasting the longest pleasure pier in the world, Gary Brooker joined the group in 1961 and brought in more American influences like Little Richard, Fats Domino, Jerry Lee Lewis, and later Ray Charles, to the live mix. (Gary told me he always wanted to sing as well as Sam Cooke, The Everly Brothers or Elvis Presley). Brooker was studying botany and zoology at College, having left school at 16. The early Paramounts established a club in the cellars below The Penguin Café, owned by guitarist Robin Trower's father Len, and named it 'Shades'. Of huge significance was the presence of two jukeboxes in 'Shades', well stocked with R&B records, which particularly impressed The Rolling Stones' Brian Jones on a visit in 1963. Robin Trower recalled, "I was very lucky! Tony Wilkinson was importing all these records from Memphis. I was getting to hear all this stuff that just wasn't available in England." **(81)**

Robin Trower's main influences at the time were Cliff Gallup, Gene Vincent's guitarist, Scotty Moore, Elvis's guitarist, Bo Diddley, Chuck Berry and Booker T & The

MG's Steve Cropper. Brooker was actually born in Hackney London in 1945 and attended primary school in the Bush Hill Park area of Middlesex before the family moved to Southend-on-Sea in 1954. Robin Trower was also born in 1945, his family having an itinerant existence with moves to Canada and New Zealand before settling in Southend in 1952. Gary explained to me how The Paramounts came about, "I was in a group called The Coasters; Robin and Chris Copping were in The Raiders and all the local groups assembled to have a big band contest. I think we came second – we were an instrumental band, we had two guitarists and a piano and we played Les Paul songs, I was the only piano player there. Robin and Chris, the drummer from the winners Mickey Law and The Outlaws, Mick Brownlee and singer Bob Scott of The Clansmen were chosen as a 'supergroup' which would be called The Paramounts – literally the 'top band'. The original Paramounts line-up was completed by bass player Grahame 'Doz' Derrick but when he left to become a bricklayer to support his young family, Barrie James Wilson successfully came through the auditions as his replacement." **(82)** The Paramounts' path collided with The Rolling Stones through Bill Wyman, whose group at the time The Cliftons were on the same bill in July, 1962. A special bond developed between The Stones and The Paramounts a year later, on 5th September, at a gig at the Strand Palais Theatre in Walmer, Kent where a fight broke out between Marines and 'east end heavies'. The two groups also recorded the same song **Poison Ivy**, The Paramounts in 1963, The Stones leaving it until January, 1964 for inclusion on their first EP. The Paramounts went on to release six 45s between 1963 and 1965; and an EP in 1964 to varying levels of critical acclaim and little commercial success. Procol Harum chronicler Claes Johansen reckons that **Bad Blood \***, an interpretation of Charles Mingus's **Freedom** and their 45s backing Duffy Power, **Parchman Farm** and **Stupidity** are fine examples of Procol Harum's embryonic sound and Robin Trower's guitar on **Cuttin' In,** a 1965 B-side is a pointer to things to come from a precocious 19 year old. Another significant development was the de rigueur status of acoustic piano and rise of the electric guitar in popular music. The days of trad jazz were passing, the force of R&B was rising, and Gary Brooker's response was to buy a Hohner Clavinet electric piano.

Lacking a breakthrough single, The Paramounts found work backing Sandie Shaw and supporting The Beatles on their final tour of Britain in 1965. [96] Robin Trower left to back Chris Andrews, was replaced by Martin Shaw and the group gradually disintegrated. **Freedom** graphically illustrated the transition that would take place from The Paramounts to Procol Harum: Claes Johansen, in his book, 'Procol Harum:Beyond the Pale' points to a seminal moment in the band's history: "Recorded less than ten months before **A Whiter Shade of Pale**, **Freedom** is the one song that most clearly links The Paramounts with Procol Harum." Johansen elaborates on the organ and guitar solos, the recited lyrics and the ascending bass line that seemed to point an arrow forward to future masterpiece 'Whaling Stories'. **(83)**

I was privileged to attend the first night of a short 50th anniversary tour of the group in the early summer of 2017. As it proved Brooker's voice has stood the test of time better than many of his contemporaries as has the music with ' **A Salty Dog'** and **'Outside The Gates of Cerdes'** rubbing shoulders with new numbers from their recently released 'Novum' album.

---

[96] The song was banned by the BBC for a supposed reference to syphilis.

**MUSICIANS:** Gary Brooker (Vocals, Piano); Matthew Fisher (Hammond Organ); Robin Trower (Guitar); David Knights (Bass); B.J. Wilson (Drums); **LYRICS:** Keith Reid; **PRODUCER:** Denny Cordell; **LABEL:** Regal Zonophone (mono); Deram in the US; **RELEASE DATE:** September, 1967 (mono)

## Track Listing/ Credits: UK Version

| | | |
|---|---|---|
| 1. | Conquistador (Gary Brooker/ Keith Reid) | 2:42 |
| 2. | She Wandered Through The Garden Fence (Brooker/ Reid) | 3:30 |
| 3. | Something Following Me (Brooker/ Reid) | 3:40 |
| 4. | Mabel (Brooker/ Reid) | 1:55 |
| 5. | Cerdes (Outside The Gates Of) (Brooker/ Reid) | 5:05 |
| 6. | A Christmas Camel (Brooker/ Reid) | 4:55 |
| 7. | Kaleidoscope (Brooker/ Reid) | 2:58 |
| 8. | Salad Days (Are Here Again) (Brooker/ Reid) | 3:45 |
| 9. | Good Captain Clack (Brooker/ Reid) | 1:30 |
| 10. | Repent Walpurgis (Fisher) | 5:05 |

## US Version

| | | |
|---|---|---|
| 1. | A Whiter Shade of Pale (Gary Brooker/ Matthew Fisher/ Keith Reid) | 4:08 |
| 2. | She Wandered Through The Garden Fence (Brooker/ Reid) | 3:20 |
| 3. | Something Following Me (Brooker/ Reid) | 3:40 |
| 4. | Mabel (Brooker/ Reid) | 1:55 |
| 5. | Cerdes (Outside The Gates Of) (Brooker/ Reid) | 5:05 |
| 6. | A Christmas Camel (Brooker/ Reid) | 4:55 |
| 7. | Conquistador (Brooker/ Reid) | 2:38 |
| 8. | Kaleidoscope (Brooker/ Reid) / Salad Days (Are Here Again | 6:30 |
| 9. | Repent Walpurgis (Fisher) | 5:05 |

According to Ronald L. Smith on the 'Beyond the Pale' website Procol Harum's 1967 debut LP is heavily preoccupied with 'portraits of youthful insecurity, mortality fears and depression'. M C Strong in his *Rock Discographies* (Canongate Press) described their style as 'gothic rock' and certainly the preoccupation with Edgar Allen Poe / HP Lovecraft horror is there for all to hear in Keith Reid's lyrics, which range from the grotesque, as someone stares at their own tombstone, to the comical as someone else expresses frustrated lust for 'Mabel' to the sound of breaking glass. *'Mabel's* humorous, infectious slapstick was the first of many 'tongue in cheek' tracks that would litter Procol albums down the years. (*Good Captain Clack* is side two's fun number [97]) **'Procol Harum'** is a precocious and substantial debut – so many musical styles and references are encompassed on the album – blues – **'*Outside the Gates of Cerdes*'**; R & B – **'*She Wandered Through the Garden Fence*'**; symphonic – **'*Conquistador*'**; classical

[97] This was the track that A Whiter Shade of Pale replaced on non-UK issues of the LP.

'*Repent Walpurgis*'. And then there's Keith Reid's often obtuse lyrics but somehow it all marries together beautifully As an interesting aside, Reid's lyrics were actually offered to an embryonic Traffic so it could have been Winwood /Reid rather than Brooker / Reid had history taken a different path!

The UK album opens with ***Conquistador***, surely one of *the* classic pop songs and certainly way ahead of its time. Paul Williams in his excellent 'Crawdaddy' article described this song as 'a lovely bit of romanticism invaded and enriched by modern anxiety.' Every track has merit but special mention must go to the brilliant '***Something Following Me***', a slower blues-inflected 'gothic horror' song with its prominent piano and fuzzed guitar. This was one of the earliest Brooker/ Reid tracks with Ray Charles cited by Brooker as an inspiration. '***Outside the Gates of Cerdes***' also gets universal accord from critics. '***A Christmas Camel***' with its 'majestic piano chords, fuzzy guitar and tricky organ' opens side two. The most striking thing about this track though is the lyric. Who else but Keith Reid would write about impersonating watering cans! Also, as with so much of Procol Harum's music it lends itself to orchestral treatment – note, for example the wonderful rendition of the song at the Hollywood Bowl in 1973 captured for posterity by KBFH FM. ***Kaleidoscope*** is described by Henry Scott-Irvine as 'a psychedelic minor masterpiece' in his sleeve notes to the remastered 30th anniversary box set on West Side Records. ***Repent Walpurgis*** is a suitably dramatic closer, is 'probably the most brilliant thing that Procol ever did' (*Zabadak*) and Trower's work on this track is 'shattering, brilliant' (*Crawdaddy*) It is Matthew Fisher's only composition and the crowning glory of an outstanding début album. As one would expect there are some Bach references but the track is so dramatic as to be almost Wagnerian in scope. 'It will shake you mercilessly and leave you aching to hear it again'.

In an interview for Acid Dragon magazine with the leader of the progressive rock group The Flower Kings, Roine Stolt revealed that, "The first LP I bought at the age of 11 was Procol Harum's first LP. I already had '***A Whiter Shade of Pale***' and I bought '**Shine on Brightly**' the week it was released in Sweden – it was even better. My friends didn't understand the greatness of this band. I was alone on this island, Rob Trower's guitar playing was an early influence on me as well as Hendrix, Gary Brooker's voice is one of the best in rock, B.J. Wilson's drumming was totally unique with cool tom fills plus they had the Hammond organ! Procol Harum's music was cool and intelligent, Imagine I was just 12 years old and into '***Repent Walpurgis***', my favourite from the first album." **(84)**

It is well documented that this album, influenced in turn by Bob Dylan, returned the compliment by providing inspiration for The Band to realise the wonderful '**Music from Big Pink**'. Procol Harum were unique and highly influential, true originators who went on to record many excellent albums which were not nearly as successful commercially as they deserved to be. As referred to earlier, it is often thought that '***A Whiter Shade of Pale***' which John Lennon played endlessly in his white Rolls Royce, forever consigned the group to be branded a 'singles group'. My first exposure to the group was the classic '**A Salty Dog**' (1969) and I worked backwards. '**Shine On Brightly**' from 1968 was another remarkable album and all three show a prodigious level of versatility and inventiveness. '**Home**' (1970) is highly underrated while **Grand Hotel** is as grandiose in places as the title suggests. Procol Harum's music has always leant itself to orchestration as the **Live in Edmonton** and the 2006 live concert at Ledreborg Castle in Denmark demonstrate. It can be truly said that, as with The Beatles, the musical roots they inherited took their music 'somewhere else' altogether, progressive in every sense of the word.

177

# The Rolling Stones

The Beatles' friends and rivals – mostly 'War babies' were to blues what The Beatles were to pop.

THE MUSICIANS: MICK JAGGER (Vocals, Harmonica); KEITH RICHARD (Guitar, Vocals); BRIAN JONES (Guitar, various other instruments, Vocals); WILLIAM PERKS AKA BILL WYMAN (Bass, Vocals); CHARLIE WATTS (Drums); IAN STEWART (Keyboards – backing musician and road manager).

THEIR FIRST RESIDENCY: Crawdaddy, Station Hotel, Richmond, Surrey; THEIR MANAGER: Andrew Loog Oldham; THEIR RECORD LABEL: Decca

THEIR FIRST RECORD: *Come On/ I Want to Be Loved* #21 UK (1964)

THEIR FIRST # 1 45: *It's All Over Now* (1964); the first of '5 in a row'*: Little Red Rooster* (1964); *The Last Time; I Can't Get No) Satisfaction; Get Off My Cloud* (1965)

THEIR FIRST #1 LP: The Rolling Stones

The Rolling Stones in 1967: 'Let's Spend The Night Together ****/ Ruby Tuesday (April #3 UK) ****; 'We Love You' (August #8 UK) ***; 'She's A Rainbow' (November) *****; 'Between The Buttons' LP (Jan/ Feb, #3 UK; #2 US) ***; 'Flowers' LP compilation (July, US #3) ****; 'Their Satanic Majesties' Request' (December #3 UK; #2 US) ***½

RECOMMENDED RELEASES/ COLLECTING: All of the above can be found on vinyl, original and reissue, although early copies will be hard to come by as they were often played to death. CDs are out there in numbers and always in demand! Apart from demos and export singles, their most sought-after '45' would be their first, *'Come On'* which can sell for up to £50. Their early LPs are all highly collectible with the first LP **'Rolling Stones'** in 1st and 2nd pressing worth a couple of hundred pounds or more as is an original **'Rolling Stones No 2'** if found in excellent condition. 1965's **'Out of Our Heads'** also fetches sizeable sums (over £100); the same with **'Aftermath'** (1966) and **'Big Hits (High Tide and Green Grass)'**, attracting collectors if its 12" x 12" picture booklet is in fine condition. Their 1967 LP **'Between The Buttons'** can go for up to £150 with mono copies around £20 more valuable than the stereo. **'Their Satanic Majesties Request'** with its 3-D gatefold sleeve is even more valuable (add up to £50 with mono again being more desirable). There are many more albums in the Record Collector Guide and, like The Beatles, The Stones are, in a word, collectible.

## The Musical History:

Michael Philip Jagger was a war baby born on 26th July, 1943, brought up in Denver Road, Dartford in the Kent Suburbs close to London's east end. He attended Dartford Grammar school and had shown a keen interest in music on the radio especially, recalled his Mum Eva, songs with a Latin American rhythm. Eschewing the rock 'n' roll of Bill Haley and Elvis Presley, his early hero was Little Richard, and he also succumbed to Buddy Holly and the Crickets after seeing them at the Granada Cinema in Woolwich in 1958. One song in particular, *'Not Fade Away'* made an impression on the young Jagger. It was the blues that really caught his attention though, thanks in part to recordings of Muddy Waters and Howling Wolf heard at his friend Dick Taylor's house.

Another important development was seeing a film documentary *'Jazz on a Summer's Day'* depicting events at the Newport Jazz Festival and in particular the hostile reception given to Chuck Berry. As Philip Norman in his seminal book 'The Stones' put it: "Each Berry song was a novel in miniature about American teenage life", (85) with Cadillacs, prom queens and the like,

A stone's throw away in Chastilian Road was Keith Richards who briefly met Jagger at the local infant school before moving to new council estate (the Temple Hill) at the other end of Dartford. Keith's early guitar hero was Elvis Presley's guitarist Scotty Moore. At Sidcup Art College, he met Dick Taylor and they listened to imported blues records. While he was mastering *'Johnny B Goode'*, Mike had changed his name to Mick, and had sent a letter to blues guru Alexis Korner with a reel to reel tape of covers by Little Boy Blue and the Blue Boys which Korner thought was 'terrible'. Undeterred, Jagger took to the stage in Korner's club opposite Ealing Broadway railway station to deliver Chuck Berry's *'Around and Around'* backed by Korner's collective of musicians and jammers, Blues Incorporated. He was taken on as a stand in for Long John Baldry.

Brian Jones also had a connection with Alexis Korner. Like the visiting American blues musicians – McKinlay Morganfield AKA Muddy Waters, Big Bill Broonzy, T Bone Walker – he would sleep on the floor of Alexis and his wife Bobbie's kitchen in Moscow Road, Bayswater. Jones was born on 28th February, 1942 and brought up in Hatherley Road, Cheltenham. His first musical love was the alto sax which he bought after hearing Charlie Parker's band. He became a member of various local groups playing trad jazz popularised by Chris Barber and Humphrey Lyttelton. Calling himself Elmo Lewis, he too became an honourary member of Blues Incorporated playing not sax but a Gibson guitar on which he played Elmore James' *'Dust My Broom'* with a metal slide, his rebellious, aggressive stage demeanour grabbing the attention of Korner. He hooked up with Paul Pond, who became Paul Jones, the Manfred Mann singer and a tape they made impressed Korner sufficiently for them to be given an interval residency at the Ealing Jazz Club. It was there that Jones came to the notice of Jagger, Richards and Taylor, and the fact that he was such a stylish, mature (He was a year older and had already fathered a child) and 'pro' musician made a deep impression on Keith especially. When Paul Pond (Jones) returned to Oxford to resume his degree, Brian recruited pianist Ian Stewart and guitarist Geoff Bradford. Mick, Dick and Keith would soon join them. Bradford was a blues purist, with an aversion to the rock 'n' roll direction the group were taking, and walked out, leaving Brian and Keith to perfect a dual guitar routine.

So on 12th July, 1962, The Rolling Stones, as they were now known (after a Muddy Waters song), with a line-up of **Mick Jagger (Vocals); Keith Richards and Brian Jones (Guitars); Ian Stewart (Piano); Mick Taylor (Bass) and Mick Avory (Drums)** played their first gig at the Marquee. Things did not start well with a hostile reaction from jazz and blues purists, Jagger, Richards and Jones living in poverty, and squalor in a flat in Edith Grove, Chelsea and their most regular gigs in the relatively modest surroundings of St Mary's Parish Hall in Hatherley Road, Richmond (alongside a fledgling group called The High Numbers who would become The Who). Their luck was no better on the personnel front with a difficulty in finding a stable, regular, suitable drummer with Taylor quitting to study at the Royal College of Art. Tony Chapman became the interim drummer and it was he who introduced **Bill Perks** to the group. The only pre-war baby Perks was born on 24th October, 1936 and brought up in Blenheim Road, Penge, attending Beckenham Grammar School. He did two years' national service as a clerk in the Royal Air Force, based near Bremen in Germany. Adopting a new surname from a fellow serviceman, he became a storekeeper in Streatham, London and by the end of 1962 was a semi-professional bass player in a group called The Cliftons, backing Dickie Pride, a starlet from the Larry Parnes stable dubbed 'Britain's Little Richard'. When the Rolling Stones saw his impressive Vox amplification equipment at the audition in the Wetherby Arms in Chelsea, any doubts they had rapidly dissipated.

The winter of 1962/1963 was reckoned to be the worst in a hundred years with The Thames regularly frozen over and Wyman, already married for three years, couldn't believe the conditions the 'nucleus' of The Rolling Stones were living in. After a failed audition for the BBC Light Programme's 'Saturday Club', Chapman left and the group saw only one possibility for a replacement: **Charlie Watts**, already familiar to them in the local scenes they had become so familiar with. Charlie was 21 when he joined, and working as a lettering and lay-out man for a Regent Street advertising agency after leaving Harrow Art College. He had recently left Blues Incorporated and, as his first love was jazz, it was perhaps a surprise that he decided to join The Stones and turn down the group Blues by Six. They quickly established a large and enthusiastic following of Mods, Rockers and art students in the Crawdaddy Club in Richmond, owned by Giorgio Gomelsky who would go on to become their manager. Gomelsky, who had worked for Chris Barber, escorting and accommodating overseas musicians, had seen the early Beatles in Hamburg and knew Brian Epstein. Philip Norman takes up the story: "As The Stones played that night, they were astonished to see all four Beatles, in expensive leather overcoats" with their manager in the front row. **(86)**, (The four Liverpudlians pronounced them 'gear' and 'fab' and John Lennon was particularly impressed by Brian Jones' harmonica playing) A rapport was struck up that night and The Stones were invited to the front row of The Beatles' Royal Albert Hall 'Pop Prom' show a week later. It took a few months but, eventually, a feature by Peter Jones of the Record Mirror stirred record label interest.

Andrew Loog Oldham had an interesting CV. He had worked for fashion designer Mary Quant and also as a PR assistant to Phil Spector and Brian Epstein and his NEMS company. Acting on a tip from Peter Jones, he visited the Crawdaddy Club, told Epstein he was leaving NEMS to manage a new R&B group, offering him a 50% share in The Rolling Stones, which Epstein declined. Gomelsky had been in Switzerland attending the funeral of his father and, in an act of cunning and stealth (also a gamble) Oldham, still just 19-years-old, and agent Eric Easton signed the group from under Gomelsky's nose with a 'sweetener' of an extra £5 a week to Brian Jones who acted on behalf of the group and signed the contract. On a suggestion from George Harrison, Dick Rowe of Decca Records, the man who turned down the Beatles, snapped the group up and the first 45 Chuck Berry's *'Come On'* b/w Willie Dixon's *'I Want to Be Loved'* was released in June, 1963. Reviewers' first impressions were not good (despite this the record very nearly made the UK top 20) with only The Record Mirror giving the record a lukewarm endorsement. A brief bottom of the bill appearance on 'Thank Your Lucky Stars' at the ABC TV studios in Twickenham, London, a week after The Beatles appeared there drew little praise. After touring, little progress had been made with an appearance at a half-filled Odeon Cinema, Liverpool on 13th October on the same bill as Bo Diddley and The Everly Brothers in stark contrast to The Beatles topping the bill on the ATV show 'Sunday Night at the London Palladium'. Nor did the choice of the Coasters' *'Poison Ivy'* with Benny Spellman's *'Fortune Teller'* as its flip for the next 45 do much to improve their fortunes.

Legend has it that a chance meeting between The Beatles and a despondent Oldham led to a gift of *'I Wanna Be Your Man'*. A couple of hours at Kingsway Sound Studios, Holborn produced the slide guitar driven Chicago blues version of a song that was to give them their breakthrough. On the B-side was an instrumental that sounded suspiciously like Booker T and The MG's *'Green Onions'*. Released on 1st November, it reached #12 in the UK charts. After that, it was uphill all the way with five #1 singles in a row as already noted. Still to follow were: *'Not Fade Away'* and *'It's All Over Now'* (1964); *'Get Off My Cloud'* (1965), *'19th Nervous Breakdown'/ As Tears Go By'*, *'Paint It Black'*. *'Have You Seen Your Mother Baby (Standing in the Shadow)'* (1966) and, in our target year *'Ruby Tuesday/ Let's Spend the Night Together'* and *'We Love*

*You'*. Moving further on there's ***Jumping Jack Flash*** (1968), *'Honky Tonk Women/ You Can't Always Get What You Want'* (1969); *'Brown Sugar'* and *'Street Fighting Man'* (1971); *'Tumbling Dice'* (1972); *'Angie'* (1973); *'It's Only Rock 'n' Roll (But I Like It)'* (1974) with *'Miss You'* and *'Respectable'* from 1978, arguably the last great singles.

On the studio albums front there was:
-   **'The Rolling Stones'** (April/ June, 1964) #1 UK; #11 US – some key tracks: *'Route 66', 'I Just Wanna Make Love to You'', 'Carol'* and *'Tell Me (You're Coming Back)'*, the only Jagger-Richards original on the album.
-   **'12 x 5'** (November, 1964) #3 US some key tracks: *'Around and Around', 'Time Is On My Side'* and *'It's All Over Now'*.
-   **'The Rolling Stones No. 2'** (January, 1965); #1 UK some key tracks: *'Time Is On My Side', 'I Can't Be Satisfied'* (Great Jones bottleneck), *'Off The Hook'*, the only semi-remarkable original of three on the album.
-   **'The Rolling Stones Now!'** (March, 1965) #5 US some key tracks *'Heart of Stone', 'Off The Hook'* and *'Little Red Rooster'*.
-   **'Out of Our Heads'** (September/ August, 1965) #2 UK; #1 US some key tracks: *'She Said Yeah', 'Heart of Stone'*, the most notable album original to date; *'The Under Assistant West Coast Promotion Man', 'I'm Free'* (another original)
-   **'December's Children (And Everybody's)'** (November, 1965) #4 US some key tracks: *'She Said Yeah', 'Get Off My Cloud', 'I'm Free', 'As Tears Go by'*
-   **'Aftermath'** (April/ July, 1966) #1 UK, #2 US some key tracks: not one cover! *'Mother's Little Helper'* (dulcimer/ detuned 12-string/ bottleneck and uncompromising; *'Under My Thumb'; 'Goin' Home'* (all 11 minutes of it!), *'Out of Time'* (clocks in at 5.5 minutes here but Chris Farlowe had a big hit with a shorter version)
-   **'Big Hits (Hide Tide and Green Grass)'** (November/ April, 1966) #4 UK, #3 US (compilation – all good)

And the 1967 albums:

## IMPORTANT ALBUMS of 1967 (17)
### Between The Buttons by the Rolling Stones

**THE MUSICIANS: Mick Jagger** (Vocals, Tambourine, Harmonica); **Keith Richards** (Guitars, Backing Vocals, Piano, Bass, Organ – 5); **Brian Jones** (Organ, Guitar-1; Piano, Trombone, Sax, Clarinet, Banjo. Marimba, Kazoo, Harmonica); **Bill Wyman** (Bass, Double Bass – 3); **Charlie Watts** (Drums, Maracas) with guests **Jack Nitzsche** on Piano (1,3,5,9) and Harpsichord (2); **Nicky Hopkins** on Piano (6,12) and **Ian Stewart** (Piano – 7,8,10,11); **PRODUCER: Andrew Loog Oldham; ARTWORK (DRAWINGS): Charlie** Watts; **PHOTOGRAPHY: Gered Mankowitz; RELEASE DATE: 20 January, 1967**, recording began in the summer of 1966, the album's title a reference to the fashion conscious Charlie Watts); **LABEL: Decca; CHART: #3 UK; #2 US.**

181

# Tracklisting/ Credits (All Jagger/ Richards)

| | | |
|---|---|---|
| 1. | Yesterday's Papers | 2:20 |
| 2. | My Obsession | 3:15 |
| 3. | Back Street Girl | 3:27 |
| 4. | Connection | 2:08 |
| 5. | She Smiled Sweetly | 2:45 |
| 6. | Cool, Calm and collected | 4:15 |
| 7. | All Sold Out | 2:17 |
| 8. | Please Go Home | 3:17 |
| 9. | Who's Been Sleeping Here? | 3:55 |
| 10. | Complicated | 3:15 |
| 11. | Miss Amanda Jones | 2:45 |
| 12. | Something Happened to Me Yesterday | 4:55 |

The US version replaced 'Back Street Girl' and 'Please Go Home' with 'Let's Spend the Night Together' and 'Ruby Tuesday' which started the album with 'Yesterday's Papers' in between, inevitably strengthening it. ****

## The Music Track by Track

- **Yesterday's Papers:** Jagger sings about the uselessness of yesterday's papers drawing an analogy with yesterday's girls and, no wonder, for the bed hopping that saw Chrissie Shrimpton (yesterday's girl) in the arms of Steve Marriot of the Small Faces and Jagger with Marianne Faithful, a highlight of the LP with great reverb and echo rich song with Brian Jones on mellotron and marimba;
- **My Obsession:** on which, Charlie Watt's drumming impresses as he unleashes a 'ricochet of stun gun effects'**(87)**
- **Back Street Girl:** Jones swaps harpsichord for French accordion and plays dulcimer on a song in waltz time which contrasts prostitution with illicit 'respectable' sex;
- **Connection:** Keith sings lead vocals and the song makes reference to sleep prohibiting non-prescription drugs ('uppers') famously used by The Beatles and others during gruelling stints in Hamburg;
- **She Smiled Sweetly:** This saccharine song didn't dissuade Love Affair who released it as an unsuccessful A-side. It has no guitar at all with Richards on organ and guest Jack Nitzsche on keyboards;
- **Cool, Calm and Collected**: the longest number thanks to a Nicky Hopkins honky-tonk piano coda invoking English music hall in 'the good old days' and Jones playing an unlikely combination of sitar and kazoo;
- **All Sold Out:** not a bad little song but it seems incomplete and could do with a proper guitar break instead of illusive snatches of what might have been as it fades out;
- **Please Go Home** takes a leaf out of The Beach Boys' song book, Jones uses a theremin in what has been described as a psychedelic number with a Bo Diddley beat

- **Who's Been Sleeping Here?:** Nitzsche guests on keyboards again in a Dylan inspired song, Dylan's harmonica style is even mimicked;
- **Complicated** is stylistically similar to 'All Sold Out';
- **Miss Amanda Jones** is a good humoured song with strong lead guitar supposedly about disco jet-setter Amanda Lear, it has a Chuck Berry feel with Jones on harpsichord and Wyman doubling on bass and organ as he frequently did on the album;
- **Something Happened To Me Yesterday:** Jones is in overdrive on overdubbed instruments including brass and woodwinds, Vaudevillian with Jagger offering road safety advice in a closing five minutes that points to an artistic direction of travel.

Enjoyed by Frank Zappa but thought of by Brian Jones as a stop gap between **'Aftermath'** and the group's response to **'Sergeant Pepper'**, Jones had reason to be unsettled as five albums in, including two albums of all original Rolling Stones songs, not one of his own had made it onto vinyl although plenty of his ideas were tortuously worked on with studio cutting tape. The uninspiring cover has contributed to the notion that **'Between the Buttons'** is a less than endearing album and they were certainly capable of a lot more, only to be achieved after the misstep of **'Their Satanic Majesties Request'**. It is, if nothing else, a fascinating glimpse into the unravelling of the relationship between Jones and the others which finally imploded by 1969 when Jones was only sporadically present to add some percussion to *'Midnight Rambler'* during the sessions for **'Let It Bleed'** as drug use took its toll.

The US version of **'Between the Buttons'** released on 11 February, 1967 was strengthened by the addition of *'Let's Spend the Night Together'* and *'Ruby Tuesday'*. It reached #2 on the US album charts. Another album, *'Flowers'*, a compilation of songs with two tracks from **'Between The Buttons'** and four tracks from the **'Aftermath'** album was released in the US in July, 1967

Not normally held in great esteem by pop and rock cognoscenti, Philip Norman's view of **'Between The Buttons'**, while not atypical, is particularly scathing, citing "a lack of ideas combined with overproduction to produce a curious, limply echoing effect, like a vaudeville show in an almost empty hall." **(88)**

## IMPORTANT ALBUMS oF 1967 (18)
## THEIR SATANIC MAJESTY'S REQUEST by THE ROLLING STONES

**THE MUSICIANS:** Mick Jagger (Vocals, Percussion, Tambourine, Maracas, Glockenspiel – 2); Keith Richards (Guitar, Vocals, Bass); Brian Jones (Mellotron, Flute, Dulcimer, Organ, Percussion, Sax, Vibraphone, Acoustic guitar, Jew's Harp, Recorder, Harp, Harmonica); Bill Wyman (Bass, Percussion, Lead Vocal – 3; Piano, Organ – 3; Mellotron,); Charlie Watts (Drums, Percussion, Congas, Tabla, Claves, Tambourine) with guests Nicky Hopkins (Piano – 1, 5-7, 9, 10); Ronnie Lane and Steve Marriott (BackingVocals-3); Eddie Kramer (Claves-9); John Paul Jones did the string arrangement for track 6 and also played Sitar and Mandolin on track 8; PRODUCER: The Rolling Stones; ENGINEER: Glyn Johns; ARTWORK/ COVER: 'Artchie', Michael Cooper, Pictorial Productions in association with The Rolling Stones; Tony Meeviwiffen (back cover); RELEASE DATE: Released in the

## Tracklisting/ Writing Credits

| | | |
|---|---|---|
| 1. | Sing This All Together (See What Happens) (Jagger/ Richards) | 3:45 |
| 2. | Citadel (Jagger/ Richards) | 2:50 |
| 3. | In Another Land (Bill Wyman) | 3:15 |
| 4. | 2000 Man (Jagger/ Richards) | 3:05 |
| 5. | Sing This All Together (See What Happens) (Jagger/ Richards) | 8:35 |
| 6. | She's A Rainbow (Jagger/ Richards) | 4:35 |
| 7. | The Lantern (Jagger/ Richards) | 4:25 |
| 8. | Gomper (Jagger/ Richards) | 5:10 |
| 9. | 2,000 Light Years From Home (Jagger/ Richards) | 4:45 |
| 10. | On With The Show (Jagger/ Richards) | 3:40 |

## The Music Track by Track

**Side One:** *Sing This All Together (See What Happens)*: Brian Jones is back on brass and woodwinds having already played alto sax on The Beatles' '*Baby, You're A Rich Man*' and '*You Know My Name*'. Camaraderie performed an oxymoronic dance with rivalry as Lennon and McCartney return the favour with some background vocals on The Stones' answer to '*All You Need Is Love*'. It's an infectious if unsubstantial opener. '*Citadel*' was apparently inspired by the Franz Fritz film from 1926, '*Metropolis*', its inherent dissonance is a brave move in juxtaposition to the opening sing-a-long; **In Another Land**: A no show by Jagger and Richards (They didn't get a message from Glynn Johns – no mobile phones in those days!) led to Stevie Marriot being recruited from an adjacent studio to play guitar and Wyman writing and singing with Nicky Hopkins playing piano and Mick and Keith adding backing vocals later. Wyman would find an outlet for his other songs on The End's LP '**Introspection**' which he produced. **2000 Man** takes an electro/ acoustic approach, Nicky Hopkins, the '*Session Man*' of The Kinks song helping Brian Jones with the keyboards. '*Sing This All Together (See What Happens)*' is an eight minute existential reprise that seems self-indulgent now (as it probably was then).

**Side Two: '*She's A Rainbow*':** With strings arranged by John Paul Jones, later to join Led Zeppelin, this is by far the best song on the LP; '*The Lantern'*: An unconvincing metaphysical 'sea of light' evocation with church organ and funereal bells, this is pretty spaced out; '*Gomper'*: Jones plays mandolin and sitar while a fledgling monophonic Moog synthesiser is heard in the instrumental section of a number inspired by Jagger's frequenting of the Indica bookshop. Watts temporarily vacates his drum stool for a tabla and Martin Elliott suggested that the 'weirdness and freakiness' of the sessions were epitomised by 'Gomper'.(89); '*2,000 Light Years from Home*' is one of the successes of the LP with Keith's searing electric guitar and Brian's spooky mellotron. It is seen by some as proto space rock; '*On with The Show*' is thought to be the forerunner of the '**Rock 'n' Roll Circus**' concept that came to fruition in 1968 (The Stones' equivalent to '**Magical Mystery Tour**' perhaps).

The Rolling Stones took a different trajectory to The Beatles and fans would sometimes (as with Blur and Oasis much later) take sides. Personally, I have always enjoyed the music of both but have to say that The Beatles had more influence on The Stones than the other way. Still, both bands produced some astounding music.

## The Searchers

The Searchers in 1967: 'Popcorn Double Feature' (Pye 45) ****, 'Western Union' (Pye 45) ***, 'Second-hand Dealer' (Pye 45) ****

THE MUSICIANS: The original line-up was John McNally and Mike Pender (Guitar and Vocals), Tony Jackson (Bass and Vocals) and Chris Curtis (Drums and Vocals) (see below for more details)

## Recommended Listening/ Collecting:

Very much a singles band so that is what I would recommend. Extensively compiled and reissued on CD. Regular radio play and revival tours ensure The Searchers remain a famous '60s' group. Notable among the compilations are the 'Ultimate Collection' CD on Castle; the '30th Anniversary Collection', a 3 CD set covering Pye singles from 1963-1967, album tracks and rarities including solo 45s from Chris Curtis and Tony Jackson; 'The EP Collection' on See For Miles; and 'The Pye Anthology' 1963-1967 (2 CDs). The Searchers' 1967 single 'Second-hand Dealer' is well worth looking out for.

THE MUSICAL HISTORY: The Searchers stayed within the safe parameters of what is affectionately known as a 'beat boom band' without the desire or ambition, it would appear, to extend their boundaries as their more famous Liverpool contemporaries The Beatles did. Taking their name from a John Ford western movie, The Searchers, like The Beatles, spent some time honing their craft in Hamburg. The group was discovered by song writer/ impresario Tony Hatch who provided them with the Pomus/ Schuman song 'Sweets for my Sweet' which launched their recording career with a #1 hit in the UK. After a stall with follow-up 'Sweet Nothin's', they reached the penultimate chart position with Hatch's 'Sugar and Spice'. Next they turned a minor Jackie De Shannon hit in the US into a major #1 hit in the UK, a song by Sonny Bono and Jack Nitzsche called 'Needles and Pins'. It also provided them with their top 20 US breakthrough as did the song that completed the 'hat trick' of number ones 'Don't Throw Your Love Away'. In 1964, they had another top 10 hit, Jackie De Shannon's 'When You Walk in the Room' (#3) and a couple of top 20s ('Someday We're Gonna Love Again' and 'What Have They Done to The Rain?'). They also had a top 10 in the US with 'Love Potion #9'. During 1963-64 they charted with no fewer than 4 top 10 LPs: 'Meet The Searchers', 'Sugar and Spice', 'It's The Searchers' and 'Sounds Like the Searchers' their debut reaching #2 in the UK album chart.

Early in 1964, Tony Jackson left to be replaced by Frank Allen from Cliff Bennett and the Rebel Rousers with Pender taking over the lead vocals. In 1965, 'Goodbye My Love' reached #4 UK followed by their first self-penned hit 'He's Got No Love' (#12). Their last top 20 hit was P.F. Sloan's 'Take Me for What I'm Worth'. This was as good as it got, so by 1967, The Searchers had become more of a peripheral figure living on past glories. As Vernon Joynson put it, "As the beat boom declined, so did The Searchers popularity."(90) This is a wasted opportunity perhaps for in 1967 they released three singles including 'Western Union' which was a hit for The Five Americans in the US but did not push their musical boundaries to keep in step with the developing psychedelic and progressive rock scene.

In 1967, they released one of their best 45s *'Popcorn Double Feature'* with an intriguing lyric, prominent bass line and empathic strings that don't overpower the psych feel. *'Western Union'* is a country rocking Monkees style version of the Five Americans hit with a twangy guitar break. The hair is getting longer and so is the length of the record, at more than 4 minutes, plenty of space to demonstrate what a good band The Searchers were, *'Second Hand Dealer'* is very much in Kinks vogue (with echoes of mid-sixties Beatles), the dealer meeting an unfortunate end.

The Searchers have continued for many decades on the '60s' revival circuit and their music remains popular on commercial radio stations.

## The Shadows/ Cliff Richard

**The Shadows in 1967: 'Maroc 7' (Columbia 45, #24 UK) \*\*\*\*; 'Tomorrow's Cancelled' \*\*\*\* (Columbia 45); 'The Shadows on Stage and Screen' (Columbia EP) \*\*\*; 'Jigsaw' (Columbia LP, #8 UK) \*\*; 'From Hank, Bruce, Brian and John' (Columbia LP) \*\*\***

**THE MUSICIANS: Hank Marvin and Bruce Welch (Guitars) Terry 'Jet' Harris (Bass) and Tony Meehan (Drums).**

## Recommended Listening/ Collecting:

Compilations and '45s' are recommended. Their most collectible '45' is their first *'Saturday Dance'* (Columbia, 1959) which was also released on a '78' which is very hard to find. As far as EPs are concerned, it would be **Thunderbirds Are Go!** (Columbia, 1966) (with Cliff Richard) and **'The Shadows on Stage and Screen'** (Columbia, 1967). Their EPs have general appeal for collectors mainly because of the picture sleeves. Their LPs are not particularly collectible except perhaps the first, **The Shadows** (Columbia, 1961) in stereo.

## The Musical History:

Although more a group associated with the early '60s, The Shadows were still releasing music in 1967 and beyond with five 45s and an album in that year. Their continuing influence on other musicians, especially guitarist Hank Marvin, guarantees them a prominent and permanent place in any pop or rock history. If **The Ventures** were the USA's top instrumental group, **The Shadows** were Britain's answer. Hank Marvin and Bruce Welch were pupils together at Rutherford Grammar School in Newcastle-upon-Tyne. Enthused about the surge of skiffle in the UK, they played in **The Railroaders** and met the two Tony's, Harris and Meehan. By the end of 1958, they were the touring band for **Cliff Richard and The Drifters**, changing their name to avoid confusion with the famous US vocal harmony group of the same name, and calling themselves The Shadows because they felt like they were always 'in the shadow' of Cliff. Session men were used on Cliff's early 45s but they did back him on his big hit *'Living Doll'* and EMI's A&R man Norrie Paramor was sufficiently impressed to offer them a recording contract of their own. So it was that they recorded their first 45, still as The Drifters, *'Feeling Fine'* in 1959. Unusually, their follow-up *'Jet Black'* featured Jet Harris on bass as the lead instrument and its B-side the Marvin penned *'Driftin'* was covered by US band The Standells. The 45 had to be released under the name The Four Jets in the US as the US Drifters had filed a court injunction.

Their first single as The Shadows *('Saturday Dance')* had doo-wop vocals but it was to be 1960 before their big breakthrough would come. And what a breakthrough it was!

Song writer Jerry Lordan had demonstrated '*Apache*' on his ukulele to the group on a UK tour in April, 1960. The Shadows recorded their version of it with Cliff on bongos and it went on to reach #1, become a million seller and was voted record of the year by New Musical Express readers. It also went on to become an established all-time classic, and along with Fleetwood Mac's '*Albatross*' eight years later probably the most recognisable instrumental to come out of the UK. The group had certainly come out of the shadow of Cliff Richard!

The Shadows' next single was a double A side '*Man of Mystery/ The Stranger*' which made #5 UK. In 1961, '*F.B.I*', a Marvin, Welch and Harris original also made the top 10 and The Shadows, after touring in their own right, backed Cliff once again on a tour of Africa, Australasia and the Far East. '*The Frightened City*', an unused Paramor track for a film score, edged to #3 but the real mark of the Shadows' impact was their first eponymous album released in September, 1961 which spent 6 weeks at the top of the UK LP chart. A single was released in the same month and was one of their best, giving them their second #1. Written by Michael Carr and called '*Kon-Tiki*', after Thor Heyerdahl's raft it featured some interesting rhythm playing by kettle drums, tympani and bass.

During a six weeks' residency in Blackpool, Tony Meehan announced he was going to quit to work as an A&R man for Decca Records and was replaced by Brian Bennett. Two tracks from '*The Young Ones*' film were then released '*The Savage/ Peace Pipe*' before a third #1 was achieved (both recorded with Meehan) '*Wonderful Land*', one of the best in The Shadows' canon, topping the UK singles chart for 8 weeks. Like '*Apache*', this was written by Jerry Lordan and was embellished with a Norrie Paramor orchestration.

Jet Harris was next to leave The Shadows after well documented differences with Brian Welch. His replacement **Brian 'Liquorice' Locking** was reunited with **Brian Bennett** who was his rhythm section partner backing **Vince Taylor** and **Marty Wilde**. In May, 1962 The Shadows with their new rhythm section departed for Greece where they filmed '*Summer Holiday*' with Cliff Richard. As a mark of their growing song writing confidence, Welch and Bennett wrote the title track. 1962 provided another two big hits, the flamenco styled '*Guitar Tango*' complete with castanets and cornets, and another chart-topper (in 1963), '*Dance On*'. Following hot on its heels in 1963, was another #1 '*Foot Tapper*' from the '*Summer Holiday*' soundtrack. Meanwhile, a second album '**Out of the Shadows**' and an EP '*The Boys*' had topped their respective charts and a compilation, '*The Shadows' Greatest Hits*' was only prevented from doing so by The Beatles' '**Please, Please Me**' LP. Another Jerry Lordan penned number '*Atlantis*' should have provided him with the kudos of a 'hat trick' of number ones but only reached #2. The Shadows were still playing summer seasons with Cliff Richard so, in a sense, had two identities. '*Shindig*' and '*Geronimo*' provided two more 1963 hits.

Locking left to become a Jehovah's Witness and was almost replaced by John Paul Jones, later of Led Zeppelin, ex Interns bassist **John Rostill** getting the job instead. 1964 began with two further hits, Welch's '*Theme for Young Lovers*' from the '*Wonderful Life*' soundtrack and '*The Rise and Fall of Flingel Bunt*'. By now, The Shadows were a top 10 band at best although their albums still threatened the top of the charts – '**Dance with The Shadows**' made #2 in 1964; '**The Sound of the Shadows**' #4 in 1965; '**Shadow Music**' #5 in 1966 and '**Jigsaw**' #8 in 1967. They ended 1964 writing the score and starring in (with Cliff) 'Aladdin' at the London Palladium just as they would in 'Cinderella' in 1966. In the same year they released an EP with Cliff and The Shadows' four tracks on the '*Thunderbirds Are Go!*' soundtrack, a Gerry Anderson movie which featured likenesses of the group as puppets, a nice bit of nostalgic memorabilia if you can track it down. An EP *'The Shadows on Stage and Screen'* would also appear in 1967 with a single *'Thunderbirds Are Go!'*, a rare collectors' item, a one sided advance promo; and *'Maroc 7'* their last top 30 hit, the title track to a spoof spy thriller composed by Paul Ferris. A 45 *'Chelsea Boot/ Jigsaw'* from their forthcoming album **'Jigsaw'** was issued only as a demo and is thus highly collectible. *'Tomorrow's Cancelled'*, a 45, and **'From Hank, Bruce, Brian and John'** (LP) were also released in '67, the former showing that The Shadows' star was on the wane, the latter a rushed effort, about as lacking in inspiration as its title would suggest.

The influence of The Shadows, and Hank Marvin's guitar playing in particular is incalculable for generations of musicians. Music changed irrevocably because of groups like The Shadows, The Ventures and, later on, Booker T. & the M.G.'s.

By 1967 though, the music on their LP **Jigsaw** showed that they had no answer to the expansive, creative music emerging all around them despite a few game attempts such as on the title track which threatens to get heavy, but inevitably relies on old standards and covers, restricting themselves to two or three minute long instrumentals. Nevertheless, they were very good at what they did. Of the 45s, *'Maroc 7'* is an intriguing number with drum rolls and percussion, sounding quite James Bond-ish. *'Tomorrow's Cancelled'* is a real groovy number with great minor piano chords, bass, drums/ vibes and dreamy guitar. The 1967 EP starts with a medley of *'Finders Keepers', 'My Way', 'Paella'* and *'Fiesta'* followed by *'Autumn', 'The Flyder and the Spy'* and, lastly a more extensive exposition of *'My Way'* – not the Frank Sinatra song with organ and (rather corny) vocal. There is an interesting variety of styles and the four track 'medley' consists more of vignettes than substantial parts of a whole, starting and stopping quite abruptly. *'Autumn'* is more standard Shadows, an upbeat catchy piece with that classic Marvin tone and use of whammy bar. The arpeggios and lead line accompaniment of the third track is very beautiful with strings adding to the visceral effect. The group's second 1967 LP with the parcel sleeve starts well with a Booker T Stax sound on *'Snap, Crackle and How's Your Dad?'* a group original; while *'Evening Glow'* is a country 12 bar with harmonica at the end. *'Naughty Nippon Nights'* has the fantasy and imagination of construction to fulfil the promise of the title! There are fourteen tracks in all including covers of *'Last Train to Clarksville'*, the summer of love classic *'San Francisco'*, The Box Top's *'The Letter'* (with vocals – the guitar sound on the latter is pretty weird!) and *'The Day I Met Marie'*.

Ultimately though, however influential they were, The Shadows must have felt very much 'out of time' in the heady flower power summer of 1967. Even so, as their 2004 final tour proved their popularity has endured and the level of musicianship has not lost any of its potency over the years with Bruce a great foil on rhythm to Hank's lead guitar. Perhaps Duane Eddy got there first but Hank did as much to influence generations of guitar players.

## Sandie Shaw

**Sandie Shaw in 1967: January: 'I Don't Need Anything' \*\*\*/ 'Keep In Touch' \*\*\* (Pye 45 #50 UK); March 'Puppet on a String' (Pye 45, #1 UK) \*\*\*\*/ 'Tell The Boys' \*\*\*; July: 'Tonight in Tokyo' \*\*\*\*/ 'You've Been Seeing Her Again' \*\*\* (Pye 45, #21 UK); 'You've Not Changed' (Pye 45, #18) \*\*\*/ 'Don't Make Me Cry' \*\*\*; 'Sandie Sings' (Golden Guinea LP) \*\*\*; 'Puppet on a String' (Pye LP) \*\*; 'Love Me, Please Love Me' (Pye LP) \*\*; May: 'Tell The Boys' EP ('Tell The Boys'/ 'I'll Cry Myself To Sleep' \*\*\*/ 'I Had A Dream Last Night' \*\*\*/ 'Ask Any Woman'.**

# Recommended Listening/ Collecting

45s, EPs and compilations are recommended. For me the albums are a bit inconsistent even though there is some great music within them (see comments below). Her most collectible '45' is *'As Long as You're Happy Baby'* (Pye, 1964) and the intriguing LP: **'Reviewing the Situation'** (Pye, 1969) is also sought after.

**THE MUSICAL HISTORY:** Born Sandra Goodrich in 1947 in Dagenham, Essex, the scene of the famous women's walk-out at the Dagenham Ford car plant so brilliantly depicted in the film on which she sang the title track. Sandie, as she was known, was not backward in coming forward, singing to Adam Faith and his group The Roulettes after a concert in April, 1964. Her early demos with producer Tony Hatch were rejected but it wasn't long (July, 1964) before she released her first 45 for Pye, *'As Long as You Are Happy'*. Promoter Eve Taylor suggested the Burt Bacharach/ Hal David song *'(There's) Always Something There to Remind Me'*, a 'smash' for Dionne Warwick in the States, as her next single and her instinct proved correct as it sailed to number one. [98] Her next 45 *'Girl Don't Come'* (originally the B-side of a Chris Andrews' number *'I'd Be Far Better Off Without Him'*) made #3 (and the top 50 in the US later); and, moving into 1965, her first album **'Sandie'** was released, a #3 success, and she embarked on a package tour with headliners Adam Faith. There were two further hit 45s in 1965: *'I'll Stop at Night'* (Chris Andrews again), originally offered to Faith (#4) and her second number one *'Long Live Love'* which failed to build on the minor success of *'Girl Don't Come'* in the States despite an appearance on the Ed Sullivan show. Another Andrews song *'Message Understood'* made #6 in the fall of 1965. Her meteoric rise came to a bit of a halt in 1966 with just one top ten hit *'Tomorrow'*. Increasingly committed to cabaret and the European market, her star began to ascend again in April, 1967 after victory with Martin and Coulter's *'Puppet on a String'* in the Eurovision Song Contest. Sandy herself was somewhat ambivalent, even hostile towards the song ("I hated the whole thing at the time") and was generous in gifting what she was sure would be a #1 (She was right!) to newcomer Tom Jones whom she had met at a Royal Command Performance – that song was Les Reed/ Gordon Mills' *'It's Not Unusual'*, also a top 10 record in the USA. Prior to that Sandy finds true love in the orchestrated ballad *'I Don't Need Anything'* and holds onto the notes in classic Shaw style. Another Martin-Coulter song, *'Tonight in Tokyo'* sounds a bit like a soundtrack number but has a certain cheeky charm through its infectious chorus. On *'You've Not Changed'*, which reunites Sandy with Chris Andrews, Shaw's delivery is jaunty and childlike and continued a series of creditable singles if a bit on the short side. The 1967 **'Sandie Sings'** LP was a budget Pye Golden Guide record released in January of that year. A review on the All Music website by Rob Flanagan also makes the point that Shaw's star was temporarily on the wane and with its 12 tracks covering 1964 to 1967 it was largely ignored at the time and is certainly redundant now. The **'Puppet On a String'** LP on Hallmark, presumably to cash in on Eurovision success, was also a compilation with only 10 tracks this time. The 'bona fide' LP in 1967 did not impress Richie Unterberger: "The program focused on songs by Jacques Brel, Antônio Carlos Jobim, Cole Porter and the like, with only two contributions by her long-time songwriter Chris Andrews…and the results held little charm either for her fan base or the larger adult market that she may have been trying to reach. The CD reissue is made more palatable by the addition of both sides of four 1967-68 singles, almost all of which were written by Andrews." **(91)**

---

[98] It was Taylor who suggested that Shaw appear on stage barefoot.

Some interesting records followed, notably '*Monsieur Dupont*' (1969) and Cat Stevens' '*Father and Son*' and two albums '**The Sandie Shaw Supplement**' (1968) and an intriguing set of covers on '**Reviewing The Situation**' in 1969 which has become a bit of a collectors' cult item.

The Record Collector article 'Made in Dagenham' offers many insights. It reminds us that Sandie presented her own TV show 'The Sandie Shaw Supplement' and launched her own fashion label. Her staunch independence continues to this day with the launch of her own self-controlled website sandieshaw.com. She sued the Pye label for the rights to her recordings and chaired the Featured Artists Coalition which included Blur and Billy Bragg. '**Long Live Love: The Very Best of Sandie Shaw**' was issued on 6 May, 2013 by the Salvo label with all the songs chosen by Sandie. Going back to 1967 for a moment it should also be remembered that Sandie was unique in venturing beyond the iron curtain to perform in Czechoslovakia. Also, like her contemporary Dusty Springfield she collaborated with artists coming to prominence in the eighties, her Smiths being the ying to Dusty's yang, The Pet Shop Boys. She also performed the song '*Cool About You*' from her 1988 LP '**Hello Angel**' with the Reids from The Jesus and Mary Chain. "They (The Smiths) gave me three songs which were quite difficult to learn because the songs didn't have any tunes really and so I had to make a tune," she said.[99]

At one time The Paramounts were Sandie's backing band (see Procol Harum) and she recalled that "I have fond memories of sitting by Gary Brooker's piano singing with him." Brian Poole and The Tremeloes and Tony Rivers and The Castaways also backed her.

It is quite an irony that her most famous song was '*Puppet On a String*' considering that seems to be the way Sandie must have thought about her career before she regained artistic control and struck out on a limb with 1969's covers album '**Reviewing the Situation**'.

The reissue of '**Love Me, Please Love Me**' by the Salvo label merits a separate consideration with its 16 bonus tracks of A and B sides. Sandie seems most comfortable on the opening title track and on Jacque Brel's '*Ne Me Quitte Pas*' which (She was comfortable singing in French or Italian and Sandie's version was before Scott Walker's), '*Time After Time*' and the only decent Chris Andrews' song on the album '*That's Why*'.

As for the rest, there is a samba, a nice version of the Charlie Chaplin co-write '*Smile*' but the trad jazz of '*Yes, My Darling Daughter*' and the big band sound of '*I Get a Kick Out Of You*' simply don't work for me and another Cole Porter song '*Every Time We Say Goodbye*' doesn't suit the artist. Of course, Sandie's manager Eve Taylor was brought up in the traditions of music hall but the options of actress, cabaret star or panto ('I would rather be dead') did not appeal to Sandie. Worried about her artistic credibility, nor was the Eurovision Song Contest an appealing prospect: "Think of all the people watching me make a fool of myself." It was Adam Faith who finally persuaded her. '*I Had a Dream Last Night*' which can be heard on the '**Tell The Boys**' EP did not make the televised UK qualifiers so '*Puppet On A String*' was chosen instead. And so history was changed in more ways than one!

---

[99] The songs were 'I Don't Owe You Anything', 'Hand In Glove' and 'Jeanie'.

# Small Faces (Known as The Small Faces): The Darlings of Wapping Wharf

Small Faces in 1967: 'I Can't Make It' ****/ 'Just Passing' ***(Decca 45 #26); 'Patterns' ***/ 'E Too D' **** (Decca 45 unauthorised); 'Here Comes the Nice' ****/ 'Talk To You' *** (Immediate 45 #12 UK); 'Itchycoo Park' *****/ 'I'm Only Dreaming' *** (Immediate 45 #3 UK; #16 US) ; 'Tin Soldier' ***** 'I Feel Much Better' *** (Immediate 45 #3 UK; #73 US) ; 'From The Beginning' **** (Decca LP #17 UK);'Small Faces' (Immediate LP #12 UK) ****

THE MUSICIANS: Ronnie Lane (Bass), Kenney Jones (Drums), Ian McLagan (Keyboards), Stevie Marriot (Vocals)

RECOMMENDED RELEASES/ COLLECTING: A good way to explore the music of The Small Faces in general is through the Immediate Years Box set '**Here Comes the Nice**' released in 2013 on the Charly label with a sleeve note by Pete Townshend of The Who. This contains three CDs and includes mono versions of the Immediate 45 A and B sides, alternative versions, backing tracks and overseas mixes including '*Green Circles*' sung in Italian. The review in Mojo magazine picked out some of the curiosities: the instrumental '*Wide-Eyed Girl*', '*Fred*' which later would become Humble Pie's '*Wrist Job*', a version of Tim Hardin's '*Red Balloon*' and a jam entitled '*Mind the Doors, Please*'. Of specific albums I'd say the second LP with the title '**Small Faces**' and the classic '**Ogden's Nut Gone Flake**' are the pick of the crop. Finding the former in excellent condition on LP will be a real challenge with a ball park figure of £200+ if you do. The latter 1st pressing had a round sleeve and there were a few near mint copies on Discogs last time I looked with prices ranging from £200+ to £400. Cheaper alternatives are the '**Small Faces**' 2 x CD remastered CD set on Immediate/ Universal (2012) which has the original mono LP and stereo LP mixes and a whopping 10 bonus mono and 7 bonus stereo tracks; and the '**Ogden's Nut Gone Flake**' 3 x CD remastered CD set on Immediate (2012) with both stereo and mono mixes of the original album plus 14 unreleased tracks. There have been vinyl LP reissues of course and the group announced a ½ speed mastered replica '**Ogden's Nut Gone Flake**' on their Facebook page which, predictably, sold out fast. Particularly collectible Small Faces '45s' are '*Patterns/ E Too D*' (Decca, 1967) – £50+ for UK versions, twice that for export picture sleeve versions; perhaps even higher prices for copies of the picture sleeve edition of '*Tin Soldier*' (Immediate, 1967).

## The Musical History:

Ronnie Lane formed **The Outcasts** in 1964 switching from guitar to bass after trying the four stringed version at the Selmer music shop in Holborn, London. Kenney Jones joined Lane in The Outcasts playing drums to Shadows records. Ian McLagan was playing guitar in **The Muleskinners**, an R&B group who had backed The Rolling Stones and touring blues singers Sonny Boy Williamson and Howling Wolf. They released the 45 '*Back Door Man*' on the Fontana label in 1964 then Booker T Jones appeared on McLagan's radar (the '*Green Onions*' moment) and he switched to the trademark Hammond organ sound for which he became famous in his own right. The flamboyant Jimmy Winston (born Langwith) had been the keyboard player up until their first 45 '*What 'Cha Gonna Do About It*' made the UK top 20 but after the group met singer Stevie Marriott, a former child actor who'd appeared as a street urchin in the London stage production of Lionel Bart's 'Oliver' [100], working at the time in a music shop in East Ham, his fate was sealed. This was not necessarily all for musical reasons but by dint of the fact that he was too tall! You see the others had two things in common: they all liked Booker T and the MGs and they were all 5"6" tall! As far as the group's name is concerned, it may be no coincidence that the line, "In places small faces abound" appears in The Byrds' song *'Eight Miles High'*. The Small Faces were nearly called The Nice but their manager Andrew Loog-Oldham didn't think it appropriate it for them giving the name instead to P.P. Arnold's backing band!

It would be 1966 before The Small Faces would break into the big time with *'Sha La La La Lee'*, a number written by Kenny Lynch (who added falsetto vocals) and Mort Shuman of the New York Brill Building 'Hit Factory', which reached #3. (The group hated it). Their next 45, in 1966 *'Hey Girl'* just made the top ten but was also notable for it was written by Marriott and Lane. These songs were not entirely representative of the group's style or musical ambition as evidenced on their eponymous debut album which reached #3 and spent six months on the album chart. *'All or Nothing'* was to rectify that situation (and make #1 into the bargain sharing the top spot with The Beatles' *'Yellow Submarine'*) although this artistic and commercial success was somewhat sullied by the group being banned from touring in the USA because of a McLagan drug conviction.

Watch out for a clip from The Morecambe and Wise BBC comedy show and a high octane performance of *'I Can't Make It'* in 1967. Stevie Marriot's movements and vocals are as energetic as Mick Jagger's or anyone around at the time (although more soulful than most). It was banned by the BBC as being too suggestive. The B-side *'Just Passing'* is another strong song, the only problem being its short length. *'Patterns'* with Ronnie Lane on lead vocals was only released under obligation to fulfil their commitment and without the band's consent – they even went as far as telling their fans not to buy it. Its B-side is a four minute gem with Marriott protesting that 'sometimes I feel like a frustrated child', it's a classic song of having everything and yet still being disillusioned, bluesy and guttural with a Bo Diddley beat, the thrashing guitar and drums making it sound more like The Who than typical Small Faces. A demo of *'My Mind's Eye'* had also been released against the wishes of the group. Although it did make #4 in the charts the group's confidence in their label was undermined. This, despite the fact that their manager Don Arden had set the group up in a house at 22 Westmorland Terrace, Pimlico with their own maid, cook and chauffer! Arden did not approve of the group spending so much of their money on drugs and reputedly sold the group to Tony Calder for £25,000. Decca's loss was Immediate's gain as Andrew Loog Oldham snapped them up for his new label (Calder was his business partner). The times they were are a changin' to paraphrase Bob Dylan and the Immediate label had been set up to allow artists to break free from the mantle of being 'hit machines' and to allow the full expression of their creativity to flourish. *'Here Come the Nice'* captured the spirit of 1967 perfectly (the drug culture part of it anyway and ironically was NOT banned by the BBC despite the telling line 'I need more speed'). It restored the group's fortunes nearly making the top 10 and confirmed the Mod scene's drug of choice.Of course, it was not just that but a great number of its time with enduring qualities. Its B-side, the groovy *'Talk to You'*, a live favourite, mines the roots of soul underpinned by a derivative piano and organ line is great but frustratingly short. Decca rushed out on a collection of early material called

---

[100] He would also appear uncredited as Jack in the film **'Heavens Above'** (1963) starring Peter Sellers. **Steve Marriott: All Too Beautiful: It's All So Beautiful – The Life and Times of Steve Marriott'** by Paolo Hewitt and John Hellier (2004) gives the lowdown on Marriot's rags to riches to rags story before he tragically died in a house fire aged 44.

'**From The Beginning**' and, in response Immediate released the 'official' album '**Small Faces**'. Both made the top 20 with 'Small Faces' marginally the more successful of the two reaching #12, five places higher than '**From The Beginning**'. The fact that two albums released so close to each other did so well is testimony to the high regard in which the group was held by the record buying public. The former was released in June and was a mixture of Marriott/ Lane compositions and covers. Their 1966 singles were included. Many people assume that '*Itchycoo Park*', a 'Mod anthem' made #1 whereas, in fact, it only reached #3 in the UK singles chart. However, the record did mark their US breakthrough where it made top 20. Its phased drums, ground-breaking use of echo, stoner observations, irresistible hook and memorable vocal combined to produce a rock classic still admired and revisited. The downside was that its effects were difficult to reproduce on stage. [101] Its B-side '*I'm Only Dreaming*' is a nostalgic ballad perfectly encapsulated in a great You Tube video with some classic 'rinky dink chords' exposing the Booker T connection. The follow-up was '*Tin Soldier*', also an excellent record further reinforcing the transition from 'Mod'/ pop/ R&B' to 'psychedelic rock' which made the top 10 in the UK and consolidated the group's position in the US by reaching #63. Ostensibly inspired by model Jenny Ryland, Ian McLagan retrospectively described '*Tin Soldier*' as "3 minutes 20 seconds of goose bumps." Incidentally, Immediate stable mate P. P. Arnold, Marriot's girlfriend at the time sings on the track. By the time of the release of The Small Faces album Chrissie Shrimpton, Mick Jagger's ex is on Marriot's arm! Another great video is to be found on You Tube depicting guys and gals on Vespa scooters providing the perfect diaspora for '*I Feel Much Better*' which reprises a Spencer Davis riff *('Gimme Some Lovin')* in its raucous ending which dies out too soon.

Despite a pretty disastrous tour of the United States with The Who in January, 1968, the rising standard of music was continued on further brilliant singles '*Lazy Sunday*' (#2, 1968), '*The Universal*' (#16) and my personal favourite, the burningly intense '*Afterglow (of Your Love)*' which surely deserved a much higher finish than #36 in 1969. Then, of course, there was the seminal album '**Ogdens' Nut Gone Flake**' which appears on every critic's list for 1968. But now we have strayed beyond our time boundary.

## IMPORTANT ALBUMS OF 1967 (19)
### THE SMALL FACES by THE SMALL FACES

**THE MUSICIANS: Steve Marriott (Vocals, Guitar, Piano), Ronnie Lane (Bass, Vocals), Ian McLagan (Keyboards, Bass – 12; Guitar & Bass – 13), Kenney Jones (Drums, Percussion) with guests Eddie Thornton (Trumpet) and Speedy Acquaye (Congas); PRODUCERS: Ronnie Lane, Steve Marriot; RELEASE DATE: 23 June, 1967; COVER DESIGN: Stephen Hill (Photography by Stephen Bobroff); LABEL: Immediate; CHART #21 UK**

---

[101] It should have been mired in controversy but wasn't after the BBC failed to get the overt drug reference in '*Itchycoo Park*' and 'bought' the cover story video showing children high on swings in a fictional park which was, in fact, a bombsite area in Ilford.

# Track listing/ Credits

## The Music Track by Track

**Side One:** *Tell Me (Have You Ever Seen Me?)* is a strong opener with powerhouse drumming; *Something I Want to Tell You* is one of the best songs on the album, Ronnie Lane delivering the aching vocal about the pathos of a broken relationship. Has nice piano and organ fills and extended organ at its conclusion; *Feeling Lonely* is a very short song continuing the theme while *Happy Boys Happy* is a short Booker T style instrumental; *Things Are Going To Get Better* has a strong, soulful lyric and chorus; *My Way of Giving* is a strong ballad written by Marriot and Lane for Chris Farlowe with great drumming again; *Green Circles* has a strange psych feel with subdued vocals, harpsichord and a repetitive chorus (personally I prefer alternate take 2 on the CD)

**Side Two:** *Become Like You* is a spooky song about imagining being like brick or wood with organ, tambourine, a druggy feel and strings at the end; *Get Yourself Together* has a fine vocal performance from Marriot, the chunky beat, prefacing The Jam and percussion/ piano accentuating the rhythm (It is a favourite of Paul Weller); *All Our Yesterdays* is a 'cheeky chappy' song that would emerge fully formed on 'Lazy Sunday, Vaudevillian Musical Hall style, with brass; *Talk To You* is a short soulful song issued as a B-side 45 which has a tantalisingly elusive but familiar piano/ organ line; *Show Me The Way* is no relation to Peter Frampton's famous song later but has that warm, familiar, cosy Small Faces stamp with harpsichord used once again; on *Up The Wooden Hills To Bedfordshire* McLagan sings lead vocal and depicts the chaotic, unhealthy urban lifestyle and yearning to find a healthy creative environment. Intense organ/ electric piano provide gravitas – this song could have taken them into Traffic territory but ends all too quickly like a lot of the numbers did; *Eddie's Dreaming*, essentially a McLagan song, has a Caribbean rhythm with Eddie Thornton of Georgie Fame's group on trumpet. Congas (Speedy Acquaye) and flute also feature. Keyboards used are a mellotron, harpsichord, celeste, Steinway grand piano, Wurlitzer electric piano and Hammond M 100

The US version of the LP was called **'There Are but Four Small Faces'** and was released in 1968. The track listing was as follows:

**Side One:** *Itchycoo Park; Talk to You, Up The Wooden Hills ; My Way of Giving; I'm Only Dreaming; I Feel Much Better*; **Side Two:** *Tin Soldier, Get Yourself Together, Show Me The Way, Here Comes The Nice, Green Circles*.

In his liner notes to the 2CD edition Mark Paytress observes: "Far from alone in suffering from acute musical schizophrenia during 1967, the band did seem to lack a killer punch in producing an album that will stand up as a creative entity in its own right – it would be their next and greatest challenge." As I have mentioned before, my frustration listening to the music is that many songs were curtailed to not much more than 2 minutes and when the band got to the launch pad the take out was quickly aborted. This is brought home by some of the bonus tracks on the 2 CD release. For example, there is a version of *'I Feel Much Better'* which fades in and fades out and threatens to produce a truly progressive moment when it stops again at 3:55. There is also a great out take that would have graced the album (***Don't Burst My Bubble***) with fine organ, bass and percussion and a fine vocal from Marriot. Released in the same month as **'Sergeant Pepper'**, **'Small Faces'** is a great listen that will appeal to fans of Stax/ Volt artists such as Sam and Dave, Booker T and Otis Redding but the group were not yet stretching the psychedelic boundaries the way they would on their apogee, **'Ogden's Nut Gone Flake'**.

# Dusty Springfield

**Dusty Springfield in 1967: 'I'll Try Anything' (Philips 45 #13) ****; 'Give Me Time ***/ The Look of Love' **** (Philips 45 #24); 'What's It Gonna Be?' ****/ 'Small Town Girl' ***; (Philips 45); 'Where Am I Going?'**** (Philips LP #40); 'Dusty Definitely' (Philips LP #30) ******

**RECOMMENDED LISTENING/ COLLECTING:** You can't go far wrong with the **'5 Classic Albums'** series on Spectrum/ Universal/ Mercury in the case of Dusty Springfield with **'A Girl Called Dusty'**, **'Everything's Coming Up Dusty'**, **'Dusty…Definitely'**, **'Dusty in Memphis'** and **'From Dusty – with Love'**. There are numerous CD compilations as you might expect but go for ones that show the full range of her talent or that are judicious in their selection of songs. Her records don't command particularly high values except for the most sought after, her classic **'Dusty in Memphis'**.

**THE MUSICAL HISTORY**: Born Mary O'Brien in Hampstead, London in 1939, 'Dusty Springfield' left a vocal trio The Lana Sisters (with whom four singles were released on Fontana) to join her brother Dion and Tim Field in a trio called The Springfields. Brother Dion also adopted the name 'Springfield' and the Dion changed to Tom. Achieving a string of hits in the UK and some success in the US (with *'Silver Threads and Golden Needles'*), Dusty became captivated by the music on the Motown label when The Springfields were singing in Nashville and decided to pursue a new musical direction.

Many assume *'I Only Want to Be with You'*, much admired and covered and successfully revived by The Tourists, was a debut #1 for Dusty but, in fact, it reached #4. The fact that it also made #12 in the US was probably more significant given that it gave her early success on both sides of the Atlantic and, straight away, she was a 'name' in America, a notoriously difficult market to crack for many British singers. Her second single *'Stay Awhile'* didn't do quite so well but it was a steady follow-up and she toured the UK with The Searchers and the US, where she appeared on the Ed Sullivan show. Her first LP '**A Girl Called Dusty**' in 1964 was a good effort with songs like '*Mocking Bird*', '*Wishin' and Hopin'* and, best of all '*Anyone Who Had a Heart*' which Cilla Black had a big hit with. '*Wishin' and Hopin'* was a hit for The Merseybeats here and for Dusty herself in the US. Another powerful performance on a Bacharach/ David song '*I Just Don't Know What to Do With Myself*' was another potential #1 that made #3 and Dusty's profile was established enough in the States for Philips to release albums specifically for that market: '**Stay Awhile**' and '**Dusty**'. This tradition continued with the release of different 45s in the UK and the US, an expensive dichotomy for collectors!

Dusty had two further top ten hits in the UK in 1964, '*Losing You*' and '*In The Middle of Nowhere*', as well as a Christmas record for the Barnardo's Homes charity, a #6 album '**Everything's Coming Up Dusty**' with an award as best female singer in the NME poll and a deportation from South Africa for refusing to perform before segregated audiences. The brilliant song writing team of Gerry Goffin and Carole King provided further hits in 1965 with '*Some of Your Lovin'* and '*Little by Little*' but it was a marvellous arrangement of an Italian ballad by Simon Napier-Bell and Vicki Wakeham that gave Dusty her only #1 hit: the classic '*You Don't Have To Say You Love Me*'. Her first 45 in 1966 was a great version of '*Goin' Back*', another Goffin-King song already well covered by The Byrds.

1967 brought a marvellous version of '*The Look of Love*' for the James Bond film '**Casino Royale**', a world tour and a third album '**Where Am I Going?**', re-titled '**The Look of Love**' for the American market. '*I Close My Eyes and Count to Ten*' and '*Son of a Preacher Man*' were still to come (1968) as well as her most critically acclaimed album '**Dusty in Memphis**'. She would also team up with The Pet Shop Boys in 1987 on '*What Have I Done to Deserve This?*' and '*Nothing Has Been Proved*' (the theme to the film 'Scandal' starring John Hurt about the John Profumo affair)

As far as the rest of 1967 is concerned, Dusty can be seen on You Tube singing the perky '*I'll Try Anything*' on her TV show on 15 August while '*Give Me Time*' gets the big booming ballad treatment. '*What's It Gonna Be*' is more direct with a more prominent rhythm section and twanging guitar/ strings and spirited backing vocalists. Its B-side is charming even if the orchestration is a bit overbearing. '*Where Am I Going?*' is from the 'Sweet Charity' musical and Dusty sings its clever lyric wonderfully with good orchestration and arrangement.

Dusty's influence on generations of female singers is phenomenal right up to and including Amy Winehouse, the best of a modern generation of soul singers.

## Status Quo

The Status Quo in 1967: *Pictures of Matchstick Men* (Pye, November) ****/ *Gentleman Joe's Sidewalk Café* **; (as The Spectres) *(We Ain't Got) Nothing Yet* (Piccadilly, February) ****; (as Traffic Jam) *Almost but Not Quite There* (Piccadilly, June) **

THE MUSICIANS – THE FIRST STATUS QUO: Francis Rossi (Lead Guitar, Vocals), Rick Parfitt (Rhythm Guitar, Vocals), Alan Lancaster (Bass, Vocals), John Coghlan (Drums, Percussion) (Roy Lynes – Keyboards, Vocals as Traffic Jam)

RECOMMENDED LISTENING/ COLLECTING: Status Quo did make some fine albums post 1967 such as '**Piledriver**' but, in our target year they were transiting from psychedelic rock to blues rock and are probably best explored through 45s. There are some good compilation CDs that include their early years e.g. The Castle 2 CD collection compiles the A and B sides of every Pye 45 the group released as well as tracks from the vaults of The Spectres, Traffic Jam and early Status Quo. With covers of Goffin-King's *Walking with My Angel* and The Bee Gees' *'Spics and Specs'* the listener may well conclude that some of these tracks would have been better left in the vaults although, to be fair, their version of *'Spics and Specs'* is pretty good. Although latterly Status Quo sold in bucket loads some of their releases are highly prized by collectors. These relate to the post 1967 period but to give a flavour they include: *Technicolor Dreams'* (as The Status Quo, Pye, 1968) and their first 2 LPs for Pye **'Picturesque Matchstickable Messages'** (the mono version valued at up to £200) and **'Spare Parts'** (I saw a VG+ mono copy on Discogs for £140 recently). More relevant to our timeframe is The Spectres whose 1966-1967 '45's' on the Piccadilly label *'I (Who Have Nothing); 'Hurdy Gurdy Man'* and *'We Ain't Got Nothing Yet'* occasionally appear on Discogs at prices over £100. Similarly, Traffic Jam's 1967 single rarely, if ever, appears for sale.

THE MUSICAL HISTORY: Status Quo is here under consideration mostly because of their releases as **The Spectres** and **Traffic Jam**. As The Spectres they released the Shirley Bassey show stopper *'I (Who Have Nothing)'*, a not altogether successful attempt to rock up the song with an embarrassing spoken ending.[102] At least it brought them to the attention of song writers Ronnie Scott and Marty Wilde who in turn brought it to the attention of in-house producer and A&R man for the Piccadilly (later Pye) label. The B-side *'Neighbour, Neighbour'* with its heavy bass line is better. Released in September, 1966 it was followed by the pretty dreadful *'Hurdy Gurdy Man'* (no relation to the Donovan song). Struggling into 1967 The Spectres next attempt at the charts was a cover of a top ten hit by The Blues Magoos in the US. Later this very same song *'(We Ain't Got) Nothing Yet'* would be transformed into *'Black Night'* by Deep Purple. The main riff is virtually identical! This was a quantum leap forward for the nascent Status Quo with an even heavier bass line than *'Neighbour, Neighbour'*.

Francis Rossi's revealing account of The Spectres in *The Status Quo Autobiography: XS All Areas* offers us an insight into those early years: "We just used to play covers to begin with, mainly instrumentals by The Shadows and The Tornados: the stuff in the charts basically."''(93) A local business man Pat Barlow became their manager and 'benefactor' eventually securing them a residency at Butlin's in Minehead. On signing to Pye in the summer of 1966 the group quickly realised they had to come up with some original songs. As Rossi said, "Up to then you went to Tin Pan Alley based companies and bought songs from them like sweets from the tuck shop. The Beatles changed all that." **(94)**

As Traffic Jam they got into hot water with Steve Winwood's Traffic (adding the Jam) and the BBC for the 'suggestive' lyrics of *'Almost but Not Quite There'*. Francis Rossi was involved in the writing of this song while keyboard player Roy Lynes wrote the B-side *'Wait a Minute'*.

Settling on a line-up of Francis Rossi, Rick Parfitt, Alan Lancaster (a greatly underestimated bass player) and drummer John Coughlan, Status Quo **[103] rose to prominence in 1968 when Francis Rossi's *Pictures of Matchstick Men* made its big breakthrough in the January of that year. The Kinks-like *Gentleman Joe's Sidewalk Café* was originally intended as the A-side but was flipped at the last minute. The follow-up *Black Veils of Melancholy* was a little too similar to *Pictures of Matchstick Man* and failed to make the same impact. The progress from third 45 *Ice in The Sun* was quite staggering. Mega stardom awaited.

---

[102] An 'absurd choice', according to Francis Rossi **(92)**
[103] Manager Pat Barlow suggested the name.

# Traffic

Traffic in 1967: 'Paper Sun' (Island 45 #5 UK) ****; 'Hole in My Shoe' (Island 45 #2 UK) *****; 'Here We Go Round The Mulberry Bush' (Island 45 #8) ***; 'Mr. Fantasy' (Island LP #16 UK) ****; 'Heaven Is In Your Mind' **** (Island 45) then 'Mr Fantasy' (different version) **** (January, 1968 # 88 US)

THE MUSICIANS: Steve Winwood (Keyboards, Guitar, Vocals); Dave Mason (Guitar, Vocals); Chris Wood (Flute, Sax); Jim Capaldi (Drums, Vocals, Keyboards)

RECOMMENDED LISTENING/ COLLECTING: The 1967 albums 'Mr Fantasy' in the UK and 'Heaven Is in Your Mind' in the US are essential. In the UK it was first released in mono in a gatefold sleeve but to find one in any better than VG+ condition will be a challenge and could cost you a couple of hundred pounds. Even a 2nd pressing on the famous Island label will cost big bucks. There have been many LP reissues all round the world e.g. Simply Vinyl (1999). A non-budget-busting option are the CD reissues with bonus tracks. All Traffic music is well worth investigating with the 'John Barleycorn Must Die' album a genre defining moment (See below).

THE MUSICAL HISTORY: Traffic formed in April, 1967 following Stevie Winwood's departure from The Spencer Davis Group, Dave Mason and Jim Capaldi were in Birmingham group Deep Feeling and Chris Wood was in Locomotive. A six month long 'bonding session' in a cottage in Berkshire (the song *'Berkshire Poppies'* references this) got the creative juices flowing and what emerged was pretty startling, three top ten hits (*'Hole in My Shoe'* the highest at #2) and a top ten album in 1967 alone. Eastern influences, jazz, rock and psychedelia all collided in a potent new sound with Winwood's remarkable voice at the centre.

Traffic released seven studio albums, one part live, part studio ('Last Exit') and one live double LP 'On The Road' during their eight-year lifespan. 'Traffic' (1968, #9 UK) was superb but 'John Barleycorn Must Die' (#11 UK) was their greatest creative achievement practically inventing a new style of jazz, rock and folk. They were only starting out in 1967 but went on to leave an indelible mark on rock music. Rob Young attributes the extreme creativity that emerged in the spring and summer of 1967, "to the remoteness of the cottage near the hamlet of Aston wouldn't have been possible in London, where the streetlight glow shut off the stars." (95)

The CD remaster of 'Mr Fantasy' is an ideal opportunity to compare the UK stereo album with the US mono version. The reconfigured American version was released under the title 'Heaven Is in Your Mind'.

## IMPORTANT ALBUMS OF 1967 (20)
## MR FANTASY by TRAFFIC

MUSICIANS: Steve Winwood (Vocals, Organ, Guitar, Bass, Piano, Percussion, Harpsichord); Dave Mason (Vocals, Guitar, Mellotron, Bass, Sitar, Tambura, Shakkai); Chris Wood (Flute, Saxophone, Vocals, Organ); Jim Capaldi (Drums, Percussion, Vocals) with guests Jimmy Miller (Maracas – 5); The Small Faces – Backing vocals, Percussion – 2); PRODUCER: Jimmy Miller; ENGINEER: Eddie Kramer; SLEEVE (DESIGN: CCS Advertising Associates/ Chris Wood); PHOTOGRAPHY: John Benton – Harris);RELEASE DATE: 8th December, 1967; LABEL: Island; CHART: #8 UK

198

# Track listing/ Credits:

1.  Heaven is in your Mind (Jim Capaldi/ Steve Winwood/   4:15
    Chris Wood)
2.  Berkshire Poppies (Jim Capaldi/ Steve Winwood/ Chris   2:55
    Wood)
3.  House for Everyone (Dave Mason)   2:05
4.  No Face, No Name, No Number ((Jim Capaldi/ Steve   3:35
    Winwood)
5.  Dear Mr Fantasy (Jim Capaldi/ Steve Winwood/ Chris   5:45
    Wood)
6.  Dealer (Jim Capaldi/ Steve Winwood)   3:35
7.  Utterly Simple (Dave Mason)   3:15
8.  Coloured Rain (Jim Capaldi/ Steve Winwood/ Chris Wood)   2:45
9.  Hope I Never Find Me There (Dave Mason)   2:10
10. Giving To You (Jim Capaldi/ Steve Winwood/ Chris Wood/   4:20
    Dave Mason)

The US VERSION had the following track listing:

1.  Paper Sun (Jim Capaldi/ Steve Winwood)   3:25
2.  Dealer (Jim Capaldi/ Steve Winwood)   3:15
3.  Coloured Rain (Jim Capaldi/ Steve Winwood/ Chris Wood)   2:45
4.  Hole in My Shoe (Dave Mason)   3:05
5.  No Face, No Name, No Number (Jim Capaldi/ Steve   3:40
    Winwood)
6.  Heaven Is In Your Mind (Jim Capaldi/ Steve Winwood/   4:20
    Chris Wood)
7.  House for Everyone (Dave Mason)   2:05
8.  Berkshire Poppies (Jim Capaldi/ Steve Winwood/ Chris   2:55
    Wood)
9.  Giving To You (Jim Capaldi/ Steve Winwood/ Chris Wood/   4:20
    Dave Mason)
10. Smiling Phases (Jim Capaldi/ Steve Winwood/ Chris Wood)   2:45
11. Dear Mr Fantasy (Jim Capaldi/ Steve Winwood/ Chris   5:35
    Wood)
12. We're A Fade, You Missed This (Jim Capaldi/ Steve   0:55
    Winwood)

## The Music Track by Track

Here's a track-by-track of the UK version: In terms of broadening musical horizons, *Heaven Is In Your Mind* is an ideal start as a new kind of funkiness emerges with Capaldi's drums high up in the mix; *Berkshire Poppies* is an ode to country life as opposed to city life where high rises block the view, distinctly Bonzo Doggish in places; *House For Everyone*, a Dave Mason song, the strange noise at the start is an old clock being wound with a key, a fantasy song like *Hole In My Shoe; No Face, No Name, No Number* is, quite simply, one of the best, if not the best 'pop' ballad ever written – the beauteous acoustic guitar, harpsichord, organ, mellotron and flute, and Winwood's aching delivery, cannot fail to make the hairs on the back of your neck stand up; *Dear*

*Mr Fantasy* features a brilliant guitar solo very similar in tone and style to Robin Trower's playing with Procol Harum, some fantastic rhythm (Winwood played the bass in style as well) and wailing harmonica. Soft Machine's *'You Did It Again'* wordless riff features (not terribly original in itself so definitely no plagiarism) rounding off a 5 minute plus number ripe for extended blues jamming; *Dealer* has a Flamenco style guitar in some ways belying the deadly serious vocal with Wood's beguiling, wistful flute adding a touch of the sinister, a Capaldi/ Winwood number with a slightly over fussy arrangement; *Utterly Simple*, Dave Mason is the writer and uses sitar to accompany his own song as well as tambura and shakkai, an eastern meditation with obvious comparisons to *Within You, Without You* on 'Sergeant Pepper's*,*'; *Coloured Rain:* Winwood's soulful tones return on this song; organ, sax and strident bass to the fore, dynamic drumming once again; *Hope I Never Find Me*, overtly psychedelic, this Mason song refers to atomic factories built on children's playgrounds and warns of an apocalyptic future filtered through a whiff of nostalgia; *Giving To You,* the only song credited as a whole group composition, it starts with 'chatter' with the words 'I mean jazz' sparking a jam you can easily imagine gestating under the stars in the cottage in Berkshire, flute solos first, rather too low in the mix, an electric guitar solo to three basic organ chords with some slight variations, a jaunty theme keeps returning keeping the improvisation well rooted, no surprise that an organ solo is next, 'jazz is where it's at'.

**US version: 'Heaven Is in Your Mind' (1st pressing); 'Mr Fantasy' (2nd & subsequent pressings) (and some further observations)**

1) **Paper Sun,** a classic psychedelic 45, no more, no less;
2) **Dealer**, comments as before;
3) **Coloured Rain,** Winwood sings as organ, manic sax, cowbell and strident bass come to the fore, dynamic drumming;
4) **Hole in My Shoe,** introduced by Dave Mason's sitar, a tramp with a hole in his shoe is also mentioned in **Berkshire Poppies**; big mellotron, organ, piano, flute, a child's voice, irresistible, another psych classic;
5) **No Face, No Name, No Number,** doesn't lose any of its impact in mono;
6) **Heaven Is in Your Mind**, funky in places, pointing the way to **Empty Pages** on the 1970 **John Barleycorn Must Die** album;
7) **House for Everyone,** with one door marked truth and another lies, is a fantasy not quite of Lewis Carroll proportions!
8) **Berkshire Poppies,** refers to a sinister park where murderers stalk girls in the park, in sharp contrast to Berkshire and its poppies; pure vaudeville at the end with a rather fine burp;
9) **Giving to You,** a jazz rock romp of Graham Bond proportions as previously described, always better in stereo where there are solos involved;
10) **Smiling Phases**, the B-side to **Hole in My Shoe** ; Blood, Sweat and Tears recognised the potential of the song and would produce the definitive (extended) version in 1968;
11) **Dear Mr Fantasy,** a very similar guitar riff would appear on the title track to The Kinks' **Village Green Preservation Society** album the following year;
12) **We're A Fade You Missed This,** the ending of the full length version of **Paper Sun** and segues back to **Paper Sun** again – time for another listen!

**Mr Fantasy** didn't gain much more than a cult following for Traffic at the time. Critics seemed to like the album and (agreed) that Steve Winwood and Traffic were good at putting together semi-mainstream psychedelic rock, except this album wasn't quite mainstream enough. This album features even more horns, flutes and less rock style instruments. The sitar is used much more undoubtedly because of Dave Mason's influence.

As regards the US version this was originally called **Heaven Is in Your Mind** with a different cover featuring the group without Dave Mason. The title was quickly changed back to **Mr Fantasy** but the new cover remained until Island Records re-issued the UK version in the late 1970s. For the original US edition, the song order was changed and a short looping snippet of *'Here We Go Round the Mulberry Bush'* was added between most of the songs. The US LP also added three new songs from the group's UK singles, *Paper Sun, Hole in My Shoe* and *Smiling Phases* while deleting two Dave Mason songs *Hope I Never Find Me There* and *Utterly Simple*. The final track on the US album *We're a Fade, You Missed This* is actually the ending of the full length version of *Paper Sun*. For most of the songs there are significant differences between the stereo and mono mixes.

The All Music Guide's verdict on **Mr Fantasy** is that "The band's musical approach was eclectic, combining their background in British pop with a taste for the comic and dance hall styles of **Sgt Pepper**, Indian music, and blues rock jamming."**(96)** And on the American version: "The result (of reconfiguration) de-emphasised Traffic's pop-psychedelic style (a hangover from the influence of **Sgt Pepper***)* and promoted its abilities as a jamming blues rock outfit, talents that were abetted by Jimmy Miller's production and that helped launch them as an album act in the US."

My verdict is that there were two Traffics: the psychedelic pop one of *Hole In My Shoe, Paper Sun* etc. and the one that wanted to veer in a more explorative jazz rock direction culminating in the jazz section of **John Barleycorn Must Die.** Dave Mason left after **Mr Fantasy** to make some fine albums of his own.

## The Tremeloes

The Tremeloes in 1967: 'Here Comes My Baby' ****/ 'Gentleman of Pleasure' ** (CBS 45, #4 UK, #13 US) ; 'Silence is Golden' ****/ 'Let Your Hair Hang Down' ** (CBS 45 #1 UK, 11 US) ; 'Even The Bad Times Are Good' (CBS 45 #4 UK) *****/ 'Jenny's Alright' **; 'Be Mine' (CBS 45 #39 UK) ***/ 'Suddenly Winter' ***; 'Here Comes the Tremeloes' (CBS LP #15 UK); 'Suddenly You Love Me' (CBS LP)

THE MUSICIANS: Original line-up: Alan Blakely (Guitar, Keyboards, Vocals), Ricky West (Westwood) (Guitar), Mick Clark (Bass) and Dave Munden (Drums)

RECOMMENDED LISTENING/ COLLECTING: Probably best explored through 45s which shouldn't be too hard to find (although their first Decca 45 *'Blessed'* has a high market value due to its scarcity) or decent CD compilations which may be the better option as a lot of the B-sides were not too spectacular!

THE MUSICAL HISTORY: The Tremeloes were, of course, formerly Brian Poole and The Tremeloes, the group continuing after Brian Poole left to carve out a solo career (They were once Tommy Steel's backing band). The group went on to have massive commercial success eclipsing anything that had gone before. After a failed 45 on Decca they switched to CBS but a version of The Beatles' *'Good Day Sunshine'* failed to impress. Clark left and was replaced by **Len 'Chip' Hawkes** bringing a second vocalist into the group. Their breakthrough came in 1967 with an up-tempo cover of a Cat Stevens' song' *Here Comes My Baby'*. The Tremeloes was a band that enjoyed success on both sides of the Atlantic and The Four Seasons' song *'Silence is Golden'* nearly made the top 10 in the US as well as topping the UK charts. The jaunty Caribbean beat styled *'Even The Bad Times Are Good'* was a true sixties classic. A succession of hits was completed in 1967 with an Italian ballad written by The Scooters, *'Be Mine'*, which had a more interesting B-side, *'Suddenly Winter'*, a tentative expedition into psychedelia. The Tremeloes song *'Hard Times'* was included on the A Monstrous Psychedelic Bubble Exploding in Your Mind vol.3 "The 3rd Ear" CD by **Amorphous Androgynous**.

That aside The Tremeloes didn't exactly keep up with the times and were basically a good time vocal harmony pop band and very good at it. The would go on to enjoy further success with *'Suddenly You Love Me'*, #6 in 1968; *'(Call Me) Number One'* and *'Me and My Life'*, #2 and #4 respectively in 1970. They might have had another #1 in 1970 but hesitated when offered Jeff Christie's *'Yellow River'* and Christie himself recorded it with backing from The Tremeloes!

## The Who

The Who in 1967: *'Pictures of Lily'* (Track 45, #4 UK, #51 US) **** (The Lily referred to was Lily Bayliss, a pin-up in the 1920s); *'The Last Time'* (Track 45, #44 UK) ****; *'I Can See for Miles'* (Track 45, #10 UK) *****; *'The Who Sell Out'* (Track LP, #13 UK; #48 US in 1968) ****

THE MUSICIANS (basic instrumentation): Pete Townshend (Guitar, Vocals), Roger Daltrey (Vocals), John 'The Ox' Entwistle (Bass) and Keith Moon (Drums) (see below for further details)

RECOMMENDED LISTENING/ COLLECTING: Taking **The Who Sell Out** as an example the definitive CD release to date is the Polydor 2 CD remastered version from 2009. Recent LP reissues of the album are the mono 2012 version on Track/ Polydor and the remastered 180g European LP edition also on Track/ Polydor (2015). **The Complete Chronicle of the Who 1958-1978(Neill/ Kent) (113)** has a comprehensive selected US/ UK discography. (My copy, the 2nd edition, is from 2007 but it may have been revised since then). The Who is a great band to listen to on either 45s, LPs, live (e.g. **Live at Leeds**) or on certain compilations (e.g. **Meaty Beaty Big and Bouncy**). Their records are much sought after by collectors including: copies of their Brunswick singles (*'I Can't Explain'*, *'Anyway, Anyhow, Anywhere'*, *'My Generation'*, *'The Kids Are Alright'*, *'A Legal Matter'* and *'La-La-La Lies'*); *'The Last Time'* (on Track); the **'Rock Steady Who'** EP (on Reaction). While the singles won't completely break the bank the following LPs in excellent condition will: **'My Generation'** (Brunswick, 1965, mono originals on sale for up to £800 on Discogs); **'A Quick One'** (£125+ – if it's the 500 limited copy with stickered sleeve and poster probably best forget it!); first pressings of all '60s' albums including **'Tommy'** and **'Live at Leeds'** from 1970, the latter not as expensive.

## The Musical History:

The Detours [104] became **The High Numbers** and The High Numbers became The Who. Their recording career started off with a top 10 UK song (top 100 US), *'I Can't Explain'* in 1965, ahead of its time with Jimmy Page and The Ivy League drafted in to

---

[104] The Detours did a version of Edvard Grieg's *'In the Hall of the Mountain King'* from his 'Peer Gynt Suite' based on an arrangement by Johnny Kidd and The Pirates. A similar version was recorded by The Who in 1967 and eventually appeared as a bonus track to **'The Who Sell Out'** CD in 1995.

help with the guitar and vocals. Once he found his feet Pete Townshend, would become one of the world's premier guitarists, the session men could be dispensed with and *'Anyhow, Anytime, Anywhere'* proved to be a good follow-up and another top 10 hit but was surpassed by the classic *'My Generation'*, another #1 that never was, falling just one place short of that elevated spot.

The Who's first album *'My Generation'* (also on Brunswick Records like their first two 45s) contained some cracking stuff like *'The Kids Are Alright'*, *'A Legal Matter'*, *'The Good's Gone'* and *'The Ox'*, a guitar excursion named after bassist John 'The Ox' Entwistle. The group signed for the Reaction label in March, 1965 for whom they released the classic **'Substitute'**, **'I'm A Boy'**, their biggest ever single hit (#2 UK) which escaped a ban despite dealing with transvestitism and *'Happy Jack'*, their first US top 30 single and a #4 in the UK. In the winter of 1966 they re-recorded songs played in October on a *'Ready, Steady, Go'* TV special and released it as the *'Ready Steady Who'* EP which is much sought after by collectors. Included on the EP were a stirring version of The Beach Boys' *'Barbara Ann'* and *'The Batman Theme'*.

Their second LP **'A Quick One'** did very well in the UK reaching #4 but less well in the States (where it was entitled **'Happy Jack'**). Of particular interest was a precursor of *'Tommy'* in Pete Townshend's mini rock opera on the subject of infidelity, *'A Quick One While He's Away'*. *'Boris the Spider'* was also a weirdly fascinating song written by John Entwistle.

As 1967 dawned Kit Lambert and Chris Stamp, The Who's managers, started their own record label, Track which was, in fact, a subsidiary of Polydor.[105] The Who were automatic signings and were rapidly followed by the first new signing, one Jimi Hendrix. Pete Townshend, Eric Clapton and John Entwistle saw The Jimi Hendrix Experience perform at The Bag O' Nails on 11th January, the very evening Hendrix put pen to paper. What is less known is that Lambert and Stamp put each member of The Who to work as talent scouts to try to find budding acts in different genres and Pete Townshend very nearly signed The Bonzo Dog Doo Dah Band and actually did sign The Crazy World of Arthur Brown. A half hour appearance at the Monterey Festival in June, 1967 [106] helped to further establish The Who in the US as a new force in rock with a spectacular if violent stage act (Townshend smashed his Strat and Moon kicked over his drum kit to the surreal background of coloured smoke bombs). The following month they supported Herman's Hermits, who at that time were the most successful British invasion band despite being a proverbial case of 'chalk and cheese'! On the back of this, on 15th September, the group went to CBS TV studios on Sunset Boulevard, Hollywood to record their US TV debut on the Smothers Brothers Comedy Hour after Tommy Smothers had seen them perform at Monterey.

On the recording front a Rolling Stones cover *'The Last Time/ Under My Thumb'* in support of the infamous Stones 'drug bust' followed but these were just a warm-up for another milestone record *'I Can See for Miles'* which gave them their first top ten hit in the US.

---

[105] The launch party for Track Records didn't take place until 16th March, at The Speakeasy in London. The guests included actor Michael Caine, model Jean Shrimpton, the World Cup winning England football team captain Bobby Moore and American singer song writing duo Simon and Garfunkel.;
[106] The complete set can be heard on the Rhino 4 CD set **The Monterey International Pop Festival.**

# IMPORTANT ALBUMS OF 1967 (21)
## SELL OUT by THE WHO

THE MUSICIANS: Pete Townshend (Electric and Acoustic Guitar, Vocals, Keyboards, Banjo, Penny whistle, Sonovox – 1); Roger Daltrey (Vocals, Percussion), John Entwistle (Bass, Vocals, Horns, Sound Effects), Keith Moon (Drums, Percussion, Backing Vocals, Sound Effects) with guests Al Kooper (Keyboards, Organ), Speedy Keen (Co-Lead Vocals – 1); PRODUCERS: Chris Stamp (Executive); Kit Lambert (Engineer, 1 of 4); DESIGN: David King, Roger Law; photography: David Montgomery; psychedelic poster design: Adrian George; Richard Evans – design and art direction (RELEASE DATE: 15th December, 1967; LABEL: Track; CHART: #13 UK, #48 US. (The first 500 mono LPs were issued with a 6 panel fold out poster – as rare as hen's teeth now I would imagine!)

## Tracklisting/ Credits

| | | |
|---|---|---|
| 1. | Armenia, City in the Sky (Speedy Keen) | 3:50 |
| 2. | Heinz Baked Beans (John Entwistle) | 1:00 |
| 3. | Mary Anne with the Shaky Hand (Pete Townshend) | 2:30 |
| 4. | Odorono (Pete Townshend) | 2:35 |
| 5. | Tattoo (Roger Daltrey/ Pete Townshend) | 2:50 |
| 6. | Our Love Was (Pete Townshend) | 3:25 |
| 7. | I Can See For Miles (Pete Townshend) | 4:05 |
| 8. | Can't Reach You (Pete Townshend) | 3:05 |
| 9. | Medac (John Entwistle) | 0:57 |
| 10. | Relax (Pete Townshend) | 2:40 |
| 11. | Silas Stingy (John Entwistle) | 3:05 |
| 12. | Sunrise (Pete Townshend) | 3:05 |
| 13. | Rael (1 and 2) (Pete Townshend) | 5:45 |

## The Music Track by Track

1. **Radio London Jingle/ Armenia City in the Sky**: The beginning of the music is surely an unconscious (at least) inspiration for Thin Lizzy's '*The Boys Are Back in Town*' and the whole song hints at psychedelia through the extensive use of electronic phasing, written by John (Speedy) Keen – indeed the 'freak out' at the end cold be intended as a send-up of psychedelia! Roger Daltrey's lyrics owe a debt to The Beatles' '*Tomorrow Never Knows*' On the album Pete Townshend's guitar would be filtered through a Leslie Cabinet with backwards guitar overdubbed by Kit Lambert.
2. **Radio London Jingle/ Heinz Baked Beans**: A John Entwistle song with brass (of course), a brief parody of sorts not quite as far out as the Bonzos but close;
3. **More Music/ Mary Anne with the Shaky Hand / Premier Drum Jingle**: Supposedly a female masturbation fantasy in the same way that '*Pictures of Lily*' referred to male fantasies, this quirky Townshend song has an enduring if perplexing appeal;

4. **Radio London Jingle/ Odorono** projects forward to the *'See Me, Feel Me'* theme of 'Tommy', the story line centres around a girl who take an audition but fails because of her prominent body odour;

5. **Radio London Jingle/ Tattoo**, a forlorn song of teenage angst and one of Townshend's finest – the clever lyric is delivered well by three-part vocal harmonies;

6. **Radio London Jingle/ Our Love Was**, a tender Pete Townshend love song with the first guitar solo on the album, it references The Beach Boys own *'You're So Good To Me'*;

7. **Radio London/ Speakeasy/ Rotosound Strings/ I Can See for Miles**, credited to Pete Townshend, the 'piece de resistance', Townshend described it as 'the ultimate Who record' – few would disagree. The final mixing and mastering of *'I Can See for Miles'* was done in Los Angeles' Gold Star Studio famous for its echo;

8. **Charles Atlas/ I Can't Reach You**, a bit of a west coast American influence, the development of Pete Townshend's lyric writing is becoming increasingly obvious, a lot of piano on this one as well;

9. **Medac**, another wry John Entwistle vignette about acne;

10. **Relax/ Rotosound Strings**, organ is prominent in quite a heavy psych tinged Townshend song which was completed on an eight-track machine in New York;

11. **Silas Stingy** is an **Entwistle** song about a miser with French horn and, again, organ plays throughout, similar to *'Uncle Ernie'* on 1968's **'Tommy'**;

12. **Sunrise**, played on 12 string, has a classical guitar touch and a jazzy feel, another Townshend song marking his continuing evolution as a writer;

13. **Rael 1:** Credited to Townshend once again, *Rael 1* is the most ambitious song on the album recalling what The Beach Boys were doing in 1967 in their aborted 'Smile' project. It has organ by **Al Kooper** and features Keith Moon at his most dynamic – its central theme would be revisited on **'Tommy'**, the use of acoustic guitar and thunderous tympani pointing the way to THE rock opera. The 'Track Records… Track Records' heard at the end of the LP was recorded in the studio from a telephone speaker dictated by Entwistle and Moon who were in a pub near Kingsway Studios.

Dave Marsh in his liner notes for the CD reissue describes it as the 'complete' rather than the 'extended' **'Sell Out'** album so let's take a look at the other material that was recorded at the time:

14. **Rael 2/ Top Gear**, an interesting short additional section to Townshend's mini rock opera followed by a 12 bar jingle;

15. **Glittering Girl/ Coke 2**, a strong Townshend song that was never officially released to that point, Kinksian in its verve;

16. **Melancholia/ Bag O'Nails**, NB this worthy Townshend song was not recorded until 1968;

17. **Something's Coming/ John Mason's Cars**, unusual in that Daltrey sings the vocal on an Entwistle song with a full brass arrangement, *'Something's Coming'* was the B-side of *'I Can See for Miles'* followed by another Who concocted jingle in the hope perhaps of being given a car or two?;

18. **Jaguar/ John Mason's Cars (Reprise)**, surprisingly omitted from the original album (the inclusion of the song in Mojo Magazine contributors' top 50 greatest Who songs support this contention). There is a little tip of the hat to Hendrix, a spirited performance by Moon (as always!) this may be the kind of car the lads were after! Mojo's verdict on 'Jaguar' was that "Townshend's version of acid-rock was sulphuric not lysergic, answering the psychedelia of the summer of love with warped visions of rampant consumerism"**(97)** Once again thundering tympani is in evidence

19. **Early Morning Cold Taxi/ Coke 1,** a Daltrey co-write, this is the most Beatle-ish sounding number I think, great bass playing by Entwistle and a neat little guitar break by Townshend;

20. **Hall of The Mountain King/ Radio One (Boris Mix)**, a popular classical number by Edvard Grieg, the Norwegian composer taken from his 'Peer Gynt Suite' covered by many '60s' groups but not quite as The Who did it! The guitar and vocal shenanigans are wild This is followed by a very brief *'Boris The Spider'* jingle;

21. **Girl's Eyes**, a respectable rare excursion into song writing by Keith Moon with great drumming and guitar, concerning a fan staring out at him from her front row seat;

22. **Odorono (Final Chorus)**, clipped from original LP;

23. **Mary Anne with The Shaky Hand (alternative version)** with **Al Kooper** on organ this appeared the B-side of the US 45 of *'I Can See For Miles'*;

24. **Glow Girl/ Track Records Jingle**, described by Pete Townshend in the sleeve notes to The Who's **'Odds and Sods'** album as 'a rock 'n' roll airplane crash song with a real Pop Art plane crash and a happy reincarnation ending.' 'It's a girl, Mrs Walker' is how it ends pointing directly to the momentous **'Tommy'**.

It should be noted that many of the 'bonus' tracks on the CD 'The Who Sell Out' appeared on the **'Thirty Years of Maximum R&B'** LP.

Still to come were the double album **'Tommy'** (and film), the seminal concert album **'Live at Leeds',** the classic **'Who's Next'** and another double album **'Quadrophenia'** telling the story of mods and rockers; and, of course, timeless classics such as *'Pinball Wizard'* and *'Won't Get Fooled Again'*. 1967 was a high water mark as their song writing matured to the extent that they could confidently put together a concept album as strong as **'The Who Sell Out'**. This came 'against all odds' as Pete Townshend describes in his revealing book 'Who I am'. Townshend paints the picture: the usual scenario. Chris Stamp pushes The Who for another LP. Pete doesn't think they have enough material. He reconsiders and presents *'Tattoo'* and *'Odorono'*. Kit Lambert suggests jingles to form bridges between songs, John and Keith begin making these up. The LP was still short so John unveiled *'Silas Stringy'* and Speedy Keen's *'Armenia'* was also presented. But it was two advertising men David King and Roger Law (later the co-creator of the Spitting Image satirical puppet-show) who came up the title **'The Who Sells Out'** and the idea that each group member would advertise a product.

On their summer into autumn tour of America the group listened to **Sergeant Pepper's Lonely Hearts Club Band,** a lot. The tectonic plates of rock music seemed to be shifting and the bar had been raised higher than ever- it was doubted if even The Beatles theselves could improve upon it. What the album lacked in social or political protest it more than compensated in terms of the songs themselves, songs that seemed to exist of themselves and for themselves, creating a world of light and shade that only The Beach Boys' **Pet Sounds** had come close to. (The Who were also well aware of the impact of **Pet Sounds**). Andy Neill in his liner notes for the Deluxe Edition double CD of '**The Who Sell Out**' takes a look from the outside: In 1967 "The Who felt disassociated from the prevailing mood, this ambivalence to the zeitgeist was unconsciously reflected in **The Who Sell Out**. While Townshend had experimented with LSD and was aware of the innovative gauntlet The Beatles' **Sergeant Pepper** had laid down, **The Who Sell Out** contains the period's forward-thinking spirit yet somehow stands curiously aloof." **The Who Sell Out** is a difficult album to categorise, as Neill points out, only four of its tracks could reasonably be dubbed 'psychedelic' and the lack of continuity of style (not necessarily a bad thing at all) almost fragments the concept (in my view it hangs together 'by the skin of its teeth') stops it short of becoming a 'classic' and the time pressure the group was under to come up with material was definitely a factor that undermined the whole foundations of the project. Considering this, **The Who Sell Out,** createdin the shadow of two albums, **Sergeant Pepper** and **Pet Sounds**, albums that created a 'shockwave' that redefined and set a new standard for pop and rock music as Pete Townshend freely admits, is a remarkable achievement.

## The Yardbirds/ Jimmy Page

**The Yardbirds in 1967:** '*Little Games*'/ '*Puzzles*' (Columbia 45) (March) ***/*** (Jimmy Page's soloing on 'Little Games' is much admired); '**Over, Under, Sideways Down**' (Over, Under, Sideways Down/ Jeff's Boogie/ Mr Zero/ Knowing (Columbia EP) (January) ***; '**Yardbirds With Sonny Boy Williamson**' (Fontana) (May); '*Little Games*' (*US only LP released August, 1967 and in the UK in 1985)* *** (A successive run of 5 straight top 10 hits between 1965 and 1966 was behind them by 1967 but their story has a lot of relevance not only in what they achieved but in respect of the destinations of the component musicians).

**THE MUSICIANS: A moveable feast, with Tony 'Top' Topham, Eric Clapton then Jeff beck then Jimmy Page on guitar; Keith Relf, Paul Samwell-Smith Chris Dreja, Jim McCarty.** (Read on!)

**RECOMMENDED LISTENING/ COLLECTING:** A Record Store Day 2,500 copy limited run of **Little Games** on coloured vinyl was issued in 2014. In 2015 Parlophone released the LP again directly cut on 180g vinyl from the 1967 stereo master tapes, including an MP3 download code. There are numerous compilations of Yardbirds music with varying stature. A significant compilation of **The Yardbirds Live at The BBC** was released on Repertoire in the summer of 2016 and represents good value with 40 tracks, all in mono, over 2 CDs recorded for 'Top Gear', 'Saturday Club' etc. It authenticity is reinforced by the cooperation of Jim McCarty and Paul Samwell-Smith in the project and interviews with Keith Relf, Jimmy Page and Samwell-Smith himself. In reverse chronological order other CDs and LPs include **Shapes of Things: The Best of the Yardbirds** a 2 CD 40 track compilation released on Music Club Deluxe in 2010. I like **As, Bs and Eps** sets for their completeness and continuity and Repertoire Germany issued a 2 CD set with a whopping 50 tracks in 2007. Again 45s and early LPs are a good option for the serious but it might be difficult to find these in reasonable condition and at a reasonable cost. However, speaking from personal experience there is nothing like a thick early vinyl pressing to reveal the true sound of The Yardbirds! Be warned though that '**The Five Yardbirds**' EP may set you back nearly £100 and you can double that for the '**Over Under Sideways Down**' EP while the '**Five Live Yardbirds**' LP 1st pressing may cost a couple of hundred, a much cheaper option is the 1969 2nd pressing, probably a quarter of that or less. Things settle down with '**The Yardbirds**' LP (Columbia, 1966) where an original copy may be had for as little as £50. The '**Shapes**

of Things' LP box released on Charly in 1984 is valued higher but I wouldn't expect to pay much more than £30–£40 for it (It is a nice collection though). Collectible singles are: *'I Wish You Would'*, *'Good Morning Little Schoolgirl'*, *'Happening Ten Years' Time Ago'* and *'Little Games'* all around £25 in excellent condition. As with all vinyl it depends on how much you want it and how much you are prepared to pay for it and, of course, these ballpark figures do not tell the whole complicated story of valuing an album, all of which will be in different condition.

## The Musical History:

Jimmy Page grew up on a diet of Elvis, Chuck Berry, Buddy Holly and his guitar heroes were James Burton, Rick Nelson's guitarist, whose string bending solos he much admired, Cliff Gallup who backed Gene Vincent and, on the acoustic side, Bert Jansch (especially *'Alice's Wonderland'* and *'Finches'* from Jansch's first album). He did the usual sort of things for budding musicians – joined a local group called Neil Christian and the Crusaders whose musical diet was dominated by Chuck Berry and Bo Diddley and attended art school. He also played at blues nights in the Marquee Club in Oxford Street, London where Alexis Korner and Cyril Davies of the Blues Incorporated project played alongside three men who would go on to find fame (and fortune) of their own: Mick Jagger, Charlie Watts and Jack Bruce. Page decided that session work rather than a group role was for him and joined the likes of Big Jim Sullivan as a session guitarist. Among his contributions were: for Jet Harris and Tony Meehan on *'Diamonds'*; for The Who on *'I Can't Explain'* (rhythm guitar with fuzz lead on the B-side); for Sonny Boy Williamson (with organist Brian Auger and drummer Mick Waller). Other artists on whose records Page played included Donovan, Tom Jones, Joe Cocker and Cliff Richard. His role on The Kinks' *'You Really Got Me'* is hotly disputed with Ray Davies insisting that Page played tambourine on the record and that his brother Dave played the guitar (see The Kinks).

Page was a friend of Eric Clapton who quit The Yardbirds after refusing to play on the pop oriented *'For Your Love'* (ever the blues purist!) but he (Page) refused Giorgio Gomelsky's offer to replace Clapton and the gig was offered to another of Page's friends, Jeff Beck who was in The Tridents at the time (see Jeff Beck). Page was hired by Andrew Oldham as staff producer for the Immediate label whose roster of artists included **John Mayall's Bluesbreakers** with Eric Clapton and Chris Farlowe. He also released a single of his own in 1965 on the Fontana label entitled *'She Just Satisfies'* with *'Keep Movin'* on the B-side. He saw and was influenced by The Byrds and Buffalo Springfield while holidaying in Los Angeles and in 1966 developed his bowing technique on the electric guitar (also being perfected contemporaneously by Eddie Phillips of the band **Creation**). Eventually (in 1966) Page did join The Yardbirds after a bust-up within the band.

The seeds of the Yardbirds were actually sown in 1963, founder members Keith Relf [107] and Paul Samwell-Smith appearing as an acoustic blues combo called the Metropolis Blues Quartet. They were joined by Chris Dreja, Jim McCarty and Tony 'Top' Topham.

---

[107] Keith Relf released two solo 45 rpm records. The Julian Cope 'Head Heritage' site has a review by David Furgess of '*Shapes In My Mind/ Blue Sands* (November, 1966). He says, *"Shapes* is a 'dead ringer' for Procol Harum circa **Shine On Brightly,** a song of immense commercial appeal while *Blue Sands* is a low key blues instrumental that recalls Lovin' Spoonful numbers like *Night Owl Blues. Mr Zero/ Knowing* (The poetic A-side was written by Bob Lind who wrote *Elusive Butterfly*). Relf also recorded the 5 minute plus of *All the Falling Angels* which has a similar quality to George Harrison's *Isn't It A Pity.*

All were part of the thriving pub scene in Kingston and played in a Chicago style blues and rhythm and blues covering artists like Bo Diddley and Howlin' Wolf. Topham was replaced by Eric Clapton and The Yardbirds became less R&B and more blues oriented.

The Yardbirds moved in high circles with Giorgio Gomelsky persuading the legendary Sam Phillips (Chess Records) to supervise a session in Memphis where they recorded *'Train Kept A-Rollin'* (which would miraculously undergo a metamorphosis into *'Communication Breakdown'* on Led Zeppelin's first album) and then in the Chess Studios in Chicago, *'Shapes of Things'* and *'I'm A Man'*. Despite their growing status, ruptures were appearing within the group and, indeed Gomelsky had sold them to Simon Napier-Bell. Beck was desperate for Page to join the group as a twin guitarist but, as it transpired, Samwell-Smith [108] quit after Relf got outrageously drunk at a show at Queen's College, Oxford on 18th May, 1966 (ironically Page was in the audience) and Page joined the group, on bass, joining them at a gig at the Marquee Club on 21st June, 1966 and then on theirAmerican tour in August, 1966 which included gigs at The Whiskey in LA and the Carousel Ballroom in San Francisco where they were at the peak of their powers. The next twist of fate was when Jeff Beck felt ill before a show and Dreja shifted to bass letting Page in on lead guitar. –Beck did get his wish of playing dual lead with Page but this was captured on record only on *'Stroll On'*, a variation of *'Train Kept A-Rollin'* for the **'Blow Up'** documentary on the swinging sixties culture in London, starring David Hemmings.

A package tour of the UK followed in September with The Rolling Stones and Ike and Tina Turner, the apotheosis occurring at a Royal Albert Hall appearance on 23rd September, 1966 which was heard by Michelangelo Antonioni, the director of the aforementioned **'Blow Up'**. Meantime Beck was working with producer Mickie Most and recording *'Beck's Bolero' (*yes, it was inspired by Ravel) with Jimmy Page, Nicky Hopkins, Keith Moon and John Paul Jones. In October the Yardbirds embarked on a US Dick Clark 'Caravan of Stars' package tour which turned out to be a bit of a disaster with long distance travel, sharing a crowded bus with other artists and sometimes two shows in the one night. Beck dropped out of the tour and disappeared to LA. Although not present anyway he was unceremoniously fired and The Yardbirds continued as a four piece. Napier-Bell sold the group to Mickie Most and business partner Peter Grant as they were about to embark on a tour of Australia and Singapore. Page was concerned at Most's reputation (his association with 'pop' artists like Herman's Hermits, Lulu and Donovan) and didn't want to record 3 minute singles. He had heard the emerging Californian groups and wanted more of a psychedelic edge to the music: "Rumours of a new Beatles masterpiece called **'Sergeant Pepper's Lonely Hearts Club Band'** were flying so Jimmy was horrified when the Yardbirds were given the Mickie Most treatment." **(98)**

Indeed much of the material recorded at this time was unremarkable compared to some of what had gone before with the exception of *'Glimpses'* which features Page on bowed guitar and sitar [109] and *'Think About It'* on which Page's solo later translated into his second solo on Led Zeppelin's *'Dazed and Confused'*. Ritchie Yorke goes as far to say: "The first (US only) Most made album *'Little Games'* released in August, 1967 was

---

[108] Samwell-Smith went on to become a record producer – Cat Stevens, Carly Simon, Paul Simon and Jethro Tull were among his clients. By 30th November, Simon Napier-Bell also announced his departure to be replaced by Peter Grant.

[109] Page liked numbers like *'Eight Miles High'* and was most impressed by George Harrison's *'Within You, Without You'*

without question the worst Yardbirds album ever**(99)** [110] A lot of the tracks were first takes and the growing feeling was that all Mickie Most was interested in were hit singles, as Page had feared. How else would you explain the inclusion of a cover of Manfred Mann's *'Ha, Ha Said the Clown'*?

Another remarkable thing that happened around this time, was when, during an American tour, the group saw Jake Holmes play *'Dazed and Confused'* at the Café Au Go Go during a free night in New York. The descending bass line and tale of a paranoia inducing acid trip gone bad would, of course, be portrayed to maximum effect on the uncredited song of the same name on Led Zeppelin's debut album. There is no doubt that this was a deliberate act of plagiarism as the group purchased *'The Underground Sound of Jake Holmes'* LP shortly afterwards, Relf reinventing the lyrics, Page adding the guitar lick from *'Think About It'* and the group laying down *'I'm Confused'* for the first time in late 1967 at Madison Square Garden in New York but it is good to see Holmes has finally got the recognition he deserves.

After a final US tour The Yardbirds played their final gig at Luton Technical College in July, 1968. A New Yardbirds with John Paul Jones fulfilled the contractual obligation and toured Scandinavia but that was effectively that. Relf and McCarty quit and formed Renaissance while the Jeff Beck Group went on to record various albums with various line-ups (see Jeff Beck). Some of The Yardbirds personnel were undoubtedly influenced by The Beatles but their music still has a unique, uncompromising edge that sounds like no one else. Perhaps the best description I have heard is 'psychedelic blues trance'. Equally interesting is that there was a symbiosis between the music of The Yardbirds and emerging Californian groups like The Byrds and The Buffalo Springfield.

It is a sobering thought that the only Yardbirds numbers you are ever likely to hear on commercial radio are *'For Your Love'* and *'Heart full of Soul'*, both written by Graham Gouldman who went on to write so many classic songs with 10CC.

Their recorded legacy is much more considerable than that: the mono only 1966 45 *'Happening Ten Years' Time Ago'* is a melodically memorable psychedelically tinged experimental song complete with police siren and great guitar work (and bass rumoured to have been played by John Paul Jones). It was backed with **Johnny B Goode'** delivered Beach Boys style with the attack of a Status Quo (not even fully in existence at that point!) The 1966 album 'Yardbirds' that has become known as 'Roger The Engineer' (after Roger Cameron who engineered the LP) was completed in less than a week, a remarkable achievement considering the wealth of good material on it starting with the powerful *'Lost Women'* with its great bass riff and harmonica, a great early example of heavy blues rock. *'Over Under Sideways Down,* a 45 from the album is one of The Yardbirds' best numbers, Jeff Beck's memorable guitar line and the expansive bass playing combining a repetitive chorus with a hint of psychedelia. *'The Nazz Are Blue'* with Beck on vocals is a 12 bar blues in a style that Taj Mahal would make his own. *'Rack My Mind'* was typical of the fare on albums like John Mayall's Bluesbreakers album with Eric Clapton (the 'Beano' album). Rightly Jim McCarty in the original album sleeve note points to the fine lyrics in *'Farewell'* and experimental flourishes like the wobble board on the next track; and promising signs of progressive song writing on side

---

[110] This is perhaps a slightly harsh assessment for, apart from the aforementioned *'Glimpses'* and *'Think About It'* the LP did contain other pointers to Led Zeppelin (the Indian influenced *'White Summer'* and Renaissance (*'Only The Black Rose'*). *'Little Games'* was fine musically with bowed cello by John Paul Jones and two all too brief guitar breaks from Jimmy Page, but the harmonica was mixed too high and the song was melodically and lyrically rather nondescript.

two, as on *'What Do You Want?'* and *'Ever Since the World Began'* which could have been a prototype Black Sabbath song (until the 'hip' chorus kicks in that is!).

IMPORTANT ALBUMS OF 1967 (22)

LITTLE GAMES by THE YARDBIRDS

**THE MUSICIANS:** Jimmy Page (Guitar); Nicky Hopkins (Keyboards); Keith Relf (Vocals, Harmonica, Percussion); John Paul Jones/ Chris Dreja (Bass); Clem Cattini (Drums); Jim McCarty (Drums, Percussion, Backing vocals); **PRODUCERS:** Micky Most and Paul Samwell-Smith; **LABEL:** CBS/ Epic; **RELEASE DATE:** July, 1967 (US only); **CHART:** #80

# Tracklisting/ Credits

| | | |
|---|---|---|
| 1. | **Little Games (Harold Spiro/ Phil Wainman)** | 2:25 |
| 2. | **Smile on Me (Chris Dreja/ Jim McCarty/ Jimmy Page/ Keith Relf)** | 3:15 |
| 3. | **White Summer (Jimmy Page)** | 3:56 |
| 4. | **Tinker, Tailor, Soldier, Sailor (Jimmy Page/ Jim McCarty)** | 2:50 |
| 5. | **Glimpses (Chris Dreja/ Jim McCarty/ Jimmy Page/ Keith Relf)** | 4:25 |
| 6. | **Drinking Muddy Water (Chris Dreja/ Jim McCarty/ Jimmy Page/ Keith Relf)** | 2:54 |
| 7. | **No Excess Baggage (Roger Atkins/ Carl D'Errico)** | 2:30 |
| 8. | **Stealing, Stealing (Gus Cannon)** | 2:40 |
| 9. | **Only The Black Rose (Keith Relf)** | 2:50 |
| 10. | **Little Soldier Boy (Jim McCarty/ Jimmy Page/ Keith Relf)** | 2:40 |

# The Music Track by Track

1. **Little Games:** The clattering guitar at the start sound incongruous when the trite lyrics kick in. Beck's searing guitar and vigorous percussion elevate this little song. John Paul Jones can be heard on bowed cello;
2. **Smile On Me** is a rattling Bo Diddley beat blues; great heavy rock blues guitar again;
3. **White Summer** is a progenitor of 'Black Mountain Side' on Led Zeppelin's first LP. Originally entitled 'Arabic #' it was inspired by Davey Graham's reading of 'She Moved Through the Fair'. The longest track on the album at 4:35 it showcases Page's considerable ability on acoustic guitar with tabla backing;
4. **Tinker, Tailor, Soldier, Sailor:** again the trite lyrics are somewhat out of synch with what is going on in the background especially the bowed guitar and reversed effects which seems to come from another dimension. It is also reckoned to be the forerunner of the Led Zeppelin song 'The Song Remains the Same';

5. **Glimpses** is an intriguing, raga based, trancelike number, an instrumental (with pronounced Jimmy Page 'wah-wah') apart from some 'ahh' vocal harmonies and field recordings, Keith Relf apparently reciting a poem over the 'drone';

6. **Drinking Muddy Water** is, unsurprisingly a raucous Muddy Waters blues with Hopkins (or Ian Stewart by some accounts) on honky-tonk piano and lashings of harmonica, it all sounds pretty cluttered and unconvincing;

7. **No Excess Baggage** is a Brill building 'Tin Pan Alley' song written by the song-writing partnership of Roger Atkins/ Carl D'Errico, who also penned 'It's My Life' by The Animals;

8. **Stealing, Stealing** credited to Dreja/ McCarty/ Page/ Relf, was originally recorded by The Memphis Jug Band, a stomper with kazoo;

9. **Only The Black Rose** is a rather gloomy, acoustic number, quite touching in many ways;

10. **Little Soldier Boy**, one of the few psych songs on the LP, of course, carrying a message (almost in nursery rhyme style like 'Little Games') with explosions at the end

Dave Thompson, writing in the 'All Music Guide' gives an overview: "By 1966-1967 The Yardbirds had developed into quite an excellent experimental rock combo, marred only by an appalling lack of self-belief."**(100).** He describes the number of takes to make the album subsequently revealed in CD packages as a 'gruelling marathon'. Inevitably it is the schizophrenic nature of the recording that lets it down. It does have its moments but it is too incongruous and inconsistent to attract many plaudits and a group that has fostered so much talent and has even been described as "in the vanguard of progressive rock" was surely capable of so much more. Mickie Most has taken criticism for this but the group collectively and individually must share the responsibility. The fact that there seemed to be little or no progression – its predecessor **The Yardbirds ('Roger the Engineer')** having gathered more positive reviews. Indeed, Keith Relf recalled, when interviewed in 1974, that "Towards the end of 1967 we were playing The Fillmore. We were more into the psychedelics… we were getting off on sound and feedback and letting it go," confirming that the ambitious, experimental spirit was alive and well even if it didn't always translate onto records where 2 to 3 minute 'pop' songs were often the driver.[111] Perhaps the best way to sum up is another quote from Record Collector "The Yardbirds entered 1968 in a state of (dazed) confusion."**(101)** The rumours that Page, Beck, Hopkins, Jones and Moon forming a 'super-group' prompted the famous comment from Moon that this would probably "go down like a lead balloon". It is likely that this comment registered with Page when considering a name for his next project.

---

[111] The Yardbirds live act at the time included *I'm A Man* featuring Page using his famous violin bow on electric guitar and The Velvet Underground's *Waiting For The Man*

# The Band Digest
## Over 100 Other Artists of 1967

The only reason some of these artists are not included in the main section is because either: they were very much of their time or they would come to prominence later on.

**The Accent,** Yorkshire,
**The Action,** London
**The Artwoods/ St. Valentine's Day Massacre,** London
**The Attack,** London
**Band of Joy,** West Bromwich, Birmingham
**The Beatstalkers,** Glasgow
**Madeline Bell,** New Jersey to London
**Dave Berry,** Sheffield
**The Birds,** London
**Bluesology,** Middlesex
**David Bowie,** London
**Alan Bown,** London
**The Bunch,** Bournemouth,
**The Bystanders,** Merthyr Tydfil
**The Californians/ O'Hara's Playboys,** Midlands/ Glasgow
**Chicken Shack,** Birmingham area
**Joe Cocker,** Sheffield
**Dantalian's Chariot,** London
**David and Jonathan,** Bristol
**Dave Davies,** London
**Dave, Dee, Dozy, Beaky, Mick and Tich,** Salisbury
**The Deviants,** London
**Simon Dupree and The Big Sound,** Portsmouth/ Glasgow
**The Easybeats,** Australia, England
**Eire Apparent,** Belfast
**Episode Six,** Harrow
**Eyes of Blue,** Swansea
**Fairport Convention,** North London (Muswell Hill)
**The Fairy Tale,** Warrington
**Marianne Faithfull,** London
**Family,** Leicester
**Chris Farlowe and The Thunderbirds** Islington, North London
**Bill Fay,** London **Felius Andromeda,** London
**Fleetwood Mac,** London
**(Les) Flur De Lys,** Southampton
**Flowerpot Men,** London/ Sussex/ Middlesex
**Wayne Fontana and The Mindbenders,** Manchester

**The Fortunes,** Birmingham
**The Foundations**, London/ West Indies/ Sri Lanka
**Freddie and the Dreamers,** Manchester
**Elmer Gantry's Velvet Opera,** London
**Roy Harper,** Manchester
**Alex Harvey Soul Band**, Glasgow
**The Herd,** London
**Herman's Hermits,** Manchester
**Honeybus,** London
**The Idle Race,** Birmingham
**The Ivy League,** Birmingham to London
**John's Children,** Surrey
**Paul Jones,** Portsmouth
**Kaleidoscope,** London
**Kippington Lodge,** Kent
**The Koobas,** Liverpool
**Alexis Korner and his Blues Incorporated**, London
**Billy J Kramer/ Dakotas,** Lancashire, England
**Liverpool Scene,** Liverpool
**Locomotive,** Birmingham
**The Loot,** Hampshire
**The Love Affair,** London
**Lulu**, near Glasgow
**Manfred Mann,** London
**Marmalade,** Glasgow
**John Martyn,** Glasgow
**David McWilliams,** Belfast
**The Merseybeats/ Merseys,** Liverpool
**The Mickey Finn,** London
**The Misunderstood,** London
**The Mojos,** Liverpool
**Zoot Money's Big Roll Band,** Bournemouth
**The Nashville Teens,** Surrey
**The New Vaudeville Band,** London
**Nirvana,** Eire, Greece
**The Nite People,** Bournemouth, Cornwall
**The Orange Bicycle,** Weymouth
**The Outer Limits,** Leeds
**Piccadilly Line**, London
**Pinkerton's Assorted Colours,** Rugby
**Plastic Penny,** Scotland/ England/ Republic of Ireland
**The Poets,** Glasgow
**Brian Poole/ The Tremeloes,** Essex
**Duffy Power,** London
**Alan Price Set,** Durham
**John Renbourn,** Richmond
**The Renegades,** Birmingham
**The Riot Squad,** London
**The Rockin' Berries,** Birmingham
**The Rokes,** London

**The Roulettes,** Hertfordshire
**Paul and Barry Ryan**, Leeds
**Crispin St. Peters,** Kent
**Savoy Brown,** London
**The Scaffold,** Liverpool
**Skip Bifferty,** London
**The Smoke,** Yorkshire
**The Sorrows,** Coventr
**Sounds Incorporated,** London
**Sounds Orchestral,** London
**The Spectres,** London
**The Spectrum**, London
**Cat Stevens,** London
**Al Stewart,** Glasgow, Bournemouth
**The Swinging Blue Jeans,** Liverpool
**The Syn,** London
**Ten Years After,** Nottingham
**Them/ Van Morrison/ Belfasy Gypsies,** Belfast
**Timebox,** Southport
**Tomorrow,** London
**The Troggs,** Hampshire
**Gary/ Scott Walker/ The Rain,** London
**Wimple Winch,** Liverpool
**Wynder K Frog,** Bolton, Lancashire
**The Young Idea**, London
**The Zombies,** Hertfordshire

## The Accent

**INSTRUMENTS: Vocals (John Hebron), Guitars (Rick Birkett and John Hebron), Bass (Alan Davies), Drums (Pete Beetham)**

**ORIGIN:** Yorkshire, England as The Blue Blood Group then moved to London

**NOTABLE RECORDINGS: Red Sky at Night/ Wind of Change **** 45** rpm (Decca F 12679) 1967/valued at £200 mint

**REISSUES: 'Red Sky at Night' – LP: Rubble Volume 6 – The Clouds Have Groovy Faces (Past & Present)**; *CD –* **Rubble Vol 4; 'Chocolate Soup For Diabetics'** *compilation;* **'Wind of Change'** *– LP:* **Rubble Volume 11;** *CD –* **Rubble Vol 6**

**DESCRIPTION:** The Accent drew the attention of producer Mike Vernon during a residency at the Upper Cut Club and made only one record for Decca but what a record! An absolute stand-out, trippy hard rock with great spaced out guitar, electric and acoustic and, yes, it does relate the old farmer's tale of 'red sky at night shepherd's delight' but in a menacing kind of way like someone coming down from a bad trip, indeed a 'red glow' and 'shaking' are mentioned in the lyrics. Bruce Eder on the All Music website reckons that the melody anticipates Emerson, Lake and Palmer's *'A Time and a Place'* piece on their **'Tarkus'** LP. Rick Hayward was later a member of **The Zombies.**

# The Action

**INSTRUMENTS:** Vocals (Reg King/ Alan King – backing vocals), Guitars (Alan King and Pete Watson – rhythm/ lead), Bass (Mike Evans), Drums (Roger Powell)

**ORIGIN:** Kentish Town London, 1963, became The Action in 1965

**NOTABLE RECORDINGS:** *I'll Keep On Holding On* ***; *Baby You've Got It* ****/ *Since I Lost My Baby* **** (Parlophone, 1966); *Never Ever* **** and *Shadows and Reflections* *** (Parlophone, 1967);

**REISSUES (a selection):** 'The Ultimate Action' has been released by Edsel on LP and CD; 'The Action: Action Packed' is on Edsel CD, 2001. *I'll Keep Holding On* is on **Nuggets II: Original Artefacts from the British Empire and Beyond** CD 1; in 1998 'Rolled Gold' came out after acetates of the master tapes of an album planned for release by Polydor, and shelved, were found. This superseded 'Brain – The Lost Recordings 1967/68' on the Dig The Fuzz label in 1995, a second generation recording with dubious sound quality; 'Rolled Gold' inspired an interesting 2017 release of The Sidewalk Society playing an entire LP of Action numbers capturing perfectly the spirit and letter of a group that is at last receiving the kudos it deserves (on the Fruits de Mer label). What makes this recording all the more remarkable is that it consists of late '60s' demos reissued in the early 1990s reimagined and played by a group from Long Beach, California. In 2014, 'Uptight and Outasight', a large collection of TV and BBC radio broadcasts from 1966/67, and live tracks from a gig at The Boston Arms, London in 1988 was released. Finally, 'The Singles Box Set', a limited edition collection of 8" x 7" singles was issued on Record Store Day, 2014 for Demon Records.

**DESCRIPTION:** Signed by George Martin's AIR Production Company, The Action was a soul, R&B and 'mod' group, They released five singles on Parlophone between 1965 and 1967. Paul Weller: "The Action were one of the few bands to not only capture the Tamla/ soul sounds, but actually shape it into their own style and sound. Alongside Steve Marriott, I reckon Reg King stands as one of the best of the white soul singers." (Phil Collins is also a fan).

Their first 45 was a confident, super charged version of the Chris Kenner/ Fats Domino song *Land of 1,000 Dances* which name checks just about every dance craze of the time. Fine vocal harmonies and a powerful rhythm section demarcated the Action sound. A strong interpretation of The Marvelettes' *I'll Keep on Holding on* was an advancement, musically and harmonically. *Baby You've Got It* is even better, largely thanks to the addition of a doomy upright piano, pure Motown, as is the B-side *Since I Lost My Baby* which Alan Robinson describes as "a strong contender for one of the finest Brit re-toolings of a Motown song recorded in the era" in the liner notes to the 'Action Packed' Edsel CD compilation. 12-string guitar was deployed on this single.

The group changed their style to include flirtations with American west coast music and harmony pop as on their fourth 45 *Never Ever* with parping trumpet, a great effort for a group original, and on their final 45 *Shadows and Reflections* which has harpsichord and trumpet, a song that shows The Action were prepared to move with the times. The B-side *Something Has Hit Me* sounds a bit like The Mamas and Papas. Whatever they tried, The Action failed to break through, never made an album and eventually became **Mighty Baby**.

Of this transformation, John Blaney, writing for Shindig magazine, comments:

"In the summer of 1969, The Action emerged from its mod pupae a brightly coloured hippy butterfly. Now calling themselves Mighty Baby, they had been transformed by pot and jazz, both mainstays of the modernist scene." Mod anthems were replaced by puzzling improvisations that baffled their existing audience but probably endeared them to more progressively inclined listeners. **(102)**

A biography **In the Lap of the Mods** based on Ian Hebditch's recollections on their formation to their reformation in 1998, co-authored by Jane Shepherd and with an introduction by George Martin has been published. A special hardback edition, limited to 400 copies, with a one-sided 45 of a 1965 Decca acetate and a diary, listing every recording session, gig and media appearance, an extended family tree (roots would extend to pub-rockers **Ace,** and **Chilli Willi and The Red Hot Peppers** and even to **Elvis Costello and The Attractions** and **Mike and The Mechanics**), a discography and some additional memorabilia was also published.

## (The) Artwoods

**INSTRUMENTS: Vocals (Arthur Wood – elder brother of Ronnie Wood of the Faces and The Rolling Stones); Guitar (Derek Griffiths); Organ (Jon Lord); Bass (Malcolm Pool); Drums (Keef Hartley)**
**ORIGIN:** London, 1964
**NOTABLE RECORDINGS: in 1967 '*What Shall I Do?*' \*\*\*\*/ '*The Deep End*' \*\*\*\***(Parlophone) ('*What Shall I Do*' is their most collectible 45 (£120 for a mint copy); EP '**Jazz In Jeans**' ('*These Boots are Made for Walkin*' \*\*\*\*/ *A Taste of Honey* \*\*\*/ *Our Man Flint* \*\*\*\*/ *Routine* \*\*', Decca France (1966 but identified by the Repertoire CD as 1967 so considered here) (£500 for a mint copy*!*); *Brother Can You Spare A Dime* \*\*\*\*/ *Al's Party* \*\*\*\*(Fontana, 1967); LP on Decca '**Art Gallery**' (1966) \*\*\*\*(£100 mint valuation so pretty hard to come by!)
**REISSUES:** Cheaper options! – Compilation LPs: '**The Artwoods**' (Spark label, 1973) with 8 tracks from '**Art Gallery**' and '*Our Man Flint*', '*A Taste of Honey*' and '*Routine*' from '**Jazz in Jeans**'; ''**100 Oxford Street**' (Edsel, 1983) with all Decca A and B sides except '*Molly Anderson's Cookery Book*' the 1966 B-side of '*I Feel Good*''; CD-'**Art Gallery**' 26 track compilation on Repertoire and, for completists, '**Steady Getting' It: The Complete Recordings 1964-1967**' 3 CDs (RPM) released in 2014, the third CD is a live set from 1967 in Denmark with dubious sound quality but a priceless archaeological archive; a Record Collector release, 'Live at Klook's Kleek' is described by curator Ian Shirley on the magazine's website. **(103)** A live, numbered, double LP '**Live at The Klooks Kleek**' was released by Record Collector magazine as part of their rare records series in 2016.
**DESCRIPTION:** Art Wood's vocals were described by Chris Welch as 'sturdy and unpretentious' in the context of a group style grounded in soul and rhythm and blues. Their only LP '**Art Gallery**' was produced by Mike Vernon and includes the soulful '*Can You Hear Me?*', and the funky strut of '*Down in the Valley*' with its choppy Hammond organ lines and Hartley's excellent drum fills. Booker T and The MGs were a big influence, and they covered a couple of their songs including the instrumental '*Be My Lady*' featuring some nice interplay between Lord and Griffiths. A standout is '*Walk On The Wild Side*' which is given the Jimmy Smith treatment in an expansive 5:32, the 'jazzy section' three minutes in finding the group sounding very much like The Nice on '*Little Arabella*' as Lord breaks free from his restraints, bringing out the best in the rhythm section. '*I Keep Forgetting*' was later covered on the Leiber-Stoller produced '**Procol's Ninth**' by Procol Harum while Freddie and The Dreamers' '*If You Gotta Make a Fool of Somebody*' is an unlikely, if successful, choice of covers (although it does sound a bit incongruous in this company). Better still is the rendition of '*Keep Lookin*' with its introductory church organ and its mock ecclesiastical 'sermon' by Jon

Lord in what is essentially prime driving beat. *'One More Heartache'* is similarly accomplished as is a slow take on *'Work, Work. Work'* with its concise, aching guitar break – the more familiar Lee Dorsey hit is still a favourite. For me Wood's best (and earthiest) vocal performance is on *'Stop and Think It Over'*. Their take on *'Don't Cry No More'* sounds very much like Lulu's big hit *'Shout'* in structure but is much more adventurous including a little wig out at the end. Overall, **'Art Gallery'** is a very fine album deserving of an acclaim and success that was not forthcoming

Regarding their numerous 45s, a rather earnest cover of Huey Ledbetter's *'Sweet Mary'* was the first in 1964 backed with *'If I Ever Get My Hands on You'*, sounding very 'un PC' now but uplifted by a couple of nifty organ and guitar breaks. Their second 45 is of interest because of a Jon Lord composition on the B-side (*'Big City'*). Also, in 1965, *'Three Sisters'* was released but was not distinctive enough to make a breakthrough. Better was the 12 bar Booker T inflected *'She Knows What to Do'*. In 1966, two further attempts were made on the charts: *'I Take What I Want'* and *'I Feel Good'* both with novelty title B-sides *'I'm Looking for a Saxophonist Doubling French Horn Wearing Size 37 Boots'* and *'Molly Anderson's Cookery Book'*. Even the insistent guitar riff and agile bass work of *'I Take What I Want'*, a hit for Sam and Dave, failed to impress in sufficient numbers to provide any kind of hit – surprising! *'What Shall I Do'* is a nice ballad with a memorable guitar figure while *'In The Deep End'* advances into Procol Harum territory musically. The covers on the ultra-rare *'Jazz in Jeans'* EP are just great proving there was a lounge jazz alternative to Herb Alpert's magnificent take on *'A Taste of Honey'*! *'Our Man Flint'* was the title of a most entertaining 'alternative Danger Man' spy spoof. *'Routine'* was another Jon Lord original which is, to be honest, pretty routine! The final 45 was as *St Valentine's Day Massacre*, a great version (Has Griffiths been listening to Robin Trower or vice versa?) of *'Brother Can You Spare A Dime'*. On the B-side, *'Al (Capone's) Party'* Griffiths' guitar is once again a revelation and Lord delivers a short piano break.

Despite having, in Jon Lord, an organ hero to compete with Steve Winwood in the Spencer Davis Group, The Artwoods ultimately made little impact at the time although they have since been given a critical reappraisal. One claim to fame is an early appearance on the first live 'Ready, Steady Go!' TV shows and they did get plenty of live work including an Oxford Street residency but a lack of commercial success led them to being dropped by Decca. There was one last attempt at a hit single as **St Valentine's Day Massacre** dressed as gangsters! Keef Hartley joined the group from **Rory Storm and the Hurricanes** (to replace Ringo who joined The Beatles!) but was sacked. He was also sacked by John Mayall as the first track of his first album as The Keef Hartley Band (*'Sacked'* on the **'Halfbreed'** LP) depicts. He formed his own band and achieved quite a bit of success and later reunited with Derek Griffiths in **Dog Soldier**. Griffiths himself played with **The Mike Cotton Sound, Alan Bown** and **Satisfaction**. Jon Lord, of course, went on to fame as the organ player with **Deep Purple**. Art Wood went onto the short-lived **Quiet Melon** eventually resurfacing in a revived version of **Downliners Sect.** Pool joined **Colosseum** and played with **Don Partridge**, of *'Rosie'* fame.

## (The) Attack

INSTRUMENTS: Guitar (Davy O'List and Bob Taylor then Taylor with John Du Cann), Vocals (Richard Shirman), Keyboards (Bob Hodges), Bass, Clarinet (Gerry Henderson), Drums (Alan Whitehead then Barny Barnfield then, briefly Brian Davison),

**ORIGIN:** London (1966)

**NOTABLE RECORDINGS: in 1967, all on Decca: 45s** *'Try It'* \*\*\*/*'We Don't Know'* \*\*\*\*; *'Any more Than I Do* \*\*\*/ *Hi Ho Silver Lining* \*\*\*\*; *'Created by Clive* \*\*\*\*/ *'Colour of my Mind'* \*\*\*\* An excellent condition copy of the first single if you can find one would be over £100; I have seen an EX copy of the second single for £90, half that if you're less fussy about the condition; the third one is also valued at around £100 with twice that for a Dutch export only picture sleeve copy. You're probably looking at nearer £150 for their 1968 '45' *'Neville Thumbcatch'*.

**REISSUES:** There is a 1990 compilation LP **'Magic in the Air'** (Reflection) which should be obtainable at a reasonable price. This has rarities including a different version of *'Hi Ho Silver Lining'* and is recorded mostly from acetates. This plus 3 bonus tracks appear on **'The Complete Recordings from 1967–1968'** (Acme CD, 2000). **'About Time: The Definitive MOD-POP Collection 1967–1968'** (RPM CD, 2006) has all their '45' sides plus BBC sessions including a cover of Jagger/ Richard's *'Sympathy For The Devil'*; **'Final Daze',** an Italian LP on the Get Back label has a bonus 7" *'Magic in the Air* (unplugged)/ *'Go Your Way'* (demo) (The LP could cost around £40 but was released on Angel Air Records in 2001 on CD). The Attack also appears regularly on psych/ mod/ freakbeat compilations.

**DESCRIPTION:** Richard Shirman and Bob Taylor were previously in The Sound System whom Davy O'List (late of **The Nice**) hooked up with. They were joined by Bob Hodges, Gerry Henderson and Alan Whitehead to form The Attack. Whitehead soon left to join **Marmalade**. Their first '45' was a copy of **The Standells** song *'Try It'* that, despite providing a hit for **Ohio Express** in The States, did nothing in the UK. The strident drumming and bass work were to become a defining feature but The Attack sounded more at home the B-side *'We Don't Know'* a groovy, soulful ditty and protest song of sorts (although more of a song of confused youth agonising over the H Bomb, marriage and sex – "What the hell is going on, we're in a mess"). The articulate bass work and superb drumming with an extended Hammond organ passage near the end all combine well to get the message across. There was real controversy surrounding *'Hi Ho Silver Lining'* which provided a hit for **Jeff Beck** but could have gone to The Attack if only Decca had pressed the record in time. (Group Manager Don Arden was already aware of the memorable Weiss/ English song). The Attack's version is similar to Beck's only a bit slower and less of an air puncher! The clarinet and vibes give it a different feel and it is well worth checking out. Its A-side is a Shirman/ Henderson/ O'List song *'Any More Than I Do'* and also has vibes and some fine guitar from O'List. The third single *'Created By Clive'* was given to Deram group **The Syn** although neither had a hit with it. This is an s acerbic dig at the fashion culture around the King's Road in London in similar 'fashion' (!) to **The Kinks' 'Dedicated Follower of Fashion'**: Its B-side, *'Colour of My Mind'* a Shirman original is a heavy, eastern sounding psychedelic/ pharmaceutical kind of record with organ and vibes and well worth hearing (as is all The Attack music). **John Du Cann**, later of **Five-Day Week Straw People, Andromeda** and **Atomic Rooster**, joined but another single *'Magic in the Air'* was rejected as being too heavy and *'Neville Thumbcatch/ Lady Orange Peel'* was released instead. An LP called **'Roman Gods of War'** was mooted and is believed to have been scheduled for a March, 1968 release but this never materialised. Another proposed single *'Feel Like Flying/ Freedom for You'* also never appeared. Bob Taylor went on to join **The Downliners Sect** and **Elmer Gantry's Velvet Opera.**

# (The) Band of Joy/ Robert Plant

**INSTRUMENTS: Vocals (Robert Plant), Guitar (Vernon Pereira then Kevin Gammond and, briefly, Dave Pegg later bass player with Fairport Convention and Jethro Tull), Bass (Paul Lockey), Keyboards (Chris Brown), Drums (John Bonham)**

**ORIGIN:** West Bromwich near Birmingham in 1966

**NOTABLE RECORDINGS:** *Hey Joe* \*\*\*\* (a five minute plus full on version with Plant's vocal delivery as impassioned as Joe Cocker's at the time, Gammond doing sterling work on guitar), *For What It's Worth* \*\*\* (Doesn't really justice to the song, Gammon's guitar is all over it like a rash and the pace is too laboured), *Adriatic Sea View (I Got to Find My Baby)* \*\*\* (a straight blues rock but a fine vocal performance by Plant which presaged what was to come) – demos from Regent Sound Studio sessions between 1967 and May, 1968. Two LPs were recorded by a reformed Band of Joy: **The Band of Joy** (Polydor, 1978) and **24K** (Thunderbolt, 1983)

**REISSUES:** *'Hey Joe'* and *'For What It's Worth'* are on the Robert Plant compilation **'Sixty-Six to Timbuktu'** (2 x CD, Atlantic, 2003).

**DESCRIPTION:** Although Robert Plant was just starting out with his Band of Joy in 1967, it is worth taking some time on his development as a singer as he was and remains, such an important figure in rock, world and other genres of music. As a very young man, Plant was an Elvis acolyte who flirted with the blues (he was particularly taken with a performance by Sonny Boy Williamson in 1965), jamming with the Delta Blues Band in Stourbridge aged just 15, and went Mod after seeing The Who and The Small Faces in Birmingham. He was also influenced by the vocalist Steve Winwood then with Traffic.

Next came a transition from Mod to Rocker to Hippy. Plant's first recording was with a band called **Listen** with a cover of The Rascals *'You Better Run'* and in late 1966/ early 1967, other singles followed under his own name. Next up was **The Band of Joy**, completing the transition with painted faces, beads and hippy clothes, the flavour of the day. Plant plunged into the San Francisco sound getting his hands on the debut LPs by Buffalo Springfield and Moby Grape.

Love's **'Forever Changes'** was apparently another influence and The Band of Joy also performed Jefferson Airplane songs. Then Plant went to London, and backed Tim Rose and worked with Alexis Korner. Jimmy Page first saw Plant singing *'Somebody to Love'* in a kaftan and beads, and thought Plant's voice was a 'good white man's blues voice, like Rod Stewart but wilder'.

Plant wanted to put a band together and went to Oxford to find **John Henry 'Bonzo' Bonham**, a drummer in the Keith Moon/ Ginger Baker mode but who actually became even more thunderous in approach. He faced competition in recruiting Bonham who was also wanted by Joe Cocker and Chris Farlowe who were aware of his prowess as a backing drummer for American singer/ songwriter Tim Rose while touring in Britain. The New Yardbirds were disintegrating although their setlist on their Scandinavian tour was interesting featuring three numbers that would appear on Led Zeppelin's first album *'Train Kept a Rollin'* (which became *'Communication Breakdown'*), *'Dazed and Confused'* and *'I Can't Quit You Baby'* as well as a cover of Spirit's *'Fresh Garbage'* and some soul numbers, a mixed bag indeed! John Paul Jones was their bass player and he had played in the Jet Harris – Tony Meehan band aged just 17 (with John McLaughlin as the guitarist). He was influenced by the styles of Motown bass players like James Jamerson, especially the Stevie Wonder record **'I Was Made to Love Her'** on which he described the playing as 'incredible' He had done sessions for Donovan (*Sunshine Superman* and *Mellow Yellow*) and with Jimmy Page on *Hurdy Gurdy Man*. He also arranged '*She's a Rainbow*' and worked with The Rolling Stones on their album '**Their Satanic Majesties Request**'.

Opinions were mixed on Plant but Page thought he fitted perfectly into the concept of a new group with Jones and Bonham, and after ditching the name Mad Dogs (already taken by Joe Cocker), an idea already mooted by John Entwistle and Keith Moon was adopted with a slight misspelt variation Led Zeppelin instead of 'Lead Zeppelin'. One of the finest albums of all time in the heavy progressive blues rock genre was less than a year away.

Robert Plant went on to release some outstanding albums as a solo artist during the 1980s right through to his 2014 album with The Sensational Space Shifters **Lullaby and the Ceaseless Roar** on Nonesuch Records including a 2010 album with, you guessed it, **The Band of Joy**, on Rounder Records.

## (The) Beatstalkers

**INSTRUMENTS: Ronnie Smith (Guitar, Vocals), Eddie Campbell (Organ,** later of **Tear Gas, Guitar), Davie Lennox (Vocals), Alan Mair then Joe Gaffney (Bass), 'Tudge' Williamson then Jeff Allen,** later of **East of Eden (Drums)**

**ORIGIN:** Glasgow, Scotland, 1965

**NOTABLE RECORDINGS:** The strident *You Better Get a Better Hold on* (B-side of '*Left Right Left*' (Decca, 1966); three 45 rpms for Decca in 1965-66 in total, and four 45 rpms for CBS between 1967 and 1969; their 1967 45s were '*My One Chance to Make It ***/ Ain't Got No Soul (Left in These Old Shoes) *** and '*Silver Treetop School for Boys' ***/ 'Sugar Coated Man' *** (all singles are collectible and fetch between £60 and £80 in mint condition).

**REISSUES:** You can hear '*You'd Better Get a Better Hold on*' on 'The Freakbeat Scene' CD. The 16 track **'Scotland's No 1 Beat Group'** remastered CD on Ika Records (2005) with a 24 page booklet with visual memorabilia and liner notes is recommended as an overview.

**DESCRIPTION:** They were, as their name suggests, a beat group who used a lot of fuzz guitar in their live act. Alan Mair ran a boutique in Kensington selling hand-made clothes including coats of many colours and platform boots, and had Freddie Mercury working for him for a while. Their first single '*Everybody's Talking About My Baby*' sold well in Scotland where they were sometimes known as the Scottish Beatles although, in fact, they included more obscure Rolling Stones songs in their repertoire. Their debut 45 was similar in some ways to The Small Faces largely because of its organ riff. Their second 45 '*Left, Right, Left*' was more poppy and its B-side 'the Joe South song '*You'd Better Get a Better Hold on*' was more typical of their live sound with its overdriven fuzz guitars. The next A-side '*A Love Like Yours*', a Holland-Dozier-Holland cover was unremarkable and its B-side '*Base Line*' was, I am reliably informed, an instrumental version of the Troggs '*I Can Only Give You Everything*'. Their 1967 singles were *My One Chance to Make It/Ain't Got No Soul (Left in These Old Shoes)* The A-side is a ballad – without being particularly ear-catching, it has a cleverly constructed lyric and prominent bass. The B-side became a popular Northern Soul number with some interesting guitar lines. Their next single was *Silver Treetop School for Boys/Sugar Chocolate Machine.* The A-side is a **David Bowie** song on which he contributes backing vocals. It has been described as 'English whimsy psychedelia' with the singer recounting his days at a public school, Kinks like nostalgia, a little clumsy but with a nice little chorus at the end. A Bowie songs website uses the word 'awkward' about the lyrics which is fair enough. There was also a reference to everyone loving the grass at Silver Treetop School for Boys! The B-side is an original and, again captures the psychedelic vibe in 1967, about time spent in café bars with a nice piano outro and interesting changes in tempo. The group's dabbling with psych continued in 1968 with *'Rain Coloured Rose'* and another Bowie composition *'Everything is You'*. A Bowie song made the A-side of their 1969 CBS single, *'When I'm Five',* backed with an unreleased Action song, **Little Boy**. The fuzz guitar and organ are notable.

At a fiftieth anniversary reunion in Glasgow, their repertoire consisted of a few covers – Donnie Elbert's *'Little Piece of Leather'*, the old blues *'Stagger Lee'*, Otis Redding's *'Mr Pitiful'* and the like; but also a fair sprinkling of originals including the A and B sides of their first single.

# Madeline Bell

**ORIGIN:** Newark, New Jersey then London

**NOTABLE RECORDINGS/ DESCRIPTION:** Madeline Bell moved from the USA in 1962, having toured with the gospel show 'Black Nativity' and worked as a session musician providing backing vocals for the likes of Scott Walker and Dusty Springfield (who was also the President of her fan club!) After a series of singles, she arrived in 1967 with a creditable 45 *'Picture Me Gone'* \*\*\* (Philips, 1967) which was to become a Northern Soul favourite and a memorable LP **'Bell's a Poppin'** \*\*\*\* (also on Philips). The LP includes a terrific version of *'Can't Get Used to Losing You'*, a #2 hit for Andy Williams in 1963 perfect for Bell's clear enunciation and silky voice. There are also strong versions of John Sebastian's *'Didn't Want to Have to Do It',* and Tamla number *'I'm Gonna Make You Love Me'* which was originally recorded by Dee Dee Warwick and was a #3 hit for Diana Rossand The Supremes and The Temptations in 1969. A lot of credit must go to Dave Greenslade's Dad Arthur for his arrangements on the album. Madeline would enjoy a #3 hit herself in 1969 as part of Blue Mink with the number *'Melting Pot'* and in the same year, provide backing vocals for two brilliant tracks, The Rolling Stones' *'You Can't Always Get What You Want'* and Joe Cocker's *'Bye, Bye Blackbird'* with Jimmy Page on guitar.

# Dave Berry

**INSTRUMENTS:** Berry was backed by **The Cruisers** playing a repertoire made up largely of Chicago blues at the Esquire Club in Sheffield. However, it took them so long to record the debut 45 that Mike Smith, the Decca recording manager hired session musicians for future records (although The Cruisers remained the group for live recordings). Among these session men were **Jimmy Page, John Paul Jones** and **'Big Jim' Sullivan**. The Cruisers' line-up consisted of **John Fleet (Bass and Piano), Roy Barber (Rhythm Guitar), Frank Miles then Frank White then Roy Ledger (Lead Guitar) and Kenny Slade (Drums)**. Local musicians **Johnny Riley, Alan Taylor** and **Pete Cliff** were also in the second generation of The Cruisers.

**ORIGIN:** Sheffield, England (Dave Berry was born David Holgate Grundy)

**NOTABLE RECORDINGS/ DESCRIPTION:** Dave Berry was still operating in 1967, although his most productive days were by then over. In fact, his last single was released in 1972. Mickie Most supervised the recording of a demo tape at Decca and their debut 45, a cover of Chuck Berry's *'Memphis, Tennessee'* with The Cruisers made the lower reaches of the UK top 20. His breakthrough record was *'The Crying Game'* (1964) with guitar by Jimmy Page which made UK #5. A cover of Bobby Goldsboro's

US hit *'Little Things'* gave him another #5 UK hit in 1965. He subsequently became more appreciated by record buyers in European countries than in his own country. For example, his 1965 single *This Strange Effect* was a cover of a Ray Davies song and made #1 in Belgium and Holland. He released two 45s in 1967 *Stranger ***/ Stick By The Book ** and **Forever ***/ And I Have Learned to Dream*. ***/ *'Forever'*, written by The Gibb brothers (see The Bee Gees). Sadly, his contribution to popular music has been reduced by many to *'The Crying Game'* and little else. Of course, as always that doesn't tell the whole story! Those around at the time will remember him hiding his face in the collar of his jacket when singing live and his gestural hand movements when handling the microphone as if it were a cobra!

REISSUES: *'The Crying Game'* can be heard on numerous sixties compilations and *'Don't Gimme No Lip Child'*, subsequently covered by The Sex Pistols can be heard on the **'R&B Scene' CD**. There are two comprehensive double CD compilations: **'This Strange Engine: The Decca Session 1963-1966'** and **'Picture Me Gone: The Decca Years 1966-1974'** on the RPM label.

## The Birds

INSTRUMENTS: **Ronnie Wood and Tony Munroe (Guitar, Vocals), Ali McKenzie (Vocals, Harmonica), Kim Gardner (Bass, Vocals), Bob Langham and Pete McDaniels (Drums)**

ORIGIN: West London, England, 1964. The Birds was originally named Thunderbirds after the Chuck Berry song *'Jaguar and the Thunderbird'* but changed their name when Chris Farlowe and his Thunderbirds hit the charts. The Birds fan club was receiving angry letters protesting that, instead of receiving copies of the 1965 record *'Leaving Here'* (a cover of a Holland-Dozier-Holland song later covered by Motorhead!), they were receiving copies of *'Mr Tambourine Man'* by The Byrds instead. The Birds' manager Leo De Clerk instituted legal action over the name and The Byrds arriving in Heathrow Airport, hyped up as America's answer to The Beatles, were served with writs in the Heathrow arrival hall!

NOTABLE RECORDINGS: Their rarest recording is *'Say Those Magic Words'* released on the Reaction label in 1966 as The Birds with guest guitar by Jeff Beck on the B-side *'Daddy, Daddy'*. (They also recorded a version of Jack Bruce's *'N.S.U.* which appeared on Cream's first album). There is one unreleased track from March, 1967, *'Granny Rides Again'* *** written by Ronnie Wood

REISSUES: The definitive collection is a 2005 Deram CD called **'The Collectors' Guide to Rare British Birds'** with all their singles, demos and unreleased material, and a treasure trove of information. Look out for tracks on **Nuggets, Perfumed Garden, Mod** and **Freakbeat Scene** compilations. There is also a 12 track LP entitled **'Say Those Magic Words'** (The Beat Records Company, 1997)

DESCRIPTION: The Birds was a Tamla Motown and R&B influenced group who branched into psychedelia. Bass player Kim Gardner left in 1966 and joined Creation, and was later part of Ashton, Gardner and Dyke (*'Resurrection Shuffle'* et al). **Ronnie Wood** was their most famous member, currently still in The Rolling Stones where he arrived via The Jeff Beck Group and The Faces. Taken on by Dick Rowe of Decca Records, the man who famously rejected The Beatles, The Birds had a minor hit top 50 hit with *'Leaving Here'*, their second 45 and described in the liner notes to the CD compilation as a 'full on guitar thrash'. After four singles, the group ceased to exist in 1967 and never made an album.

# Bluesology

**INSTRUMENTS: Caleb Quaye, Neil Hubbard, Stuart Brown (Guitars); Reg Dwight (keyboards); Elton Dean, Mark Charig (sax/ brass); Rex Bishop (Bass) and Mick Inkpen (Drums).**
**ORIGIN:** Middlesex, England, 1961
**NOTABLE RECORDINGS:** Bluesology released their last single in 1967, a cover of Kenny Lynch's *'Since I Found You Baby' *,* an undistinguished effort. None of their three singles between 1965 and 1967, two on Fontana, one on Polydor made much impact. *'Come Back Baby'* their first single was written by Reg Dwight (Elton John) and is worth £300 in mint condition as is their 1966 single *'Mister Frantic'*. I am not aware of any reissues.
**DESCRIPTION:** A blues and R&B band notable (and collectible) because of launching the careers of musicians who went on to achieve artistic and commercial success. Apart from **Elton John,** group members went on to become members of **Hookfoot, Cochise**, **Heads, Hands and Feet, The Grease Band** and **Soft Machine** They allegedly took their name from a Django Reinhardt album **'Djangology'** but a Modern Jazz Quartet piece entitled *'Bluesology'* may have had something to do with it.

# David Jones Aka David Bowie

Why is David Bowie here? Well, it was not until *Space Oddity* in 1969 that David Bowie took off. Of course, he had a lot more in his locker (pun entirely intentional).
**INSTRUMENTS**: **David Bowie (Vocals, Acoustic Guitar, Saxophone)** and as part of various groups (see below).
**ORIGIN:** Brixton, London
**NOTABLE RECORDINGS:** David Bowie as a part of the Kon-Rads (1962–63) then Davie Jones and the King Bees (1964), then The Manish Boys who released one 45 *I Pity the Fool* on Parlophone in 1965. Next came The Lower Third with one 45 *You've Got a Habit of Leaving* also on Parlophone. David Jones' first 45 as David Bowie, *Can't Help Thinking About Me,* got much airplay on Radio London. This and two subsequent 45s on Pye in 1966 failed to make much impact. *Rubber Band/ The London Boys* was Bowie's first 45 for his new label Deram. The A-side was a novelty song, its flip, an interesting parody of swinging London. His first 1967 single *The Laughing Gnome *** has been compared in style to Anthony Newley and was seen as a novelty record at the time but did chart in 1973 (#6 UK) as a 'cash in' on Bowie's mega success. This was the year of **'Aladdin Sane'** and it couldn't be more different to the challenging metamorphic music Bowie was producing in the process of transforming from a stranded spaceman to Ziggy Stardust to a 'Young American', not to mention **'Low'**, famously interpreted by minimalist composer **Philip Glass**. *Love You till Tuesday ****, a 1967 '45', was an orchestrated number with Bowie chuckling at the thought of a 'burning desire' that would probably only last from Sunday to Tuesday and would maybe make it until Wednesday evening. Bowie couldn't get any more songs accepted for release by Deram and his manager Ken Pitt terminated his contract. *Space Oddity* (on Philips) was two years away, and subsequent singles on Mercury failed to register. It was a move to RCA that coincided with Bowie's emergence as a top song writer and performer (the prophetically titled *Changes* in 1972). In between was a stint with **Turquoise** (see separate entry). Some LPs were also released in 1967, an eponymous one and a compilation called **'The World of David Bowie'** (part of a series on Decca).

224

# Alan Bown

**INSTRUMENTS:** Alan Bown (Trumpet); Jeff Bannister (Lead vocals, Organ), Dave Green (Sax, Clarinet, Flute) replaced by John Helliwell (Sax), Pete Burgess (Guitar) replaced by Tony Catchpole, then Derek Griffiths (ex The Artwoods), Stan Haldane (Bass) replaced by Andy Brown, then Dougie Thomson and Vic Sweeney (Drums) with Jess Roden added as a lead vocalist in 1966 replaced by Robert Palmer in The Alan Bown Set! (then by Gordon Neville). Mel Collins (Sax) joined in. In 1972, Bown convened a short lived final line-up including Dave Lawson, later of Greenslade on keyboards.

**ORIGIN:** London, England

**NOTABLE RECORDINGS:** *Can't Let Her Go / I'm the One* their first 45 for Pye Records in 1965*; Emergency 999* (1966) later became a Northern Soul club anthem (two further 45s were released in 1966). Three singles were released in 1967 on three different labels (Pye, Disques Vogue, and MGM): *Gonna Fix You Good (Every time You're Bad)* **; *I Really, Really Care* ***; *Jeu De Massacre*** and *Technicolour Dream* ***. The notable LP 'Outward Bown' was released on Music Factory and had a version of Bob Dylan's *'All Along the Watchtower'* that impressed Jimi Hendrix sufficiently for him to include it in his stage set and take it into the recording studio himself. *'We Can Help You'* (1968) provided them with a top 30 UK single and an appearance on the 'Top of The Pops' BBC TV show (which can be viewed on You Tube). Four further 45s were released before the group's dissolution in 1972. A collectible group, Pye singles are worth between £25 and £80, and a mint copy of 'Outward Bown' might cost £80. There is one other interesting curiosity, an early example of a split LP (with Jimmy James and the Vagabonds) called 'London Swings Live at the Marquee Club' on Pye Records.

**REISSUES: Emergency 999** (2002, Sequel) is a compilation. 'Kick Me Out' on See For Miles Records was an LP compilation of tracks from 1969. Their 1970/71 albums have been remastered on CD on the Esoteric label (Cherry Red).

**DESCRIPTION**: The Alan Bown Set was later known as 'The Alan Bown!' then just plain old Alan Bown. Their music incorporated elements of jazz, blues, rhythm, and blues and soul with psychedelic and progressive elements as the years went on. Alan Bown started off as a gigging musician in The Embers who played conterminously with The Beatles in The Star Club in Hamburg. Bown's next group was The John Barry Seven (until 1965). Bown formed The Alan Bown Set in the summer of 1965 with three members of the defunct John Barry Seven. In 1967, Bown reformed the band as The Alan Bown, appearing on John Peel's 'Top Gear' radio show and on a BBC session hosted by Bryan Matthew (playing the Beatle-ish *'Penny for Your Thoughts'*). Also in 1967, they contributed to a curious soundtrack to the French film 'Jeu De Massacre' with a chaotic piece entitled *'The Killing Game'* ** for the International Cannes Film Festival. Despite the fetching cartoon cover of the 'Disques Vogue' and a three part piece by Jacques Loussier on side one, The Alan Bown do little to settle the nerves of the listener with the primitive vocal impersonations of an automatic weapon – but then again, that was probably the intention! Better was their second 45 on Pye *'I Really, Really Care'* which has been described as 'Mod Soul meets Freakbeat', a strident number with catchy organ, psych guitar and pounding drums. An album 'Outward Bound' was recorded for Verve Records followed by a 'Second Album' on MGM. By 1969, they were recording for the Deram label releasing an album 'The Alan Bown!' and in 1970, they changed labels once again to Island Records for whom they recorded two very listenable albums 'Listen' and **Stretching Out** in 1970 and 1971 (pity about the horrible cover), and both of these have been remastered as CDs on the Esoteric label. During 1967, they shifted style from R&B/ soul in the rather derivative un PC *Gonna Fix You*

*Good (Every time You're Bad)* to *Toyland* which starts with children playing and flute but sounds like The Bee Gees, and is pretty if rather twee b/w *Technicolour Dream* which is equally 'psych' but has a bit more edge to it. In between, there was *We Can Help You* (a cover of a Nirvana song from 'The Story of Simon Simopath') which starts off like a medieval folk song then bursts into action with strings and woodwind as "you suddenly discover you are a member of happiness society!" (Ah, those were the days!)

## The Bunch

INSTRUMENTS: **John Sherry (Vocals, Drums); John Huntley (Lead Guitar); Alan Willoughby (Rhythm Guitar); Mo Lake (Bass) then Peter Beckett (Vocals); Chris Redwood (Guitar); Dave Cooper (Organ); Dave Potter (Tenor Sax); Mike Berry (Baritone Sax) and John King (Bass)**

ORIGIN: Bournemouth, England.

RECORDINGS IN 1967: *'We're Not What We Appear to Be \*\*\* / You Never Came Home' \*\*\*; 'Don't Come Back to Me \*\* / You Can't Do This' \*\*; 'Looking Glass Alice' \*\*\*\*/' Spare a Shilling' \*\** (all CBS, 1967)

REISSUES: *'We're Not What We Appear to Be'* can be heard on the LP **'Yellow Elektric Years'** and *'Looking Glass Alice'* on the CD **'We Can Fly: UK Psychedelic Obscurities'** and **'Artefacts From The Psychedelic Dungeon'**. There is a nicely presented LP/ double CD compilation of songs on Tenth Planet featuring *'Spare A Shilling'* called **'The Upside Down World of John Pantry'** released in 1999 and showcasing the work of songwriter John Pantry. Record Collector magazine has released an imagined LP including the 3 singles and unreleased demos and live performances.

DESCRIPTION: Their 1967 debut single is catchy heavy soul/pop with a strong backbeat and prominent bass (both sides). There is some dodgy miming on a black and white video of *'You Can't Do This'* on You Tube – this one has a sax break. *'Looking Glass Alice'* was their best record as they turned psychedelic with flute and references to 'high', 'trip', 'lotion' and 'potion', and nothing new in the use of Lewis Carroll imagery. There is a BBC London Transcription Service recording on YouTube which is somewhat different sounding more like Georgie Fame. Its B-side is less successful – although catchy – the vocal harmonies and harpsichord do not save the lyric. Hammond organ underpins all their records. The Bunch released a final single in 1968, *'Birthday'*, like *'Spare A Shilling'* another John Pantry song. Striving for 'a big American sound' The Bunch initially went down the soul/ Tamla route, backed Edwin Starr and toured with Ike and Tina Turner.

Not to be confused with the Fairport Convention off-shoot, The Bunch formed by Trevor Lucas after the breakup of Fotheringay who released an album in 1972.

## (The) Bystanders

INSTRUMENTS: **Vic Oakley (Vocals), Micky Jones (Guitar), Clive John (Keyboards), Ray Williams (Bass), Jeff Jones (Drums)** (all operating under pseudonyms, **Lynn Mittell** was also an early member)

ORIGIN: Merthyr Tydfil, Wales, c.1966

NOTABLE RECORDINGS: *'98.6'* \*\*\*\* A top 50 UK hit but a bigger hit for Keith and equally good is the stirring arrangement of Gaye, Stevenson and Gordy's *'Stubborn Kind of Fellow'* \*\*\*\* on the flip with a powerful vocal by Vic Oakley and an early Micky Jones guitar break. The Beatles/ Hollies/ Kinks influenced Ronnie Scott and Marti Wilde penned *'Royal Blue Summer Sunshine Day/ Make Up Your Mind* (a Los Brincos cover, Beatles in style)' is a less successful 45 (\*\*) and *'Pattern People'* \*\*\* (a Jim

Webb penned Fifth Dimension song from their 'Up, Up and Away' LP) is given a Beach Boys treatment/ *'Green Grass'* ***(similar in style to The Fortunes, The Tremeloes and Unit 4+2) (all Piccadilly, 1967) and *'When Jesamine Goes/ Cave of Clear Light'* – both ****(a great orchestrated version of The Casuals' top 3 hit as *'Jesamine'* written once again under pseudonyms by Ronnie Scott and Marti Wilde: the latter, a marvellous example of psychedelic pop, gave its name to a CD box set retrospective of the Pye Dawn label on Esoteric Recordings) (Pye, 1968). The infectious Albert Hammond song *'This World is My World'* and the country flavoured *'Painting the Time'* were their last releases on 45. 'Record Collector Rare Record Price Guide' lists a 1965 '45' on Pylot *('That's the End')* as being worth up to £150. All singles are collectible with *'When Jesamine Goes'* worth up to £50.

**REISSUES:** CD compilation '**Ripples Present the Bystanders**'; '*Cave of Clear Light*' on '**We Can Fly Vol 2**'; '*Royal Blue Summer Sunshine Day*' and '*98.6*' on '**Ripples Vol 1**' CD; '*Pattern People*' on '**Ripples Vol 2**'

**DESCRIPTION:** Mainly, a US styled vocal harmony group, The Bystanders had **Micky** and **Jeff Jones**, **Clive John** and **Ray Williams** (who went on to form **Man**) in their original line-up. The falsetto sound perfected by the likes of The Tokens and The Beach Boys was in early evidence (*'**The Little Girl I Once Knew**'*), and also the sound of The Four Seasons (the B-side of their first single '**(You're Gonna) Hurt Yourself** which was a Frankie Valli solo number (as was the unreleased at the time '**You're Ready Now'**). Later, the stylistic inclinations of The Fifth Dimension, The Strawberry Alarm Clock and The Turtles were assimilated by the group. They were more than that though, taking a lead like most other groups from The Beatles and dipping their toes into psychedelia. For me, their finest moment was a John/ Jones original *'**Cave of Clear Light**'*, the B-side of *'**When Jesamine Goes**' while 'This World is My World'* wouldn't have seemed out of the place on the promising Bee Gees debut album (released the year before in 1967). Group members were getting increasingly into west coast American groups such as The Doors, Love and The Steve Miller Band' and were getting increasingly ambitious, attempting a version of *'**I Am the Walrus**'* (I'd love to have heard that). As Kingsley Abbot observed in the liner notes to the Castle Music CD compilation: "The age was dominated by new and conflicting records, from '**Sergeant Pepper**' and Procol Harum to Engelbert Humperdinck, destroying all opposition – and the band's radio friendly pop, good as it was, just wasn't distinctive enough." However, The Bystanders were more than a footnote in history, did lead to Man, an enduring 'jam' band in the seventies, and leave much to be proud of in the 23 track Castle compilation.

# The Californians/ John O'Hara and The Playboys Aka O'Hara's Playboys

**THE MUSICIANS: The Californians: (John O'Hara: Lead Vocals, Tenor Sax; Mick Brooks: Guitar, Vocals; Pete Habberley: Bass, Vocals; Keith Evans (Drums, Vocals); O'Hara's Playboys: (John O'Hara: Lead Vocals, Tenor Sax; Barry Herd (Guitar, Vocals); Bobby Campbell (Organ, Vocals); Peter Green (Sax), Bill Mathieson (Bass) and Dave McHarg (Drums)**

**ORIGIN:** Wolverhampton area/ Glasgow

**1967 RECORDINGS:** The Californians: *'Golden Apples'* **** (CBS, 1967); *'Follow Me/ What Love Can Do'* ****' (Decca, 1967); *'Sunday Will Never Be The Same* ***/ Can't Get You Out of My Mind* ***' (Decca, 1967); '; O'Hara's Playboys: *'Spicks and Specks'* ** *'Ballad of the Soon Departed'* ***; *'Island In The Sun'* *** (all Fontana, 1967)

REISSUES: '*Golden Apples*' is on **Rubble LP volume 17** and **Rubble CD volume 10**; '*Follow Me*' is on various compilations including Rubble; '*The Cook of Cakes and Kindness*' is on **Rubble volume 4 LP** and **Rubble volume 3 CD**.

DESCRIPTION: The Californians were not from California at all, although you could be forgiven for thinking so. There are two flashing, trippy videos of '*Golden Apples*' on You Tube, hookah pipes, sitars and all and the song itself has a lot packed into just over two minutes. '*Follow Me*' is more up-tempo and is a cover of a **Warren Zevon** number (performed with Lyme and Cybelle); '*What Love Can Do*' has brass and there is a rather corny, if touching black and white video; '*Sunday Will Never Be the Same*' is a strong cover of a song by American west coast group **Spanky and Our Gang** and has a strong B-side '*(I) Can't Get You Out of My Mind*'. In total, The Californians recorded nine 45s between 1967 and 1969 for CBS, Decca, Fontana and Chapter One (the latter a slower version of The Fortunes' big hit '*You've Got Your Troubles*'. '*The Cooks of Cake and Kindness*', released on Fontana in 1968, was a rather lacklustre song also in the repertoire of The Flowerpot Men.

John O'Hara was also in O'Hara's Playboys who recorded eight 45s for Fontana between 1966 and 1969 including two Bee Gees' songs '*Spicks and Specks*', *and* '*I Started a Joke*'. '*Ballad of the Soon Departed*' with its spectral organ and rasping sax is the best of their 1967 singles. The Harry Belafonte song '*Island in the Sun*' was the last of the three. The group was popular in Germany where they released a '**Party Album**' and also released one UK album for Fontana called '**Get Ready**' in 1968. This consisted mainly well-known covers such as '*Respect*', '*I Was Made to Love Her*' *and* '*(I Can't Get No) Satisfaction*'. It also has a rather dodgy cover with a shot of the guys ogling a glamorous croupier at a roulette table! The '**Playboys Party No. 1**' LP had a 'Mashed Potatoes' medley and dance floor fillers like '*Twist and Shout*' and '*La Bamba*'.

## Chicken Shack

THE MUSICIANS: **Stan Webb (Guitar, Vocals); Christine Perfect (Piano, Vocals); Andy Silvester (Bass); Dave Bidwell (Drums)**

ORIGIN: **Birmingham area**

NOTABLE RECORDINGS: **in 1967 '*It's OK with Me, Baby*' \*\*\*/ '*When My Eye Left Jumps*' \*\*\*; '*I'd Rather Go Blind*' #14 and '*Tears in the Wind*' #29 (Both 1969), LP: '40 Blue Fingers Freshly Packed and Ready to Serve' #12, 1968 (all Blue Horizon)**

REISSUES: Their 'classic' album '**40 Blue Fingers**' has been reissued on Music on Vinyl (2010) – expect to pay around £20. It has also been reissued on CD (around £8): if it is an original mono you want you will probably be looking at between £75 and £100 in excellent condition. My recommendation for a compilation would be '**The Complete Blue Horizon Sessions**' 3 CD set.

DESCRIPTION: Chicken Shack was another group that thrived in the reflected light of the '60s' blues boom inspired by the arrival of US musicians en masse. Mike Vernon signed them for his Blue Horizon label with Fleetwood Mac and it was while touring with them that Christine Perfect met her future husband John McVie. The '45' with 1967 on the label had one foot in 1967 and one foot in 1968 when their first, very successful LP was released in January – much of the material for their '**40 Blue Fingers**' must have been in preparation in our target year.

# Joe Cocker

It goes without saying that Joe Cocker would be in the main section of this book, had our target year been a year later but, after releasing a single *'I'll Cry Instead'/'Precious Words'* on Decca in 1964, Cocker's career stalled until his seminal albums **'With a Little Help from My Friend'**(1968), **'Joe Cocker!'** (1969) (both on Regal Zonophone) and **'Something to Say'** (1972) (Cube), with his **'Mad Dogs and Englishmen'** caper (1970) (A&M) in between. By this time, Cocker had gathered the cream of the crop in terms of musicians around him to become one of the great soul rock singers of all time.

# Dantalian's Chariot

**THE MUSICIANS: Andy Summers (Guitar); Zoot Money (Keyboards); Pat Donaldson (Bass); Colin Allen (Drums)**
**ORIGIN:** London
**NOTABLE RECORDINGS:** *'The Madman Running Through the Fields/ Sun Came Bursting Through My Cloud'* **** 45 rpm (Columbia, 1967) Zoot Money related to Nick James of Record Collector magazine: "*Madman* was a description of our personal experience and the subsequent self-revelations brought about by hallucinogenics. It was based around the observations we made once we returned to 'normal'. The verse is the voice of the taker (of acid) and the chorus is him being observed by a second party."

**REISSUES: 'Chariot Rising'** is the main reference point for the group. It was an album pieced together with both sides of their only single release along with previously unreleased material recorded for the CBS Direction label. It was released on vinyl on the Tenth Planet label in 1995 with a CD release on Wooden Hill the following year with the addition of an extra track *'This Island'*. Pieces of note were the west coast American sound of *'High Flying Bird'*, the Cold War paranoia guitar dominated song *'World War Three'*; the Beatles influenced *'Four Penny Bus Ride'* and the instrumental *'Soma'* in two parts with **Andy Summers** on sitar. CBS did release a hotch-potch album of songs from various studio sessions, mostly covers, entitled **'Transitions'** in March, 1968 but this was unrepresentative of the group's music at the time and was mislabelled as a release by Zoot Money and The Big Roll Band. *'The Madman Running Through the Fields'* 45 may be heard on the eighth **'Rubble'** LP and the fifth **'Rubble'** CD and other compilations.

**DESCRIPTION:** There were high hopes and expectations for Dantalian's Chariot, a group that arose from the embers of The Big Roll Band, Georgie Fame, and The Blues Flames' replacement as the resident band in Soho's popular Flamingo Club who had a top 30 single, *'Big Time Operator'*. Acid entered the group's lives and the blues/ soul/ jazz of The Big Roll Band seamlessly metamorphosed into a more mind expanding trippy, psychedelic, progressive brand of acid rock and a name change. Dantalian's Chariot made their debut on 12th August, 1967 at the Windsor National Blues Festival with The Crazy World of Arthur Brown, The Nice and Ten Years After on the bill. Their repertoire was all new with Money mostly writing the lyrics and Summers the music. They became regular performers at the Middle Earth, The Roundhouse and the UFO Club in London. Appearing all in white with an impressive light show, Dantalian's Chariot was a big live draw. Dropped by EMI, the group appeared in the film **'Popdown'**, bankrolled by American entrepreneur Fred Marshall, which also featured Blossom Toes and The Idle Race (Brian Auger, Julie Driscoll and the Trinity also feature in the soundtrack).

229

Eric Burdon recorded a version of *'The Madman Running through the Fields'* on his **'Love Is'** LP. Money became musical director for Burdon's New Animals. Summers had struck up a friendship with Robert Wyatt and briefly joined Soft Machine then Kevin Ayers' band and later found fame with The Police; Colin Allen went on to join John Mayall's Bluesbreakers then Stone the Crows and had a stint in Focus; Pat Donaldson joined Fotheringay.

Sadly, the full potential of Dantalian's Chariot was never realised but their legacy is a very real and lasting one. Within six months of rubbing shoulders with future greats like Pink Floyd and The Soft Machine, their trip was over.

## David and Jonathan

**THE MUSICIANS:** The group comprised **Roger Cook (David)** and **Roger Greenaway (Jonathan)**, song-writers and session singers.

**ORIGIN:** Bristol, England, they were named after the Biblical characters in the Book of Samuel.

**NOTABLE RECORDINGS:** Their cover of the Beatles' *'Michelle'* made #11 in the UK charts in 1966 (and #18 US Billboard), *'Lovers of the World Unite'* provided them with an even bigger hit in, later, in 1966 (#7). A rather earnest cover of *'She's Leaving Home'* \*\*\* with an interesting orchestral arrangement didn't make any impact on the charts in 1967 but will be of interest to collectors. One other single was released in 1967, a rather cloying number with a pretty melody *'Softly Whispering I Love You'* \*\*\*. *'You've Got Your Troubles'* which was a big hit for The Fortunes was included on a See For Miles CD compilation (see below). David and Jonathan released one eponymous LP in 1967. All recordings (nine singles and one album between 1965 and 1968) were released on Columbia.

**REISSUES:** A See For Miles CD compilation of 20 tracks was released in 1984

**DESCRIPTION:** Roger Greenaway (sometimes with Cook) wrote many successful songs e.g. *'You've Got Your Troubles'* for The Fortunes and *'Something's Gotten Hold of My Heart'*, a big hit for Gene Pitney. They also wrote novelty songs such as *'I Was Kaiser Bill's Batman'*, a hit for Whistling Jack Smith as well as *'Gilly Gilly Ossenfeffer Katzenellenbogen by the Sea'* in 1966.

## Dave Davies (See The Kinks)

**INSTRUMENTS: Guitar, Vocals**
**ORIGIN:** Muswell Hill, London
**NOTABLE RECORDINGS:** The Dylanesque *'Death of a Clown'* \*\*\*\* (#3 UK) and *'Susannah's Still Alive'* \*\*\*\* (#20 UK), both on Pye in 1967. Other 1967 songs included on **'Hidden Treasures'** (see below) are *'Love Me till the Sun Shines'* \*\*\*\*, the B-side of *'Death of a Clown'* (the supercharged BBC live version is superior to the studio version with Mick Avory outstanding on the drums and organ pushed up the mix near the end) and *'Funny Face'* (sounds more like The Who than The Kinks) \*\*\*\*, the B-side of 'Susannah's Still Alive', and also on The Kinks' 'Something Else' LP. There is also a rare studio version of *'Good Luck Charm'* (a countrified ditty of 1:45 with honky-tonk piano and crude 12 bar, great fun though!) \*\*\* from July, 1967.

**REISSUES:** 'Hidden Treasures' is a well compiled Sanctuary CD from 2011. The first 13 of the 27 tracks replicate the acetate of the 'lost' Dave Davies LP.

**DESCRIPTION:** Famed for his genre defining guitar solo on *'You Really Got Me'*. While seemingly in the shadow of his brother Ray, Russell Smith, an ex co-Director of

The Kinks Fan Club, is one of many who extol the virtues of brother Dave, in playing a major part in the style and fashion as well as the music. **(104)** Dave's first writing credit, *'One Fine Day'*,had been passed over by The Kinks but was released by Shel Naylor in 1964. It was the year 1967 when Dave Davies came into his own but, as he told music writer Lon Goddard, "I finished a solo album I'd started, but after hearing it a few times, I never had it released." The album in question was rumoured to include covers of blues numbers by **Big Bill Broonzy** and **Lead Belly** as well as *'Good Luck Charm'*, a reworking of **'Spider' John Koerner's** *'Good Luck Child'*. The prospect of a solo album was revisited in 1968 when Dave somewhat reluctantly entered Polydor Studios to record some songs with Ray as producer. From these sessions, *'Hold My Hand/ Creeping Jean'* would be released as a single in January, 1969. Disappointed that this excellent record didn't trouble the charts, Dave reconvened with The Kinks to record some more songs in the 8-track Pye Studios that same month. It was late February before the tracks for the album would be brought close to completion after Dave fractured a finger on 3rd February. One song *'Mr Shoemaker's Daughter'* emerged from a playful backwards tape playing of *'Death of a Clown'* while *'Mr Reporter'*, credited to brother Ray, had been in the group's repertoire for a while but they had never managed before to successfully capture it in the studio. The release of a new Kinks' single *'Plastic Man'* and the departure of bassist Pete Quaife served to delay the ill-fated album. A final song *'Mindless Child of Motherhood'* was written specifically with the group **Turquoise** in mind (the group's Ewan Stevens was a friend) and, indeed the original demo was recorded with them (The song ended up as the B-side of The Kinks' 45 *'Drivin'*). A further delay occurred when The Kinks focused on their next project **'Arthur and the Decline and Fall of the British Empire'** in May, 1969. The 12-track tape was finally delivered to Warner Brothers in July. Dave called the album "a mish mash of the Pye and Polydor material". The songs were: *'I Am Free'* from 'The Kink Kontroversy', *'Love Me till the Sun Shines'* and *'Funny Face'* from 'Something Else', *'Death of a Clown'* and **Susannah's Still Alive'** 45, *'Good Luck Charm'*, a cover first issued on 'Hidden Treasures', *'Lincoln County'*, a 1968 '45', *'Hold My Hand'* and *'Mindless Child of Motherhood'* 'from the 'Arthur' album, *'Creeping Jean'* from the 'Village Green Preservation Society' album, *'This Man He Weeps Tonight'*, a 1969 single and *'Strangers'* from the 'Lola' LP.

## Dave Dee, Dozy, Beaky, Mick & Tich

**THE MUSICIANS: Dave Harman AKA Dave Dee; John Dymond AKA Beaky and Michael Wilson AKA Mick (Guitars); Trevor Davies AKA Dozy (Bass); Ian Amey AKA Tich (Drums)**
**ORIGIN:** Salisbury
**1967 RECORDINGS:** *'Zabadak'* *** in 1967 but *'The Legend of Xanadu'* **** was their finest three minutes.
**REISSUES:** Prominent on '60s' compilations and there is a four CD Dutch box set. The group has probably not been that well served on compilations. An example is the sparsely annotated Cedar CD compilation, 12 songs only – fair enough but hardly matches the liner note: "1966 was a vintage year: 50 weeks in the charts with their 4 singles outselling rock legends Elvis, The Beatles and The Rolling Stones. 1967 brought yet another 3 top 20 hits and in 1968 came the ultimate accolade of a Number One chart topper – the whip cracking *Legend of Xanadu*."
**DESCRIPTION:** Cutting their teeth in Hamburg like so many other groups, they were fronted by Dave Dee (David Harman), their first big hit coming in 1966 with *'Hold*

*Tight'*. Other high points in their run of fifteen 45s on the Fontana label as well as eight albums including 3 compilations were: **'Bend It'** (#2); *'Zabadak'* (#3), **'The Legend of Xanadu',** their only number one – pure drama whipcracks and all!; the rather good **'Last Night in Soho'** (#8) and **'The Wreck of the Antoinette'** (#14). After 1968, the group lost their grip on the charts but did have two further top 30 hits in 1969 with **'Don Juan'** and **'Snake in the Grass'.** Of their albums, their eponymous debut nearly made the top ten while the cutely entitled **'If Music be the Food of Love... Prepare for Indigestion'** made the top 30. Both albums were released in 1966 but they were, in essence, an archetypal singles band. *If Music Be the Food of Love* was reissued on CD on Repertoire Records in 2003, the number of bonus tracks (14) outnumbering the tracks (12).

Colin Larkin's take is: "with songs provided by Howard and Blaikley they presented a veritable travelogue of pop, filled with melodramatic scenarios." **(105)**

## The Deviants

**THE MUSICIANS: Mick Farren (Vocals), Sid Bishop and Clive Maldoon (Guitar), Michael McDonnell, Pete Monroe and Cord Rees (Bass), Russell Hunter (Drums) and later Dennis Hughes (Keyboards), Paul Rudolph (Guitar and Vocals) and Duncan Sanderson (Bass and Vocals)**

**ORIGIN:** London (Notting Hill area)

**NOTABLE RECORDINGS: 'PTOOF!'** LP (Impresarios, 1967, reissued Decca, 1969), a significant album of 1967\*\*\*; **Disposable** LP (Stable, 1968); The **Deviants** LP (Transatlantic, 1969); *You Got to Hold On/ Let's Loot The Supermarket'* 45 Stable, 1968) (A-side fine psychedelia; B-side anarchic) The original **'Ptooff!'** LP is very rare as only 8,000 copies were pressed and distributed through 'underground music' retailers and magazines like 'Oz' and 'International Times'. Thereafter, it was reissued on the Decca label in 1968.

**REISSUES:** Their albums have been remastered for CD by Esoteric. [112] LP reissues on the Psycho label and on CD in 1992 on Dropout Records.

**DESCRIPTION:** Originally, The Social Deviants: The Deviants have been described asthe British equivalent to The Fugs, with touches of The Mothers of Invention, "a bad-tempered Jefferson Airplane", and the British R&B based rock of The Yardbirds and The Pretty Things." **(106)** [113]

The Deviants' 1967 debut album **'Ptooff!'** is seen by Dave Thompson) **(107)** as representing the 'underbelly of Britain's psychedelic sixties, a seething mass of discontent and rancour which would eventually produce the likes of Hawkwind, the Pink Fairies and the Edgar Broughton Band' (in fact, three Deviants would become Pink Fairies). Psych authority Jim De Rogatis considers **'Ptooff!'** to be the best of The Deviants albums, although perversely, he justifies this by saying that it proudly flaunts 'both its freakishness and its incompetence, the group's former manager dubbing it the worst record in the history of man'! **(108)**

---

[112] The Esoteric release of *'PTOOFF!'* includes a fold-out reproduction of the futuristic comic strip and a raft of quotations with the liner notes by John Peel that appeared on the original sleeve

[113] The MC5 were another influence

MUSICIANS: Mick Farren (Lead Vocals, Piano), Sid Bishop (Guitar, Sitar and Vocals), Cord Rees (Bass, Spanish Guitar, Vocals), Ross Hunter (Drums, Vocals); PRODUCER: Johnathon Weber; ENGINEERS: John Pantry, Victor Gamm; COVER DESIGN: Kipps; LINER NOTES: John Peel; LABEL: Underground Press then Decca in 1968

## Tracklist/ Credits:

| 1. | Opening (Rees, Farren, Hunter, Bishop, Sparkes) | 0:05 |
|---|---|---|
| 2. | I'm Coming Home (Farren, Hunter, Bishop) | 4:50 |
| 3. | Child of the Sky (Rees, Hammond, Farren) | 4:25 |
| 4. | Charlie (Farren, Bishop) | 3:50 |
| 6. | Nothing Man (J. Henry Moore, Farren) | 4:20 |
| 7. | Garbage (Farren, Hunter, Bishop) | 5:30 |
| 8. | Bun (Rees) | 2:35 |
| 9. | Deviation Street (Farren) | 9:10 |

*'PTOOFF!'* has savage social commentary: *'Nothing Man'*, a collage of percussion, narrative and noise bordering on musique concrete; *'Deviation Street'*, whose political sloganising has not dated well; a reworking of 'Gloria' called *'I'm Coming Home'*; psychedelic jamming (the end of *'Deviation Street'*); blues riffs (the country blues of *'Charlie'*); and pretty acoustic ballads; *'Child of the Sky' and 'Bun'* mostly Cord Rees on Spanish guitar. Add in the Bo Diddley beat meets psych of *'Garbage'* returned to on *'Deviation Street'* and corruptions of popular ditties, and you are left with a pretty eclectic mix. John Peel said, "There is little that is not good, much that is excellent and an occasional flash of brilliance."

I don't subscribe to the theory that *'PTOOFF!'* was The Deviants' best album although its honest primitivism does have a certain attraction. By the time we get to **'The Deviants ',** the one with the infamous picture of a nun sucking a Lyons Maid rocket ice lolly, the line-up of Farren and Paul Rudolph backed by a more confident and inventive rhythm section of Duncan Sanderson and Russell Hunter, is much more professional as demonstrated on the five minute long **'Rambling B(l)ack Transit Blues'**, with Rudolph's superior guitar playing bringing out the best in everybody. Skip Jansen, writing again for the All Music Guide reckons that this 'straightforward heavy psychedelic rock album almost reaches the explosive magnitude of the Stooges' **'Funhouse'** and is 'an absolute classic of proto-punk UK psychedelic rock'. **(109)**The addition of Tony Ferguson on organ here and elsewhere is also welcome and the interplay between organ and guitar allows Hunter to stretch out a bit as well. Going back a step my own personal favourite Deviants album is **'Disposable'** once described by Farren as a 'methedrine monster' (Have a listen to **'Let's Loot the Supermarket'**).

The success of **'Disposable'** lies. I think in the continuing development of musicians like Sid Bishop and drummer Russ Hunter and, although it runs out of steam towards the end, it contains some of The Deviants' best songs

By the time we get to the fourth esoteric release, actually a solo Mick Farren album released in 1970, the game is over. It's no joke when somebody says (presumably Mick)

that 'this is the best bit' as the full version of a cover bookending the album (*'Mona'*) draws the Deviants saga to a conclusion – for now! Peter Doggett says: "The British rock audience preferred Edgar Broughton's orthodoxy to the almost psychopathically uncommercial approach of '**Mona – The Carnivorous Circus**'." **(110)**

## Simon Dupree and the Big Sound

**THE MUSICIANS: Ray Shulman AKA Simon Dupree (Vocals); Phil Shulman (Sax); Eric Hine (Keyboards); Ray Shulman – Pete O'Flaherty, then Geary Kenworthy who were also bass players in the group: Guitar, Bass, Vocals; Tony Ransley then Martin Smith (Drums)**

Drums **ORIGIN:** Portsmouth, England (although two of the Shulman brothers were born in Glasgow)

**NOTABLE RECORDINGS:** Singles-*'Reservations'* \*\*\* is a Hammond driven rocker written by Albert Hammond, *'Day Time, Night Time'* \*\*\*\* written by Manfred Mann drummer Mike Hugg is a decent piano/organ driven ballad with occasional brass, its B-side *'I've Seen It All Before'* has some cheesy organ and prominent walking bass and almost strays into Ska \*\*\*; *'Kites'* \*\*\*\*\* UK (#9) and a staple of '60s compilations features gongs, mellotron and vibraphone and was recorded at Abbey Road (all Parlophone, 1967); *'Like the Sun, Like the Fire'* \*\*\* is another song that responds to the gauntlet thrown down by '**Sergeant Pepper**', slightly comical in the brass arrangement possibly *'(For the Benefit of) Mr Kite'* influenced. The group had one more top 50 chart success with *'For Whom the Bell Tolls'* in 1968 (written by sister Eve Shulman). *'Part of My Past'*, also written by Eve, was another notable 1968 recording. They released one album '**Without Reservations**' \*\*\* in 1967 which contained various singles and soul covers.

**REISSUES:** Your best port of call is probably the two CD anthology 'Part of My Past: The Simon Dupree and The Big Sound Anthology' (EMI, 2004) As far as is vinyl is concerned, there hasn't been a lot of activity to date but there is a 12 track German Odeon label LP called '**The Best of Simon Dupree**'.

**DESCRIPTION:** Originally, The Howlin' Wolves and The Road Runners, Simon Dupree and The Big Sound went from a soul and R&B band, such as on their first 45 *'I See the Light* (A **Five Americans** song) */ It is Finished'* (Parlophone, 1966), to embrace psychedelia, most successfully with *'Kites'* then the three Schulman brothers and drummer Martin Smith went on to form highly influential, ground breaking progressive rock group, the incomparable **Gentle Giant**, certainly one of the most enduring top ten prog groups in terms of originality and influence along with likes of E.L.P, Yes, Genesis, Jethro Tull and Van Der Graaf Generator. The group supported The Walker Brothers and were part of the support for the first Beach Boys tour of the UK. An appearance on German TV alongside Jimi Hendrix is recalled in an interview with Record Collector magazine by Derek Shulman who describes Hendrix as "a complete gentleman, great guy and very humble." Brother Ray was so impressed, he bought a Marshall Amplifier stack shortly afterwards) **(111)**. The story behind their most famous song *'Kites'* is an interesting one: written by a pair of Broadway show tune hit churners, Hal Hackady and Lee Pockriss, Dupree hated the song which explains his deadpan vocal delivery. The song repeated the trick in Traffic's *'Hole in My Shoe'* by using a spoken passage in the middle eight delivered by actress Jacqui Chan which, along with the mellotron and xylophone, adds to its enduring charm. After some relatively unsuccessful records in 1968 and struggling to get airplay after the demise of pirate radio, manager John King came up with a scam releasing a seven-minute song called *'We are the Moles'* credited to The Moles who were actually Simon Dupree and The Big Sound! Now managed by Gerry Bron, they eventually incarnated into Gentle Giant and signed a four album deal with Vertigo.

## The Easybeats

**THE MUSICIANS: John Bell** then **The Starfighters** then **Stevie Wright (Vocals); Johannes Van Der Berg** then **Harry Vanda and George Young (Guitar); Dick Diamonde, real name Dingeman Van Der Slice (Bass) and Gordon 'Snowy' Fleet** then **Tony Cahill (Drums)**, a backbeat 'veteran' – at 24 – Liverpudlian who played the same circuit as The Beatles and suggested the name with The Beatles in mind.

**ORIGIN:** Like The Bee Gees, The Easybeats started making records in Australia where they had four #1 hits (although two of their members were Dutch). They returned to England in 1966.

**NOTABLE RECORDINGS:** *'Friday on My Mind'* (United Artists, 1966) #6 UK, #16 US, still a staple of radio shows to this day. Their 1967 singles were *'Who'll Be the One/ Saturday Night'* **; *'Heaven and Hell'* **** which has interesting guitar work and sounds like a template for David Bowie and Mott the Hoople/ *Pretty Girl'* and the soul searching *'The Music Goes Round My Head'* ***/ *'Come in, You'll Get Pneumonia'*, all on the United Artists label. They also released an album **'Good Friday'** in 1967 on the United Artists label. The original on vinyl could cost £50 upwards in excellent condition. A cheaper alternative is the reissue on the Varèse Sarabande label. The Easybeats also released quite a few EPs in 1967 and released LPs on an annual basis until 1969: **'Easy'** (1965, Parlophone); **'It's 2 Easy'** and **'Vol 3'** (1966, Parlophone); **'Vigil'** (1968, United Artists); **'Friends'** (1969, Polydor). They also released a split 45 with **Strawberry Alarm Clock** in 1968.

**REISSUES:** There are numerous compilations and **'The Singles As and Bs'** is a Repertoire double CD set with all their UK and Australian A and B sides. *'Friday On My Mind'* and *'Heaven and Hell'*, another 1967, A-side are included on the 'Nuggets' CD.

**DESCRIPTION:** An unusual inclusion this as The Easybeats were Australian and were as big as The Beatles in Australia, unlike The Bee Gees, who found 'their mojo' when emigrating with the hope of emulating The Beatles. When they went to London, they had to start all over again with an unacquainted public. Like The Bee Gees, they also dabbled in psychedelia (although descriptions vary from rock 'n' roll to beat to garage). Guitarist George Young's brothers were Angus and Malcolm of AC/DC fame. *'Heaven and Hell'* aside the real development musically came in 1968 with songs like *'Good Times'*, predating the Primal Scream sound. Their 1967 album has their 1966 hit *'Friday on My Mind'* and covers of *'Hound Dog'* and *'River Deep, Mountain High'*. There is an excellent video on YouTube called 'Friday on My Mind: The Story of The Easybeats' ('a couple of Poms, a Scot and two Dutchmen'), a tale of immigration, a hostel collective and an unlikely success story. John Bell describes how easily they could imitate The Beatles. Mop top Stevie Wright was preferred to Bell not because he was a better singer but because he had better stage presence and threw himself all over the stage and 'out-Jaggered Jagger' – 'a little guy with a huge ego'. A gig at The Beatle Village Club in Sydney got them started then they were discovered by Ted Albert who went on to produce their records. *'She's So Fine'* (1965) was their real breakthrough record (a #1 in Australia – three more were to follow in 1966 – *'I'll Make You Happy'* was not only heavy but risky) when they discovered that playing rock 'n' roll got people dancing more than Bo Diddley beat blues. Thus 'Easy Fever' was born. In July, 1966, the 'fab five' reversed the British invasion and headed for London where they saw The Kinks and The Who. A promised session with George Martin was cancelled. Young and Vanda started writing songs, and *'Friday on My Mind'* emerged (influenced by jazzy The Swingle Sisters!). Recorded at Abbey Studio, this was the group's breakthrough in the UK. They met Paul McCartney at his house in St John's Hill. *'Who'll Be the One?'* didn't emulate the success of their famous hit. In May, 1967, they returned to Sydney after another bout of 'Easy Fever' when *'Friday on My Mind'* impacted on Oz. *'Heaven and Hell'* was a better record and a top 10 Australian hit but failed to impress anywhere else. By 1969, it was all over.

## Eire Apparent

**THE MUSICIANS:** Ernest Graham (Vocals); Michael Cox/ Henry McCullough/ Jimi Hendrix/ David Taylor/ Peter Tolson/ Steve Jolly (Guitar); Chris Stewart (Bass) and Dave Lutton (Drums)

**ORIGIN:** Belfast, Northern Ireland

**NOTABLE RECORDINGS:** *'Follow Me/ Here I Go Again'* (Track, 1968); **'Sun Rise'** LP (Buddah, 1969) (although their first single was not released until January, 1968, they were in existence throughout most of 1967 and of great relevance, not only because of some of the fine music they produced (listen for example to the heavy guitar of *'Here I Go Again'* and the twitchy rhythms of its more psychedelic A-side *'Follow Me'*), but also because of their association with Jimi Hendrix.

**DESCRIPTION:** The reason for the inclusion of Eire Apparent is because of his association with Jimi Hendrix and other 1967 illuminati. The significance of Hendrix in a book about music in the UK in 1967 will become apparent in the chapter dedicated to him at the end of his book. The group started off as Tony and The Telstars with Stewart and Lutton as founding members. They were joined by Ernie Graham in 1965 and then they became The People. Henry McCullough joined on guitar in 1967, and they played gigs in places like Blackpool and Dublin. After they moved to London, they were signed by Chas Chandler and Mike Jeffrey and changed their name to Eire Apparent. They recorded one single for Track Records, *Follow Me/ Here I Go Again* in 1967 but it wasn't released until January, 1968. They toured North America with The Animals in February and March, 1968. McCullough was busted for possession of marijuana in Vancouver and deported to Ireland. That is where Mike Cox comes in. The tour continued with The Jimi Hendrix Experience and Soft Machine in 1967, and Hendrix played on several Eire Apparent tracks: *'Captive in the Sun'* (the bridge), *'The Clown'*, *'Yes, I Need Someone'* (lead guitar) and *'Let Me Stay'* (alternate lead with Michael Cox) as well as producing their only LP, which was mostly recorded in Los Angeles, in October, 1968. The group recorded one final 45 *'Rock 'n' Roll Band'* in 1969 with David 'Tiger' Taylor on guitar and toured Europe with Hendrix, recording a John Peel Session in April, 1969. Taylor left and was replaced by Peter Tolson then Steve Jolly. A mooted second LP failed to materialise and in May, 1970 Eire Apparent split up for good.

Ernie Graham went on to join **Help Yourself** who produced some very creditable music. Peter Tolson joined **The Edgar Broughton Band** and **The Pretty Things**; Henry McCullough was in **The Grease Band**, then **Wings**. Dave Lutton was in **Heavy Jelly**, then in **Ellis** (Steve Ellis's band), and finally, he worked with **Marc Bolan** and **Chris Spedding**. Chris Stewart played with **Frankie Miller, Joe Cocker, Eric Burdon, Jim Capaldi** and **Spooky Tooth**. David Taylor formed **Anno Domino** who released one folksy, Byrds influenced album **'On This New Day'** on Deram in 1971. Steve Jolly hooked up with Bobby Harrison, original Procol Harum drummer and joined **Freedom** for their 1972 album **'Freedom is More Than a Word'** on Vertigo. Michael (Mick) Cox formed **Magnet** who in 1969 released two songs from the **'Sunrise'** album as a single, *'Let Me Stay/ Mr Guy Fawkes'*, played on Van Morrison's **'Common One'** LP (1983) and reputedly was behind the release of tapes of a Hendrix jam session released on Red Lightnin' Records called **'Woke Up This Morning and Found Myself Dead'**.

## Episode Six

THE MUSICIANS: The original line-up was **Ian Gillan (Vocals)** and **Roger Glover (Bass)**, both later in **Deep Purple** with **Sheila Carter-Dimmock (Organ, Piano and Vocals),** her brother **Graham Dimmock** on **Rhythm Guitar and Vocals, Tony Lander** on **Guitar and Vocals** and **Harvey Shields** on **Drums and Vocals**.

ORIGIN: Harrow, England

NOTABLE RECORDINGS: Starting as Sheila Carter and Episode Six in 1966 with a Pye '45' *'I Will Warm Your Heart',* The Beatles were an obvious influence on the group's first record as just Episode Six *'Put Yourself in My Place'* (Pye, 1966) and there was a cover of *'Here, There And Everywhere'* later that year; the west coast American sounding version of the much recorded *'Morning Dew'* \*\*\*\* by Tim Rose was released in 1967 as were the trippy, psychedelic *'I Can See Through You'* \*\*\*\* and *'Love, Hate, Revenge'* \*\*\*\*. *Morning Dew', 'I Can See Through You'* and *'Love, Hate, Revenge'* (all on the Pye label) are collectible records, especially the latter two which are very hard to find.

REISSUES: Episode Six feature on numerous compilations and there are also a few featuring the group exclusively including '**The Roots of Deep Purple: The Complete Episode Six'** (Sequel, 1991) and **'Love, Hate and Revenge'**, a 44-track 2-CD set on Castle/ Sanctuary.

DESCRIPTION: Episode Six never quite managed to carve out a niche for themselves over the years between 1966 and 1969. Their *'Time and Motion Man'* 45, which can be heard on **Ripples volume 8 ('Butterfly')** has American West Coast vocal harmony based leanings like **The Association** or **The Mamas and The Papas**. *'I Can See Through You'* has a pleasant psych feel to it, nice vocal harmonies, jangly guitars, folky flute, a nice bass led (and unexpected) variation near the end, written by Roger Glover. There is a great You Tube video of the group playing a spirited version of *'Morning Dew'* for German TV in 1967 showing the group's predilection for hats, face paint and harmony vocals! *'Love, Hate, Revenge'* has a creepy lyric about controlling another's subconscious mind, a touch of voodoo perhaps! It is an inventive psych song with some early electronics and vocal harmonies owing much to groups like **The Mamas and The Papas**. It fades out all too quickly unfortunately. Gillan and Glover certainly did carve out a niche for themselves in Deep Purple.

## The Eyes of Blue

THE MUSICIANS: **Gary Pickford Hopkins (Vocals), Ritchie Francis (Guitar), Phil Ryan (Keyboards), Ray Williams/ Ray Bennett (Bass), Wyndham Rees then John Weathers (Drums)**

ORIGIN: Swansea, Wales

NOTABLE RECORDINGS: The Eyes of Blue released just two singles prior to 1968 and so are beyond the scope of our radar in terms of their later albums. Their 1967 single *'Supermarket Full of Cans'* \*\*\* may be heard on the CD **'The Mod Scene'** (although it is perhaps more 'Northern Soul' than anything else and not representative of what the group was to achieve on **'In Fields of Ardath'**). Expect to pay upwards of £50 for an excellent copy of their 1967 single, more for Mercury originals of their two albums (although these have been reissued on Wah-Wah Records).

**REISSUES:** Both albums ('**The Crossroads of Time'** and '**In Fields of Ardath'**, 1969, on Mercury Records) have been reissued on CD with Esoteric Recordings (2015) in remastered editions with bonus and recollections by drummer John Weathers. '**In Fields of Ardath'** is highly recommended as a neglected classic of progressive and psychedelic rock.

**DESCRIPTION** Eyes of Blue were not only the antecedents of the great Welsh rock band **Man** but also released a very creditable album as **Big Sleep ('Bluebell Wood')** in 1971 (also remastered by Esoteric Recordings). In between times they backed **Buzzy Linhart** as session men to good effect on his solo album which is now widely available on CD. Their first LP '**Crossroads of Time'** is very much a band feeling its way with the outstanding tracks mostly covers, of Graham Bond's '**Love is the Law'**, Love's '**7+7 Is'** and an interesting take on McCartney's '**Yesterday'**, '**Q III'**, a single B-side being the strongest original presaging the quantum leap forward that was '**In Fields of Ardath'**. Their second album was much more confident, progressive and experimental than its predecessor, sounding at times like the group was listening to **Procol Harum** and **Robin Trower** in particular. Ritchie Francissaid, "We were a lot more organised and we were keen to push the envelope", while John Weathers opined, "We weren't afraid of taking risks"

## Fairport Convention/ Sandy Denny

**THE MUSICIANS: Judy Dyble (Vocals and Recorder), Simon Nicol and Richard Thompson (Guitars), Ashley Hutchings (Bass), Martin Lamble (Drums)** and later **Ian MacDonald** (who changed his working name to **Iain Matthews** to avoid confusion with the King Crimson musician of the same name- see below)

**ORIGIN:** London

**NOTABLE RECORDINGS:** Fairport Convention started to make a big impact in 1968 but ,in 1967, recorded '**If I Had a Ribbon Bow/ If (Stomp)'** \*\*\* 45 (Track);

**DESCRIPTION:** Although, obviously, a major player in the development of folk rock Fairport Convention didn't release their first album until 1968 but, as this was actually completed in October, 1967 it is certainly on our radar. They produced a series of terrific albums including '**Unhalfbricking'** (1968) and ground breaking folk rock evergreen '**Liege and Lief'** (1969). Going back a bit, 1967 was a significant year for the group as they played their first gig in a church hall in Golders Green on 27 May, 1967 and, among their repertoire at that time were shrewd choices of covers like Emmitt Rhodes song for Merry Go Round, '**Time Will Show The Wiser'** (soon to appear on their first album) and Love's '**Seven And Seven Is'**. Joe Boyd discovered the group playing at Happening 44, a club in Gerrard Street, Soho and booked them to play in the UFO club where they supported Pink Floyd. Within their orbit was Sandy Denny, surely, one of the greatest female singers to walk the planet, who had, by 1967, featured on two LPs, '**Alex Campbell and His Friends'** (Eros/ Saga 22/03/67) and '**Sandy and Johnny'** (24/04/67). Sandy sang lead on three songs on the first of these albums: '**This Train'**, '**The False Bride'** and the most distinguished of the three, a cover of Jackson C Frank's '**You Never Wanted Me'**. The second album was made with Johnny Silvo with whom she worked with until the summer of 1967 either as a duo or as part of The Johnny Silvo Four. She fronted six songs (interchanging tracks with Silvo, she the odd, he the even)*:* '**Milk and Honey'** (another Jackson C Frank song); '**The Last Thing on My Mind'** (popularised by Tom Paxton); '**3.10 to Yuma'** (Frankie Laine's 1957 soundtrack hit);

*'Make Me a Pallet on the Floor'; 'Pretty Polly'* and *'Been on the Road So Long'* (an Alex Campbell favourite). 1967 also saw Sandy become a member of **The Strawbs**, collaborating with her musical muse Dave Cousins on developing original song writing on an album called **'All Our Own Work'** which remained in suspended animation, until six years later, when it was officially released (on the budget Hallmark label) in the wake of Denny's and The Strawbs' success. On the strength of some demo tapes recorded at Cecil Sharp House, Karl Knudsen invited the group to Copenhagen to record the album for his Storyville label. The group alternated a season in Tivoli Gardens with recording sessions in the Vanløse Bio cinema. The album was aimed at the pop market with strings arranged by local jazz trumpeter Svend Lundvig [114] The most significant thing was not only the emergence of the immortal *'Who Knows Where the Time Goes'* as Denny's first recorded original but the fact that she took lead vocal on seven of the twelve songs. Despite interest in the album from Polydor and the Major Minor label, to paraphrase Ray Davies, Denny got 'tired of waiting' especially as Polydor wanted the group to re-record it. In the summer of 1967, she also met Joe Boyd and her direction (and fortunes) began to change. Boyd admired Denny for having the strength of character to turn down The Strawbs seeing her as an ideal fit for folk rock group Fairport Convention. [115] Although they were being billed as 'England's Top West Coast Group' and described as 'the English Jefferson Airplane', Judy Dyble's vocals were not considered strong enough (even with the recruitment of Ian MacDonald to strengthen this department) and she was unceremoniously told by de facto group leader Ashley Hutchings that her singing was not always in tune.

Joe Boyd has vivid recollections of "one evening in the eventful month of June, 1967": "I went to hear Sandy Denny at Les Cousins in Soho. I still wasn't convinced: she insisted on performing songs by her American ex-boyfriend Jackson C Frank and other undistinguished singer-songwriters. Her voice seemed more big than expressive." However, after talking about music all night, and listening to a tape of Radio Luxembourg's preview of **'Sergeant Pepper's'** at Sandy's parents' home in Wimbledon, Sandy convinced Boyd that she was ambitious to leave the folk circuit and front a band. .**(112)**Boyd was astonished to hear how good Denny's voice sounded on record on her LP with The Strawbs and was aware that Judy Collins was about to make Denny's *'Who Knows Where the Time Goes'* the title track of her new LP. The rest is history as the orbits of Sandy Denny and Richard Thompson converged.

## The Fairy-tale

**THE MUSICIANS: Malcolm (Mally) Rabbit (Keyboards), John Weston (Guitar), Chaddy Penketh (Bass) and Billy Fagg (Drums)**
**ORIGIN:** Warrington, Lancashire
**NOTABLE RECORDINGS:** The Fairy-tale released two singles on Decca in 1967 the best of which was the slightly psychedelic *'Guess I Was Dreaming'* *** (nice piano) and its flip side *'Run and Hide'* *** (cheesy organ and earnest tom-toms). The other was *'Lovely People ***/ Listen to Mary Cry'* *** (both Decca). The A-side has been eulogised by some as a hippy anthem and considered by others as not as good as its predecessor. As for me, I think it is on a par with the first although perhaps a little one-

---

[114] The strings were not actually part of the final mix used for the LP release but can be heard on the CD **'Sandy Denny and the Strawbs'** released on Joe Boyd's Hannibal label in 1991.
[115] Boyd saw the potential in Sandy's song *'Who Knows Where The Time Goes'* in the hope that songs of equal quality whould emerge which they did.

paced despite efforts to embellish with a little harpsichord and woodwind. Its B-side has nice vocal harmonies and organ.

**REISSUES:** Their songs are comprehensively covered on **Rubble LPs (volumes 5 & 11)** as well as CDs including **'The Freakbeat Scene'.**

**DESCRIPTION:** Psychedelic pop/ rock with the emphasis on pleasant melody such as on *'Lovely People'* their existence was short-lived which makes them very collectible and well worth hearing.

## Marianne Faithfull

**ORIGIN: London**

**NOTABLE RECORDINGS:** (all Decca) *'As Tears Go By'* (1964) #9 UK, #22 US; *'This Little Bird'* (1965) #6 UK, #31 US; LPs: 'Come My Way' #12 UK and 'Marianne Faithfull' #15 UK, #12 US (both **1965**) in 1967 'Loveinamist' **\*\*\*\*** LP

**REISSUES:** Most recent compilations include 'Come and Stay with Me- the UK 45s 1964-1968' (Ace, 2018); 'North Country Maid/ Loveinamist' (BGO, 2016); the most comprehensive a 4 CD set, 'The Decca Years, 1965-1967 (Decca, 2007, Japan- very expensive!) All of these are on CD.

**DESCRIPTION:** Girlfriend of John Dunbar, Marianne met Andrew Loog Oldham, the Rolling Stones manager at a party hence her early breakthrough with a Jagger/ Richards song. She enjoyed early success on both sides of the Atlantic, became Mick Jagger's girlfriend and was involved in the notorious drug bust (see **The Rolling Stones**). Despite this commercial success her early LPs are collectible with prices of £50+ not unusual. Faithfull enjoyed a resurgence in the late '70s and early '80s with two creditable top 50 albums, **Broken English (1979),** and **Dangerous Acquaintances (1981).** Her 1967 album has many great moments mixing 'standards' (McCartney's *'Yesterday'*) with songs by up and coming songwriters (John D Loudermilk's *'This Little Bird'*), which provided her with a big single hit); two lesser known Donovan songs perfectly suited to her quavery voice, *'Young Girl Blues'* and *'Good Guy'* (as indeed is a heartfelt reading of Bob Lind's *'Counting'*). Then there is chanson (the charming *'Coquillages'* and Jacques Brel's *'Ne Me Quitte Pas'*). Mix in interpretations of Tim Hardin's *'Reason to Believe'* and *'Don't Make Promises You Can't Keep'* and, all-in-all you've got a pretty strong album with sensitive string arrangements that are not overbearing.

## Georgie Fame (Clive Powell)

**THE MUSICIANS:** (as **The Blue Flames**); **Georgie Fame (Vocals, Piano), Colin Green (Guitar), Mick Eve (Sax), Tony Makins (Bass) and Red Reece (Drums)**

**ORIGIN:** Leigh, Lancashire

**NOTABLE RECORDINGS:** *Yeh Yeh* (Columbia, 1964) #1 UK; *Get Away* (Columbia, 1966) #1; *Ballad of Bonnie and Clyde* **\*\*\*\*** (CBS, 1967) #1; two further 45s: *Because I Love You* **\*\*\*** and *Try My World* **\*\*\*\*** and two LPs, **Hall of Fame \*\*\*** and **Two Faces of Fame \*\*\***were released in 1967/1968 (reissued as a 2 on 1 CD on Beat Goes On, 2006).

**DESCRIPTION:** Larry Parnes took Powell under his wing on a recommendation by Lionel Burt and gave him the name Georgie Fame. He would join Billy Fury's band The Blue Flames in 1961 and when Fury brought in The Tornadoes, Fame took over the leadership of The Blue Flames. Combining jazz and beat, they gained a reputation and a following in The Flamingo Club in London's west end and signed to the Columbia label in 1963, A live album **'Rhythm and Blues at the Flamingo'** was released but Georgie and The Flames made their breakthrough with the 1964 album 'Fame At Last' (#15 UK). The 45 breakthrough also came in 1964 with 'Yeh Yeh' which hit the top spot in the UK and nearly made the US top 20 becoming a million-seller. Further hits followed, including two number ones. He parted company from The Blue Flames in the autumn of 1966 and went more pop than R&B, working with musicians like Jon Hiseman, John McLaughlin and Mitch Mitchell. A collaboration with ex Animals organist Alan Price was less successful. TV work followed and he became Van Morrison's musical director for a while.

As far as 1967 goes, the jazzy brass driven 'Because I Love You' is a little light on melody but interesting musically. Imagine an early version of Chicago. 'Try My World' is a dreamy, enchanting song with string and harp backing and a nice muted staccato trumpet line. Over 1967 and 1968, two LPs were released that are great favourites of fans and are seen as a two-part concept of swinging jazz and soul. The first LP was half live, a mixture of jazzy 'big band' soul like Duke Ellington's 'Things Ain't What They Used to Be' and pure soul (Percy Mayfield's 'River's Invitation'). The second part is almost all jazz based except for the southern soul of 'El Pussycat'. 'Third Face of Fame' has the blues ballad 'St James Infirmary'; 'The Ballad of Bonnie and Clyde'; 'When I'm 64' and closes with an expansive jazzy version of Donovan's 'Mellow Yellow'.

# Family

Family fall into the same category as Fairport Convention above albeit in a different musical context with their distinctive throaty singer **Roger Chapman** and their unique take on psychedelic/ progressive rock. **Chapman** was ably assisted by **John 'Charlie' Whitney** (guitars), **Jim King** (sax, vocals, harmonica), **Ric Grech** (bass, violin, vocals) and **Rob Townsend** (drums) in the original line-up of a band that was to develop a unique sound, a dedicated following and great commercial success with singles and albums. Their first album **'Music in a Doll's House'** was released in 1968 but, as a foretaste, they released a single on Liberty in 1967, a psych classic called **'Scene Through the Eyes of a Lens'** **** (which ends with a quotation from Gustav Holst's 'Mars, The Bringer of War') backed with the bluesy **'Gypsy Woman'** ****. Unaccountably, Family's first 45 does not appear on Family compilations but can be found on the **Electric Sugar Cube Flashbacks CD**. It should be noted that Family were gigging heavily in 1967 so this was a significant year for their future development.

# Chris Farlowe and The Thunderbirds

**THE MUSICIANS: John Deighton AKA Chris Farlowe (Vocals); Dave Greenslade, Pete Solley (Keyboards); Albert Lee (Guitar); Ricky Chapman** then **Bugs Waddell (Bass); Johnny Wise,** then **Ian Hague** then **Carl Palmer (Drums)**

**ORIGIN:** Islington, London

**NOTABLE RECORDINGS:** 'Think', a Mick Jagger/ Keith Richard composition which reached #37 in 1966; 'Out of Time', another Jagger/ Richard number was a #1 UK hit for Immediate in the same year; 45s released in 1967 were *My Way of Giving* ****/ *You're So Good to Me'* ****#48 UK; *'Yesterday's Papers ***/ Life is But Nothing'* ****; *'Moanin' ****/ What Have I Been Doing?'* #46 UK; *'Handbags and Gladrags ****/ Everyone Makes a Mistake'* *** deserved better than #33 in 1967.

**REISSUES:** Loads of compilation coverage for *'Out of Time',* and *'Handbags and Gladrags'* which provided bigger hits for Rod Stewart and The Stereophonics whose version was the title song of the long running UK sit com 'The Office'.

**DESCRIPTION:** Chris Farlowe is probably too well-known to be included in this section of the book but he is sometimes considered a one hit wonder which is unfair. He was a steady recipient of Jagger/ Richard songs – for example *'Yesterday's Papers'* in 1967 and *'Paint It Black'* in 1968 without the same success. Farlowe released records under his own name from 1962 to 1971, and became the singer with **Colosseum** and **Atomic Rooster** until a revival in 1975 when he released a live album. He reunited with Dave Greenslade in providing music for a BBC TV show entitled 'Gangsters'. His 1967 repertoire included *'My Way of Giving'*, a big production with strings and some Hammond, and great power-house drumming, this record shows Farlowe right up there with the Joe Cockers, the Tom Joneses and the Rod Stewarts. Its more balladic B-side is a life-affirming prime slice of northern soul. *'Yesterday's Papers'* is a highly charged, over busy version of one of the better songs on The Rolling Stones' **'Between the Buttons'** with Farlowe sounding unusually strained. Its B-side is better with Farlowe more at home on the stripped down arrangement with strong drumming, brass parps and restrained strings. At four minutes, it was unusually long for a 45 of the time. *'Moanin'* is a remarkable song in Farlowe's repertoire with Big Jim Sullivan on sitar and a tabla player. Brass and strings still adorn the record while Jimmy Page's brief fuzz guitar was removed for the final cut. *'Handbags and Gladrags'* is one of Farlowe's most famous numbers, of course, and its B-side is also of merit with a more basic groove than most of his 1967 cuts. It's a pity the Hammond couldn't have been extended to allow the number to pass the two minute mark.

## Bill Fay

**INSTRUMENTS: Bill Fay (Vocals, Piano), Ray Russell (Guitar), Daryl Runswick (Bass) and Alan Rushton (Drums)**

**ORIGIN:** London

**NOTABLE RECORDINGS:** Bill Fay started recording in 1967 with a brilliant Deram single *'Some Good Advice* \*\*\*\*\*/ *Screams in the Ears'* \*\*\*\*\*. His early albums **'Bill Fay'** (Deram Nova, 1970) and **'Time of the Last Persecution'** (Deram, 1971) come highly recommended.

**REISSUES:** Fay's 1970 and 1971 albums have been reissued on CD on Esoteric Recordings.

**DESCRIPTION:** In recent years, Fay has garnered some long overdue attention thanks in part to an appearance with Jeff Tweedy (who is a fan) at a Wilco concert. His 2013 recording **'Life is People'** is brilliant, and the passing of the years has not dimmed his musical and lyrical perceptiveness making for some haunting music that sounds quite unlike anything else. He also released another highly acclaimed album **'Who Is the Sender?'** (2015).

## Felius Andromeda

**THE MUSICIANS: Bill Haine (Vocals); Denis Couldry (Organ); Pete Parks (Guitar), Alan Morgan (Bass) and Mick Richardson (Drums)**

**ORIGIN:** London

**NOTABLE RECORDINGS:** Felius Andromeda are included because of their **Procol Harum** influenced 1967 Decca single *'Meditations'* \*\*\*\* b/w *'Cheadle Heath's Delusions'* \*\*\*\*.

**REISSUES:** *'Meditations'* is on the **'Psychedelic Scene'** CD and the 4-CD box set **'Acid Drops, Spacedust & Flying Saucers'**. The group is also included in the extended **Rubble** CD box set.

**DESCRIPTION:** The group had great faith in their ambitious four minute long debut 45 and dressed in monks' robes to accompany the meditative chanting on their *'Meditations'* recording. When it failed to make any impact, they drifted apart and Alan Morgan, who had co-written *'Meditations'* doggedly tried to continue, with Steve Webber (organ) and Pete Banks of **The Syn** (guitar-see separate entry). Pete Parks went to **Warhorse** whose Vertigo album is now highly collectible. The B-side references a neighbourhood in the Stockport area and is an accomplished piece of psych rock.

## Fleetwood Mac

Another group falling into the category of Fairport Convention and Family above, just outside the remit of this book's time period – one of the planet's most famous and enduring groups – their first album wasn't released until 1968 but they did release a blues 45 *'I Believe My Time Ain't Long ****/ Rambling Pony'* *** on the Blue Horizon label in 1967. The line-up at that time was **Jeremy Spencer (Guitar and Vocals), Peter Green (Guitar and Harmonica), Bob Brunning (Bass)** and **Mick Fleetwood (Drums)**. Originally entitled *'I Believe I'll Dust My Broom',* the A-side originates with Robert Johnson in 1936, Elmore James doing a slide guitar version in 1951 and shortening the title to *'Dust My Broom'* which Fleetwood Mac emulate, changing the title again. Credited to Peter Green, the riff is taken from Muddy Waters' (and others) *'Rollin' and Tumblin'*, stripped back with a drum beat that sounds very machine-like. Breakthrough instrumental hit *'Albatross'* was just a year away.

## (Les) (The) Fleur De Lys/ Rupert's People

**THE MUSICIANS:** Frank Smith→ Chris Andrews→ Tony Head (Vocals); Frank Smith→ Phil Sawyer→ Bryan Haworth→ Graham Maitland (Guitar); Alex Chamberlain→ Pete Sears (Keyboards); Gary Churchill → Gordon Haskell→ Tago Byers (Bass); Keith Guster (Drums)

**ORIGIN:** Southampton

**NOTABLE RECORDINGS:** *'Circles'* (Immediate, 1966); *'Mud in Your Eye/ I've been Trying'* (Polydor, 1966-Bryn Haworth's guitar work on *'Mud in Your Eye'* is notable); *'Reflections of Charles Brown'* ****/ *'Hold On'* **** (Atlantic, 1967) as Rupert's People, the B-side with Sharon Tandy; *'Stay with Me'* ****/ *'Hold On'* **** (with Sharon Tandy, Atlantic, 1967, the A-side is the same song as 'Stay with Me, Baby' that Lorraine Ellison had a hit with; the B-side has a great Haworth guitar solo and made #5 in Germany); **I Can See a Light** ****/ **Prodigal Son** *** (Polydor, 1967); *'Gong with the Luminous Nose'* (Polydor, 1968); *'Liar'* (Atlantic, 1969)

**REISSUES:** **'Les Fleur De Lys: Reflections'** compiles all Fleur De Lys studio recordings, and records made with John Bromley, Donnie Elbert, Sharon Tandy and others; and under the names **Shyster, Chocolate Frog, Waygood Ellis** and **Rupert's People**. As Rupert's People: **'The Major World of Rupert's People'** (Circle CD, 2002) includes the 45s and predecessor group **Sweet Feeling**'s only 45 *'All So Long Ago/ Charles Brown'* on Columbia, 1967, concert tracks and some reunion tracks; *'Reflections of Charles Brown'* appears on a **Perfumed Garden** CD and on the **Nuggets II** box set. Other songs appear on **Rubble**. Likewise, Fleur De Lys songs can be found on various 'psychedelic' compilations.

**DESCRIPTION:** As Les Fleur De Lys, a version of Buddy Holly's *'Moondreams'*, produced by Jimmy Page, was released on Immediate in November, 1965. Only drummer Keith Guster remained from that original line-up with Gordon Haskell coming in on bass, Phil Sawyer on guitar and Pete Sears on keys when, as The Fleur De Lys, they released Pete Townsend's *'Circles'* (The Who's original version was called *'Instant Party'*) which got much pirate radio attention but was ignored by the BBC. Chris Andrews, who came to the public's attention as a child actor playing The Artful Dodger in the London production of 'Oliver' in 1964 and having narrowly missed out on becoming a Monkee, joined the group in 1966 when they were signed by Polydor. Sears left the group, and eventually, joined Jefferson Starship while Phil Sawyer, having previously been a member of The Cheynes and Shotgun Express, joined the Spencer Davis Group. Continuing as a 3 piece in their 'STAX/VOLT phase' [116](recruiting Bryn Haworth) they issued a single *'Mud in Your Eye'*, backed by a cover of the B-side of The Impressions' *'People Get Ready'*, *'I've Been Trying'* in November, 1966. During this period, they backed **Aretha Franklin, Isaac Hayes** and **Sharon Tandy**. They released four singles in 1967 as Fleur De Lys: *'I Can See a Light'/ 'Prodigal Son'*, the former a dreamy psychedelic ballad, the latter an all too short ballad with nice guitar; *'This Land is Mine/ What the World Needs Now is Love'* (as Debrah Aire, a pseudonym for Sharon Tandy); *'Stay with Me'/'Hold On'*; *'Our Day Will Come/ Look and Find'* (the latter two also with Sharon Tandy) and guested on John Peel's 'Top Gear' (with **Cream, Traffic** and **Vanilla Fudge**) in October, 1967, doing three numbers of their own and backing **Sharon Tandy** on three of hers. They released three further singles on Polydor then Atlantic between 1968 and 1969 the best remembered of which is probably *'Gong with the Luminous Nose'* written by Gordon Haskell and based on the nonsense rhyme of Edward Lear. Haskell joined **King Crimson** in 1969.

Regarding Rupert's People (actually Les Fleur De Lys) on the 45 *'The Reflections of Charles Brown'* resemblance to the summer of love masterpiece *'A Whiter Shade of Pale'* is obvious and, coincidentally, Pete Solley, who would later join **Procol Harum**, played organ on the record. It was a big hit across parts of Europe but not in the UK. On hearing the level of plagiarism, Les Fleur De Lys wanted nothing to do with it, and while they recorded it, refused to promote it. So it was a different group that continued as Rupert's People. The B-side *'Hold On'* was written and recorded by The Fleur de Lys with Sharon Tandy. *'I Can Show You'*, their third and final single released in 1968 makes obvious reference to The Beatles' *'Ticket to Ride'*. Group member John Tout went on to join **Renaissance** and **Wishbone Ash**.

The nearest Les Fleur De Lys came to a hit was when they backed **Tony Head** and **Sharon Tandy** on a song that led to a 'Top of the Pops' appearance but not a hit, *'Two Can Make It Together'*. Unfortunately, the BBC producers did not want the group to play on the TV!

---

[116] Bryn Haworth told Record Collector magazine that the group were 'into' Motown and Atlantic stuff. "We were really a soul band, Gordon, Chris and I would sing three part harmonies." The group's manager Frank Fenter (who was married to singer Sharon Tandy whom The Fleur De Lys backed) had contacts and influence that provided opportunities for the group to take Aretha Franklin shopping when she was in London and jam with musicians like Isaac Hayes, Sam and Dave and an (in) famous all night session with Vanilla Fudge.

# (The) Flowerpot Men

**THE MUSICIANS:** Tony Burrows, Perry Ford, Neil Landon, Peter Landon **(Vocals)** with backing musicians who included **Jon Lord** on **Organ** (who replaced **Billy Davidson** briefly in 1968) and **Nick Semper/ Gordon Haskell** on bass.

**ORIGIN:** London, Sussex, Middlesex

**NOTABLE RECORDINGS:** *'Let's Go to San Francisco parts 1 & 2'* \*\*\*\*\* (Deram, 1967) #4 UK; *'A Walk in the Sky'* \*\*\*\* (Deram, 1967) – very similar to the Beach Boys with a Beatle-ish ending which flopped in the UK but was big hit in Holland.

**REISSUES:** **'Let's Go to San Francisco'** (Repertoire, 1993) is more comprehensive than 1988's compilation of the same name on C5 Records and includes an eight minute track *'Children of Tomorrow'*. **'Peace Album/ Past Imperfect'** consists of two albums never released in 1969 (Repertoire, 2000) while **'Midsummer Dreaming (Let's All Go to San Francisco)'** with its striking psychedelic cover, compiles rarities and B-sides.

**DESCRIPTION:** According to J F Lilburn's liner notes to the CD reissue, singer songwriter team John Carter and Ken Lewis (who go back to the early 1960s when as Carter-Lewis and the Southerners they had a top 20 hit in November, 1963 with *'Your Momma's Out of Town'*) formed a vocal trio with Perry Ford to provide vocal backing for records such as The Who's *'I Can't Explain'* and as The Ivy League produced a number of hit singles including *'Funny How Love Can Be'* and *'Tossing and Turning'*.

"Then along came the summer of love… Carter and Lewis write a paean to the genre, cut a demo of *'Let's Go to San Francisco'*, overdub additional backing vocals (using session men), creating a sound which fitted the era perfectly coined the name The Flowerpot Men, leased the track to Deram, and it became a smash hit." (A group was hired to mime to the record on 'Top of the Pops').

After the follow-up dived (except in Holland), they released two other unsuccessful 45s for the Deram label in 1968 and 1969. Neil Landon joined **Fat Mattress** and Robin Shaw and Peter Nelson became members of **White Plains** and **Brotherhood of Man**, who enjoyed 'middle of the road' chart success. Burrows' voice can also be heard on **Edison Lighthouse**'s 1970 #1 hit *'Love Grows'*. As far as their name is concerned, it was taken from the popular BBC 'Watch with Mother' TV programme featuring Bill and Ben with Weed. The drug connotations and flower power reference are obvious.

# Wayne Fontana and the Mindbenders/ The Mindbenders

**THE MUSICIANS:** Glyn Ellis AKA Wayne Fontana (Vocals), Eric Stewart (Guitar), Bob Land (Bass), Rick Rothwell (Drums)

**ORIGIN:** Manchester, England

**NOTABLE RECORDINGS:** *'The Game of Love'* (Fontana, 1965) later used in the film 'Good Morning, Vietnam'; *'A Groovy Kind of Love'* (The Mindbenders, Fontana, 1966); three singles were released by Wayne Fontana and three by The Mindbenders in 1967 including a two minute cover of The Box Tops *'The Letter'* (#42 UK) \*\*\*, Graham Gouldman's first record as a producer, the catchy, string laced, wah-wah guitar of *'Schoolgirl'* \*\*\*\* (clever lyric and arrangement although the strings are unnecessary and detract from the psych feel, suggestive of what was to come for Gouldman as a writer) and its freaky psych B-side *'Coming Back'*. Wayne Fontana's nostalgic tale of innocence *'Pamela, Pamela'* \*\* (#11 UK) has a nice melody but the syrupy strings and trite lyrics do it no favours and it hasn't aged well. Les Reed and Barry

Mason's *'24 Sycamore'* \*\*\* was also sang by Gene Pitney and is a nice ballad. *'From a Boy to a Man'* \*\* is in similar vein and again sounds dated now.

**REISSUES:** The group's better known songs can be found on various '60s' compilations. *'The Morning After'* their B-side to the Rod Argent song *'I Want Her, She Wants Me'* released on Fontana in 1966 can be found on **'The Psychedelic Snarl'** (Rubble Vol 1).

**DESCRIPTION:** It is arguable that Wayne Fontana should not be in the 'lesser known' section of this book. However, as he split from his Mindbenders (thought to be named after a 1963 horror movie) in November, 1967, the relevance of his music is limited in terms of the 'age of Sergeant Pepper'. Discovered (as The Jets) by a Fontana Records talent spotter (pure coincidence!) at Manchester's Oasis Club, their 1963 debut single, a cover of Bo Diddley's *'Hello! Josephine'* reached the UK top 50. The B-side was *'Road Runner'* which became a big Motown hit for Junior Walker and The All Stars.

Between 1964 and 1965, Wayne Fontana and the Mindbenders released two albums, four EPs and eight singles on the Fontana label and the most successful of these were a cover of Curtis Mayfield's *'Um, Um, Um, Um, Um, Um'*, a US hit for Major Lance, and the million selling *'The Game of Love'*, a Hank Ballard Junior song (#2 in the UK, #1 in the US). They passed up on another Ballard song which provided The Hollies with a #1 hit (*I'm Alive*). Their first album, issued in 1964 as **'Wayne Fontana and the Mindbenders'** in the UK (where it reached #18 on the album charts) and **'The Game of Love: Wayne Fontana and the Mindbenders'** in the US (where it only reached #58) consisted of cover versions except for an Eric Stewart co-write. The liner notes of my US copy make no attempt to praise the album referring only to how the group came about and the success of *'The Game of Love'* single. The Beatles are mentioned in the first paragraph but there was nothing here that suggested a glittering creative career – their version of Chuck Berry's *'Jaguar and Thunderbird'* clocked in at 1:03 and the whole album barely lasts half an hour.

After two further attempts on the singles charts, the group split in November, 1965. Wayne Fontana went solo and released a succession of singles mostly between 1965 and 1969, the most famous one being *'Pamela, Pamela'* which nearly made the top ten in the UK and featured in the revivalist Old Gold series in 1985. The Mindbenders without Fontana suffered the same fate as their predecessors despite getting off to a spectacular start with what would become a sixties classic *'A Groovy Kind of Love'* and reaching #2 in the UK in 1966. A lack of original material and lack of innovative defining features in the crowded arena of early to mid-sixties pop music would prove their undoing but they did provide a breeding ground for the likes of Eric Stewart and Graham Gouldman who would go on to form **Hotlegs** which became **10CC**.

## The Fortunes

**THE MUSICIANS: Shel McRae (Vocals), Glen Dale→Barry Pritchard/ Shel McRae (Guitar); David Carr (Keyboards); Rod Allen (Bass)** and **Andy Brown (Drums)**

**ORIGIN:** Birmingham, England

**NOTABLE RECORDINGS:** *'You've Got Your Troubles'* (Decca, 1965); *'Here It Comes Again'* (Decca, 1965); *'Our Love Has Gone'/ 'Truly Yours'* (Decca, 1967) \*\*\*; *'The Idol'/ 'His Smile Was a Lie'* (United Artists, 1967) \*\*\*\*/ \*\*\*\*; *'Fire Brigade'* (UA, 1968 – US only) (a cover of The Move hit)

**REISSUES:** Concentrating on singles, the most comprehensive compilation I have found is '**The Complete Decca Singles 1963-67**' on Dynamic Voice (2015) (UK & Europe) with 31 tracks.

**DESCRIPTION:** The Fortunes released only two singles in 1967 (out of a total of twenty-four in their entire career): *Our Love Has Gone/ Truly Yours* and *The Idol/ His Smile Was a Lie* on Decca and United Artists respectively. The Decca A-side is a lachrymose ballad with the mandatory sixties strings (orchestras must have been in regular employment back then), very well done but rather cloying. The UA single was a thoughtful, incisive and unusual number well worth (re)exploring with a definite Beatles influence in its coda. Its B-side is a definite 'nugget' contender, an interesting psych/pop song with mellotron and piano. After switching from Decca to the United Artists label, their heyday of 1965 was by then well and truly over. However, they did have a revival in chart success in 1971 and 1972 with '*Freedom Come, Freedom Go*' and '*Storm in a Teacup*' (Both top 10 hits in the UK), by that time, recording for Capitol Records.

Starting off as The Cliftones, they provided the theme tune for Radio Caroline (*'Caroline'*) in 1964 but it was '*You've Got Your Troubles*' that provided their big chart breakthrough and gave them a #2 UK and #7 US hit. '*Here It Comes Again*' was a strong follow-up which made #4 on the UK charts. In 1967, they recorded advertising jingles including the '*It's the Real Thing*' for Coca-Cola. Their next hit was a cover of Pickettywitch's '*That Same Old Feeling*' which nearly made the top 60 on the US. Employing songwriters Roger Cook and Roger Greenaway improved their fortunes (!) once more, and gave them another purple patch in 1971/72. As far as I am aware, they only released two albums both called **The Fortunes** (in 1965 and 1972) and one EP in 1980 called '**You've Got Your Troubles**' in the UK. There were some European releases and an LP '**That Same Old Feeling**' in the US.

## The Foundations

**THE MUSICIANS:** Mike Elliot→ Pat Burke (Sax), Eric Allendale (Trombone), Clem Curtis→ Allan Warner/ Colin Young (Vocals), Tony Gomez (Organ), Allan Warner, Colin Young (Guitar); Peter Macbeth (Bass) and Tim Harris (Drums)

**ORIGIN:** London with membership from Barbados, Dominica, Jamaica and Sri Lanka (then known as Ceylon)

**NOTABLE RECORDINGS:** '*Baby, Now That I've Found You*' (Pye, 1967) ****; '*Build Me Up, Buttercup*' (Pye, 1968)

**REISSUES:** Lots of examples of their most famous songs on '60s' compilations and Sequel compiled two of their albums '**From the Foundations**' (1967) and '**Digging the Foundations**' (1969).

**DESCRIPTION:** The Foundations burned brightly but briefly between 1967 and 1971, releasing nine singles on Pye, and one on MCA as well as four albums and one EP on Pye. They got off to a meteoric start with '60s' classic the infectious soul of '*Baby, Now That I've Found You*' in 1967 and nearly made the number one spot again in 1968 with '*Build Me Up, Buttercup*', an enduring song whose inclusion during the closing credits of memorable spoof film 'There's Something About Mary' sparked a revival of interest in the group. '*In the Bad, Bad Old Days*' from 1969 provided another top ten UK hit and was another catchy song but from then it was downhill all the way.

# Freddie and the Dreamers

THE MUSICIANS: Freddie Garrity (Vocals), Roy Crewdson (Guitar), Derek Quinn (Guitar, Vocals), Peter Birrell (Bass), Bernie Dwyer (Drums) with session man Big Jim Sullivan (Guitar) on certain releases.

ORIGIN: Manchester

NOTABLE RECORDINGS: (All on Columbia except *) 45s: *'If You Gotta Make a Fool of Somebody'* (1963) #3, *'I'm Telling You Now'* (1963) #1 UK (1965) (Tower) #1 US, *'You Were Made for Me'* (1963) #3

COLLECTING/ REISSUES: Their first three singles are great fun and a nice addition to a sixties jukebox. A 'greatest hits' CD would be a suitable alternative.

DESCRIPTION: A bit of a 'novelty' act with gimmicky stage antics like 'the Freddie dance' they became part of 'the British invasion' ironic since Capitol Records dropped them when' *I'm Telling You Now'* came out and this subsequently topped the US charts when released by Tower Records. Paul McCartney reckoned that *'If You Gotta Make a Fool of Somebody'* sounded similar to a number The Beatles had played at the Cavern but there were no hard feelings with Freddie, and the Dreamers invited to entertain the crowd at The Beatles Christmas show in 1964. Concentrating on 45s and EPs, the obligatory long playing records were also released with titles like '**Sing Along Party**' confirming the group was content to be in the light entertainment business rather than part of the psychedelic scene!

# Elmer Gantry's Velvet Opera/ Velvet Opera

THE MUSICIANS: Colin Forster→ Dave Terry AKA Elmer Gantry→ Paul Brett as Velvet Opera (Guitar); James Horrocks (Organ and Piano); Elmer Gantry→ John Joyce as Velvet Opera (Vocals), John Ford (Bass) and Richard Hudson (Drums, Sitar).

ORIGIN: London

NOTABLE RECORDINGS: '**Elmer Gantry's Velvet Opera**' (Direction, 1968 LP); *'Flames'* ****/ *'Salisbury Plain'* **** 45 (Direction, 1967-the B-side was *'What's The Point of Leaving'* in the US); *'Talk of the Devil'* (from an obscure film of the same name); also of interest are versions of *'Eleanor Rigby'* and *'All Along The Watchtower'*.

REISSUES: '**Elmer Gantry's Velvet Opera**' 1968 LP with non-album singles has been released on the Repertoire and Arkama labels. The second album, under the name **The Velvet Opera**, has also been reissued on CD on Arkama. A See for Miles compilation '**The Very Best of Elmer Gantry's Velvet Opera**' has selected tracks from their two albums and 4 previously unreleased including *'Talk to the Devil'*; A double CD set '**Stretch: The Story of Elmer Gantry**' is on Repertoire. There is also a single CD of their 1967 LP on Repertoire with 6 bonus tracks; **The Psychedelic Dungeon:** *'Flames'* & *'All Along the Watchtower'* (John Peel's Top Gear, 1968)

DESCRIPTION: Although straying beyond the boundaries of our 1967 target year, it is important to include Elmer Gantry's Velvet Opera because of their famous 45 *'Flames'* which was released in '67. Not an American band as the name would suggest, Elmer Gantry's Velvet Opera (named after a fictional preacher in a 1960 film based on a novel by Sinclair Lewis) started off as a soul/ blues group called The Five Proud Walkers. After supporting Pink Floyd, they went in a more experimental direction and acquired a new 'psychedelic' name. 'Elmer' was also listening to John Cage and experimenting with reel-to-reel tape and tone generators. They played the London circuit in 1967 – the Marquee, the Electric Garden, the Speakeasy etc.- where they jammed with **Jimi Hendrix**. They generated some controversy on the University circuit for using strobe lighting and 'brainwashing' their audience. In fact, a newspaper headline of the time read, "Banned – Elmer Gantry's Audience Brainwashing!" They also sparked controversy with their second single *'Mary Jane'* banned by the BBC when they realised it was a slang term for marijuana. A third single, a song from the Howard/ Blaikley hit machine called *'Volcano'* in 1969 failed to make much impact. *'Flames'* gained popularity partly thanks to its inclusion on the CBS sampler LP **'The Rock Machine Turns You On'** and also because **Led Zeppelin** included it in their early live shows. Its UK B-side *'Salisbury Plain'* is also a strong number much in keeping with times. The rhythm section was Richard Hudson and John Ford who were later in **The Strawbs** and also recorded as Hudson-Ford and had some UK hits like *'Burn, Baby, Burn'* and *'Pick Up the Pieces'* as well as the 1979 novelty song *'Nice Legs, Shame About the Face'* (under the pseudonym The Monks). The eponymous debut album released on CBS Direction in 1968 encompassed a variety of styles from pop/ psych to hard rock to Motown to **Beatles** and eastern influences, a real hybrid. There is much to enjoy from John Ford's in your face bass playing on *'Mother Writes'*; *'What's the Point of Leaving?'* which sounds like a Paul McCartney ballad; the moving *'Long Nights of Summer'* (a lament for the passing of summer and lost love but hope still lingers on after the winter has gone) with similar sentiments to *'Now She's Gone'* which also has mellotron as does *'Reaction of a Young Man'*, with its memorable organ motif, brooding lyric and subtle vocal harmonies, quite **Gentle Giant** like; and *'Dream Starts'* (the start of Hudson-Ford's recorded song writing team), an intriguing song with phasing effects, strange vocals, kazoo and trumpet and excellent drumming/ piano sounding almost like **Family.** The transition between R&B band and 'progressive' is highlighted in the contrast between an inspired cover of a little known Oscar Brown song *'I Was Cool'* and *'Walter Sly Meets Bill Bailey'* a combination of an original Bach like, progressive sounding instrumental coupled with the traditional *'Bill Bailey'*.[117]

They shortened their name to The Velvet Opera and without Elmer Gantry recorded a second album entitled **'Ride a Hustler's Dream'** in 1969. Gantry went on to take a lead role in 'Hair' and work with **Alan Parsons, Cozy Powell** and **Jon Lord.** Prior to that he infamously led a supposed manifestation of **Fleetwood Mac** brought to an abrupt end by litigation. He then formed **Stretch** which had a #16 hit in 1975 with a song about the botched attempt to 'overthrow' Fleetwood Mac, *'Why Did You Do It?'*

# Roy Harper

**INSTRUMENTS: Vocals/ Guitar with various backing musicians**
**ORIGIN:** Manchester, England
**NOTABLE RECORDINGS:** His first LP was *'Sophisticated Beggar'* in 1966. *'Come Out Fighting Genghis Smith'* *** was his 1967 album but it took until 1974 and 1975 for him to achieve a degree of commercial success with one top 30 and one near top 30 UK album (**'Valentine'** and **'H.Q'** respectively). (See below)
**REISSUES:** 'Sophisticated Beggar' has been reissued four times on LP, on Youngblood in Italy and Germany in 1970 and again on Birth Records in the UK in 1973, as **'Return of the Sophisticated Beggar'** with a short extra track and as **'The Sophisticated Beggar'** (strangely enough the title of the original cassette version on Big Ben in 1967) enhanced for stereo on the Big Ben/ Polydor label in 1977 and again, in edited version, reverting to its original title on the Sundown label in 1990. Original copies

---

[117] The album seems to have one foot in 1967 and one in 1968, the All Music guide giving its release date as 1967 while Wikipedia and Discogs say 1968.

have been known to change hands for hundreds of pounds. A good cheap alternative is the Birth label reissue. *'Come Out Fighting, Genghis Smith'* was released on Harper's own Science Friction label on CD in 1991 but I am not aware of any LP reissue so expect to pay at least £50 for an excellent copy on vinyl. Most of Harper's music has been released on CD and is readily available while a double CD **'Counter Culture'** summarises his career to 2005 in chronological order (on Science Friction)

**DESCRIPTION:** Roy Harper was a bohemian folk troubadour who hitch-hiked his way around Europe and North Africa in 1964 translating his experiences into distinctive original songs. On his return to the UK, he was a participant in London's coffee house folk scene taking up residence in the legendary Les Cousins club revealing his rhythmic acoustic guitar style and poetic refrains to appreciative audiences. By his own account, he started writing long poems in the 1950s firstly inspired by *'Endymion'* by John Keats. He is by no means a lesser known artist now and was popular at the regular Hyde Park concerts prior to moving to the progressive Harvest label but his best known works like **'Flat Baroque and Berserk'** are firmly rooted in the late 1960s and 1970s. In 1966 though he released **'Sophisticated Beggar'** on the Strike label and in 1967 *'Come Out Fighting Genghis Smith'* on CBS.

At over 51 minutes, **'The Sophisticated Beggar'** was lengthy for a solo 'folk' album but maintained a consistent quality of writing and was not reliant on covers, Harper penning all 13 songs. Described by the artist as "a wild journey into deepest space", Harper pulls no punches and produces a highly personal yet accessible and intimate debut, baring his soul on a song about electro convulsive therapy entitled *'Committed'* which has Ritchie Blackmore, later of Deep Purple on guitar and a field recording of the crowd at the legendary Manchester City team of the time. The sophisticated beggar title is probably a reference to his time as a London busker. *'Goldfish'* shows Harper's early intent as a serious poet/ singer/ songwriter sounding very much like Donovan on this number. It's as if the artist had emerged fully formed, a butterfly with no pupation stage. *'Black Clouds'* showed Harper's intent as an acoustic guitar player in the **Bert Jansch** mould.

**'Come Out Fighting, Genghis Smith'**, produced by Shel Talmy, was released in our target year and *'Nobody's Got Any Money in the Summer'* will be familiar to many because of its inclusion on the second CBS sampler LP, **'Rock Machine: I Love You'**. It's a clever and catchy song with a wry lyric, similar to Peter Sarstedt in style. At the other extreme *'Highgate Cemetery'*, an 'a capello' vocal performance finds Harper in 'monastic' mode, demonstrating his inventiveness and versatility. His second album is not generally as highly regarded as the **'Sophisticated Beggar'** – indeed one reviewer commented that the third track *'In a Beautiful Rambling Mess'* summed up the album. On his website Harper says, "In the past I have tended to berate this record because I felt it was made too quickly on a tight budget but I have now got to like it from a distance." The overt promotion of dope smoking on songs like *'You Don't Need Money'* would raise eyebrows then and, even if erratic, the ambition of the lengthy title track is to be applauded and his expansive approach is further demonstrated on the ten-minute-long *'Circle'*. The album shows why Harper was labelled progressive, underground and folk. Indeed, he was managed and produced by Peter Jenner and signed to EMI's progressive imprint, Harvest, for his **'Flat Baroque and Berserk'** on which he was backed by members of **The Nice** on one track (*'Hell's Angels'*)

In 1968 a further album **'Folkjokeopus'** was released as, ever the wanderer, he moved from CBS to Liberty. This anti-establishment album contained the epic song *'McGoohan's Blues'* with reference to cult 1967 TV series **'The Prisoner'** and its main protagonist Patrick McGoohan. Many of Harper's subsequent albums were released on

EMI's progressive imprint Harvest. His latest album **'Man and Myth'** is a highly recommended recording. He has written many memorable songs including *'Tom Tiddler's Ground'* and *'I Hate the White Man'*. **Jimmy Page** guested on Harper's **Stormcock** (1971 – as S. Flavius Mercurius!) and **Lifemask** albums and Led Zeppelin dedicated a song *Hats Off to Harper* to him on their third LP. Harper was seriously ill with circulatory problems and *The Lord's Prayer* on **Lifemask** was his 'last testament'. However, he recovered to fill the Royal Albert Hall and the Rainbow in London where he was backed by an orchestra. Dave Gilmour guested on his 1975 LP **'H.Q,'** and Harper returned the compliment by singing lead vocals on *'Have A Cigar'* on Pink Floyd's **Wish You Were Here** album. 'Stormcock' utilised the recording facilities of the Abbey Road studio to great effect over four longitudinal tracks covering a diversified range of topics from 'eye of the storm' social malaise to the pleasures of the unspoilt English countryside. Moving ever further into rock territory, Harper worked live and in the studio with a bewildering array of musicians including **David Gilmour, Chris Spedding, John Paul Jones, Ronnie Lane** and **Keith Moon.** Although now far beyond our time zone it is worth noting that Kate Bush guested on Harper's 1980 LP **'The Unknown Soldier'**. Roy has an active website which is a great source of information and recordings.

## Alex Harvey Soul Band

**THE MUSICIANS: Alex Harvey (Vocals, Guitar) Howie Casey→ Bill Patrick (Sax); Bill Patrick (Flute); Kingsize Taylor (Guitar); Bobby Thompson→ Jimmy Grimes (Bass); Gibson Kemp→ Billy Law (Drums)**
**ORIGIN:** Glasgow, Scotland
**NOTABLE RECORDINGS:** The group's first two singles were standards like *I Just Wanna Make Love to You* and *Got My Mojo Working* on the Polydor label in 1964. His psych period produced two 45s in 1967: *The Sunday Song/ Horizons* **\*\*\*\*** and *Maybe Some Day* **\*\*\*\***/ *Curtains for My Baby* on Decca.
**REISSUES:** I would recommend the double CD compilation **'Considering the Situation'** (Universal, 2003) which traces Harvey's musical history. There are, of course, numerous reissues/ remasters of Sensational Alex Harvey Band albums. There is an incredible 14 CD retrospective on Universal entitled **'The Last of the Teenage Idols'** with an abridged 4 CD version. If it is vinyl you want **'The Alex Harvey Soul Band'** was reissued on the Polydor label in January, 1967. An original copy in excellent condition may cost around £100 but there are much cheaper reissues. **'The Blues'** his other 1964 album is even harder to find and will cost at least twice that. The 45s are hard to come by as well.
**DESCRIPTION:** Like Roy Harper, Alex Harvey could hardly be described as 'lesser known' but his most famous works began in 1972 with the Vertigo album, **'Framed'**. From thereon in The Sensational Alex Harvey Band had four top 20 albums and one top 10 album as well as a top 10 single with **'Delilah'** in 1975 and a top 20 UK hit with **'Boston Tea Party'** in 1976. Like many others, Harvey spent some time in Hamburg and he also, with his soul band, backed Eddie Cochran and Gene Vincent. (He formed his band in 1959). Alex Harvey and his Soul Band released two albums on Polydor in 1964 and one on Fontana in 1969. On the 1964 album, recorded live at the Star Club in Hamburg, his 'Soul Band' was replaced by King Size Taylor and The Dominoes. It includes *'Framed'* and covers of standards like *'Reeling and Rocking', 'I Got My Mojo Working'* and *'Let The Good Times Roll'*. 'The Blues' trawls traditional solo acoustic guitar folk blues such as on *'T.B. Blues'*. Also included are versions of *'Big Rock Candy Mountain', 'St. James Infirmary', 'Strange Fruit', 'Trouble In*

*Mind'*, *'Nobody Knows You When You're Down and Out'* and even *'Waltzing Matilda'*. Eight singles were released between 1964 and 1969, mostly blues and soul standards, but in 1967, Harvey, in keeping with the times, tried some psychedelic numbers with a short-lived group, **Giant Moth** which were released on Decca. Between this and his 'sensational band', Harvey released a jazz based album with **Rock Workshop (Roman Wall Blues,** 1969) and was a member of the pit band in the London version of the **'Hair'** musical and appeared on the original cast album on Polydor in 1969. Of the 1967 records *'Maybe Someday'* is a game, if clumsy psych song with flute and sitar like guitar, quite weird and chaotic but engaging and pointing an arrow forward to the 'sensational' band at their most exuberant. The first B-side *'Horizons'* has flute again and is similar vein with phased drums and hand drums, pretty spaced out! The two '45s' were actually by Harvey's 'flower power' group **Giant Moth** but released under his own name.

## The Herd

**THE MUSICIANS: Andy Bown then Lewis Rich (Keyboards); Peter Frampton (Guitar); Peter Frampton (lead)/ Andy Bown/ Gary Taylor/ Terry Clark (Vocals); Louis Cennamo then Gary Taylor (Bass); Tony Chapman then Andrew Steele then Henry Spinetti then Mike Underwood (Drums)**

**ORIGIN:** South London

**NOTABLE RECORDINGS:** The Herd's 1967 singles are well worth checking out – *'I Can Fly'* \*\*\*\*/ *'Diary Of A Narcissist (I'm So Pretty)'* \*\*\* *'(Understand Me'* \*\*\*\* in the US) ; (April); *'From The Underworld'* \*\*\*\*\* / *'Sweet William'* \*\*\* (August); *'Paradise Lost'* \*\*\*\* / *'Come On, Believe Me'* \*\* (November) (all on the Fontana label) as well as their big 1968 hit *'I Don't Want Our Loving To Die'* and a 1968 LP **'Paradise Lost'** on Fontana in mono and stereo (called **'Paradise And Underworld'** in Germany and entitled **'Lookin' Thru You'** in the US with a very different track listing – in effect a compilation of single and album tracks). Two promos were released in 1967 of *'From the Underworld'* and *'Paradise Lost'* on Double-R Productions and these are now very collectible. Expect to pay around £10 for an excellent copy of the *'I Can Fly'* 45; £5 for *'From The Underworld'* and £5 or £15 for *'Paradise Lost'* depending on whether you want the picture sleeve or not.

**REISSUES: 'Paradise & Underworld'** (Repertoire CD, 1992) (26 tracks from 1967 to 1969 including the German LP); **'Underworld'** (Recall 2-CD compilation, 2000). The most recent CD compilations are **The Complete Herd Singles As and Bs** (Repertoire, 2006) and **'The Complete Herd'** is also on Repertoire, 2005; **'Paradise Lost: The Complete UK Fontana Recordings'**, issued as a 2-CD set by the Grapefruit label in 2011. Vinyl LP reissues include **'Lost in Paradise'** (a compilation on Subway); **'The Fontana Years'** (Vinyl Lovers 2 LP, 2009)

**DESCRIPTION:** In 1967 The Herd hit a purple patch with the promise of the psychedelic rock of *'I Can Fly'* attracting much interest but failing to chart, however the otherworldly psych ballad *'From The Underworld'* (based on the legend of Orpheus and Eurydice) made #6 UK. In 1968 *'Paradise Lost'* made #15 followed by their biggest hit of all – *'I Don't Want Our Loving to Die'* in 1968 (#5).

Herd records were well produced often incorporating brass, strings and wispy flutes, the latter on *'I Can Fly'* which starts with a big Pete Townshend like guitar chord. *'From The Underworld'*, is very melodramatic, starting with doomy bells and piano before guitar, bass and drums, excellent vocal harmonies and sharp lines (e.g. 'escaping the ghosts of yesterday'), a clever brass arrangement propelling the song onwards, one of

1967's genuinely classic three minutes. *'Paradise Lost'* starts off like **David Rose**'s *'The Stripper'*, big band sleaze, before abruptly changing to a fine string led melodious song in the vein of *'From the Underworld'*. Brass again takes the song forward before innocent childlike piano and more strings and, somewhat incongruously back to the sleazy bit, in 3:30 of inventive pop. All three were written by Ken Howard and Alan Blaikley. They also penned *'Diary of a Narcissist (I'm So Pretty')'*, a 'Kinksian' 2-minute ditty.

Bown and Frampton had a go at writing on two 1967 B-sides, *'Sweet William'*, a nice two-minute slice of sunshine pop with organ (as was their *'Sunshine Cottage'* a year later) and *'Understand Me,* a marvellous slab of soulful rock with a powerful rhythm. The Herd's 1968 Fontana album *'Paradise Lost'* made the UK top 40 and they appeared as one of the support acts for The Jimi Hendrix Experience at the Savile Theatre on 8th October, 1967. In 1968 they split with their managers, song writing duo Howard and Blaikley. Peter Frampton went on to form **Humble Pie** with **Steve Marriott** of **The Small Faces** and then have phenomenal success with his *'Frampton Comes Alive'* album. **Andy Bown** became a member of **Status Quo** and **Gary Taylor** and **Henry Spinett**i became part of **Gerry Rafferty**'s band.

# Herman's Hermits

**THE MUSICIANS: Peter Noone (Vocals, Guitar, Keyboards), Keith Hopwood (Guitar, Vocals), Derek Leckenby (Guitar, Vocals), Karl Green (Bass, Vocals), Barry Whitwam (Drums)**

**ORIGIN:** Manchester

**NOTABLE RECORDINGS: (All Columbia) 45s:** *I'm Into Something Good* **(1964) #11;** *A Must To Avoid* **(1965) #6 UK, #8 US,** *No Milk Today* **(1966) #7 UK,;** *There's A Kind of Hush* **(1966) #7 UK, #4 US;** in 1967 *Museum* *** **#37 US** – for the US market (on **MGM**)

**DESCRIPTION:** Peter Noone (Peter Kovak) had been in Manchester beat group The Heartbeats but his Hermits got off to a flier after being signed by Mickie Most with a Goffin/ King song *'I'm into Something Good'*. They did less well with another Goffin/ King song *'Show Me Girl'* in 1964 but it did reach the top 20. The most lucrative market for the group was the USA and a cover of Sam Cooke's *'Wonderful World'* did even better there than in the UK (#4/ #7). A song from their first eponymous LP, which was trumpeted by a US DJ, *'Mrs Brown, You've Got a Lovely Daughter'*, spent 3 weeks at #1, selling in truck loads worldwide and earning a gold disc. Thus started a highly profitable trend of stereotypically English nostalgic songs for US release including *'I'm Henry The 8th I Am'*, a 1911 music hall song. Even a cover of The Kinks' *'Dandy'* seemed to fall into the same category sounding like a novelty song. The 'one tricky pony' approach couldn't last forever and it took a Graham Gouldman song, *'No Milk Today'*, to revive their flagging fortunes and restore their credibility somewhat. Their straight rendering of Donavon's *'Museum'* was one of a baffling assortment of records released all over the world in 1967.

# Honeybus

**THE MUSICIANS: Peter Dello, Ray Cane, Colin Hare, Jim Kelly (Vocals); Ray Cane, Colin Hare, Jim Kelly (Guitars); Ray Cane (Keyboards); Colin Hare (Bass); Peter Kircher (Drums)**

**ORIGIN:** London

**NOTABLE RECORDINGS:** *'The Breaking Up Scene'* **** (B-side of first Deram single *'Delighted to See You'* ***, 1967); *'(Do I Figure) In Your Life'* ****/ *'Throw My Love Away'* **** (Deram, 1967); *'I Can't Let Maggie Go'* **** (Deram, 1968)

**REISSUES:** *'I Can't Let Maggie Go'* can be found on '60s' compilations, of course, (and was reissued on Decca in 1986). There is a 2002 anthology **'She Flies Like a Bird'** (2 x CD, Castle Music/ Sanctuary Records) and a Repertoire compilation **'The Honeybus Story'** (1999). On vinyl there is **'At Their Best'** (See for Miles, 1979).

**DESCRIPTION:** Honeybus struck gold with *'I Can't Let Maggie Go'* which became a perennial of sixties compilations and commercial radio stations. Its use in the Nimble bread TV commercial also helped ensure the immortality of this number. Of the 1967 singles the risky *'Delighted to See You'* has the nice Honeybus harmonies and kazoo (!) The B-side *'The Breaking Up Scene'*, another Pete Dello song (He was the main song writer), is a different kettle of fish with heavy-ish guitar and driving drums and deep bass, more bluesy and ballsy, at least a match for *'I Can't Let Maggie Go'*. *'(Do I Figure) In Your Life'* is one of the group's best songs, if not the best version, it was improved upon by Joe Cocker whose version remains the definitive one turning it into a pleading soulful ballad (although Dave Stewart and Barbara Gaskin did a multi-layered vocal version). The string quartet used was a good idea but neither it nor the vocals do the song justice. *'Throw My Love Away'* repeats the trick of *'The Breaking Up Scene'*, strong vocal, bluesy guitar (nice break), tinkling piano, there's even a walking bass line which fades the song out, puzzling as this should have been much longer. The first 2 singles' estimated value is £10 for an excellent copy – like The Herd well worth investing in for the juke box if you're lucky enough to have one!

## The Idle Race

**THE MUSICIANS: Jeff Lynne/ Dave Pritchard/ Mike Hopkins (Guitars), Jeff Lynne and, later, Roy Cullom then Dave Walker (Vocals); Greg Masters (Bass), Roger Spencer (Drums)**

**ORIGIN:** Birmingham

**NOTABLE RECORDINGS:** *'The Imposters of Life's Magazine ****/ Sitting in My Tree'* **** (Liberty, 1967); *'Here We Go Round the Lemon Tree ****/ My Father's Son *****, the A-side is a Roy Wood song (Liberty, 1967 not UK). For collectors, Idle Race singles will set you back a bit: expect to pay at least £25–£30 for an excellent copy of *'Imposters of Life's Magazine'* and upwards of £40 for a copy of their 1968 LP **'Birthday Party'** (more for a mono copy), at least £60 for their 1969 LP **'The Idle Race'** (also on Liberty) and a whopping £120 or more for **'Time Is'** from 1971 on Regal Zonophone.

**REISSUES:** Idle Race songs appear on various compilations and there is a career retrospective double CD **'Back to the Story'** (Zonophone, 1990) that is still widely available. There have been quite a few vinyl reissues: **'Imposters of Life's Magazine'** (Daffodil, 2 x LP, 1974); **'Sea of Dreams'** (Raven, 1983); **'Light at The End of The Road'** (See For Miles, mono, 1985); **'Best of The Idle Race'** (See For Miles, 1990). **'The Birthday Party'** was reissued on the Sunset label in 1976 and there is a CD 'twofer' (2 on 1) on Retro Disc International (2006) of **'The Idle Race'** and **'Time Is'** albums.

**DESCRIPTION:** The Idle Race had self-confessed Beatles nut Jeff Lynne in their ranks and released two singles in 1967, only one of which was released in the UK. *'Imposters of Life's Magazine'* is a psych classic with improbable lyrics, one of Jeff

Lynne's first songs, if not the first. The B-side was a bit of a catchy throwaway but up there with The Beatles musically, presaging some of the frivolous stuff to appear a year later on their white album. A more psychedelic version of *'Here We Go Round the Lemon Tree'* than The Move's was released in the US with *'My Father's Son'*, which has Moody Blues type harmonies and heavy bluesy guitar playing, a fine period piece. (The *'Lemon Tree'* 45 was pulled by Liberty in the UK after The Move's version attracted airplay as the B-side of their *'Flowers in The Rain'*).

Their concentrated period of activity was in 1968 and 1969 with the release of two albums **'The Birthday Party'** and **'Idle Race'** on the Liberty label and no fewer than five singles which failed to impact on the charts. The post Lynne Idle Race achieved some commercial success in various European countries with Mungo Jerry's *'In The Summertime'* and Hotlegs *'Neanderthal Man'*. They must have been an interesting live act to see and included long versions of songs by **The Doors, Tyrannosaurus Rex, Moby Grape** and **Steppenwolf.** Lynne was later in **The Move** and **Electric Light Orchestra**. He worked closely with Roy Wood and, indeed The Move's *'Blackberry Way'* bears a resemblance, in parts, to The Idle Race's 1969 '45' *Days of Broken Arrows*.

## The Ivy League

THE MUSICIANS: **John Shakespeare AKA Carter/ Brian Pugh AKA Perry Ford/ James Hawker AKA Ken Lewis/ Tony Burrows and Neil Landon in second line-up plus backing group Division Two (Multi-part Vocals); Mike O'Neill (Keyboards); Mickey Keen (Guitar); Clem Cattini (Bass) and Dave Wintour (Drums)**

ORIGIN: Various parts of England

NOTABLE RECORDINGS: *'Funny How Love Can Be'* and *'Tossin' and Turnin'* (Piccadilly, 1965); in 1967 *'Four and Twenty Horses'* ***/ *'Arrivederci Baby'*\*\*\*; *'Suddenly Things'* *** / *'Tomorrow Is Another Day'* ** (both on Piccadilly); *'Thank You for Loving Me'* ** / *'In The Not Too Distant Future'* **** (Pye); **'Sounds of The Ivy League'** (Marble Arch LP) *** The Ivy League probably work best on 45s and EPs. Their 1965/1966 EPs are quite collectible (around £15 for an excellent copy, less for **'The Holly and Ivy League'**) while the LP **'This is the Ivy League'** on Piccadilly is worth over £20.

DESCRIPTION: In the mists of time, The Ivy League is perhaps remembered by the few rather than the many although their two big hits *'Funny How Love Can Be'* and *'Tossin' and Turnin'* do get exposure from time to time on commercial radio stations. They released two LPs, four EPs and eleven singles between 1964 and 1967. In 1967 itself they released **'Sounds of The Ivy League'** on the budget label Marble Arch and three 45s, two on Piccadilly, one on Pye. The first Piccadilly release *'Four and Twenty Hours'* is the second song listed after *'Tossin' and Turnin'* and, despite its clumsy title is a pleasant enough affair with organ backing and the group's trademark 'sunshine pop' vocal harmonies. Its B-side has lovely Beach Boys type harmonies and interesting percussive backing. *'Suddenly Things (Began to Happen When I looked Into Your Face)'* (adding the rest of the first line makes sense of the title!) is, again standard 'sunshine pop' with orchestration and optimism. Its B-side is a sickly, sweet romantic song. The group goes into saccharine love-in overdrive on their third 1967 45 *'Thank You for Loving Me'*, indebted once again to The Beach Boys but when it gets to 'sugar and spice' it all gets too much for me I'm afraid. Mercifully it's only two minutes long but is very well done! At least the B-side *'In The Not Too Distant Future'* has an inclination towards beat and a nice cello part. During 1967 they underwent a metamorphosis into **The Flowerpot Men**, songs of peace and love rather than romance and love. (See separate entry).

## John's Children

THE MUSICIANS: Andy Ellison/ Marc Bolan in second line-up (Vocals); John Hewlett/ Geoff McClelland/ Marc Bolan/ Chris Townson (Guitars); John Hewlett (Bass), Chris Townson then Chris Colville (Drums)

ORIGIN: Surrey as The Few and The Silence

NOTABLE RECORDINGS: *'Desdemona ****/ Remember Thomas A Beckett'* *** (Track, 1967*); Sara Crazy Child' ***** (B-side of *'Midsummer Night's Scene'* ***/ *'Come and Play with me in the Garden'* *** (Track, 1967-withdrawn); also released in 1967 were *Go Go Girl ****/ Jagged Time Lapse ***** (Track); *Just What You – Just What You'll Get ****/ But She's Mine ****and an album **Orgasm** *** both on Track. If you want originals of records by John's Children's then you are talking hundreds of pounds for the early singles, up to £500 or more for *'The Love I Thought I'd Found'* with the rare picture sleeve. The withdrawn 45 *'Midsummer Night's Dream'* will literally set you back thousands (probably at least £4,000). As for the other 1967 records, *'Come and Play with me in the Garden'* will cost up to £200 in a picture sleeve probably around one third of that without while *'Go Go Girl'* may also cost around £70, all estimated and in excellent condition. The title of the **'Orgasm'** LP didn't appear on the sleeve or the labels to spare people's blushes I suppose. Expect to pay over £100 for an excellent copy of this.

REISSUES: There has been a **'Complete'** double CD including BBC session with a booklet on Voiceprint. **'A Midsummer Night's Scene'** is a Bam-Caruso collection with a spring 1967 BBC session and is well packaged and informative; *Desdemona* has been widely compiled on, for example **The House That Track Built** and **Backtrack 7**, both samplers and the 4-CD **'Nuggets'** box set. It was later covered by **Marsha Hunt**. **'John's Children: The Legendary Orgasm Album'** has been released on CD and LP by Cherry Red (1982). There is also an EP, **'Smashed Blocked'**, on the Acid Jazz label (2014) and a remastered 2 CD **'A Strange Affair: The Sixties Recordings'** on Grapefruit (2013)

DESCRIPTION: Managed by Simon Napier Bell (who had earlier overseen the affairs of The Yardbirds), John's Children's first single was actually backed by Californian session men and among studio tricks to disguise the weakness of the vocals was a sound-byte of Arsenal football club supporters. Its title was *'Smashed Blocked'* but due to record company sensitivities this was changed to *'The Love I'd Thought I'd Found'* and released on Columbia in 1966. The US release scraped into the top 100 chart. Their delayed 1967 album **'Orgasm'** is described by Vernon Joynson as "one of the worst albums ever recorded. Much of the music was eminently forgettable and drowned by screaming girls." (113)Napier-Bell had used the soundtrack to the Beatles film '**A Hard Day's Night'** for the screaming. Joynson is right about that but much of the music stands up to my ears. Napier-Bell also hired session men for their second single released in 1967 and, although it is the group on its B-side the guitar part was overdubbed with one by Jeff Beck. The guitarist in question, Geoff McClelland, was replaced not by a guitarist as such but by none other than Marc Bolan. John's Children was one of the groups who played in the 14-Hour Technicolour Dream all-nighter in 1967. Bolan wrote the group's best known number **'Desdemona'**. This was banned because of suggestive lyrics about Toulouse Le Treque bedding some 'chick' on the roof anda reference to skirt lifting. . It starts with a lift of the *'Jailhouse Rock'* riff but much heavier with fuzz bass (John Hewlett) and strident guitar with Andy Ellison on lead vocals embellished by Bolan's wailing back-up. Apparently, one of Bolan's heroes **Eddie Cochrane** covered the number. (*'Come and Play with me in the Garden'* is similar apart from no 'Thomas A Beckett' part). A cello and psychedelic effects add to the weirdness and the strident drumming is most efficacious! Bolan left soon afterwards to form **Tyrannosaurus Rex.** *'Sara Crazy Child'* signals the mythical lyrics Tyrannosaurus Rex would perfect but it's Ellison on lead vocal, an intriguing song with Bolan faintly in the background near its conclusion and strange, otherworldly guitar songs, very daring. *'Go Go Girl'* is a dance floor filler with great rhythm playing and Hammond organ. *'Jagged Time Lapse'* is ostensibly about a dodgy drug trip with reference to mysterious shapes deceiving the mind. and is also very bold, putting John's Children with their unique sound and experimental tendencies (similar to label mates **The Who),** in among the top notchers of 1967 in their own right. Their final 1967 single, released on Columbia was *'Just What You Want – Just What You'll Get'*. With its phasing and military drumming and aggressive vocal and primitive organ it sounds almost like a precursor of punk (UK style that is), the 'ba b aba ba' vocal harmonies juxtaposing with the 'in your face' chanting. Its B-side *'But She's Mine'* is a powerful rock number sounding very much like **The Who**'s *'I Can't Explain'*, and features a mini guitar duel.

The withdrawn single *'Midnight Summer's Dream'* is pretty weird in a nice sort of way with strange 'bottleneck' guitar and Bolan's vocal quite distinctive. Sadly, their music was largely overlooked but more and more people are recognising its significance. Marc Bolan was a sad loss to music when he died in a car accident aged just 29.

As a postscript it is worth recalling the notoriety that stalked and eventually exterminated the band. Hounded by self-inflicted ignominy, John's Children was determined to make an impact on a tour of Germany supporting The Who. Whether it was scattering hotel room pillow feathers or staging mock fights the Who manager Kit Lambert's patience was running short and he threatened to throw them off the tour if their crowd-baiting antics continued. Refusing to curb their antics, John's Children, in the words of drummer Chris Townson declared, "Bollocks, let's do it!" The result was unbridled mayhem. As Townson hammered out an incessant beat and Bolan began thrashing his guitar with chains, Ellison and (Bassist) Hewlett threw punches. After showering the place in feathers and running wild among the throng – chased by a pack of fuming security guards – Ellison began chanting "Sieg Heil!" Then he started smashing up chairs. The crowd went wild. Suddenly, chairs were flying through the 12,000-seater auditorium like missiles. **(114)**This was at a gig in Ludwigshafen on 12 April, 1967. Townson and the group escaped through a back door into manager Simon Napier-Bell's Bentley leaving scenes of mayhem and water cannons. The group's equipment was confiscated by German police. They were thrown off the tour and Marc Bolan left two months later.

# Paul Jones

**THE MUSICIANS: Paul Pond AKA Paul Jones (Vocals, Harmonica)** with various backing musicians.

**ORIGIN:** Portsmouth

**NOTABLE RECORDINGS:** *'High Time'* (HMV, 1966 #5); *'I've Been a Bad, Bad Boy'* ****/ *Sonny Boy Williamson* *** (HMV, 1967 #5); also in 1967: *Thinkin' Ain't For Me* ****/ *Softly (La Vita)* *** (HMV #32); *Three Sisters* **/ *Sons And Lovers* ** (Columbia).

**REISSUES:** RPM and Repertoire have reissued Paul Jones music on CD. For those who want something comprehensive there is a 5 CD Paul Jones and Manfred Mann original album series box set on the Parlophone label (2014). Probably best collected through 45s which should be a reasonably affordable pastime! His most collectible LPs are **'Privilege'** (soundtrack recording with George Bean group and Mike Leander) (around £30) and **'Crucifix in A Horseshoe'** from 1971 on Vertigo (£50 or more). A one-sided demo of *'Privilege'* from 1967 (HMV PSR 5307) is worth around £15-£20 in excellent condition.

**DESCRIPTION:** Paul Jones was a part of the 'scene' in 1967 albeit on the blues/ soul rather than rock spectrum – having turned down an offer **by Keith Richards and Brian Jones** to be the lead singer of the group that was to become **The Rolling Stones** his career got off to a good start as the singer for **Manfred Mann**. He left Manfred Mann in 1966 to launch a solo career and his first two singles were very successful. The EP **'Privilege'**, the soundtrack of a film he starred in with Jean Shrimpton, topped the UK EP charts. He stopped recording for a while to concentrate on acting, including a role in **'Joseph and the Amazing Technicolour Dreamcoat'**, **'Cats'** and **'Evita'**. He also did a lot of TV work including appearances in 'Z Cars' and 'The Sweeney' and as a presenter of children's shows. In 1979 he formed **The Blues Band** and has played on many sessions. He has continued to tour with a Manfred Mann roadshow (The Manfreds) and has been presenting an award winning R&B radio show for Radio 2 for more than twenty-five years. At the time of writing this section he had released a new album **'Starting All Over Again'** and was touring with Dave Kelly. There is a video of Jones and Kelly on You Tube at the Lowdham Festival in 2007. Jones tells the story of nearly backing **Sonny Boy Williamson** during his Manfred Mann days where they fell out about how many bars there are in 12 bar blues ('any number the singer wants'). **The Yardbirds** got the gig. The B-side of his 1967 hit *'I've Been a Bad Bad Boy'* was a poignant tribute to Sonny Boy Williamson who died the previous year. ('There ain't nobody played harp the way he's done'). *'Thinkin' Ain't for Me'* was a creditable follow-up and the arrangement, while slightly awkward rhythmically, is intriguing, a mixture of orchestration and beat with gorgeous flute and piano/ organ accompaniment. Its B-side shows the versatility of Jones as a singer turning his hand to a saccharine ballad.

Paul Jones' influence is as much in terms of what he has done to promote others, a recent example being his endorsement of blues prodigy **Joanne Shaw-Taylor**, in my view the best blues rock/ soul writer and guitarist for a generation.

## Kaleidoscope

**THE MUSICIANS: Peter Daltrey (Vocals, Keyboards); Eddie Pumer (Guitar, Keyboards), Steve Clark (Bass, Flute), Danny Bridgman (Drums)**

**ORIGIN:** West London, 1964 as The Sidekicks, then The Key

**NOTABLE RECORDINGS:** *'Flight from Ashiya \*\*\*/ The Murder of Lewis Tollani'* \*\*\*\* (Fontana, 1967); *'A Dream for Julie'* \*\*\*/ *Dive Into Yesterday* \*\*\*\* (Fontana, 1968); **'Tangerine Dream'** LP \*\*\*\* (Fontana, 1967); *'The Sky Children'* from 'Tangerine Dream' \*\*\*\*\* Big bucks are required for original pressings in excellent condition: around £50 for the first single *'Flight from Ashiya'* and at least £30 more for the same record in a picture sleeve; things calm down a bit with subsequent singles (between £30 and £40) but it is the LPs that are the most collectible: between £300 and £400 for the first LP and at least £100 more for the second (only £150–£200 with a watermark at the beginning of each side!) The last time I looked on Discogs VG+ copies of their LPs could be on offer from £800 to £1,750 while a reissued version was obtainable for less than £20.

REISSUES: 'Dive into Yesterday' compilation (Fontana, 1996) (the Repertoire reissue with 6 bonus tracks); the albums can be found on LP (on the 5 Hours Back label, 1987), 'Faintly Blowing', not in gatefold unfortunately), on Sunbeam and on Tapestry and on CD, some unofficial and from various parts of the world; 'Please Listen to the Pictures' on Circle Records is a 22 track compilation including BBC sessions of Kaleidoscope and Fairfield Parlour. The 1967 A-sides can be heard on the 'Rubble' volume 4: 49 Minute Technicolour Dream LP and on the 4 CD 'Nuggets' box set. The 'Tangerine Dream' LP was reissued on Sunbeam Records in 2011 with a 12-page booklet and a recording history by Peter Daltrey.

DESCRIPTION: Despite two promising early singles, it was their 1967 LP 'Tangerine Dream' with its striking 'psych' cover, that attracted the public eye. They released a second album 'Faintly Blowing', also on Fontana in 1969. In all Kaleidoscope released a further three singles between 1968 and 1969 before changing their name to Fairfield Parlour and signing for the Vertigo label. At this stage they were being managed by Radio 1 DJ Dave Symonds and released an LP 'From Home to Home'. Unreleased recordings finally surfaced in 1991 as 'White Faced Lady'.

Peter Daltrey, talking to MOJO magazine prior to Kaleidoscope's reunion gig at London's Le Beat Bespoke festival on 3 April, 2013, related his memories of the group's early days as The Sidekicks playing numbers by The Beatles, The Rolling Stones, Chick Berry and Muddy Waters in youth clubs, securing a contract with Fontana in January, 1967, simultaneously changing the group's name. He also alluded to the broad landscape in 1967 beyond music, specifically films, fashion and painting, identifying The Beatles' Revolver as a seminal 60s album.

Unfortunately, Fontana's distribution was 'pathetic' and they never played in the big venues, they had no manager and an ineffective agent. Nevertheless, Daltrey was proud to be associated with "that whimsical English brand of psychedelia" (although believing that, by 1968, its days were numbered).

## IMPORTANT ALBUMS OF 1967 (24)
## TANGERINE DREAM by KALEIDOSCOPE

THE MUSICIANS: Peter Daltrey (Vocals, Keyboards); Eddie Pumer (Guitar. Keyboards); Steve Clark (Bass, Flute); Dan Bridgman (Drums, Percussion); PRODUCER: Dick Leahy; DATE: 24 November, 1967; LABEL: Fontana

TRACK LISTING/ CREDITS (All songs written by Eddie Pumer (music) and Peter Daltrey (Lyrics):

| | | |
|---|---|---|
| 1. | Kaleidoscope | 2:15 |
| 2. | Please Excuse My Face | 2:10 |
| 3. | Dive into Yesterday | 4:45 |
| 4. | Mr Small, The Watch Repairer Man | 2:40 |
| 5. | Flight from Ashiya | 2:40 |
| 6. | The Murder of Lewis Tollani | 2:45 |
| 7. | (Further Reflections) In The Room of Percussion | 3:17 |
| 8. | Dear Nellie Goodrich | 2:45 |

| | | |
|---|---|---|
| 9. | Holidaymaker | **2:28** |
| 10. | A Lesson, Perhaps | **2:40** |
| 11. | The Sky Children | **8:00** |

**THE MUSIC:** The poetic lyrics referring to people talking abut the hereafter while puffs of white cotton clouds pass by are unusual for the opening of a single, even in 1967, and you have to admire the ambition of *'Flight from Ashiya'*. It's also the penultimate track of side one of their 1967 LP with its B-side *'The Murder of Lewis Tollani'* closing the side, similar in style to The Who at the time (or perhaps The Zombies), a song about repentance with a lachrymose lyric that changes into a fleeting nursery rhyme ending then disappears, a strange, compelling piece with arpeggiated guitars. Kaleidoscope reunited for a tour in 2015 and a performance of their second 45 *'A Dream for Julie'*, "a great, little psych pop song", can be seen on You Tube. *'Dive into Yesterday'* is nearly five minutes long, a psych fest about tambourines tickling your ears and Shakespeare floating in wild roses, water pistols filled with lemonade, very 'out there'! The LP itself includes the single A and B sides and starts off with their 'theme song' I suppose (*'Kaleidoscope'*). *'Please Excuse My Face'* is a gentle, sad ballad with acoustic guitar. The ringing guitar tone so prevalent in the group's sound introduces *'Dive into Yesterday'*. Some comical flute introduces *'Mr Small Watch Repairer Man'* which is right down Kinks street. Side two opens with *'Dear Nellie Goodrich'* which has a piano that sounds like an out of tune harpsichord and is a charming little love song. The next song *'Holiday Maker'* starts with sounds of the seaside and has Mariachi trumpet backing, well observed.

'**Tangerine Dream**' has the feel of a concept album where the whole is more than the sum of the parts – they obviously weren't a singles band (although this was mandatory at the time!) and searching for the hit can be such a demoralising process. Suddenly, we are transported to medieval times (*'A Lesson Perhaps'*) with kings and castles, and a Peter Daltrey narration. Had Procol Harum heard this before they did *'In Held 'Twas in I'*? This is a moral tale about a 'king with conscience' with nice acoustic guitar which gives way to a lovely long song about a 'million white flowers in a field in the sky', very dreamlike about tiny minds being amazed, a porcupine captain in a coat of needles who looked very fine and fire breathing dragons, very Alice in Wonderland/ Peter Pan, a sky land instead of a kingdom through a rabbit hole. It ends fittingly with the sound of a musical box.

## Kippington Lodge

**THE MUSICIANS: Barry Landerman then Bob Andrews (Keyboards, Vocals); Brinsley Schwarz (Guitar, Vocals); David Cottam then Nick Lowe (Bass, Vocals). Peter Whale (Drums)**

**ORIGIN:** Kent, England (formerly Sounds 4+1 and Three's A Crowd)

**NOTABLE RECORDINGS:** one 45 in 1967: *Shy Boy* \*\*\*\*/ *Lady on a Bicycle* \*\*\*\* The *'Shy Boy'* 45 is quite collectible (c. £30) as are all their 45s most of all *'In My Life'* from 1969 (£70). An EP from 1978 is quite affordable.

**REISSUES:** *'Lady on a Bicycle'* can be heard on the '**We Can Fly**' CD and *'Shy Boy'* which was written by Keith West of Tomorrow on '**A Teenage Opera – The Original Soundtrack Recording**'. There is also a 2 CD compilation '**Shy Boy: The Complete Recordings: 1967–1969**' on RPM (2011) (This has 10 single sides, 5 bonus tracks, 2 alternate takes and 2 BBC performances).

**DESCRIPTION:** Kippington Lodge is of interest mainly because they became the inimitable Brinsley Schwarz and featured both Schwarz and Nick Lowe. They released five singles on the Parlophone label between 1967 and 1969. Their final single was a cover of The Beatles *'In My Life'*. Written by Keith Hopkins/ Keith West and given to Kippington Lodge by EMI producer Mark Wirtz *'Shy Boy'* is a great song with a neat little bass riff. The B-side is another one to add to the collection of songs about bicycles and this is one of the better ones with terrific drums/ percussion, spiky guitar and prominent bass. They later transmogrified into The Rumour.

## The Koobas

**THE MUSICIANS: Roy Morris (Lead Guitar), Stu Leatherwood (Guitar, Vocals), Pete Williams then Keith Ellis (Bass), Tony O' Reilly (Drums)**

**ORIGIN:** Liverpool

**NOTABLE RECORDINGS:** in 1967: *Sally ****/ Champagne and Caviar \*\*\** and *Gypsy Fred ****/ City Girl \*\*\*\** (Columbia) The Koobas 1969 Columbia LP is as rare at hen's teeth with a valuation of close to £1,000 (but I suspect it will change hands for more). Their 45s are valued at between £30 and £60.

**REISSUES:** BGO CD of 'The Koobas' LP on CD with eight bonus tracks (2008).

**DESCRIPTION:** The Koobas were managed by Brian Epstein and toured with The Beatles in 1965. Their 1969 album **The Koobas** (on Columbia) is worth a listen. Bass player Keith Ellis went on to join **Van Der Graaf Generator** Mark One. *'Sally'* was the old music hall number with the group sounding more like The Bonzo Dogs or The Temperance Seven than anything else! The whistling and ghostly Wurlitzer sounds are both marvellous. The Beatles, of course, reinvented music hall in their own original songs like *'Honey Pie'*. The flip side takes a smooth jazz turn, tongue in cheek but taking a sideways swipe at the 'jet set'. I can't think of many songs that have the word 'oblivious' in them and the use of it with reference to the 'credit squeeze' is ostensibly a comment on the 'never never' credit culture of the time that persists, in exaggerated form, today. *'Gypsy Fred'* is a salutary tale of an outsider who becomes famous and 'found his new life very strange' longing for 'the fields and the trees and the doors without keys'. *'City Girl'* showed just how much touring with The Beatles had rubbed off on them. The theme of isolation and disillusionment is similar to the A-side as 'the concrete skyline' gets her down. Roy Morris's guitar playing is particularly noteworthy.

## Alexis Korner and Blues Incorporated

**THE MUSICIANS:** Alexis Korner's Blues Incorporated was a veritable 'revolving doors' endeavour with members including all four of the original **Rolling Stones**, **Ginger Baker, Dick Heckstall-Smith, Graham Bond** and **Eric Burdon**.

**ORIGIN:** Alexis Korner was born in Paris, moved to England in 1939, his musical career starting with The Chris Barber Jazz Band in 1948.

**NOTABLE RECORDINGS:** Released in 1967 were two LPs: **'I Wonder Who'** *** (Fontana) and **'Blues Incorporated'** *** (Polydor Special) and as a 45 rpm *'Rosie ****/ Rock Me'* **** (also Fontana). The records are highly collectible with his 10" LP as The Alexis Korner Breakdown Group from 1957 running into thousands if you want a copy and of his 1967 LPs **'I Wonder Who'** is valued at over £100 for a mono copy and £150 for a stereo one in excellent condition while **'Blues Incorporated'** comes in at £60+ for a first issue (4 tracks listed on side one on label) and £40+ for a second issue (5 tracks listed). Korner's **'At the Cavern'** live LP with laminated sleeve and flipbacks attracts over £300 (Oriole, 1964). His most collectible 45s are the first *'I Ain't Gonna Worry No More'* as The Alexis Korner Skiffle Group) (£80+) (also on 78 rpm at only half the value) and *'Blaydon Races'* as Blues Incorporated with Alexis Korner, given free with a women's magazine (similar price). His EPs from the late '50s and early '60s are also highly collectible, the Topic label ones featuring folk acoustic guitarist Davy Graham.

REISSUES: *'I Got My Mojo Working'* can be heard on the **'R&B Scene'** CD (Deram) while quite a few albums have been released on CD. Doxy issued a vinyl LP/CD **'R&B from the Marquee'** with Long John Baldry (the original will set you back £100) in 2012. There is also a 2 CD compilation **'Kornerstoned 1954-1983'** on Sanctuary (2008). There are various compilations – please refer to Korner's website for a full list.

DESCRIPTION: Alexis Korner formed Blues Incorporated with **Cyril Davies** in 1961. They were the resident band at the Ealing Blues Club then the Marquee. Their first of thirteen albums between 1962 and 1975 was **'R&B from the Marquee (Live)'** on the Ace of Clubs label. They also recorded an album called **'At the Cavern'** (Oriole, 1964). Alexis Korner worked for many years as a broadcaster before his death in 1984. For more on Alexis Korner please refer to the narrative on **The Rolling Stones**. Korner's 1967 album **'I Wonder Who'** opens with a blues version of Herbie Hancock's *'Watermelon Man'*. The rolling drums (**Terry Cox**, later of Pentangle) and cool guitar playing (Korner himself throughout the album) are most effective but it is hard to say that it does justice to the original. Ricky Nelson's *'Streamline Train'* follows, a straight ahead 12 bar. The album is mostly covers like *'Rollin' Pete'*, **Ma Rainey**'s *'See See Rider'* and **Jimmy Smith**'s *'Chicken Shack Back Home'*, another jazz blues crossover. *'Rock Me'*, Korner's 1967 B-side is a somewhat lascivious slow blues with slide guitar and double bass (Danny Thompson), much covered. *'Rosie'* is a nice shuffle blues with a **Bo Diddley** feel, similar to the direction **Captain Beefheart and his Magic Band** was taking in 1967. Its rather chaotic arrangement is what singles it out for me as one of my favourites from Korner's catalogue. When he sings *'Oh, Rosie'*, you can almost hear Robert Plant a couple of years later.

The **'Blues Incorporated'** LP ranges from *'Long Black Train'* (similar in vein to Jack Bruce's take on *'Traintime'* in Cream but less frenetic) to the slow, acoustic blues of *'Louise'* and the upbeat *'Wee Baby Blues'*. It also has *'Rock Me'* and a line-up of **Danny Thompson/ Terry Cox** (bass and drums), **Duffy Power** (mouth harp), Alexis himself on electric and acoustic guitar and vocals and, on some tracks like *'Wee Baby Blues'*, **Alan Skidmore** on tenor sax and **Chris Pyne** on trombone.

## Billy J. Kramer and The Dakotas/ Billy J. Kramer

THE MUSICIANS: **Billy J Kramer (Vocals), Mike Maxfield then Mick Green (Guitar), Robin MacDonald (Bass), Tony Mansfield then Frank Farley (Drums)**

ORIGIN: Liverpool and Manchester; NOTABLE RECORDINGS: *'Do You Want To Know A Secret?'*, *'Bad To Me'* and *I'll Keep You Satisfied'* (Parlophone, 1963); *'Little Children'* and *'From A Window'* (Parlophone, 1964); *'Trains and Boats and Planes'* (Parlophone, 1965); Billy J Kramer (solo) *Sorry ****/ Going Going Gone* (Parlophone, 1967) and *The Town of Tuxley Toymakers *** / Chinese Girl ***** (Reaction, 1967) For collectors this artist's records do not attract particularly high values except for the **'Billy J Plays The States'** EP (Parlophone, 1965) (£40+)

REISSUES: There are numerous compilations including **'The Best of'** (Charly LP, 1984), **'The Definitive Collection'** and **'Best of The EMI Years'** (both EMI CDs from

1991), **'The EP Collection'** (See For Miles CD, 1995) and **'Billy J Kramer With The Dakotas At Abbey Road. 1963-1966'** (EMI, 1998)

**DESCRIPTION:** The Dakotas were teamed up with Billy Kramer (real name William Howard Ashton) by Brian Epstein who arranged them to play a residency in The Star Club, Hamburg. The name 'Kramer' was picked at random from a telephone directory while **John Lennon** suggested the addition of the 'J' to give the pseudonym more bite. Their first four singles were phenomenally successful and, again, there is a case for including them among the mainline artists. However, their first three hits (#2, #1 and #4 respectively) were all written by **John Lennon** and **Paul McCartney**. The best remembered one is probably *'Do You Want to Know A Secret?'* which was on **The Beatles** debut LP. However, it was a **John Lennon** song *'Bad to Me'* which topped the charts. Their third hit was *'I'll Keep You Satisfied'*. Their next hit was not written by Lennon/ McCartney but by **John McFarlane**. This was *'Little Children'* possibly their most memorable 45. It topped the UK charts and reached #7 Stateside, becoming a million-seller worldwide. *'Bad to Me'*, which was the flip side of *'Little Children'* in the US, became a top 10 hit in its own right there. Reverting back to recording **Beatles** songs, *'From A Window'* provided another top tenner in 1964. This and a US only album *'Little Children'* made #23 and #48 respectively in the US. They had one other big hit with *'Trains and Boats and Planes'* written by **Burt Bacharach** (in 1966). This nearly made the top 10 in the UK and just made the top 50 in the US. Kramer went solo in 1966 but enjoyed no further chart success not even with a **Bee Gees** song in 1967, *The Town of Tuxley Toymakers* – Kramer doesn't feel comfortable on this or its B-side *'Chinese Girl'*, a big departure from his previous style, nor on a version of **Lennon/ McCartney**'s *'World Without Love'* in 1968 without The Dakotas (a bit late with this one – see Peter and Gordon). He was then consigned to the club and nostalgia circuit. Also in 1967 Kramer recorded *'Sorry'* with a balalaika making it sound vaguely Russian and a bit mysterious, co-written by Chip Taylor who wrote *'Wild Thing'* for **The Troggs**.

# Locomotive

**THE MUSICIANS: Norman Haines (Keyboards, Vocals), Mike Taylor/ Henry Lowther (Trumpet), Lyn Dobson/ Dick Heckstall-Smith/ Bill Madge/ Chris Mercer (Sax), Chris Wood (Woodwinds), Mark Hincks (Bass, Vocals) and Bob Lamb (Drums) ORIGIN:** Birmingham

**NOTABLE RECORDINGS:** *'Rudy, A Message to You'* \*\*\*\* (Direction, 1967); *'Rudi's In Love'* (Parlophone, 1968 reissued 1971, 1979 – on EP – and 1980 in picture sleeve); *'Mr. Armageddon'* (Parlophone, 1969) and the classic album **'We Are Everything You See'** (Parlophone, 1969)

**REISSUES: 'We Are Everything You See'** (Esoteric CD); LP reissued first on the Zap label in 1988 then on 180-gram vinyl on the Radioactive label in 2006 *'Rudi's In Love'* on various '60s compilations *and* *'Mr. Armageddon'* on various compilations including **'Psychedelia at Abbey Road'** CD.

**DESCRIPTION:** The Ska style of top 30 UK hit *'Rudi's in Love'* is atypical of their output with the progressive powerhouse, *'Mr. Armageddon'* more representative. The group featured some notable names: Norman Haines, Chris Wood, later a founder member of Traffic, Dick Heckstall-Smith, Henry Lowther. Their album included a cover of ? and the Mysterians' *'I'm Never Gonna Let You Go'*. In 1967 Rudy appeared in another single *'Rudy, A Message to You'*, a rather plodding but catchy ska predecessor to *'Rudi's In Love'* which was later covered by Judge Dread and Amy Winehouse. The Norman Haines band went on to produce some fine music.

An original copy of '**We Are Everything You See**' on Parlophone PCS 7093 with a laminated front sleeve fetches prices in excess of £400 and even the CD reissue on the Shoestring label in 1995 is valued at £25 or more.

## The Loot

**THE MUSICIANS: Chris Bates (Vocals), Bruce Turner and Dave Wright (Guitars), Jeff Glover (Bass), Roger Pope (Drums)**

**ORIGIN:** Andover, Hampshire, England

**NOTABLE RECORDINGS:** *'Baby Come Closer'* (Page One, 1966); *'Don't Turn Around'* (CBS, 1968); in 1967 *Whenever You're Ready \*\*\*/I Got What You Want \*\*\** (CBS), *I've Just Gotta Love You \*\*/ You Need Someone to Love \*\** (Fontana) On the subject of collectability, The Loot's 45s are all estimated at between £15 and £40 (their final single *'Try To Keep It A Secret'*, 1969).

**REISSUES:** 'The Loot: Singles As and Bs' CD (Radioactive, 2005)

**DESCRIPTION:** Pop/ psych. Guitarist Dave Wright had been an early member of **The Troggs** and their first single released in 1966 sounds rather Trogg like. The Loot released six singles between 1966 and 1969 but no album. They had a typical 'summer of love' psychedelic look but by 1968 they were singing not about where the flowers have gone but what is going to happen after the flowers are thrown away. on *'Don't Turn Around'*. *'Whenever You're Ready'* has organ backing, heavy bass and driving drums and finds the group in exuberant mood. The B-side is in similar vein. There is no variation in subject matter, all the records seem to be about chasing girls, typical of the times – it all gets a bit wearing by the second 1967 single. Often labelled psych/ freakbeat – I hear the beat although I don't think it's particularly freaky or psychedelic apart from the odd (very) brief instrumental break. **Roger Pope** became **Elton John**'s drummer.

## The Love Affair

**THE MUSICIANS: Steve Ellis then Gus Eaden (Vocals), Rex Brayley (Guitar), Morgan Fisher then Pete Bardens then Lynton Guest (Keyboards), Mick Jackson (Bass), Maurice Bacon (Drums)**

**ORIGIN:** London

**NOTABLE RECORDINGS:** *'She Smiled Sweetly' \*\*\*\*/ Satisfaction Guaranteed \*\*\** (Jagger/Richard) (Decca, 1967); *'Everlasting Love' \*\*\*\*\*/ Gone Are the Songs of Yesterday \*\*\** (CBS, 1967 #1 UK); *Rainbow Valley* (CBS, 1968 #5 UK); *'A Day Without Love'* (CBS, 1968 #6 UK); *'One Road'* (CBS, 1969); *'Bringing On Back The Good Times'* (CBS, 1969 #9) Their first 45 *'She Smiled Sweetly'* is their rarest record, changing hands for prices in excess of £50.

**REISSUES:** 'Everlasting Hits' (actually the first album) on CD (Columbia, 1992) with *'One Road'* as a bonus; '**The Everlasting Love Affair**' (Repertoire), a well remastered CD with 8 bonus tracks and a booklet with liner notes by Chris Welch and quotes from Steve Ellis. '**No Strings**' on Angel Air is a compilation released in 2000. '**Singles As and Bs**' (Arcadia, 2002) includes hitherto unreleased Ellis solo and 1966 Love Affair tracks.

**DESCRIPTION:** Fronted by outstanding soul/ rock singer Steve Ellis, who left fame and fortune to form **Ellis** although by the time 1969 came around The Love Affair's star was in the descendant. The group hit big with covers of two **Robert Knight** songs *'Everlasting Love'* (which hit #1 UK in January, 1968) and *'Rainbow Valley'*. They released a dozen singles for different labels and a couple of albums, notably '**The**

**Everlasting Love Affair'** in 1968 before calling it a day. The aforesaid album contained their first three CBS singles plus some other originals plus covers of *'Tobacco Road', 'The First Cut is the Deepest'* and *'Handbags and Gladrags'. 'She Smiled Sweetly',* their first single, in 1967, was a ballad with organ backing written by **Mick Jagger/ Keith Richard** as was its B-side, *'Satisfaction Guaranteed'*, which has little organ and drum-breaks, not as good a song though, with prominent bass. The B-side of *'Everlasting Love', 'Gone Are the Songs of Yesterday'* has orchestral backing and is, as the title suggests, a ballad.

In summary, The Love Affair relied too much on other writers: their last three hits were written by **Philip Goodhand-Tait** and they could not sustain their excellent start as a pop band. **Pete Bardens** was briefly in the group and drummer **Maurice Bacon** and keys player **Morgan Fisher** left in 1971 to form **Morgan**. Later Fisher joined **Mott the Hoople**.

## Lulu (Marie McDonald McLaughlin)

**THE MUSICIANS:** Lulu's backing band **The Luvvers** included **Jim Dewar** (later of **Stone the Crows** and **Robin Trower**) and (allegedly) **Jimmy Page** (**John Bonham** certainly played drums on her *'Everybody Clap'* single for Atlantic in 1971).

**ORIGIN:** Lennoxtown, near Glasgow

**NOTABLE RECORDINGS:** *'Shout'* (Decca, 1964 #7 UK); *'I Can't Hear You No More'* (Decca, 1964); *'Here Comes The Night'* (Decca, 1964 #50 UK); *'Leave A Little Love'* (Decca, 1965 #8 UK); *'Try To Understand'* (Decca, 1965 #25 UK); *'The Boat That I Row'* **** (Columbia, 1967 #6 UK); *'Let's Pretend/ To Sir With Love'* **** (Columbia, 1967 #11 UK); *'I'm A Tiger'* (Columbia, 1968 #9 UK); *'Boom-Bang-A-Bang'* (Columbia, 1969 #2 UK); *'The Man Who Sold The World'* (Polydor, 1974 #3 UK); *'The Man With The Golden Gun'* (Chelsea, 1974); **'Something To Shout About'** LP (Decca, 1965); **'Lulu!'** (Ace of Clubs, 1967); **'The World of Lulu'** (Decca, 1967) ****; **'To Sir with Love** (soundtrack) (Fontana, 1967); **'The Most of Lulu'** (MFP, 1969)- this budget label album was the only one to chart reaching UK #15. Lulu's 1965 **'Something to Shout About'** LP (Decca) and **'To Sir with Love'** soundtrack with Ron Grainger and The Mindbenders (1967, Fontana) are quite rare in decent condition (around £50)

**REISSUES:** **'Shout'** widely compiled and re-issued; **'To Sir with Love: The Mickie Most Years'** 2 CDs remastered (EMI, 2005); **'Shout!'** CD (RPM Retrodisc, 2009)

**DESCRIPTION:** Lulu is an enigma in the sense that she found fame and success early on (at 16) and had such a great R&B voice that never quite managed to garner artistic success. When she turned (or was turned) to pop material like *'I'm A Tiger'* (which she allegedly disliked but which actually wasn't bad) and joint Eurovision Song Contest winner *'Boom-Bang-A-Bang'* (can't say the same here), she found her greatest success but this could not have been satisfying artistically. When she married **Maurice Gibb** of **the Bee Gees**, she switched labels to Atlantic's Atco subsidiary and her *'New Routes'* LP had **Duane Allman** on guitar. The title track of her next album **'Melody Fair'** originated on **The Bee Gees'** Album **'Odessa'**. Following her divorce from Gibb, **David Bowie** arranged and produced his own *'The Man Who Sold the World'* for Lulu. The theme for the James Bond film *'The Man with The Golden Gun'* was a surprise flop. She gained her first #1 hit in 1993 in conjunction with **Take That** (*'Re-light my Fire'*) and appeared in the hilarious send-up sitcom 'Absolutely Fabulous'. Her enduring appeal is illustrated by her well received appearance at 'T in the Park' in 2000. In 1967

*'The Boat That I Row'* was performed effervescently by Lulu (sometimes in frills!), nice organ. *'Let's Pretend'* was a ballad with orchestration, piano and organ and doesn't suit her style as well, I think (more **Dusty Springfield** territory I would say) although it was a well-produced and performed single. Its B-side was from the soundtrack of the film starring Sydney Poitier, playing a school teacher, in a racially backwards era. It was the A-side in the US where it topped the charts.

## Manfred Mann

**THE MUSICIANS: Paul Jones (+ Harmonica) then Mike d'Abo (Vocals); Manfred Lubowitz AKA Mann (Keyboards), Mike Vickers/ Tom McGuinness (Guitar); Dave Richmond/ Klaus Voormann/ Tom McGuinness then Jack Bruce (Bass); Mike Hugg (Drums)**

**ORIGIN:** London, 1962 as The Mann-Hugg Blues Band

**NOTABLE RECORDINGS:** *'5-4-3-2-1'* (HMV, 1964 UK #5); *'Do Wah Diddy Diddy'* (HMV, 1964, UK #1); **'The Five Faces of Manfred Mann'** (LP, HMV, 1964, #3 UK – mono only in UK); *'If You Gotta Go, Go Now'* (HMV, 1965, #2 UK); *'Pretty Flamingo'* (HMV, 1966, #1 UK); *'Just Like a Woman'* (Fontana, 1966, #10 UK); *'Semi-Detached Suburban Mr. James'* (Fontana, 1966, #2 UK); in 1967 *'Ha! Ha! Said The Clown'* ****/ *'Feeling So Good'* *** (Fontana, #4 UK); *Sweet Pea* ***/ *One Way* **** (Fontana) #36); *So Long, Dad* ***/ *Funniest Gig* **** (Fontana – didn't chart), *'Mighty Quinn'* (Fontana, 1968 #1 UK); *'My Name Is Jack'* (Fontana, 1968 #8 UK); *'Fox on the Run'* (Fontana, 1968 #5 UK) Many Manfred Mann records can be bought at a reasonable price. The most elusive are: **'The Five Faces of Manfred Mann'** (HMV CLP 1731) (£60+), **'Soul of Mann'** (HMV CSD 3594) especially the stereo pressing (£50+) and **'Up the Junction: Original Soundtrack Recording'** (Fontana (s) TL 5460)

**REISSUES:** Numerous including **'World of Mann: Very Best of Manfred Mann and Manfred Mann's Earth Band'** (2 CD, Universal Music TV, 2006), **'Down The Road Apiece: Their EMI Recordings, 1963-1966'** (4 CD, EMI, 2007), **'The Manfred Mann Album'** (LP, Sundazed, 2013), **'Manfred Mann and Paul Jones'** Original Albums Series (5 CD box set, 2014).

**DESCRIPTION:** South African Manfred Mann (real name Manfred Lubowitz) studied piano in an Austrian university and was also tutored in jazz piano. His musical career started when he sat in (alternating with **Graham Bond**) for a jazz quartet whose drummer was **Mike Hugg**. As the Mann-Hugg Blues Brothers the pair played with a horn section in tow at The Marquee and the Johnny Dankworth Jazz Club. **Paul Jones** (Pond) also joined on vocals and harmonica after the break-up of The Roosters following the departure of **Brian Jones** for the newly formed **Rolling Stones**. As Manfred Mann top 10 success was achieved with their third 45, *5-4-3-2-1*, in 1964. As can be seen from the selective list of notable recordings Manfred Mann, the group, made quite an impact as a pop group with Mann himself returning to his jazz roots in the much more musically ambitious **Chapter Three** and **Earth Band**, who made some outstanding music in the 1970s. Mann prodigiously recorded the songs of Bob Dylan beginning with *'With God On Our Side'* on **'The One in the Middle'** EP in 1965, including *'If You Gotta Go, Go Now'* (later successfully recorded by Fairport Convention in French as *'Si Tu Dois Partir'*), *'Mighty Quinn'* from The Basement Tapes as Manfred Mann and *'Father of Day, Father of Night'* with his Earth Band. The B-side of sixties staple *'Ha! Ha! Said The Clown'*, *'Feeling So Good'* sounds a bit contrived but, musically, it is quite ambitious. *'Sweet Pea'* starts with organ and recorder and is an instrumental (apart from a spoken 'sweet pea' which is a bit annoying), very infectious as the vibes develop the theme. Its B-side *'One Way'* is near 4 minutes of lethargic instrumental late night jazz with piano, organ and guitar breaks. Paul Jones is in good vocal form on *'So Long, Dad'*, a 'vaudevillian' sketch of the times about a lad bringing his girlfriend home for the first time complete with 'pub piano', great fun. In complete contrast *'Funniest Gig'* is pure psychedelia reprising previous songs and singing about strawberries and bananas and chocolate soldiers on stage, well you know!

# Marmalade

THE MUSICIANS: Dean Ford/ Mikel Japp in last line-up (Vocals); Junior Campbell then Hugh Nicholson on Lead Guitar, Par Fairlie on Rhythm Guitar; Mike Japp (Guitars), Graham Knight then Joe Breen (Bass); Raymond Duffy, Alan Whitehead, Dougie Henderson then Howie Casey (Drums)

ORIGIN: Glasgow, Scotland

NOTABLE RECORDINGS: *'It's All Leading Up To Saturday Night'* (CBS, 1966 – their first release); *'I See The Rain'* (CBS, 1967 – their first self-penned 45, a top 30 hit in Holland) ***** ; *'Man In A Shop'* *** (CBS, 1967); *'Lovin' Things/ Hey Joe'* (CBS, 1968 #6 UK); *'Ob-La-Di Ob-La-Da'* (CBS, 1968 #1 UK); *'Reflections of My Life'* (Decca, 1969 #3 UK); *'Rainbow'* (Decca, 1970 #3 UK; #51 US); *'Cousin Norman'* (Decca, 1971 #6 UK*); 'Radancer'* (Decca, 1972 #6 UK); **'There's A Lot of It About'** – especially *'Kaleidoscope'* (CBS, 1968 LP); **'Reflections of The Marmalade'** issued as **'Reflections of My Life'** in the US (Decca, 1970)

REISSUES: *'Ob-La- Di Ob-La-Da'*, *'Lovin' Things'* and *'Reflections of My Life'* extensively. Quite a few compilations including **'The Best of the Marmalade'** (CBS, 1969); **'I See the Rain: The CBS Years'** (Sequel); **'Rainbow – The Decca Years'** (2 CDs); **'The Reflections of The Marmalade'** (Sanctuary) (The 2 CDs cover much of the CBS and Decca output and four A-sides as Dean Ford and The Gaylords); **'Ultimate Collection'** (3 CD box set with previously unissued demos); **'BBC Sessions'** (includes a cover of Crosby, Stills and Nash's *'Suite: Judy Blue Eyes'*). Some of their more psychedelic songs are heard on compilations like **'Nuggets'** (like *'I See the Rain'* on Nuggets II) and **'Psychedelic Pstones Volume 2'**

DESCRIPTION: Formerly The Gaylords then Dean Ford and the Gaylords, Marmalade peaked commercially between 1968 and 1972. They stood apart from contemporaries like The Love Affair in that they did write much of their own material but it was a cover of The Grassroots *'Lovin' Things'* that provided their commercial breakthrough. *'Reflections of My Life'* was co-written by the group's guitarist Junior Campbell who went on to have a big hit with *'Hallelujah Freedom'* but it is for a cover of **The Beatles'** *'Ob-La- Di Ob-La-Da'* from the 'White Album' that they are probably best remembered. *'I See the Rain'* is probably the best song Marmalade recorded (and one of the best psych records of all time). It not only inspired **Led Zeppelin's** *'Whole Lotta Love'* but was a great favourite of **Jimi Hendrix**. Junior Campbell played a white Stratocaster left handed and had a perm and small moustache like Hendrix at this time. On the release of *'I See the Rain'* Hendrix was at the beginning of his rise to success having just released his *'Hey Joe'* 45. *'Man in A Shop'* sounds like **The Bee Gees**, the orchestration is a little overdone but, at its heart, it's a good song, a song in a long line of songs about loneliness and alienation based on local characters. I'd like to hear this re-recorded. Marmalade records can usually be picked up for reasonable prices.

# John Martyn (Iain David McGeachy)

**THE MUSICIANS: John Martyn (Acoustic/ Electric Guitar and Vocals) with supporting musicians**

**ORIGIN:** Glasgow, Scotland

**NOTABLE RECORDINGS:** All LPs **'London Conversation'** *** (Island, 1967- his debut LP); **'The Tumbler'** (Island, 1968); **'Stormbringer'** and **'The Road to Ruin'** (Island, 1970 with Beverley Martin née Kutner); **'Bless the Weather'** (Island, 1971); **'Solid Air'** (Island, 1973); **'Inside Out'** (Island, 1973). His **'Live at Leeds'** with extended versions of some of his classic songs and a virtuoso performance by **Danny Thompson** on bass is also well worth checking out. There are two very collectable records in John Martyn's back catalogue, the first pressing of the 1967 LP 'London Conversation' (expect to pay over £100) and the first pressing of 1968's 'The Tumbler' (also £100++), both on Island Records.

**REISSUES: 'Live at Leeds'** 2 LP with triple g/f sleeve and 12 page booklet on Turning Point Records; John Martyn's website offers **'The Island Years'** 18 CD box set, 'Best of the Island Years' 4-CD box with out-takes from the full set, **'Ain't No Saint'**, a 4 CD box set, **'I'd Rather Be The Devil'** 4 CDs/ 2 DVDs and much more. Universal is releasing a ½ speed mastered vinyl of one of Martyn's most popular LPs **'Solid Air'** with a recommended retail price of £32. His CDs are readily available as are vinyl reissues.

**DESCRIPTION:** John Martyn cut his teeth on the London folk circuit, straying into jazz on his second album **'The Tumbler'** with **Harold McNair** on flute and produced by **Al Stewart**. Martyn's brand of jazz fusion was also very much in evidence on **'The Road to Ruin'** when he began his musical relationship with bassist **Danny Thompson** to be joined by the other Thompson, **Richard Thompson** on **'Bless the Weather'**. This album marked the first appearance of Martyn's distinctive echo unit guitar sound to join his unmistakeable voice. The title track of **'Solid Air'** was written in tribute to **Nick Drake**, a friend and label mate. **'Inside Out'** brought his jazz experimentations to its apotheosis. A concert at Leeds University in 1975 with **Danny Thompson**, drummer **John Stevens** and Free guitarist **Paul Kossoff** was sold by mail order from his home and limited to 1,000 making it a collectible item. Martyn released over 20 studio albums and many live recordings until his death in 2009 and also worked with artists like **Eric Clapton**, **Phil Collins** and **David Gilmour**, The Times once described him as "an electrifying guitarist and singer whose music blurred the boundaries between folk, jazz, rock and blues".

# David McWilliams

**THE MUSICIANS: David McWilliams (Vocals, Acoustic Guitar) with Bass, Drums, Flute, Harp, Harmonica, Tympani, Brass, Orchestration**

**ORIGIN:** born Belfast, Northern Ireland, moved to Ballymena, aged 3.

**NOTABLE RECORDINGS:** *'The Days of Pearly Spencer****/ Harlem Lady* ** (Major Minor, 1967); **'Singing Songs by David McWilliams'** **** (#38 UK) and **'David McWilliams Volume 2'** *** (#23 UK) and **'David McWilliams – Vol 3'** compilation (all LPs on Major Minor, 1967) David McWilliams vinyl should be obtainable for between £10 and £20 or less. **REISSUES/ COMPILATIONS: 'Days of Pearly Spencer'** (Starline, 1971); **'Days at Dawn'** (Castle 2 CD); **'The Best of the EMI Years: The Days of Pearly Spencer'** (EMI CD); **'The Days of David McWilliams'** (RPM CD, 2014); *Days of Pearly Spencer* is on the 4 CD set **Acid Drops, Spacedust & Flying Saucers** and other more mainstream '60s' compilations.

**DESCRIPTION:** Under the mentorship of famous Irish songwriter **Dominic Behan** and with the support of **Phil Solomon** who had managed **The Bachelors** and **Them**, McWilliams released an unsuccessful 45 in 1966 entitled *'God and My Country'* on the CBS label. David McWilliams then released *'Days of Pearly Spencer'* one of the greatest number ones that never was in the UK at least despite two reissues! It was #1 in France and Holland but the song had to wait until 1992 for Marc Almond to hit UK #4 in 1992 with a cover version. The comparative lack of success of the song in the UK as opposed to the rest of Europe is perhaps due to the BBC refusing to play it because of Phil Solomon's business association with the pirate radio station, Caroline. Much of the appeal of *'Days of Pearly Spencer'*, a song about a homeless man in Ballymena, derives from the fact that McWilliams used a megaphone much like **The New Vaudeville Band** with *'Winchester Cathedral'*. The vocal was actually recorded in a telephone booth near the recording studio and **Mike Leander**'s orchestral arrangement also adds to the finesse of this recording. It did sell a million copies worldwide. Six albums, two compilation albums, seven 45s McWilliams was a trier and wrote some great songs for the Major Minor and Dawn labels but never got the breakthrough to extend his career beyond 1974. *'Lord Offaly'*, the title track of McWilliams' 1972 LP was the song selected for the Cherry Red Dawn label box set **'Cave of Clear Light'** in 2010.

His 1967 LP **'Singing Songs by David McWilliams'** contains the excellent social justice song *'Redundancy Blues'*. *'Hiroshima'* is another touching song about the infamous atrocity. Another 1967 LP **'David McWilliams Volume 2'** goes more into a **Cat Stevens** or **Peter Sarstedt** kind of direction, more personal 'pop' then 'protest', as on *'Lady Helen of the Laughing Eyes'* and *'Brown Eyed Gal'*. The vocal style of *'Can I Get There by Candlelight'* is similar to **Bill Fay** and a musical and lyrical highlight (although McWilliams' music was sometimes a bit overpowered by strings – more piano might have been more effective on this number). The lead-off song on the album was *'Days of Pearly* **Spencer***'. There was yet another album in 1967 on Major Minor entitled **'David McWilliams – Vol 3'**.

## The Merseybeats/ The Merseys

**THE MUSICIANS: Vocals (all group members sang apart from the drummer); Frank Sloane/ Tony Crane then Tony Crane and Aaron Williams with Bob Garner then Johnny Gustafson (Guitars); Billy Kinsley (Bass); David Elias then John Banks (Drums)**

**ORIGIN:** Liverpool

**NOTABLE RECORDINGS (to 1967):** *'It's Love That Really Counts'* (Fontana, 1963 #24 UK, a Shirelles cover); *'I Think of You'* (Fontana, 1963 #5 UK); *'Don't Turn Around'* (Fontana, 1964 #13 UK); *'Wishin' And Hopin'* (Fontana, 1964 #13 UK); *'I Stand Accused'* (Fontana, 1965 #38 UK); **'The Merseybeats'** LP (Fontana, 1964 LP #12 UK); *'Sorrow'* as The Merseys (Fontana, 1966 #4 UK); *'Love Will Continue'* and *'Is It Love?'* (Fontana B-sides, 1966); and in 1967: *'The Cat'* ** / *Change of Heart* *** (Fontana, 1967); Tony Cranc solo *'Anonymous Mr Brown ***/ In This World'* (Pye, 1967) It is the 1964 Eps on Fontana that are collectible (£25–£30 or more) and 'The Merseybeats' LP on Fontana TL 5210 (£60+ for an excellent copy).

**REISSUES/ COMPILATIONS: 'The Merseybeats Greatest Hits'** (Look, 1977); **'Beats and Ballads'** (Edsel, 1982); **'I Think of You/ Wishin' and Hopin'** (Fontana, 1969); **'Sorrow/ I Think Of You'** (Philips, 1973); **'The Very Best of The Merseybeats'** (Spectrum Audio CD, 1998)

**DESCRIPTION:** The Merseybeats released eight singles, three EPs and 2 LPs between 1963 and 1965. *'I Think Of You'*, a cover of a song by Peter Lee Stirling [118], was not only their biggest hit but much praised by **The Beatles** when they appeared on the TV show 'Juke Box Jury'. *'I Stand Accused'* was covered by **Elvis Costello** in 1980. Guitarist/ singer Tony Crane and bassist/ singer Billy Kinsley formed **The Merseys** in 1966 out of the ashes of The Merseybeats and immediately made an impact with *'Sorrow'* (previously a B-side for **The McCoys**) with **Jimmy Page, Jack Bruce** and **Clem Cattini** all playing on the record. **David Bowie** later made *'Sorrow'* his own going one place higher with the song in 1973 and included it on his covers album '**Pin Ups**'. The success of *'Sorrow'* was not repeated and, after six singles on Fontana the group called it a day in 1968. A Pete Townshend song *'So Sad About Us'* was the follow-up to *'Sorrow'* but could not build on its success while its B-side *'Love Will Continue'* was an original composition with **John Entwistle** adding French horn. They were also offered a song by **John Lennon**, *'I'll Be Back'*, from '**A Hard Day's Night**' but it never came to pass.

Billy Kinsley still vividly recalls the rift in **The Who** in 1966 when **John Entwistle** and **Keith Moon** approached Tony Crane and himself to form a group with them and **Jimmy Page**, called **Led Zeppelin**! The Merseys were on tour with **The Who** and **Cream** at the time (**Jack Bruce** would play on some of their records). The following year, in January, they supported **The Four Tops** on a UK tour and played at the Royal Albert Hall. After touring again with **The Who** and **Cream**, the lacklustre Cook/ Greenaway song *'The Cat'* was issued in 1967 and the group felt their managers Chris Stamp and Kit Lambert were investing too much of their efforts on The Who. *'Change of Heart'*, its B-side, had more character with its choppy beat and barrelhouse piano. In August Brian Epstein took over as manager but died the same month. Despite releasing a creditable 45 *'Penny in My Pocket'* written by **Jimmy Campbell** (then of the Kirkbys, another Liverpool group), the end was near. After a final 45 whose B-side was once again written by **Jimmy Campbell** the group split with Crane and Kinsley becoming The Merseybeats again (only for Kinsley to go and work for Apple) but reassembled over four decades later as part of a '60s' revival package tours. Tony Crane also released five solo 45s on four different labels between 1965 and 1968. His *'Anonymous Mr Brown'* was covered by Dutch group **The Cats**.

## Mickey Finn (And The Blue Men)/ The Mickey Finn

**THE MUSICIANS:** Alan Anthony/ Alan Marks (Vocals); Micky Waller (Guitar); John Cooke/ 'Fluff' (Organ); John Birkitt/ Mick Stannard (Bass); Richard Brand (Drums).

**ORIGIN:** Bethnal Green, London

**NOTABLE RECORDINGS:** *'Tom Hark'* (Blue Beat, 1964); *'Pills'* (Oriole, 1964); *'Reelin' And Rockin'* (Oriole, 1964) *'Night Comes Down'* (B-side, Columbia, 1965 as The Mickey Finn); *'Garden of My Mind \*\*\*\*\*/ Time to Start Loving You'* \*\*\*\* (Direction, 1967) If you want a vinyl copy of the \*\*\*\*\* *'Garden Of My Mind'* you

---

[118] Actually christened Peter Charles Green, Stirling wrote songs for, among others, **Wayne Fontana and the Mindbenders, Frankie Vaughan, Duffy Power, Kathy Kirby** (the 1965 *'Song for Europe'*), *Kiki Dee's 'Stop and Think'* from 1967; and also *'The Mulberry Tree'* for **The Dave Clark Five**. He also wrote *'Don't Turn Around'*, the successor to *'I Think of You'*.

may have to part with as much as £200. Make sure it's a Direction original (58-3086) and not an unofficial copy, has *'Time to Start Loving You'* and is by 'The Mickey Finn'.

**REISSUES:** 'Keep Movin!' (1997 CD on LCD) with eight tracks by the **Jimmy Page All Stars**; there are no shortage of Mickey Finn tracks (mostly *'Garden of My Mind'* on compilations like the **'Nugget II' box set** (Rhino); **'Chocolate Soup For Diabetics'** 5 CD box set (Past & Present); **'Rare '60s' Beat Treasures Vol 1'** CD (Gone Beat); **'We Can Fly' 2** CD and **'English Freakbeat Vol 2'** CD. James Patrick Page compilation CDs are also a source – see below.

**DESCRIPTION:** Named after a spiked drink and formerly called The Strangers, The Mickey Finn, as they eventually became known, changed from a ska band to a mod sound. *'Pills'* is a reference to the discovery of purple hearts by guitarist Micky Waller stashed in his amp and featured **Jimmy Page** on harmonica. In 1965 they toured with **The Hollies, The Kinks** and **The Yardbirds.** Page plays guitar on *'Night Comes Down'.* The group played for **Brigitte Bardot** at a private party in St. Tropez in 1966. Ironically they had nothing released after their nadir, the much compiled freakbeat song *'Garden of My Mind'* with its pounding bass and guitar. **Jimmy Page**'s guitar playing is wild (Micky Waller does the backup) and surely must have influenced **Jimi Hendrix**'s *'Purple Haze'.* Its B-side is a love song with similar heavy backing but more organ and an informal helping of count in, whistles and hooting and hollering – great fun!

## The Misunderstood

**THE MUSICIANS: Rick Brown then Steve Hoard (Vocals); George Phelps and Greg Treadway then Tony Hill then Neil Hubbard then Davy O'List (Guitars); Steve Whiting then Nic Potter (Bass); Rick Moe then Guy Evans (Drums); Steel Guitar Glenn Ross Campbell (Steel Guitar); Chris Mercer (Sax-final line-up)**

**ORIGIN:** Riverside, California as surf group The Blue Notes changing to The Misunderstood in 1965. John Ravenscroft AKA Peel [119] took them back to London. Treadway had to return to the States to be drafted and Tony Hill from Newcastle band The Answers was recruited.

**NOTABLE RECORDINGS:** *I Can Take You to The Sun/ Who Do You Love?* (Fontana, 1966); *Children of The Sun/ Unseen* (Fontana, 1968), **The Lost Acetates** compiled by Mike Stax of 'Ugly Things' was pressed on a limited edition run of 1,500 copies on 180-gram vinyl – the four songs featuring Tony Hill – *My Mind, Find The Hidden Door, Children of the Sun* and version 2 of *I Unseen* show just how great The Misunderstood could be; there are also two versions of the fuzz laden *She Got Me* and the jingly jangly *Don't Break Me Down.* Misunderstood singles on the Fontana label could set you back from as much as £30 to £60+.

**REISSUES:** Two LPS (and CDs) one called **Before The Dream Faded** (Cherry Red's 1982 compilation of the group's earlier material), the other **Golden Glass** originally released on the Time Stood Still label in 1984; **The Legendary Goldstar Album** is a 2 CD set from 1997 which contains 'Golden Glass' plus other material from

---

[119] John Peel in 2003, in an interview with Steve Lafreniere, described The Misunderstood's performance in Hollywood in 1966 as the greatest he'd seen in his life. "They weren't getting anywhere in California so I said to them: Why don't you go to London? They did and stayed with my mother." Unfortunately vocalist Rick Brown was drafted into the US army fighting in Vietnam and the American band split up only to be reincarnated on the same record label (Fontana) with a different line-up that included Nic Potter and Guy Evans who would go on to form a rhythm section for **Van Der Graaf Generator**.

1966; **The Lost Acetates 1965-1966** (Ugly Things, 2004) which sparked a resurgence of interest in the group and which included four acetates of four songs from the band's psychedelic era; *I Can Take You To The Sun* is on '**Acid Drops, Spacedust and Flying Saucers'**; *Children of the Sun* is on the '**Nuggets II: Original Artyfacts from the British Empire and Beyond'** 4-CD box set; other songs like *Never Had A Girl (Like You Before)* from 1969 are on **Rubble** compilations

DESCRIPTION: The Misunderstood are something of a one-off in terms of their rapid metamorphoses, originating in the US as a surf group, their first two 45s were blues numbers, their John Peel era coinciding with two of the best psych 45s ever. In fact, *I Can Take You to the Sun* was listed by Record Collector magazine as one of the 100 greatest psychedelic records of all time coming out in December, 1966, the same month as Jimi Hendrix's version of *Hey Joe* and two months before '*Strawberry Fields Forever'*. As if that were not enough the 1969 reformed version of The Misunderstood released two R&B 45s. Despite being a popular live group in places like The Marquee in 1967, The Misunderstood did not survive for long and a successor band (if there was such an entity) was **Turquoise** (see separate entry) with Tony Hill on guitar and vocals who included an early version of '*Space Oddity'* in their repertoire. In the end Glenn Campbell and Neil Hubbard became members of **Juicy Lucy** and Tony Hill formed the incomparable **High Tide**. **Adrian (Ade) Shaw**, bassist with **Hawkwind, Bevis Frond** etc. said of Tony Hill's guitar playing, "He's not blues, not jazz although his technique is easily good enough for that discipline and he's certainly not out and out rock. He plays scales in his solos I've never heard before and his song writing combines beautiful obtuse lyrics with highly structured psychedelic arrangements." **(115)**

## The Mojos

THE MUSICIANS: Stuart Slater AKA Stu James (Lead Vocals); Adrian Wilkinson then Nicky Crouch (Backing Vocals); Adrian Wilkinson then Nicky Crouch (Guitar); Terry O'Toole (Piano); Keith Alcock AKA Keith Karlson then Lewis Collins (Bass); John Konrad then Aynsley Dunbar then Steve Snake (Drums)

ORIGIN: Liverpool evolving from The Nomads

NOTABLE RECORDINGS: '*Everything's Alright'* (Decca, 1964 #9 UK*); 'Why Not Tonight?'* and '*Seven Daffodils'* (Decca, 1964 – #25 and 30 respectively). They released one album in 1964 '**The Mojos'** and one 45 in 1967: '*Goodbye, Dolly Gray ** /I Just Can't Let Her Go'* ** (Decca) The scarcest Mojos 45 is '*Until My Baby Comes Home/ Seven Park Avenue'* from 1968 (Liberty LBF 15097) valued at £50 or more while the group's EP released in 1964 on the Decca label is valued at £60 upwards.

REISSUES: There is an Edsel compilation (1982); '**The Complete Recordings'**, a CD compiled in 2009 with 20 tracks and contributions from group members in the liner notes.

DESCRIPTION: A lot of early sixties groups had a similar sound to **The Beatles**, absorbing American influences before in turn invading the US with their own brand of rock 'n' roll. This is particularly true for **The Mojos** who started off life as The Nomads. Their rhythm section at one time included Lewis Collins who was to become a professional actor most famous for his role in the TV series 'The Professionals' and Aynsley Dunbar destined to join **John Mayall** and then form his own group **Retaliation**.

In the liner notes to the Edsel LP compiling most of their recorded work, Stuart (Stu) James says: "We were in the second generation of Liverpool groups. I'd often gone down to The Cavern at lunch time when I was at school, and **The Beatles** and **The Big Three** were the best of the first generation" As The Nomads they were very much into American

R&B and blues copying songs by the likes of **Muddy Waters** and **John Lee Hooker** and the group's eventual name was derived from a McKinlay Morganfield song *'Got My Mojo Working'*.

Like The Beatles The Mojos went to Hamburg (early in 1964). On returning to the UK the group undertook a 43 date tour of England supporting (with **The Kinks**) **The Hollies** and headline act **The Dave Clark Five**. They also supported **The Rolling Stones**. There were accusations that The Mojos were Beatles copyists and this is evident on several of their numbers. Lead guitarist Nick Crouch admitted, "The similarity is deliberate. I think every group wanted to do something that was Beatles flavoured." Their biggest 45 hit was *'Everything's Alright'*, recorded in a church hall when the group were in Hamburg, which made #9 in the UK in 1964. Their fourth single *'Seven Daffodils'* was based on a **Lonnie Donegan** song originating with **Lee Hayes**, a member of The Weavers folk group. It was apparently their response to The Animals *'House of The Rising Sun'* but, ironically Mickie Most who produced that very record decided to record it with another group **The Cherokees** with both vying for a place in the UK top 30.

The group splintered early in 1965 and a mark II version which included **Aynsley Dunbar** on drums soldiered on until 1968. In an interesting interview with Paul Du Noyer for his book 'Liverpool: Wondrous Place: Music from the Cavern to the Coral' Stu James describes his experience of going to The Cavern (and anywhere else The Beatles were playing): "I was absolutely obsessive about The Beatles and I could recite their set list to you." **(116)**. On touring with The Mojos and the way it all ended, wishing they'd remained a blues band, James was sitting by the pool in a residency by the Mark II Mojos when he was thinking he was 23 years old and the music wasn't going in the right direction and that was basically that.

As far as 1967 is concerned the group released a rather corny single *'Goodbye, Dolly Gray'* about a soldier leaving for the front with big production, bugle and backing choir. Its B-side has orchestral backing and suffers again from the corny lyric and overwrought production.

## Zoot Money's Big Roll Band

**THE MUSICIANS: Vocals and Organ (Zoot Money), Piano (Al Kirtley – mark 1 only), Guitar (Roger Collis then Andy Somers then Mike Moody), Sax (Kevin Drake then Nick Newell and Johnny Almond then Clive Burrows), Trumpet/ Flute/ Flugelhorn (Jeff Condon – mark V only, Mike Cotton – trumpet – mark VI only), Trombone (John Beauchamp – mark VI only), Bass (Johnny King then Paul Williams – also Backing Vocals – then Lem Lubin), Drums (John Hammond and Mike Montgomery then Pete Brooks then Colin Allen then Bernie Berns)**

**ORIGIN:** Bournemouth, England

**NOTABLE RECORDINGS:** *'It Should've Been Me'* LP (Columbia, 1965); *'Zoot! Live at Klooks Kleek'* LP (Columbia, 1966 #23 UK); *'Uncle Willie'* (Decca, 1964); *'Big Time Operator'* (Columbia, 1966 #25 UK); and in 1967 *'I Really Learnt How to Cry'* \*\*\*/ *'Nick Nack'* \*\*\* (Columbia) The **'Big Time Operator'** EP is rare and a copy in excellent condition could cost £200 or more. The most valuable LP is '**It Should Have Been Me**' (Columbia, 1965 – £100+) followed by **'Transition'** (Direction, 1968 – £60+); then **'Zoot! Live at Klooks Kleek'** (£50 for a mono, £60 for a stereo copy) and finally **'Zoot Money'** (Polydor, 1970) (£40). The Columbia singles will set you back between £15 and £30+.

**REISSUES:** **'A's and B's Scrap Book'** CD on Repertoire; **'A Big Time Operator'** 2 CD on Castle; **'Zoot! Live at Klooks Kleek'** has been remastered for CD (Repertoire) as has the first album; both have also been reissued on vinyl.

**DESCRIPTION:** As you can see from its membership Zoot Money's Big Roll Band was a revolving doors collective. An R&B/ soul/ jazz crossover sound demarcated Money's (real name George Bruno) music. Group members had pedigrees in **Georgie Fame**'s group and, in Money's case, with Alexis Korner in **Blues Incorporated** in 1964. In 1967 organist/ vocalist Money, guitarist Andy Somers/ Summers (later of **The Police**) and drummer Colin Allen (later of **Stone the Crows**) formed the excellent psych rock group **Dantalian's Chariot** (see separate entry) when, in a classic case of transmogrification, 'walking the dog' turned into a 'madman running through the fields'. Bassist Paul Williams joined **John Mayall** then **Juicy Lucy**. Money went on to join **Eric Burdon and the New Animals**, as did Somers later. Money would also become a member of **Centipede** and **Ellis** in the early 1970s. There is an excellent video of the group Live at Klooks Kleek, Hampstead in January, 1967 (with loads of reminiscences), Money leading from the front with the full power of the group revealed. Some of the audience seem reluctant to participate but others are right into the swinging big R&B band sound. **'I Really Learned How to Cry'** is a doleful, soulful song with lethargic organ, acoustic guitar and drums embellished by brass and a piano and guitar break. The B-side **'Nick Nack'** originates from 1964 EP and is a catchy novelty song about drunkenness which is based on 'nick nack paddy wack give the dog a bone'!

## The Nashville Teens

**THE MUSICIANS:** Vocals (Arthur Sharp – lead, Ray Phillips – backing and Terry Crow in mark III), Guitar (Michael Dunford in mark I then John Allen), Piano (John Hawken), Bass (Pete Shannon and Ray Phillips), Drums (Roger Groom then Pete Lace then Barry Jenkins then Roger Groom again)

**ORIGIN:** Weybridge, Surrey

**NOTABLE RECORDINGS:** *'Tobacco Road'* (Decca, 1964 #6 UK, #14 US); *'Goggle Eye'* (Decca. 1964 #10 UK); *'All Along the Watchtower'* (Decca, 1968); **'The Nashville Teens'** EP (Decca, 1965); and in 1967: **'I'm Coming Home ***/ Searching ***'** and **'The Biggest Night of Her Life ***/ Last Minute ***'** (both Decca). The Nashville Teens Decca EP from 1965 and the group's LP on New World in 1975 are valued at £50 and £30 respectively for excellent copies.

**REISSUES:** *'Tobacco Road'* features on numerous sixties compilations; **'Tobacco Road'** (Repertoire CD) contains their 1975 album plus 14 bonus tracks.

**DESCRIPTION:** Another group that spent time in Hamburg where they backed **Jerry Lee Lewis** (**Live At The Star Club,** on **Philips,** released in 1965), their main claim to fame, apart from backing **Chuck Berry** on his 1964 UK tour, was a raucous version of **John D Loudermilk**'s *'Tobacco Road'*, establishing it as a rock standard. The follow-up *'Goggle Eye'*, about a trout of all things, was also written by Loudermilk. Their R&B credentials were also established by their version of *'Parchment Farm'* on the EP. Their version of a third Loudermilk song *'This Little Bird'* was trumped by Marianne Faithfull's more successful version as was the case with Dylan's *'All Along the Watchtower'* where they lost out to **Jimi Hendrix**. Pianist John Hawken was to join Keith Relf in **Renaissance**. 1967's *'I'm Coming Home'* has a **Tremeloes** feel to it but is demarcated by an all too short blazing guitar break emerging unexpectedly from the vocal 'na nas' and 'ch chs'. There is a full discography on their.com website. *'The*

*Biggest Night of Her Life'* has honky tonk piano and a choppy beat, quite psych, quite Beatle-ish although it sounds a little awkward at times.

## The New Vaudeville Band

**THE MUSICIANS: Vocals (Geoff Stephens joined by Alan Klein in mark II), Keyboards (Ian Green then Stan Haywood), Guitar (Mick Wilsher), Sax and Trombone (Bob Kerr, Hugh Watts also on trombone), Bass (Neil Korner), Drums (Henri Harrison)**

**ORIGIN:** North London

**NOTABLE RECORDINGS:** *'Winchester Cathedral'* and *'Peek-A-Boo'* (Fontana, 1966 – #4 and #7 UK respectively – *'Winchester Cathedral'* **** made #1 US in 1967); *'Finchley Central'* (#11 UK), *'Green Street Green'* (#37); **'Winchester Cathedral'** and **'Finchley Central'** LPs (all on the Fontana label)

**REISSUES:** *'Winchester Cathedral'* is pretty much a staple on compilations of '60s' music. LPs of their music are not too hard to get.

**DESCRIPTION:** Not surprisingly brass player Bob Kerr had been in **The Bonzo Dog Doo Dah Band** as the spoof of 1920s/30s Charleston era jazz music would suggest. Success was short-lived as their humour was not as diverse as the Bonzo Dogs and the **Temperance Seven** had got there first. *'Winchester Cathedral'* was a phenomenal success on both sides of the Atlantic and, after much speculation, the singer has been confirmed as **John Carter** of **The Ivy League** and **The Flowerpot Men**. On dissolution Korner joined **The Nashville Teens**, Kerr formed his Whoopee Band and Haywood briefly joined a US band with ex-Animals **Hilton Valentine**.

## Nirvana

**THE MUSICIANS:** see appreciation of **'The Story of Simon Simopath'**

**ORIGIN:** Eire/ Greece

**NOTABLE RECORDINGS/ REISSUES***:* 'The Story of Simon Simopath' **** and **'All of Us'** (both Island LPs from 1967 and 1968); *'Tiny Goddess ****/ I Believe in Magic'* *** and *'Pentecost Hotel ****/ Feelin' Shattered'* *** 45s (Island, 1967) *'Rainbow Chaser'* (Island 45, 1968 #34 UK). If you want to explore further **'Dedicated to Markos III'** although out with our timeframe (1969 US/ 1970 UK) is quite progressive, well worth seeking out and has been released on CD (Island, 2003). Similarly: released as Nirvana **'Local Anaesthetic'** (1971) was effectively a Patrick Campbell-Lyons solo project in conjunction with P. J. Kelly following the departure of Alex Spyropoulos. 1972 brought **'Songs of Love and Praise'** with a more song oriented approach and a completely reworked version of *'Rainbow Chaser'* and *'Pentecost Hotel'*. Both LPs are highly collectible and decent copies will cost between £150 and £250. The Esoteric CD remasters (2017) are great sounding and cheaper alternatives – that is not to say I wouldn't want a copy of 'Local Anaesthetic' myself! I have never come across **'Dedicated to Markos III'** on LP but there is an Italian LP reissue on 'Get Back' (1998). The 1967 singles are valued at around £15 in excellent condition but their 1967 LP will cost between £150 and £200 for an excellent copy (if you are lucky) depending on whether it is mono or stereo. **'The Story of Simon Simopath'** and **'All of Us'** was released on Island remastered with bonus tracks in 2003 while the **'Simon Simopath'** LP was issued on the Bell label in 2014. As mentioned above the other albums are harder to get and only expensive imported copies were available when I checked.

**DESCRIPTION:** The combination of Patrick Campbell-Lyons and Alex Spyropoulos produced intriguing, and at times brilliant, music and two very decent albums. Songs like *'Pentecost Hotel'*, *'We Can Help You'* and *'Satellite Jockey'* graced their promising first sci-fi concept album about Simon Simopath (see below) while '**All Of Us**' included the group's first 45 released on Island in 1967, *'Tiny Goddess'* (which deserved better and sounds like the direction ELO would take – its B-side *'I Believe In Magic'* sounds a bit like **The Kinks**, quite trippy with tinkly piano and chimes and a catchy chorus), the orchestrated *'Melanie Blue'*, the title track and *'Rainbow Chaser'* with its powerful phasing effects which deserved a higher chart placing. The B-side of *'Pentecost Hotel'*, *'Feelin' Shattered'* is a jolly pub piano kind of affair. The third album **'Dedicated to Markos III'** is very rare with only 500 copies known to be in existence while '**Local Anaesthetic**', on Vertigo (1971) had just two long tracks. There was one final album **'Songs of Love and Praise'** (Philips, 1972) and the group released a total of 11 singles on 4 different labels between 1967 and 1971.

## IMPORTANT ALBUMS OF 1967 (25)
## THE STORY OF SIMON SIMOPATH by NIRVANA

**THE MUSICIANS: Patrick Campbell Lyons: Guitar and Vocals; Ray Singer: Guitar; Alex Spyropoulos: Piano, Keyboards and Vocals; Michael Coe: French horn and Viola; Brian Henderson: Bass; Peter Kester, David Preston and Patrick Shanahan: Drums; Sylvia A. Schuster: Cello; PRODUCER: Chris Blackwell; DATE: October, 1967; LABEL: Island; CONDUCTOR: Syd Dale**

**TRACK LISTING/ WRITING CREDITS (All songs credited to Patrick Campbell-Lyons and Alex Spyropoulos)**

| | | |
|---|---|---|
| 1. | **Wings of Love** | 3:20 |
| 2. | **Lonely Boy** | 2:30 |
| 3. | **We Can Help You** | 2:00 |
| 4. | **Satellite Jockey** | 2:35 |
| 5. | **In The Courtyard of the Stars** | 2:35 |
| 6. | **You Are Just The One** | 2:05 |
| 7. | **Pentecost Hotel** | 3:05 |
| 8. | **I Never Found A Love Like This** | 2:50 |
| 9. | **Take This Hand** | 2:15 |
| 10. | **1999** | 2:10 |

**THE MUSIC:** A futuristic story (based in 1999!), Simon Simopath is unhappy at school and has a nervous breakdown when working as a computer operator. A mental hospital doesn't help his plight so he boards a rocket, meets a centaur who befriends him and falls in love and marries a tiny goddess named Magdalena (the title of Nirvana's first single) who works at Pentecost Hotel (the title of their second single) – as you do! Track by track:

1. **Wings of Love:** Simon fantasises at school about wanting to be in love and to fly;
2. **Lonely Boy:** Some orchestration, organ, the story continues in Beatles ballad mode , the music is drowning in melancholy then there is hope;
3. **We Can Help You:** A typical catchy '60s' chorus, the bit about the Earth being in the sky bringing Simon peace of mind in the verse gives a clue that some strange things are about to happen;
4. **Satellite Jockey:** a strong track in true '60s' 'intelligent pop' tradition (i.e. not churned out by a 'hit factory' with commercial success the overriding ambition);
5. **In the Courtyard of the Stars:** If it weren't for the rather twee organ this is stylistically similar to early Marc Bolan;
6. **You Are Just the One:** An up-tempo beat number;
7. **Pentecost Hotel:** a syrupy, string laden Baroque style ballad (with prominent harp) with a darker edge in the lyrics referring to 'cobwebs', 'insanity' and 'seven sirens' which sets it apart from the standard orchestrated pop of the time;
8. **I Never Found a Love Like This** is a beguiling ballad that could have originated in the 1930s – all that's missing is the megaphone or could be from a classic musical;
9. **Take This Hand:** you can guess what happens here!
10. **1999** is a Vaudevillian number with its 'come on in, have a drink and be merry', a stark contrast to the despair felt by the central character at the beginning.

**REVIEW:**

Subtitled, 'A Science Fiction Pantomime', 'The Story of Simon Simopath' is a tenuous concept album, sounding more like a collection of songs linked by a fantasy story line. It is short in length (25 minutes) and, while lacking the grandeur and ambition of a 'Sergent Pepper's' or a 'Pet Sounds', has an enduring charm. Transcending beyond 'bubblegum pop' or even 'pop' itself to include elements of psychedelia and orchestration, the melodious, infectious nature of songs like 'Wings of Love', 'Pentecost Hotel' and 'Satellite Jockey ensure that the album has come to be increasingly regarded as an important period piece.

# The Nite People

**THE MUSICIANS:** Vocals (Jimmy Warwick), Guitars (Christopher Ferguson and Francis Gordon), Keyboards and Recorder (Barry Curtis), Tenor sax (Patrick Bell), Bass (Martin Clark then Scott Kirkpatrick), Drums (Chris Ferguson)
**ORIGIN:** Bournemouth, Cornwall and Weymouth, England
**NOTABLE RECORDINGS:** in 1967: *Trying to Find Another Man/ Stay as Sweet as You Are* and *Summertime Blues ****/ In the Springtime* (both on Fontana); *'Morning Sun'* (Fontana, 1968) I have seen the *'Summertime Blues'* 45 advertised for £150 for a near mint copy which is twice the book price. Their 1969 Page One LP 'P.M.' is listed at £200+ so the reissued version is a good option at around £15.
**REISSUES:** There is a 2012 limited edition LP on a Spanish label Sommor entitled *'P.M.'*; their version of *'Hot Smoke and Sassafras'* appears on '**Glimpses Volume 1**' a psych and beat compilation on the Spiral Groove LP also from 2012; *'Love, Love, Love,*

*Love'* is on **We Can Fly** a 2001 compilation on Past and Present (2001) and the song *'P.M.'* appears on '**We Can Fly 5**' (2004).

**DESCRIPTION:** Releasing their first single in 1966, The Nite People covered a **Righteous Brothers** number *'Trying to Find Another Man'* in 1967. *'Morning Sun'* was produced by **Spencer Davis** and is reckoned to be their finest number. Mostly they were a covers group – *'Summertime Blues'* (a stirring Mod Hammond rendition sure to fill dance floors*), 'Hot Smoke and Sassafras'* were others among the seven singles they released on Fontana and Page One between 1966 and 1969. They released one album '**P.M.**' on Page One in 1969 which veers towards heavy organ based rock and is well worth checking out with interesting originals like the title track, a funky version of 'Rock Island Line' (Nice guitar), a rather good 'Delilah' and a version of **Frank Zappa**'s *'Peaches en Regalia'* from his '**Hot Rats**' LP.

7 Inch Records.com have an interesting 'rare beat, garage rock and psychedelic' section and has this to say about The Nite People. "Their sound is best described as stoned and funky psych with fuzz, pounding rhythms and raw vocal delivery."

## Orange Bicycle

**THE MUSICIANS: Vocals (R.J. Scales-Lead; Wil Malone – Backing); Guitar (Bernie Lee); Piano, Organ, Harpsichord, Mellotron (Wil Malone); Bass (John Bachini); Drums (Kevin Curry)**

**ORIGIN:** London

**NOTABLE RECORDINGS:** in 1967 *'Hyacinth Threads'* (#1 France) ***/ *Amy Peate* ***\*; *'Sing This All Together'* (Jagger/ Richard) (Columbia, 1968); '**The Orange Bicycle**' LP (Parlophone, 1970). Expect to pay £100+ for their 1970 LP, the most costly 45 is *'Hyacinth Threads'*, at least £30.

**REISSUES:** '**The Orange Bicycle**' LP was reissued in the limited edition Record Collector vinyl series (Blue Morgan Town). There is a two CD Edsel compilation, **Hyacinth Threads: The Morgan Blue Town Recordings**.

**DESCRIPTION:** Recently coming to prominence as a Record Collector limited edition orange vinyl reissue LP, The Orange Bicycle's music has been re-evaluated. A mixture of light psych-pop originals and diverse cover versions of songs such as **Bob Dylan**'s *'Tonight I'll Be Staying Here with You'*, **Lennon/ McCartney**'s *'Carry That Weight/ You Never Give Me Your Money'*, **The Rolling Stones**' *'Sing This All Together'*, **Denny Laine**'s *'Say You Don't Mind'* and **Elton John**'s *'Take Me To The Pilot'* failed to impress at the time but have been rediscovered in this modern age of search for nostalgic obscurities. Led by fine, husky vocalist R.J. Scales (almost in the Roger Chapman mode) the Record Collector album leads off with two **John/ Taupin** numbers *'Lady Samantha'* (fine electric guitar by Bernie Lee on this) and *'Country Comforts'* (fine keyboards by Wilson (Wil) Malone and busy bass by John Bachini). Malone's originals are funky, country honk type numbers similar to **The Grease Band**, much better than they're often given credit for. Ian Shirley's description of Malone's songs on side one is: "*The Sweet Thing Is* has its base in the blues, with some great playing and spot on backing harmony vocals (thought to be Bachini who sang the soprano parts) while *'Hallelujah Moon'* opens with a beautiful electric piano figure before blossoming like a rose, as fantastic multi-tracked vocals kick in." I'd like to put a word in also for *'Make It Rain'*, with rich interplay between drums, bass and piano.

As far as 1967 is concerned *'Hyacinth Threads'* is Beach Boys meets the harpsichord and, while full of energy, is a bit heavy handed. I prefer its B-side, the psychedelic *Amy Peate. Laura's Garden*, which is still fixated on US west coast harmony vocals, and has harpsichord and swirling strings, in keeping with the sound of the summer of love.

## The Outer Limits

**THE MUSICIANS: Vocals, Guitar, Bass (Jeff Christie), Guitar (Gerry Layton then Steve Isherwood), Bass (Gerry Smith), Drums (Stan Drogie then Rod Palmer)**
**ORIGIN:** Leeds
**NOTABLE RECORDINGS: *'When The Work Is Through'* (split single), The Elephant label, Leeds Student Charity Rag (1965), *'Just One More Chance'* ****/ 'Help Me' *** (Deram, 1967), *'Great Train Robbery'*/ 'Sweet Freedom' (withdrawn by Immediate and released later on Instant, 1968), *'(I'm Not) Your Stepping Stone'*/ 'Great Balls of Fire' (Snow)**
**REISSUES: *'Just One More Chance'* on 'The Mod Scene' CD and various '60s' comilations; *'Help Me'* on Rubble 12 'Staircase to Nowhere' LP, Rubble volume 7 CD and 'The Freakbeat Scene' CD**
DESCRIPTION: As documented in the video 'Death of a Pop Group' group members were disillusioned with lack of success and promoters'/ record companies interest in their music after a promising start on Deram with ***'One More Chance'*** which, while not successful at the time would become a great Northern Soul favourite at the Wigan Casino. Jeff Christie's breakthrough came with *Yellow River*. (see **The Tremeloes**).

## Piccadilly Line

**THE MUSICIANS: Vocals (Rod Edwards, Roger Hand then Jan Barber and George Butler); Guitars (Rod Edwards and Roger Hand); Keyboards (Rod Edwards); Bass (Norrie McLean); Drums (Keith Hodge then George Butler)**
**ORIGIN:** London
**NOTABLE RECORDINGS:** *At The Third Stroke* ***/ *How Could You Say (You're Leaving Me)* **** and *Emily Small (The Huge World Thereof)* ***/ *Gone, Gone, Gone* **** (1967, CBS 45s); **The Huge World of Emily Small** LP *** (CBS, 1967) The LP book price is £300+ for an original and their 45s value at about £25
**REISSUES:** CD reissue of LP (Lightning Tree, 2005); Cherry Red CD reissue with bonus. There is a 2016 limited edition LP on the Radiation label.
DESCRIPTION: Pop-psych in style, Piccadilly Line released two further 45s: *Yellow Rainbow* (written by **Graham Nash**) and *Evenings with Corinna* on CBS in 1968 – **Bob Dylan** is an obvious influence. The music may be too lightweight and whimsical but the album hangs together well in much the same way as **Nirvana**'s Simon Simopath concept work and the classic period cover of the album is a joy to behold.

IMPORTANT RECORDS OF 1967 (26)

THE HUGE WORLD OF EMILY SMALL by PICCADILLY LINE

**THE MUSICIANS: Roger Hand (Vocals, Acoustic Guitar); Ron Edwards (Vocals, Organ, 12-string Guitar); Alan Parker, Colin Green (Guitars); Alan Hawkshaw, Roger Coulam (Keyboards); Harry Stoneham (Organ); Harold McNair (Flute); Brian Hodges, Herbie Flowers, Mo Foster (Bass); Danny Thompson (Acoustic Bass); Barry Morgan, Dougie Wright, Tony Carr (Drums);**

PRODUCER: John Cameron; DATE: 17 April, 1967; LABEL: CBS; ARTWORK: The Sons of Saturn.

## Track Listing/ Writing Credits

| | | |
|---|---|---|
| 1. | Emily Small (The Huge World Thereof) (Edwards/ Hand) | 2:30 |
| 2. | Silver Paper Dress (Edwards/ Hand) | 2:40 |
| 3. | At The Third Stroke (Edwards/ Hand) | 3:00 |
| 4. | Can You See Me? (Edwards/ Hand) | 2:10 |
| 5. | Your Dog Won't Bark (Edwards/ Hand) | 2:55 |
| 6. | How Could You Say You're Leaving Me? (Edwards/ Hand) | 2:35 |
| 7. | Gone, Gone, Gone (Phil & Don Everly) | 2:18 |
| 8. | Twiggs (Edwards/ Hand) | 3:45 |
| 9. | Tumble Down World (Edwards/ Hand) | 2:50 |
| 10. | Visions of Johanna (Bob Dylan) | 6:10 |
| 11. | Come and Sing a Song (Edwards/ Hand) | 3:00 |
| 12. | Her Name is Easy (Edwards/ Hand) | 3:25 |

## The Music Track by Track

1. **Emily Small (The Huge World Thereof)** Not sure about the organ and brass but pleasant enough and grows on you;
2. **Silver Paper Dress** – absolutely charming with nice flute;
3. **At the Third Stroke** has more punch musically but allusion to the circus is a bit corny and the cello backing is rather melodramatic, the speaking clock is good though!
4. **Can You See Me?** Nice multi-part vocals and arrangement with brass, wind, strings, harpsichord and bells;
5. **Your Dog Won't Bark** starts with parping brass, a catchy tune about looking so pretty in a house of straw and a dog that won't bark when the postman comes despite the protagonist saying it will bite him;
6. **How Could You Say (You're Leaving Me)** sounds quite west coast American, a nice little ballad with fine orchestration, some of the singing and thoughtfulness in the lyrics also reminds me of Bill Fay at the time;
7. **Gone, Gone, Gone** An uptempo Everly Brothers cover with muted trumpet and parping brass, great fun despite the subject matter;
8. **Twiggs** Edwards and Hand do a bit of a Simon and Garfunkel on this one;
9. **Tumbledown World:** A lovely dreamy number beautifully arranged;
10. A good version of Bob Dylan's **Visions of Johanna**;
11. **Come and Sing A Song:** Not so keen on the arrangement or the overused sentiment of singing songs with the Sun;
12. **Her Name Is Easy** 'Easy Sometimes, Happy Good Times' is another jolly kind of summer of love chorus and the number chugs along anticlimactically.

Overall, this is an album I'd like to hear re-recorded with less orchestration, I don't know if they were available at the time but *Rosemary's Bluebell Day* and *Country Girl* would be good alternatives for the final two tracks. Although not on the original LP these are bonuses on the Cherry Red CD remastered from a Japanese edition. The "We only said what we wanted her to believe" part of the lyric in *Rosemary's Bluebell Day* encapsulates the bittersweet mood which is what makes the album, on the whole, work.

It is heavier than the tracks that made the album and it's pity the organ wasn't allowed to drive it all the way though as the strings become overbearing. Harold McNair's flute is given room to breathe on the excellent *'Country Girl'*.

'The Huge World of Emily Small' is among the growing number of pop psych albums being re-discovered by collectors, high vocal harmonies exaggerating the innate sentimentality of a music populated with fanciful and capricious workaday British characters and settings, sometimes embellished by minor baroque orchestrations.

Similarities are drawn with **Simon & Garfunkel, The Beatles**, '60s' and California pop.

## Pinkerton's Assorted Colours

**INSTRUMENTS: Guitars (Tom Long and Tony Newman then Steve Jones in mark II), Vocals and Autoharp (Samuel' Pinkerton' Kemp), Autoharp, Bass (Barrie Bernard then Ian Coleman), Drums (Dave Holland)**
**ORIGIN:** Rugby, England as the Liberators in 1964 then Coventry.
**NOTABLE RECORDINGS:** *Mirror Mirror (*Decca, 1965 #9 UK); *Don't Stop Loving Me, Baby* (Decca, 1966 #50 UK); *Magic Rocking Horse* (Decca, 1966); in 1967 *Mum and Dad \*\* / On A Street Car \*\*\** and, in 1968, *There's Nobody I'd Sooner Love/ Look at Me* (both on Pye) thereafter known as Pinkertons
**REISSUES: Flight Recorder** (A 2 CD retrospective on Sequel spanning Pye recordings from 1967 to 1971 with no less than 50 songs of Pinkerton's Assorted Colours and successor group The Flying Machine). A few songs compiled on **Rubble** and other more obscure collections.
**DESCRIPTION:** Pop, although *'Magic Rocking Horse'* was covered by a US psych group Plasticland. Bass player Ian Coleman AKA Stuart Colman became a Radio London DJ. Samuel 'Pinkerton' Kemp was the autoharp player and singer. *'Mum and Dad'* is a straight ahead pop song, recognising, unfashionably perhaps, that things haven't changed that much and Mums and Dads used to, perish the thought, be in love! *On A Street Car* was better, short countrified ditty with a west coast guitar sound and more than a hint of **The Lovin' Spoonful**.

## Plastic Penny

**INSTRUMENTS: Vocals (Brian Keith – lead with Nigel Olsson and Paul Raymond), Guitar (Mick Grabham), Organ (Paul Raymond), Bass (Tony Murray then Chris Lain), Drums (Nigel Olsson)**
**ORIGIN (band members):** Various parts of England, Scotland, Republic of Ireland
**NOTABLE RECORDINGS:** *Everything I Am \*\*\*\** (Page One, 1967 #6 UK); *Your Way to Tell Me Go* (Page One, 1968); **Two Sides Of** (Page One 1968 LP) especially *Genevieve, Mrs Grundy, So Much Older Now* and *Make Me Up*; **Currency** (Page One 1969 LP) especially *Baby You're Not To Blame* B-side of 1968 45; an interesting version of *Hound Dog* and the 8 minute long *Sour Suite*.
**REISSUES:** First two albums released on CD by Repertoire in 1993 along with a Best of & Rarities CD, also on Repertoire. Their classic *'Everything I Am'* 45 should not be difficult to find.
**DESCRIPTION:** A highly underrated group with guitarist par excellence Mick Grabham later to ply his trade with **Cochise** and step into the unenviable role of succeeding **Robin Trower** in **Procol Harum** with aplomb. Indeed, most of the group went on to further achievement in **Chicken Shack** (organist Paul Raymond), **The**

Spencer Davis Group (drummer Nigel Olsson), **The Troggs** (bass player Tony Murray), **Savoy Brown** (Raymond again) and **Elton John** (Olsson again). They also covered '*Strawberry Fields Forever*' on their first album and '*MacArthur Park*' on their second. '*Everything I Am*' is a classic visceral sixties ballad and I have a well-worn '45' to prove it!

## The Poets

THE MUSICIANS: **Vocals (George Gallagher – Lead Vocal with Hume Paton then Andy Mulve, Guitars (Hume Paton – Lead with Tony Myles and Fraser Watson then Norrie McLean and Ian McMillan with Hughie Nicholson), Organ (Johnny Martin), Bass (John Dawson), Drums (Alan Weir then Jim Breakey then Dougie Henderson)**

ORIGIN: Glasgow, Scotland

NOTABLE RECORDINGS: *Now We're Thru'* (Decca, 1964 #31 UK); *That's The Way It's Got to Be (*Decca. 1965); in 1967 *Wooden Spoon \*\*\*\*/ In Your Tower \*\*\*\* (Decca)* The Poets is a highly collectible group. Copies of their first single are not as hard to get as you might imagine although they tended to be well played so excellent copies may prove illusive – £10 or less should buy a VG+ copy. It is not the same story for their second single *I Am So Blue* whose value pushes beyond the £50 mark. Their 1965 single for Immediate *Call Again* could cost three figures while their Decca 1965 single is very hard to find. When it comes to the Immediate 1966 '45' *Baby Don't You Do It*, you could be talking a couple of hundred! Their great 1967 single could also prove illusive!

REISSUES: **The Poets** (Immediate, 1995 LP); **In Your Tower** (Strike, 1995 CD version of The Poets); **Scotland's No. 1 Group** (Dynovox covering 1964 to 1968); **Wooden Spoon: The Singles Anthology 1964-67** CD compilation (Grapefruit, 2011); *That's The Way It's Got To Be* on '**Circles' The Mod 45s box set 1965-67** (various artists – Universal Music Operations, 2013).

DESCRIPTION: The Poets had a distinctive rocking minor key sound demarcated by 12-string guitar. '*That's the Way It's Got to Be*', a rousing rocker, is the hit that never was. The Poets were thought by many to be capable of going further but alas success eluded them although guitarist Hughie Nicholson went on to join Marmalade. '*Wooden Spoon*' is a smart beat number about inequality (with a touch of optimism "gotta lose it soon") with a strong vocal, driving drums and bursts of wailing guitar. Its B-side *In Your Tower* has a hypnotic beat and recorder.

## Brian Poole and the Tremeloes

INSTRUMENTS: **Vocals (Brian Poole), Guitars (Alan Blakely with Graham Scott then Rick West), Bass (Alan Howard), Drums (Dave Munden)**

ORIGIN: Dagenham, Essex, England

NOTABLE RECORDINGS: *Twist and Shout/ We Know* (Decca, 1963 #4 UK); *Do You Love Me?* (Decca, 1963 #1 UK); *Candy Man* (Decca, 1964 #6 UK); *Someone, Someone* – a Crickets song (Decca, 1964 #2 UK; top 100 US); *I Want Candy* (Decca, 1965 #25 UK)

REISSUES: Various compilations including '**The Very Best of Brian Poole and The Tremeloes**' (Spectrum, 1998) and reissues of '*Do You Love Me*' in 1978 and '*Twist And Shout/ Do You Love Me/ Candy Man/ Someone Someone* in a picture sleeve in

1980, an item for collectors. *'Keep on Dancing'* their fourth 45 appears on the Decca compilation CD **'The Beat Scene'**.

DESCRIPTION: **Buddy Holly** obsessed Barking born Brian Poole cut his teeth playing at US airbases and Butlin's Holiday Camp in Ayr. Their main claim to fame may well be beating **The Beatles** to a recording contract with Decca on New Year's Day, 1962. Wind back to a young lad of primary school age in 1963 trying to buy his first record in a long extinct electrical/ record shop in Carnoustie, famous for its hosting of the World Open Golf Championships. The Beatles' version of **The Isley Brothers'** **'Twist and Shout'** EP had come out and sold out so the little boy had to settle for a 45 by Brian Poole and The Tremeloes. However, the joy of discovering its splendid B-side' *We Know'* was some compensation and Brian Poole's version of *'Twist And Shout'* seemed just as good. It was actually the group's fifth attempt at the charts since the first single *'Twist Little Sister'* released in 1962. Their only number one came with another copy, this time of a song by Motown's **The Contours**. Their final top 30 hit was another copy, this time of **The Strangeloves'** *'I Want Candy'*, later revived by **Bow Wow Wow** in 1982. Their final 45 *'Good Lovin'* (an Olympics' number this time) did not chart despite **The Young Rascals** later having a #1 hit with the same song in the US. The group split in January, 1966 and, while they fall short of our target year of 1967, Brian Poole did continue to release records as a solo artist from 1966 to 1969 including two orchestrated ballads for CBS in 1967 neither of which was particularly remarkable. Also, out of the ashes of Brian Poole and The Tremeloes came The Tremeloes which is why I'm giving them a mention here. None of their records are particularly collectible, the highest values going to the first 45, EPs and LPs.

## Duffy Power

INSTRUMENTS: **Guitar, Piano, Harmonica and Vocals backed by session musicians.**

ORIGIN: Fulham, London

NOTABLE RECORDINGS: *It Ain't Necessarily So, I Saw Her Standing There* and *Hey Girl* (all Parlophone 45s, 1963); *Parchman Farm/ Tired, Broke and Busted* and *'I Don't Care'* (both Parlophone, 1964); in 1967 as Duffy's Nucleus *'Hound Dog'***/ 'Mary, Open the Door'* *** (Decca) and *'Davy O'Brien'* ***/ *July Tree'* ** (Parlophone)

REISSUES: **Lovers and Sleepers** (2 CDs on RPM, 34 tracks, including A-s and B-s of his Parlophone 45s and many unreleased, a good, informative package); **Just Stay Blue** (RPM Retro, 1995 CD with best of '60s; 1971 unreleased and a 1965 US only 45). His **'Duffy Power'** album was reissued as **'Blues Power'** with extra tracks on the See For Miles CD reissue label in 1992.

DESCRIPTION: Duffy Power started recording for the Fontana label in 1959 but it was not until he signed for Parlophone that he began to establish a reputation as a blues singer. On his version of **The Beatles'** *'I Saw Her Standing There'* he was accompanied by the **Graham Bond Quartet** including **Jack Bruce** on bass and **John McLaughlin** on guitar. On *'Tired, Broke and Busted'* his backing group was **The Paramounts**, forerunner to **Procol Harum**. After a spell of touring with The Fentones Duffy suffered from depression but came back to release two singles in 1967. These were *'Hound Dog/* *'Mary, Open the Door'* as Duffy's Nucleus (January) on Decca and *'Davy O'Brien (Leave That Baby Alone)'/ 'July Tree'* in October on Parlophone. The version of *'Hound Dog'* is worth checking out on You Tube, a 'chunky' rhythm powered by harmonica reverting to a slow-ish blues although a bit passé for 1967. The B-side is self-penned with brass backing and a soulful leaning – a desperate heartfelt plea, in fact, again worthy of investigation. *'Davy O'Brien'* is more in singer-songwriter vein staring **Randy Newman** like at the sheet music on his piano on the You Tube video. There is no harmonica on this one. Its B-side *'July Tree'* is a cover, an orchestrated ballad. Power also released LPs on different labels in the early 1970s starting with **'Innovations'** on the Transatlantic label and **'Duffy Power'** on the Spark label reissued as **'Blues Power'** on CD in 1992 and had a career as a session harmonica player in the sixties. Most of his 45s for Parlophone are quite collectible along with his Transatlantic album.

## The Alan Price Set

**INSTRUMENTS: Vocals and Keyboards (Alan Price), Sax and Flute (Clive Burrows and Steve Gregory), Trumpet (John Walters), Bass (Ray Slade), Drums (Ray Mills).**

**ORIGIN:** Fairfield, County Durham, England

**NOTABLE RECORDINGS:** *I Put A Spell On You* (Decca, 1966 #9 UK); *Simon Smith and the Dancing Bear* \*\*\*\* and *The House That Jack Built* \*\*\*\* (Decca, 1967 both #4 UK); *Don't Stop The Carnival* (Decca, 1968 #13 UK); *Jarrow Song* (Warner Brothers, 1974 #6 UK)

**REISSUES: Performing Price (live at the Royal Theatre, London, 1975)**, 1975 Polydor double LP on Edsel CD in 2000; **I Put A Spell On You** – The Decca/ Deram Singles As & Bs (Connoisseur CD, 2000); **The House That Jack Built: The Complete '60s' Sessions** (Castle Music, 2005)

**DESCRIPTION:** After leaving The Animals in 1965 Price had hits with covers of Screamin' Jay Hawkins' *'I Put a Spell on You'*, Randy Newman's *'Simon Smith and His Amazing Dancing Bear'*, Sonny Rollins' *'Don't Stop the Carnival'* and the self-penned *'The House That Jack Built'*. Two albums and one EP were released: **'The Price to Pay'** (1966) **'A Price on his Head'** (1967) and **'The Amazing Alan Price'** (1967) all on Decca. The Alan Price Set split up in 1968 and Price joined forces with Georgie Fame then had a big hit with *'Rosetta/ Bonnie and Clyde'* in 1971 on CBS (#11 UK) with an album **'Fame and Price'** in the same year. Price wrote the music for the film **'O Lucky Man'** released on Warner Brothers in 1973. Further albums followed but nothing notable for this study. Alan Price Set trumpeter John Walters' became DJ John Peel's producer.

## John Renbourn

**INSTRUMENTS: Acoustic Guitar, Vocals, Sitar** (on **'Sir John a Lot of Merrie England's Music Thynge and Ye Greene Knight'**, 1968)

**ORIGIN:** Richmond, England

**NOTABLE RECORDINGS:** To 1967 three LPs **'John Renbourn, 'Bert and John'** (with Bert Jansch) (both 1965) and **'Another Monday'** (1966).

**REISSUES:** CD reissues of the first two albums/ Renbourn had been extensively recompiled and shouldn't be hard to find. On vinyl they will be a bit more expensive in excellent condition

**DESCRIPTION:** Folk/ medieval music, Renbourn was a contemporary of **Davy Graham** and **Bert Jansch** and, while he didn't release anything in 1967 his main commercial impact would come in the extraordinary **Pentangle** which doesn't detract from the great music he was involved in before that.

# The Renegades

INSTRUMENTS: Guitars (Kim Brown – lead and Denys Gibson then Joe Dunnett then Mick Wembley), Vocals (Kim Brown), Bass (Ian Mallet), Drums (Graham Johnson)

ORIGIN: Birmingham

NOTABLE RECORDINGS: *Cadillac* (Scandia, 1964 #1 Finland; Polydor, 1966); *Thirteen Women* (President, 1966); *Take a Message* \*\*\* (Parlophone, 1967); *John Fitzgerald Kennedy* \*\*\* (Arison, 1967, Italian release)

REISSUES: There is a CD compilation on Fazer entitled **The Renegades**

DESCRIPTION: Their 1960s albums and 45s were released on the Scandia label in Finland so this is not an easy group to track down especially *'Thirteen Women'* which may cost you a couple of hundred pounds. What success they had was in Finland and Italy where their records were also released on various labels, mostly Ariston. Some songs like *'Uomo Solo'* were recorded in Italian. This is over 4 minutes long, and a pleasant, catchy ballad. *'Take a Message'* is a light, country rock, pleasant but rather lightweight. Their song about JFK was also sung in Italian.

# The Riot Squad

INSTRUMENTS: Guitar (Graham Bonney); Organ (Mark Stevens and Jon Lord); Vocals, Sax, Flute (Bob Evans); Bass (Brian Davies then Mike Martin); Drums (Mitch Mitchell then Bob O'Brien) (David Bowie fronted the group from February to May, 1967).

ORIGIN: London, 1964

NOTABLE RECORDINGS: *Cry Cry Cry; I Take It We're Through, It's Never Too Late to Forget* (all Pye, 1966); *Gotta Be a First Time* \*\*\*/ *Bitter Sweet Love* \*\* (Pye, 1967)

REISSUES: The Riot Squad has been extensively compiled and re-released. The last time I looked there were over 200 entries on Discogs mostly CD mod and Joe Meek compilations. Among these is the 4 CD box **'Real Life Permanent Dreams: A Cornucopia of British Psych 1965-1970** (Castle, 2008) with *I Take It We're Through* and **'Let's Go Down and Blow Our Minds: British Psychedelic Sounds of 1967'**, a 3 remastered CD mono box set on Grapefruit Records (2016) which has The Riot Squad featuring David Bowie singing one of Bowie's early songs, *Toy Soldier*. **'Jump'**, a Castle CD, compiles their 7 singles and unreleased, including 15 Joe Meek productions. When you consider the cumulative value of the 45s to collectors runs into hundreds of pounds (Most attracting a market value of £40 for excellent copies with *I Take It We're Through/ Working Man* (Pye, 1966) fetching over £100 this must constitute good value – although I have seen near mint copies of *Cry, Cry, Cry* on Discogs for £25). A Bam-Caruso LP **'The Riot Squad – Anytime'** (1988) also compiles the complete singles. Also of interest is a mono EP picture disc released in 2013 entitled **'Toy Soldier'** on Acid Jazz Records which has three songs by David Bowie on it: *Toy Soldier, Silly Boy Blue and Silver Treetop School for Boys* as well as a cover of Lou Reed's *Waiting for the Man*. Record Collector released a colourful 750 copy limited edition compilation LP in 2013: **'Making Up For Lost Time'** with remasters of lost acetates and various cover versions including Bob Dylan's *Like A Rolling Stone*, and soul classic *Ain't No Mountain High Enough*.

DESCRIPTION: The Riot Squad became a nursery for the likes of drummer **Mitch Mitchell,** later of **Georgie Fame and The Blue Flames** and **The Jimi Hendrix Experience; Jon Lord**, formerly of **The Artwoods**, and later of **Deep Purple**, and

David Jones (Bowie). Also, **Joe Meek** produced quite a few of their records. They appeared on the British TV talent show contest 'Opportunity Knocks', an early forerunner of 'The X Factor' or 'The Voice' and, despite finishing last, grabbed the attention of American producer Lee Magid and two sessions were recorded which have recently been released on a Record Collector LP after the discovery of an acetate in 2012 (see above). As far as their 1967 releases is concerned *'Gotta Be a First Time'* doesn't quite live up to the name of the group which perhaps promises something a bit more raucous! Its B-side is typical '60s' saccharine pop. Under Joe Meek's production *'How It Is Done'* with its squealing sax and driving beat from the year before is better. This was the B-side of *'Cry, Cry, Cry'* which, arguably, should have been the A-side. By 3 February, 1967, tragically, Joe Meek was dead, having shot his landlady then himself.

## The Rockin' Berries

**INSTRUMENTS: Vocals (Chris Lea – Lead Vocal with Geoff Turton), Guitars (Chuck Botfield – Lead and Geoff Turton then Pete Spooner), Bass (Roy Austin then Bobby Thompson), Drums (Terry Bond then Kenny Redway)**

**ORIGIN:** Birmingham (1961)

**NOTABLE RECORDINGS:** A succession of six top 50 UK hit singles between 1964 and 1965 on the Piccadilly label. Their two top ten hits were *He's In Town*, a lush cover of **The Tokens** hit in the US (played to them by Hollywood producer Kim Fowley) (#3 UK) and *Poor Man's Son*, a cover of a number by a US group called **The Reflections**. In 1967: **Sometimes \*\*\*/ Needs to Be \*\*\*; Smile \*\*\*\* / Breakfast at Sam's \*\*\*** (Piccadilly); *Dawn (Go Away)* **\*\*\* / She's Not Like Any Girl \*\*** (Pye)

**REISSUES: 'A Bowl of Rockin' Berries'** (PRT); **'They're In Town'** (Sequel 2 CD compilation); **'The Water Is Over My Head'** has been variously compiled including **'The Beat Scene'** CD; The Rockin' Berries can also be heard on **'Ripples'** CDs. There is also a Repertoire compilation (1991).

**DESCRIPTION:** Distinguished by guitarist Geoff Turton's falsetto vocals this group's star was in the descendent by the year 1967 although they went on to record for Pye until the mid-1970s. Turton became Jefferson who had a UK hit with Paul Ryan's *'The Colour of My Love'* in 1969, a Gene Pitney style ballad. Yes, *'Smile'* is a cover of the Charlie Chaplin song. The vocal harmonies on songs like *'Dawn (Go Away)'* give The Four Seasons a run for their money.

## The Rokes

**INSTRUMENTS: Vocals (all four), Guitars (Johnny Charlton and Norman Shapiro), Bass (Bobby Posner), Drums (Mike Roger Shepstone)**

**ORIGIN:** London

**NOTABLE RECORDINGS:** *When You Walk in the Room* (in Italian, 1965, ARC) #11 Italy; in 1967 *Let's Live for Today* **\*\*\*\* / Ride On \*\*\***; *Hold My Hand* **\*\*\* / Regency Sue \*\*\*** *(RCA); Bisogna Saper Perdere, Eccola Di Nuovo, Cercate Di Abbracciare Tutto Il Mondo Come Noi* (ARC); *When The Wind Arises* (RCA, 1968)

**REISSUES:** An RCA anthology has been released on CD

**DESCRIPTION:** The Rokes fall into a similar category to The Renegades finding success abroad, in Italy. In fact, they released no fewer than 18 singles on the ARC label between 1964 and 1970 as well as 5 albums. Norman Shapiro had cut his teeth with Gene Vincent's backing group **The Blue Caps** and had played the Hamburg circuit. Their first 45 was a version of *'Shake, Rattle and Roll'* in 1964. A cover of **Jackie de Shannon**'s

*'When You Walk in the Room'* sung in Italian nearly made the top ten in Italy. *'Piangi Con Me' (Let's Live for Today)'* was covered by **The Living Daylights** and was a big hit in the US for **The Grassroots**. It should be a staple of sixties compilations with a slight **Kinks** edge and an infectious chorus. Its B-side *'Ride On'* is a bubbly number that starts with backwards guitar with nice bass and guitar throughout. *'Hold My Hand'* has some weak lyrics (a common failing back then) but a really interesting arrangement, like *'Ride On',* with a **Beatles** influence. *'Regency Sue'* (with brass) also has a big Beatles influence. In 1967 *'Bisogna Saper Perdere'* reached #2 in the Italian charts.

## The Roulettes

**INSTRUMENTS: Guitars (Russ Ballard and Pete Salt), Vocals (Russ Ballard), Bass (John Rodgers then John 'Mod' Rogan), Drums (Bob Henrit)**
**ORIGIN:** Hertfordshire, England
**NOTABLE RECORDINGS:** *The Tracks of My Tears* (Parlophone, 1966); in 1967 *Rhyme Boy, Rhyme ** / Airport People ***; Help Me to Help Myself ***/ To A Taxi Driver* (Fontana)
**REISSUES:** 'Russ, Bob, Pete and Mod' (Edsel, 1983) includes all the Parlophone A-sides – 8 between 1963 and 1966 – and most of the B-sides and 2 tracks from their rare 1965 punning and highly collectible (could be £500 or so!) LP 'Stakes and Chips'.
**DESCRIPTION:** Originally **Adam Faith**'s backing band they included Russ Ballard, later the guitarist, singer and song writer in **Argent** and drummer Bob Henrit also later in Argent. Prior to that the pair were in **Unit Four Plus Two**. Their final two singles were released on Fontana in 1967. *'Airport People'* has a psychedelic edge with meaningful lyrics, much better than its A-side in my opinion.

## Paul and Barry Ryan

**INSTRUMENTS: Paul and Barry Ryan (Vocals) with session and orchestral backing.**
**ORIGIN:** Leeds
**NOTABLE RECORDINGS: in 1967:** *Keep It Out of Sight ***/ Who Told You? ** #30 UK;; Claire/ I'll Make It Worth Your While #47 UK* (both Decca); *Heartbreaker **/ Night Time *** (MGM); LP: The Ryans: Two of a Kind* (Decca, 1967) **
**REISSUES:** The only one I know of is a best of 2 CD on the Repertoire label (1988)
**DESCRIPTION:** Identical twin sons of '50s' pop singer Marion Ryan, Paul and Barry released lots of singles from 1965 onwards under the guidance and production of Mike Leander and Les Reed who also provided them with some songs in their Leander/ Mills and Reed/ Mason songwriting partnerships (etc.) which provided some of their 3 top 20 hits and one near miss between 1965 and 1966. Unfortunately, by 1967, the big '60s' orchestrated productions were becoming a bit 'passé' with only the Cat Stevens penned *Keep It Out of Sight* and the superb vocal harmonies of the ballad *Night Time* showing them at anywhere near their best. The best was yet to come though as Paul Ryan penned the giant hit *Eloise* for brother Barry to have a number two hit with. The Damned also enjoyed success with the song in 1986 reaching number 3 in the charts.

## Crispian St. Peters

**INSTRUMENTS: Vocals with backing musicians**
**ORIGIN:** Swanley, Kent, England

NOTABLE RECORDINGS: *You Were On My Mind* (Decca, 1965 #2 UK); *The Pied Piper* (Decca, 1966 #5 UK); in 1967 *Almost Persuaded* **** and *Free Spirit* *** (Decca)

REISSUES: The Anthology CD (Repertoire, 1997); the two hits have been reissued together on the Virgin and Old Gold labels.

DESCRIPTION: Real name Robin Peter Smith, a cover of the big We Five US hit *'You Were On My Mind'* propelled him to fame in 1965 followed by the much played *'The Pied Piper'* the following year. There were a couple of albums and fifteen 45s between 1963 and 1975. *'Almost Persuaded'* is a clever country bar room song about infidelity with a fine vocal performance (a distinctive Elvis lint). Three good A-sides in three successive years is not a bad achievement. The 1967 B-side *'Free Spirit'* echoes the lack of political correctness of the times "she comes on to everyone" (!) but the song's protagonist doesn't seem too bothered stoically regarding it as a sign of the times!

## The St. Valentine's Day Massacre (See The Artwoods)

INSTRUMENTS: Guitar (Derek Griffiths), Organ (Jon Lord), Vocals (Art Wood), Bass (Malcolm Pool), Drums (Colin Martin)

ORIGIN: see The Artwoods (the same group under a different name)

NOTABLE RECORDINGS: just one 45 issued: *Brother Can You Spare a Dime* **** *(Fontana, 1967)*

REISSUES: None that I know of.

DESCRIPTION: A strong performance of the depression era standard *'Brother Can You Spare a Dime'*.

## Savoy Brown

INSTRUMENTS: Guitars (Kim Simmonds throughout, Martin Stone then Dave Peverett); Vocals (Bruce Portius then Dave Peverett and Chris Youlden then Dave Walker then Miller Anderson and Stan Webb); Piano (Bob Hall until 1969), Keyboards (Paul Raymond); Bass (Ray Chappell then Rivers Jobe then Tone Stevens then Andy Pyle, Andy Silvester and Jimmy Leverton); Drums (Leo Mannings then Roger Earl then Dave Bidwell then Ron Berg then Eric Dillon); Harmonica (John O'Leary mark 1 1967 only); guest Brass

ORIGIN: London (1966)

NOTABLE RECORDINGS: 45s *Taste and Try Before You Buy* **** (Decca, 1967); *Train To Nowhere* (Decca, 1969); various albums like **'Looking In'** (Decca, 1970), their only charting LP; an LP was released in 1967 entitled **'Shake Down'**.

REISSUES: Hellbound Train (Castle 2 CD covering the years between 1969 and 1972). There are also compilations covering the period between 1968 and 1971 on the Decca and See for Miles labels. Savoy Brown featured on blues sampler LPs like **World of Blues Power**.

DESCRIPTION Emerging from the British blues boom the Savoy Brown lynchpin was guitarist Kim Simmonds with an apparent revolving door of musicians like Bob Hall, veteran of blues weekends around the country, who played piano on the first three albums; fellow guitarist Martin Stone who went on to **The Action** and **Mighty Baby**; and Miller Anderson, who would become a valued meber of The Keef Hartley Band, in its final formation. Simmonds and his group relocated to the US where they enjoyed more success than in the UK. After a long hiatus Simmonds re-formed the group to release the splendid album in 2011 entitled 'Voodoo Moon' on Ruf Records. *'Taste And*

*Try Before You Buy'* is a concise electric blues with a strong salutary message. Their best days were still ahead with some accomplished blues rock LPs.

## Scaffold

INSTRUMENTS: Vocals (Mike McGear and Roger McGough then John Gorman and Helen Cox); Guitar (Andy Roberts in final incarnation (Mk. 3) in mid 1970s); Keyboards (Zoot Money Mk. 3); Piano (John Megginson Mk. 3 and, allegedly Elton John on *Lily the Pink*); Sax (Brian Jones – Mk. 3); Bass (Dave Richards); Drums (Gerry Conway and Rob Townsend)

ORIGIN: Liverpool; NOTABLE RECORDINGS: *Thank U Very Much* ****/ *Ide B the First* ** (Parlophone, 1967 #4 UK); *Do You Remember* and *Lily the Pink* (Parlophone, 1968 #34 and #1 UK)

REISSUES: There are compilations on EMI and See for Miles including an LP.

DESCRIPTION A novelty group in the finest English tradition with a Liverpudlian twist, of course, featuring Mike McGear, Paul McCartney's brother, the Penguin modern poet Roger McGough, Zoot Money and, as with The Liverpool Scene, Andy Roberts on guitar.

## Skip Bifferty

INSTRUMENTS: Vocals (Graham Bell), Guitar (Jon Turnbull), Keyboards (Micky Gallagher), Bass (Colin Gibson), Drums (Tom Jackman) with orchestral backing

ORIGIN: London

NOTABLE RECORDINGS: *On Love* ***/ *Cover Girl* ***; *Happy Land* ***/ *Reason to Live* *** (RCA, 1967), *Men in Black/ Mr Money Man* (RCA, 1968) and their highly regarded psychedelic 1967 eponymous album ****; *I Keep Singing That Same Old Song* **** (as Heavy Jelly) which appeared on Island's 'Nice Enough To Eat' sampler. Excellent copies of early singles will cost in the £50 region.

REISSUES: The Skip Bifferty album has had numerous CD reissues and tracks appear on various psychedelic compilations including Rubble 10 and 20 CD boxes which should contain pretty much everything of note discussed in this section of the book. The Story of Skip Bifferty (Castle 2 x CD) is a worthwhile compilation. While an original RCA Victor Skip Bifferty album will cost a fortune the LP has been reissued twice and should be available at normal LP price on the Tapestry label (2007) and a bit more with a bonus 7" single on Essex Records and the latest Acme Label version (2015).

DESCRIPTION An essential part of any '60s' collection their fine album had a memorable psychedelic design and sleeve notes by John Peel. Very much of its period, it normally attracts festival flower power films to accompany the music on You Tube. Lead instrumentalists Jon Turnbull and Micky Gallagher joined singer Graham Bell in Bell and Arc who released a good album which started in high style with *'High Priest of Memphis'*. Bell 'n' Arc played on the famous 50p Charisma tour supporting Genesis and Van Der Graaf Generator (sometimes it was Lindisfarne).

## The Smoke

INSTRUMENTS: Vocals (Mick Rowley), Guitar (Mal Luker), Bass (Zeke Lund), Drums (Geoff Gill)

ORIGIN: Yorkshire, England

**NOTABLE RECORDINGS:** In 1967 *My Friend Jack \*\*\*\* / We Can Take It \*\*\** (Columbia #45 UK); *If the Weather's Sunny \*\*\* / I Wish I Could but I Can't \*\*\*; It Could Be Wonderful \*\*\*\* / Have Some More Tea \*\*\*\**; **It's Smoke Time'** LP \*\*\*\* (Metronome, 1967 – Germany only but now reissued on vinyl)

**REISSUES: It's Smoke Time** (2012 Limited to 500 copies on Record Collector label); **High in the Room: The Smoke Anthology** (Castle, 2002) They have been extensively compiled including the 4 CD box '**Acid Drops, Spacedust & Flying Saucers', 'Perfumed Garden Volume 1', 'We Can Fly Volume 1'** and the '**Nuggets II** 4 CD box set.

**DESCRIPTION** An R & B group turned acid/ psychedelic pop, The Smoke's only hit single was banned by the BBC for 'drug connotations'. Their album is being exposed to a new audience by the Record Collector label. They went on to record two unreleased 45s for Island including a cover of **Traffic**'s *'Utterly Simple'* in 1968, produced by **Dave Mason** of Traffic and **Jeff Beck**. They also covered **Nirvana**'s *'Girl in the Park'*. Their 1967 'nuggets' classic is an overt drugs song about Jack a 'sugar man' who "doesn't have a care" and has "been travellin' everywhere" (LSD was administered on sugar cubes at the time). It features great tremolo guitar and is in the style of **The Who** or **The Yardbirds**. Its B-side is a cry of resilience with its reference to 'coolest chicks' might sound most unhip nowadays but, at the time, was a big statement. *'If The Weather's Sunny'* with its brutal separation of maracas, hand bells and keyboards and superficial similarity to **The Lovin' Spoonful**'s *'Daydream'* is pleasant enough but its B-side with lots of laughter and conversation, although featuring some nice guitar work is a step too far. *'It Could Be Wonderful'* is much more mature in composition and arrangement with a short snatch of what sounds like a banjo and insistent guitar towards its brief conclusion. Oh, no, not another song about tea – ah, but what's in the tea to make it 'groovy' and lead to 'crimson faces', something innocent changed into something else perhaps, clever!

## The Sorrows

**INSTRUMENTS: Guitars (Philip Whitcher, Wes Price), Vocals (Don Maughan AKA Fardon), Bass (Philip Packham), Drums (Bruce Findlay), Organ/ Guitar (Chris Fryers)**

**ORIGIN:** Coventry; **NOTABLE RECORDINGS:** *Take a Heart* (Piccadilly, 1965 #21 UK); **Take a Heart** (Pye, 1965 LP); *Pink, Purple, Yellow and Red* \*\*\*\* (Piccadilly, 1967)

**REISSUES: Pink, Purple, Yellow and Red** (Bam Caruso CD compilation, 1987)

**DESCRIPTION** The Sorrows' first recording was allegedly made in Joe Meek's bathroom! Their first and only 'hit' was in R & B style but they developed a harder edged 'freakbeat' style. They can be seen on You Tube playing a pounding version of *'Take a Heart'* to frenetic drumming by Bruce Findlay (tom toms covered by towels). The singer was Don Fardon who later had a hit with *'Indian Reservation'*. *'Take A Heart'* has been described by Richie Unterberger as 'one of the best obscure British invasion records' (All Music.com) Like a few of the groups we have considered The Sorrows couldn't find success in the UK and reconvened with **The Clouds**' Roger Lomas on board on a package tour of Italy where they had a big fan base and released three 45s in Italian. By 1967 they had fallen out of favour. "Sorrows penniless after a sweet life" read the newspaper headline! This, despite a game effort in their single of that year with its drug references, a psych edged piece of freakbeat with good drumming. A further album, a mixture or originals was released on the Miura label in 1968. The covers included two

Family songs *'Hey Mr Policeman'* and the title track and two **Jim Capaldi/ Steve Winwood** songs written for **Traffic** *'Heaven is in your Mind'* and *'Mr Fantasy'*.

## Sounds Incorporated/ Sounds Orchestral:

**INSTRUMENTS: SOUNDS INCORPORATED: Guitar (John St John AKA John Gilliard), Keyboards (Barrie Cameron then Trevor White – Keyboards and Vocals), Tenor Sax (Griff West), Flute, Sax (Alan Holmes), Bass (Wes Hunter), Drums (Tom Newman then Terry Fogg)**

**ORIGIN:** based in London

**REISSUES: Sounds Incorporated/ Studio 2 Stereo (BGO CD) (2005)** contains their big Australian hit *William Tell* with 25 tracks in total; if it's vinyl you're after some of their 45s and LPs could be up to £20 but most shouldn't prove that expensive.

**DESCRIPTION:** Sounds Incorporated backed Gene Vincent when he toured the UK after his group The Blue Caps were refused work permits and other 'claims to fame' are opening for The Beatles at New York's Shea Stadium and the horn section appearing on *Good Morning, Good Morning* from **The Beatles' 'Sergeant Pepper's Lonely Hearts Club Band'** album. They had been drawn to the attention of Brian Epstein by the early Beatles when Sounds Incorporated was playing in Hamburg in 1963. One of their records *Keep Movin'*, a 1963 B-side and one of their most collectible, was produced by Joe Meek and they used a unique keyboard instrument at the time, the 'clavioline', which was also used by The Tornados. They shortened their name to Sounds Inc. in 1967 and released a pretty good 45 with vocals, *How Do You Feel?* \*\*\*

**INSTRUMENTS: SOUNDS ORCHESTRAL: Piano (Johnny Pearson), Violin (Tony Gilbert), Bass (Tony Reeves, Peter McGurk, Frank Clark, Russ Stapleford), Drums (Kenny Clare, Ronnie Verrell) with The John Schroeder Orchestra**.

**ORIGIN:** based in London

**NOTABLE RECORDINGS: 45s** *Cast Your Fate to the Wind* **(1964) #5 UK #10 US;** *Moonglow (Introducing Theme from Picnic) (1965)* **(both Piccadilly), LPs: Thunderball – Sounds Orchestral Meets James Bond (Pye, 1965), Cast Your Fate to the Wind (Piccadilly, 1965)**

**REISSUES:** None that I can knowingly recommend. However, an LP on the PRT label **Cast Your Fate to the Wind: The Best of Sounds Orchestral (1988)** shouldn't cost you more than £5.

**DESCRIPTION:** Sounds Orchestral was formed as a competitor for Sounds Incorporated to reap the benefits of a healthy easy listening and soundtrack market in the sixties. They got off to an auspicious start with a Vince Guaraldi Trio number (famous for their musical accompaniment to Charlie Brown cartoons) *Cast Your Fate to the Wind* which was a hit on both sides of the Atlantic and secured them a gold disc. They never repeated this success however and their 1967 releases were either numbers from films like *Un Homme Et Une Femme* or covers of pop standards like *Black Is Black, God Only Knows* and *Pretty Flamingo*.

## The Spectres

**INSTRUMENTS: Vocals (Francis Rossi), Guitars (Francis Rossi and Alan Lancaster), Keyboards (Rod Lynes), Bass (Rick Parfitt), Drums (John Coghlan)**

**ORIGIN:** London

**NOTABLE RECORDINGS***: I (Who Have Nothing)* and *Hurdy Gurdy Man* (Piccadilly, 1966) and *We Ain't Got Nothin' Yet* \*\*\*\* (Piccadilly, 1967)

**REISSUES:** Status Quo CD compilations are not difficult to find with Spectres tracks on them. Their early singles are very hard to find in decent condition. (Already covered under '**Status Quo**')

**DESCRIPTION** The Spectres were the prototype Status Quo prior to the short-lived Traffic Jam. Their three singles were covers of numbers sung by **Shirley Bassey, Donovan** and **The Blues Magoos** respectively. '*We Ain't Got Nothin' Yet*' has the template for the bass riff that Deep Purple later used on their hit single '*Black Night*', a 'manufactured hit' (as related by Deep Purple's Jon Lord to DJ Bryan Matthew) with the band wasting a day in the studio trying to come up with ideas only for '*Black Night*' to emerge during the 'wee small hours'. The rest of it is really good too, a spirited heavy rock record from a band so young. You hear the kind of quirky guitar lines that would soon provide Status Quo with their early 'psych' hits.

# The Spectrum

**INSTRUMENTS: Guitar (Tony Atkins, John Beattie), Organ (Bill Chambers then Peter Wood), Vocals (Colin Forsey), Bass (Tony Judd), Drums (Keith Forsey)**
**ORIGIN:** London
**NOTABLE RECORDINGS: In 1967:** *Samantha's Mine* \*\*\*\*: *Portobello Road* \*\*\*\* and *Headin' For A Heatwave* \*\*\*\* which was #1 in Spain (RCA Victor); *Ob-La-Di Ob-La-Da* (RCA, 1968 top 20 Germany); **The Light Is Dark Enough** LP (RCA, 1970)
**REISSUES: The Light Is Dark Enough** has been reissued on CD
**DESCRIPTION:** The Spectrum was another group who were bigger in Europe than in the UK, The Spectrum's second 45, the jaunty curio '*Portobello Road*' was a pirate radio favourite but failed to chart. Their LP was essentially a best of, had a peculiar cover with a gravestone on a hill set against a rainbow and is very rare. '*Samantha's Mine*' has a harpsichord sound and is a really good pop song and a hit in Spain and Portugal. Their well-arranged and produced final 1967 single (about the Heatwave) is also worth checking out (surprised this didn't catch on in the States).

# Cat Stevens

**INSTRUMENTS: Acoustic guitar, vocals with session musicians and backing bands.**
**ORIGIN:** Real name Steven Georgiou, born Soho, London
**NOTABLE RECORDINGS:** *Matthew and Son* (Deram, 1966 #2 UK); in 1967 *I'm Gonna Get Me A Gun* \*\*\*\*/ *School Is Out* \*\*\* *#6 UK, A Bad Night* \*\*\* / *The Laughing Apple* \*\* #20 UK, *Kitty* \*\*\*\*/ *Blackness of the Night* \*\*\*\* #47 UK (all Deram*); Lady D'Arbanville* (Deram, 1970 #8 UK); *Peace Train (*Island, 1971 top 10 US); *Morning Has Broken* (Island, 1972 #9 UK); LPs – **Matthew and Son** (Deram, 1967); **New Masters** (Deram, 1967) **Tea for the Tillerman** and **Teaser and the Firecat** LPs (Island, 1971 #20 and #3 UK/ #2 US respectively); **Foreigner** (Island, 1973 #3 UK)
**REISSUES:** Cat's early hits were all reissued in the early 1980s with *Matthew and Son* a particular favourite. A comprehensive 4 CD US compilation '**On the Road to Find Out**' was released in 2001. It shouldn't be difficult to find copies of his 1967 records but expect to pay a bit more for his two 1967 LPs (perhaps around £15 in excellent condition). A better bet might be **The World of Cat Stevens** which compiled

the pick of his 1966-1969 singles. Comprehensive CD compilations shouldn't be hard to find.

**DESCRIPTION** Eyebrows might be raised at Cat Stevens not being included in the main section but his major artistic success falls slightly out with our timeframe. He was operating and successful in 1966 and 1967 but a bout of tuberculosis early in 1968 sidelined him for the best part of a year. It should not be forgotten that Stevens also wrote successful songs that others gained success with like *'Here Comes My Baby'* (The Tremeloes); *'The First Cut is the Deepest* (**P.P. Arnold**) and *'Wild World'* (**Jimmy Cliff**). In 1967 itself he released two LPs which contained eight of the ten songs on his first five singles.

In December, 1977 Stevens converted to Islam and changed his name to Yusuf Islam. It has been said (including the artist himself) that some of Cat's early songs were too patchwork, disjointed and certainly *'School Is Out'* and *'A Bad Night'* fall into this category (There's a film of a 19 year old Cat in frilly shirt singing this on You Tube with the audience clapping before the end of the song!) He always had big backing in those days but this doesn't always work as on the novelty song *'The Laughing Apple'* that brings you back to the image of Cat surrounded by children on the **'World of Cat Stevens'** compilation LP. *'Kitty'* is one song where it does work, a dynamic arrangement with Cat sounding a bit like Donovan, a really 'groovy' number with brass backing. On its B-side Stevens broke free from the 'show biz performer' image to a protest song, pity it ends so abruptly as he sings "I'm alone and there's no one on my side" – this would prove prophetic with a near death experience (TB) and two years in limbo before the seminal albums **'Teaser and the Firecat'**, **'Tea and the Tillerman'** and (musically) **'Foreigner'**.

## Al Stewart

**INSTRUMENTS: Vocals, Acoustic Guitar with various backing musicians.**
**ORIGIN:** Glasgow, Scotland moving to Dorset, England
**NOTABLE RECORDINGS: The Elf/** *Turn Into Earth* (Decca, 1966, the B-side was a Yardbirds song on which Jimmy Page played guitar); **Bedsitter Images *** ½** (CBS 1967 LP); **Love Chronicles** (CBS 1969 LP); **Zero She Flies** (CBS 1970 LP #40 UK); **Past Present and Future** (CBS 1973 LP); **Year of the Cat** (RCA 1976 LP #38 UK – the title track as a 45 made #31 UK and the only one you're likely to hear on commercial radio). His first two '45's *The Elf* (Decca) and *Bedsitter Images* are hard to find. The former sold less than 500 copies which would be a lot nowadays but back then classifies it as an 'obscurity'.

**REISSUES: Just Yesterday** (5-CD box set, EMI); Al's early albums were big sellers (counting re-issues) and there are plenty of them on the market at low prices but an original excellent copy of 'Bedsitter Images' might set you back three figures

**DESCRIPTION** The same remarks apply as to Cat Stevens as Al Stewart could just as easily have been included in the main section were it not for the fact that it took a while for him to get established. Stewart's personal and expansive music began with his very first, heavily orchestrated album. For me, while he enjoyed a good level of success and acknowledgement there is much to discover in Stewart's extensive catalogue. I still think of him more as a '70s than '60s' artist.

# The Swinging Blue Jeans

**INSTRUMENTS: Guitars (Ray Ennis and Ralph Ellis then Terry Sylvester then Mike Pynn); Vocals (Ray Ennis with Ralph Ennis then Les Braid); Bass (Les Braid then Mike Gregory then Les Braid again); Drums (Norman Kuhlke then John Laurence)**

**ORIGIN:** Liverpool

**NOTABLE RECORDINGS:** *Hippy Hippy Shake* (HMV, 1963 #2 UK); *Good Golly Miss Molly* and *You're No Good* (HMV, 1964 #11 and #3 UK respectively); in 1967 *Tremblin' \*\*/Something's Coming Along \*\*\*; Don't Go Out Into The Rain \*\*/ One Woman Man \*\*\** (HMV POP)

**REISSUES:** Mostly *Hippy, Hippy Shake* as a 45 and some sixties and Merseybeat CD compilations including **'Shake'** and **'At Abbey Road: 1963 to 1967'** which includes a cover of *'This Boy'* and **The Lovin' Spoonful**'s *'Do You Believe in Magic'*.

**DESCRIPTION** The Swinging Blue Jeans' moon was waning by 1967 as the demands of the industry helped them lose their rock 'n' roll mojo (How long could they go on like that, anyway?) although they did release two undistinguished 45s in 1967 and continued releasing singles until 1974 latterly as The Blue Jeans. *'Tremblin'* is fairly standard pop fare, by this time rock 'n' roll having become orchestrated in true de rigueur sixties fashion. The B-side is more subtle as the group re-emerges with the inexplicably subtitled *'You're Gonna Melt'*, *'Don't Go Out into the Rain'* is a lightweight effort and the rhyming of 'miserable' and 'kissable' is, thankfully, unrepeated. Its B-side is better. Personally, I'll stick to *'Hippy, Hippy Shake'*. Their main significance to our study is as part of the Merseybeat phenomenon.

# The Syn

**INSTRUMENTS: Guitars (Steve Nardelli with John Painter then Peter Banks), Vocals (Steve Nardelli), Keyboards (Andrew Jackman), Bass (Chris Squire), Drums (Gunnar Hákonarson then Chris Allen then Ray Steele)**

**ORIGIN:** Wembley, England

**NOTABLE RECORDINGS:** *Created By Clive \*\*\* / Grounded \*\*\*\** (Deram, 1967, also recorded by The Attack*); Flowerman \*\*\* / 14-Hour Technicolour Dream \*\*\*\** (Deram, 1967). Original copies of their 1967 singles could cost you up to £100 for the first and £50 for the second in excellent condition.

**REISSUES: The Original Syn 1965-2004** (2-CD); their two singles can be found on psych compilations such as **Perfumed Garden, Rubble** and **Nuggets**. The Syn released a number of CDs on Umbrellos Records between 2005 and 2016 with only Nardelli (and Squire early on) remaining of the original group.

**DESCRIPTION** The Syn has become legendary for not only releasing two very decent singles but, in a surreal moment of notoriety, for dressing up as flowers when presenting their psych operas at the Marquee Club in London. Their best remembered and most compiled record concerned a certain multi-media all-night event at the Alexandra Palace in London on 29th–30th April, 1967. They also included Peter Banks and Chris Squire later of **Mabel Greer's Toyshop** then **Yes**, and in Banks' case **Flash**. *'Created by Clive'*, with its public school boy accented singing and 'toy shop' organ, sounds almost like a **Bonzo Dog** send-up. Its B-side is better, a Nardelli original sounding as powerful as **The Small Faces**, Squire's bass style he would later develop in Yes emerging, powerhouse drumming, great song covered by **The Lyres**. Taking the Bill and

Ben theme tune introduction [120]a little too far *'Flower Man'* fails with its lyrics but is redeemed somewhat by its psych pop quirkiness. The B-side was again better with drumming of near **Keith Moon** like proportions, nice vocal harmonies, bass and a nice ending.

## Ten Years After

In 1967 Ten Years After had just started out a journey that would, within a couple of years see them take Woodstock by storm and have two top ten albums under their belts.
**INSTRUMENTS: The classic line-up: Guitar, Harmonica, Vocals (Alvin Lee); Keyboards (Chick Churchill); Leo Lyons (Bass), Ric Lee (Drums); the current line-up (2018): Marcus Bonfanti, Chick Churchill, Colin Hodgkinson and Ric Lee.**
**ORIGIN:** Nottingham
**NOTABLE RECORDINGS: LPs (all Deram): Ten Years After (1967) \*\*\*½; Undead (1968) UK #26; US #115; Stonedhenge (1969) UK #6; US #61; Ssssh (1969) UK #4; US #26; Cricklewood Green (1970) UK #4; US #14; Recorded Live (1973) UK #36; US #39; 45s (Deram):** *Love Like A Man* **(1970) UK #10**
**REISSUES:** Most recently there is an expensive 10 CD box set, **Ten Years After: 1967-1974** (Chrysalis, 2018) limited to 1500 worldwide but the live 1973 album is not included. The **Original Album Series**, also on Chrysalis, has 5 CDs from **Ssssss** onwards. Their 1967 LP has been reissued from the original master in mono on Sundazed Music. (For further details see below).
**DESCRIPTION:** Organist Chick Churchill (ex Sons of Adam) met Alvin Lee, then in The Jaybirds, whose main claim to fame was backing **The Ivy League**. Bassist Leo Lyons and drummer Ric Lee quickly came on board and, after a gig at The Marquee supporting **The Bonzo Dog Band** as The Bluesyard, Ten Years After was born. There are two possibilities for the name: it was Alvin Lee's idea to acknowledge the tenth year since his hero Elvis's big breakthrough in 1956 or Leo Lyons' idea inspired by the title of a book he saw advertised called 'Ten Years After the Suez'. Known as "the fastest guitar in the west" Alvin Lee was a super talented, talesmanic guitarist influenced by the likes of **Big Bill Broonzy, Chuck Berry, Chet Atkins** and **Scotty Moore.** He was also into some jazz players like **George Benson** and **Wes Montgomery** (indeed TYA played at the Windsor Jazz Festival in 1967 and the Newport Jazz Festival in 1969) and was inspired by the achievements of contemporaries like **Peter Green** and **Eric Clapton.** Latching onto the late '60s' blues boom Ten Years After toured the US extensively and played at Woodstock and The Isle of Wight (In fact Ric Lee has written a book about his experiences entitled 'From Headstocks to Woodstock') Their debut LP is reviewed below and they followed it with a live album, **Undead**, recorded at the famous Klooks Kleek Club in London featuring their Woodstock 'signature' tune *I'm Going Home,* a 10 minute jazz blues jam *I May Be Wrong But I Won't Be Wrong Always* and a version of Woody Herman's *Woodchopper's Ball.* **Stonedhenge** was a more experimental album, Alvin Lee and Churchill both playing piano, Lyons playing bowed bass and string bass and Ric Lee adding tympani to his drums. Sound effects were also added on the 8-minute *Untitled* and album closer *Speed Kills.* **Ssssss** has a brilliant lead off rock song *Bad Scene* but blues and boogie are still the order of the day. **Cricklewood Green** has the big hit single *Love Like A Man* in extended version as it was on the B-side of the single (at 33 rpm!) and is arguably the group's most varied album with sci-fi sound

---

[120] For the unacquainted 'Bill and Ben, The Flowerpot Men, were literally sharing a garden with 'Weed' on the BBC children's programme 'Watch With Mother'.

effects, another memorable riff based song in *Working On The Road* and a fine Churchill piano solo in the jazzy *Me and My Baby* 1971's **A Space In Time** on the Chysalis label was a platinum album and the group's best seller due to the big American hit singles *I'd Love To Change The World* and *Baby Won't You Let Me Rock 'n' Roll You.* The highest value among collectors is accorded to the first LP with an excellent copy commanding a price of between £40 and £50 depending on whether it is stereo or mono. Despite selling well their subsequent albums up to 1971's **Watt** may cost anywhere between £25 and £30 except for **Cricklewood Green** in mono with poster and **Watt** with poster (£50+). Vinyl reissues tend to be compilations but the most comprehensive 10 CD box set came out in 2018 and has all their albums up to **Rock & Roll Music Music to the World** plus **Positive Vibrations** (an LP in a style similar to ZZ Top who supported them live at the time) and **The Cap Ferret Sessions.** Cheaper options are **Original Album Series**, also on Chrysalis, (2014) with 5 CDs from **Sssssh** to **Rock & Roll Music Music to the World** and **Think About the Times: The Chrysalis Years, 1969-1972**, a 3 CD set which includes all their albums from that period plus the A-sides of their 1970 and 1971 singles.

## IMPORTANT RECORDS OF 1967 (27)
## TEN YEARS AFTER by TEN YEARS AFTER

**THE MUSICIANS: Guitar, Vocals, Harmonica (Alive Lee), Organ, Piano (Chick Churchill), Bass (Leo Lyons), Drums (Ric Lee); PRODUCERS: Mike Vernon and Gus Dudgeon; DATE: 27 October, 1967; LABEL: Deram**

**TRACK LISTING/ CREDITS:**

1. **I Want To Know(Paul Jones) 2:10**
2. **I Can't Keep From Crying Sometimes (Al Kooper) 5:25**
3. **Adventures of A Young Organ (Alvin Lee, Chick Churchill) 2:35**
4. **Spoonful (Willie Dixon) 6:05**
5. **Losing the Dogs (Alvie Lee, Gus Dudgeon) 3:05**
6. **Feel It For Me (Alvin Lee) 2:40**
7. **Love Until I Die (Alvin Lee) 2:05**
8. **Don't Want You Woman (Alvin Lee) 2:40**
9. **Help Me (Raph Bass, Willie Dixon, Sonny Boy Williamson) 9:50**

**THE MUSIC:** *I Want to Know* is a fast paced blues boogie loosener with some tinkling of the ivories and on *I Can't Keep From Trying Sometimes* guitarist Lee demonstrates he is not all 'flash' with a subtle touch like Rory Gallagher's playing with Taste or Robbie Krieger's with the early Doors. *Adventures of A Young Organ* is a particular favourite of mine with terrific laid back jazz drums in what is essentially a walking blues with great organ and jazz guitar chording. *Spoonful* gives Cream a run for their money while there is an enormous tip of the hit to Chuck Berry on *Losing the Dogs*. On *Love Until I Die* Lee gets his harmonica going while **Help Me** ends the album with a 12-bar and some mesmerisingly ambitious guitar solos to the accompaniment of Churchill's brooding organ. All in all an important first step for a highly successful band whose live shows were riveting.

# Them/ Van Morrison/ Belfast Gypsies

**THEM: INSTRUMENTS:** Vocals: George Ivan Morrison (Van Morrison) (+ Harmonica and Sax) then Ken McDowell; Guitar: Bobby Harrison then Joe Boni then Jim Armstrong then Jerry Cole then Jim Parker; Keyboards: Eric Wrixton (piano) then Pat McAuley (Organ and Drums) then Jackie McAuley (organ) then Pete Bardens then Ray Elliott (Organ, Sax and Flute); Bass: Alan Henderson; Drums: Ronnie Millings then Terry Moore then John Wilson then Dave Harvey then Billy Bell then Johnny Stark.

**ORIGIN:** Belfast

**NOTABLE RECORDINGS:THEM: 45s:** *Gloria/ Here Comes the Night* and *Baby, Please Don't Go / Gloria* (Decca, 1964); *Mystic Eyes* (Decca, 1965); *Richard Cory* (Parrot, 1966); in 1967 *Gloria/ Friday's Child* *****/**** (Major Minor); **LPs:** The Angry Young Them (Decca, 1965); Them Again (Decca, 1966)

**VAN MORRISON: 45s:** *Brown Eyed Girl* ****/ *Goodbye Baby (Baby Goodbye)* ***; in 1967 **Blowin' Your Mind LP** (Bang) ***

**BELFAST GYPSIES: 45s:** Portland Town/ People (Let's Freak Out) (Loma, Us, 1966); *Gloria's Dream* ***/ *Secret Police* **** (Island, 1966 then on Disques Vogue EP, France, 1967); *Portland Town* ***/ *Boom Boom* *** (Sonet, 1967); LP: Them Belfast Gypsies (Sonet, 1967) ***; **REISSUES/ DESCRIPTION:** There are a baffling number of releases in the USA and Europe as numbers were recycled (with 'Gloria' in particular popping up regularly) with different packagings encompassing a psych phase after Morrison left e.g. the LP **Time Out, Time In For Them** (1968) released only in the USA on Tower Records and the blues inflected psych of **Now and Them** reissued on CD on labels like Rev Ola (2003) and LPs on the Klimt label (2013). Aside from the classic 'hits' *Mystic Eyes* is a fascinating number with a Bo Diddley beat, Jimmy Page on guitar and Van blowing his 'harp' as if there were no tomorrow That Bo Diddley beat (*Not Fade Away* in particular would continue on numbers like *Midnight Train* and *People(Let's Freak Out)* which would appear on **Belfast Gypsies** one and only LP along with a version of Donovan's *Hey Gyp (Dig The Slowness),* the paranoia fuelled *Secret Police* and the anti-war Kim Fowley produced ballad *Portland Town.* The Belfast Gyspies was basically Them after Van Morrison left to pursue a solo career with Pat and Jackie McAuley from Them, Ken McLeod and Mike Scott. As you might imagine records are pretty hard to find. Of course, Van Morrison would be included in the main digest if it were not for the fact that he was just starting out in 1967 releasing an inauspicious Bert Berns co-write with a 'La Bamba' beat, 45 *Chick A Boom* **. *Ro Ro Rosey* *** (Bang, 1967), its superior B-side has nice guitar work and harmonica. There was no way Mossion's own *Brown Eyed Girl* was going to be bettered by its B-side but *Goodbye Baby (Baby Goodbye)* is a decent slice of female singer backed soul written by the Berns/ Farrell songwriting team. All of these were on Van's first LP **Blowin' Your Mind** except *Chick-A-Boom,* its centrepiece being the rather unsettling 9:45 of *T.B. Sheets,* a one-paced funky R&B number with prominent organ and Van's distinctive semi-spoken, semi-sung 'poetic' musings (when he was not blowing his harmonica that is). The LP was released in the USA, Canada, Germany and South Africa in 1967 but not until 1968 in the UK on the London label. It has been reissued as a Troubadour CD in 2008 and an LP on Simply Vinyl in 2006. Worldwide stardom lay ahead with 1968's LP **Astral Weeks** his early breakthrough album, an acquired taste but to most listeners a triumph ant fusion of world jazz, Afro Celtic blues and street poetry. The soulful jazz of **Moondance** followed in 1970, the countrified **Tupelo Honey** in 1971 (**Hank Williams** and **Jimmy Rodgers** were early influences) and collaborations with artists as diverse as Georgie Fame, Roger Waters and Mose Allison followed,. In the case of Allison this was an album of Mose's songs for the Verve label. In 2017 he returned to his blues roots with Jeff Beck, Paul Jones and Chris Farlowe on **Roll with the Punches** revisiting a lasting fascination with artists like **Bo Diddley, Lead Belly, Lightning Hopkins** and **Muddy Waters**. At the time of writing Van was at it again bringing some exceptional playing from some stellar musicians on his album with **Joey De Francesco, 'You're Driving Me Crazy'**. As for Them they continued for ten years revealing a harder edge on 1971's **Them In Reality** LP on Happy Tiger Records (USA) including a 6 minute version of *Gloria* and a re-booting of *Baby, Please Don't Go*. They reunited between 1978 and 1979 releasing an album of blues rock witheringly entitled **Shut Your Mouth** for a German label in 1979. As far as collecting is concerned Them's first 45 *Don't Start Crying Now* is their most collectible with prices of £60 upwards. Their 1965 **Them** EP with the unboxed Decca logo may set you back more than £100 in excellent condition with the export only 'band on ladder' picture sleeve potentially changing hands for 5 times that amount! Them's first LP **(The Angry Young) Them** is also highly collectible £100+) and double that for the flickback sleeve (similar figures apply to the second LP **Them Again**. Even the 1970 repressings of these two albums with the boxed Decca logo may change hands for £40–£50. You see **The World of Them**, an early compilation (Decca, 1970) around quite often is a much more affordable alternative. As for CDs there is a 3 CD set on Sony entitled **The Complete Them 1964-1967** with 45 tracks plus 24 demos, sessions and rarities. For Van Morrison's early work a 3-CD **The Authorised Bang Collection** was released in 2017 with 'original masters, sessions, rarities' and a 'contractual obligation session'!

## Timebox

**INSTRUMENTS: Guitar, Organ and Vibes (Pete 'Ollie' Halsall); Piano (Chris Holmes); Vocals (Mike Patto and Ollie Halsall); Bass (Clive Griffiths); Drums (John Halsey)**

**ORIGIN:** Southport, England

**NOTABLE RECORDINGS:** *I'll Always Love You* ** / *Save your Love* *** (Piccadilly, 1967); *Soul Sauce* ***/ *I Wish I Could Jerk Like My Uncle Cyril* *** (Piccadilly, 1967); *Walking Through The Streets of My Mind* *** / *Don't Make Promises* **** (Deram, 1967); *Beggin'* and *'Girl Don't Make Me Wait/ Gone is the Sad Man'* (Deram, 1968 – *'Beggin'*, a Four Seasons cover reached #38 in the UK chart but was expected to go higher); *Baked Jam Roll In Your Eye* (Deram, 1969)

**REISSUES: Timebox: The Deram Anthology** (Deram CD); songs included on **The Mod Scene** and **The Freakbeat Scene** Decca CDs as well as **Nuggets** and **Acid Drops, Spacedust & Flying Saucers** box sets.

**DESCRIPTION** A collection of formidable musicians who later became the fantastic **Patto** they recorded two singles for Pye in 1966 then became increasingly adventurous and at times outright strange on their journey from soul and beat to psychedelic. Their 1967 single '*Walking Through the Streets of My Mind*' is a nice soul ballad but the strings adhered to it don't do anything for it. The B-side is a cover of a **Tim Hardin** song, very soulful again with Ollie on guitar, organ and vibes! Their first two 1967 45s are rare and an excellent copy will probably edge to the three figure mark, especially the second which sold poorly. The first of these is a pretty straightforward soul number with chiming vibes and ponderous organ. *'Save Your Love'*, its B-side is an instrumental typical of the style Booker T & The MGs but without the spark – its redemption is in a great little vibes solo by Halsall. *'Soul Sauce'*, another instrumental, is worth seeking out especially the You Tube clip with the saucy little video, a perfect fit for the music. Here the group stretch out more in Booker T style with organ and vibes. Its B-side is real little swinger, the only voices to be heard hootering and hollering approval in the background as fluent and organ vibes solos are unleashed to a walking bass line.

## Tomorrow

INSTRUMENTS: **Guitar (Steve Howe), Vocals (Keith West real name Keith Hopkins); Bass (John Wood AKA Junior); Drums (John Alder AKA Twink) with Keyboards by producer Mark Wirtz**

ORIGIN: **London**

NOTABLE RECORDINGS: *My White Bicycle* \*\*\*\*/ *Claramount Lake* \*\*\*\*; *Revolution*\*\*\*\*/ *Three Jolly Little Dwarves* \*\*\*\* (all Parlophone, 1967); *Real Life Permanent Dream* \*\*\*\*; **Tomorrow** LP (Parlophone, 1968), the songs for which were written by Keith (West) Hopkins and his old school friend Ken Burgess who was the original guitarist with **The Teenbeats**, forerunners to **Four + One** (Keith West and John 'Junior' Wood were members) which became **The In Crowd** *Excerpt from a Teenage Opera/ Mark Wirtz Orchestra Theme From a Teenage Opera* \*\*\*\*\* #2 UK

REISSUES: **'Tomorrow Featuring Keith West'** with the whole album, singles, unreleased and tracks by **The Aquarian Age** (Twink and Junior and solo Keith West) on EMI is pretty much essential for any '60s' collector. Tomorrow's releases are extensively represented on psych compilations, '*My White Bicycle*' in particular but also their tracks that didn't make the '**Blow Up'** film soundtrack. If you insist on a vinyl original of their 1968 Parlophone LP expect to pay big money. It will be a similar story for their two 45s.

DESCRIPTION Preceded by Tamla oriented band **The in Crowd** who had a top 50 hit in 1965 with a cover of **Otis Redding**'s *'That's How Strong My Love Is'*, Tomorrow was one of the most popular groups playing in the UFO Club in London sharing the stage with **Jimi Hendrix** on one famous occasion. Steve Howe had previously been in **The Syndicats** and John 'Twink' Alder in **The Fairies.'** *My White Bicycle'* (inspired by the proliferation of environmentally friendly bikes for hire in Amsterdam) must rank as among one of the best songs that didn't chart and provided success for **Nazareth** as well as being (in)famously covered/ parodied by Neil of The Young Ones. Its B-side *'Claramount Lake'* is just as good with great rhythm and a progressive guitar solo by Howe, the shape of things to come with **Yes**. The line-up included Steve Howe later of **Bodast** and **Yes**; singer Keith West whose concurrent project *'Teenage Opera'* was not completed but is well known for the song *'Excerpt'* that made #2 in the UK; and Twink who later joined **The Pretty Things**. Tomorrow made many interesting recordings during their short existence including the song *'Real Life Permanent Dream'* (which can be heard on the 4 CD box set '**Acid Drops, Spacedust & Flying Saucers'**) and a straightforward cover of *'Strawberry Fields Forever'*. *'Revolution'* is not the Beatles number, a bit early for that but an idealistic psychedelic song about 'flower children spreading love' with interesting effects, flutes and strings. 'Have your own little revolution....NOW!' There is also a phased mono version (as well as a speedier version of *'Real Life Permanent Dream'*) on the EMI CD. If you think *'Revolution'* is freaky try the acid-drenched B-side *'Three Jolly Little Dwarves'*! Tomorrow used to start their concerts with a strong version of Roger McGuinn's song for **The Byrds**, *'Why'* (Steve Howe brings out the best in the rhythm section in a whirlwind performance and this number would stretch to 10 minutes as Howe freaked out on guitar) and this is also on the CD compilation.

For those who want to know everything the most comprehensive article I have read on the group appeared in Flashback magazine **(117)** and interviews down the years by Steve Howe and Keith West point to 1967 as a pivotal year, led by the innovative music of The Beatles so much so that no one believed 1968 could be as good!

Tomorrow also has a claim to fame in appearing on the first John Peel Radio One show on 21st September, 1967.

## The Troggs

**INSTRUMENTS: Guitars (Chris Britton then Barry Lee then Richard Moore then Colin Fletcher); Vocals (Reg Ball AKA Presley); Keyboards (Barry Lee); Bass (Pete Staples then Tony Murray); Drums (Ronnie Bullis AKA Bond),**

**ORIGIN:** Andover, Hampshire, England

**NOTABLE RECORDINGS:** *Wild Thing* and *With A Girl Like You (*Fontana, 1966 #2 and #1 UK); *I Can't Control Myself* and *Any Way That You Want Me* (Page One, 1966 #2 and #8 UK); *Give It To Me \*\*\*, Night of the Long Grass \*\*\*\** and *Love Is All Around \*\*\** (Page One, 1967 #12, #17 and #5 UK), other records in 1967: *You're Lyin' \*\*\** (B-side of *Give It To Me*), *My Lady \*\*/ Girl In Black \*\*\*; Hi Hi Hazel \*\*/ As I Ride By \*\*, When Will The Rain Come \*\*\*\** (B-side of *Love Is All Around*) (all Page One)

**REISSUES:** Apart from **'The Best of'** on Page One in 2 volumes (1967) there were other compilations into the 1970s. Some of their 45s were reissued in the ensuing decades mostly with *'Wild Thing'* as the lead-off track. In 1975 the reformed Troggs actually released a reggae version of *'Wild Thing'* on the Penny Farthing label. Their first two LPs have been reissued on one CD (BGO, 1997) **'Trogglodynamite'** has been reissued on a Repertoire digipak with 8 bonus tracks along with **'Cellophane'** (with 12 bonus) and **'Mixed Bag'** (as **'Hip, Hip, Hooray'** – not sure why?). Repertoire has also released the definitive **'Singles A's and B's'** collection from the 1966-1969 period on 3 CDs.

**DESCRIPTION** The Troggs are another case in point of a group that may well have been included in the main chapter. However, they tend to be associated with one number *'Wild Thing'* which, ironically only reached #2, and many consider *'I Can't Control Myself'* rather than *'Wild Thing'* as their finest moment. *'Love Is All Around'* seemed pretty innocuous at the time until Wet, Wet, Wet sat at the top of the UK chart with it for such a long time that even singer Marti Pellow seemed to get fed up with it. Interestingly, although ostensibly a singles band, their albums did well and **'From Nowhere – The Troggs'** which reached #6 in 1966 (on Fontana) was an apposite title for they literally did come 'from nowhere' when **Kinks** manager Larry Page took control after hearing their version of *'You Really Got Me'*, they changed their name from The Troglodytes and singer Reg Ball changed his name to Reg Presley! The Troggs shifted to the label set up by Larry Page and their debut 45 for Page One, the aforementioned *'I Can't Control Myself'* with its risky lyrics about a young lady's hips showing above her slacks was banned in Australia. Their second LP **'Trogglodynamite'** was their first for Page One and just made the UK top 10. *'Cousin Jane'* and *'Evil Woman'* are particularly highly regarded tracks. Their 1967 LP was entitled **'Cellophane'** and included a different version of *'Night of the Long Grass'*, *'Love Is All Around'* and *'Little Girl'*, their last UK 45 hit when released the following year. Of other 45s released in 1967 *'Give It to Me (All Your Love)'* was catchy enough but all too short and repetitive. The best of them was the mysterious, psych tinged *'Night of the Long Grass'*. **'Mixed Bag'** (1968), the next LP, introduced a more psychedelic flair on some tracks. The original Troggs split up in the Easter of 1969. Their final LP **'Contrasts'** (apart from numerous compilations)

300

was recorded and released on DJM Silverline with the core of the original line-up but no Reg Presley or Chris Britton. During their reunion in 1975 (with Larry Page and his Penny Farthing label) they covered *'(I Can't Get No') Satisfaction'* and **The Beach Boys'** *'Good Vibrations'*. Britton eventually re-joined the group later on in the seventies when they signed to US label Basement Records. In a classic case of milking the cow dry Reg Presley recorded yet another version of *'Wild Thing'* with Suzi Quatro in 1986 and an album with The Troggs **'Wild Thing'**. (**'Big Wave'** followed in 1989). In 1992 they collaborated with REM on an album called '**Athens and Andover'** from which two 45s were released.

As far as 1967 is concerned songs like *'Night of the Long Grass'* and *'You're Lyin'* are typical of the hard edged, rhythmical Troggs sound, similar to **The Kinks** on this one with a little twangy guitar break. *'Girl in Black'* is more like The Who as Ronnie Bond flails around on the drums to some heavy guitar chords. *'When Will The Rain Come'* has a west coast American sound and was more mature than most of the compositions at that time, a nice guitar and bass line carrying it along.

## Wimple Winch

**INSTRUMENTS:** Guitars (John Kelman – Lead; Demetrius (Dee) Christopolus – Rhythm); Vocals (Demetrius Christopolus); Bass (Barry Ashall); Drums (Lawrence Arendes AKA Larry King)
**ORIGIN:** Liverpool
**NOTABLE RECORDINGS:** *What's Been Done/ I Really Love You Save My Soul* and, in January, 1967, *Rumble on Mersey Square South ****/ Atmospheres ***** (Fontana – withdrawn) then c/w *Typical British Workmanship *** REISSUES: The Wimple Winch Story '63–'68 (Bam Caruso CD, 1998); *Save My Soul* is on the 4 CD **Nuggets II** box set and on the Rubble **'Psychedelic Snarl'** LP. Other songs are on **Rubble** and **Chocolate Soup for Diabetics** compilations. If you can find any of the group's singles you will need a lot of spare cash!
**DESCRIPTION** Formerly Just Four Men, at their best Wimple Winch was a superlative Freakbeat group. The excellent Bam Caruso compilation gives a comprehensive Phil Smee history including a family tree. Smee credits *'Save My Soul'* as being the first example of 'freak beat'. Beginning as Dee Fenton (Christopolus) and The Silhouettes they played the Merseyside beat circuit including The Cavern sometimes on the same bill as **The Beatles** (they were also on a package tour with **The Rolling Stones** later, in 1965) and changed their name to The Four Just Men after a weekly TV serial of the same name. John Kelman bought George Harrison's guitar when he returned from Hamburg. They were forced to change their name to Just Four Men after it came to light that the name was already registered. They did record the **Bacharach/ David** number *'Trains and Boats and Planes'* but Billy J Kramer and the Dakotas had the hit with it. It was a pretty good version with piano and guitar but not as assertive as Kramer's version. As The Four Just Men they produced some pretty standard testosterone fuelled songs and a **Shadows** styled instrumental *'Four Just Men Theme (Laura Norder)'*. The first single as Wimple Winch, *What's Been Done*, created a bit of a stir and drew comparisons with **The Creation** and **The Action**. The follow up *'Save My Soul'* had a tougher edge and was remarkable for its memorable guitar riff and Larry King's crisp drumming. There were two 45s in January, 1967 but the first was withdrawn: *'Rumble on Mersey Square South* b/w *Atmospheres* (A fine 4:30 excursion into **Who** territory with a gutsy vocal and strong riff) only to reappear with a new B-side. Unfortunately the next B-side *'Typical British Workmanship'* was a not altogether successful attempt at a

301

**Ray Davies** wry commentary on British idiosyncrasies and perceived characteristics predictive of the collapse of British industry with a 'made in Japan' reference. '*Rumble on Mersey Square South*, all 4:30 of it **has** great heavy bass and drumming, guitar fills (and a solo rather low down in the mix) with whistles providing rather a poor substitute for a police siren! It would have been great to have heard a concept album based on the promise shown on the withdrawn 1967 single but as it turned out Fontana dropped them but demos survive from 1968 with titles like '*Lollipop Minds*' (**Beach Boys** influenced), '*Marmalade Hair*' and '*Coloured Glass*', not as adventurous as they sound. They went on to become **Pacific Drift** who released what has become a highly collectible LP 'Feelin' Free' on the Deram Nova label.

## Wynder K. Frog

INSTRUMENTS: Guitar (Neil Hubbard then Mike Liber); Keyboards (Mick Weaver AKA Wynder K Frog); Sax (Chris Mercer); Bass (Alan Spenner); Drums (Bruce Rowland); Congas (Rebop Anthony Kwaku Baah)

ORIGIN: Manchester

RECORDINGS: Very active in 1967/1968 with famous covers like *Turn on your Lovelight, Sunshine Superman \*\*\*, Green Door \*\*\*/ Dancing Frog and I'm A Man* and *Jumpin' Jack Flash*, all on Island. They released two LPs: **Sunshine Superfrog** \*\*\* in 1967 and **Out of the Frying Pan** in 1968 and a posthumous LP **Into the Fire** in 1969.

REISSUES: First LP on the Valhalla label with *I'm a Man* single as a bonus; second LP on Edsel in 1995 and also on Valhalla.

DESCRIPTION With blues and jazz roots and led by Hammond B3 player Mick Weaver, Wynder K. Frog's made copious use of other's material including songs like '*Baby, I Love You*', '*The House That Jack Built*' and even '*Alexander's Rag Time Band*'! A good original, '*Gasoline Alley*', was picked for the Island sampler 'You Can All Join In'. The 1967 album '**Sunshine Superfrog**' started the process but it is '**Out of The Frying Pan**' that cemented the group's reputation and if you can get past the disgusting fry up photo of the sleeve pictured on a white label acetate pressing of '**Out of the Frying Pan**' I recommend you watch and listen to tracks like '*Green Door*' on You Tube. This is fairly typical, has frantic Hammond, parping sax and lots of hooting and hollering. Like the cover of Donovan's '*Sunshine Superman*' and just about everything else it was ideal material for the coming Northern Soul scene. In their early days they opened for Island teammates **Traffic**. Spenner, Rowland and Hubbard all went on to become part of Joe Cocker's **Grease Band**. Rebop played with Traffic and Mercer found no shortage of session work. Following the group's dissolution, Island released a posthumous album '**Into the Fire**' in 1969.

## Young Idea

INSTRUMENTS: Guitar (Tony Cox and Douglas Macrae-Brown); Piano (Tony Cox); Vocals (Tony Cox and Douglas Macrae-Brown)

ORIGIN: London University

NOTABLE RECORDINGS: *Peculiar Situation* – a song given to them by The Hollies whom they supported on tour b/w *Just Look at the Rain* – and *With a Little Help from My Friends \*\*\*\* / Colours of Darkness \*\*\*\** – #10 UK (Columbia, 1967) Also in 1967 *Mister Lovin' Luggage Man \*\*\*/ Room With a View \*\*\**

**DESCRIPTION** A talented duo, their first two 45s for Columbia in 1966 failed to make much impact, but a tour with **The Hollies** raised their profile, and they produced a good version of **The Beatles'** classic with a pretty good B-side. The Music for Pleasure label released an album in 1968 not surprisingly entitled '**With a Little Help from My Friends'** (which surprisingly omits *Colours of Darkness*) *Mister Lovin' Luggage Man'* was a Reed-Masson song with good orchestral backing.

## The Zombies

**INSTRUMENTS: Keyboards (Rod Argent); Guitar (Paul Atkinson); Vocals (Colin Blunstone); Bass (Paul Arnold then Chris White); Drums (Hugh Grundy)**

**ORIGIN:** Hertfordshire, England

**NOTABLE RECORDINGS:** *She's Not There* (Decca, 1964 #12 UK, #2 US); *Tell Her No* (Decca, 1965 #42 UK top 10 US); **Odessey and Oracle** LP (CBS, 1968); in 1967 *Goin' Out of My Head **** / She Does Everything For Me **** * (Decca)

**REISSUES: In the Beginning** (Demon, 2019) is a 5 different coloured LP box set with A-sides, B-sides and EP tracks on LPs 2 and 3 and their unreleased album on LP 4 bookended by the LPs 'Begin Here' and 'Odessey and Oracle'. **The Complete Studio Recordings** (Varèse Sarabande, 2019) is similar with the 'R.I.P.' unreleased album, 'Odessey and Oracle' and lots of 'oddities and extras'.

**DESCRIPTION** Known as Britain's brainiest beat band because of the accumulation of certificates group members achieved at school, The Zombies had the likes of Rod Argent, Chris White and Colin Blunstone within their ranks. They did not enjoy as much success in the UK than in the US, their all-time classic debut single failing to reach the top 10 in the UK while selling a million across the Atlantic where they undertook a 10-day tour in December, 1964. Things were not going too smoothly until 1967 when they left Decca for CBS and fate intervened when they made the first non-EMI recording in Abbey Road Studio Two following **The Beatles'** 'Sergeant Pepper'. They certainly used their heads when using some of George Martin and The Beatles' innovations such as coupling two eight tracks and multi-layering vocals. The result was the classic '**Odessey and Oracle'.**

As has been noted, The Zombies were one of those curious cases of a group who sold more records in the US than the UK When asked by Background magazine about why this was Rod Argent had no explanation, "I really don't know. We were certainly much more popular there." *'Tell Her No'* got just outside the top 5 in the US and just outside the top 40 in the UK *Time of the Season,* which went on to sell 2 million copies, didn't even chart in the UK. **(118)** As far as 1967 is concerned *'I Think I'm Going Out Of My Head'* was originally done by Little Anthony and The Imperials and was also cut by **Dionne Warwick**. The Zombies' version is pretty good and can be found on their 'Singles As and Bs' compilation. The B-side is unusual for The Zombies in that the rhythm section and guitar take centre stage in a psychedelic mix that would be perfect if only it had a stronger lyric.

Although not released until April, 1968 **'Odessey and Oracle'** is very much an album of 1967. Rod Argent told Background magazine "We made it clear we were going to split up, so we asked if we could be left alone to make our own album. They gave us £1000 and it was interesting because this was at the time when things were starting to come out in stereo. They said that if we wanted a stereo mix we would have to pay £200 out of our own money. So it was a much more home grown album." And so, in the first week of June, 1967, the very week *Sergeant Pepper* was released, The Zombies entered Abbey Road to make their own album, their own way, two three-hour sessions separated by a two-hour dinner break. Colin Blunstone reckoned The Zombies were, if not the first, then one of the first to self-produce there. Anyway, The Zombies produced a work of fragile beauty that has stood the test of time. Inspired early on by **Elvis Presley** and **The Beatles** it was after seeing the likes of **The Nice** and **Yes** in concert that Rod Argent went on to spearhead the progressive group of the same name. However, as Rod himself said, in answer to a question about the move away from beat music and straightforward rock and pop towards progressive rock, "like most music in the sixties it was following on from The Beatles."

Please note that 'odyssey' is spelt 'odessey' on the most famous Zombies LP. Given the connotation of the word 'ode' this may have been intentional.

## Beyond Rock and Pop

## Ska, Reggae, Jazz, Blues and the Myriad of Other 'Genres' Percolating In 1967

While genres are useful for organisational purposes, in record shops and so on, there was such a cross-fertilisation of ideas and influences percolating away in 1967 and the years leading up to it that it would be remiss of me not to make reference to at least some of these before concluding.

### REGGAE EXPLOSION

When around 500 Jamaicans, mostly men, disembarked from the 'SS Empire Windrush' ship on 23rd June, 1948, society and music irremovably changed in Britain's capital city and points north. They had paid their own passage, £24, and came from a variety of backgrounds bringing different skills to a war ravaged country crying out for nurses, transport workers and even milkmen. As has been seen what the Jamaican immigrants had left behind was a terrible hurricane that had destroyed crops and dwellings in 1944 and the world war depressing the price of their country's main export, sugar.

"For many, when they arrived, the reality was somewhat different from that presented in the cheery posters they had seen back home; they found chilly summers and bitter winters and were housed in inner-city streets full of bleak, untended tenement lodgings or Victorian and Edwardian bay-fronted middle-class houses." (119) They were exploited by unscrupulous landlords charging rents above the going rate for what were, in effect, little better than hovels, with one room per family and 'no coloured signs' prominently displayed, in bombed-out inner cities like Notting Hill Gate. By 1958 there were an estimated 125,000 West Indians in the UK in places like Bristol, Birmingham, Nottingham and, of course, London. There was racial tension, stoked by right-wing fascists like Oswald Mosley, especially when unemployment rose to 500,000 in that same year, which was inevitably blamed on immigration by some, instead of the root cause, economics.

I have already documented the troubles in Nottingham and Notting Hill over that period with Jamaican Prime Minister, Norman Manley, coming to the UK, as a kind of peace ambassador to try to smooth the trouble waters. The musical response to the troubles was documented on a 45 rpm record on Melodisc's Calypso label, *'Carnival Boycott'* by **Mighty Sparrow**. As the '60s approached artists like Laurel Aitken and Lord Kitchener were releasing records like *'Boogie In My Bones'*, a stirring rocker with vibrant piano, sax and a guitar solo thought to be the work of **Ernest Ranglin**.

By 1962 the dominant Blue Beat label, who released singles by **Laurel Aitken**, were beginning to face their first serious competition from Chris Blackwell's Island label.

Blackwell imported records to satisfy music lovers in the growing Caribbean communities in the UK.[121]

Cecil 'Prince Buster' Campbell was emerging as a Blue Beat star and he and Derrick Morgan went over to London for live gigs backed by Georgie Fame and The Blue Flames. Notable records were Prince Buster's *'Madness'* and the instrumental *'Al Capone'* with his 'All Stars' on Melodisc Records, a steady seller in the UK eventually reaching the top 20 of the UK charts in 1967 despite being released in 1965! High tempo ska dance music was all the rage but by 1967 a slower variation called rocksteady emerged epitomised once again by Prince Buster on *'Judge Dread'*. To mark Prince Buster's passing on 8 September, 2016 Record Collector's Laurence Cane-Honeysett wrote a comprehensive tribute. It tells of his *'The Ten Commandments (From Man To Woman)'* which made #81 on the Billboard charts and a succession of releases in the UK in 1967 with a 17 day tour backed by The Bees (later The Pyramids and Symarip).

The influence on UK music in the '70s was considerable: "While Jamaica remained preoccupied with roots and dub, in the UK a number of British groups had come to the fore playing ska infused with punk. All cited Buster and his music as a major source of inspiration." (120)

These included Madness with *'One Step Beyond'*, the B-side of *'Al Capone'* which in turn inspired The Specials *'Gangsters'*, the first record on the 2 Tone label in 1979. The Beat also recorded Buster's *'Rough Rider'* and *'Whine and Grine'*.

It was not until 1968 and after that reggae labels and records started to emerge in considerable numbers and labels like Trojan started to become household names.

## 3 Very Different and Very Notable Reggae Legends (Pre Bob Marley)

NB These are my own personal recommendations based on my own listening. It makes no claim to be comprehensive but hope this is a useful, selective 'rough guide'.

CECIL BUSTAMENTE CAMPBELL AKA PRINCE BUSTER: No reggae collection would be complete without the prolific 'Buster' Campbell AKA Prince Buster. Influential to the ska/ 2-Tone revival of The Specials/ Madness etcetera he even found top 30 success in the UK charts three decades after his 'heyday' with an update of 1968's *Whine and Grind* in 1998 followed by successful sell-out tours. In the early 1960s Buster not only fronted his own group but produced other budding artists. One of them, Derrick Morgan, abandoned ship to link up with produced Leslie Kong, who released *Forward March* on his Beverley label. Morgan also had a big hit with the 1963 '45' *Housewife's Choice* leading to a charge of plagiarism when Buster heard one of his own instrumental breaks. [122] Buster even appeared on TV pop show 'Ready, Steady, Go' and, while in England, joined Georgie Fame and His Blue Flames on stage at the Flamingo Club, inviting Fame to add vocals and organ on a remake of 1962's *Wash Wash*. As noted by Dave Thompson: "The song signposts the direction which ska would soon be taking, as

---

[121] Blackwell flew Millie Small, then just 14 years old, to London to record *'My Boy Lollipop'* which became a huge international hit. The record "marked a pivotal moment in the evolution of Jamaican culture" and helped the upward trajectory of the Island Records business in an old church in Basing Street, Notting Hill.

[122] The 'feud' continued with Morgan's *Blazing Fire* 45, Buster's *Thirty Pieces of Silver* riposte and Morgan's *Praise Without Raise*. Eventually even the Jamaican government got involved arranging a truce and a public reconciliation.

the frenetic rhythms and juvenile energies of the sound were smoothed and cooled on the road to rock steady and the languorous dance steps preferred by the rude boys." **(121)**

In 1964 Buster released notable singles on a regular basis (easily reaching double figures over a year) including *Wings of a* **Dove** and *ABC Ska* which was a commentary about poverty and illiteracy in Jamaica. The following year brought *Float Like a Butterfly*, *One Step Beyond* (which was to lend its title to a Madness album) and a calypso cover of Lord Invader's *Rum and Coca Cola.* The most commercial single in 1965 was *Al Capone* eventually reaching #18 on the UK chart in February, 1967. 1966 saw a preoccupation with rude boy culture in many of his releases which brought some criticism and accusations of sympathising with what was not always a peaceful movement! The likes of **Desmond Dekker** and **The Wailers** were already making similar references, of course, but Buster 'repented' with his *Judge Dread* alter ego delivering his 'courtroom sentences' which attracted antipathy and 'anti Dread' sentiments in turn.

Of his 1967 releases, *Shaking Up Orange Street* is not as difficult to find as some of the other 45s listed here but still worth around £25, this was a dancehall favourite with classic sing/ speak vocal delivery, it's on the FAB label. Then there's *Rock and Shake:* I think this is from '67, a dub style dance record with a spoken vocal delivery, also on FAB. Buster released at least 20 collectible singles on the Blue Beat and FAB labels in 1967 alone including *Judge Dread/ Waiting for My Rude Girl* with The All Stars on Blue Beat.

An economical way of getting into Campbell's music might be through his albums (although finding them in decent condition at affordable prices will prove a challenge). Starting in 1963 with **I Feel the Spirit** (Blue Beat), always ahead of his time, Campbell even writes about those who are 'jealous' of his progressive ideas and is not afraid to tackle overtly political issues as on *Blackhead Chinaman* "a song about freedom and racial problems" according to the sleeve notes but referring to Derrick Morgan's alleged perfidy.

In 1964 there was *I Got a Pain* (Blue Beat) where Campbell appears with The All Stars who include **The Maytals, Tommy McCook** and **The Skatalites**. The brass playing on this album is particularly enjoyable. Also in 1964 Blue Beat released *Free Flying Ska* (subtitled *'Come Fly With Me'*), a collaboration with **The Skatalites, Millie Small**, **The Maytals, Don Drummond** etc. on which Buster used the others' material as well as his own – the title track (actually *Wings of a Dove* is a well-known tune and *Ska War* with **The Maytals** sounds advanced for 1964).

1967 brought **Prince Buster Sings His Hit Song Ten Commandments** on the RCA Victor label with a ripost to Campbell's sexist, and materialistic 'commandments' on the dress and behaviour he expected from women by a 'Princess' (Lucile Pearce?) who says she's married to 'His Royal Highness Prince Buster'. Besides all that there is a great little song, *'Is Life Worth Living?'* with its catchy rhythms and sax solo and another *Wings of a Dove*. A live album **Prince Buster on Tour** was also released in '67 on the Blue Beat label on which old favourites like *007 (Shanty Town)*, *Al Capone* and *Madness* (the one the 2-Tone group took their name from) are delivered in style. Finally, **Judge Dread Featuring Prince Buster** – Jamaica's Pride, also on Blue Beat, has a rocksteady version of *A Change Is Gonna Come,* courtroom shenanigans on *Judge Dread Dance (AKA Barrister Pardon)*, staccato guitar and trumpet on the infectious *Raise Your Hands* while *Sweet Beat* is just that.

Buster would continue through the sixties and cultivate a fascination with The Beatles on covers of songs like *Ob-La-Di, Ob-La-Da* and *Hey Jude.*

## Desmond Dekker

The best known of the reggae stars on British commercial radio in the '60s was **Desmond Dekker** born Desmond Dacres in Kingston, Jamaica. He had a #1 hit with *The Israelites* but this was in 1969. He was also signed to Stiff Records in the 1970s and recorded the covers album **King of Kings** with **The Specials** in 1993. Prince Buster's old adversary **Leslie Kong** produced Dekker's self-written 45 *Honour Your Father and Mother*, in 1963, a very reverential song for an emerging 'rude boy'! He swept all before him in his native Jamaica with no fewer than twenty #1 hits during the mid to latter part of the '60s. His success was not limited to his homeland though with *007 – Shanty Town* giving him a top 20 in the UK in 1967, *Unity* in the same year providing a stirring rallying point and the effervescent *Rude Boy Train* keeping his train firmly on the rails! Like Lulu, he even covered the movie soundtrack song *To Sir with Love*. Most of Dekker's success is out with our 1967 time frame but his significance to the '60s with other great songs like *It Mek* is remarkable.

## Lord Kitchener

In 1954 a Jamaican disc jockey **Count Suckle** played Jamaican music around The Grove and Notting Hill areas of London, including all-nighters at the Apollo public house on All Saints Road and at cafes in Talbot Road and Blenheim Crescent. There was even an annual 'battle of the sound systems' at Lambeth Town Hall!

One of those whose music would be resonating from the giant speakers was 'The King of Calypso' **Aldwyn Roberts** AKA **Lord Kitchener** ('Kitch') from Port of Spain, Trinidad and Tobago sings *'London is the Place for Me'*, painting a rosy picture of a place that was not without prejudice in the year he sang, 1963. "They take you here and they take you there and make you feel like a millionaire" sings Kitch but references to living in Hampton Court perhaps give the game away as the 'chimes' take you out. Nevertheless, the record is unforgettable and utterly convincing in its vocal and musical delivery. *Is Trouble* paints a different picture about being held and beaten suggesting police brutality. In 1948, after some success in America, Kitch and his friend **Egbert More AKA Lord Beginner** sailed via Curacao, Aruba and Jamaica (for performances) aboard the Empire Windrush (following in the wake of SS Almazora in 1947). It turns out *London is the Place for Me* was especially written as a tribute to London on his arrival and was filmed for Pathé News. Kitch's obsession with cricket was demonstrated with his on field celebration, dancing and singing *Walcott, Weekes and Worrell* (three West Indian players) after The West Indies defeated England at Lords Cricket Ground in 1950. "I'm asking you please, don't put the blame on the West Indies," he sang, "The appeal for Hutton was disallowed – they let him continue, he made 202," and "the umpire's decision was a big disgrace as the ball was at the level of his lace" with regards to another contentious decision (all with good humour and best wishes to the MCC for their Australian tour). Serious issues outside sport were also covered on songs like *If You're Not White, You're Black* and Kitchener's snapshots of London life on songs like *The Underground Train* ('never again' as he loses his way in the underground station – great guitar on this!) are a joy to listen to. It also turns out that Princess Margaret was a fan and rumour has it she purchased multiple copies of Lord Kitchener's *Kitch Come to Bed* on a visit to Trinidad and Tobago. Signed to Melodisc Records he released *Rock 'n' Roll Calypso* on which the new dance craze was given the full swing treatment, "on her wedding day we danced the modern way" Kitch sings as he teaches the lady in question how to 'rock 'n' roll'.[123] Lord Kitchener released an LP on RCA entitled **67 Kitch** and continued recording into the 1990s but it is his early observations of '60s' London life that are the most endearing.

## 33 Or So Notable Reggae Records from the 1960s
### (122)/(123)

- *Boogie in my Bones* by **Laurel Aitken** (1960) (Starlite) (Chris Blackwell production) (Brilliant R&B based dance number recorded in 1958)
- *Rock 'n' Roll Calypso* by **Lord Melody** with **The Caribbean AllStars** (1960) (Calypso) (Great fun, not the same song as Lord Kitchener's, a humorous response to Harry Belafonte's hit version with great trumpet)
- *Carnival Boycott* by **Mighty Sparrow** (1960) (Calypso) (Calypso with a message, "The Queen does nothing for carnival, she is history that is all!" and "Keep the calypsos on the shelf – If you want to go you can but we ain't going nowhere!" – also anger at allegations about violence at the carnival)
- *Lover Boy* by **Derrick Morgan** (1960) (Blue Beat) (Duke Reid production) (Off kilter boogie with great solo and trumpet solos) (also *Forward March* (1962) (Island) (Leslie Kong production), like The Skatalites record, a celebration of Jamaican independence)
- *Hey Bar Tender* by **Laurel Aitken** (1961) (Blue Beat) (Ken Khouri production) (Sounds like in some ways The Jordanaires, fun R&B with fairly manic sax break for the time) (also *Mighty Redeemer* (Duke Reid production) (Reckoned to be the first openly Rastafarian recordings by a major artist).
- *Hurricane Hatty* by **Jimmy Cliff** (1962) (Beverley / Island) (Leslie Kong production) (Rocksteady beat with harmonica depicting the tragic destruction of Stann City in Honduras, now Belize, to be rebuilt as Hattieville).
- *Minutes to Go* by **Duke Reid & His Group (The Skatalites)** (1962) (Blue Beat) (Duke Reid production) (a suave instrumental)
- *Independent Jamaica* by **Lord Creation** (1962) (Island) (Vincent Chin production) (optimistic swinger following the Jamaican independence referendum)
- *They Got To Go* by **Prince Buster** (1962) (Blue Beat) (Prince Buster production) (An attack on inequality and personally at Coxsone Dodd and Duke Reid, this was co-written with Derick Morgan after they settled their differences, Morgan going on to make a version called *Blazing Fire* before Prince's definitive version *Madness)*
- *Judge Not* by **Robert Marley** (1962) (Island) (A young Bob Marley belts out this moralistic song to recorded accompaniment and trumpet)
- *Royal Flush* by **Don Drummond** (1963) (Coxsone/ R&B) (Coxsone Dodd production) (Walking bass and trombone led instrumental, one B-side has **The Maytals** skanking on *Matthew Mark* to a chorus of 'hallelujahs')
- *Victory Test Match* by **Lord Beginner** (1963) (Calypso) (Lord Kitchener's companion aboard the Windrush, this is cricket commentary as you may not have heard it before!) (**Laurel Aitken** released yet another one in 1964 – *West Indian Cricket Test/ Three Cheers for Worrell* (JNAC Records)

---

[123] His late 50s, 78s and 45s were collected on two LPs **'Calypso too Hot to Handle'** (Melodisc UK) (1961) followed by **'Volume 2'** in 1962

- *Hallelujah* by **The Vikings (AKA the Maytals)** (1963) (Island) (Coxsone Dodd production) (The band pin their faith to the mast as they do on *Never Grow Old* in the same year, a joyous celebration of faith and life).
- *149 Eastern Time* by **Don Drummond** (1964) (Island) (Duke Reid production) (A haunting song in a far Eastern style).
- *My Boy Lollipop* by **Millie** (1964) (Fontana) (Chris Blackwell production) (A multi-million seller that reached #2 in the UK mainstream chart, the original was sung by **Barbie Gay** in R&B style but Millie's brilliant ska vocals and **Ernest Ranglin**'s orchestration ensured this would become an evergreen classic) (*Sweet William* was the gutsy follow-up along with *Oh, Henry* from Millie's LP **The Blue Beat Girl**)
- *Pieces of Silver* by **Prince Buster** (1964) (Blue Beat) (Prince Buster production) (A great upbeat number with brass and harmonica, a salvo against Dereck Morgan and Leslie Kong)
- *Down by the Riverside* by **The Vikings aka the Maytals** (1964) (Black Swan) (Coxsone Dodd production) (A spiritual rendition of the old classic with great vocal harmonies and The Skatalites, of course)
- *Never You Change* by **The Maytals** (1965) (Island) (Ronnie Nasralla/ Byron Le production) (With its B-side *What's on Your Mind* a classic up tempo 45 with great vocal harmonies, guitar and brass)
- *Al Capone/ One Step Beyond* by **Prince Buster** (1965) (Blue Beat) (With sax by Val Bennett and Dennis Campbell, jazzy beat with The Skatalites incognito as The All Stars – already discussed)
- *Guns of Navarone* by **The Skatalites** (1965) (Island) (Coxsone Dodd production) (A Caribbean rendition of a war movie theme with yelps by Lee Perry) (The group also used a TV theme *Dr Kildare* for another Island release in the same year).
- *It Hurts to be Alone* by **The Wailers** (1965) (Island) (Coxsone Dodd production) (A fine vocal performance by Junior Braithwaite on this ballad with guitar by **Ernest Ranglin**)
- *Put It On* by **The Wailers** (1966) (Island) (Coxsone Dodd production) (One of the group's most memorable songs reportedly played at Bob and Rita Marley's wedding)
- *007 (Shanty Town)* by **Desmond Dekker** (1967) (Pyramid) (Leslie Kong production) (an alternative 'summer of love' song that takes a swipe at the rude boys who adopted Dekker as one of their own)
- *I've Got A Date* by **Alton Ellis and the Flames** (1967) (Dr Bird) (Duke Reid production) (Doctor Bird) (Written by Ellis, a soulful number, up tempo ska with rocksteady bass)
- *Rudy, A Message to You// 'Til Death Us Do Part* (1967) (Ska-Beat) by **Dandy (Livingstone)** (made famous by The Specials later with a B-side about the BBC sitcom)
- *Train to Skaville* by **The Ethiopians** (1967) (Rio) (Coxsone Dodd production) (singing, rhythm, horns all excel in what is considered a ska classic)
- *Dedicated to You* by **The Jamaicans** (1967) (Trojan) (Duke Reid production), a cover of The Impressions' *Dedicate My Song to You*, soulful with great falsetto vocals and horns, some think this outdoes the original.
- *Tonight* by **Keith and Tex** (Keith Rowe and Tex Dixon) (1967) (Island) (Derek Harriott production) (a nice rocksteady ballad with a memorable bass line that is highly valued by collectors, part of a split 45 with **Lynn Tait and The Jets**)

- *This Music Got Soul* by **Hopeton Lewis** (1967) (Island) (Sam Mitchell-Keith Scott production) (catchy piano hooks, ska rhythms, rocksteady beat) (*Cool Collie* the B-side of Lewis' first 45 *Rock Steady* is also worth checking out with its choppy piano and offbeat percussion, very collectible)
- *Queen Majesty* by **The Techniques** (1967) (Treasure Isle) (Duke Reid production) (Written by **Curtis Mayfield** for The Impressions as *Minstrel and Queen* in 1962. "Classic rocksteady in every sense of the word" says The DanceCrasher website).
- *It's Raining* by **The Three Tops** (1967) (Treasure Isle-Jamaica; Trojan-UK) (Duke Reid production) (uptempo ska almost as soulful as **The Four Tops**)
- *Won't You Come Home, Baby?* By **Delroy Wilson** (1967) (Island) (a Coxsone-Dodd production) (Has nice piano and upper register bass and can be heard on the CD/ 2 LP **Studio One Kings** on the Soul Jazz label).
- *The Russians Are Coming* by **Val Bennett** (1968) (Island) was actually released in 1968 but is of interest to us from a sociological perspective musically it was a great rocksteady instrumental and a reworking of **Dave Brubeck's** *Take Five* from 1959 with reference to the hilarious 1966 cold war paranoia satire. Val Bennett was the tenor saxophonist and this was a split single with **Lester Sterling** on the B-side. As with many reggae singles (a) You will be lucky if you find an original in anything better than VG condition and (b) You may need to pay up to £100.

## The Blues

We have seen the influence American bluesmen had on many musicians and groups in the UK. What follows is merely an overview. [124]

## Some Notable Blues Legends

**Mose Allison** was influenced equally by jazz and blues. "They both come from the same place" he famously once said. **Louis Armstrong, Nat King Cole, Duke Ellington, Errol Garner, Thelonius Monk** and **Fats Waller** were all on his musical radar as singers and piano players. He was not your archetypal Mississippi bluesman either, having been educated at two universities graduating in Economics, English and Philosophy. He became, with his trio, a major influence on groups like **The Who, Cream, The Kinks** and **The Rolling Stones** as well as artists like **Georgie Fame** and **Van Morrison** who recorded a whole album of Allison's songs (**Tell Me Something** on Verve). John Mayall covered *'Parchman Farm'* while The Who played his *'Young Man Blues'*.

**Otha Elias Bates,** adopted name **Elias McDaniel AKA Bo Diddley**: Famed for his rectangular shaped guitar Bo Diddley was another Mississippi man who took his music in yet another direction, neither blues nor R&B. **John Lee Hooker** was a big influence on his electric guitar style. **The Rolling Stones** took the 'Bo Diddley beat' to a different level on **Buddy Holly's** *'Not Fade Away'*. There are too many songs that have been covered to list here but try this for starters: *'Mona'* by **The Deviants** and *'Who Do You Love?'* by **Juicy Lucy. The Pretty Things** even took their name from a Bo Diddley

---

[124] Please note that space does not allow me to cover every blues artist and I have selected those I consider of most relevance to the overall purpose of this book. Also, what follows are merely thumbnail sketches with some reading recommendations for those inclined to delve further.

favourite *'Pretty Thing'*, actually written by **Willie Dixon**. **The Animals, The Kinks, Manfred Mann** and **The Yardbirds** all used Bo Diddley songs. It is worth reflecting that the 'Bo Diddley beat' is actually based on African musical traditions with Cuban/Latin elements incorporating maracas as an integral part of the sound (although Bo Diddley himself cited gospel music as an inspiration). Musicologists associate the beat with the 'hambone' style of slapping body parts while chanting, literally using the body as a form of percussion.

**Willie Dixon** was enormously influential as a musician and a writer. He was the main writer, producer and arranger for Chess Records honing what was to become a recognisable Chicago blues sound. His original career aspiration was to be a heavyweight champion boxer and he did gain some success in this regard but once he formed **The Five Breezes** musical group in 1940 the die was cast. A conscientious objector, Dixon was imprisoned in 1941 and formed **The Four Jumps of Jive** then **The Big Three** on his release from jail. His close association with Phil and Leonard Chess began in 1948 and by 1957 he had become the label's 'main man'. Definitive Chicago blues songs that he wrote included *'Hoochie Coochie Man'*, *'I Just Want To Make Love To You'* (both hits for **Muddy Waters**), *'Backdoor Man'*, *'Little Red Rooster'* and *'Spoonful'* (for **Howlin' Wolf**), *'I Can't Quit You, Baby'* for **Otis Rush**, *'Bring It On Home'* (**Sonny Boy Williamson**) and *'Big Boss Man'* (later covered by **The Grateful Dead** and **Elvis Presley**), quite a list! His *'You Need Love'* was the source of Led Zeppelin's *'Whole Lotta Love'* and **The Rolling Stones** and **Cream** were just two of the groups to cover his songs. In a dispute over pay and song writing copyright Dixon left Chess for Cobra Records in 1957 but the label folded in 1959.

**Champion Jack Dupree,** a New Orleans man, was an entertainer as well as a boogie woogie pianist. Like **Willie Dixon** he was a boxer for a while earning the nickname 'champion'. His life changed when he came across musicians like **Big Bill Broonzy** and **Tampa Red,** moving to New York after World War II where he developed his repertoire of music, jokes and stories in the famous Cotton Club, the Rick Wakeman of his day perhaps. He too became part of the European blues invasion releasing albums on Mike Vernon's Blue Horizon label and recording with the likes of **John Mayall** and **Eric Clapton**. Dupree's **Blues From The Gutter** (Atlantic Records, 1958) includes versions of 'standards' like *'Stack of Lee'* and *'Frankie and Johnny'* as well as his own *'Junker Blues'* which dealt with the subject of drug addiction and was adapted by **Fats Domino** for his *'Fat Man'* song.

**Buddy Guy:** Louisiana man George 'Buddy' Guy signed for the Chess label in 1960 and was a session man to the likes of **Willie Dixon, Howlin' Wolf** and **Muddy Waters**. Ironically Leonard Chess was not a big fan and it was an uncredited appearance on **Junior Wells**' Delmark album **'Hoodoo Man Blues'** in 1965 that cemented Guy's reputation. **Eric Clapton** credited Guy with giving him the idea for Cream on hearing Guy's electric trio playing at the American Folk Blues Festival. **Jimmy Page** and **Jeff Beck** were similarly impressed and **Jimi Hendrix** even adapted Guy's 'party trick' of playing the guitar with his teeth and behind his back. Buddy Guy and **Junior Wells** are thought to have been part of the inspiration for The Blues Brothers. In 1970 **Eric Clapton** produced their LP **'Buddy Guy and Junior Wells Play the Blues'** and they supported The Rolling Stones on tour. After a fairly dormant period Guy played with Clapton at The Royal Albert Hall and released arguably his best album **'Damn Right I Got the Blues'** for the Silvertone label the following year. We have strayed well out with our time period but my main recommendation would be **The Complete Chess Studio Recordings** released in 1966. There are many fine tracks on the album including a cover of **Little Brother Montgomery**'s *'First Time I Met The Blues'* and sax, organ and backing vocalists are also used to produce a blues soul crossover on *'Hard But Fair*. The slow blues **'When My Left Eye Jumps'** was played by Fleetwood Mac. The vocal performance on *'Stone Crazy'* recorded in 1961 is superb and this number sounds ahead of its time with sharp guitar playing, lazy sax backing, tinkling piano and prominent bass. The style was much emulated later in the sixties by groups such as **Fleetwood Mac**. *'Leave My Girl Alone'* (1966) is sheer brilliance with trebly rhythm guitar (of sorts), brooding organ and walking bass lines and Guy hollering like **Little Richard**. Surely singers like **Robert Plant** were listening! On the next track the music was more like Stax soul with a vocal that **Otis Redding** would have been proud of. Guy's expert guitar fills and overt showmanship drew legions of fans making him one of the most popular blues artists selling in excess of 5 million records. Buddy Guy's relevance to the mid-sixties is immense.

**John Lee Hooker** was born in Clarksdale, Mississippi but in his twenties worked in a Detroit car factory honing his skills by night in the clubs around Hastings Street. It was at this time he wrote *'Boogie Chillen'.*This foot tapper sounded like a new kind of blues and sold a million. Hooker's idiosyncratic style was further developed due to unusual odd numbered bar structures, the use of open guitar tuning and his famous foot stomp. Recording under many pseudonyms he finally released classic songs such as *Dimples'*, *'Crawling King Snake'* (later recorded by **The Doors**) and *'Boom Boom'* and recorded under his own name for the Vee Jay label. He was supported by an emerging young artist named **Bob Dylan** in Greenwich Village, touring Europe in 1962 with the American Folk Blues Festival. **The Animals** and **The Yardbirds** were two of the groups who covered his songs and, later he recorded with the exceptional blues boogie group **Canned Heat** on **Hooker n' Heat'**. In an extraordinary comeback he recorded what many regard as one of the best blues crossover albums of all time – **The Healer** – in 1989 with guest players such as **Keith Richards** and **Carlos Santana**. In 1991 he followed it with another excellent fusion album **Mr Lucky**, recording this time with the likes of **Ry Cooder, Albert Collins** and **Van Morrison**. A succession of recordings with celebrity players followed almost right up until his death in 2001 at the age of 83. His music has been variously described as 'primal' and 'erotic' (**Bonnie Raitt** and others). I commend to readers Charles Shaar Murray's extensive biography of Hooker, **Boogie Man: The Adventures of John Lee Hooker in the American Twentieth Century'** (Viking, 1999)

**Elmore James** died in 1963 before the '60s' blues beat revival came into full force but, even so, he was highly influential on the nascent blues rock movement justifying the epithet 'king of the slide guitar' and influencing new generations of musicians such as **Stevie Ray Vaughan, Eric Clapton** and Finnish blues guitarist **Erja Lyytinnen**. The Rolling Stones' **Brian Jones** even adopted the alter ego of Elmo Lewis in deference to the blues legend. **John Mayall**'s tribute was to record a song of homage, *'Mr James'*, while Fleetwood Mac's **Jeremy Spencer** emulated Elmore's slide guitar style on songs like *'Shake Your Moneymaker'*. Elmore's in-house band consisted of **Little Johnny Jones** on barrelhouse piano, **J.J. Brown** on sax and a rhythm section of **Homesick James** and **Odie Payne** and they were commercially successful, having a top ten hit in the R&B charts with one of the most iconic blues numbers, period, *'Dust My Broom'*, in 1951. He is also closely associated with another **Robert Johnson** song *'Crossroads'* and passionate vocal performances as in his rendition of **Tampa Red's** *'It Hurts Me Too'*. **'The Ultimate Collection: 60 Electric Blues Classics by the King of the Slide Guitar'** tells you pretty much all you need to know including evidence of a twangy guitar style adopted by **Duane Eddy**.

**Howlin' Wolf:** Chester Burnett (AKA Howlin' Wolf) came from Mississippi and was performing alongside the likes of **Robert Johnson** and **Sonny Boy Williamson** by the time he was in his early twenties. An imposing 'bull' of man he stood more than six feet tall and weighed more than twenty stones. His first recordings for Philips' Records included *'How Many More Years'* (later covered in much reconstructed and extended form by Led Zeppelin on their brilliant 1969 album of progressive blues as *'How Many More Times?'*) but he moved to Chicago and opted for Chess Records for whom, working with **Willie Dixon**, he released classic electric blues records like the Dixon penned *'Spoonful'* (popularised by **Cream**); *'The Red Rooster'* (adapted by The Rolling Stones as *'Little Red Rooster'*); and *'Back Door Man'* (later covered by **The Doors**) between 1960 and 1961. Burnett also wrote some of his own hits like *'Smokestack Lightning'* (1956) demonstrating his unmistakeable gruff, growling vocal style) and the much covered *'Killing Floor'* (1964) with **Buddy Guy** and **Hubert Sumlin** on guitars.

**Robert Johnson: King of the Delta Blues Singers:** First heard on LP in 1962, guitarist and slide guitarist Robert Johnson's anguished vocals resonated with many and among songs covered by or inspired musicians in the sixties, seventies and beyond were *Crossroads Blues (1936 –* **Cream**'s *Crossroads), Come On In My Kitchen (1936 –* **Eric Clapton with Delaney and Bonnie***), Travelling Riverside Blues* (*1937 –* **Led Zeppelin**'s *Lemon Song), Love In Vain* (1937 – **The Rolling Stones**). It is hard to believe that this musician from the Mississippi Delta only released eleven 78 rpm recordings during his short life (He was another to die at the fated aged of 27). **Bob Dylan** first heard him on an acetate of the compilation cited above on the label he had just signed for (CBS/ Columbia) in 1961. Legendary staff producer **John Hammond** no doubt had something to do with this. . The legend that Johnson sold his soul to the devil in exchange for his music as depicted in songs like *Hellhound On My Trail, Me And The Devil Blues* and, of course, *Crossroads Blues*, was ingenuously presented to cinema audiences in the Coen Brothers film *Oh Brother Where Art Thou?*

**'We Three Kings'**

**Albert King**, like **B.B. King** (no relation – his real name was Albert Nelson) was born in Indianola, Mississippi. Like **Jimi Hendrix** he played left-handed on a right-handed guitar strung upside down. Although a couple of years older than B.B. King he was a relatively late starter and his stage name became King when B.B's *'Three O'Clock Blues'* became a big hit. He even called his Gibson Flaming V guitar 'Lucy' in honour of 'Lucille', B.B's guitar and constant travelling companion **Willie Dixon** arranged an audition for Parrot Records. His first hit was on the national R&B chart with *'Don't Throw Your Love on me So Strong'*. An *Ike Turner* produced album, **Big Blues**, was released in 1963. His big breakthrough came on signing to Stax Records in 1966 where he hooked up with house band **Booker T and The MGs**. Booker T Jones and William Bell wrote *'Born Under a Bad Sign'* for him and this was covered by **Cream** on their **Wheels of Fire** album. King's powerful voice, rhythmic guitar fills, clear tone and comprehensive use of note-bending demarcated a modernised form of the blues that appealed to hippy music lovers who would attend his concerts at venues such as The Fillmore West in San Francisco. Fans included myself who went to see him play at Glasgow's Barrowland later in his career when, after a dalliance with soul and funk he had returned to his blues rock roots. Other famous Albert King numbers include *'The Hunter'*, released in our target year of 1967 and covered by **Free** a few years later; *'Laundromat Blues'*, a **Rory Gallagher** favourite and *'Cross Cut Saw'* which **Eric Clapton** used to deconstruct and reconstruct his solo on **Cream's** *'Strange Brew'*.

**Riley B. King AKA Blues Boy King** hitchhiked to Memphis, Tennessee in 1946 to team up with his cousin **Bukka White** but his busking did not earn him any real money so he went back to being a tractor driver in Indianola. Much radio coverage and constant touring during the 1950s raised his profile and B B's big break eventually came with the release of **Live at the Regal** in 1964. His most famous song *'The Thrill Is Gone'* with its Bill Szymczyk produced strings (and with divorce from his second wife on his mind) was not actually written by B.B. but by **Roy Hawkins** in 1951 and was not released until 1969, the year he toured with **The Rolling Stones**. He has subsequently recorded with many rock luminaries such as **Joe Cocker, David Gilmour, Eric Clapton** and **Van Morrison**. King once said that **T-Bone Walker's** *'Stormy Monday'* was the prettiest sound he had ever heard. And it is true that King named his guitar Lucille' after rescuing it from a bar fire started during a fight over a woman called Lucille! The record I keep coming back to is **Now Appearing at Ole Miss**, a double album from 1980 on MCA records recorded live at Mississippi University.

Freddie **Christian AKA King** was a Texan who had a big influence on the development of blues rock. He broke through in 1960 after signing to the Federal label (a subsidiary of King Records) and recorded Billy Myles' *'Have You Ever Loved a Woman?'* which was later covered by Eric Clapton with **Derek and The Dominoes**. Freddie King was mainly known for instrumental numbers with his *'Hideaway'* covered by **John Mayall's Bluesbreakers** on their famous 'Beano' album in 1967. Freddie was particularly influential on **Eric Clapton, Peter Green** and **Chicken Shack's Stan Webb**.

**Lead Belly: The Library of Congress Recordings:** First released on LP in 1966, 17 years after his death, Texan Huddie Ledbetter was physically a giant of a man who played 12-string guitar and was a 'blues hollerer'. A contemporary of **Blind Lemon Jefferson**, Lead Belly's songs were captured for posterity by renowned blues chroniclers John and Alan Lomax. Among these songs were: *Goodnight Irene (1933), Pick A Bale of Cotton (1935) and Rock Island Line (1937/ 1948)*, the latter re-recorded for **Lead Belly's Last Sessions**.

**Lightnin' Hopkins:** Like Lead Belly, Texan Hopkins learned from **Blind Lemon Jefferson** (He sang about it in *Reminiscences of Blind Lemon)* and apparently got his nickname because of his musical association with **Wilson 'Thunder' Smith**, the pianist. The first part of his career was in the 1940s when he recorded songs like *Katie Mae (1946).* He was tempted back into recording by **Sam Charters** and **The Roots of Lightnin' Hopkins** was released on Folkway Records in1959 with *Penitentiary Blues* and *Mojo Hand* as two of the key songs. The tracks are mostly solo with some group ones which sound rushed and fade out abruptly. However, Hopkins' prowess on acoustic guitar and vocal range are there for all to hear. Hopkins enjoyed celebrity status touring Europe with the American Folk Blues Festival in 1964, opening for **The Grateful Dead** and **Jefferson Airplane** and appearing in 'The Blues According to Lightnin' Hopkins' an award winning documentary at the Chicago Film Festival.

**Otis Spann** came from Jackson, Mississippi and was another who died tragically young in 1970, aged 40. He was the pianist in **Muddy Waters'** band performing on *Hoochie Coochie Man* and also recorded with **Bo Diddley** and **Howlin' Wolf** and many others as the house Chess pianist. His first recording as Otis Spann was *It Must Have Been the Devil* which had both **B.B. King** and **Robert Lockwood** on guitar! Spann can be heard at his best on the Chess album **Muddy Waters at Newport** (the jazz festival). His first album **Otis Spann Is the Blues** was released in 1960 on the Candid label and is highly regarded. Nigel Williamson says, "Only **Robert Lockwood**'s guitar backed Spann, so he enjoyed plenty of space to indulge in the florid runs and two-handed rhythmic attack that characterised a style connecting Delta barrelhouse with modern Chicago." (124) He released a number of albums, his final studio LP in 1968 **The Biggest Thing since Colossus** with Fleetwood Mac's **Peter Green** on guitar. This included the brilliant *Bloody Murder*, the number selected for the Blue Horizon sampler LP. Sadly,

Otis did not have long to live when he recorded 'Last Call: Live at the Boston Tea Party, April 2, 1970'.

T-Bone Walker was a Texan who is regarded as the father of electric blues guitar dating from 1942 when he recorded *'Mean Old World'*, He is best known for *'Stormy Monday Blues'* (1947) which inspired B B King to go out and buy an electric guitar. His 1960 album T-Bone Blues (Atlantic, 1960) is highly regarded.

McKinley Morganfield aka Muddy Waters was yet another Mississippian. He was first recorded on a plantation in the Mississippi Delta by acclaimed musicologist Alan Lomax who, legend has it, found Waters looking for Robert Johnson who he didn't realise was already dead. Like B B King Muddy was anxious to swap tractors for a living in music and moved to Chicago in 1942, was befriended by Big Bill Broonzy and played guitar backing Sonny Boy Williamson. Muddy had mastered the harmonica as a teenager and this with his gruff, primeval vocal style and edgy guitar helped redefine the sound of the blues from a country mode to an electric and electrifying taxonomy. This can be heard on songs like *'I Can't Be Satisfied'* (1948 – a ground breaking moment in electric blues), *'(I'm) Your Hoochie Coochie Man'* (1954) and *'Mannish Boy'* (1955), all recorded for the Chess label. Nigel Williamson shoots the arrow straight in the target in his summation that Waters "vital, visceral and earthy, the bedrock of the electric blues, continuing to resonate to this day with the same thrilling force they must have packed at the time." (125)Those who played in Muddy Waters' bands reads like a 'who's who' of the blues: Buddy Guy, Little Walter, Junior Wells, Memphis Slim, Luther Johnson and a guitarist I had the great pleasure of listening to playing live atop piles of milk crates in a Brussels bar – Luther Tucker – until the police intervened following complaints about the noise at that late hour!

The Rolling Stones, of course, took their name from one of Muddy's songs and Mick Jagger lamented that Muddy was more appreciated in Europe than he was in his own country. Chess tried to reinvent him back to his roots as a country blues singer with Muddy Waters: Folk Singer in 1964 but artist and label performed a volte face with 1968's Electric Mud which was royally slated by many reviewers at the time but has since been re-evaluated in more positive terms.

The inverse invasion occurred with blues music, US bluesmen coming over here to be saluted as heroes by fans who became some of the most influential musicians of their generation. The same thing happened in the US, of course, especially in the form of Bob 'The Bear' Hite whose collection of blues 78s was legendary and whose Canned Heat were the principle players across the Atlantic in terms of competing with a host of superb blues/ boogie bands operating in the UK.

# Recommended Listening (For Starters)

**(Got The Blues) I Can't Be Satisfied** by **Mississippi John Hurt**
**Serves Me Right to Suffer** by **John Lee Hooker**
**Hound Dog** by **Big Mama Thornton**
**That's All Right** by **Arthur Big Boy Crudup**
**Crossroads and Dust My Broom** by **Robert Johnson**
**The Red Rooster** by **Howling Wolf**
**I Can't Quit You Baby** by **Otis Rush**
**Bo Diddley** by **Bo Diddley**
**Born Under a Bad Sign** by **Albert King**
**Did You Ever Love a Woman** by **B.B. King**
**Irene** by **Lead Belly**

Vietnam by **J.B. Lenoir**
Me and My Chauffeur Blues by **Memphis Minnie**
Chicken Shack Boogie by **Amos Milburn**
Bad Luck Blues by **Ma Rainey**
Careless Love by **Bessie Smith**
Statesboro Blues by **Taj Mahal**
Stormy Monday Blues by **T-Bone Walker**
(I'm) Your Hoochie Coochie Man by **Muddy Waters**
Messin' With The Kid by **Junior Wells**
Baby, Please Don't Go by **Big Joe Williams**
Don't Start Me Talking by **Sonny Boy Williamson**

## All That Jazz

In all time lists of jazz albums you will find **Miles Davis,** you will find **John Coltrane, Duke Ellington, Thelonius Monk, Louis Armstrong, Billie Holiday, Charles Mingus, Count Basie, Stan Getz, Bill Evans, Sonny Rollins, Ornette Coleman, Jimmy Smith, Larry Young, Ella Fitzgerald, Coleman Hawkins, Horace Silver, Keith Jarrett** and jazz fusion artists like **The Mahavishnu Orchestra, Herbie Hancock** and **Pat Metheny.** What they all have in common is that they are all largely American. The UK had a peculiarly British form of jazz often referred to as 'trad' with roots in ragtime and Dixieland music, its chief exponents included **Chris Barber, Ken Colyer, Humphrey Lyttelton, Acker Bilk** and **Kenny Ball**. This was usually dominated by brass instruments with no equivalent of **Bill Evans, Horace Silver** or **Thelonius Monk** in sight. As the Guardian newspaper pointed out 'trad jazz' was often regarded as "unloved, untrendy and underappreciated, British traditional jazz has a chequered history."[125] Skiffle music, most famously exemplified by **Lonnie Donegan**, was often as the 'errant child' of trad jazz and blues.

The UK was just on the cusp of jazz rock in 1967 with artists like **Graham Bond, Alan Price, Alan Bown, Brian Auger** and **The Nice** incorporating jazz elements into their music and the **Bonzo Dog Doo Dah Band** and **The New Vaudeville Band** doing great send-up jobs. Jazz rock outfits like **Colosseum, If, Traffic** and **Soft Machine** wouldn't start emerging until the late 1960s.

There are not many essays on The Beatles and jazz and I refer the reader to the brilliant article in allaboutjazz.com. This adds greatly to the stock of knowledge as well as offering wonderful insights (although perhaps trying a little too hard at times to make connections). In summary **Paul McCartney** was a long-time admirer of George Gershwin's music (His Dad Jim would play *I'll Build a Stairway To Paradise'* on the family 'Joanna') and **Brian Jones** of The Rolling Stones was once described by Mick Jagger as 'an old traddy'. (Of course, Stones' drummer Bill Watts' passion for jazz is well documented). I'd forgotten until I read the article that McCartney had played **Duke Ellington's** *'I Don't Get Around Much Anymore'* on his Russian tour. And, of course, an early Beatles recording of *'Ain't She Sweet'* sung willingly enough by John Lennon, is typical of the trad jazz/ skiffle approach minus the brass. At another angle, *'A Taste of Honey'*, included by The Beatles on their first album, was an example of 'Latin Jazz' that would be memorably performed by **Herb Alpert and His Tijuana Brass**. The group also played a number recorded by both **Benny Goodman** and **Artie Shaw** (*'Moonglow'*)

---

[125] Philip Clark, 8 September, 2016 "Trad Jazz: Don't Mock It, It's Part of British pop's DNA."

during their Hamburg residency. Novelty jazz such as **Fats Waller's *'Your Feet's Too Big'*** and ***'The Sheik of Araby'*** also featured. Although not overtly jazz, songs like ***'She Loves You'*** follow a Gershwin chord structure (***'Embraceable You'*** and ***'I Got Rhythm'*** in particular*). The authors also point out that The Beatles' breakthrough in America ***'I Want to Hold Your Hand'*** is a close relative of **Fats Waller's *'Honey Hush'*.** And then, of course, there is Humphrey Lyttelton's ***'Bad Penny Blues'*** as the template for ***'Lady Madonna'*** and in our target year ***'When I'm 64'*** which surely qualified as somewhere within the realms of jazz.

If truth be told The Beatles were a melting pot of influences and no musical style was excluded.

## 55 Recommended Jazz Albums 1960–1967: A Selective List

**1960**

**Kind of Blue** by **Miles Davis**
**My Favourite Things** by **John Coltrane**
**The Shape of Jazz to Come** by **Ornette Coleman**
**Mingus Ah Um** by **Charles Mingus**
**Open Sesame** by **Freddie Hubbard**
**We Insist!: Max Roach's Freedom Now Suite by Max Roach**
**The World of Cecil Taylor** by **Cecil Taylor**
**The Incredible Jazz guitar** by **Wes Montgomery**
**Sketches of Spain** by **Miles Davis**

**1961**

**Blues and the Abstract Truth** by **Oliver Nelson**
**Waltz for Derby** by **Bill Evans**
**Impressions** by **John Coltrane**
**Oh Yeah** by **Charles Mingus**
**Mosaic** by **Art Blakey**
**Bluesnik** by **Jackie McLean**
**A Night in Tunisia by Art Blakey and The Jazz Messenhers**

**1962**

**Portrait of Sheila** by **Sheila Jordan**
**We Free Kings** by **Roland Kirk**
**Nefertiti** by **Cecil Taylor**
**Go** by **Dexter Gordon**
**Night Train** by **Oscar Peterson**
**The Bridge** by **Sonny Rollins**
**Let Freedom Ring** by **Jackie McLean**

**1963**

**The Black Saint and the Sinner Lady** by **Charles Mingus**
**Impressions** by **John Coltrane**
**Idle Moments** by **Grant Green**
**Criss Cross** by **Thelonious Monk**
**Midnight Blue** by **Kenny Burrell**
**Getz/ Gilberto** by **Stan Getz and João Gilberto**

**1964**

> Out to Lunch by Eric Dolphy
> The Sidewinder by Lee Morgan
> Maiden Voyage by Herbie Hancock
> A Love Supreme by John Coltrane
> Life Time by Tony Williams
> The Cat by Jimmy Smith
> Point of Departure by Andrew Hill
> Four for Trane by Archie Shepp
> Speak No Evil by Wayne Shorter

**1965**

> Spirits Rejoice by Albert Ayler
> ESP by Miles Davis
> Organ Grinder Swing by Jimmy Smith
> Behind the 8 Ball by Baby Face Willette
> Song for My Father by Horace Silver Quintet
> A Charlie Brown Christmas Soundtrack by Vince Guaraldi
> Ascension by John Coltrane
> Heliocentric Worlds of Sun Ra by Sun Ra
> Jazz Suite inspired by Dylan Thomas' Under Milk Wood by Stan Tracey
> Indo-Jazz Suite by Joe Harriott and John Mayer

**1966**

> Meditations by John Coltrane
> Unity by Larry Young
> Unit Structures by Cecil Taylor
> Far East Suite by Duke Ellington
> Dream Weaver by Charles Lloyd
> The Jody Grind by Horace Silver

**1967**

> Atlantis by Sun Ra
> Electric Bath by Don Ellis
> Nefertiti by Miles Davis
> Sorcerer by Miles Davis
> The Real McCoy by McCoy Turner

Still to come were **Miles Davis** with *Bitches Brew* and *In a Silent Way* which would be hugely influential on the development of progressive jazz fusion rock music.

## Conclusions

So just how influential were The Beatles at the pinnacle of their creative powers in 1967 and the years preceding 'the summer of love'? And how big a say did they have in the development of popular music both at home and in the USA?

There is an old maxim – never trust academics for they have a habit of producing 'self-fulfilling prophecies'. 'I think therefore I am' becomes 'I predict therefore it is'. Give them a computer and this effect can be exacerbated. And I think this applies to a study by computing academics at London universities who attempted to find scientific proof of who were the true pop innovators. Jimi Hendrix, the subject of the last chapter of this book as a 'bridge across the Atlantic' is disregarded. So are Jim Morrison and The Doors. And most tellingly the role of The Beatles is underplayed. They do figure in one of the best years, defined as 1963 and 1975. 1963, because it is seen as the breakthrough year for 'pop', Tamla Motown and the folk boom (The Beatles, The Beach Boys, Marvin Gaye, Stevie Wonder and Bob Dylan); 1975 because it is 'the high-water mark of pop's expansive diversity with so many landmark albums pointing in different directions: stadium rock, progressive rock, Krautrock, art-rock sophistication, confessional song writing, psychedelic funk, and even jazz (the list is comprehensive with numerous albums cited). The subjective nature of what began earnestly as an objective exercise concerns me. It will not surprise you to learn that I am somewhat bemused why 1967 did not figure as a critical year. Perhaps Andy Gill and other media observers get it right when he says, "The study's greatest failing is its chart-oriented purview, when it is clear that most innovations take place at the margins." [126] Gill's observation leads him in one direction: punk and hip-hop, mine in another: progressive and psychedelic. [127]

In an analysis of The Beatles' contemporaries it is noticeable how many were either provided material by Lennon, McCartney and Lennon/ McCartney or covered that material or were influenced by the lyrical and musical innovativeness of that material. We have touched upon this effect as part of the 'British invasion' or the 'beat boom' in the USA but a thorough analysis will be left until a future volume perhaps. It is hard to imagine much serious opposition to the idea that 1967 was a watermark year for The Beatles and 'popular' music (or more accurately the harder edged 'rock' music). In 1968 the group would begin to implode but produced what has become many people's favourite Beatles album 'The Beatles', otherwise known as 'The White Album'. While the recordings made in 1967 might be considered their most innovative and creative the same innovation and creativity was delivered in 1968 in a more fractured and schizophrenic way.

I will not re-conjure the number of artists who cited 'Sergeant Pepper' as the catalysing moment, this is evident from the preceding text. But, without claiming to be a modern day Nostradamus when I started on this project ten years ago, I reflected that 2017 would be the 50th anniversary of The Beatles' most influential work and provide an ideal opportunity for re-appreciation and re-evaluation. I have done my best to trace the context and musical evolution that occurred during those heady, idealistic days and been amazed at just how much happens in one year of human existence (even if I did not finally complete the book until 2019!)

I hope you have enjoyed the journey we have made together and our probing of the context in which The Beatles and other '60s' musicians grew up and developed. I hope also that this book has illuminated how music, in the broader context of film, literature, social and cultural changes, and politics, made 1967 such a fertile and creative period in musical history. The arrival of SS Windrush and other ships from the West Indies brought a ready audience for imported reggae records; blues records brought not only the sounds into living rooms but the musicians themselves onto our stages while jazz, potentially the most creative format of all, brought a myriad of styles and experimentations that would inspire and challenge musicians to attain ever greater heights of creativity and sow

---

[126] "An academic breakdown of the charts got it badly wrong," argues Andy Gill in 'I' newspaper on 9th May, 2015 p 37.

[127] Although I must make it clear that I do listen to a lot of 'electronic' music, the category accorded by Discogs to describe a wealth of modern musical styles and am always discovering new music on Bandcamp and elsewhere.

the seeds for progressive rock, jazz fusion and experimental music of all hues and colours. Psychedelic rock, progressive rock, heavy metal and just good old fashioned rock thrived and developed in 1967 and would continue to do so throughout the sixties and much of the seventies and is as relevant and inspiring now as it was 50 years ago today. Long may it continue!

# Appendix One

What follows is a selective discography and chronology of the year 1967, what singles I would recommend you listen to and what significant albums were released, also a very selective look at what was happening. I make no claims that this appendix is fully comprehensive but I hope you will find it useful. I am indebted to the Marmalade Skies website in refreshing my memory, and thoroughly recommend you look at and listen to it at regular intervals.

I welcome the recollections of readers of any of the following, and comments on any aspects of the book, via e-mail at phil7jackson@madasafish.com

## 1967 Month by Month – A Selective Discography
### January

**45s**
**THE ATTACK-Try It/ We Don't Know (Decca)**
**THE BYSTANDERS-98.6/ Stubborn Kind of Fellow (Piccadilly) #45**
**THE CYMBALINE-I Don't Want It/ Where Did Love Go Wrong (Mercury)**
**SPENCER DAVIS GROUP-I'm a Man/ Can't Get Enough of it (Fontana) #9**
**CHRIS FARLOWE-My Way of Giving/ You're So Good for Me (Immediate) #48**
**THE KOOBAS-Sally/ Champagne and Caviar (Columbia)**
**THE LOOT-Baby Come Closer/ Baby Come Closer (diff. Version) (Page One)**
**THE MOODY BLUES-Life's Not Life/ He Can Win (Decca)**
**ROLLING STONES-Let's Spend the Night Together/ Ruby Tuesday (Decca) #3**
**THE SEARCHERS-Popcorn Double Feature/ Lovers (Pye)**
**THE TREMELOES-Here Comes My Baby/ Gentlemen of Pleasure (CBS) #4**
**WIMPLEWINCH-Rumble On Mersey Square South/ Typical British Workmanship*(Fontana) (*Some B-sides play 'Atmospheres').**
**LPs**
**MANFRED MANN-Soul of Mann (HMV) #40**
**VARIOUS ARTISTS-ORIGINAL SOUNDTRACK-The Family Way (Decca)**
**ROLLING STONES-Between the Buttons (Decca) #3**

In the year that album sales overtook singles sales for the first time, it is interesting to analyse what that meant in popular, if not artistic, terms. In truth tastes were still 'conservative' with albums by artists like The Seekers, Cliff Richard, The George Mitchell Minstrels, Val Doonican and Mrs Mills still proving popular and little sign of the rock and pop groups apart from The Beatles, The Rolling Stones and The Who. US artists populating the UK top 20 album charts included The Beach Boys, The Supremes, The Monkees, Bob Dylan and The Walker Brothers with Jim Reeves and Herb Alpert and his Tijuana Brass proving consistently popular. Soundtracks like 'The Sound of Music' and 'Doctor Zhivago' were particularly big sellers. Soul music, in its broadest sense (and blues), was represented by the likes of Dusty Springfield, Geno Washington and his Ram Jam Band and The Four Tops and, as the year wore on, John Mayall's Bluesbreakers, The Temptations and Otis Redding. Extending the analysis to the top 30 we find artists like The Hollies, The Kinks, The Spencer Davis Group and, later The Small Faces and Donovan breaking through.

As we move to the release of 'Sergeant Pepper's Lonely Hearts Club Band' and 'the summer of love' there is still a mix of rock and pop, represented principally by The Beatles, Jimi Hendrix, The Monkees and emerging groups like Cream and Pink Floyd but also a large representation of 'easier listening' artists such as The Dubliners, James Last and sountracks such as 'Fiddler on the Roof'. While 'Sergeant Pepper' holds the record for an album repeating its initial #1 success 50 years later (on its re-release in June, 2017 to commemorate its 50th anniversary), it is a sobering thought that 'The Sound of Music' has spent more weeks in total in the UK albums chart.

## What Was Happening in January, 1967?

**In summary: Prog rock is born, The Bee Gees arrive and the Jimi Hendrix Experience works its socks off.**
**Specifically:**

- ➢ The Beatles shoot promo films for the forthcoming *Strawberry Fields Forever/ Penny Lane* single.
- ➢ The Rolling Stones appear on the Ed Sullivan Show, playing a censored version of their latest single *Let's Spend The Night Together* ('some time' instead of 'the night') (A 'Top of the Pops' appearance would reveal Jagger gyrating around, Wyman standing stone faced, Watts similarly disinterested, Richard hardly visible and a hatted Jones miming on the piano).
- ➢ Prog rock groups Genesis and The Family were both conceived as, respectively, The Anon (who send a demo tape to Charterhouse fellow boy Jonathan King), and The Farinas from Leicester who decant to London with a new name and become regulars at the UFO club.
- ➢ The Bee Gees arrive in London from Australia and sign a five-year management deal with Robert Stigwood.
- ➢ Artists at the Marquee Club include The Herd, The Syn, Pink Floyd, The Bunch, Cream, Al Stewart, Marmalade and The Jimi Hendrix Experience.
- ➢ Five days later, on the 29th, Jimi Hendrix appears, along with The Who and The Koobas at Brian Epstein's Saville Theatre. Earlier in the month (the 11th), he had appeared, famously at The Bag O'Nails pub. Other gigs for the prolific Hendrix ensemble included: in the London area – the 7½ Club (4 nights); The Speakeasy, Tiles on Oxford Street and also a single night at The Upper Cut (see below); and elsewhere gigs included Bromley (twice), The Country Club, Kirklevington, Yorkshire, the New Century Hall, Manchester, the Toll Bar in Sheffield, the Beachcomber Club in Nottingham, and the Orford Cellar in Norwich.
- ➢ Pink Floyd has a weekly engagement at the UFO club and play at the Seymour Hall, W1 as part of the 'Freak Out Ethel' extravaganza. They also play at Reading University on the 14th; the Institute of Contemporary Arts,

London on the 16th; the Commonwealth Institute, Kensington on the 17th, the Birdcage Club, Portsmouth on the 21st and the Benn Memorial Hall, Rugby on the 23rd.

- The little remembered 'Upper Cut Club' run by Billy Walker boasts some top names including The Move, The Small Faces, Pink Floyd and The Jimi Hendrix Experience. The club was located in the Forest Gate Centre in Woodgrange Road (London E7)
- Soft Machine has dates at the Zebra Club and The Roundhouse.
- Donovan appears at The Royal Albert Hall on the 15th.
- Going around the country, The Move cut their teeth in the Leicester Corn Exchange, at Worcester College, at the Black Cat in Gravesend, at Wolverhampton Queen's, at Bristol University, Salisbury City Hall and the Nottingham Dungeon. North of the border, they visit Aberdeen University, and do two nights in Glasgow (Maryland) on the 21st and 22nd.
- The Cream appears at the Guild Hall, Southampton, the Bristol Corn Exchange, Stourbridge Town Hall and Leicester Granby Hall.
- Who gigs include the Bristol Locarno, the Central Pier, Morecombe, Leeds University, the Festival Hall in Kirkby-in-Ashfield, in Folkestone, the Ilford Palais and Hadleigh at the Kingsway Theatre on the 25th which also hosted The Small Faces who are in Hull the following night.
- The Spencer Davis Group appears at the Coventry Matrix, at Redcar in the Coatham Hotel, in Ipswich, at Queen Mary's College, London and Toft's in Folkestone
- Eric Burdon and the Animals play in the Coventry Locarno, Liverpool University, at the Stevenage Locarno, the Club A Go-Go, Newcastle and the Birdcage Club, Portsmouth
- The Incredible String Band appear at the Dunfermline Kinema on the 17th.

# February, 1967

### 45s
**THE ACTION**-Never Ever/ Twenty-Four Hours (Parlophone)
**THE BEATLES**-Penny Lane/ Strawberry Fields Forever (Parlophone) #2
**THE BEE GEES**-Spicks and Specks/ I am the World (Polydor)
**GRAHAM BOND ORGANISATION**-You've Got to Have Love Babe/ I Love You (Page One)
**PETULA CLARK**-This is My Song/ The Show is Over #1
**DONOVAN**-Mellow Yellow/ Preachin' Love (Pye) #8
**ENGELBERT HUMPERDINCK** – Release Me/ Ten Guitars (Decca) #1
**EPISODE SIX**-Love-Hate-Revenge/ Baby Baby Baby (Pye)
**THE EYES of BLUE**-Supermarket Full of Cans/ Don't Ask Me to Mend Your Broken Heart (Deram)
**THE HOLLIES**-On A Carousel/ All the World is Love (Parlophone) #4
**THE IVY LEAGUE**-Four and Twenty Hours/ Arrivederci Baby (Piccadilly)
**JOHN'S CHILDREN**-Just What You Want/ But She's Mine (Columbia)
**THE KNACK**-Marriage Guidance and Advice Bureau/ Dolly Catch Her Man (Piccadilly)
**LOVE AFFAIR**-She Smiled Sweetly/ Satisfaction Guaranteed (Decca)
**THE POETS**-Wooden Spoon/ In Your Tower (Decca)

THE SMOKE-My Friend Jack/ We can Take it (Columbia) #45
SOFT MACHINE-Love Makes Sweet Music/ Feelin', Reelin', Squeelin' (Polydor)
THE SPECTRES-We Ain't Got Nothin' Yet/ I Want it (Piccadilly)
TIMEBOX-I'll Always Love You/ Save Your Love (Piccadilly)
THE TROGGS-Give it to Me/ You're Lying (Page One) #12
THE VIPs-Straight Down to the Bottom/ In a Dream (Island)
LPs
THE TROGGS-Trogglodynamite (Page One) #10

## What Was Happening?

In summary: The infamous Stones' drug bust, Pink Floyd gigging hard and Jimi Hendrix playing in a sinking ship, the dawn of the 'pop opera'.
Specifically:

➢ Mick Jagger and Keith Richard are arrested on drugs charges after a police raid on Richard's home, Redlands.

➢ Pink Floyd record their debut single *Arnold Layne* at Abbey Road.

➢ Monkee Mickey Dolenz drops in on a Beatles recording session and also visits Paul McCartney's home during a promotional visit to London. He recalls the visit in the lyrics to the Monkees' hit single *Alternate Title (AKA Randy Scouse Git)*

➢ Pete Townsend reveals that he is writing a pop opera, "purely as a musical experiment".

➢ The Marquee hosts, among others, Al Stewart, The Action with the Marmalade, The Herd, the Spencer Davis Group, The Syn (weekly residence), the Bonzo Dog Doo Dah Band, The Birds, Cat Stevens and the Alan Bown Set.

➢ The UFO has Soft Machine (twice), the Bonzo Dog Doo Dah Band and Pink Floyd.

➢ The Roundhouse has Cat Stevens, Soft Machine (twice) and Jimi Hendrix.

➢ The Tiles venue (79-89 Oxford Street) has Family, the Move and Cat Stevens.

➢ Cream play at the Saville Theatre, London, Tofts in Folkestone, the Pavilion Baths in Matlock, the City Hall in Salisbury, the Starlight Ballroom in Greenford and the Bromel Club, Bromley

➢ Pink Floyd also play at Blaises with The Majority, at Cadenna's in Guildford, at the University of Sussex with Alan Bown, and The Wishful Thinking, in the New Addington Hotel in Surrey, the Guild Hall, Southampton, at Leicester Technical College, in the grandly named California Ballroom in Dunstable, the Ricky Tick Club in Hounslow, the Thames Hotel in Windsor, the Adelphi, West Bromwich and St Catherine's College, Cambridge.

➢ The Yardbirds appear at Barnsley Civic Hall, Tofts in Folkestone, the Glasgow Locarno, another Locarno in Coventry and at Sophia Gardens, Cardiff.

➢ The Jimi Hendrix Experience also plays in the Imperial Hotel in Darlington, Pavilions in Bath and Worthing, the Ricky Tick Club in Hounslow (they must have done OK as they were invited for a return visit), the Star in Croydon, the Civic Hall, Grays in Essex, the Sinking Ship in Stockport, the

Plaza in Newbury, the Blue Moon, Cheltenham, the New Cellar Club in South Shields, the Bromel Club, Bromley, the Dorothy Ballroom, Cambridge, at Leicester and York Universities, the Bristol Locarno and the Corn Exchange, Chelmsford. They also played at the Cliffs Pavilion, Southend with the Nashville Teens, The Koobas and Force Five on the 26th.

➢ The Move visit the Town Hall, Battersea, the Lotus Ballroom, Forest Gate, the Town Hall, High Wycombe, the Mojo in Sheffield, the Top Spot in Ross-On-Wye, Manchester University and the Locarno, Coventry.

➢ The Birmingham Plaza hosts The Moody Blues and The Attack.

➢ The Spencer Davis Group are at the Starlight Ballroom, Boston, at a Radio London event in the Kingsway Theatre in Hadley (with among others Sounds Incorporated and The Fourmost), at the Sherwood Rooms in Nottingham and the Top Deck in Purfleet.

➢ Who gigs include the Locarno, Coventry, the Birdcage Club in Portsmouth, the Grimsby Gaiety, the Starlight Ballroom in Greenford and the Royal Links Pavilion in Cromer.

➢ Manfred Mann, Family, Cat Stevens and the Wilde Flowers are also doing their fair share of touring.

➢ The Graham Bond Organisation does one of their famous sessions in the Klooks Kleek club in Hampstead.

➢ Both Cream and Pink Floyd are on the bill at an all-night rave in the Queen's Hall, Leeds (3rd).

## March, 1967

**45s**
**THE ATTACK-Hi-Ho Silver Lining/ Any More Than I Do (Decca)**
**JEFF BECK-Hi-Ho Silver Lining/ Beck's Bolero (Columbia) #14**
**ALAN BOWN SET-Gonna Fix You Good/ I Really Care (Pye)**
**JIMI HENDRIX EXPERIENCE-Purple Haze/ 51st Anniversary (Track) #3**
**MANFRED MANN-Ha Ha Said the Clown/ Feeling So Good (Fontana) #4**
**MARMALADE-Can't Stop Now/ There Ain't No Use in Hangin' on (CBS)**
**THE MINDBENDERS-We'll Talk About it Tomorrow/ Far Across Town (Fontana)**
**THE MOVE-I Can Hear the Grass Grow/ Wave The Flag and Stop The Train (Deram) #5**
**PINK FLOYD-Arnold Layne/ Candy and a Currant Bun (Columbia) #20**
**SMALL FACES-I Can't Make it/ Just Passing (Decca) #26**
**CAT STEVENS-I'm Gonna Get Me a Gun/ School is Out (Deram) #6**
**THE ZOMBIES-Going Out of My Head/ She Does Everything for Me (Decca)**
**LPs**
**CAT STEVENS-Matthew and Son (Deram) #7**

# What Was Happening?

In summary: Traffic hit the road, Pink Floyd continue to gig prodigiously and record their first album; Cream and Who fly to the States; Small Faces are in action.

**Specifically:**

- Steve Winwood quits The Spencer Davis Group, and forms a new group, Traffic with Jim Capaldi, Chris Wood and Dave Mason.
- Pink Floyd sign to EMI and begin recording their first album at Abbey Road where they meet the Beatles (21st). Paul McCartney says some encouraging words to Syd Barrett. They also make a promotional film for the *Arnold Layne* 45.
- At the end of March, the Jimi Hendrix Experience begins a month long tour with The Walker Brothers, Cat Stevens and Engelbert Humperdinck.
- Meanwhile, The Small Faces tour with Roy Orbison, and appearances include the ABCs in Edinburgh and Carlisle, the Glasgow and Leeds Odeon, Newcastle City Hall, and both the Doncaster and Wolverhampton Gaumont.
- Cream and The Who are in New York as part of DJ Murray the K's 'Music in the Fifth Dimension'.
- The Marquee hosts Al Stewart, Pink Floyd, Skip Bifferty, The Herd, Marmalade (thrice), the Bonzo Dog Doo Dah Band, Savoy Brown, Cream, Family and The Amboy Dukes from the States (spoiled for choice as they say).
- Pink Floyd are as busy as ever with gigs at the Saville Theatre (which also hosts The Bee Gees), the Canterbury, Kingston, Rotherham and Enfield Techs, the Ricky Ticks in Hounslow and Windsor, a hall in Little Titchfield St, London – the Corn Exchange, Bristol, the Winter Gardens in Malvern, the Agincourt Ballroom, Camberley. The Top Spot Ballroom, Ross-on-Wye, Market Hall, St Albans, the Assembly Rooms in Worthing and twice at Eel Pie Island, Twickenham.
- The Middle Earth Club has a succession of progressive acts including Family, Pink Floyd, The Moody Blues and the Crazy World of Arthur Brown.
- The UFO Club hosts the Soft Machine three times, once with the Pink Floyd and the Crazy World of Arthur Brown.
- Soft Machine also has a weekly residency at the Speakeasy and play at the London School of Economics and Padworth Hall, Reading.
- At The Tiles, The Move, Amen Corner, The Easy Beats, John's Children with their new lead guitarist Marc Bolan and Eyes of Blue all play along with a lot of lesser known acts.
- The Upper Cut has Episode Six, The Herd, Alan Bown and The Syn.
- Jimi Hendrix also plays at the Assembly Hall in Aylesbury, the International Club, Leeds the Starlight Room in Boston, the Giro Club, Ilkley, the Skyline Ballroom in Hull, the Club A Go-Go, Newcastle, the Orchid Ballroom, Purley, the Guild Hall, Southampton and the Tabernacle Club, Stockport.
- The Troggs are at the Bournemouth Winter Gardens, the California Ballroom, Dunstable, Coventry Theatre and the Cardiff Capitol.
- The Top rank in Cardiff hosts The Who and The Herd.
- The Who are also in the California Ballroom in Dunstable, Exeter University and Granby Halls in Leicester.
- Cream opens the month with gigs at the Belfast Ulster Hall and Queen's University.

- ➤ The Hollies and Family are gigging extensively, and Brian Auger and The Trinity are also starting to put themselves about a bit.
- ➤ Sheffield University hosts an excellent evening of folk on the 15th with Bert Jansch, John Renbourn and the Incredible String Band.

## April, 1967

45s

ARTWOODS – What Shall I Do/ In the Deep End (Parlophone)

BEE GEES – New York Mining Disaster 1941/ I Can't See Nobody (Polydor) #12

DAVID BOWIE – The Laughing Gnome/ The Gospel According to Tony Day (Deram)

CHRIS FARLOWE – Yesterday's Papers/ Life is but Nothing (Immediate)

THE HERD – I Can Fly/ Diary of a Narcissist (Fontana)

DENNY LAINE – Say You Don't Mind/ Ask the People (Deram)

THE OUTER LIMITS-Just One More Chance/ Help Me Please (Deram)

THE PRETTY THINGS – Children/ My Time (Fontana)

PANDEMONIUM – No Presents for Me/ The Sun Shines from His Eyes (CBS)

PURPLE GANG – Granny Takes a Trip/ Bootleg Whiskey (Big T)

THE QUIK – Love is a Beautiful Thing/ Bert's Apple Crumble (Deram)

TERRY REID AND THE JAYWALKERS – The Hand Don't Fit the Glove/ This Time (Columbia)

THE ROKES – Let's Live for Today/ Ride On (RCA)

THE SEARCHERS – Western Union/ I'll Cry Tomorrow (Pye)

SANDIE SHAW – Puppet on a String/ Tell the Boys (Pye) #1

SHOTGUN EXPRESS – Funny 'Cos Neither Could I/ Indian Thing (Columbia)

TIMEBOX – Soul Sauce/ I Wish I Could Jerk Like My Uncle Cyril (Piccadilly)

TWICE AS MUCH – Crystal Ball/ Why Don't They All Go and leave Me Alone (Immediate)

WARM SOUNDS – The Birds and Bees/ Doo Dah (Deram)

THE WHO – Pictures of Lily/ Doctor Doctor (Track) #4

YARDBIRDS – Little Games/ Puzzles (Columbia)

## What Was Happening?

In summary: The 'summer of love' beckons in the month of the 14 Hour Technicolour Dream; 'A Whiter Shade of Pale'; The Marquee and UFO are doing a roaring trade.

Specifically:

- ➤ Gary Brooker with lyricist Keith Reid advertises in the Melody Maker for musicians to play their new songs. Thus, The Paramounts R&B group become the proto progressive Procol Harum with *'A Whiter Shade of Pale'* and the 'summer of love' on the horizon.
- ➤ The 14 Hour Technicolor Dream all-nighter is held at London's Alexandra Palace on the 29th.
- ➤ Donovan plays two dates at the Saville Theatre in London.

- Cream, The Move, The Kinks and The Troggs all appear at the Daily Express newspaper Record Star Show at Wembley Empire Pool on the 16th.
- The Syn and The Herd both have weekly gigs at The Marquee. The Marmalade, Family, Skip Bifferty, The Action, Chris Farlowe and The Jeff Beck Group are also among those that appear.
- The UFO hosts Soft Machine, Tomorrow (with whom Jimi Hendrix did a cameo on bass), The Crazy World of Arthur Brown and Pink Floyd.
- Tim Buckley and Roy Harper (on the same bill), Family, Soft Machine, Brian Auger and The Trinity with Julie Driscoll and Fairport Convention all play at the Electric Garden.
- The Roundhouse hosts Pink Floyd, Soft Machine (three times), Creation and the Sam Gopal Indian Group (three times).
- Soft Machine also plays a weekly residency at the Speakeasy.
- Pink Floyd are still gigging hard along with all the 'usual suspects' and emerging acts such as Traffic, with 'Paper Sun' about to grab attention.

## May, 1967

**45s**

THE BEATSTALKERS – My One Chance to Make it/ Ain't Got No Soul (CBS)

THE BRAIN – Nightmares in Red/ Kick the Donkey (Parlophone)

ERIC BURDON/NEW ANIMALS – When I Was Young/ A Girl Named Sandoz (MGM) #45

DAVE CLARK 5 – Tabitha Twitchit/ Man in a Pin-Striped Suit (Columbia)

JIMI HENDRIX EXPERIENCE – The Wind Cries Mary/ Highway Chile (Track) #6

HOLLIES – Carrie-Anne/ Signs That Will Never Change (Parlophone) #3

JOHN'S CHILDREN – Desdemona/ Remember Thomas a Becket (Track)

THE KINKS – Waterloo Sunset/ Act Nice and Gentle (Pye) #2

THE KOOBAS – Gypsy Fred/ City Girl (Columbia)

MANFRED MANN – Sweet Pea/ One Way (Fontana) #36

THE MIRAGE – The Wedding of Ramona Blair/ Lazy Man (Phillips)

MONOPOLY – House of Lords/ Magic Carpet (Polydor)

MOODY BLUES – Fly Me High/ Really Haven't Got the Time (Decca)

PROCUL HARUM – A Whiter Shade of Pale/ Lime Street Blues (Deram) #1

SMALL FACES – Patterns/ E Too D (Decca)

TOMORROW – My White Bicycle/ Clermont Lake (Parlophone)

TRAFFIC – Paper Sun/ Giving to You (Island) #5

THE TREMELOES – Silence is Golden/ Let your Hair Hang Down (CBS) #1

THE TROGGS – -Night of the Long Grass/ Girl in Black (Page One) #17

**LPs**

JIMI HENDRIX EXPERIENCE – Are You Experienced? (Track) #2

THE KINKS – Live at Kelvin Hall (Pye)

THE PRETTY THINGS – Emotions (Fontana)

# What Was Happening?

**In summary: Brian Jones becomes the third stone to be arrested, Sergeant Pepper's is premiered and The Move gets into trouble; some tapes are lost.**
Specifically:

➤ Brian Jones is arrested on drug charges.

➤ **Sgt Pepper's Lonely Hearts Club Band** is premiered at a party thrown by manager Brian Epstein. Paul McCartney meets photographer Linda Eastman for the second time at the party (the first occasion being in the Bag O'Nails club).

➤ The Move's penchant for publicity seeking and zany antics leads to threatened action by a member of the audience at a gig at the Civic Hall in Nantwich who slips on a banana thrown from the stage, and injures himself. This follows a five month 'sentence' for setting the stage on fire at the Marquee. The tapes of the first album which had apparently been stolen the previous month are found on a building site. Steve Winwood also loses the tape of the first Traffic album at an NME Poll winners' concert at Wembley (The Small Faces, The Yardbirds, The Move, The Troggs, The Spencer Davis Group, Cat Stevens and Cream all appear at the concert).

➤ Ex-T Bones members Keith Emerson (organ) and Lee Jackson (bass) put together a group to back American soul singer PP Arnold. Guitarist Davy O'List and drummer Ian Hague. Brian 'Blinky' Davison will soon come in on drums to form another 'proto progressive' group, The Nice, who will become a massive success for the Immediate label.

➤ An event called 'Barbeque 67' takes place at the unlikely venue of the Tulip Ball Auction Hall in Spalding, Lincolnshire on 29th May. The Jimi Hendrix Experience, Cream, Reno Washington and The Ram Jam Band, Pink Floyd, The Move and Zoot Money all appear for a total admission cost of £1! Considering things agricultural rather than botanical, the Royal Agricultural College, Chippenham may not be a household name for concert goers but they did host Cream, The Yardbirds and The Mindbenders on the 6th.

➤ Soft Machine begins a weekly residence at London's Theatre Royal in Stratford and play weekly at The Speakeasy which also hosts Brian Auger, and The Trinity and Amen Corner. The Tiles Club hosts weekly performances from Amen Corner.

➤ Soft Machine also plays at the UFO Club which includes The, Crazy World of Arthur Brown, The Move and Tomorrow among its other acts.

➤ The Marquee hosts The Herd, Skip Bifferty, Alan Bown, Marmalade (three times), Creation, The Syn (three times), the Bonzos, Family, Cream, the Spencer Davis Group and Bluesyard, about to change their name to Ten Years After.

➤ The Roundhouse at Chalk Farm has the Jeff Beck Group, Simon Dupree, and the Big Sound and Sam Gopal.

➤ Appearing at the Saville Theatre is the Jimi Hendrix Experience.

➤ The Upper Cut has a varied line-up of groups including The Herd, The Merseys, The Kinks and The Troggs.

➤ A bit of Scottish history is made by the appearance of The Bee Gees at Galashiels Town Hall on the 26th.

## June, 1967 The Month of Pepper-The Summer of Love Arrives

**45s**

THE ACTION-Shadows and Reflections/ Something Has Hit Me (Parlophone)

THE ATTACK-Created by Clive/ Colour of My Mind (Decca)

THE BYSTANDERS-Royal Blue Summer Sunshine Day/ Make Up Your Mind (Piccadilly)

CREAM-Strange Brew/ Tales of Brave Ulysses (Reaction) #17

THE EASYBEATS-Heaven and Hell/ Pretty Girl (UA)

EPISODE SIX-Morning Dew/Sunshine Girl (Pye)

CHRIS FARLOWE-Moanin'/ What Have I Been Doing (Immediate) #46

PICCADILLY LINE-At the Third Stroke/ How Could You Say You're Leaving Me (CBS)

PINK FLOYD-See Emily Play/ Scarecrow (Columbia) #6

SMALL FACES-Here Comes the Nice/ Talk to You (Immediate) #12

THE SYN-Created by Clive/ Grounded (Deram)

TRAFFIC JAM-Almost but Not Quite There/ Wait Just a Minute (Piccadilly)

THE YOUNG IDEA-With a Little Help from My Friends/ Colours if Darkness (Columbia) #10

**LPs**

THE BEATLES-Sgt Pepper's Lonely Hearts Club Band (Parlophone) #1

DAVID BOWIE-David Bowie (Decca)

DONOVAN-Sunshine Superman (Pye) #25

HOLLIES-Evolution (Parlophone) #13

SMALL FACES-Small Faces (Immediate) #21

## What Was Happening?

In summary: Butterflies break on a wheel; All You Need is Love makes history; Hendrix and The Who head the Monterey Pop Festival; Sergeant Pepper!
Specifically:

➤ Mick Jagger and Keith Richard are jailed for drug offences, their sentences three months and one year respectively. They only spend one night in prison and are released pending appeal. The Times runs a story incorporating the famous phrase about the folly of breaking a butterfly on a wheel.

➤ The Beatles, along with some celebrity guests, sing *All You Need is Love* on the first worldwide live satellite TV broadcast, entitled **Our World**. As if **Sergeant Pepper** and **Magical Mystery Tour** were not enough, it is revealed that a full length animated film is to be made to be called **Yellow Submarine.**

➤ The Jimi Hendrix Experience and The Who star at the Monterey International Pop Festival.

➤ The Beatles watch the Jimi Hendrix Experience at Brian Epstein's Saville Theatre in London's west end. Procol Harum and Denny Laine's Electric String Band are the support. Manfred Mann, The Yardbirds and The Zombies are on the bill later in the month.

- ➢ The Crazy World of Arthur Brown and Tomorrow appear at the Electric Garden. For Marc Bolan, memories of the venue are not so good as he quits John's Children after a disastrous gig there.
- ➢ Among the acts playing at the UFO Club this month are Pink Floyd, Procol Harum, The Graham Bond Organisation, The Crazy World of Arthur Brown, Soft Machine and Tomorrow,
- ➢ Popular groups at The Marquee include Marmalade, The Herd, Timebox and The Syn, The Jeff Beck Group, Denny Laine and the Electric String Band, Procol Harum, Family, Ten Years After, The Creation, Terry Reid, and The Action while Al Stewart and Piccadilly Line have a weekly residency.
- ➢ The Tiles Club hosts Amen Corner and The Pink Floyd
- ➢ Soft Machine and The Crazy World of Arthur Brown play at the London School Of Economics 'Midsummer Night's Dream' on the 24th

# July, 1967 – Post Pepper

### 45s
ART-What's that Sound/ Rome Take Away Three (Island)
THE BEATLES – All You Need is Love/ Baby You're a Rich Man (Parlophone) #1
JEFF BECK – Tallyman/ Rock My Plimsoul (Columbia) #30
BEE GEES – To Love Somebody/ Close Another Door (Polydor) #41
DAVE DAVIES – Death of a Clown/ Love Me Till the Sun Shines (Pye) #3
SPENCER DAVIS GROUP – Time Seller/ Don't Want You No More (Fontana) #30
NIRVANA – Tiny Goddess/ I Believe in Magic (Island)
RUPERT'S PEOPLE – Reflections of Charles Brown/ Hold On (Columbia)
SHARON TANDY – Stay with Me/ Hold On (Atlantic)
KEITH WEST – Excerpt from 'A Teenage Opera' Parts 1&2 (Parlophone) #2

### LPs
BEE GEES – First (Polydor) #8
THE INCREDIBLE STRING BAND – 5000 Spirits or The Layers of The Onion (Elektra) #26
THE SHADOWS – JIGSAW #8

# What Was Happening?

In summary: The Who show their solidarity with Jagger and Richard; the International Love-In signals that the 'Summer of Love' has come to the UK and Jeff Beck dons a fur coat on stage; an attempt is made to 'free the pirates'; Pink Floyd go to Scotland.

Specifically:
- ➢ Keith Richard gets an unconditional discharge and Mick Jagger a conditional one after the appeal against drugs charges, The Who show their solidarity by covering two Stones' songs including *The Last Time*.

- Old Paramounts members Robin Trower and Barry (BJ) Wilson replace Ray Royer and Bobby Harrison in Procol Harum, and set about recording their classic debut album.
- There is a major event at Alexandra Palace called 'The International Love-In Festival' (the summer of love has truly arrived!). Pink Floyd, Eric Burdon, Brian Auger, Julie Driscoll and The Trinity, The Crazy World of Arthur Brown, Blossom Toes, Tomorrow and Creation are on the bill. There is also an event called 'Free The Pirates' in support of the radio stations under threat from the British establishment with The Move and The Pretty Things providing the music.
- A charity event in aid of the St John's Ambulance Service is held at the British Woodstock in Oxfordshire with Manfred Mann, The Nice and PP Arnold, The Jeff Beck Group, and Simon Dupree and The Big Sound on the bill.
- At The Roundhouse 'Angry Arts Festival' are The Social Deviants, Procol Harum, The Crazy World of Arthur Brown, The Yardbirds, Pink Floyd, Moody Blues and The Outer Limits.
- The Who begins their first full US tour on the 14th supporting Herman's Hermits and The Blues Magoos.
- Jeff Beck wears a fur coat but no shoes at a gig at the Saville Theatre.
- The Happening 44 club (44 Gerrard St) appearances include The (Social) Deviants, Fairport Convention and Roy Harper,
- Among those appearing at The Electric Garden in Covent Garden, are The Crazy World of Arthur Brown Fairport Convention and Marc Bolan's new group Tyrannosaurus Rex.
- At the UFO are The Pretty Things, Denny Laine, The Crazy World of Arthur Brown, Tomorrow, Pink Floyd and Fairport Convention.
- The Marquee is as busy as ever with weekly appearances by Al Stewart, Marmalade, Piccadilly Line, The Tribe; and also, gigs by The Herd, Ten Years After, Nite People, Family, Creation, The Move, The Bonzo Dog Doo Dah Band, The Syn, The Iveys and The Amboy Dukes.
- Scottish music fans have a visit by Pink Floyd to The Beach Ballroom in Aberdeen on the 22nd.
- Jimi Hendrix Experience didn't appear to have as easy a time of it on a US tour supporting strange bedfellows The Monkees as they did at Monterey but it turned out that their removal from the tour after complaints was an orchestrated publicity coup.
- The 'International Love-In Festival' is held at Alexandra Palace in London (29th). Eric Burdon, Pink Floyd, Crazy World of Arthur Brown, Tomorrow, Blossom Toes, Brian Auger, Julie Driscoll & the Trinity, Apostolic Intervention and The Creation are the main attractions.
- 'Free The Pirates' takes place at Alexandra Palace, featuring The Move and The Pretty Things (22nd).
- Cream and The Moody Blues appear in the Uppercut Club. Cream also appears at the Kinema in Dunfermline.
- The Blenheim Palace Pop Festival on the 23rd has The Jeff Beck Group, Manfred Mann, PP Arnold with The Nice and Simon Dupree's Big Sound.
- Pink Floyd is as well-travelled as ever including a visit to The Isle of Man to play at The Palace in Douglas. They are also on tour in Scotland playing

the Two Red Shoes Ballroom in Elgin, the Greenock Palladium, the Ballerina Ballroom in Nairn and the Maryland, Glasgow.

➢ At Les Cousins Club in Soho, eminent folk/ rock artists such as Bert Jansch, Pete Brown and his Poetry Band, Roy Harper and Davy Graham make appearances.

➢ Family are gigging heavily in Newcastle (and area), Manchester and the south. Ten Years After and Wages of Sin are also added to the list of groups putting themselves about a bit.

## August, 1967

45s

**ERIC BURDON AND THE ANIMALS – Good Times/ Ain't That So (MGM) #20**

**THE BYSTANDERS – Pattern People/ Green Grass (Piccadilly)**

**DANTALIAN'S CHARIOT – Madman Running Through the Fields/ The Sun Came Bursting Through My Cloud (Columbia)**

**THE FAIRYTALE – Guess I Was Dreaming/ Run and Hide (Decca)**

**BILL FAY – Some Good Advice/ Screams in the Ears (Deram)**

**THE FLOWERPOT MEN – Let's Go to San Francisco Parts 1 & 2 (Deram) #4**

**JIMI HENDRIX EXPERIENCE – Burning of the Midnight Lamp/ The Stars That Play with Laughing Sam's Dice (Track) #18**

**THE HERD – From the Underworld/ Sweet William (Fontana) #6**

**THE LOOT – Whenever You're Ready/ I Got What You Want (CBS)**

**THE MOVE – Flowers in the Rain/ (Here We Go Round) The Lemon Tree (Regal Zonophone) #2**

**THE ORANGE BICYCLE – Hyacinth Threads/ Amy Peate (Columbia)**

**THE ROLLING STONES – We Love You/ Dandelion (Decca) #8**

**SKIP BIFFERTY – On Love/ Cover Girl (RCA)**

**THE SMALL FACES – Itchycoo Park/ I'm Only Dreaming (Immediate) #3**

**THE SMOKE – If The Weather's Sunny/ I Would If I Could but I Can't (Columbia)**

**THE SPECTRUM – Portobello Road/ Comes the Dawn (RCA)**

**TRAFFIC – Hole in My Shoe/ Smiling Phases (Island) #2**

**THE TREMELOES – Even The Bad Times are Good/ Jenny's Alright (CBS) #4**

**WARM SOUNDS – Sticks and Stones/ Angeline (Immediate)**

**THE WHO – The Last Time/ Under My Thumb (Track) #44**

**LPS**

**PINK FLOYD – Piper at the Gates Of Dawn (Columbia) #6**

# What Was Happening?

In Summary: Brian Epstein passes, the tide turns against pirate radio, The Who cause havoc in America and Pink Floyd release their first LP but lose Syd Barrett; John Peel leaves the perfumed garden to present Top Gear on Radio One; The Electric Garden becomes The Middle Earth; The Festival of the Flower Children weekend costs £1.50; The National Blues and Jazz Festival reaches its seventh year; the ballrooms are busy!

Specifically:

> This month sees the tragic death of NEMS entrepreneur and Beatles manager Brian Epstein. The group hear the news in Bangor, North Wales where they are attending a course run by the Maharishi Mahesh Yogi.

> A marathon last 'Perfumed Garden' show on the 14th presented by John Peel marks the end of Radio London. Peel, subsequently, becomes the co-presenter of BBC Radio 1's 'underground' station's 'Top Gear'. Many of the other DJs also find jobs with Radio 1. Radio Caroline defiantly vows to carry on broadcasting from Dutch waters.

> Pink Floyd's prolific touring is stopped temporarily in its tracks as Syd Barrett collapses from exhaustion.

> The Who creates havoc on the US TV comedy show 'The Smothers Brothers' when an explosion at the climax of their act wrecks Keith Moon's drum kit and Pete Townsend's hearing.

> The Electric Garden club at 43 King Street, Covent Garden folds to be replaced by Tolkien inspired The Middle Earth. Among those appearing are The Crazy World of Arthur Brown, Fairport Convention and The Soft Machine.

> The UFO Club move into the new, improved Roundhouse premises at 31 Tottenham Court Road reassuring its members that all will be well. There are some pretty good bills to choose from including Family, The Crazy World of Arthur Brown, The Incredible String Band and The Pretty Things.

> "By kind permission of His Grace the Duke of Bedford", a 3 day non-stop happening called The Festival of the Flower Children is held in Woburn Abbey over three days starting on the 26th. On the bill are The Small Faces, The Bee Gees, The Jeff Beck Group, Marmalade, Eric Burdon, Denny Laine, Alan Price, Family, Al Stewart, Dantalian's Chariot, Blossom Toes, The Syn. Tintern Abbey and Breakthru'. The cost of a day ticket is £1 and a weekend ticket £1.50 (or I should say 30 shillings old money).

> Hastings also hosts a festival of music with a varied line-up including The Kinks, Dave, Dee, Dozy, Beaky, Mick & Tich and the hard gigging Crazy World of Arthur Brown, Unit 4+2 play on Hastings Pier as a replacement for Pink Floyd.

> The 7th National Jazz and Blues Festival takes place at Windsor Race Course. Cream, Jeff Beck, Donovan, Fleetwood Mac Small Faces, The Move, Paul Jones, Eric Burdon, Amen Corner, John Mayall, Denny Laine, PP Arnold & The Nice, The Syn, The Nite People, Marmalade, Tomorrow, Timebox, Zoot Money, Ten Years After, Al Stewart, Piccadilly Line, Alan Bown, Blossom Toes and The Pentangle and Arthur Brown who was rescued from serious injury when his flaming hat was doused by beer. The coloured fibre glass futuristic design of the stage proved not to be robust enough and had to be supported with scaffolding. Cream commences their second U.S tour with two weeks at the Fillmore West in San Francisco (22nd).

> It is a sad conclusion to the month at the Saville Theatre but it hosts The Jeff Beck Group, The Jimi Hendrix Experience and The Crazy World of Arthur Brown.

334

- Appearing at the London Speakeasy, are Les Fleur de Lys with Sharon Tandy, Cream, Fairport Convention and Dantalian's Chariot.
- At the Tiles, are Tomorrow, The Bee Gees, Downliners Sect, Zoot Money and Dantalian's Chariot, Human Instinct and The Amboy Dukes.
- There are some great acts at the Uppercut Club this month like Eric Burdon and The Animals, The Small Faces, Rupert's People and The Bee Gees.
- Among those appearing at The Marquee, are The Action, The Creation, Family, Eric Burdon and The Animals, The Jeff Beck Group, The Iveys, Terry Reid, Amen Corner with Al Stewart, Studio Six, The Tribe and The Syn playing multiple gigs, and Piccadilly Line, Marmalade and Timebox enjoying a monthly 'residence'.
- The California Ballroom in Dunstable attracts some top acts in The Bee Gees, The Small Faces, The Jeff Beck Group and The Move. As does the Starlite Ballroom in Greenford which hosts The Bee Gees, The Small Faces, The Syn, Jeff Beck and Human Instinct while Toft's in Folkestone has Chicken Shack, The Amboy Dukes and The Jeff Beck Group,
- The Small Faces also play at the Beach Ballroom in Aberdeen and Perth City Hall and visit the Isle of Man. Following Pink Floyd they also agree to play in at the Nairn Ballerina but don't turn up (Did they get lost?). Dantalian's Chariot do manage to fulfil their engagement in Nairn on the last day of the month.

# September, 1967

**45s**

BEE GEES – Massachusetts/ Barker of the UFO (Polydor) #1

CRAZY WORLD OF ARTHUR BROWN – Devil's Grip/ Give Him a Flower (Track)

THE FAIRYTALE – Lovely People/ Listen to Mary Cry (Decca)

FLEUR-DE-LYS – I Can See the Light/ Prodigal Son (Polydor)

HOLLIES – King Midas in Reverse/ Everything is Sunshine (Parlophone) #18

THE IDLE RACE – Imposters of Life's Magazine/ Sitting in My Tree (Liberty)

KALEIDOSCOPE – Flight from Ashiya/ Holidaymaker (Fontana)

MARMALADE – I See the Rain/ Laughing Man (CBS)

DAVID MCWILLIAMS – Days of Pearly Spencer/ Harlem Lady (Major Minor)

THE MINDBENDERS – The Letter/ My New Day and Age (Fontana) #42

THE MOODY BLUES – Love and Beauty/ Leave This Man Alone (Decca)

NIRVANA – Pentecost Hotel/ Feelin' Shattered (Island)

THE PEEP SHOW – Your Servant, Stephen/ Mazy (Polydor)

PICCADILLY LINE – Emily Small (The Huge World Thereof)/ Gone Gone Gone (CBS)

PROCUL HARUM – Homburg/ Good Captain Clack (Regal Zonophone) #5

RENAISSANCE – Mary Jane/ Daytime Lovers (Polydor)

SANDS – Mrs Gillespie's Refrigerator/ Listen to the Sky (Reaction)

THE SYN – Flowerman/ 14 Hour Technicolour Dream (Deram)

**TANGERINE PEEL** – Every Christian Lion-Hearted Man Will Show You/ Trapped (UA)
**TOMORROW** – Revolution/ Three Jolly Little Dwarfs (Parlophone)
**23RD TURNOFF** – Michael Angelo/ Leave Me Here (Deram)
**THE ZOMBIES** – Friends of Mine/ Beechwood Park (CBS)
LPs
**THE KINKS** – Something Else (Pye) #35
**AL STEWART** – Bedsitter Images (CBS)

## What Was Happening?

**In Summary:** The Magical Mystery Tour film is made, Radio One plays its first record, the Stones sack their manager, Pink Floyd tours in Ireland and Scandinavia, and The Soft Machine has passport problems.
**Specifically:**

➢ The **'Magical Mystery Tour'** film is shot in Kent, London and parts of the West Country.

➢ Andrew Loog Oldham is sacked as the Rolling Stones manager.

➢ The first record to be played on Radio 1 is *'Flowers in the Rain'* by The Move.

➢ On returning from France to Britain, Soft Machine's Daevid Allen is refused re-entry. Allen returns to France to eventually form Gong while The Soft Machine plays at the Edinburgh Festival as a trio.

➢ The Moody Blues undertake a 3-month US tour performing **'Days of Future Passed'** at the Hollywood Bowl with the Stan Kenton Orchestra.

➢ John Peel does just one Sunday spot of his 'Perfumed Garden' show at the Tiles Club before it closes down. The Fortunes, Chicken Shack, The Graham Bond Organisation, Simon Dupree and The Big Sound, The Gass, Tangerine Peel and Pink Floyd have all passed through its doors.

➢ The UFO Club hosts a two-day festival featuring Pink Floyd, The Crazy World of Arthur Brown, Tomorrow, The Move, Denny Laine and Soft Machine.

➢ The Middle Earth continues to attract top and upcoming acts like Soft Machine, Tyrannosaurus Rex (their debut concert on the 23rd), Fairport Convention, Graham Bond and The Third Ear Band.

➢ Among those appearing at the Marquee, are the Bonzo Dog Doo Dah Band, Syn, Denny Laine and the Electric String Band, The Gods, the Social Deviants with John Peel, The Move, Mud, Ten Years After and The Orange Bicycle, The Jeff Beck Group and in longer 'residencies' The Dream, The Crazy World of Arthur Brown, Piccadilly Line and Marmalade. Appearing at The Saville Theatre, are Eric Burdon and The Animals with Denny Laine and Dantalian's Chariot at a concert on the 10th; John Mayall's Bluesbreakers and Fleetwood Mac with Long John Baldry on the 17th and Traffic with Nirvana, The Smoke and Wynder K Frog on the 24th.

➢ Appearing at the UFO at the Roundhouse, are Eric Burdon and The Animals with The Aynsley Dunbar Retaliation; Soft Machine with Family; Dantalian's Chariot with Exploding Galaxy and The Social Deviants; and The Jeff Beck Group with Ten Years After.

➢ Mabel Greer's Toyshop, Sam Gopal, The Third Ear Band and The Social Deviants all appear at Happening 44.

- ➢ Pink Floyd visits Northern Ireland – the Flamingo in Ballymena and the Starlight Ballroom, Belfast and go on a short Scandinavian tour of Denmark and Sweden.
- ➢ Blues groups like Fleetwood Mac and John Mayall's Bluesbreakers are actively gigging. Robert Plant's Band of Joy are also on the road.
- ➢ Soft Machine visits the Barrie Hall in Edinburgh.
- ➢ The Nice play a gig at the Big C Club in Farnborough on the 1st of the month.
- ➢ The 5th Dimension Club in Leicester hosts some stellar groups including Ten Years After, Pink Floyd, Family and Amen Corner.

# October, 1967

45s

THE ACCENT – Red Sky at Night/ Wind of Change (Decca)

BLOSSOM TOES – What On Earth/ Mrs Murphy's Budgerigar (Marmalade)

ALAN BOWN – Toyland/ Technicolour Dream (MGM)

ERIC BURDON & THE ANIMALS – San Franciscan Nights/ Gratefully Dead (MGM) #7

THE CALIFORNIANS – Follow Me/ What Love Can Do (Decca)

DAVE CLARK 5 – Everybody Knows/ Concentration Baby (Columbia) #2

CREATION – Life is Just Beginning/ Through My Eyes (Polydor)

DAVE, DEE, DOZY, BEAKY, MICK AND TICH – Zabadak!/ The Sun Goes Down (Fontana) #3

DONOVAN – There is a Mountain/ Sand and Foam (Pye) #8

SIMON DUPREE AND THE BIG SOUND – Kites/ Like the Sun Like the Fire (Parlophone) #9

EPISODE SIX – I Can See Through You/ When I Fall in Love (Pye)

FAMILY – Scene Through the Eyes of a Lens/ Gypsy Woman (Liberty)

FOCUS THREE – 10,000 Years Behind My Mind/ The Sunkeeper (Columbia)

HONEYBUS – Do I Still Figure in Your Life? /Throw My Love Away (Deram)

THE KINKS – Autumn Almanac/ Mr Pleasant (Pye) #3

JACKIE LOMAX – Genuine Imitation Life/ One Minute Woman (CBS)

THE MISUNDERSTOOD – I Can Take You to the Sun/ Who Do You Love (Fontana)

MUD – Flower Power/ You're My Mother (CBS)

THE QUIK – I Can't Sleep/ Soul Full of Sorrow (Deram)

RUPERT'S PEOPLE – Prologue to a Magic World/ Dream on My Mind (Columbia)

TIMEBOX – Walking Through the Streets of My Mind/ Don't Make Promises (Deram)

THE TROGGS – Love is All Around/ When Will the Rain Come (Page One) #5

THE WHO – I Can See for Miles/ Someone's Coming (Track) #10

LPs

BONZO DOG DOO-DAH BAND – Gorilla (Liberty)

ERIC BURDON/ANIMALS – Winds of Change (MGM)

THE HOLLIES – Butterfly (Parlophone)
DAVID McWILLIAMS – Volume 2 (Major Minor)

## What Was Happening?

In summary: Bee Gees members escape extradition, The Move pre-empt MTV by a good number of years, the UFO club closes and the establishment's patience runs out.

Specifically:

➤ Brian Jones has to serve a suspended sentence following an appeal against an original nine-month stretch for the possession of cannabis resin.

➤ The Beatles are in the studio working on the soundtrack to their '**Magical Mystery Tour**' TV film.

➤ Australian members of The Bee Gees, Colin Peterson and Vince Melouney, are told they will have to leave Britain when their work permits expire on 30th November. They are given a reprieve following a campaign by Bee Gees fans and legal representations.

➤ The ever enterprising Move release what may be the first popular music video when they release an 8 mm silent movie to accompany their '*Flowers in the Rain*' single. It is a bit on the expensive side though at seven shillings and sixpence (75p) for the black & white version and £3 15s for the colour version (£3.75)

➤ Art change their name to Spooky Tooth, and American organist/vocalist Gary Wright (ex-The New York Times) joins the group.

➤ The UFO club closes.

➤ Sheffield's Beat Music Club is closed down by the city council. Owner Peter Stringfellow pledges to launch an appeal.

➤ Following 'acts of immorality' at this year's event, Windsor Council decides that the National Jazz and Blues Festival will not be staged in Windsor in 1968.

➤ Traffic headlines a package tour bill that includes Art, The Flowerpot Men, The Mindbenders, Tomorrow and Vanilla Fudge. The dates are as follows: Finsbury Park Astoria (4th), the ABC, Chesterfield (6th), City Hall, Newcastle (7th), Empire, Liverpool (8th), the ABC, Croydon (10th), Birmingham Town Hall (11th), Colston Hall, Bristol (13th), the Gaumont, Wolverhampton (14th), De Montfort Hall, Leicester (15th) and the Gaumont, Ipswich (17th).

➤ During 'Sundays at the Saville', Pink Floyd are supported by The Incredible String Band, Tomorrow, Tim Rose and Fairport Convention; The Jimi Hendrix Experience are supported by The Crazy World of Arthur Brown, The Herd and Eire Apparent; Cream are supported by The Bonzo Dog Doo Dah Band and The Action.

➤ The Nice, Neat Change and Timebox are regulars at The Marquee. Also making appearances are Nite People, The Action, Studio Six, Ten Years After, The Gods, Herbal Mixture, Alan Bown, Syn, The Third Eye, The Iveys, The Amboy Dukes, Open Mind, The Jimi Hendrix Experience and Marmalade.

➤ Appearing at The Middle Earth, are The Crazy World of Arthur Brown, Mabel Greer's Toyshop, The Action, Tyrannosaurus Rex, Soft Machine,

Blossom Toes, Eire Apparent, The Nice, The Incredible String Band and Fairport Convention.

➢ The Crazy World of Arthur Brown are regulars at The Roundhouse where Soft Machine, supported by Open Mind, also appear, Soft Machine also appear with Fairport Convention at The UFO before it closes.

➢ The Who appears at the Beach Ballroom in Aberdeen and the Kinema in Dunfermline. The Bee Gees appear in Coatbridge Town Hall, The Edinburgh Rosewell Institute and the Dundee Top Ten Club. Cream are in the Capitol, Edinburgh and Magoos in Glasgow.

➢ The Move and Jimi Hendrix Experience are at the Starlight Ballroom in Crawley.

➢ Toft's in Folkestone attracts Savoy Brown and Junior Walker and The All Stars supported by The Amboy Dukes and Wages of Sin.

# November, 1967

**45s**

LONG JOHN BALDRY – Let The Heartaches Begin/ Annabella (Who Flies to Me When She's Lonely (Pye) #1

THE BEATLES – Hello Goodbye/ I Am the Walrus (Parlophone) #1

THE BEE GEES – World/ Sir Geoffrey Saved the World (Polydor) #9

BONZO DOG DOO-DAH BAND – Equestrian Statue/ The Intro and The Outro (Liberty)

THE BUNCH – Looking Glass Alice/ Spare a Shilling (CBS)

THE CYMBALINE – Matrimonial Fears/ You Will Never Love Me (Philips)

DAVE DAVIES – Susannah's Still Alive/ Funny Face (Pye) #20

ELMER GANTRY'S VELVET OPERA – Flames/ Salisbury Plain (Direction)

THE FACTOTUMS – Cloudy/ Easy Said Easy Done (Pye)

CHRIS FARLOWE – Handbags and Gladrags/ Everybody Makes a Mistake (Immediate) #33

FELIUS ANDROMEDA – Meditations/ Cheadle Heath Delusions (Decca)

FLOWERPOT THE MEN – Walk in the Sky/ Am I Losing You (Deram)

THE FOUNDATIONS – Baby, Now That I've Found You/ Come on Back to Me (Pye) #1

GRANNY'S INTENTIONS – The Story of David/ Sandy's on the Phone Again (Deram)

MARMALADE – Man in a Shop/ Cry (CBS)

MOODY BLUES – Nights in White Satin/ Cities (Deram) #19

THE NICE – Thoughts of Emerlist Davjack/ Azrael (Angel Of Death) (Immediate)

NITE PEOPLE – Summertime Blues/ In the Springtime (Fontana)

ORANGE BICYCLE – Laura's Garden/ Lavender Girl (Columbia)

PINK FLOYD – Apples and Oranges/ Paintbox (Columbia)

THE PRETTY THINGS – Defecting Grey/ Mr Evasion (Columbia)

THE ROKES – Hold My Hand/ Regency Sue (RCA)

THE SEARCHERS – Secondhand Dealer/ Crazy Dreams (Pye)

SKIP BIFFERTY – Happy Land/ Reason to Live (RCA)

THE SMOKE – It Could Be Wonderful/ Have Some More Tea (Island)

KEITH WEST – Sam/ Thimble Full of Puzzles (Parlophone) #38
THE ZOMBIES – Care of Cell 44/ Maybe After He's Gone (CBS)
LPs
BLOSSOM TOES – We Are Ever So Clean (Marmalade)
CREAM – Disraeli Gears (Reaction) #5
KALEIDOSCOPE – Tangerine Dream (Fontana)
THE MOODY BLUES – Days of Future Passed (Deram) #27
PROCOL HARUM – Procol Harum (Regal Zonophone)
TEN YEARS AFTER – Ten Years After (Deram)

## What Was Happening?

In Summary: Further musical advances are made and rock comes more 'progressive', the Stones try to figure out how to respond to 'Sergeant Pepper', Jimi Hendrix headlines at the Royal Albert Hall, Robin Gibb has a narrow escape and Status Quo is born.

Specifically:

➢ Syd Barrett is still 'out of it' and work permits arrive late on Pink Floyd's US tour. Several concerts are cancelled and TV audiences see Barrett stare blankly into the camera.

➢ The Rolling Stones announce the release of their attempt at nudging into the psychedelic space created by The Beatles on **'Sergeant Pepper'** with an album called **'Her Satanic Majesty Requests and Requires'** (not quite the finished article as far as the title is concerned).

➢ The heavy schedule of touring takes its toll on Small Faces singer Steve Marriott who collapses with nervous fatigue during their Irish tour.

➢ Robin Gibb of the Bee Gees survives a train crash on 5th November at Hither Green in south-east London in which 49 people are killed. The group play a special show in aid of the disaster fund at Lewisham Concert Hall followed by a concert at the Saville Theatre on the 19th, supported by The Bonzo Dog Doo Dah Band and The Flowerpot Men.

➢ Traffic Jam (formerly The Spectres) change their name to The Status Quo, following the addition of rhythm guitarist Rick Parfitt and sign for the Pye label.

➢ Another important moment in the development of progressive rock when The Syn bassist Chris Squire forms Mabel Greer's Toyshop. Syn guitarist Peter Banks also joins and although two concurrent groups are intended, The Syn project is disbanded in February, 1968.

➢ The Jimi Hendrix Experience headlines a package tour at the Royal Albert Hall beginning on 14th November on a bill that includes The Move, Pink Floyd, Amen Corner, The Nice, The Outer Limits and Eire Apparent.

➢ Nice guitarist Davy O'List steps in for Syd Barrett for 15 Pink Floyd's UK gigs between 14th November (The Royal Albert Hall) and 5th December (Green's Playhouse, Glasgow).

➢ Touring together seems to be the 'in thing' with The Who, Traffic, The Herd, Marmalade and The Tremeloes concluding a two week tour on 10th November. For the record, the full list is: City Hall, Sheffield (28th Oct), Coventry Theatre, Coventry (29th Oct), City Hall, Newcastle (30th Oct), Empire, Liverpool (1st Nov), Granada Theatre, Kingston (3rd), Granada, Walthamstow (4th), Theatre Royal, Nottingham (5th), Birmingham Town

Hall (6th), Granada, Kettering (8th), Granada, Maidstone (9th), Adelphi, Slough (10th).

- ➢ As 'pop' artists get more ambitious, Al Stewart appears with group, a 35-piece orchestra and a go-go dancer at the Royal Festival Hall (struggling to visualise that one!).
- ➢ The Saville Theatre has its usual quota of top-notch acts like The Alan Price Set, David McWilliams, The Nice, Ten Years After, The Bee Gees, The Flowerpot Men, The Bonzo Dog Doo-Dah Band and Tony Rivers & The Castaways.
- ➢ At The Marquee this month are: Syn, Ten Years After, The Wild Flowers, The Nice, The Herd, Tuesday's Children, Traffic, The Remo Four, Sensory Armada, Cream, Marmalade, Open Mind, Neat Change and The Iveys.
- ➢ The Bystanders, The Web and Timebox are among those who play at the Scotch of St. James Club.
- ➢ The Middle Earth hosts various double and triple bills – Family, Herbal Mixture (3rd), The Knack, Piccadilly Line, The Third Ear (4th), Soft Machine, Zeus and Sensory Armada (10th), Dantalian's Chariot, Amalgam and Mabel Greer's Toyshop (11th), Fairport Convention (17th), Denny Laine's Electric String Band (18th), The Pretty Things, Eyes Of Blue and Tyrannosaurus Rex (24th); and Mabel Greer's Toyshop, Nervous System (25th).
- ➢ Cream are in Romano's, Belfast, Silver Blades Ice Rink in Streatham, the Central Pier in Morecambe and the Club A-Go-Go in Newcastle. Various venues in Birmingham are as busy as ever with The Troggs, Arthur Brown and The Troggs among the visitors. As the year comes to an end, the University and college circuit is also still thriving for established, up and coming, and American artists with Jimi Hendrix and Ten Years After at Sussex University in Brighton on the 11th; The Gods at Bradford University on the 3rd, Colleges and art colleges also host many gigs with The Jeff Beck Group at Lanchester and Poole Colleges, Coventry and Exeter University, Kaleidoscope at Leicester and Reading University, Dantalian's Chariot at London's West Polytechnic; The Spencer Davis Group at Southampton University and Elmer Gantry's Velvet Opera at the University of East Anglia, Norwich,
- ➢ Manchester's Free Trade Hall hosts an amazing line-up on the 11th in The Incredible String Band, Al Stewart, Bert Jansch and John Renbourn.
- ➢ The Imperial Ballroom in Nelson hosts The Who and The Troggs,
- ➢ Soft Machine cross the Channel for the Palais des Sports 'Love-In' in Paris on 17th–18th November with Cat Stevens, Dantalian's Chariot, The Spencer Davis Group and Tomorrow.

# December, 1967

You can see the beginning of the fruition of what I call 'The Pepper Factor' as more ambitious, higher quality albums become the way to get artistic street cred rather than simply having hit singles, and how original composition became the norm rather than reliance on 'tin pan alley' song writers. Although **'Sergeant Pepper'** was a loose kind of concept, nevertheless, the concept, (or what Robert Schumann called the 'Programme'/ themed approach perhaps) would become more and more popular as 1967 turned into 1968.

**45s**

THE CALIFORNIANS – Sunday Will Never Be the Same/ Can't Get You Out of My Mind (Decca)

CHERRY SMASH – Sing Songs of Love/ Movie Star (Track)

THE CHOCOLATE WATCHBAND – Requiem/ What's it to You? (Decca)

SPENCER DAVIS GROUP – Mr Second Class/ Sanity Inspector (UA) #35

EASYBEATS – The Music Goes Round My Head/ Come in, You'll Get Pneumonia (UA)

THE HERD – Paradise Lost/ Come on Believe Me (Fontana) #15

THE HUMAN INSTINCT – A Day in My Mind's Mind/ Death of the Seaside (Deram)

THE MICKEY FINN – Garden of My Mind/ Time to Start Loving You (Direction)

SMALL FACES – Tin Soldier/ I Feel Much Better (Immediate) #9

CAT STEVENS – Kitty/ Ceylon (Deram) #47

STUDIO SIX – Strawberry Window/ Falling Leaves (Polydor)

SYMBOLS – (The Best Part of) Breaking Up/ Again (President) #25

TINKERBELL'S FAIRY DUST – Lazy Day/ In My Magic Garden (Decca)

TINTERN ABBEY – Vacuum Cleaner/ Beeside (Deram)

TRAFFIC – Here We Go Round the Mulberry Bush/ Coloured Rain (Island) #8

DAVE BERRY – Stranger/ Stick by the Book; Forever/ I Have Learned to Dream (Decca)

ALAN BOWN – We Can Help You/ Magic Handkerchief

THE BEATSTALKERS – Silver Tree Top School for Boys/ Sugar Coated Man (CBS)

VALENTINE'S DAY MASSACRE (THE ACTION) – Brother Can You Spare a Dime/ Al's Party

**LPs**

ART – Supernatural Fairy Tales (Island)

JULIE DRISCOLL/ BRIAN AUGER – Open (Marmalade) #12

PICCADILLY LINE – The Huge World of Emily Small (CBS)

JIMI HENDRIX EXPERIENCE – Axis: Bold as Love (Track) #5

THE HERD – Paradise Lost (Fontana) #38

ROLLING STONES – Their Satanic Majesties Request (Decca) #3

TRAFFIC – Mr Fantasy (Island) #8

THE TROGGS – Cellophane (Page One)

## What Was Happening?

In summary: Magical Mystery tour gets 'panned', the Kensington Olympia stages an all-nighter.

Specifically:

> ➤ **'Magical Mystery Tour'** is screened by BBC1 on Boxing Day, and loses much of its impact by being screened in black and white. The critical response is not that favourable.

- The tolls of intense gigging and promotion tell on Move bassist Ace Kefford who is reported as having a breakdown during filming for promoting the *'Fire Brigade'* single.
- There is a disappointing turnout at the 'Christmas on Earth Continued', held in the vast London Olympia on the 22nd, due to inadequate publicity and bad weather.
- The Middle Earth has visitors from the States in The Electric Prunes on the 1st of the month supported by Sensory Armada. Also appearing are Blossom Toes, The Deviants, Family, Piccadilly Line, Arthur Brown, Pink Floyd, Soft Machine, Al Stewart, Paper Blitz Tissue, Eclection, Eyes of Blue, Mabel Greer's Toyshop, Fairport Convention, Tintagel and Ten Years After. The Nice play a Scandinavian tour in the middle of the month. A live Swedish Radio session tape is excavated and released on CD over three decades later.
- Appearing at London's Speakeasy are, The Moody Blues (10th), Traffic (18th), Pink Floyd (21st) and Tintern Abbey (29th)
- The Marquee has Neat Change (2nd, 9th, 16th, 23rd, 30th), Open Mind (5th, 23rd), Amboy Dukes (7th, 28th), Ten Years After (8th, 22nd), Mabel Greer's Toyshop (9th), Simon Dupree & The Big Sound (11th), Jeff Beck Group (12th), Nite People (12th, 31st), Remo Four (14th), Herbal Mixture (16th), Timebox (17th, 21st), The Nice (18th), Eric Burdon & The Animals (19th), Eire Apparent (19th), Clouds (21st), The Iveys (21st) Tuesday's Children (28th), Mud (30th) and Marmalade (31st).
- The Move and The Who are at the Upper Cut. The Who also appear at The Pavilion in Bath the Pier Ballroom, Hastings and Hull and Durham University.
- Pink Floyd do an all-nighter in the Penthouse, Constitution Hill, Birmingham and play the Pavilion in Bournemouth, the Royal College of Art, Kensington with the Bonzos and Marmalade, the Flamingo Club, Redruth and Chislehurst Caves, Kent.
- The Top Rank in Brighton starts the month with appearances by Cream and The Nice.
- Robert Plant and The Band of Joy are at the Dunfermline Kinema.
- Traffic plays at the Skyline Ballroom in Hull and Leicester and Southampton University.
- The Isle of Wight welcomes Fairport Convention, Brian Auger and The Trinity, Pandemonium, Marmalade and Skip Bifferty to the 69 Club, Ryde Castle Hotel.

# Appendix Two
## ***** System: An Explanation

***** I hesitate to say flawless as creations rarely are. However, here are some of the criteria: exemplary musicianship not to be confused necessarily with virtuosity; creativity, inventiveness, experimentation, taking established musical configurations into new dimensions and proving influential on generations of musicians; rhythmic and melodic accessibility unless 'avant-garde' in which different criteria may apply; my own personal inclinations (although I have much critical appraisal to rely on here). Production and engineering are also important, and even the sequencing of tracks, in the case of an LP, may come into play.

**** Highly recommended but in terms of an LP, perhaps a missed step or two (or a track that in hindsight might not have fitted into the project as well as intended). A '45' is more easily afforded a **** or ***** star rating – after all, it may be 3 or 4 minutes as opposed to 30 or 40. All of the ***** criteria apply although a **** record doesn't quite get there.

*** Still recommended although perhaps not essential. There will be much to enjoy and commend in such a recording but the ideas and musicianship may not attain the higher standard or be inconsistent, there may be too music genre mix-mash (a difficult thing to pull off), if an instrumental record there may not be enough variety. Perhaps, there might be more doubts in terms of originality and taking music forward than for a **** or ***** rating.

** Worth checking out for completeness sake even to compare this with a recording with a higher rating. The intentions may have been good, the musicianship and technical aspects may even be good but this is a recording that may not be returned to often!

*What Rolling Stone magazine used to accord a to! Best avoided, very few redeeming features if any.

# Epilogue
## Excuse Me While I Touch the Sky

The BBC TV programme 'Seven Ages of Rock' broadcast on 20th May, 2007 describes the pivotal moment on Saturday, 24th September, 1966 at approximately 9.00 in the morning when James Marshall Hendrix (christened Johnny Allen Hendrix) set foot on English soil for the very first time following a flight from JFK International Airport, New York to Heathrow, London. He had forty dollars in his pocket. Within 24 hours, he had acquired a girlfriend Kathy Etchingham whom he escorted to safety to his hotel after a fight broke out at the Scotch of St. James Club where he was playing. Etchingham *happened to be a tenant in Zoot and Ronnie Money's house who were also at the time the landlords of Andy Summers who eleven years later would form the Police with Gordon Sumner (Sting) and Stewart Copeland.

A friend Hendrix had left behind in New York, Linda Keith (Keith Richards' girlfriend at the time), had touted Hendrix as a possible recording artist to Andrew Loog Oldham, the Rolling Stones' manager, who was unimpressed. "He was trouble," said Oldham, "and I had enough trouble already with The Stones." Seymour Stein of Sire Records was not won over either. When Linda Keith contacted him, he did attend a gig only to see Hendrix smash his guitar in frustration. The lack of original material at that stage was probably another reason for Stein not following up his interest. **

Enter stage left the towering figure of Bryan 'Chas' Chandler, bass player of The Animals. Looking to get into record production after The Animals' 1966 tour of the US had concluded, Chandler had spotted the potential of the Tim Rose's song 'Hey, Joe'. The runes were cast when Chandler witnessed Hendrix playing *'Hey, Joe'* with his Blue Flames group in the Wha club in New York in the company of Linda Keith. In 'A Film About Jimi Hendrix', Chandler recalled his reaction, "I thought immediately he was the best guitarist I'd ever seen." He also thought there had to be a 'catch' to explain how an artist so talented could possibly be unsigned. Hendrix continued to play in Greenwich Village while Chandler completed the Animals' tour.

Meanwhile, word of Hendrix's talent was spreading and John Hammond Junior added Hendrix to his own band in a two-week residency at the Café Au Go Go. Nothing much changed for Hendrix. He was now reduced once again to the role of a backup guitarist with the benevolent concession of a solo spot during the shows. The amazing thing was that the Hammond dynasty became the third party to pass on Jimi Hendrix (the arrangement with Chandler was a 'gentleman's agreement'). ***

Chandler took four days to find Hendrix on returning to New York at the end of The Animals' tour. The Animals' manager Michael Jeffrey, Chandler's business partner in managing his newly discovered artist, paid the $ it cost to buy back Hendrix's contract at Sue Records and pulled some strings to ensure that Hendrix had the paperwork to enter the UK. As for his band, Randy California was only 15 at the time, and would not get a passport and his rhythm section, Billy Cox and Danny Taylor politely declined. Hendrix deliberated but eventually struck a deal with Chandler: part of the deal was "If you can guarantee that you'll introduce me to Clapton, I'll come to London."

Born in Seattle, Washington State on 27 November 1942, Hendrix was from a broken home with father Al often absent on army duty and mother Lucille taking off with another man. He was cared for by friends and relatives.

Charles R Cross explains the point Hendrix had reached as he was about to enter his teenage years. The year is 1955: "That summer, the welfare department again threatened to bring court action to force Jimi into foster care. As a compromise, Al agreed that Jimi could live with Al's brother Frank, who resided close by." **** **(126)** This relatively affluent environment offered Jimi care and security but it was a boarder of his dad Al (now working as a landscaper), Ernestine Benson, who ignited Jimi's interest in music that had first flourished during his neighbourhood wanderings. It was through Ernestine that Hendrix heard, for the first time, 78 rpm records by the likes of Robert Johnson, Muddy Waters and Howlin' Wolf. ***** On 1st September 1957, a historic musical event occurred that left an indelible imprint on young Jimi's mind when he watched Elvis Presley perform at Seattle's Sick's Stadium from a hilltop vantage as he couldn't afford the price of a ticket.

By the time he saw Elvis from a distance, Jimi, one of the first exponents of 'air guitar', at last, had a real guitar to experiment with bought for him by the same Erneston Benson who had introduced him to blues records on his gramophone. "He experimented with every fret, rattle, buzz and sound-making property the guitar had." **(127)**. Finally, Ernesto persuaded Al to buy Jimi a proper guitar, a white Supro Ozark which was right-handed but to which left-handed Jimi quickly adapted. Early influences on the development of Jimi's playing included Elmore James, B.B. King, Chuck Berry and Duane Eddy. He was in groups called The Velvetones, The Rocking Kings and The Tom Cats, and graduated to a Danelectro Silvertone guitar, also white.

The next significant event in Jimi's life was his arrival at Fort Ord, California to join the 101st Airborne. ***** Eventually, he became a supply clerk based in Fort Campbell, Kentucky and it was there he had a fateful meeting with bass player Billy Cox with whom he formed a five piece called The Kasuals who got weekend gigs in Nashville, and, further away, in military bases as far as North Carolina. He was discharged from the army on a fabrication engineered by Hendrix himself ('homosexual tendencies') with $400 which he managed to squander in a jazz club in Clarksville and ended up homeless with not enough money for the bus fare to Seattle, having to clandestinely sleep in his old army bunk. He did manage to rescue his guitar 'Billy Jean' ****** which he'd slept with every night during his time in the army and ended up being pawned.

Armed with a new guitar, an Epiphone Wilshire, Hendrix hooked up with Cox once he was discharged, and formed The King Kasuals with singer Harry Bachelor and rhythm guitarist Alphonso Young who could play the guitar with his teeth.

## Are You Experienced?

Hendrix's first album '**Are You Experienced?**' ***** was released on Track Records in the UK in May 1967. In the US, it wasn't released until August with three singles, *'Hey Joe'* *****, *'Purple Haze'* ***** and *'The Wind Cries Mary'* **** replacing three of the UK album tracks, '*Can You See Me?*', '*Remember*' and *'Red House'*.

Taking the UK version first, the track rundown was as follows:

Side One: *Foxy Lady; Manic Depression; Red House; Can You See Me; Love or Confusion; I Don't Live Today*:Hendrix hit the ground running with the powerhouse sexual innuendo of the opener, experimented with double-tracked vocals and guitar stereo separation on *'I Don't Live Today'* both completed in 1966 while anguished subjects like the 'frustrating mess' of *'Manic Depression'*, the crazed emotional entanglement of *'Love or Confusion'*, and what Peter Doggett describes as the 'magnificently malevolent psychic voyage' that is *'I Don't Live Today'* with its suggestion of reincarnation revealed early on that Hendrix was not afraid to tackle any subject and apparently, had 'carte blanche' to do just that. *'Red House'* was a Chicago style slow blues that would endure in Hendrix's stage act and provide an important component of his canon with a compilation album called 'Blues' eventually appearing in 1994.

**Are You Experienced?** Side two: *May This be Love; Fire; Third Stone from the Sun; Remember; Are You Experienced?* Experienced in what? Was it sex, drugs or something more esoteric or spiritual perhaps? The title track takes the album out in a swathe of phantasmagorical experimentation with backwards tapes, guitars mimicking saxophones and unhinged psychedelia. Before it, Hendrix gives us his first piece of musical science fiction *'Third Stone from the Sun'*, the irresistibly sexy chorus of *'Fire'* with drummer Mitch Mitchell excelling. *'May This be Love'* signposted early on what a melodic and inventive guitarist Hendrix was while *'Remember'* proved he could solo with the best of them.

As if this weren't enough, in October of 1966, The Experience recorded the song (with backing vocals by The Breakaways session group) that Chandler had heard Hendrix playing in New York, a night that changed the destiny of popular music. That song, of course, was *'Hey Joe'*, released as a single, and appearing on the American version of **'Are You Experienced?'**. The song has a chequered history. Written by Californian Billy Roberts, he sold it to Dino Valenti of the Quicksilver Messenger Service who copyrighted it under the name of Chet Powers and shared it with his friend David Crosby, only for Los Angeles group The Leaves to beat The Byrds in the race to release it. The slower, more bluesy version was developed by Tim Rose and this was the incarnation that Hendrix incorporated into his early stage shows in 1966.

*'Purple Haze'* and *'The Wind Cries Mary'* were recorded on the same day in January 1967. Both unique in their own way, *'Purple Haze'* would become a massive hit and garner much radio play owing a little to parts of The Beatles 'Revolver' but ultimately, a new form and direction for music with the whammy bar reaching new heights of intensity. *'The Wind Cries Mary'* is a haunting, shimmering love song.

Two other songs from the **'Are You Experienced?'** sessions emerged on the UK and US CD 'Experience Hendrix' releases: *'Highway Chile'* and *'51st Anniversary'* respectively. While neither was as strong as anything that appeared on the original albums *'51st Anniversary'* is interesting as a rueful recollection on the state of marriage presumably prompted by his own parents' relationship, and his own uncertainty as expressed in other songs musing on what love is and what love means.

**'Axis: Bold is Love'** ***** is preferred by Hendrix luminaries like Charles Cross and Noel Redding but it was a very different kind of album. I have always preferred the first although consider both to be absolutely essential, and must concede 'Axis' is more ambitious and a step forward. It is a remarkable indicator of the creativity of the artists responsible that such a strong second album flowed uninterrupted from the **'Are You Experienced?'** sessions, allowing two exceptional LPs by anyone's standards to be released in the same year within seven months of each other.

Track listing: side one: **EXP; Up from the Skies; Spanish Castle Magic; Wait Until Tomorrow; Ain't No Telling; Little Wing; If Six was Nine; You've Got Me**

**Floating; Castles Made of Sand; She's So Fine; One Rainy Wish; Little Miss Lover; Bold as Love.**

Following *'Third Stone from the Sun'* on the first album, the next most explicit manifestation of Hendrix's interest in science-fiction, that included watching Flash Gordon movies when he was a boy and reading sci-fi novels, comes *'EXP'* on which, Hendrix pretended to be a musician friend from Greenwich Village, Paul Caruso discussing UFOs on radio 'EXP'. Much use was made of Mayer's effects and stereo panning as well as some screeching guitars. On initial listening, the album tended to be dominated by certain songs like *'Spanish Castle Magic'* written about a rock club in Seattle, 'Spanish Castle' and the brilliant guitar classic *'Little Wing'* thought (like the classic song of personal doubt *'Castles Made of Sand'*) to be inspired by the playing of Curtis Mayfield (Hendrix told his brother, Leon, the song was about his mother Lucille) to which Hendrix adds glockenspiel ********. It frustratingly fades out very early (check out the version on the outtakes CD). However, in time, other songs emerge, *'If Six was Nine'*, recorded in May 1967, a fantastic song about determinism which Peter Doggett reckons "prefigured the political funk of Sly Stone in 1969", even going as far as "If the hippies cut off their hair, I don't care" but ultimately, letting his 'freak bag fly' in the face of "white collar Conservatives pointing their plastic finger at me". There's also the spoken line about facing death and living his life like he wants to do, a recurring theme in Hendrix's music. The song also marks the blossoming of Redding as a bass player (remembering he was converted from guitarist to bass player to form The Experience) and Mitch Mitchell's drumming became even more brilliant, the only comparison for freneticism surely being Keith Moon of The Who. Noel Redding sings lead vocal on his own *'She's So Fine'*, a good piece of psychedelic rock with a Pete Townshend fashioned solo in the middle eight. Elsewhere there's the soulful R&B of *'Wait Until Tomorrow'*, *'Ain't No Telling'* and *'You've Got Me Floating'*, the latter with backing vocals from members of The Move who just happened to be recording next door at Olympia Studios. The twin guitar dreamy drug imagery of *'One Rainy Wish'*, the Mitch Mitchell led testosterone charged guitar of *'Little Miss Lover'* and the title track which Doggett describes as "a typically subtle climax to an album divided between R&B dramatics and near-confessional poetry" brought a second remarkable album in the remarkable year of 1967 to a close. **(129)**

# Footnotes

*Etchingham had some famous boyfriends prior to Hendrix including Brian Jones of The Rolling Stones and Keith Moon of The Who.

**To compound matters further, the guitar belonged to Keith Richard 'borrowed' by Linda Keith for Hendrix to play.

***John Hammond Senior's signings included Billie Holiday, Bob Dylan (and later) Bruce Springsteen.

****Things were so bad that, on 30 March 1955, Al and Lucille Hendrix signed away their parental rights to Al's brothers and sisters, Alfred, Joe, Kathy and Pamela. The description of life for young Jimmy at this time was harrowing with dirt, degradation and despair as he wandered the neighbourhood unsupervised picking up on whatever music was playing from neighbouring houses on his itinerant wanderings.

*****Later on, in 1958, Ernestine would take Jimi to a local record store called 'World of Music' to pick a record.

******He completed no fewer than 26 parachute jumps during his time in the army.

******Betty Jean Morgan was Hendrix's fiancé at the time, although on his discharge from the army, he changed his mind about returning to Seattle, settling down and getting married. Hendrix's determination not to 'get hooked' became a recurring theme in songs like 'Stone Free' (his 'ode to promiscuity') and '51stAnniversary'.

*******As was the imaginative 'Castles Made of Sand'. "The song begins with a domestic spat, and the wife slams the door on her drunken husband. Another verse tells of a young boy who plays in the woods, pretending he is an Indian chief. The crippled woman eventually decides to take her own life by jumping into the sea, pleading 'You won't hurt me more' as she leaps. She lands on a 'golden winged' ship. Jimi ends the song with couplet about timelessness, using the image of 'castles made of sand' washing into the sea." **(128)**

In the BBC TV programme 'Seven Ages of Rock', Pete Townshend pays tribute, "Jimi changed the sound of the guitar. I think in many respects he changed the sound of rock far more than The Beatles."

Charles Shaar Murray says, "***Voodoo Chile*** was blues music from Mississippi transformed to the psychedelic limits of outer space." It redefined what it meant to be a guitar player, musician and artists, redefined the whole period in which he existed.

The sight of a left hander playing a right handed guitar upside down sent shockwaves through London and, according to Roger Daltrey, the guitar 'god' Eric Clapton said he was going to have to practise more.

Jeff Beck remembers Hendrix playing the bass line with his thumb, the lead with his little finger and the rhythm with the rest of them.

So 1967 was the year in which The Beatles produced an LP and EP, and Jimi Hendrix produced two LPs, not to mention the memorable 45s, a year in which music changed forever in the wake of two very different but equally tremendous creative forces. While British bands had 'invaded' the USA in the sixties, this was reciprocated by an influx of

West Indian reggae fans, American bluesmen and Jimi Hendrix who, by a quirk of fate, ended up being brought by Charles Chandler to the shores of the UK having, like The Beatles, been rejected by record labels in his formative days. A 'Pandora's Box' was opened as American groups tried to emulate British rock groups like The Beatles, The Rolling Stones and The Kinks, and British groups learned a lot from hearing the indigenous garage and psychedelic music emanating from the States. A cross fertilisation of ideas saw jazz, blues, folk, reggae, pop and rock orbit similar musical universes with mutual admiration from fans who were not narrowly focused on one particular genre, and wanted to escape from the stranglehold of the 'easy listening' their parents had endorsed and which remained hugely popular in the sixties despite the fact that, in the immortal words of Bob Dylan, 'the times they were a changing'. The visit by The Beatles to see Elvis Presley, and the threat they posed to his image confirmed that a musical and cultural revolution was indeed under way, and that kids liked to listen to a wide variety of 'underground' music, the generic term for anything that wasn't out and out pop. The term 'punk' was already in parlance in the States long before it would come along as the fierce dragon to destroy the 'prog dinosaurs' who themselves had flourished in the wake of the adventurous spirit of The Beatles, Hendrix and all the myriad other creative musical forces documented in this book. Nowadays, the tsunami has subsided, the forces of nature have re-balanced, progressive rock has enjoyed a resurgence while 'punk', 'post-punk' and 'post-rock' remain in favour among the generations following 'Sergeant Pepper'.

However, big challenges remain. While the charts have become dominated by boy and girl bands, winners of TV talent shows, and nostalgic compilations of artists of the '60s, '70s and '80s a visit to E-Bay or Discogs reveals that new forms of music are popular among those who still have that restless spirit of the '60s, and that electronic and experimental music still have wide appeal with forthright political and musical expression still evident in hip-hop and so on, and in the 'rave' culture' with trance and techno music to name but two emerging as new derivations as artists seek new paths to explore. In many ways, the music is as uncompromising as it was in the '60s and '70s but, unfortunately, there are not the record companies around to support musicians in their development, and much music is now self-produced and sold via Bandcamp and Soundcloud. The access to affordable home recording studios has opened music up to facilitate the emergence of a 'cottage industry' with, on occasion, that pot of gold at the end of the rainbow to allow artists to break through to enjoy commercial as well as artistic success and 'graduate' from 'indie' to 'establishment' (assuming they want to!). In this respect, perhaps, the world has changed for the better but music, to develop, needs funding, and, one wonders, if many of the brilliant artists documented in this book, would ever have got off the ground in this modern era where backing is difficult to find and music is sold cheaply or perhaps even given away free through downloads. In this respect, it is pleasing to see the resurgence of vinyl records and a 'cassette tape culture' as music lovers yearn for a tangible product they can see and feel. At the end of the day, good music is good music but always in the ear of the beholder.

**The End**

# References

## Overture

(1) **De Groot, Gerard: '60s Unplugged: A Kaleidoscopic History of a Disorderly Decade'** (Macmillan, 2008), p 228 (De Groot is an American and Professor of Modern History at the University of St. Andrews. A review in the Scotland on Sunday newspaper on 4 May, 2008 makes a sobering point which is relevant to my discourse: *"For too long"*, De Groot contends, *"the sixties has been a sacred zone. Throw away the rose-tinted spectacles too many of us have worn since youth and what do we find? Mindless mayhem, shallow commercialism and unbridled cruelty in much of the world. Spot the difference with any other decade."* Yoko Ono put it slightly differently speaking to Playboy magazine in 1981, saying *"I believe we will blossom in the eighties"* (She means spiritually). *"The seventies, unlike what people think, was a marvellous age, leading to the hope I feel."* And *"before the sixties, we were not allowed to tune into ourselves. We saw only form, no substance. So it's all a natural progression to the eighties."* As John Lennon said in the same interview, *"Carrying the Beatles or sixties dream around with you is like carrying the Second World War and Glenn Miller around."* (see 3 for reference)

(2) **Fraser Sandercombe, W: 'The Beatles Press Reports' (Collectors' Guide Publishing Inc, 2007)** p 305 (quoting from 'Disc and Music Echo', 25 April, 1970)

### CHAPTER ONE: SETTING THE SCENE

1. **Kynaston David: Family Britain 1951-1957** (Bloomsbury Publishing, 2010) p 544
2. **Judt, Tony: Post War: A History of Europe since 1945** (Vintage Books, 2010) p 162
3. **Ibid**
4. **Marr, Andrew: A History of Modern Britain** (Pan Books, 2008) p 65-67
5. **Marr, Andrew: The Making of Modern Britain** (Pan Books, 2010) p 307
6. **Judt, Tony: Post War: A History of Europe since 1945** (Vintage Books, 2010) p 276
7. **Ibid** p 153
8. **Independent on Sunday:** 'Günter Grass Attacks Merkel for Athens Policy' (Johnston Publications Ltd, 27 May, 2012) p 18-19
9. **Judt, Tony: Post War: A History of Europe since 1945** (Vintage Books, 2010) p 153

10. **Kynaston David: Family Britain 1951-1957** (Bloomsbury Publishing, 2010) p 309

11. **Sandbrook, Dominic: Never Had It So Good: A History of Britain from Suez To The Beatles** (Abacus Books, 2005) p 309

12. **Halliwell, Leslie and Walker, John: Halliwell's Film and Video Guide** (Harper Collins, 2004) p 744

13. **Forrest, Adam: 'Meet The Beatles: Back Better Than Ever Again'** (The Big Issue, John Hunt publisher) (12th September, 2016)

14. **(17) Ibid**

15. **(18) Pynchon, Thomas:** introduction to **Orwell, George: 1984** (Penguin Books Ltd, 2003)

16. **(19) Orwell, George- The Lion and the Unicorn: Socialism and the English Genius** (Penguin Books Ltd, 1982: introduction by Bernard Crick)

17. **(20) Kynaston David: Family Britain 1951-1957** (Bloomsbury Publishing, 2010) p 45

## CHAPTER TWO- "YOU'VE NEVER HAD IT SO GOOD"

18. **Miles, Barry; London Calling: A Countercultural History of London since 1945** (Atlantic Books, 2010) p 57

19. **Judt, Tony: Post War: A History of Europe since** 1945 (Vintage Books, 2010) p 347

20. **Ibid** p 298

21. **Johnstone, Nick: A Brief History of Rock 'n' Roll** (Running Press, 2007)

22. **Miles, Barry: London Calling: A Countercultural History of London since 1945** (Atlantic Books, 2010) p 52

23. **Dominic Sandbrook: Never Had It So Good: A History of Britain from Suez to the Beatles** (Abacus Books, 2005) p 154

24. **Ibid** p 170

## CHAPTER THREE: CONTEXT IS EVERYTHING

25. **The Beatles: The Beatles Anthology** (Apple Corps Ltd, 2000) p10

26. **Ibid** p 11

27. **Ibid** p 27

28. **Ibid** p 27

29. **Ibid** p 36

30. **Dave McAleer: Encyclopedia of Hits: The 1950s** (Blandford Press, 1997)

31. **The Beatles: The Beatles Anthology** (Apple Corps Ltd, 2000) p 21

32. **Heatley, Drew:** liner notes to 'Sun Record Company Essential Collection' boxed CD set (Metro Tins)

33. Also **Guralnik, Peter: Sweet Soul Music: Rhythm and Blues and The Southern Dream of Freedom** (Canongate, 1986, MOJO reprint, 2002) p 58 ("Big Joe Turner and Jesse Stone wrote a song (*Shake, Rattle and Roll)* that marked one of the turning points in rock 'n' roll as well as establishing Bill Haley as the first white artist to truly cross over the line in 1954.")

34. **Berry. Chuck: Chuck Berry: The Autobiography** (Harmony Books, New York, 1987) (general reference)

35. **Ibid** p 150

36. **The Beatles Anthology** (Apple Corps Ltd, 2000) p 10

37. Stanley, Bob: 'Bob the Cat issue' (The Big Issue, John Hunt Publishing July 15-21, 2014).

38. Foster, Mo: Play Like Elvis: How British Musicians Bought the American Dream (Sanctuary Publishing, 2000) p 213

39. De Rogatis, Jim: Turn On Your Mind: Four Decades of Great Psychedelic Rock (Hal Leonard, 2003) p 6

40. Hodgkinson, Will: Song Man (Bloomsbury Publishing, 2007)

## CHAPTER FOUR: THE BEATLES: CONCEPTION TO AMERICAN BREAKTHROUGH

41. Taylor, Alistair: With The Beatles (John Blake Publishing Ltd, 2011) p 19-

42. Macdonald, Ian: Revolution in The Head: The Beatles' Records and The Sixties (Pimlico, 1995) p 41

43. ibid p 52

44. Marsh, Dave: The Beatles' Second Album (Rodale Books, 2007) p 78

45. Shapiro, Peter: 'Rough Guide to Soul and R&B 1st edition' (2006) p 65

## CHAPTER FIVE: A HARD DAY'S NIGHT / HELP/ FOR SALE / RUBBER SOUL / REVOLVER

46. Macdonald, Ian: Revolution in The Head: The Beatles' Records and The Sixties (Pimlico, 1995) p 94

47. Clayson, Alan: Ringo: A Life' (Sanctuary, 2005) p 130

48. Norman, Philip: Shout! The True Story of The Beatles (Hamish Hamilton Ltd, 1981) p 393

49. Kane, Larry Ticket To Ride': Inside The Beatles' 1964 Tour That Changed The World (Running Press, 2003) p 201

50. Ibid p 246

51. Ibid p 207

52. Guralnik, Peter: Careless Love: The Unmaking of Elvis Presley (Abacus Books, 1999) p 211

53. The Beatles: The Beatles Anthology (Apple Corps Ltd, 2000) p 191

54. Macdonald, Ian: Revolution in The Head: The Beatles' Records and The Sixties (Pimlico, 1995) p 113

55. Evans, Paul in De Curtis, A and Henke, J with George-Warren, Holly The Rolling Stone Album Guide (Random House, 1979 reprinted in Straight Arrow Publishers Inc, 1992) p 44

56. Larkin, Colin: The Virgin Encyclopedia of '60s' Music (Virgin Books Ltd, 2002) p 46

57. Larkin, Colin (editor) Guinness Encyclopedia of Popular Music: All Time 1,000 Albums' Virgin Books p 23

58. Macdonald, Ian: Revolution in The Head: The Beatles' Records and The Sixties (Pimlico, 1995) p 152

59. Ibid

60. The Beatles: The Beatles Anthology (Apple Corps Ltd, 2000) p 209

61. The Beatles: The Beatles Anthology (Apple Corps Ltd, 2000) p 209

62. Crawdaddy magazine quoted in Williams, Paul (ed): The Crawdaddy! Book: Writings and Images From The Magazine of Rock (Hal Leonard Corporation, 2002) p 100-107

63. **The Beatles: The Beatles Anthology** (Apple Corps Ltd, 2000) p 208

64. **Evans, Paul in De Curtis, A and Henke, J with George-Warren, Holly The Rolling Stone Album Guide (**Random House, 1979 reprinted in Straight Arrow Publishers Inc, 1992) p 44

65. **Gould, Jonathan Can't Buy Me Love: The Beatles, Britain and America** (Harmony Books, 2007 reprinted in Piatkus Books, 2008) p 340

66. **The Beatles: The Beatles Anthology** (Apple Corps Ltd, 2000) p 11

## CHAPTER SIX: THE BEATLES: FROM SERGEANT PEPPER TO BEYOND

67. **Taylor, Alistair: With The Beatles** (John Blake Publishing Ltd, 2011 originally published 2003) p 73

68. **Hutton, Jack: Melody Maker**, 2 December, 1967 cited in Sandercombe W. Fraser: The Beatles Press Reports (Collector's Guide Publishing Inc, 2007) p 221

69. **Herbert, Ian: The Independent, 9 September, 20016**
(https://www.independent.co.uk/arts-entertainment/music/news/revealed-dentist-who-introduced-beatles-to-lsd-6231654.html)

70. **Norman, Philip 'John Lennon: The Life'** (Harper Collins Publishers, 2008) p 422-423

71. **The Beatles: The Beatles Anthology** (Apple Corps Ltd, 2000) p 177

72. **Brown, Peter and Gaines, Steven: The Love You Make** (Macmillan London Lt, 1983, quoted in 2nd edition Pan Books Ltd, 1984), p228

73. **Philip Norman: Shout! The True Story of The Beatles** (Hamish Hamilton Ltd, 1981 p303

74. **Gilbert, Martin: Challenge To Civilization: A History of the 20th Century, 1952- 1999** (Harper Collins Publishers, 2000) p 366

75. **Ibid** p 356

76. **Isaacs, Jeremy and Downing, Taylor: Cold War: An Illustrated History 1945- 1989** (Little, Brown, 2008) p 274

77. **Ibid** p 275

78. **De Groot, Gerard: '60s Unplugged: A Kaleidoscopic History of a Disorderly Decade (Macmillan, 2008)** p 249

79. **Ibid** p 247-48

80. **Neville, Richard: Playpower** (Paladin, Granada Publishing Ltd, 1971) p 47

81. **Ibid**

82. **Ibid** p 87-88

83. **Doggett, Peter: There's A Riot Going On: Revolutionaries, Rock Stars and The Rise and Fall of '60s Counter-Culture** (Canongate Books, 2007) p 103

84. **De Groot, Gerard: '60s Unplugged: A Kaleidoscopic History of a Disorderly Decade (Macmillan, 2008)** p 2

85. **Richards, Keith: Life** (W&N 1st edition, 2010) p 195-96

86. **Neville, Richard: Playpower** (Paladin, Granada Publishing Ltd, 1971) p 32

87. **Ibid**

88. **Karnow, Stanley: Vietnam: A History** (Penguin Books, 1997)

89. **Wolfe, Tom: The Electric Kool Aid Acid Test**

90. **Kercher, John: 'The Beat Lives On'** (The Big Issue, John Hunt Publishing) (4th -10th April, 2011)

91. **Hoskins, Barney: Beneath The Diamond Sky: Haight-Ashbury 1965-1970** p 33/35

92. **Ibid** p 125

93. **Ibid**
94. **Smith, Martin: John Coltrane: Jazz, Racism and Resistance** (Redwords, 2003) p 12
95. **Wolfe, Tom: The Electric Kool Aid Acid Test** p 223
96. **Walker, Harriet: The Independent**, 7 May, 2011 (https://www.independent.co.uk/life-style/fashion/news/the-fashion-god-who-brought-his-message-to-the-streets-2280351.html)
97. **Kerrigan, Michael: Modern Art** (Flame Tree Publishing, 2005) p 60
98. **Asherman, Allan: The Star Trek Compendium** (1993 3$^{rd}$ edition, Titan Books) p 88
99. **Harris, Mark: Scenes From A Revolution** (Canongate Books Ltd, 2008) p 148
100. **Cousins, Mark: The Story of Film** (BCA/ Pavilion Books, 2004) p 302
101. **Mason, Simon: The Rough Guide to Classic Novels** (Rough Guides Ltd/ Penguin, 2008) p 60-61
102. **Moorcook, Michael: The Jewel In The Skull** (Mayflower Books)
103. **Neville, Richard: Playpower** (Paladin, Granada Publishing Ltd, 1971) p 41
104. **Sandbrook, Dominic: White Heat- A History of Britain in the Swinging Sixties** (Abacus Books, 2007) p 401-42

## CHAPTER EIGHT: THE BEATLES: SERGEANT PEPPER BECKONS

105. **Sheff, David ed. Golson, G Barry: The Playboy Interviews with John Lennon and Yoko Ono** (New English Library, 1982) p131
106. **Norman, Philip: John Lennon: The Life** (Harper Collins Publishers, 2008) p481-482
107. **Macdonald, Ian Revolution in The Head: The Beatles' Records and The Sixties** (Pimlico, 1995) p172-173
108. **Heylin, Clinton: The Act You've Known For All These Years** (Canongate Books Ltd, 2007) p 60
109. **Sounes, Howard: An Intimate Life of Paul McCartney** p 161
110. **Norman, Philip: John Lennon: The Life** (Harper Collins Publishers, 2008) p483
111. **Ibid**
112. **Norman, Philip: Shout! The True Story of The Beatles** (Hamish Hamilton Ltd, 1981) p 296
113. **Macdonald, Ian: Revolution in The Head: The Beatles' Records and The Sixties** (Pimlico, 1995) p177
114. **The Beatles: The Beatles Anthology** (Apple Corps Ltd, 2000) p 241
115. **Heylin, Clinton: The Act You've Known For All These Years (Canongate Books Ltd, 2007)** p 285
116. **The Beatles: The Beatles Anthology** (Apple Corps Ltd, 2000) p 242
117. **Ibid**
118. **Shapiro, Marc: 'All Things Must Pass: The Life of George Harrison'** p 82

## CHAPTER NINE: SERGEANT PEPPER'S LONELY HEARTS CLUB BAND TRACK BY TRACK

119. **Macdonald, Ian: Revolution in The Head: The Beatles' Records and The Sixties** (Pimlico, 1995) p 184
120. **Ibid** p 197
121. **The Beatles: The Beatles Anthology** (Apple Corps Ltd, 2000) p 242

122. **Ibid** p 159
123. **Ibid**
124. **Sheff, David ed. Golson, G Barry: The Playboy Interviews with John Lennon and Yoko Ono** (New English Library, 1982) p 154
125. **Heylin, Clinton: The Act You've Known For All These Years** (Canongate Books Ltd, 2007) p 163
126. **Ibid** p 163
127. **Everett, Walter: The Foundations of Rock, Oxford University Press Inc, 2009, page 113.**
128. **Martin, George (ed): Making Music: The Guide to Writing, Performing & Recording** (Pan Books, 1983) p 78
129. **Macdonald, Ian: Revolution in The Head: The Beatles' Records and The Sixties** (Pimlico, 1995) p193-94
130. **Harrison, George: I, Me, Mine** (Weidenfeld & Nicolson, 2004) p 112
131. **Gould, Jonathan Can't Buy Me Love: The Beatles, Britain and America** (Harmony Books, 2007 reprinted in Piatkus Books, 2008) p 408
132. **Macdonald, Ian Revolution in The Head: The Beatles' Records and The Sixties** (Pimlico, 1995) p 190
133. **Wiener, John: Sergeant Pepper and Flower Power** in **Evans. Mike (ed): The Beatles: Paperback Writer: 40 Years of Classic Writing** (Plexus Publishing Ltd, 2009) p 177
134. **Macdonald, Ian: Revolution in The Head: The Beatles' Records and The Sixties** (Pimlico, 1995) p 186
135. **Heylin, Clinton: The Act You've Known For All These Years** (Canongate Books, 2007) p 124
136. **Sommer, Tim, The Observer, 15 June, 2016 (observer.com/2016/06/49-years-ago-the-beatles-sgt-peppers-sounded-much-better-in-mono/**
137. **The Beatles: The Beatles Anthology** (Apple Corps Ltd, 2000) p 248
138. **Ibid**
139. **Gould, Jonathan: Can't Buy Me Love: The Beatles, Britain and America** (Harmony Books, 2007 reprinted in Piatkus Books, 2008) p 392
140. **Heylin, Clinton: The Act You've Known For All These Years** (Canongate Books, 2007) p 173
141. **Harris, John: 'The Day The World Turned Day- Glo'** (Mojo magazine, Consumer Media Ltd, March, 2007
142. **Ibid**
143. **Ibid** p 83
144. **Ibid** p 87
145. **Barry Miles: London Calling: A Countercultural History of London since 1945** (Atlantic Books, 2010) p 246
146. **Macdonald, Ian: Revolution in The Head: The Beatles' Records and The Sixties** (Pimlico, 1995) p 199
147. **Evans. Paul** in **Rolling Stone Album Guide** (Straight Arrow Publishers Inc, 1992) p 44-45
148. **McNeill, Don** in **Williams, Paul (ed): The Crawdaddy Book!** (Hal Leonard Corporation, 2002) p 219
149. **Macdonald, Ian: Revolution in The Head: The Beatles' Records and The Sixties** (Pimlico, 1995) p 203
150. **Macdonald, Ian: Revolution in The Head: The Beatles' Records and The Sixties** (Pimlico, 1995) p 217

151. **Norman, Philip: John Lennon: The Life** (Harper Collins Publishers, 2008) p 528

152. **Taylor, Alistair: With The Beatles** (John Blake Publishing Ltd, 2011 originally published 2003) p 213

153. **The Beatles: The Beatles Anthology** (Apple Corps Ltd, 2000) p 274

154. **Macdonald, Ian: Revolution in The Head: The Beatles' Records and The Sixties** (Pimlico, 1995) p 208

155. **Ibid** p 209

156. **The Beatles: The Beatles Anthology** (Apple Corps Ltd, 2000) p 273

157. **Macdonald, Ian: Revolution in The Head: The Beatles' Records and The Sixties** (Pimlico, 1995) p 216

158. **Norman, Philip: John Lennon: The Life** (Harper Collins Publishers, 2008) p 529

159. **Nick Jones: 'Melody Maker' cited in in Sandercombe W. Fraser: The Beatles Press Reports** (Collector's Guide Publishing Inc, 2007) p 228

160. **Faithful, Marianne and Dalton, David: Faithful** (Penguin Books, 1995) p 14

## REFERENCES: THE BAND DIGEST

1. **Egan, Sean: Animal Tracks: The Story of The Animals: Newcastle's Rising Sons (**Helter Skelter Publishing, 2001) p12-14

2. **Light, Alan: Eric Burdon: Confessions of an Animal** (Mojo magazine, Bauer Consumer Media Ltd, May, 2013)

3. **Egan, Sean: Animal Tracks: The Story of The Animals: Newcastle's Rising Sons (**Helter Skelter Publishing, 2001) p 96

4. **Ibid** p 199

5. **Joynson, Vernon: The Tapestry of Delights: The Comprehensive Guide to British Music of the Beat, R&B, Psychedelic and Progressive Eras 1963-1970** (Borderline Productions, 2006, 2nd edition, 2008) p 135

6. **Jackson, Phil: 'Finally Found You Out: From Jazz to Trinity to Oblivion Express'** (Acid Dragon magazine #45, publisher- Thierry Sportouche, Lyon, France)

7. **Thompson, Dave and Leech, Jeanette: 'Julie Driscoll, Brian Auger, A Kind of Love-In'** (Shindig magazine Vol 2 Issue 12 Sept/ Oct 2009, p 56-63) (Volcano Publishing)

8. **Makowski, Peter: 'Born To Run': 'Jeff Beck: The Guitarists' Guitarist', a 50 year celebration- interview, profile, discography.'** (MOJO magazine, Bauer Consumer Media Ltd, June, 2009)

9. **Sandoval, Andrew**: liner notes to 'Bee Gees First' CD, Warner Brothers Records, 2007, p 9); also **'From Brilliant Birth to Brotherly Burnout'** (Shindig magazine #25 pages 46-63) (Volcano Publishing)

10. **Unterberger, Richie: All Music Guide To Rock** (Backbeat Books 3rd edition, 2002) p 85

11. **Rossi, Marco,** Shindig # 2 (1 Nov/ Dec, 2007) p 45 (Volcano Publishing)

12. **Unterberger, Richie: Unknown Legends of Rock 'n' Roll (**Backbeat Books, 1998) p 83

13. **Ibid** p 84

14. **Unterberger, Richie: All Music Guide to Rock 3rd Edition** (Backbeat Books, 2002) p 114

15. **Rathbone, Oregano** talks to **Brian Godding**: **'This Little Piggy'** Record Collector magazine, June, 2014, (Diamond Publishing Ltd) p 30-34

16. **Larkin, Colin: The Virgin Encyclopedia of '60s' Music** (Virgin Books Ltd, 2002) p 79

17. **Chapman, Bob**: MOJO magazine, Bauer Consumer Media Ltd, August, 2007 album review

18. **Larkin, Colin: 'The Virgin Encyclopedia of '60s' Music'** (Virgin Books Ltd, 2002) p 79

19. **Lewis, John: 'Hunting Tigers Out in Indiah',** ('Uncut' magazine. Time Inc, UK: April, 2007

20. **Ibid** p 34

21. **Welch, Chris, Spear, Roger Ruskin, Stott, Emma, Stanshall, Viv: 'The Intro and the Outro'** (Shindig magazine, issue 14, Jan- Feb, 2010, pages 48-57) (Volcano Publishing)

22. **Heckstall- Smith, Dick: Blowing The Blues Away: Playing the British Blues** (Clear Books, 2004) p 45

23. **Ibid** p 46

24. **Ibid** p 47-49

25. **Ibid** p 54

26. **Baker, Ginger: Hellraiser (**2010, John Blake Publishing Ltd.) p 42

27. **Ibid** p 101,

28. **Ibid**

29. **Paytress, Mark: 'Ginger Baker: There's A Curse On Me.'** (MOJO magazine, Bauer Consumer Media Ltd, January, 2015)

30. **Baker, Ginger: Hellraiser** (2010, John Blake Publishing Ltd.) p 101

31. **Paytress, Mark: 'Strange Brew: A Collector's History of Cream'** (Record Collector magazine, Diamond Publishing) p 80

32. **Rooksby, Ricky: Albums: 50 Years of Great Recordings** (Quantum Publishing Ltd, 2006) p 88

33. **Clapton, Eric: The Autobiography** (Century Books, 2007) p 91

34. **Thompson, Dave: Cream: The World's First Supergroup** (Virgin Books Ltd, 2005) p188-189

35. **Platt, John: Disraeli Gears (Classic Rock Albums series)** (Schirmer Books, Simon and Schuster Macmillan, 1998) p 85

36. **Williamson, Nigel: Uncut magazine, May, 2004 (TI Media Ltd)**

37. **Platt, John: Disraeli Gears (Classic Rock Albums series)** (Schirmer Books, Simon and Schuster Macmillan, 1998) p 78

38. **Leitch, Donovan: The Hurdy Gurdy Man** (Arrow Books, 2005) p 165

39. **Ibid** p 177

40. **Ibid** p 176

41. **Ibid** p 301

42. **Ibid p 300**

43. **Boyd, Joe: White Bicycles: Making Music in the 1960s** (Serpent's Tail, 2006) p 1

44. **Ibid** p 120-121

45. **Ibid** p 12

46. **Young, Rob: Electric Eden: Unearthing Britain's Visionary Music** (Faber & Faber, 2010) p 29

47. **Ibid** p 349

48. **Ibid** p 356

49. **Ibid** p 357
50. **Jackson, Phil: Mike Heron and Trembling Bells concert review** (Acid Dragon magazine #62, publisher- Thierry Sportouche, Lyon, France)
51. **Martin, Neville and Hudson, Jeff: The Kinks** (Sanctuary Publishing Ltd, 2nd edition, 2002) p 90
52. **Ibid** p 86
53. **Williamson, Nigel: The Rough Guide to the Blues** (Rough Guides Ltd, 2007) p 265
54. **Macan, Edward: Rocking The Classics: English Progressive Rock and the Counterculture** (Oxford Paperbacks) p 21
55. **Joynson, Vernon: The Tapestry of Delights: The Comprehensive Guide to British Music of the Beat, R&B, Psychedelic and Progressive Eras 1963-1976** (Borderline Productions, 2nd edition, 2008) p 581
56. **Macan, Edward: Rocking The Classics: English Progressive Rock and the Counterculture** (Oxford Paperbacks, 1997) p 21/23
57. **Macan, Edward: Endless Enigma: A Musical Biography of Emerson, Lake and Palmer** (Open Court, Carus Publishing Company, 2006) p 21
58. **Ibid** p 19
59. **Forrester, George, Hanson, Martyn and Askew, Frank: Emerson, Lake and Palmer: The Show That Never Ends** (Helter Skelter Publishing, 2008) p 23
60. **Macan, Edward: Endless Enigma: A Musical Biography of Emerson, Lake and Palmer** (Open Court, Carus Publishing Company, 2006) p 20-21
61. **Blake, Mark: Pigs Might Fly: The Inside Story of Pink Floyd** (Aurum Press, 2007) p 75
62. **Ibid**
63. **Ibid** p 88
64. **Black, Johnny: 'Across the Universe': Pink Floyd & The Story of Prog Rock** (Q Classic magazine, Bauer Media Group) p 49
65. **Harris, John: The Dark Side of the Moon: The Making of the Pink Floyd Masterpiece** (Harper Perennial, 2005) p 30
66. **Bogdanov, Vladimir, Wodstra, Chris and Erlewine, Stephen Thomas: All Music Guide to Rock: The Definitive Guide to Rock, Pop and Soul (Steve Huey)** (Backbeat Books, AEC One Stop Group Inc.) p 861
67. **Wells, David: 'Fry Your Mind and Your Ass Will Follow: A Trip Through the Greatest British Psychedelic Albums of All Time'** (Record Collector magazine, Diamond Publishing abridged quotation, May, 2003) p 30
68. **Blake, Mark: Pigs Might Fly: The Inside Story of Pink Floyd** (Aurum Press, 2007) p 91
69. **Thompson, Dave: Space Daze: The History and Mystery of Electronic Ambient Space Rock** (Cleopatra, Los Angeles, 1994) p 26
70. **Ibid** p27
71. **Dellar, Hugh: 'Are We Having Fun Yet?'** (Shindig magazine, Volcano Publishing Vol 2 #1 Nov/ Dec, 2007) p 11-21
72. **Ibid** p 13
73. **Andrews, Mark: 'The Pretty Things: Return to the Midnight Circus'** (Progression magazine, U.S., summer/ fall, 1999) p 67
74. **Helsing, Lenny: 'The British Evasion'** (Shindig magazine, Volcano Publishing Vol 2 # 9 Mar/ Apr, 2009) p 51
75. **Ibid** p 49

76. **Ibid** p 51

77. **Stax, Mike: 'The Beat Goes On'** (Shindig magazine, Volcano Publishing Vol 2 #9 Mar/ Apr, 2009) p 56

78. **Scott- Irvine: Procol Harum: The Ghosts of a Whiter Shade of Pale** (Omnibus Press, 2012) Chapter 18: 'Pale Goes To Court' 2005-2009

79. **Chapman, Rob: 'The Giant Shadow'** (MOJO magazine, Bauer Consumer Media Ltd, September, 1995) p 54

80. **Jackson, Phil: 'Play It Again, Procol Harum!'** (Acid Dragon magazine #72, publisher- Thierry Sportouche, Lyon, France)

81. **Scott- Irvine: Procol Harum: The Ghosts of a Whiter Shade of Pale** (Omnibus Press, 2012) p 7

82. **Jackson, Phil: 'Play It Again, Procol Harum!'** (Acid Dragon magazine #72, publisher- Thierry Sportouche, Lyon, France)

83. **Johansen, Claes: Procol Harum: Beyond The Pale** (SAF Publishing Ltd, 2000) p 38-39

84. **Jackson, Phil: 'Procol Harum: Beyond These Things- In Held 'Twas In I-Roine Stolt on Procol Harum'** (first published on www.procolharum.com)

85. **Norman, Philip: The Stones** (Pan Books, 2002) p 36

86. **Ibid** p 81

87. **Landau, Jon: 'Between The Buttons- The Rolling Stones'** (Review in Crawdaddy magazine reprinted in 'The Crawdaddy Book' (Ed- Paul Williams) (Hal Leonard Corporation, 2002) p154

88. **Norman, Philip: The Stones** (Pan Books, 2002) p 240

89. **Elliot, Martin: Rolling Stones Complete Recording Sessions 1963-1969** (Blandford Press, 1990) p 76

90. **Joynson, Vernon: The Tapestry of Delights: The Comprehensive Guide to British Music of the Beat, R&B, Psychedelic and Progressive Eras 1963-1976'** (Borderline Productions, 2nd edition, 2008) p 739

91. **Bogdanov, Vladimir, Wodstra, Chris and Erlewine, Stephen Thomas: All Music Guide to Rock: The Definitive Guide to Rock, Pop and Soul (Richie Unterberger)** (Backbeat Books, AEC One Stop Group Inc.) p 999

92. **Rossi, Francis: Status Quo Autobiography XS A; Areas** (Pan, 2005) p 69

93. **Ibid** p 24

94. **Ibid** p 68

95. **Young, Rob: Electric Eden: Unearthing Britain's Visionary Music** (Faber & Faber, 2010) p 286

96. **Bogdanov, Vladimir, Wodstra, Chris and Erlewine, Stephen Thomas: All Music Guide to Rock: The Definitive Guide to Rock, Pop and Soul (Steve Huey)** (Backbeat Books, AEC One Stop Group Inc.) p 1153

97. **'Various contributors (foreword by Johnny Marr): 'The 50 Greatest Who Songs'** (MOJO magazine, Bauer Consumer Media Ltd, August, 2015) p 65

98. **Ibid** p 32

99. http://www.smh.com.au/comment/obituaries/ritchie-yorke-rock-journalist-close-to-lennon-led-zeppelin-and-hendrix-20170213-guber1.html **('Ritchie Yorke, Rock Journalist Close to Lennon, Led Zeppelin and Hendrix' obituary by Glenn A Baker, Sydney Morning Hearld, 14th February, 2017)**

100. **Thompson, Dave:** https://www.allmusic.com/album/little-games-mw0000471492

101. **Lewis, Dave: 'Happenings 50 Years Time Ago'** (Record Collector magazine, Diamond Publishing abridged quotation, April, 2016) p 76

102. Blaney, John with Martin Stone 'The Buddhas of Suburbia' (Shindig magazine, Volcano Publishing, issue 25) p 28

103. Shirley, Ian: https://recordcollectormag.com/articles/klooky-art

104. www.officialkinksfanclub.co.uk

105. Larkin, Colin: The Virgin Encyclopedia of '60s' Music (Virgin Books/ Muze UK Ltd, 2002) p 155

106. Thompson, Dave: All Music Guide to Rock, Pop and Soul (Backbeat Books, 2002) p 305

107. For example, Thompson, Dave: Space Daze: The History and Mystery of Electronic Ambient Space Rock' (Cleopatra, 1994) p 47

108. De Rogatis, Jim: Turn on Your Mind: Four Decades of Great Psychedelic Rock (Hal Leonard Corporation, 2003)

109. Jansen, Skip: All Music Guide to Rock, Pop and Soul (Backbeat Books, 2002) p 305

110. Doggett, Peter: There's a Riot Going on: Revolutionaries, Rock Stars and The Rise and Fall of '60s Counter-culture (Canongate Books Ltd, 2007) p 369

111. Shulman, Derek: 'How Simon Dupree Grew Into Gentle Giant' (interview with Ray Shulman) (Record Collector magazine, Diamond Publishing, # 413, April, 2013)

112. Boyd, Joe: White Bicycles: Making Music in the 1960s (Serpent's Tail, 2006) p 165

113. Joynson, Vernon: The Tapestry of Delights: The Comprehensive Guide to British Music of the Beat, R&B, Psychedelic and Progressive Eras 1963-1976 (Borderline Productions, 2nd edition, 2008) p 451

114. Mills, Jon 'Mojo' with Rick Brown: 'Beautiful Losers' (Record Collector magazine, Diamond Publishing, February, 2012) p 36

115. Jackson, Phil: 'High Tide: Interesting Times- The History of High Tide' (Acid Dragon magazine) p 39??

116. Du Noyer, Paul: Liverpool: Wondrous Place: Music from the Cavern to the Coral (Virgin Books, 2002) p 89

117. Jack, Richard Morton: 'Tomorrow' (Flashback magazine issue #2, Winter, 2012) p 82-112

118. Halper, Phil and Segal, Charles: 'Rod Argent Interview' (Background magazine, year unknown) p 12

119. De Koningh, Michael and Griffiths, Marc: Tighten Up: The History of Reggae in the UK (Sanctuary Books, 2003) p 12

120. Case- Honeysett, Laurence (Record Collector magazine, Diamond Publishing, September, 2016) p 76

121. Thompson, Dave: Reggae & Caribbean Music' (Backbeat Books, 2002) p 220

122. With acknowledgement to Thompson, Dave: 'Reggae & Caribbean Music' (Backbeat Books, 2002) for helping to inform the choices.

123. With acknowledgement to www.dancecrasher.co.uk for free listening and helping inform the choices.

124. Williamson, Nigel: 'The Rough Guide to the Blues' (Rough Guides Ltd, 2007) p 325

125. Williamson, Nigel: 'The Rough Guide to the Blues' (Rough Guides Ltd, 2007) p 354

126. Cross, Charles R: 'Room Full of Mirrors: A Biography of Jimi Hendrix' (Sceptre, 2005) p 51
127. **Ibid** p 52
128. **Ibid** p 57